Reading Literature

Purple Level
Yellow Level
Blue Level
ORANGE LEVEL
Green Level
Red Level

Reading Literature

Orange Level

The McDougal, Littell English Program

McDougal, Littell & Company
Evanston, Illinois
New York   Dallas   Sacramento

Authors

Staff of McDougal, Littell & Company
Marilyn Sherman

Consultants

Sharon Edwards, Teacher, Woodbury Junior High School, Shaker Heights, Ohio
Anne Emmert, Teacher, Richardson Junior High School, Dallas, Texas
Yvonne Fasold, Teacher, Sheldon High School, Eugene, Oregon
Richard H. Gray, Chairman, English Department, Enfield High School, Enfield, Connecticut
Patricia West Jeffries, High school teacher and freelance writer on basic skills for the Memphis (Tennessee) City Schools
Parker Kendall, Teacher, Oxnard High School, Oxnard, California
Sandra Nash, Teacher, Salt Rock Junior High School, Huntington, West Virginia
H. Vance White, Department Chair, English, Walker Junior High School, La Palma, California

Frontispiece: *Ulysses Deriding Polyphemus,* (detail) 1829, JOSEPH MALLORD WILLIAM TURNER. The National Gallery, London.

Acknowledgments

Robert Silverberg and Agberg, Ltd.: For "The Assassin" by Robert Silverberg, from *Travels Through Time;* copyright © 1957 by Greenleaf Publications, Inc. Atheneum Publishers, Inc.: For "Thumbprint" by Eve Merriam, from *It Doesn't Always Have To Rhyme;* copyright © 1954 by Eve Merriam. Toni Cade Bambara: For "Raymond's Run," from
(continued on page 668)

ISBN: 0-86609-231-5

Copyright © 1985 by McDougal, Littell & Company
Box 1667, Evanston, Illinois 60204
All rights reserved. Printed in the United States of America

86 87 88 / 12 11 10 9 8 7 6 5 4

Contents

CHAPTER 2 *Norse Myths and Legends*   99

Great Modern Stories 265

Science Fiction Stories 305

CHAPTER 6 *Poetry*

Human Relationships

Reading Literature: More About Poetry

Handbook for Reading and Writing

Dear Educator,

Reading Literature brings to your students the greatest literature of all time. In this age of computers and VCR's, precious little of the world's great literary heritage filters through to our new generation. I don't believe you want your students to go through life without being acquainted with Homer's *Odyssey*. I don't believe you want your students to be unacquainted with the stories and poems of O. Henry, Walt Whitman, T. S. Eliot, and Leo Tolstoy. This kind of reading can provide your students with a quickened sense of life's drama and a new sense of life's possibilities. The time is now. The opportunity is here.

Your students will be reading stories, poems, nonfiction, and plays in their original form. Selections are not adapted. We have searched through the world's great literature to find selections that will stretch the students' minds, sharpen their senses, and enrich their lives.

Throughout, *Reading Literature* integrates reading and writing. Writing is presented as a process. A thorough foundation for writing is presented in a complete chapter, "How Writers Write" (see Chapter 4). The universal themes and ideas revealed by great literature make easy the task of teacher and text in guiding students to discover topics for their own writing.

I hope you will be as proud to offer *Reading Literature* to your students as we are to present it to you. I hope, too, that *Reading Literature* will assist you in helping the students to read happily, to think critically, and, above all, to meet the wondrous challenge that is life. Great writers of our time, and of earlier times, can help students in this process of growth. No other writers can do it as well.

Joseph F. Littell
Editor-in-Chief
McDougal, Littell & Company

CHAPTER **1**

Greek Myths and Legends

Aphrodite (the Bartlett Head),
325 B.C. Greek Attic sculpture.
Courtesy of the Museum of Fine Arts, Boston.

Reading Literature: Greek Myths and Legends

Myths and legends are both very old stories. They have influenced people for thousands of years. Some of the most important myths and legends are from ancient Greece. The first part of this chapter introduces Greek myths. The second part will introduce Greek legends.

What Is a Myth?

What is lightning? What causes it? What causes the sun to rise and the moon to change its shape? Today, we have scientific answers to such questions. Long ago, however, people created answers. They explained many mysteries of nature and human life with stories called **myths**.

Myths are stories from the **oral tradition**. That is, they were told and retold, passed down from generation to generation. Myths usually involve gods with superhuman powers who live forever. Myths are related to the religion of a people. Because a myth is part of the oral, or spoken, literature of a people, it has no one author. Some of the most imaginative myths come to us from the early Greeks.

Myths helped the early Greeks to understand the world, nature, life, and death. For example, one myth explained lightning this way: an angry god threw his spear down from the heavens. Myths in this chapter explain the origins of the earth, of humans, and of evil.

While most myths explain how something happened in the world, some concentrate on showing human characteristics. For example, the story of Icarus is a tale of cleverness, love of freedom, and recklessness. Other myths give moral lessons, illustrating the best way to live.

The History of the Greek Myths

Greek myths began with the people who lived in Greece 3000 years ago. Their tales were carried about by traveling singer-poets. Because the different poets added to the myths, there are many versions. Still, certain basic stories developed about the Greek gods and heroes.

After Rome conquered Greece around 148 B.C., the Roman people took over the Greek myths as their own. For the most part, they simply changed the names of the gods. For instance, the most powerful Greek god Zeus became the Roman god Jupiter. For over one thousand years, people worshiped these gods. Eventually they stopped believing in the gods. They continued, however, to enjoy stories about them.

These stories affected the way people in the western world thought. Names from the myths became words in many languages, including English. Artists created paintings and statues that showed events in myths. Stories and plays, including musicals, are based on Greek myths. Even today, myths are exciting stories, some of the best ever told.

The Elements of a Greek Myth

Characters. Some of the characters in myths are **gods** and **goddesses**. They are much more powerful than humans. However, they have human faults, such as jealousy. Another common character is a **hero** who has fantastic adventures. The hero often is born of a god and a human. Hercules, for example, is the son of Zeus and a human.

Setting. The setting of a myth is not limited to Earth. Events may occur in the home of the gods and goddesses or in the land of the dead. Myths even tell of events that occurred before the Earth came to be.

Plot. Each myth has a **plot**, a series of related events. The plot may include events that could not happen in the real world. Perseus, for example, battles a monster who turns men into stone.

How To Read a Greek Myth

1. The names may seem strange at first. Refer to the list of Greek gods and goddesses on page 9 as you read. It will be easier to understand each story if you can identify who is in it.
2. Identify anything the myth teaches or explains.
3. Read each myth twice. The first time, simply enjoy the story. The second time, look carefully at the events and characters. Discover for yourself why the story has appealed to people for 3,000 years.

Comprehension Skills: Direct Statements

Understanding Information Stated Directly

The first step in reading well is understanding what the writer states directly. From there, you can build to understanding what the writer does not directly tell about plot, setting, and characters.

Descriptions. Frequently a writer provides a direct description of a character. To understand what the character might do, you must watch for details that the writer gives. Here is an example:

> The monster Medusa lay asleep. Fastened securely to her scalp by the tips of their tails, snakes with awful breath writhed and twisted about her face and neck.

The myth states directly that the monster had smelly, twisting snakes where her hair should have been.

In addition to characters, a writer can directly describe settings, actions, and ideas.

Time Order. When a writer describes an action, he or she tries to make the order of events clear. The writer may use words such as the following to signal time order:

first	then	before	now	soon
next	when	during	later	finally

As you read, keep in mind what happened first, then what happened next, and so on. Watch for time signals that will help you. For example, notice the order of events described in these sentences:

> Odysseus clung to the raft until it fell apart. Then, plunging into the sea, he began to swim. The surf beat high on the rocks, but he soon found calmer water at the mouth of a gentle stream where he landed, breathless and nearly dead.

Here is the order, signaled by the words *until*, *then*, and *soon*.

1. Odysseus clung to the raft.
2. The raft fell apart.
3. Odysseus began to swim.
4. He found high surf.
5. He found calmer water.
6. He landed.

Cause and Effect. A writer may tell more than the order in which events occur. He or she may also state that a certain event caused a later event. Here are some words a writer can use to signal a cause and effect relationship:

because	consequently	as a result	so . . . that
since	therefore	for this reason	if . . . then

Recognizing cause and effect relationships helps you make sense out of what you read. Here is an example:

> The young men loved Helen so devotedly that they swore they would defend her from harm all her life.

The young men swore to protect Helen because they loved her. The words *so* and *that* are clues to the relationship.

Exercises: Understanding Direct Statements

A. Read this passage. Then answer the following questions.

At this time, the valley of Nemea (Nē′mē a) was inhabited by a terrible lion. It was large and fierce and had overcome all the hunters who had been sent to capture it. Hercules went alone and sought the animal in its lair. Calling it forth, he set on the beast with a club, but his blows fell in vain. Then Hercules caught it and strangled it with his bare hands.

1. The setting is   (a) in Hercules   (b) in Nemea.
2. The lion is described as   (a) inhabited   (b) terrible.
3. Hercules went   (a) with all the hunters   (b) alone.

B. Reread the passage. Then arrange these events in order.

1. Hercules called the lion out.
2. Hercules went alone.
3. He strangled the lion.
4. He hit the lion with a club.

Vocabulary Skills: Four Ways To Find Meanings

Recognizing Four Ways To Find Word Meaning

Frequently in your reading, you come across an unfamiliar word. How can you learn its meaning? It is important to realize there's more than one way to figure out a word. In this book, you will study four different ways to find word meanings. When you know several ways, you can choose the best one for any unfamiliar word.

Word Parts.　Sometimes an unfamiliar word is based on a familiar word. However, it looks different because new word parts have been added to its beginning or ending or both. The ending may have changed because of the added part. For example, look at the word below. Can you find the word *forget* in it?

unforgettable

The word part *un-* was added at the beginning of *forget*. The word part *-able* was added at the ending. If you know the meanings of those word parts and of the word *forget*, you can figure out *unforgettable*.

Both this chapter and Chapter 2 will tell about using word parts to find word meanings.

Context.　Very often the context of a word can lead you to its meaning. The **context** consists of the words or sentences around a word. Here is an example of a context clue:

Odysseus was noted for his sagacity, that is, sound judgment.

From the sentence, you learn that *sagacity* means "sound judgment." You will learn more about context clues in this chapter and in Chapters 3 and 5.

Word Origins.　English has taken many words and word parts from other languages. You may know the meaning of the word or word part in the other language. It will help you figure out the English word. For example, *solar* in English and *sol* in Spanish are based on the same Latin word. In both Latin and Spanish, *sol* means "sun." From that you can guess that *solar energy* is energy from the sun.

This chapter and Chapter 6 will discuss word origins.

The Dictionary. Sometimes you cannot use any of the first three ways to find the meaning of an unfamiliar word. Then you must use a dictionary for help. This chapter will discuss when to use a dictionary. Chapter 7 will discuss how to use one.

Exercise: Choosing the Best Way To Find Word Meaning

Read each statement below. Then tell which way you would find the meaning of the underlined word.

1. Zeus was the most <u>powerful</u> of the gods.

   a. word parts   b. the dictionary

2. The first <u>Olympic</u> games were played in the valley of Olympia in Greece.

   a. word origins   b. the dictionary

3. Nessus was a <u>centaur</u>, in other words, a creature that was half man and half horse.

   a. context clues   b. the dictionary

4. The poet sang feelingly of that <u>eventful</u> time.

   a. word parts   b. the dictionary

5. Odysseus's friend suspected a <u>ruse</u>.

   a. context clues   b. the dictionary

6. The monster was so ugly that she was <u>indescribable</u>.

   a. word parts   b. the dictionary

7. In an effort to solve his problem, the king consulted the <u>oracle</u>, who spoke for the gods.

   a. word parts   b. context clues

8. The job required <u>Herculean</u> efforts.

   a. word origins   b. context clues

Greek Myths

Do you like stories with adventure? Do you like tales of suspense, with villains or threatening monsters? Are the heroes and heroines of your favorite stories brave and faithful to their friends? The ancient Greeks would have answered "Yes!" to each of these questions. The myths in this chapter show how well the storytellers of long ago pleased their audiences. You will certainly find something to please you, too.

Apollo and the Muses on Mount Helicon, 1681, Claude Lorrain. Courtesy of the Museum of Fine Arts, Boston.

Major Greek and Roman Gods and Goddesses

This list identifies the most important Greek gods and goddesses by their Greek names. If there were Roman names, they appear in italic type after the Greek names.

The Titans—giants who sprang from the meeting of the Earth, and the heavens

Kronos (krō′ nos), *Saturn,* was the father of the gods.

Atlan (at′ lən), *Atlas,* held the heavens on his shoulders.

Prometheus (prō mē′ thē əs) created man from clay.

Epimetheus (ep′ə mē′ thē əs) gave a gift to each animal.

Themis (thā′ məs) was the goddess of law and justice.

Rhea (rē′ ə) was the wife of Kronos.

Mnemosyne (ne moz′ ih nē) was the goddess of memory.

The Rulers—children of Kronos and Rhea

Zeus (zōōs), *Jupiter,* was the ruler of all living creatures.

Hera (hir′ ə), *Juno,* was the wife of Zeus and queen of the gods and goddesses.

Hades (hā′ dēz), *Pluto,* was the ruler of the Underworld, the Kingdom of the Dead.

Poseidon (pō sī′ don), *Neptune,* was the ruler of the oceans. One of his sons was Triton. The sea nymphs were his daughters.

Separate Creations

Athene (ə thē′ nə), *Minerva,* the goddess of wisdom, sprang fully grown from Zeus's head.

Aphrodite (af′rə dī′ tē), *Venus,* the goddess of love and beauty, sprang from the foam of the sea.

Dionysus (dī ə nī′ səs), *Bacchus,* was the god of wine.

Iris (ī′ ris) was the goddess of the rainbow.

Children of Zeus and Hera

Hephaestos (hi fes′ təs), *Vulcan,* was the god of fire and metalworking. Aphrodite was his wife.

Hebe (hē′ bē), the heavenly wife of Herakles, was the goddess of youth.

Ares (er′ es), *Mars,* was the god of war.

Children of Zeus and Goddesses Other than Hera

Hermes (hʉr′ mēz), *Mercury,* grandson of Atlas, was the messenger god and the god of science, of commerce, and of sports.

Apollo (ə päl′ ō), *Phoebus,* was the god of the sun, of the lyre, of archery, and of prophecy.

Artemis (är′ tə mis), *Diane,* was Apollo's sister. She was the goddess of the moon, of wild animals, and of hunting.

The Horae (hō′ rī), the Hours, daughters of Themis, guarded the gates of heaven and were the goddesses of time.

The Moirai (moi rī′), the three Fates, were also daughters of Themis.

The Charities (kar′ ə tēs), the three Graces, granddaughters of the sea nymphs, presided over social occasions.

The Muses (myōōz′ əs), the nine daughters of Mnemosyne, had special interest in the arts and sciences.

The Beginning of the World

TRADITIONAL GREEK MYTH
Retold by Sally Benson

The ancient Greeks told stories about the gods in an effort to explain life. As you read this myth, consider how people today explain events such as thunder and fire. Are our explanations similar or different?

A long time ago, more years than anyone can count, there was no earth, no sky, sun, moon, or stars. There was only space. In this space, a huge, shapeless mass hung suspended. It was without color, and it was neither hard nor soft. There was no water on it and no land, not even a blade of grass or the tiniest of living things.

Then there was a deafening clap of thunder. Flames leapt high in the air and formed the skies. Beneath them, the air arose, while the earth, being the heaviest, sank to the bottom.

The Gods and Goddesses

As the earth and heavens met, there sprang into being a race of gigantic gods called Titans. They had as their ruler a cruel god named Kronos (krō′ nōs), who had many children. Kronos's son Zeus (zoōs), with his brothers and sisters, rebelled against Kronos and defeated him. They sentenced him to Tartarus (tär′ tər əs), which was one of the regions under the control of Hades (hā′ dēz), Lord of the Underworld.

This was a dreadful place surrounded by three impenetrable walls and the waters of the burning river. Kronos's brother, Atlas, was forced to bear the heavens on his shoulders for eternity.

Zeus and his favorite brothers, Poseidon (pō sī′ don) and Hades, divided the world into three parts. Poseidon said he would rule the ocean. Hades, who was a rather melancholy god, chose the Kingdom of the Dead. The earth was to belong to all the gods, and Zeus was chosen to reign over all living creatures: gods, men, and beasts.

Zeus chose as his kingdom the very top of a mountain in Thessaly. He called it Olympus. Here, with the exception of Poseidon and Hades, all the gods lived. They got along together as most families do, sometimes quarreling and bickering among themselves and, at other times, dwelling amicably together. They were shut off from the earth by a gate of clouds that was guarded by the goddesses known as the Horae (hō′ rī) (the Seasons). Each god had a palace of his own, but they all assembled

Morning, 1879, THOMAS DEWING. Delaware Art Museum, Wilmington.

daily in a mammoth hall in Zeus's palace. There they talked over the affairs of the day. They dined on nectar and ambrosia, drink and food so delicious that it cannot be compared with anything in the world. It was so miraculous that the tiniest sip or bite would cause the lowliest of men to become immortal. The lovely goddess, Hebe (hē′ bē), served them their food and drink, and Apollo (ə päl′ ō) played soft tunes on his lyre.

Apollo, son of Zeus, was the god of the sun. He was also the god of the lyre, of archery, and of prophecy. Every day he drove his flaming chariot across the skies, bringing the day. Apollo's sister, Artemis (är′ tə mis), pale and beautiful, was goddess of the moon.

All the Immortals had kingdoms over which they ruled. Aphrodite (af′ rə dī′ tē), for example, was the goddess of love and beauty. She sprang from the foam of the sea. As she was born, a soft breeze carried her along the waves to the Isle of Cyprus. Here she was dressed in flowing robes by the Horae and led to the palace of Zeus. She wore an enchanted sash embroidered in glowing colors, which had the power of inspiring love in all who beheld her. As she bowed before Zeus, all of the gods were enchanted by her beauty. Each one asked to have her for his wife. Zeus finally gave her to Hephaestos (hi fes′ təs) as a reward for the service of forging thunderbolts.

Hephaestos was an artist, the son of Zeus and Hera (hir′ ə). He had been born lame and, because of this handicap, had learned the art of working in metals. He was architect, smith, armorer, and chariot builder for the gods. He built them houses of shining brass. He designed golden shoes that enabled them to walk on water or air and to move from place to place with the speed of the wind. He shod the steeds that whirled the celestial chariots through the air. Most miraculous of all, he endowed the chairs and tables of his design with self-motion so that they could move themselves in and out of rooms. There is a story that his lameness was the result of a quarrel with Zeus. Angry with Hephaestos for taking Hera's part in a dispute, Zeus flung him from the heavens. He was a whole day falling, and he landed on the Island of Lemnos, which was afterwards sacred to him.

Hera, Zeus's wife, was something of a scold. She was tall and regal-looking, and she was apt to interfere in things. The goddess of the rainbow, Iris (ī′ ris), was her personal attendant and messenger. The peacock was Hera's favorite bird, because of its pride and splendor.

The nine Muses were the daughters of Zeus and Mnemosyne (ne moz′ ih nē′), who was also known as Memory. Each one of the nine had chosen one of the arts such as astronomy, history, poetry, and dance as her particular province. They all presided over song and prompted the memory, in honor of their mother. They sang when Apollo played soft tunes on his lyre.

There were the Moirai (moi rī′), the Fates, who spun the thread of human destiny. The life of a person continued until all the thread allotted to that person was spun. Then death was supposed to occur.

The Erinyes (ə rēn′ əs), or Furies, punished secretly. If criminals escaped the law, or won unjustified acquittal in the courts, they stung them throughout life. Nemesis (nem′ ə sis), too, was an avenging goddess. She represented the anger of the gods against the proud and insolent.

There were a great many lesser gods and goddesses. Pan, the god of flocks and shepherds, dwelt in Arcadia, a mountainous region where contentment reigned. The Satyrs (sāt′ ərs) were deities of the woods and fields. They were covered with bristly hair, horns grew on their heads, and they had feet like those of goats. Momus (mo′ məs), a grotesque fellow, was god of laughter, and Plutus (plōōt′ əs), cold and grasping, was god of wealth.

Athene (ə thē′ nə), the goddess of wisdom and expert in arts and crafts, had no mother. She sprang forth from Zeus's head, fully armed. She was wise and kind and chose the owl for her favorite bird, because of his sage, thoughtful expression. It was one of her tasks to weave the cloth for all the robes worn by the goddesses. Day after day she sat in the shade of the olive trees weaving soft and colorful materials. She was assisted in her work by the three Charities, who personified charm, grace, and beauty. They were frivolous, pretty girls who enjoyed presiding over banquets and other social gatherings. They were very elegant, and considered good manners and social arts extremely important.

Hermes, tall, lean, and fleet of foot, was the god of all gymnastic sports, commerce, and even thieving. He presided over everything that required skill and dexterity. He was Zeus's messenger and wore a winged cap and winged shoes. In his hand he carried a rod entwined with two serpents. He is said to have invented the lyre. Roaming about the earth one day, he found a tortoise. He stripped it of its covering. Then, in the shell he made holes through which he drew nine cords of linen, in honor of the nine Muses. He gave the lyre to Apollo.

Dionysus (dī′ ə nī′ səs) was the god of wine. He was a peaceful, jovial god, famed as a lawgiver and a promoter of civilization. He liked nothing better than to sit around in the great hall of the palace, eating, drinking, and talking.

The First Man

The beginning of the world was a time of great peace and happiness. All over the land seeds swelled and burst, and animals came into being. Horses roamed the plains, chipmunks and squirrels played in the trees and deer ran through the woods without fear. The cats lay in the sun all day and padded softly through the wet grass at night. Fish appeared in the seas and rivers, and the birds were busy building nests. Only the dog was unhappy, because there was no one on earth for him to love.

Now at this time, there lived a god named Prometheus (prō mē′ thē əs), who was one of the Titans. He had escaped punishment at the hands of Zeus. He was a gigantic creature who could step across rivers as easily as men can step across brooks. In two strides, he could reach the top of the highest mountain.

Prometheus and his brother, Epimetheus (ep′ ə mē′ thē əs), had been selected to guard the animals as they came to life. Epimetheus decided to give each animal a gift that would help it survive in the new wilderness. He gave wings to the birds, claws to the tiger, and shells to the turtles. To others he gave courage, strength, speed, and keenness of mind. Prometheus had promised his brother that he would approve these gifts after they were given. In the meantime, he had been thinking that something was missing. There was need for a nobler animal than any that had sprung from the seeds that lay in the earth and the sea.

One day, as he was resting on the shore, Prometheus scooped up a handful of earth. To amuse himself, he began to form an image in the shape of the gods. He moistened the image with water from the ocean so that it would hold together. He modeled the figure standing upright, its face uplifted, gazing at the heavens. In the handful of earth, he found a seed. It was different from any seed he had ever seen, larger and more shining. He washed it off in the sea and placed it in the exact center of the statue he had made. The sun beat down on the image, heating it, and a fresh breeze sprang from the sea, cooling it. Like a piece of pottery, it hardened and dried. Inside, the seed grew and gave the image life. The color of the earth faded from it. It took on the reflections of all around it: blue from the ocean for the eyes, gold from the skies for the hair, the color of the pale sand for the skin, and deep red from the sunset for the lips. Prometheus called it Man.

Taking Man by the hand, Prometheus led him to Epimetheus, and he asked his brother to bestow a gift, finer and more valuable than any other. Epimetheus hung his head in shame. The last gift, he said, was gone. He had given the giraffe a long neck so it could reach fruit from the tallest trees. While Man waited, Prometheus and his brother talked over what they should do. They finally decided to ask Athene, goddess of wisdom, to help them. It was quite some time before they found her. They finally came upon her seated at her loom, weaving robes for the goddesses, in the heart of an olive grove.

Hearing their problem, she agreed to accompany Prometheus to heaven. There he might find something belonging to the gods

The Great Red Spot on Jupiter. NASA.

that he could give to Man. They rode up into the sky. As they passed the chariot of Apollo, Prometheus dipped his torch into the sun. Turning, he descended quickly to earth. He handed the torch to Man and gave him fire, the most valuable gift of all. With it, men became the rulers of the world. They heated metals and formed weapons to protect themselves; they made tools to cultivate the fields; they built fires to heat their dwelling places.

When the gods learned that Prometheus, a Titan, had stolen the fire from heaven, they became enraged. He had, they said, made Man too powerful by giving him this divine gift. Zeus, hearing what Prometheus had done, ordered him chained to a rock on a mountain, face upward in the burning sun. There he lay while a vulture gnawed at his liver, which was renewed every time it was eaten.

Now, Prometheus knew a deadly secret which, if he told it, would cause Zeus's downfall. What this secret was, no one today knows. For a moment, Prometheus thought he would reveal it to save himself. Immediately, however, he acknowledged to himself that he had, indeed, stolen the fire from the gods. He accepted his punishment, scorning to tell the secret. He comforted himself with the thought that he had

Diadoumenus, 440–430 B.C. Roman copy of a Greek original by Polyklietos. The Metropolitan Museum of Art, Fletcher Fund, 1925. (25–78.56)

given a divine gift—that is, he had sacrificed himself to Man, whom he had created.

That night, Man slept in a cave. Close to him huddled a dog, growling and twitching in his sleep, while in front of the fire, which crackled and leapt in the hollow of a rock, a cat lay purring.

Developing Comprehension Skills

1. According to the myth, how did the world start? How did the gods come into being?

2. Choose any three of the gods and goddesses in this myth. For what personal quality or power was each god or goddess noted?

3. The gods were angry with Prometheus because he stole fire from the sun and gave it to Man. How did the gods think Prometheus's action would change the world?

4. Arrange the following events in the order they occurred.
   a. Prometheus dipped his torch into the sun and handed the torch to Man, giving him the gift of fire.
   b. Prometheus asked his brother to bestow on Man a valuable gift.
   c. Prometheus scooped up a handful of earth and formed an image in the shape of the gods.
   d. Prometheus was chained to a rock on a mountain.
   e. Epimetheus and Prometheus decided to give each animal a gift that would help it survive.
   f. Epimetheus said the last gift was gone.
   g. The gods became enraged.

5. Epimetheus and Prometheus gave the other animals many gifts. These included courage, strength, and keenness of mind (intelligence). However, the gods thought fire was a much more valuable gift. Why do you think fire was considered more valuable?

Reading Literature: Greek Myths

1. **Recognizing Characters.** Each of the following gods and goddesses was important to the Greeks as the explanation for something in nature. Identify the title and the most important action or job of each god or goddess.

   a. Aphrodite   d. Poseidon
   b. Zeus   e. the Horae
   c. Atlas

2. **Understanding Purpose.** Myths were told to explain nature, to teach about life, or to entertain. What is the purpose of this myth?

3. **Making Comparisons.** Modern western religions believe in one God. That God is all-powerful, all-good, and all-seeing. Compare this idea with the gods of ancient Greece described in this myth.

4. **Using Details To Make Inferences.** Sometimes facts and ideas are stated directly in a story. Other times they are not stated directly. However, you use information given in the story to guess at those facts and ideas. This is called **making inferences**. Use information in this myth to decide whether or not dogs and cats were used as pets in ancient Greece. Tell the details from the myth that led you to your answer.

Developing Vocabulary Skills

Recognizing Base Words. A **base word** is a word on which other words are based. For example, *rewrite* and *writer* are both formed from the base word *write*. Word parts may be added at the beginning of a base word, as in *rewrite*. They may be added at the end of the word, as in *writer*. Sometimes word parts are added at both the beginning and end of a base word, as in *unbelievable*. Recognizing base words will help you figure out the meaning of longer, unfamiliar words.

Each of the following words is from "The Beginning of the World." Read each word and identify the base word. Sometimes the spelling of the base word is changed slightly. For example, the base word of *miraculous* is *miracle*. On your paper, write the base word only.

1. mountainous
2. colorful
3. shapeless
4. renew
5. goddess
6. immortal
7. kingdom
8. secretly
9. valuable
10. impenetrable

Developing Writing Skills

1. **Writing an Explanation.** "The Beginning of the World" introduces many gods and goddesses in Greek mythology. Several of the goddesses are introduced in groups. Three important groups are the Muses, the Fates, and the Furies. Develop a paragraph to summarize these characters.

   Pre-Writing. Review the descriptions given in the myth for the Muses, the Fates, and the Furies. Match each group with the area of life it affected:

   conscience   destiny   art

   Then, choose two descriptive details from the following list for each group.

Moirai	spinners
Erinyes	nine
punishers	Memory's daughters

   Next, skim the story one last time. Look for any additional details about the Muses, the Fates, or the Furies. If you find any, add them to your notes.

   Last, organize your ideas. Make sure all the details in each group are about the same characters.

   Writing. Write the paragraph. Introduce only one group at a time. Name the group, and then present important details to describe its role. Keep your sentences short but complete.

   Revising. Read your paragraph to another person. Ask the person to summarize each of the three groups. Also ask the person to point out any part of your paragraph that is hard to understand. Change that sentence so that it gives a clearer picture.

2. **Putting Yourself into the Story.** Imagine that you were the first person in the Greek myth of creation. Think about what happened to you. Think about what you saw or felt. Write one or two paragraphs to describe the events. Use *I* to refer to yourself. Describe the setting and the action. Include your personal reactions to the events.

Pandora, the First Woman

The last selection described the creation of Man. This selection tells about the creation of Woman. What does this myth tell you about ancient Greek attitudes toward women?

TRADITIONAL GREEK MYTH
Retold by Sally Benson

Although Zeus had punished Prometheus for stealing the divine fire from the chariot of the sun, he was not satisfied. He felt the gods should seek retaliation against Man for accepting the stolen gift. Summoning all the gods to the great hall, he asked them what they thought would plague and torment Man the most. It was decided, after many suggestions and arguments, that a woman might harry him and plant seeds of ambition and dissatisfaction in his breast. So, in much the same way as Prometheus had made Man, they brought clay from the earth and created a woman. They named her Pandora (pan dor′ ə).

When she was given life, Pandora was endowed by the gods with every gift; Aphrodite bestowed beauty on her, Hermes gave her the art of persuasion, Apollo donated the love of music, and the Charities trained her in the social arts. Then, Hephaestos fashioned an exquisite box of pure gold into which were put all the evils that have plagued mankind ever since—disease, famine, fever, envy, greed, gluttony, hatred, and intolerance. It did not seem possible that a thing as lovely as the golden box could contain so many ills.

As they were about to close the box, the gods and goddesses regretted their hasty decision. Although they were too proud to abandon the idea altogether, they added one beautiful gift that would lessen the pain caused by all the other disasters. This gift was called Hope. The gods tucked it down into the bottom of the box. Then they cautioned Pandora not to open the box, for it was intended as an offering to the man who took her in marriage.

Then, bidding her goodbye, they gave her to Hermes, the messenger who bore her away with him to the earth. Hermes left her with Epimetheus, who was so struck by her unusual beauty and grace that he gladly took her into his home.

Seeing the golden box under her arm, he asked her what it contained. She answered that she did not know, exactly, but that she had been told to give it to the man she married. She placed it on a table and its brilliance lighted the entire room.

Epimetheus cautioned Pandora not to look at the contents of the chest until he had asked the advice of his brother. Then he left her alone. He traveled a whole day until he reached the mountain where Prometheus lay in chains. When he heard the story, Prometheus suspected a trick. He told Epimetheus to hasten back and hide the box in a place so remote that no one could ever find it.

In the meantime, Pandora explored her new home. She picked flowers and scattered their petals, which were soft and fragrant, under foot. She brought cold, sparkling water from the brook that roared over clean stones at the foot of the hill. She took honey from the bees and fruit from the trees. Each time she entered the house, the shining box caught her eye. More than once, she stopped to touch it, shake it, and wonder what it might hold. All day long she kept busy, until, as night drew near, she could find nothing else to do. Drawing a chair up to the table on which the box lay, she sat down, hypnotized by its beauty and glitter. Occasionally, she went to the door and looked in the distance to see if either Epimetheus or Man were approaching.

Finally, she took the box from the table and held it, turning it over and over, admiring its exquisite design. It was almost dark and she was all alone.

"Surely," she thought, "it can do no harm to open this lovely thing a mere crack and see what it contains. Is it a crown? A precious jewel? A magic cloak? A gift from the gods must be something both beautiful and rare."

As she thought this, Pandora opened the box a little, and peering in, saw nothing. Angry and emboldened, she opened it wider and saw what at first looked to be a brown, ugly cloud. The cloud moved and separated. Then, with a loud buzzing sound, hundreds of things resembling insects escaped into the room. Terrified, she tried to close the box, but her hands shook and she could not manage the catch. It was almost empty when she finally slammed the lid. Only one thing remained. This was Hope, which had lain on the bottom.

She hurriedly placed the box on the table again and ran to the door to see if Epimetheus or Man were in sight. She looked around the room to make sure that none of the evils remained to be seen. She shook her robe in fear that some might lurk in its folds, and she combed her hair free of them. Then, she set the table for supper, selecting the ripest fruits, the most delicious berries, and the loveliest scented flowers. Pulling her chair far away from the table, she sat down to await Epimetheus and Man.

When Epimetheus arrived with Man, they found her innocently busy mending clothes. She looked so beautiful sitting there that Epimetheus almost forgot to ask her whether or not she had looked in the box. When he asked her, she pretended for a moment to have no idea what he meant. "The box?" she queried. "Oh, that one! It

Pandora, 1910–12, ODILON REDON. National Gallery of
Art, Washington, D.C., Chester Dale Collection, 1962.

had slipped my mind entirely. Yes, I did
open it a little, and there is a lovely, irrides-
cent thing lying in it. It is more beautiful
than the rarest jewel, and it is called Hope."

"We will keep it there," Epimetheus said.

She made no mention of the ugly, brown
cloud composed of hundreds of ills that had
flown out into the world. Therefore, it was
some time before Epimetheus and Man
knew that the box had contained anything
but Hope. When they did learn, Pandora
had so endeared herself to them that they
could not punish her. They looked at her
sadly, unable to speak. Seeing the disap-
proval in their eyes, she tried to defend her
disobedience. "It is true that I opened the
box," she argued. "But it also true that I
allowed the evils to escape into the world. I
brushed them from the room. They are not
here and cannot harm us. Our house har-
bors only Hope."

Developing Comprehension Skills

1. According to the myth, was the first woman made in the same way as the first man?

2. Why was woman created?

3. Find the paragraph that describes Pandora opening the box. List the events in this paragraph in time order. Identify two words in this paragraph that signal time order.

4. Zeus and the other gods sent a box full of evils to earth. What does this action reveal about Zeus's personality?

5. Pandora disobeyed orders and opened the box. Do you think Pandora should be forgiven or punished for her action? Why?

Reading Literature: Greek Myths

1. **Analyzing Character.** Describe Pandora's character traits or qualities. Is she an evil person? Give reasons for your answer.

2. **Identifying Setting.** Describe two places where the action of this myth occurs?

3. **Identifying Characters.** Aphrodite, Hermes, and Hephaestos, among others, bestow gifts upon Pandora. Explain how each gift is particularly fitting for that god or goddess to give. Refer to the descriptions of gods and goddesses in "The Beginning of the World" if necessary.

4. **Making Inferences.** What sort of attitude did the Greeks who created this myth have toward women? Did they think of women in a positive or favorable way? Or did the Greeks view women in a negative or unfavorable way? What position do you think women held in ancient Greek society? Give reasons from this story for your answers.

Developing Vocabulary Skills

Recognizing Prefixes. A word part added to the beginning of a base word is called a **prefix**. The word part *un* is a prefix in *unusual*. A prefix has its own meaning. When a prefix is added to a base word, it changes the meaning of the word. For example, *usual* means "common or ordinary." The prefix *un-* means "not." Therefore, the word *unusual* means "not common, not ordinary."

Two other prefixes that mean "not" are *non-* and *in-*. For example, *nonfiction* means "not fiction" and *incorrect* means "not correct."

Some words seem to begin with a prefix but really do not. It is not difficult to decide if a word has a prefix. Look at what remains if you omit the beginning word part. *Unable* becomes *able*, a base word that makes sense. *Uncle*, however, becomes *cle*, a word part that does not make sense.

Read the following words. In some, a prefix meaning "not" has been added to a base word. Other words appear to begin with a prefix, but they do not. Copy each word on your paper. If the word includes a prefix, write the prefix separately from the rest of the word.

Examples: a. in complete   b. inch

1. unfair
2. inactive
3. nonstop
4. unite
5. intolerance
6. unknown
7. interest
8. nonliving
9. none
10. undo

Developing Writing Skills

1. **Developing an Argument.** Frequently the term *argument* is used to describe a planned presentation of ideas that support a belief or

statement. For example, a lawyer in court may present an argument that shows why the client was right in acting a certain way. Develop an argument to answer the following question. Make your argument from one to three paragraphs long.

According to the myth, who actually caused the evils to be set loose in the world: Pandora, Epimetheus, Prometheus, Man, or Zeus?

Pre-Writing. To organize your ideas, arrange the five names. Start with the person in the myth most responsible for the release of evil. Next to each name, list the actions that explain that person's responsibility. You may change your mind as you work. If so, rewrite the list or draw arrows to show the change in order.

Writing. Begin your argument by identifying the person at the top of your list. Tell why you hold that person most responsible. Be sure to support your statement with specific reasons from your list. Include at least three details to explain your argument. Use direct, forceful words.

Revising. Read your argument to another person. Does it convince the person of your idea? If not, ask the person to explain why. Rewrite that section of your argument.

2. **Writing a Myth.** Choose a familiar object in nature, such as a rabbit or a rainbow, or a manmade object such as scissors or a toaster. Write a myth explaining how one of the Greek gods or goddesses created that thing. Your story may be serious or funny. Use one of the gods or goddesses mentioned in the story "The Beginning of the World."

Developing Skills in Speaking and Listening

Relating a Myth. Myths began as stories told by one storyteller after another. Choose either myth: the creation of man or the creation of woman. Prepare to tell the myth in your own words. If you like, you may write short notes to remind yourself of the order of the events. Then present your myth to a group. Be sure to speak loudly enough for everyone to hear. Speak with feeling to make the story come alive.

Arcadia, 1883, THOMAS EAKINS. Hirshhorn Museum and Sculpture Garden, Smithsonian Institution, Washington, D.C.

The Flood

TRADITIONAL GREEK MYTH
Retold by Sally Benson

Mythology and religion from around the world tell about great floods. What is the cause of the flood in this myth? How do humans survive the flood?

The first age of humans was called the Golden Age. It was an age of innocence and happiness, as the evils that had escaped from Pandora's box had not grown large enough to cause any serious damage. There were no seasons, and perpetual spring reigned. All things that people needed to sustain themselves grew in the fields, and it was not necessary to sow or reap crops. Because the air was so soft and warm, people lived in the open or roamed from place to place, carefree and content.

After a time, Zeus decided to shorten the time of spring and divide the year into seasons. Then, houses became necessary to protect the young and aged from the cold. People learned to plow and cultivate their lands and to rob the forest of its trees to build homes. This was called the Silver Age.

With food growing scarcer, people became more grasping. They clung tightly to the lands they had cultivated and guarded their homes. They became suspicious of neighbors who had more than they, and their tempers flared. They began to quarrel

Composition—Storm, 1913, WASSILY KANDINSKY.
The Phillips Collection, Washington, D.C.

amongst themselves, and often blows were exchanged. This age of humans was known as the Bronze Age.

Then followed the Iron Age, a period of horror for the inhabitants of the earth. Crime burst on the world, and honor fled. People outwitted their friends and duped them for gain. They built fences around their properties and were proud of their wealth and prestige in the community. They despoiled the forests of wood to build boats, and they sailed out on the sea and robbed it of its treasures. Not satisfied with what the earth produced on its surface, they dug into it and mined ore and metals. They found iron and gold and fashioned them into weapons. With the weapons, they killed their enemies. Wars became common on the earth.

Then Zeus, burning with rage at the stupidity of people, summoned all the gods to a mighty council. They came from everywhere, taking the road to the palace of heaven. The road is still visible on clear nights stretching across the dark blue sky. It is called the Milky Way.[1]

Zeus addressed the assembly in stern, indignant tones. He told them of the frightful conditions that existed on the earth. Then he announced that he intended to destroy every person who dwelt on it and to create a new race that, unlike the first, would be worthy of life. Turning, he seized

a thunderbolt in his bare hands. He was about to hurl it to earth and wipe out all life, when he realized that such a mighty conflagration would even set heaven afire. He changed his plan and announced that he would flood the world.

With the help of all the gods, Zeus captured the north wind, which scatters the clouds, and chained it up. The south wind was sent out to blow the clouds together, and soon the sky was pitch black and threatening. There was a terrific clash as the clouds met, and rain fell in torrents. Fields were flooded, crops destroyed, and fruit was beaten from the trees.

Zeus called on his brother Poseidon to loose the rivers from their course and rout the ocean from its bed. He implored his brother, Hades, to rock the land with violent earthquakes. The sea washed over the shores. Cattle, fowl, people, and houses were swept away in the torrent. The temples of the gods, long neglected, fell into the waters. The whole world was a mighty sea. Here and there, for a while, one could see a few people who had taken to their boats or sought protection on a hilltop, but soon these disappeared in the swirl of the angry flood.

Only one mountain rose above the maddened waters, and this was called Parnassus (pär nas′səs). On this mountain a man and his wife found refuge with some of the innocent creatures of the earth. The names of the humans were Deucalion (doo kal′yən) and Pyrrha (pir′ə). They were descendants of Prometheus, who had allowed himself to

---

1. **Milky Way**, a thick band of light that crosses the sky at night. It is composed of clouds of gases and billions of stars.

Paestum, 1982, PHILIP PEARLSTEIN. Collection of the Artist. Courtesy of Hirschl and Adler Modern, New York.

be tortured through eternity for the sake of mankind. Deucalion and Pyrrha had taken no part in the warfare and hatred that had swept the earth. He was a just, honest man; she was a faithful worshipper of the gods. Looking down from Olympus, Zeus saw them clinging to the rocks on Parnassus, the water already washing about their feet and ankles. Remembering the blameless lives they had led, he unchained the north wind

to drive away the clouds, and Poseidon directed his son, Triton, to blow on his shell and sound a retreat to the waters. The sea returned to its bed, and the rivers subsided.

Then Deucalion said to Pyrrha, "O my wife, only surviving woman, you are joined to me first by the ties of kindred and marriage and now by common danger. Would that we possessed the power of our ancestor, Prometheus, and could renew the race as he first made it! But as we cannot, let us seek yonder temple and inquire of the gods what remains for us to do."

They walked toward the temple, slipping and falling on rocks covered with slime. The temple was almost in ruins, and no fire burned on its altars. There they kneeled and prayed for help. The goddess Themis (thā' məs) answered, "Depart from the temple with heads veiled and garments unbound, and cast behind you the bones of your mother."

They looked at one another in astonishment. Where could they find the bones of their mother? Also, if they found them, how could they desecrate their mother's bones by casting them to the ground?

Finally, Pyrrha spoke. "We cannot obey," she said firmly. "We dare not treat the remains of our parents with such disrespect as this."

Upon leaving the temple, they sought protection in a nearby wood and talked over what they should do. Then Deucalion said, "Either I am deceiving myself, or the command is one we may obey without impiety. The earth is the parent of all. The stones are her bones. These we may cast behind us, and I think this is what the goddess means. At least, it will do no harm to try."

They veiled their faces, unbound their garments, and, picking up stones, they cast the stones behind them. The stones, striking the earth, grew soft and began to assume shape. Slowly, they showed a vague resemblance to the human form, as a statue does when it is half finished by a sculptor. The moisture and slime that covered them became flesh. The stony part became bones. The veins in the rocks became human veins. The stones thrown by Deucalion turned into men, and those cast by Pyrrha grew into women.

Thus, a whole new race was created. It was a hardy race whose very bones contained stone from the earth, a race that owed its existence to the descendants of the hero who had first made Man.

Developing Comprehension Skills

1. List the Ages of humans from the earliest to the latest. Describe each of the Ages in your own words.

2. How does the name of each Age suggest the quality of the Age?

3. How many people survived the flood? Who were they? Why were they allowed to live?

4. Do you think the new race of humans that was created after the flood will be different from the race described in the myth? Why or why not?

Reading Literature: Greek Myths

1. **Recognizing Purpose.** What is the purpose of this myth? That is, what main idea is it trying to explain?

2. **Understanding Characters.** In "The Flood," Deucalion and Pyrrha are described only briefly. Usually the most important characters in a story are described in detail. List all the characters in "The Flood." Which characters do you think are most important in this story? Why do you suppose less important characters are also included?

3. **Understanding Figurative Language.** Writers and good storytellers try to get their audience to see and think about things in a new way. To do this, they describe familiar things in unfamiliar terms. This is called **figurative language**. For example, in this myth Deucalion states, "The earth is the parent of all. The stones are her bones." What new ideas about the earth does this statement bring to your mind? Write your ideas in one or two sentences. Can you find another example of figurative language in the myths?

Developing Vocabulary Skills

Using Context Clues. As you read, you may see an unfamiliar word. You might look up the word in a dictionary. You could also ask someone to explain its meanings. There is another method that you can sometimes use to find the meaning. You can use the **context**.

The context of a word is the sentence or group of sentences in which the word appears. Clues to the meaning of the word often are found in the context. For example, you may not know the meaning of *serpentine*. However, if you read the word in the context of the following sentence, you can figure out its meaning.

> The serpentine road twisted and wound around the mountain.

The sentence tells you that the road "twisted and wound around the mountain." From this clue, you can figure out that *serpentine* must mean "full of curves, like a serpent."

The underlined words in the following sentences are from "The Flood." Use the context clues to figure out the meaning of each word. Select the best meaning from the choices given.

1. There were no seasons, and perpetual spring reigned. The weather was always sunny and warm; flowers were always in bloom.

lasting forever	never
short	unhappy

2. During the meeting with the gods, Zeus spoke in harsh, indignant tones that showed his displeasure with human beings.

understanding	angry
joking	friendly

3. Deucalion and Pyrrha did not desecrate, or destroy the sacred memory of, the bones.

dishonor	praise	explain	break

4. People <u>despoiled</u> the forests by chopping down all the trees for wood to build boats.

    planted   used   ignored   robbed

5. The ancient Greeks did not show <u>impiety</u>, or disrespect, for the gods.

    courtesy   lack of honor
    jealousy   high regard

Developing Writing Skills

1. **Writing About Character Traits.** You have now read about Zeus in three myths. Write a paragraph explaining what you have learned about him. Compare Zeus in this story with what you already knew about him from "The Beginning of the World" and "Pandora." Support your ideas with facts.

    Pre-Writing. Review the three stories. Gather information on the way Zeus behaves. List his main traits in each myth. Then compare Zeus's actions in one story with his actions in the other two. For example, in the story of Pandora, Zeus is angry and vengeful. Does he show the same traits in the other stories? Or does his behavior change? Develop a topic sentence for your paragraph. The topic sentence must clearly state the main idea, your opinion.

    Writing. Begin your paragraph with the topic sentence. Then give at least three examples to support the idea. Include details from the chart you made. Be careful to include only those details that prove your topic sentence.

    Revising. Check your paragraph. Make sure it explains the idea you had in mind. Is the topic sentence clear? Point out the three examples that support the topic sentence. Rewrite any sentence that does not do its job.

2. **Writing a Description.** Imagine that you were a god or goddess watching the stones change into people. Describe how the change took place. Tell what you saw and heard.

Developing Skills in Critical Thinking

Recognizing Slanted Writing. Very often, a writer chooses among several ways to make a statement. One way may simply tell the facts, as in this example: "The depth of the water here is twelve feet." This statement is called a **neutral** statement.

A second way may make the reader feel good about the facts. Note the difference between the first example and this one: "At twelve feet, this water is safe for diving." This statement has a **positive** slant.

A third way of making the statement may cause the reader to feel uneasy or disturbed about the facts. This third example has a **negative** slant: "The violent water has risen to a dangerous depth of twelve feet."

Read each of these statements from "The Flood." Tell whether each statement is neutral, has a positive slant, or has a negative slant.

1. Because the air was so soft and warm, people lived in the open or roamed from place to place, carefree and content.

2. The road is still visible on clear nights, stretching across the dark blue sky.

3. On this mountain a man and his wife found refuge with some of the innocent creatures of the earth.

4. They became suspicious of neighbors who had more than they, and their tempers flared.

5. They looked at each other in astonishment.

Perseus Slays the Gorgon

TRADITIONAL GREEK MYTH
Retold by Sally Benson

In this action-packed myth, the hero Perseus fearlessly fights his enemies. As you read of his adventures, look for Perseus's reasons for fighting.

Perseus (pur sē′ əs) was the son of Zeus and Danae (dan′ə ē). When he was born, his grandfather, Acrisius (ə crē′sē us), consulted an oracle and prayed to know what the infant's fate would be. To his horror, the oracle answered that the child would one day slay him. Acrisius was terrified over this prophecy. He wanted to murder Perseus, but he was too tender-hearted to do the deed himself. He finally decided to shut up Danae and her baby in a chest and set them adrift on the sea. He secretly hoped they would be dashed to pieces on the rocks.

Clinging to her baby in the dark, hot chest, Danae huddled in terror while the box whirled and dipped in the waves. It seemed days like before they were washed upon the shores of Seriphus (ser′ ə fus), where they were found by a fisherman. He took the mother and her baby to Polydectes (po′ lē dec′ tēs), the king of the country, who took them into his own home and treated them with kindness. Here Perseus grew to manhood.

Not far from Seriphus, there lived a horrible monster named Medusa (mə dōō′ sə) the Gorgon. She had once been a beautiful maiden whose hair was her chief glory, but she had dared to vie in beauty with Athene. In a rage, Athene turned her into a horrible figure and changed her beautiful ringlets into hissing serpents. She became cruel and so frightful looking that no living thing could behold her without being turned to stone. She dwelt in a foul, dank cavern, and all around lay the stony figures of men and animals that had unfortunately chanced to catch a glimpse of her and had been petrified by the sight.

When Perseus became of age, Polydectes told him the story of the monster and begged him to attempt her conquest. Athene favored Perseus and lent him her shield to take on his journey. Hermes gave him his winged shoes so that he might travel with the speed of the wind.

As he neared the mouth of the cave where the dreadful maiden lived, Perseus turned his back lest he see Medusa and

Medusa, 1892, ALICE PIKE BARNEY.
National Museum of American Art. Gift of
Laura Dreyfus Barney and Natalie Clifford
Barney in memory of their mother, Alice Pike
Barney.

share the fate of others who had tried to kill her. Slowly and stealthily, he walked backwards, holding his shield before his eyes and guiding himself by the reflections in it. He entered the cave. Beholding Medusa's head mirrored in the shining metal, he stopped in horror. Medusa lay asleep. Fastened securely to her scalp by the tips of their tails, snakes with awful breath writhed and twisted about her face and neck. Their eyes winked evilly. Water dropped from the roof of the cave, and the air was dank. In the halflight, Perseus saw hundreds of lizards and giant toads crawling over her body. The sight was so dreadful that he almost ran from it in terror. However, remembering his vow to Polydectes who had raised him, he advanced slowly, keeping

Medusa's image reflected in the shield. Closer and closer he crept until he stood within reach. And then he struck. Her head fell to the ground.

After the slaughter of Medusa the Gorgon, Perseus, bearing with him her head, flew far and wide, over land and sea. He eventually arrived at the country of the Ethiopians, of which Cepheus (sē′ fə yo͞os) was king. Cassiopeia (kas′ ē ə pē′ ə), his queen, had been so proud of her beauty that she had dared to compare herself to the sea-nymphs. This roused their indignation to such a degree that they sent a prodigious sea-monster to ravage the coast. Fishermen and ships were destroyed by the dreadful monster. Cepheus in dismay consulted the oracle, who directed him to sacrifice his daughter, Andromeda (an dräm′ ə də), to appease the deities. Weeping and sad, Cepheus ordered his beautiful daughter to be chained to a rock where the sea-monster could find her and devour her. He kissed Andromeda tenderly and hastened away, fearing to look back.

At this moment, Perseus, flying far overhead, glanced down and saw the maiden. She was so pale and motionless, that if it had not been for her flowing tears and her hair that moved in the breeze, he would have taken her for a marble statue. As he hovered over her, he said, "O maiden, undeserving of those chains, tell me, I beseech you, your name and the name of your country. Tell me why you are thus bound."

At first she was silent, half-frightened at the sight of the hero who floated in the wind above her. But seeing that he was not going to harm her, she told him her name and that of her country, and the punishment that had fallen on the land because of her mother's pride of beauty. Before she had finished speaking, a sound was heard far off on the water. Then the sea-monster appeared, its head raised, above the surface, cleaving the waves with its broad breast. Andromeda shrieked in terror, and her father and mother who were hiding not far away, rushed back to the rock. They stood near, wretched and helpless.

Perseus flew close to them and said, "There will be time enough for tears. This hour is all we have for rescue. My rank as the son of Zeus and my renown as the slayer of Medusa might make me acceptable as a suitor. I will try to win her, if the gods will only favor me. If she be rescued by my valor, I demand that she be my reward."

The parents eagerly consented.

The monster was now within a stone's throw of Andromeda. With a sudden bound, Perseus soared high into the air. As an eagle in flight sees a serpent below and pounces on him, so the youth dropped down onto the monster and plunged his sword into its shoulder. Irritated by the wound the monster raised himself up and then plunged into the depths. Coming to the surface once more, it tried to attack Perseus, who was still on its back. Like a wild boar surrounded by a pack of barking dogs, it turned swiftly from side to side. Perseus stuck to its back and struck it time and again with his sword, piercing its sides, its flanks, and its tail. The brute spouted water and blood from its nostrils, and the wings of the hero were wet. He no longer dared trust the wings to carry his weight, and he alighted on a rock which rose above the waves. As the monster floated near, Perseus gave it a death stroke.

The people who had gathered on the shore shouted so that the hills re-echoed the sound. Andromeda's parents, wild with joy, embraced their future son-in-law. Andromeda was unchained and descended from the rock.

At the palace a banquet was spread for them, and joy and festivity ruled the land. Suddenly, a noise was heard and Phineus (fin' ē əs), who had been betrothed to Andromeda, burst in and demanded the maiden as his own. It was in vain that Cepheus reasoned, "You should have claimed her when she lay bound to the rock, the monster's victim. The sentence of the gods dooming her to such a fate dissolved the engagement, as death itself would have done."

Phineus made no reply and hurled his javelin at Perseus. It missed its mark and fell to the floor. Perseus would have thrown his in turn, but the cowardly assailant ran and took shelter. His act was a signal to his band who set upon the guests of Cepheus. They defended themselves and a general conflict ensued. The old king argued with the fighters trying to stop them, but was ignored. He called the gods to witness that he was not guilty of this terrible outrage on the rights of hospitality.

Perseus and his friends fought on, but the numbers of their assailants were too great for them. Then Perseus thought once more of the Gorgon's head. "I will make my enemy defend me," he said to himself. He called out, "If I have any friend here, let him turn away his eyes!"

He held Medusa's head high. "Seek not to frighten us with your tricks," a man cried, and raised his javelin to throw it. He was instantly turned to stone. Another was about to plunge his sword into the fallen body of his foe when his arm stiffened. Men were petrified with their mouths open as they shouted in anger. The swords of those still alive hit against the bodies of their enemies and broke.

Phineus, still hiding, beheld the dreadful result of his injustice. He called aloud to his friends, but got no answer. He touched them and found them stone. Falling on his knees, he stretched out his hands to Perseus. "Take all," he begged. "Give me but my life!"

"Base coward," Perseus cried, "this much I will grant you. No weapon shall touch you. You shall be preserved in my house as a memorial of these events."

So saying, he held the Gorgon's head in front of Phineus. In the very form in which he knelt with his hands outstretched Phineas became fixed, a mass of stone!

Developing Comprehension Skills

1. In correct order, tell the events that led up to Polydectes's kindness in taking Perseus into his home.

2. What caused Medusa to become a horrible monster?

3. Perseus attempted to kill Medusa simply because Polydectes asked him to. What does this tell you about Perseus's relationship to Polydectes and about Perseus himself?

4. Prometheus stole fire in order to make his creation, Man, become like the gods. Remember what happened to Prometheus. Then think about what happened to Medusa and Cassiopeia when they compared themselves to Athene and the nymphs. What do the fates of the Titan and the two humans tell about the nature of the gods? What are some possible reasons for the strong reactions of the gods?

Reading Literature: Greek Myths

1. **Recognizing a People's Belief in Myths.** When a myth was retold over and over by different storytellers, it changed slightly. However, all the storytellers were careful to keep those parts that they agreed were important. As a result, each time the story was told, it taught important values. With this in mind, think over the story of Perseus. Which actions are rewarded and praised? Which are punished or made to appear undesirable? Identify at least one action of each type. Explain what the rewards and punishments suggest about the early Greeks.

2. **Comparing Characters.** Which of these three women in this myth do you learn the most about: Danae, Cassiopeia, or Andromeda? Write a sentence about her.

3. **Recognizing Relationships Between Gods and Humans.** Perseus was the son of Zeus and a human. Was he a god or a human? Were there any advantages to being the child of a god? Were there any disadvantages?

4. **Identifying Themes.** This myth has more than one theme, or general statement about life. One theme is that bravery will be rewarded. Another theme is a warning against certain actions or attitudes. Compare the adventures Perseus had with the Gorgon to those he had with the sea monster. What do the two adventures have in common? By including both events, or episodes, in the same myth, the creators of the myth stressed the bad effects of a certain action. What action is being warned against?

Developing Vocabulary Skills

Deciding Whether To Use the Dictionary or Context Clues. You have learned that context clues can help you figure out the meaning of an unfamiliar word. For example, clues in the following sentence suggest that *stealthily* means "in a sneaky, quiet way."

> Perseus approached Medusa *stealthily*, holding the shield before his eyes and walking backwards toward the monster in a sneaky, quiet way.

However, many sentences do not have enough context clues to help you with an unfamiliar word. For example, there are not enough clues in the following sentence to define *stealthily*. You need to check a dictionary.

> Perseus approached Medusa *stealthily*.

The underlined words in the following sentences are from "Perseus Slays the Gorgon." There are two sentences for each word. One sentence in each pair provides context clues for the word. For that sentence, write **Context**. The other sentence does not give enough clues to explain the meaning. For that sentence, write **Dictionary**.

1. Perseus no longer dared trust the wings to carry his weight, and so he alighted on a rock that rose above the waves.

2. Perseus alighted on a rock before he killed the monster.

3. Perseus claimed that he was a son of Zeus and that he was a valorous suitor.

4. The valorous Perseus was rewarded for his bravery and courage in rescuing Andromeda from the monster.

5. In the very form in which he knelt with his hands outstretched and face half averted, Phineus became fixed, a mass of stone!

6. Perseus warned his friends to keep their eyes averted, or turned away, from Medusa's terrible head.

Developing Writing Skills

1. **Comparing Reasons.** The reasons for a character's actions are called **motives**. Write a paragraph to compare Perseus's motives for killing Medusa with his motives for killing the sea monster.

    Pre-Writing. Think of at least two reasons why Perseus killed Medusa. Did he act for others or for himself? Be sure to consider the situation in which Perseus killed the sea monster. Were his motives the same or different? What did he hope to gain? Decide whether you will compare or contrast the slayings of the monsters. Write a topic sentence to state your idea. Select the clue words you will use in your paragraph.

    Writing. Begin with the topic sentence. In your paragraph, include at least three points to show the comparison or contrast of the killings. Be sure to use clue words to signal the comparison or the contrast. You may give your opinion of Perseus's actions if you wish.

    Revising. Read your topic sentence to another person. Ask the person to restate the idea in his or her own words. If the person cannot summarize the main idea, your topic sentence may need to be rewritten. Then, find at least three words in the paragraph that signal either comparison or contrast. If you have not used clue words, add them to your paragraph. You want the ideas to be clearly connected.

2. **Writing an Explanation.** Oracles have appeared twice in this myth of Perseus. In one, two, or three paragraphs, discuss the role of the oracle in each passage. Tell how the oracle affected the events in the myth. Also tell how the people reacted to the oracle's statements.

3. **Creating a Monster.** This myth contains a vivid description of a horrible monster. Part of the horror comes from the combination of a human with animals that most people do not like to be near. Write a paragraph to describe a monster that you might imagine. Use the same approach as the myth, but use different animals.

Developing Skills in Study and Research

Improving Understanding with Maps. The settings described in the myths are based closely upon the real landscape of Greece and the surrounding areas. You may appreciate the stories more if you see a map of the area. Examine the map on pages 58 and 59 of this textbook. Then tell how seeing the map helps you to understand or appreciate the story of Perseus.

Girl with Pigeons, 5th Century, B.C., Relief. The Metropolitan Museum of Art, Fletcher Fund, 1927. (27.45)

The Labors of Hercules

TRADITIONAL GREEK MYTH
Retold by Sally Benson

In Greek the name Hercules is spelled Heracles. It means "well-known because of Hera." As you read about the hero Hercules, decide why this name is appropriate.

The day Hercules was born, Hera declared war against him. He was the son of Zeus and Alcmene (alc mē′ nə). Hera, always hostile to the offspring of Zeus by mortal mothers, sent two serpents to destroy him as he lay in his cradle. Hercules seized the snakes and strangled them with his own hands.

When all efforts to kill Hercules failed, Hera abandoned attempts to destroy him. Instead, she bound him in service to his cousin Eurystheus (yōō ris′ thē əs), King of Argos. Hercules had to perform all of Eurystheus's commands. The tasks were so dangerous that Hera hoped Hercules would be slain.

Eurystheus ordered Hercules to engage in a series of desperate adventures, which are called "The Labors of Hercules."

At this time, the valley of Nemea (nē′ mē ə) was inhabited by a terrible lion. It was large and fierce and had overcome all the hunters who had been sent to capture it. Eurystheus bade Hercules to bring him the skin of this monster. Hercules went alone and sought the animal in its lair. Calling it forth, he set on the beast with a club, but his blows fell on the lion's thick skull in vain. Then Hercules caught it and strangled it with his bare hands, as he had the serpents. He returned wearing the dead lion's skin on his shoulders. The skin was so tough that arrows could not pierce it. Eurystheus was frightened, not only by the sight of the skin but also by this proof of the awesome strength of the hero. He ordered Hercules to deliver the accounts of his exploits outside the town in the future.

Hercules's next labor was the slaughter of the Hydra (hī′drə). This monster ravaged the country of Argos, and dwelt in a swamp near the well of Amymone (am u′ mō nē′). The well had been discovered by Amymone when the country was suffering from a dreadful drought.

Poseidon, who loved the maiden, had permitted her to touch a rock with his trident, and a spring of three outlets burst forth. Here the Hydra took up its position, polluting the clear waters and devouring any person who came to fill a pitcher at the fountain. The Hydra had nine heads, and its middle head was immortal.

Accompanied by his faithful servant Iolaus (i ō lā′əs), Hercules set forth to vanquish the monster. He found the Hydra lying near the spring, and he attacked it savagely. He struck at its heads with his club, but each time he knocked off a head two new ones grew forth. At length, with the help of Iolaus, he tied up the monster and burned away its mortal heads. Then they buried the ninth and immortal one underneath a rock.

Eurystheus was so enraged that his rival had performed another task successfully that he sent him off quickly to clean the Augean (ô jē′ ən) stables. Augeas (ô jē′ əs), king of Elis (ē′ lis), had a herd of three thousand oxen, whose stalls had not been cleaned for thirty years. Filth lay piled up almost to the oxen's heads and Hercules, seeing the state of the stables, was dismayed. It did not seem possible that he could clean them before nightfall as Eurystheus had demanded. However, two rivers flowed nearby, and Hercules diverted them from their beds and brought them through the stables. The clear rushing waters swept all the dirt before them, and by sundown the stables were washed and in order.

The next labor of Hercules was of a more delicate kind. Admeta (ad mē′ tə), the daughter of Eurystheus, longed to own the magic belt of the queen of the Amazons,

and Eurystheus ordered Hercules to go and get it for her. The Amazons were a nation of women. They were very warlike and ruled several flourishing cities. It was their custom to bring up only their female children. The boys were either sent away to neighboring cities or put to death. On this adventure, Hercules was accompanied by a number of young men who had volunteered to aid him on his quest. They finally arrived at the country of the Amazons. Hippolyta (hi pöl′ i tə), the queen, received him kindly, and consented to give him her belt. However, Hera was enraged that the hero was accomplishing his labor so easily. She took the form of an Amazon and persuaded the powerful women of the country that Hercules was carrying off their queen. They armed themselves and came in great numbers down to the ship. There Hercules, thinking that Hippolyta had betrayed him, killed her and took her magic belt back to Eurystheus.

Then, Eurystheus asked Hercules to bring him the oxen of Geryon (jir′ē ən). Geryon was a monster with three bodies who dwelt on the island of Erytheia (er′ē thē′ə) the Red. It lay at the west under the rays of the setting sun.

The oxen were guarded by the giant Eurytion (yōō rit′ē ən) and the two-headed dog, Ortheus (ôr thē′ əs). Hercules strangled the giant and the dog, then crushed Geryon to death, and brought the oxen safely to Eurystheus.

The most difficult labor of all for Hercules was getting the golden apples of the

Hesperides (hes per′ ə dēz), because he did not know where to find them. These were the apples that Hera had received at her wedding from the goddess of the Earth. She had entrusted them to the keeping of the daughters of Hesperus, who were assisted by a faithful dragon. After searching throughout the world, Hercules finally arrived at Mount Atlas in Africa. Atlas, who bore the weight of the heavens on his shoulders, was related to the Hesperides. Hercules thought that, if anyone, the Titan might be able to find the apples and bring them to him. Yet how could he send Atlas away from his post, and who would bear up the heavens while he was gone? In his mighty strength, Hercules took the burden on his own shoulders and sent Atlas to seek the apples. The giant Titan was only too pleased to be released from his eternal punishment and gladly went on the search. He called to the Hesperides, and they gave him the precious apples. Atlas reluctantly returned and took the heavens on his shoulders once more, and Hercules took the apples back to Eurystheus.

On his travels, Hercules encountered Antaeus (an tē′əs), the son of the Earth. He was a mighty giant and wrestler, whose strength was invincible so long as he remained in contact with his mother Earth. Antaeus compelled all strangers who passed through his country to wrestle with him. If conquered, which they all were, they were put to death. Hercules fought Antaeus and found that it was of no use to throw him, for he always rose with renewed strength from every fall. Finally Hercules lifted the giant Antaeus up from the earth and strangled him in the air.

Still another of Hercules's tasks was to bring Cerberus (sər′ bər əs) from the lower world. Cerberus was a gigantic, three-headed dog who guarded the gates of Hades's realm. Hades gave his permission to carry the beast to the upper air, providing Hercules could do so without the use of weapons. Accompanied by Hermes and Athene, Hercules journeyed to the realms of darkness. There, in spite of the monster's struggling, he seized it, held it fast, and carried it to Eurystheus. Afterwards, he took the dog back again.

Worn out by his adventures, which had taxed his strength to the utmost, Hercules became nervous and easily roused to anger. One day, in a fit of madness, he killed his friend Iphitus (ə fē′ təs). For this offense, he was condemned to become the slave of Queen Omphale (äm′ fə lē′) for three years. While in this service, the hero's spirit seemed broken. He refused to talk of his exploits and was content with the company of the hand-maidens of Omphale, assisting them in their spinning. Hercules even allowed their queen to wear his lion's skin.

When this service was ended, he married Dejanira (dā′ jan ir′ ə) and lived happily with her for three years. Once, when he was traveling with his wife, they came to a river. The Centaur Nessus (nes′ səs), half-man, half-horse, carried travelers across the river for a stated fee. Hercules forded the river himself but gave Dejanira to Nessus to be

Hercules Leading Cerberus to Eurystheus, 525 B.C., Greek vase.
The Louvre, Paris. Courtesy of Giraudon/Art Resource, New York.

carried across. Nessus attempted to run away with her. Hercules heard her cries and shot an arrow into the heart of Nessus. The dying Centaur told Dejanira to take a portion of his blood and keep it as a charm to preserve the love of her husband.

Dejanira did so, and before long thought she had occasion to use it. In one of his conquests, Hercules had taken prisoner a fair maiden named Iole (ī′ ō lē). When he was about to offer sacrifices to the gods in honor of his victory, he sent his wife for a white robe to use. Dejanira was jealous of Iole. Thinking this a good opportunity to try her love spell, she soaked the garment in the blood of Nessus. She took good care to wash out all traces of it, but the magic power remained. As soon as the garment became warm on the body of Hercules, the poison penetrated into all his limbs and caused the most intense agony. In his frenzy, he seized Lichas (lī' kəs), who had brought him the fatal robe, and hurled him into the sea. He wrenched off the garment. It stuck to his flesh, and he tore away whole pieces of his body. In this frightful state, he embarked on a ship and sailed for home. Dejanira, on seeing what she had unwittingly done, hanged herself. Hercules, realizing that he was dying, ascended Mount Etna. He built a funeral pyre of trees and laid down on the pyre, his head resting on his club, and his lion's skin spread over him. With a serene face, he commanded his friend Philoctetes (fil' ăk tē' tēz) to apply the torch to the pyre.

The gods felt troubled at seeing the champion of the Earth brought to his end. Zeus addressed them. "I am pleased to see your concern," he said, "and glad that my brave son enjoys your favor. But now I say

to you, fear not! He who conquered all else is not about to be conquered by those flames which you see blazing on Mount Etna. Only his mother's share in him can perish. What he derived from me is immortal. I shall take him to the heavenly shores, and I ask of you all to receive him kindly. If any of you feel grieved at his attaining this honor, no one can deny that he has deserved it."

The gods all gave their consent. Hera heard the words with some displeasure, yet not enough to make her question the decision of her husband.

So when the flames had consumed the mother's share of Hercules, the divine part rose from the flames with an awesome dignity. Zeus enveloped him in a cloud and took him up in a chariot drawn by four horses to dwell among the stars. As he took his place in heaven, the shoulders of Atlas bent lower with the added weight. Hera, now reconciled to him, gave him her daughter Hebe (hē' bē) in marriage. He dwelt, a hero among gods, until the end of time.

Developing Comprehension Skills

1. List the labors of Hercules that are described in this myth. Write them down in the order in which they are reported. There are seven labors reported here.

2. On page 36, in the first five paragraphs of the myth, identify three words or phrases that signal time order.

3. Give the character's reason for each action listed below. If the myth does not state a reason, figure out one that fits the information given in the myth.

   a. Hera tried to kill the infant Hercules.
   b. Hercules killed Hippolyta, the queen of the Amazons.
   c. Atlas returned and took back the burden of holding up the heavens.
   d. Nessus lied to Dejanira, telling her that his blood was a love potion.
   e. Dejanira sent Hercules a robe steeped in the poisonous blood of Nessus.
   f. The gods consented to accept Hercules into the heavens.

4. In the course of his adventures, Hercules killed several evil people, including the giant Antaeus and the Centaur Nessus. He also killed several innocent people, including Queen Hippolyta, his friend Iphitus, and the messenger Lichas. He was punished for only one of these actions. Should he have been punished for any other killings? Give reasons for your answer.

Reading Literature: Greek Myths

1. **Examining Setting.** One interesting quality of myths is their wide range of settings. The story of Hercules, for example, takes place not only on Earth, but also in heaven and in the underworld, the house of Hades. Identify episodes that take place in each of these three settings.

2. **Understanding Character Traits.** Hercules is shown to have both good and bad qualities, or character traits. Name some of each type. Which traits do you believe caused him to be considered a great hero?

3. **Understanding the Greek Gods.** Each of the myths you have read gives more information about the gods on Olympus, particularly

Hercules slaying the lion, 6th Century, B.C., Attic terra cotta black-figure amphora. Katherine K. Adler Fund.
© The Art Institute of Chicago. All rights reserved.

Zeus and Hera. Considering all the facts given so far, describe either Zeus or Hera. Mention both good and bad traits.

Developing Vocabulary Skills

Discovering the Meanings of Number Words. In the episode of the Hydra, the myth describes a spring with three openings. The *trident* of Poseidon had caused the spring to burst forth. The word parts in *trident* explain what this pitchfork looks like. *Trident* is from the Greek word part meaning "three," and *dent*, from Latin, means "tooth." Many other English words concerning numbers make use of Greek prefixes for these numbers. The following chart lists several Greek prefixes and their meanings. Use the information in the chart to answer the following questions.

Greek prefix	English meaning
mono-	one
di-, dia-	two
tri-	three
tetra-	four
penta-	five
hex-	six
hept-	seven
oct-, octa-	eight
dec-, deca-	ten
poly-	many

1. How many years are there in a *decade*?

2. How many musicians play in an *octet*?

3. How many angles are there in a *heptagon*? an *octagon*? a *polygon*?

4 How many athletic events are there in the *pentathlon*?

5. How many choices does a *dilemma* offer?

6. How many wheels are on a *tricycle*?

7. What number is a *decimal* system of counting based on?

8. How many gods does a *monotheist* worship?

Developing Writing Skills

1. **Comparing Characters.** Both Perseus and Hercules were sons of Zeus, each with a human mother. Was there anything similar in their characters or their situations? From the information given about Perseus and Hercules in this chapter, which hero seemed to be favored by Zeus? Write one or two paragraphs comparing the two heroes.

2. **Rewriting a Story with Details.** In this story you read about seven labors of Hercules. Choose one of the labors. Rewrite the story of the labor adding your own details.

   Pre-Writing. Outline the events in the labor you select. Keep the actions in order. Add details to the outline to include the following information:

   a. a clear description of the setting

   b. a description of the appearance of the person or object Hercules must fight

   c. an explanation of the amount of work involved

   d. comments about Hercules's feelings

   You may need to use your imagination to provide details not given in the myth.

   Writing. In two or three paragraphs, retell the labor. Write about events in the order they occur. Select words to make the ideas in your outline clear and lively.

   Revising. Read your account to another person. Ask if there is anything else the person would want to know about the story. Add those details to your explanation.

Theseus and the Minotaur

TRADITIONAL GREEK MYTH
Retold by Sally Benson

In this myth, the hero Theseus faces several conflicts. As you read, try to decide an important reason for the successes of Theseus.

Theseus (thē′ syoos) was the son of Aegeus (ē′ joos), king of Athens, and of Aethra (ē′ thrə), daughter of the king of Trœzen (trē zān′). He was brought up at Trœzen and, when he reached the age of manhood, was to proceed to Athens and present himself to his father. Before the birth of Theseus, Aegeus had placed his own sword and shoes under a large stone. He told his wife to send his son to him when the boy became strong enough to roll away the stone and take the sword and shoes from under it. When she thought that the time had come, his mother led Theseus to the stone, and he rolled it aside with ease.

The roads to Aegeus's country were infested with robbers. Therefore, Theseus's grandfather, the king of Trœzen, urged Theseus to take the shorter and safer way, which was to go by sea. However, the youth felt in himself the spirit and soul of a hero. He was eager to imitate Hercules, with whose fame all Greece then rang. Theseus wished to destroy the evil-doers and monsters that oppressed the country. For this reason, he took the more perilous and adventurous journey by land.

His first day's journey brought him to Epidaurus (ep′ ə där′ əs). There dwelt Periphetes (per′ ə fē′ tēs), who was the son of Hephaestos. This ferocious savage always went about armed with a club of iron, and all travelers stood in terror of his violence. When he saw Theseus, Periphetes set upon him viciously, but the giant soon fell beneath the blows of the young hero. Theseus took possession of his enemy's club and carried it ever afterwards as a memento of his first victory.

Several similar contests with the petty tyrants and marauders of the country followed, in all of which Theseus was victorious. One of these monsters was called Procrustes (prō krus′ tēz), or the Stretcher. He had an iron bedstead on which he tied all travelers who fell into his hands. If they were shorter than the bed, he stretched their limbs to make them fit it; if they were longer than the bed, he cut off their feet and ankles. Theseus tied Procrustes to the bed and cut off his head to make him fit.

Having overcome all the perils of the road, Theseus reached Athens at last, where new dangers awaited him. The sorceress Medea (mē dē′ a), had become the wife of Aegeus, the father of Theseus. She discovered by her magic arts who the newcomer was. Fearing the loss of her influence with her husband if Theseus should be acknowledged as his son, she filled the mind of Aegeus with suspicions of the young stranger. She whispered to Aegeus that the youth had come to poison him and that he, in turn, should administer a cup of poison to Theseus. When Theseus stepped forward to take the poisoned wine, Aegeus caught sight of his own sword hanging at the hero's side. Striking the fatal cup to the floor, he embraced the boy and called upon everyone to witness that he had found his son. Medea, detected in her villainy, fled the country and went to Asia. The country later called Media received its name from her.

The Athenians were at that time in deep suffering because of the tribute that they were forced to pay to Minos, king of Crete. Every year seven youths and seven maidens were sent to be devoured by the Minotaur, a monster with a bull's head and a human body. The horrid beast, strong and fierce, was kept in a labyrinth that had been constructed by Daedalus (ded′ ə ləs). The labyrinth was so artfully designed that whoever entered it could never find the way out unassisted. Paths led into paths, and all of them seemingly led nowhere. Here in the labyrinth the Minotaur roamed and was fed with human victims.

Every year when the time came for the youths and maidens to be delivered to the monster, Athens was plunged into mourning. Mothers trembled lest their beautiful daughters or brave sons should be chosen to feed the dreadful creature. After the victims had been chosen, the houses of the entire populace were draped in black as the procession of young people bravely set out for the labyrinth. When Theseus arrived in Athens, the time was approaching for the sacrifice. He noticed the sad faces of the people and asked his father to tell him the cause of their sorrow. Aegeus reluctantly told him the story. Theseus, indignant at the cruel and useless sacrifice, resolved to deliver his countrymen from the calamity or die in the attempt. The youths and maidens were drawn by lot every year, but Theseus, in spite of the pleas of his father, offered himself as one of the victims.

The morning for their departure dawned, and Theseus joined the weeping, shivering group. They were dressed in deep black, but Theseus had arrayed himself in bright colors, confident of victory. The ship that was to carry them to their destination had black sails, and Theseus promised his father that he would change the sails to white if he returned victorious.

When they arrived in Crete, the youths and maidens were exhibited before Minos. There, Ariadne (ar ē ad′ nē), the daughter of the king, saw Theseus and fell in love with him. She furnished him with a sword and with a spool of thread. She instructed him to fasten the thread to a stone as he entered the labyrinth. He was to unwind the spool as he made his way into the maze. As long as he kept one end firmly grasped in his hand, he could guide himself back to the daylight once more.

Cheered by these gifts, the young people entered the dark, wet caves. They clung together while Theseus fastened the thread securely to a jutting rock. Then, walking one behind the other, they followed the first path. Around and around they traveled, their ears alert for the slightest sound to warn them of the approach of the monster. It was pitch dark, and Theseus was careful of the thread lest it catch on a sharp corner and break off. They wandered for hours, too cold and frightened to sit down. Their eyes became accustomed to the darkness and they could make out the tall grey walls and hundreds of paths winding in the half-light. There was an odor of decay in the air, and on the ground were the white bones of the victims of other years.

Suddenly, they heard a tremendous bellowing and the stamping of angry feet. It was the Minotaur, ravenous from his year's fast and anxious to partake of the sweet blood of the youths and maidens. At the sound, there were screams of horror from the victims. Theseus begged them to be calm and ordered them to a place of comparative safety in the rocks. Then he advanced alone to meet the Minotaur. He saw the monster's head as it turned the corner.

Theseus, 1942, JACQUES LIPCHITZ.
Courtesy of Marlborough Gallery, Inc., New York.

Its mouth dripped in anticipation of the feast that awaited it. It uttered wild cries that resembled the bellowings of a bull and the roars of an insane human. As it caught sight of Theseus, it charged forward, ready to crunch him in its powerful jaws and devour him. With one quick movement, Theseus stepped forward and plunged his sword into the creature's breast. When the monster lay dead, the young people threw their arms around one another in a frenzy of joy. Following the precious thread, they made their way out of the labyrinth.

They silently crept to their ship, which lay in the harbor, and, with Ariadne, set sail for Athens. On their way home, they stopped at the island of Naxos (näk′ sôs). There Theseus dreamed that Athene commanded him to abandon Araidne. He awoke and roused his companions, leaving Ariadne asleep on the island.

On approaching the coast of Greece, Theseus forgot the signal and neglected to raise the white sails. Aegeus, thinking his son had perished, put an end to his own life. Thus, Theseus became king of Athens.

Developing Comprehension Skills

1. Put the following events in order:
   a. Medea told Aegeus to poison Theseus.
   b. Theseus decided to fight the Minotaur.
   c. Aegeus hid his sword and shoes under a stone.
   d. Aegeus saw that Theseus had his sword.
   e. Theseus fought Periphetes, son of Hephaestos.
   f. Theseus rolled aside the stone with ease.

2. What country demanded tribute from Athens? What was the tribute required? How did Theseus plan to end the tribute?

3. Name at least two ways in which Theseus was like his hero, Hercules. You may list events that happened to him as well as character traits.

4. You have read about three heroes: Perseus, Hercules, and Theseus. Which seems the most believable to you? Is any one of them described so well that you can imagine what he would do in situations outside the myth? Give reasons for your answer.

Reading Literature: Greek Myths

1. **Identifying Details of Plot.** The first enemy Theseus defeats is Periphetes, the son of Hephaestos. Who is Hephaestos? If necessary, refer to the chart on page 9. What

does Periphetes have that connects him with his father?

2. **Recognizing History in Myth.** In addition to explaining the origin of natural things, myths sometimes told the history of cities and countries. The Greek story of Theseus and the Minotaur, for example, has a connection to the real history of Athens. The real city of Athens had more than one conflict with Crete. On the real island of Crete, the people were fascinated by the symbol of the bull. Many ancient pieces of art from Crete show heads of bulls. There are also drawings of people "dancing" with bulls, that is, facing bulls in a bull ring without weapons.

What possible happening could be represented by Minos's demand that Athenian youths and maidens be sacrificed yearly to the Minotaur? What might Theseus's conquest of the Minotaur stand for?

3. **Recognizing Theme.** What part did Medea play in the story of Theseus? What lesson might be drawn from her story? What details in the story support your answer?

4. **Identifying Conflict.** Conflict appears in a story in several ways. First, the conflict may be a struggle between two persons. Second, the conflict may be a struggle between a person and a force in nature, such as the weather. Third, the conflict may be a struggle between a person and a supernatural force, such as a goddess. Finally, the conflict may be a struggle within a character. For example, a character may feel both the desire to fight a bully and a strong fear of the bully.

What kinds of conflict are there in the story of Theseus?

Developing Vocabulary Skills

Recognizing Suffixes. A word part added at the end of a base word is called a **suffix**. For example, in *helpless,* the base word is *help* and the suffix is *-less.* Sometimes the spelling of a base word changes slightly when a suffix is added. For example, in *happiness,* the last letter of the base word *happy* changes.

Read the following list of words from the myth "Theseus and the Minotaur." In each, a suffix has been added to a base word. Identify each suffix and base word.

1. traveler	6. silently
2. perilous	7. securely
3. viciously	8. dreadful
4. adventurous	9. useless
5. powerful	10. reluctantly

Developing Writing Skills

1. **Examining Literary Techniques.** Some of the happenings and characters in the story of Theseus may remind you of more recent stories. Write a paragraph to describe ways in which this myth is like another story you have read or a movie you have seen.

Pre-Writing. Try to find parts of the Theseus myth that are similar to another story you know. For example, Medea is like the wicked stepmother in fairy tales. The use of white sails on a ship to signal good news is common in other legends. You may know adventure stories in which long-lost children are recognized and saved because they carry some object belonging to the family. List at least three similarities between the Theseus myth and one or more other stories. Be sure to include the story titles.

Writing. You are writing a comparison. Use signal words, such as *more* and *less,* to connect the ideas in your paragraph. Include at least three examples to support the comparison of the stories.

Revising. Check your paragraph to be sure you included an accurate title for the story. Underline book titles, movie titles, and play titles. Use quotations marks to enclose titles of short stories, poems, and television programs. Be sure you have spelled characters' names correctly.

2. **Writing a New Solution.** Can you think of a way that Theseus could have conquered the Minotaur and saved his companions without Ariadne's help? Write at least one paragraph explaining your solution to the problem.

Developing Skills in Study and Research

Comparing Two Encyclopedias. You can get additional information on a research topic by using encyclopedias. Most sets of encyclopedias have indexes. All the topics covered in the encyclopedia are listed in alphabetical order in the index. The index tells which articles discuss each topic.

1. Use at least two different encyclopedias to learn more about the labyrinth on Crete. You might begin by looking up *labyrinth* and *Crete* in the index of each encyclopedia. On your paper, list the facts reported in each reference work. Compare the lists of facts. Then decide which encyclopedia gave you the most information.

2. Next, you can determine which facts are the most important. Compare the information given by each of the encyclopedias. Circle the facts about the labyrinth that were included in both encyclopedias. Both encyclopedia publishers included these facts. Therefore, the experts must agree that these are the most important ideas about the labyrinth. By checking more than one source for your research, you confirm the information you find. That is, you make sure it is correct and worth knowing.

Head of a Bull, 1500 B.C. Heraklion Museum, Crete. Courtesy of Scala/Art Resource, New York.

The Flight of Icarus

TRADITIONAL GREEK MYTH
Retold by Sally Benson

This myth is a sequel to the story of Theseus and the Minotaur. It also explains how something came to be. As you read, look for what is explained.

When Theseus escaped from the labyrinth, King Minos flew into a rage with its builder, Daedalus (ded′ ə ləs). He ordered the builder shut up in a high tower that faced the lonely sea. In time, with the help of his young son, Icarus (ik′ ə rəs), Daedalus managed to escape from the tower, only to find himself a prisoner on the island. Several times he tried by bribery to stow away on one of the vessels sailing from Crete but King Minos kept strict watch. No ships were allowed to sail without being carefully searched.

Daedalus was an ingenious craftsman and was not discouraged by his failures. "Minos may control the land and sea," he said, "but he does not control the air. I will try that way."

He called his son Icarus to him and told the boy to gather up all the feathers he could find on the rocky shore. As thousands of gulls soared over the island, Icarus soon collected a huge pile of feathers. Daedalus then melted some wax and made a skeleton in the shape of a bird's wing. The smallest feathers he pressed into the soft wax and the large ones he tied on with thread. While his father worked, Icarus played about on the beach happily. He chased the feathers that blew away in the strong wind that swept the island and sometimes took bits of the wax and worked it into strange shapes with his fingers.

It was fun making the wings. The sun shone on the bright feathers, the breezes ruffled them. When they were finished, Daedalus fastened the wings to his shoulders and found himself lifted upwards where he hung poised in the air. Filled with excitement, he made another pair for his son. They were smaller than his own, but strong and beautiful.

Finally, one clear, wind-swept morning, the wings were finished. Daedalus fastened them to Icarus's shoulders and taught him how to fly. He bade him watch the movements of the birds, how they soared and glided overhead. He pointed out the slow, graceful sweep of their wings as they beat the air steadily, without fluttering. Soon the

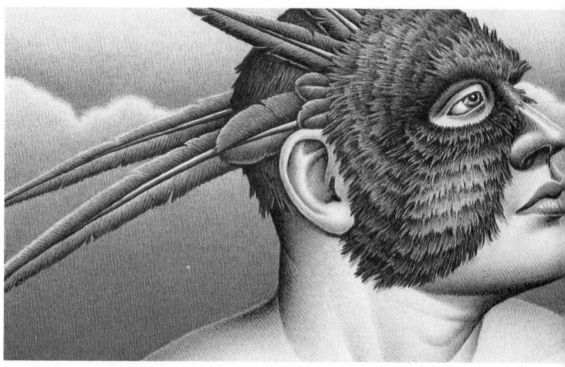

Violet-Tailed Sylph and Crimson Topaz, 1983, ROBERT LOSTUTTER. Courtesy of Dart Gallery, Chicago.

boy Icarus was sure that he, too, could fly and, raising his arms up and down, skirted over the white sand and even out over the waves, letting his feet touch the snowy foam as the water thundered and broke over the sharp rocks.

Daedalus watched him proudly but with misgivings. He called Icarus to his side. Putting his arm round the boy's shoulders, he said, "Icarus, my son, we are about to make our flight. No human being has ever traveled through the air before, and I want you to listen carefully to my instructions. Keep at a moderate height. If you fly too low, the fog and spray will clog your wings. If you fly too high, the heat will melt the wax that holds them together. Keep near me and you will be safe."

He kissed Icarus and fastened the wings more securely to his son's shoulders. Icarus, stood in the bright sun, the shining wings drooping gracefully from his shoulders. His golden hair was wet with spray and his eyes were bright and dark with excitement. He looked like a lovely bird. Daedalus's eyes filled with tears and turning away he soared into the sky, calling to Icarus to follow. From time to time, he looked back to see that the boy was safe and to note how he managed his wings in his flight.

Icarus, beating his wings in joy, felt the thrill of the cool wind on his face and the

clear air above and below him. He flew
higher and higher into the blue sky until he
reached the clouds. His father called out in
alarm. He tried to follow, but he was heavier and his wings would not carry him. Up
and up Icarus soared, through the soft
moist clouds and out again toward the glorious sun. He was bewitched by a sense of
freedom; he beat his wings frantically so
that they would carry him higher and higher
to heaven itself.

The blazing sun beat down on the wings
and softened the wax. Small feathers fell
from the wings and floated softly down,
warning Icarus to stay his flight and glide to
earth. But the enchanted boy did not notice

them until the sun became so hot that the
largest feathers dropped off and he began
to sink. Frantically he fluttered his arms,
but no feathers remained to hold the air. He
cried out to his father.

Daedalus, crazed by anxiety, called back
to him, "Icarus! Icarus, my son, where are
you?" At last he saw the feathers floating
from the sky and soon his son plunged
through the clouds into the sea. Daedalus
hurried to save him, but it was too late. He
gathered the boy in his arms and flew to
land, the tips of his wings dragging in the
water from the double burden they bore.
Weeping bitterly, he buried his small son
and called the land Icaria in his memory.

Developing Comprehension Skills

1. What did Daedalus build? Why did King Minos get angry with him?

2. Why did Daedalus want to fly? Why did his son Icarus fly so high?

3. The story says that Daedalus with pride watched Icarus fly but also "with misgivings." What misgivings do you think Daedalus had? Give a reason for your answer.

4. Do you think that Daedalus would have flown if he had known what would happen to Icarus? Give a reason for your answer.

5. This myth explains the origin of the name for an area. Do you think that is the major reason why this story continues to be told? What other element in the story may cause people to like it even today?

Reading Literature: Greek Myths

1. **Appreciating Setting.** What is the setting of this myth? Why is that important?

2. **Making Inferences About a Character.** What kind of a man do you think Daedalus was? This story began long after Daedalus built the labyrinth. It does not describe that job. However, it describes Daedalus's behavior as he worked at an escape. From what you learn about Daedalus here, do you think he enjoyed building the labyrinth? What statements in this story led to your answer?

3. **Recognizing Realistic Details.** Many of the myths tell about impossible happenings, such as fights with monsters or humans flying with birds' feathers. However, we are willing to believe in the story as long as some parts of it are possible. The story of Icarus seems more real than some of the other myths. One reason is that it includes more details that are possible. For example, Daedalus's attempt to bribe his way off the island sounds more possible than Hercules's trip to the underworld. List at least five other details that make the myth of Icarus seem real.

4. **Examining Elements of Myths.** What typical element of myths is absent from this story?

5. **Finding Cause and Effect Relationships.** Events are often related by cause and effect. However, a writer will not always provide signal words. The relationship may be implied, or suggested. Here is an example:

I can't think. There is too much noise.

The cause is too much noise. The effect is inability to think.

As you read, you cannot rely only on signal words. You must think about each event and how it connects with other events.

The following passage is from "The Flight of Icarus." Several events in the passage are related by cause and effect. Signal words are not always used to connect the events. Sometimes the cause and the effect are in separate sentences. Read the passage. Find at least two cause and effect relationships that do not use signal words. For each, write the cause and the effect on your paper.

Up and up Icarus soared, through the soft moist clouds and out again toward the glorious sun. He was bewitched by a sense of freedom; he beat his wings frantically so that they would carry him higher and higher to heaven itself.

The blazing sun beat down on the wings and softened the wax. Small feathers fell from the wings and floated softly down, warning Icarus to stay his flight and glide to earth. But the enchanted boy did not notice them until the sun became so hot that the largest feathers dropped off and he began to sink. Frantically he fluttered his arms, but no feathers remained to hold the air. He cried out to his father.

Developing Vocabulary Skills

Determining the Meaning of a Word. You have studied three ways to find the meaning of an unfamiliar word. First, you could find clues in the context, or the sentence around the word. Second, you could identify word parts. You could look for base words, prefixes, and suffixes that you already know. Third, you could look up the word in a dictionary.

Read each of the following sentences about "The Flight of Icarus." Decide how to figure out the meaning of the underlined words.

Select the best answer from the choices provided. Write it on your paper.

1. Keep at a <u>moderate</u> height.

   dictionary   context

2. When they were finished, Daedalus fastened the wings to his shoulders and was lifted upwards, where he hung <u>poised</u> in the air.

   word parts   context

3. Daedalus did not become <u>discouraged</u> by his failures.

   dictionary   word parts

4. Daedalus gathered the boy in his arms and flew to land, the tips of his wings dragging in the water from the double burden they <u>bore</u>.

   context   dictionary

5. He <u>bade</u> him watch the movements of the birds and told him to study their actions.

   context   dictionary   word parts

6. Daedalus, crazed by <u>anxiety</u>, called back to Icarus.

   dictionary   context   word parts

Developing Writing Skills

1. **Analyzing a Story.** Many of the myths you have read involved children and parents. Do you think the relationship between Daedalus and Icarus was more realistic than the father-son relationships in other myths, or less? How does the absence of gods and goddesses affect the way Daedalus and his son are presented?

   Write at least one paragraph explaining your opinion of this father-and-son relationship. First, state your opinion. Then, list the reasons for your opinion.

2. **Describing Feelings.** Imagine yourself in Icarus's place, flying above the sea. You are so excited and delighted by flying that you have forgotten all the warnings you have heard about dangers. You are aware only of the pleasures of flying. Write one to three paragraphs telling what you see and hear and sense.

   Pre-Writing. Make a chart with headings for the five senses: sight, hearing, smell, touch, and taste. Under each heading try to list two or three details about the flight. For example, you might *smell* the salty sea air. Then, expand, or add to, each detail in your list with an adjective describing it. Choose words that suggest how thrilled you feel during the flight.

Writing. Combine the descriptive details into sentences. Include details about each of the five senses.

Revising. Read your description. Does it make you feel the emotions Icarus felt? Can you feel the excitement of the flight? If, not, change your words to ones that are more alive.

Developing Skills in Speaking and Listening

1. **Expressing Emotions.** Choose one of these three sections of the myth of Icarus:

   paragraphs 1 through 4
   paragraphs 5 through 6
   paragraphs 7 through 9

   Prepare to read the section in a way that brings out the feelings of that part of the story. You may need to read fast to suggest excitement, slowly to show sadness, or softly to suggest warning. Practice trying to make your voice show the emotions the characters feel in the story.

2. **Evaluating a Presentation.** Work with a group of three or four other students. Listen to each group member read one of the sections of the myth. Discuss which speaking techniques were most successful in expressing emotions.

   Some questions to consider include the following:

   Did the person speak loudly enough?
   Were all the words clear and easy to understand?
   Did the speaker stress words that helped listeners feel the emotions of the story?

   You may think of other techniques that could be judged.

Greek Legends

In these legends, the gods and goddesses often disagree with each other. They change their minds. They help the humans they like and cause problems for humans they dislike. Yet the legends are not about the gods and goddesses. The legends are about the humans. They tell how the humans face every danger, whether from human enemies, strange monsters, or angry gods. Whether they win or lose, these human heroes show a great deal about being human.

The Building of the Trojan Horse, about 1760, GIOVANNI BATTISTA TIEPOLO.
Wadsworth Atheneum, Hartford, Connecticut. The Ella Gallup Sumner and Mary Catlin Sumner Collection.

Reading Literature: Greek Legends

What Is a Legend?

Like myths, legends are very old stories. They developed over many years as they were told and retold by storytellers. Legends probably started with facts. The facts gradually became less clear and less important as storytellers added more and more made-up details. However, the ideas suggested by the legends became more and more important.

For example, there is an American legend about George Washington as a child. According to the legend, George chopped down a cherry tree without permission but later admitted it. The story is not true, but its hero is a historical person. The made-up story became popular because it illustrates an important American ideal, honesty.

Every country has its own legends. They reflect the attitudes and goals of the people who tell them. They are part of a people's folklore, that is, all the stories, songs, and guidelines passed from one generation to the next. They last because they tell something about the people.

In this chapter you will read the most famous Greek legends. They are about the Trojan War and the fantastic adventures of the hero Odysseus on his way home from that war.

The History of Greek Legends

The legends you will read in this chapter are about 3,000 years old. They are based on events that happened even earlier.

Historians believe that the Trojan War actually happened around the middle of the 13th century B.C. Troy was an actual city in what is now Turkey. The Greeks and Trojans probably fought over trade rather than over a beautiful woman, as the legend says.

For hundreds of years after the Trojan War, poet-singers kept alive the memory of Greeks who had taken part in the battle. These warriors became the heroes of legends. Eventually many of the separate legends were combined in the poetry of Homer, who lived around 850 B.C.

Homer wrote *The Iliad* and *The Odyssey*, long poems about the Greek heroes. *The Iliad* is about the Trojan War itself. *The Odyssey* tells of the struggles of one warrior, Odysseus, to return home from the war.

The Elements of a Greek Legend

Characters. The major characters of legends are humans rather than gods. The heroes and heroines represent the ideals of their people. They often have high rank or special traits that set them apart. Odysseus, King of Ithaca, is the typical Greek hero, clever and brave.

Setting. The setting of a legend is usually the distant past. Most legends say the events occurred on Earth, but some picture fantastic places. The legends explain that these places no longer exist or have been lost. The setting is often broad in time and location. Odysseus's wanderings, for example, last ten years and take him to many lands.

Plot. The plot, or series of events in a story, concerns a struggle. This struggle, or **conflict**, may be between heroes. It may be between a hero, representing good, and a monster, representing evil. It may be inside a hero. For example, Odysseus must frequently fight despair.

Theme. In a story or poem, the **theme** is the main idea or statement about life. Greek legends present moral guidance. The legend of the Odyssey shows that the early Greeks believed in moderation and in hospitality. Legends also point out truths about human nature. Odysseus's struggles, for example, represent human determination.

How To Read a Greek Legend

1. Look for actions and words that show each character's traits.
2. Pay attention to the names of characters. To keep them separate in your mind, identify an important character trait with each name.
3. Watch for the role of gods and goddesses from Greek mythology. If necessary, review the chart on page 9.
4. Focus on the customs and ideas discussed in the legends. Try to draw some conclusions about the ancient Greek outlook on the world. Try to see the events as the ancient Greeks did.

Map of the Mediterranean Area

Adriatic Sea

SCHERIA

GREECE

▲ MT. OLYMPUS

THESSALY

▲ MT. PARNASSUS

ITHACA

• Aulis

ELIS

• Athens

• Nemea

Argos •

• Epidaurus

Troezen •

ARCADIA

SERIPHUS

• Sparta

Mediterranean

Sea

▲ MT. IDA

CRETE

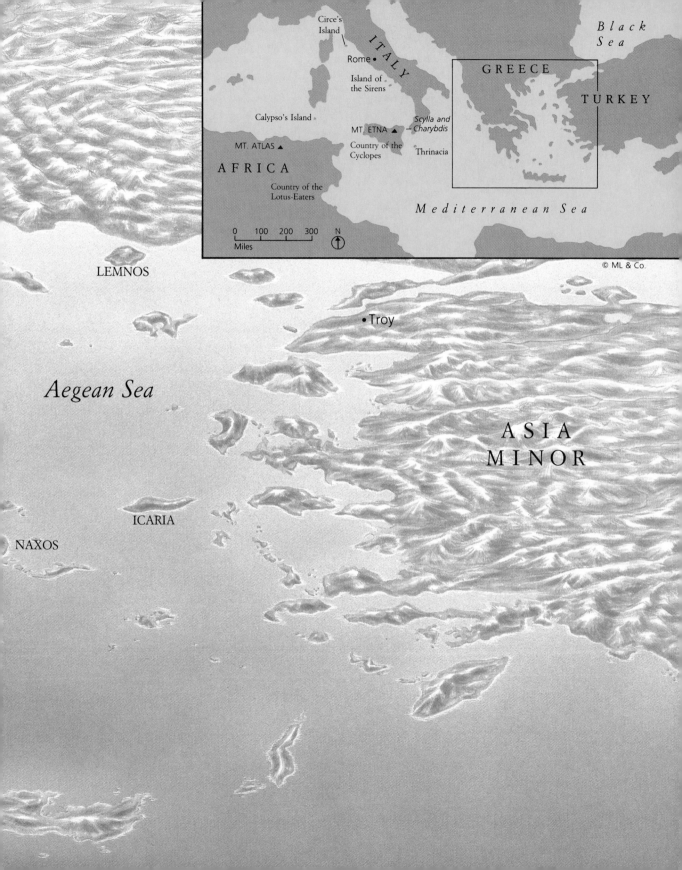

LEMNOS

Aegean Sea

• Troy

ASIA
MINOR

ICARIA

NAXOS

Circe's Island

ITALY

Rome •

Island of
the Sirens

Calypso's Island

MT. ETNA ▲

MT. ATLAS ▲

*Scylla and
Charybdis*

AFRICA

Country of the
Cyclopes

Thrinacia

Country of the
Lotus-Eaters

*Black
Sea*

GREECE

TURKEY

Mediterranean Sea

0   100   200   300
Miles

N
↑

© ML & Co.

The Trojan War

TRADITIONAL GREEK LEGEND
Retold by Sally Benson

According to this legend, gods and humans meddled in each other's affairs. As you read, notice who pays for the meddling.

When Peleus (pā′ lē əs) was married to Thetis (the′ təs) all the gods and goddesses were invited to the wedding feast with the exception of Eris (er′ is), goddess of Discord. Enraged at the slight, Eris threw a golden apple among the guests. The golden apple bore the inscription: "For the fairest."

Hera, Aphrodite, and Athene each claimed the apple. Soon they were quarreling bitterly. Zeus was not willing to make a decision on so delicate a matter. He sent the goddesses to Mount Ida, where the beautiful shepherd Paris, the son of Priam (prī′ əm), King of Troy, was tending his flocks. Paris was asked to make the decision about the goddesses.

The goddesses gathered around Paris, each extolling her own charms. Each one promised to reward him if he gave her the prize. Hera promised him power and riches; Athene told him that she would see that he gained glory and renown. Aphrodite whispered that he should have the fairest woman in the world for his wife. Paris decided in favor of Aphrodite and gave her the golden apple, thus making the other two goddesses his enemies.

Under the protection of Aphrodite, Paris sailed for Greece, where he was hospitably received by Menelaus (men′ ə lā′ əs), King of Sparta. Now Helen, the wife of Menelaus, was the very woman whom Aphrodite had destined for Paris.

Helen was the daughter of Zeus and a mortal, Leda. Helen was the most beautiful woman in the world and had been sought as a bride by hundreds of suitors. The young men loved her so devotedly that they swore that, no matter which of them she chose to wed, the others would defend her from harm all her life. She married Menelaus and was living with him happily when Paris became their guest.

Paris, aided by Aphrodite, persuaded Helen to elope with him, and he carried her away to Troy. Overcome by grief, Menelaus called upon his brother chieftains of Greece

Judgment of Paris, 15th Century.
Museo Nationale, Florence, Italy.
Scala/Art Resource, New York.

to fulfill their pledge and join in his efforts to recover his wife. Only one of them held back. His name was Odysseus (ō dis′ ē əs). He had married a woman named Penelope (pə nel′ ə pē) and was happy with his wife and child. He had no wish to embark on such a troublesome affair. One of his friends, Palamedes (pal′ ə mē′ dēs), was sent to beg him to join the quest.

When Palamedes arrived at Ithaca where Odysseus lived, Odysseus pretended to be mad. Seeing Palamedes approaching, he hastily yoked a donkey and an ox together to the plough and began to sow salt. Palamedes, suspecting a ruse, placed Odysseus's child before the plough, whereupon the father turned the plough aside, showing plainly that he was no madman. After that, Odysseus could no longer refuse to fulfill his promise.

Now, although Paris was the son of Priam, King of Troy, he had been brought up in obscurity because of a prophecy. The oracle had warned that he would one day be the ruin of the state. As he entered Troy with Helen, these forebodings seemed likely to be realized. The army that was being assembled in Greece was the greatest one that had ever been known. Agamemnon (ag ə mem′ nän), brother of Menelaus, was chosen as the commander-in-chief. Achilles (ə kil′ ēs) was the most illustrious Greek warrior; after him came Odysseus, famous for his wisdom and cleverness.

On the other hand, Troy was no feeble enemy. Priam was now an old man, but he had been a wise ruler and had strengthened his state by governing well at home and keeping peace with his neighbors. The principal support of his throne was his son Hector, a brave, noble young man. Hector feared danger when he realized the great wrong his brother Paris had done in bringing Helen to Troy. He knew that he must fight for his family and country, yet he was sick with grief at the foolish circumstances that had set hero against hero.

After two years of preparation, the Greek fleet and army assembled in the port of Aulis (ô′ lis). Here they suffered more delays: disease broke out in the camps, and there was no wind to fill their sails. Eventually, they set out for the coast of Troy and plunged at once into a battle with the Trojans. For nine years they fought, neither side winning over the other. The Greeks began to despair of ever conquering the city. Finally they decided to resort to a trick thought of by Odysseus. They pretended to

Athena Building the Trojan Horse, 470–460 B.C. Attic red-figure kylix. Archeological Museum of Tuscany, Florence, Italy.

be preparing to abandon the siege, and most of the ships set sail with many warriors on board. They did not head for home, however, but sailed to a nearby island, where they hid in a friendly harbor. The Greeks who were left in the camp built a huge horse of wood that, they said, was to be a peace offering to Athene. Instead, at night, they filled it with armed men and left it in their camp. The remaining Greeks then sailed away.

When the Trojans saw that the encampment had broken up and the fleet had gone, they threw open the gates to the city, and everyone rushed forth to look at the abadoned camp grounds. They found the immense horse and wondered what it could be. Some thought it should be carried back to the city and put on exhibition as a trophy of the war, but others, more cautious, were afraid of it. One of the people, Laocoon (lā äk′ ə wən′) the priest of Poseidon, tried to warn them against it. "What madness, citizens, is this?" he exclaimed. "Have you not learned enough of Greek fraud to be on your guard against it? For my part, I fear the Greeks even when they offer gifts."

As he spoke, he threw his lance at the horse's side. It struck, and a hollow sound like a groan came forth from it. The people were almost ready to take his advice and destroy the horse, when a group of people appeared, dragging a young man with them. He appeared to be a Greek prisoner, and he was brought before the Trojan chiefs. They promised him that they would spare his life on one condition; he was to answer truly the questions they asked him.

He told them that he was a Greek named Sinon (sī′ non), and that he had been abandoned by his countrymen, betrayed by Odysseus for a trifling offense. He assured them that the wooden horse had been made as a offering to Athene, and that the Greeks had made it so huge to prevent its being carried into the city. Sinon added that the Greeks had been told that, if the Trojans took possession of the horse, the Greeks would lose the war.

Then the people began to think of how they could move the enormous horse into the city. Suddenly, two immense serpents advanced from the sea. The creatures crawled up on the shore, and the crowd fled in all directions. The serpents slithered to the spot where Laocoon stood with his two sons. First they attacked the children, crushing their bodies and breathing their pestilential breath into the faces of the boys. Laocoon tried to drag his children away, and the serpents wound their bodies around his. He struggled pitifully to free himself, but they soon strangled him and his sons. In awe, the people crept back to the camp. They decided that the gods had taken revenge on Laocoon for talking against the wooden horse, which must be a sacred object. They began to move it into the city in triumph. All day, the Trojans feasted and sang around the horse, which they had placed in the main square of Troy. At last, exhausted from the festivities, they went to their homes and fell asleep.

When the city was quiet, the armed men who were hidden in the body of the horse were let out by Sinon. They stole to the gates of the city, which were closed for the night, and let in their friends, who had returned under the cover of darkness. They set fire to the city, and the people, overcome with feasting and sleep, were ruthlessly killed. Troy had fallen.

King Priam was the last to be slain, and he fought bravely to the end.

Menelaus hastened to the palace and found his wife, Helen. Not even Aphrodite could save Paris from the wrath of his enemies. He was killed, and Menelaus carried his wife safely back to Sparta.

Developing Comprehension Skills

1. Why did Paris take Helen to Troy?

2. How did Odysseus try to avoid going to war? What was his reason for not wanting to aid Menelaus?

3. Why did the Greeks resort to trickery in order to conquer Troy?

4. The Trojans believed Sinon when he said the wooden horse was an offering to Athene. Why did they believe him?

5. The oracle had prophesied that Paris would be the ruin of the state. Paris did play a part in the start of the Trojan War. Who else shared in the blame for the war?

Reading Literature: Greek Legends

1. **Connecting Characters and Plot.** Paris is offered one of three rewards. Why do you suppose he chooses the one he does? What does his choice tell you about his character?

2. **Identifying Conflict.** A story can tell about a conflict, or struggle, between a person and other people or outside forces, such as a flood. Such conflicts are outside a person, so they are called **external conflicts**. A story may also tell about a struggle within a person. For example, a person may want to be a good citizen but may not have the time to work in the community. The person must decide how to meet this responsibility. Such struggles are called **internal conflicts**. Identify three conflicts in this story. Who or what is involved in each of the conflicts?

3. **Putting Events in Time Order.** Explain how the Greeks use the Trojan Horse to conquer Troy. List the steps in proper time order.

4. **Identifying Setting.** The setting changes several times in the story of the Trojan War. List the settings in the order in which they occur.

Developing Vocabulary Skills

Determining the Meanings of Words. Each of the following sentences uses a word from "The Trojan War." Some of the sentences give context clues to the meaning of the word. For those words, write your own definition. The other sentences do not give enough context clues. For those, write **Dictionary**.

1. Palamedes was sent to beg Odysseus to join Menelaus's quest, the search for his wife.

2. Odysseus had no wish to embark on the quest of Menelaus.

3. Odysseus tried to play a ruse on Palamedes to escape joining the war, but Palamedes figured out the trick.

4. The Greeks built the Trojan horse as a ruse to defeat Troy.

5. They found the immense horse of wood and wondered what it could be.

6. The Trojan horse was immense, so huge that it could hardly fit through the city gates.

Developing Writing Skills

1. **Explaining a Saying.** In modern times, people sometimes use the statement, "Beware of Greeks bearing gifts." They are not really talking about Greeks or the Trojan War. However, the meaning of the warning is based on the story about Laocoon. Write a paragraph explaining your idea about the meaning of the phrase.

2. **Examining Motives.** The reason for a person's action is called a **motive**. A detective trying to prove that a certain person is guilty of a crime must establish a motive. That is, the detective must find a likely reason for the person to commit the crime. In "The Trojan War," it is obvious that Odysseus had no desire to help Menelaus. Neither did Hector wish to fight for his brother's cause. Yet both heroes joined the battle. What might have been their motives for doing so? Write three paragraphs explaining possible reasons for their actions.

   Pre-Writing. Think about the reasons that Odysseus and Hector decided to fight. For each character, try to answer the following questions. Refer to the story for details.

   Was he expected to fight? By whom?
   Why didn't he want to fight?
   What would he lose if he refused to fight?

   Then, organize your ideas. Write one topic sentence that summarizes why Odysseus joined the battle. Also, write a topic sentence that summarizes why Hector decided to fight.

   Writing. Begin the first paragraph with the topic sentence you developed about Odysseus. Then, present details that explain why he joined the war. Write one paragraph about Odysseus.

   Begin the second paragraph with the topic sentence you wrote about Hector. Then, give the reasons why Hector fought.

   For the final paragraph, explain whether the motives of the heroes were similar or whether they were different.

   Revising. Ask another person to read your assignment. Then have the person tell you the main motive for each hero's decision to fight. If the person cannot summarize the ideas you had in mind, then you have not written clearly. Ask the person to point out any sentences that are confusing. Rewrite those sections to make your ideas stronger.

3. **Making a Decision.** In this legend, Paris was forced to make a decision. His choice led to the start of a war. Imagine what it would be like to make such an important decision. Write a paragraph about being in such a situation. Describe your thoughts about responsibility as well as your feelings of power. Write in the first-person point of view. Use *I* and *me* to refer to yourself.

Developing Skills in Critical Thinking

Defining a Personal Hero. You have read many myths about heroes. A hero is a character who represents the ideals in a society. The ancient Greeks told of heroes such as Odysseus. Greek heroes fought against evils, had respect for the powers of the gods, and were not afraid to die. You might agree or disagree with the Greek view of heroes. Try to develop your own definition of a hero.

Establish your own standards for a hero. Think about real men and women whom you respect. What is it about them that makes them special? List at least five qualities that define your ideal hero. You might include the traditional values of bravery or physical strength. You might choose values important to your own everyday life, such as friendship and honesty.

Then, summarize the standards you choose. Write from two to three sentences defining a personal hero.

The Voyage of Odysseus

TRADITIONAL GREEK LEGEND
Retold by Sally Benson

Odysseus encounters many adventures that delay his return home. As you read, think about how Odysseus reacts to each conflict. What patterns do you see in his actions?

When Troy had fallen, Odysseus with his men set sail for home. No sooner were they out of the harbor than a dreadful storm blew up and drove their ship from its course. For nine days they were hopelessly lost at sea. Finally they sighted a small island, the country of the Lotus-eaters. Almost dying of thirst, the men first set out to look for water. When they had refreshed themselves, Odysseus told them to explore the island and find out who the inhabitants were. Soon the men came upon a group of people who received them hospitably and offered them some of their own food, the lotus plant, to eat.

Odysseus's men did not know the power of the lotus leaf. Anyone who ate one immediately forgot all about home and family and wanted to remain forever on the island. Half-starved and flattered by the attentions shown them by the islanders, the men from the ship were only too happy to sit down at the table and eat. Odysseus waited a while for his soldiers and then went in search of them. He saw them feasting and saw what they were eating. Knowing what effect the sweet-tasting lotus would have on them, he begged them to come with him. The men, who were by this time in dreamy half-sleep, did not even hear him. By force, he dragged them away and tied them to the benches of the ship until he hoisted the sails and got under way. The sea air soon cleared their heads, and they sailed on.

After many days they sighted the country of the Cyclopes (sī clō′ pēz). These huge giants each had but one eye which was placed in the middle of the forehead. They lived in caves and tended their flocks, eating whatever roots and wild grasses grew on the rocky shores. Odysseus left the main body of his ships at anchor and went with one vessel to the Cyclopes' island to search for supplies. He and his companions landed, carrying with them a jar of wine for a present. They wandered about until they

Cyclops, 1947. WILLIAM BAZIOTES. Walter M. Campana Memorial Prize. Oil on canvas, 48″ × 40″.

came to a large cave, which they entered. Finding no one about, they explored it. They found quantities of cheese, pails of milk, lambs and kids in wooden pens, and dried and salted meat. They ate some of the cheese, drank a few pails of milk, and were about to cook a roast of meat when they heard dreadful noises outside of the cave. Peering out they saw a frightful giant called Polyphemus (päl′ ē fē′ məs). He carried an immense bundle of firewood, which he threw to the ground at the mouth of the cave. Then he drove his flock of sheep and goats into the cavern to be milked, and, when they were safely in, he moved a large stone, closing the entrance. It was so large a stone that twenty oxen could not move it.

As the men quaked with terror, Polyphemus sat down and milked his goats. When he had finished, he turned his great eye around and saw the men who huddled in the shadows of the pens. He spoke to them, and his voice was a dreadful growl that echoed from the dripping walls. "Who are you?" he asked. "And where do you come from?"

Odysseus stepped forward and answered him humbly. "We are Greeks," he said, "returning from a great expedition. We have lately won much glory in the conquest of Troy. We are now on our way home, but we are lost. And, if you will offer us your hospitality, in the name of the gods, we will restock our larders, and be on our way."

Polyphemus did not answer. He reached out his great hand and seized two of the Greeks as easily as a man picks a handful of grass. He hurled them against the side of the cave and dashed out their brains. As their companions stood watching in horror, he pulled the men apart and ate them up, clothes and all. Then, having made a hearty meal, he stretched himself out on the floor and went to sleep.

Odysseus drew forth his sword and was about to kill the giant as he slept. Then he remembered the huge rock that blocked the entrance to the cave. He realized that, if he killed the giant, he and the rest of his men would be hopelessly imprisoned and would eventually die of starvation. All night, the men huddled in fright in the dark, damp cave. They were unable to decide what to do. When morning came, they were sunk in hopeless despair. The giant awoke, lazily stretched out his hand, and grabbed two more of the men. He hurled them against the walls and feasted on their flesh until there wasn't a fragment left. Then the giant moved the rock away from the entrance, drove out his flocks, and replaced the rock.

When he was gone, the men came out from their hiding places. Odysseus tried desperately to plan how he might avenge the death of his companions and make his escape with his friends. Searching the cave for a weapon, he found a massive tree trunk that had been cut by the Cyclops (sī′ kläps) for a staff. He ordered his men to sharpen the end of it to a fine point. When that was done, they seasoned it in the fire and hid it under the straw on the floor. Then four of the boldest were selected, and Odysseus told them of his scheme.

It was almost evening when they had finished their tasks, and they soon heard the Cyclops approaching. He rolled away the stone and drove his flock in as usual. After milking his sheep and goats, he seized two more men, dashed their brains out, and made his evening meal. After the giant had supped to his content, Odysseus approached him and handed him a bowl of wine, saying, "Cyclops, this is wine. Taste it and drink after eating your meal of man's flesh."

The giant was delighted with the taste of the wine and called for more. Odysseus

Ulysses and Polyphemus, 1982, EARL STALEY. Courtesy of Phyllis Kind Gallery, New York and Chicago. Photograph by William H. Bengtson.

gave him bowl after bowl of the heady drink, and this pleased the giant so much that he promised Odysseus that he would be the last of his party to be devoured. He asked his name, and Odysseus replied, "My name is No-man."

When he had drunk the last of the wine, the giant lay down to sleep. Then Odysseus called to his four friends and, lifting the staff, they thrust the end of it into the fire until it was red hot. Then they plunged it into the Cyclops's one eye.

The monster roared in pain. Odysseus and his men sprang back and hid themselves in the cave. Polyphemus bellowed

and called out to the other Cyclopes to help him. Hearing his cries, they came from their caves and flocked around his den. "What hurt," they asked, "has caused you to sound an alarm?"

"O friends, I die," he answered, "and No-man gave the blow."

"If No-man gave the blow," they said, "then you have been killed by a blow from Zeus, and you must bear it."

They turned away from the cave, leaving him groaning on the ground. He was not dead, only wounded, and in the morning he rolled the huge stone aside and let his flocks out to pasture. Although he couldn't see, he stood at the entrance of the cave to feel everything that passed him, so that Odysseus and his men should not escape. Earlier, Odysseus had told his companions to harness the rams of the flock three abreast with willow branches, which they found on the floor of the cave. To the middle ram of each group of three, one of the Greeks hung, protected on either side by the other two rams. One by one, the men swung from the shaggy coats of the rams. As they passed the giant, he felt the animals' backs and sides, but he never thought to feel their bellies. So all the men escaped. Odysseus was the last one who passed.

Once outside the cavern, the men released themselves and ran to the ship, driving the flock before them. They hastened aboard and pushed off from shore. When they seemed to be at a safe distance way, Odysseus shouted out, "Cyclops, the gods have repaid you for your atrocious deeds! It is Odysseus to whom you owe your loss of sight."

The Cyclops, hearing this, bellowed in rage and, seizing a huge rock from the side of the mountain, he hurled it with all his might in the direction of the ship. Down it came, just clearing the vessel's stern. The ocean heaved and threw the ship once more toward the land, and it barely escaped from being dashed against the shore. The sailors pulled away with the utmost difficulty. Odysseus was about to call to the giant again, but his friends begged him not to do so. He waited until they were far out at sea. Then, unable to resist taunting the Cyclops, he called out again. The giant answered him with curses, but his men pulled at their oars and soon reached the rest of the fleet. At once they set sail again.

Developing Comprehension Skills

1. What did Polyphemus do to two of the men after Odysseus asked for hospitality?

2. Why did Odysseus offer the Cyclops wine?

3. Explain why Odysseus told Polyphemus that his name was No-man.

4. How did Odysseus and his men finally get out of the cave?

5. Polyphemus was a mean character in the myth. Why do you think he acted that way?

Reading Literature: Greek Legends

1. **Understanding Time Order.** One way to see the order of major events in a story clearly is to arrange them on a time line. Events in the story are shown as dots on the line:

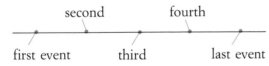

Draw a time line to represent Odysseus's voyage. Include five important events. Begin with the time when Odysseus and his men leave Troy. Next to each of the five dots, identify the event briefly.

2. **Analyzing Character Traits.** After his departure from the land of Cyclopes, Odysseus taunts Polyphemus. What does this tell you about Odysseus's character?

3. **Identifying Elements of a Legend.** The elements of character, setting, plot, and theme are important in a legend. Review the elements of a Greek legend on page 57. Then, think about "The Voyage of Odysseus." Identify in it at least two elements of a legend. Explain your answers.

Developing Vocabulary Skills

Recognizing Greek Word Origins. In the legends you have read, several Greek names form the base for English words. Match each English word below with the Greek name that is its origin. Then use the dictionary to find the meaning of each English word. Think about what each English word and its Greek origin have in common. Write a sentence to explain the similarities you see.

polyphemus moth   odyssey   Spartan

Developing Writing Skills

1. **Analyzing Character.** A hero is a human with special traits who fights in a conflict of good against evil. A hero defends ideas or habits valued by his or her people. For example, Odysseus fights in the Trojan War to defend the honor of Greece. He battles Polyphemus to defend the lives of his men.

   Although Odysseus is a Greek hero, he also displays weaknesses, just as other humans do. Review the actions of Odysseus in the legends you have read. Find at least two times when his behavior is more human than superhuman. Write a paragraph to describe Odysseus's human side. Do you think his human weaknesses make Odysseus more heroic or less heroic? Include your opinion in your paragraph.

2. **Identifying with a Character.** In the legend, Odysseus and his men explore Polyphemus's cave. At first, it seems strange to them. It is a new place and they are unsure what to do. Imagine a situation in which you are exploring an unfamiliar place. Write an account of how you think you would feel and how you would try to make sense of the situation.

Pre-Writing. Plan what you will write. List information on the following points:

Exactly where are you?

Where were you before arriving there?

Why are you there?

Who is with you?

Describe the physical surroundings.

Is there the possibility of danger?

How long do you expect to be there?

Will you leave on your own or will you need help?

Also, add any other important information you would use in the description.

Writing. Organize your account to explain the details of the situation. Use your notes for ideas. Present your descriptions in an order that makes sense. Be sure to include your feelings. Write from one to three paragraphs about the situation.

Revising. Ask someone else to read your description. Can the reader clearly understand where you were? Can the reader understand how you felt? Ask the reader to point out any sentence that could be changed to present a clearer idea.

Developing Skills in Critical Thinking

Analyzing Character Description. Sometimes a writer tells about a character with direct descriptions. At other times the writer may let the reader draw conclusions about the character. In the legends of Odysseus, we learn directly about Odysseus's character from his actions.

Below are listed three characters from the Greek myths and legends you have read. Also, three ways of describing a character are listed. If you were writing about each character, which way would you use? Why?

1. Medusa   a. character is described mostly through his or her own thoughts and only one major action

2. Prometheus   b. character is directly described by details of physical appearance

3. Hercules   c. character is mainly described through his or her own actions

Then review the myths to find out whether the methods used match yours.

Circe, the Enchantress

In this adventure, Odysseus makes a mistake that causes a series of problems. Will Odysseus be able to rely on his own strengths to overcome his mistake? Read to find out.

TRADITIONAL GREEK LEGEND
Retold by Sally Benson

Near the island of the Cyclopes lay the island of Aeolus (ā′ ə ləs). Aeolus ruled the winds, and he sent them forth to fill the sails of ships or kept them chained as he chose. Odysseus and his men landed at the beautiful little island, and Aeolus greeted them in a friendly manner. When they were ready to leave, Aeolus gave them a leather bag tied with a silver string. The bag held all the winds that might be harmful or dangerous. Aeolus warned Odysseus not to open the bag until he had reached home. Until that time, the god of the winds promised that he would send forth only his pleasantest breezes.

For nine days the ships sped before the swift breezes of Aeolus. All that time, Odysseus stood at the wheel, without sleep. At last, exhausted, he lay down to rest. While he slept, the crew approached him and, seeing the leather bag lying by his side, wondered what it could contain. They decided that it must hold some rare treasure that the hospitable King Aeolus had given their commander. They loosed the string, and the winds rushed forth with a dreadful sound. The ships were driven from their course again, back to the island they had left. Here Aeolus, indignant at the folly of the sailors, refused to help them again. They were obliged to row away from the island.

For weeks they sailed the seas until they came to the Aeaean (ā ē′ ən) isle where Circe (sur′ sē), the daughter of the sun, dwelt. After landing on the sloping beach, Odysseus climbed a high hill and, gazing about, saw no signs of life except in one spot on the center of the island. There he saw a palace, surrounded by lovely trees.

He ordered one half of his crew under the leadership of Eurylochus (yoo ril′ ə kus) to go to the palace and ask for hospitality. The men set forth, and, as they approached the palace, they found themselves surrounded by wild beasts—lions, tigers, and wolves. These animals were not at all fierce, and the men looked at them in wonder. They did not know that these animals had once been men. These men had been changed into the forms of beasts by Circe's enchantments.

The men drew near the palace, and soon they heard soft music and a sweet woman's voice singing. Eurylochus called aloud, and the goddess herself came forth and invited them in. The men gladly followed her, all, that is, but Eurylochus, who suspected danger. He hid himself in a tall tree where he could look over the hedges and see what befell his men.

The goddess led them to a banquet table and served them with wine and other delicacies. When they had feasted heartily and were stuffed like pigs with rare food and drink, she touched them with her wand and changed them into swine. Their bodies only were changed; they retained their human minds. Then she shut them up in sties and supplied them with acorns and other things that swine love.

Eurylochus climbed down from the tree and hurried back to the ship where he told his tale to Odysseus. Angered by the loss of his men, Odysseus determined to go himself and see if he could find any means to set

his companions free. He went alone and, as he walked, he met a youth who addressed him familiarly and who seemed to know all about him and his adventures. He told Odysseus that he was the god Hermes. He warned Odysseus of the magic arts of Circe and of the danger of approaching the palace. Odysseus would not heed the warning. Hermes gave him a sprig of a plant that had the power to resist sorceries. He then advised Odysseus how best to resist the charms of the lovely goddess.

Odysseus thanked him and went on his way. When he reached the palace, he was received by Circe, who entertained him as she had done his companions. After he had eaten and drunk, she touched him with her wand, saying, "Hereafter, seek the sty and wallow with your friends."

Instead of obeying, he drew his sword and rushed at her, furious. She fell to her knees and begged for mercy. He told her that he would spare her only if she swore to release his companions and practice no further arts against them. She led him to the pens and changed the swine back to humans once more. Odysseus was so grateful to her that he accepted her invitation to stay on the island for a while and rest from the tiresome voyage. Odysseus would have forgotten his native land entirely had not his companions reminded him of his duty. Sadly, Circe saw the Greeks to their ships and instructed them how to pass safely by the Sirens. The Sirens were sea-nymphs who charmed unhappy mariners by their songs until the travelers could do nothing else but throw themselves into the sea. Circe told Odysseus to fill the ears of his sailors with wax so that they could not hear the music. Odysseus himself should be bound to the mast with stout ropes.

"Warn your men," Circe said. "No matter how you plead to be released, they must refuse. They must not release you until you have passed the Sirens' island."

It was well that Odysseus followed her advice. When they reached the island, the sea was calm, and over the waters came the notes of music so lovely that Odysseus cried to be set free. The men, obedient to his first orders, bound him still tighter and held to the course. The music grew fainter and fainter and soon faded in the distance.

The Sirens, 1875, EDWARD BURNE-JONES.
John and Mable Ringling Museum of Art, Sarasota, Florida.

Developing Comprehension Skills

1. What did Aeolus give Odysseus?

2. How did the god Hermes help Odysseus?

3. The Greek hero defends good against evil. He always is willing to fight, no matter how great the danger. He is a good warrior with superhuman strengths. Name one action Odysseus took in this legend that proves he was a hero.

4. The story does not tell why Hermes offered help to Odysseus. Can you suggest any possible reasons?

Reading Literature: Greek Legends

1. **Identifying Details of the Plot.** By the time Eurylochus arrived at Circe's palace, he suspected danger. Review the details of the story. Try to figure out what alerted Eurylochus to danger.

2. **Analyzing Character.** Odysseus has weaknesses as well as strengths. Sometimes Odysseus is not careful. Sometimes he does not think before he acts. Name one weakness shown by Odysseus in the legend of Circe. Explain how it causes trouble for his men.

3. **Comparing Stories.** The myth about Pandora's box and the legend about Aeolus's bag are similar. Compare the two stories. For each story, answer the following questions.

   a. Is the gift a reward or punishment?
   b. What is contained inside?
   c. When opened, what is the gift's effect on the immediate situation?
   d. What is the long-term effect on the world?
   e. What lesson is learned from the gift?

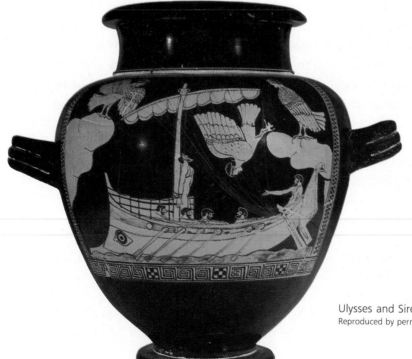

Ulysses and Sirens, 475 B.C., Red-figure Greek vase.

The Perils of Odysseus

TRADITIONAL GREEK LEGEND
Retold by Sally Benson

In this legend, Odysseus faces several dangers. As you read, decide whether the perils are caused by Odysseus's weaknesses or are the result of bad luck.

In a cave high up on a rocky cliff, near a narrow passage through which Odysseus's ships had to pass, lived Scylla, who had once been a lovely water nymph. She had spurned the love of Glaucus (Glä′ kəs), a sea deity and a favorite of Circe. To punish her, Circe had changed her into a monster. Serpents and barking monsters surrounded her, and, more horrible, they were attached to her, and she could not drive them away. In shame, she turned from the green waters of the sea she loved and hid herself on the lonely rock. As the years passed, she grew into a beast at heart and preyed on the mariners who sailed too near her. She had six heads, and, from every vessel that passed, she seized six of the crew and devoured them.

Near the cave where Scylla dwelt was a bottomless hole named Charybdis (kə rib′ dis). Three times each day the water rushed into it with terrific force, and three times the tide rushed back. Any ship coming near the whirlpool when the tide was rushing in was carried down to the blackest depths of the ocean where not even Poseidon could save it.

Circe had warned Odysseus of these two dangers. As they approached the dreadful places, he kept strict watch. The roar of waters from Charybdis could be heard from a distance, but Scylla could not be seen. While Odysseus and his men watched the dreadful whirlpool with anxious eyes, they were not on guard from the attack of Scylla. She darted her snaky heads down, caught six of his men from the deck of the ship, and bore them away, shrieking, to her den. It was the saddest sight Odysseus had yet seen, as he felt powerless to save them. Soon their cries were stilled, and Scylla, sated with human blood, allowed the ship to pass.

After passing Scylla and Charybdis, the sailors came in sight of Thrinacia (thri na′ sē ə). On this island the cattle of the Titan Hyperion (hī pir′ ē ən) were pastured, tended by his daughters. Circe had warned Odysseus that these flocks must not be molested, no matter what the needs of the voyagers might be. She cautioned him that, if her warning was not heeded and the flocks were touched, destruction was sure to fall on the entire crew.

Odysseus would gladly have passed the island without stopping, but his companions begged for rest and refreshment. As Odysseus yielded, he made them swear that they would not touch one animal of the sacred flocks and herds. They would have to be content with the provisions that remained on board the ships. They landed. As long as the provisions lasted, the men kept their oath. However, when their food was gone, they were forced to rely on what birds and fishes they could catch near the shores. Driven reckless by hunger, they killed some of the cattle and tried to make amends for their deed by offering a portion of the kill to the gods.

Odysseus had been overseeing some repairs to his ships when the cattle were slain. When he returned to land, he was horrified at what his men had done. The men were already preparing the meat to eat. Odysseus, looking down at the skins of the animals, saw the hides creep along the ground and heard the joints of meat moaning plaintively as they turned on the spit.

He bade his men make haste to set sail. They hurried away from the island, thinking that they had escaped punishment. No sooner were they at sea than the fair weather changed. A storm blew up. A stroke of lightning shattered the mast and killed the pilot. At last the vessel, beaten by the waves, fell to pieces.

The keel and mast floated side by side, and Odysseus made them into a raft to which he clung. The rest of the crew perished in the waves. Through the night Odysseus held to the raft. By morning he had drifted to Calypso's island.

Calypso (kə lip′ sō) was a sea nymph, and she saw Odysseus on the raft just as he was about to be dashed to death on the rocks. She pulled him from the sea and brought him food and drink. For many days he lay near death while she nursed him back to health. She made him a bed of fragrant violets and would have kept him with her, had not Zeus bade her to send him on his way. Together they built a sturdy raft and provisioned it well. Calypso sadly saw Odysseus sail out to sea.

He journeyed for many days and, when he was in sight of land, another storm broke out. His mast fell and great cracks appeared beneath his feet. Calypso, learning of his plight, sent a sea-nymph to him who took the form of a cormorant and lighted on his sinking raft. The cormorant gave Odysseus a scarf and told him to bind it around his chest so that it would buoy him up as he swam to land.

Odysseus clung to the raft until it fell apart. Then, plunging into the sea, he began to swim. Athene smoothed the waves before him and sent him a wind that carried him toward shore. The surf beat high on the rocks, but he soon found calmer water at the mouth of a gentle stream where he landed, breathless and nearly dead. He kissed the soil and lay down to sleep.

Developing Comprehension Skills

1. Why was Scylla changed into a monster?

2. How did the men try to make amends for killing Hyperion's cattle?

3. Odysseus stopped at Thrinacia, even though Circe had warned him to avoid the place where Hyperion's cattle were kept. Because his men killed the cattle for food, Hyperion caused a storm that wrecked the ship. All of Odysseus's men died at sea. Do you blame Odysseus for what happened, or do you think the events were out of his control?

4. Myths and legends were told to explain nature, to teach ideas about life, and to entertain. For example, the myth you just read explains that storms might be the result of the gods becoming angry. Name one lesson that you think "The Perils of Odysseus" teaches about life.

Reading Literature: Greek Legends

1. **Understanding the Effect of Setting.** Surroundings often affect the way a character behaves. Compare the surroundings in which Polyphemus and Scylla live. How are the two settings alike? Can you think of a way in which the creatures' surroundings might affect their personalities?

2. **Understanding Character.** Early in Odysseus's adventures, Odysseus escapes from Polyphemus. Odysseus then taunts Polyphemus. At a later point in the voyage, Odysseus escapes from Scylla. Odysseus simply sails away and takes no action against the monster. Why does he react differently? What can you tell about his feelings from the way he acts?

Developing Vocabulary Skills

Identifying Meanings of Suffixes. As you know, a suffix is a word-part added to the end of a base word. It changes the meaning of the base word. Each of the words listed below is from one of the selections you have just read. List each word on your paper, being sure to underline the suffix. From what you know of the word and its base, you can figure out the meaning of the suffix. Next to each word, write the suffix meaning from the list provided.

Words	Suffix Meanings
danger<u>ous</u>	without
friend<u>ly</u>	female
travel<u>er</u>	in that way
black<u>est</u>	most
god<u>dess</u>	full of
bottom<u>less</u>	a person who does something

Developing Writing Skills

1. **Using Details To Support Main Idea.** One main idea of the last two selections is that a human cannot always control what happens. Write a paragraph about one of Odysseus's adventures to support this idea.

   Pre-Writing. From the legends, select a situation that Odysseus could not control. Gather information to answer the following questions:

   What is the exact problem?
   Is there a warning given?
   Does he try to control the situation?
   What happens?
   Is the outcome a result of the gods, the forces of nature, or luck?

   Use your ideas to develop a topic sentence, one that clearly states the main idea.

Writing. Begin your paragraph with the topic sentence. Use at least three details collected during your pre-writing to support the topic sentence.

Revising. Show your paragraph to another person. Tell the person that the first sentence of your paragraph is the topic sentence. Ask the person to find three different details that help explain the topic sentence. If the person cannot find three supporting details, then you need to change one or more of your sentences.

2. **Imagining Your Reaction.** Circe turns the bodies of Odysseus's men into pigs, but she leaves them with the minds of men. The legend tells this story in a serious way, but there are other approaches that might be taken. How would you react if—for one day—your body was turned into the form of a pig, but your mind remained the same? Would you laugh, or would you be upset? Write a paragraph about the experience. Tell about the emotions and thoughts you would have.

Developing Skills in Study and Research

1. **Recognizing How Ideas Are Organized.** You have studied two ways to show the relationship of ideas: *time order* and *cause and effect*. Review these skills in the introduction to this chapter. A third way to present ideas is by **comparison and contrast**. A writer may use comparison words to signal the reader that the two items have something in common. Some of these words are *both*, *similar*, and *like*. Contrast words such as *more than*, *but*, and *on the other hand*, signal that two items are different. Each of the following sentences shows a comparison or a contrast. Use the underlined signal words to identify which relationship is used in each sentence.

a. Odysseus was <u>both</u> god-like and human.
b. Circe warned Odysseus of evil, <u>but</u> she could not prevent it.
c. Scylla and Charybdis were the <u>same</u> in certain ways.
d. Odysseus knew the gods were <u>more</u> powerful <u>than</u> he was.

2. **Learning How To Organize Your Own Thoughts.** You have studied three ways to show the relationship of ideas. They are: time order, cause and effect, or comparison and contrast. You can use these relationships to organize your ideas easily and quickly. Suppose you were given a speaking or writing assignment on each of the following topics. Select the relationship you would use to organize your ideas into an outline.

a. a biography of the author, Jack London
b. a description of two paintings by an American artist
c. the instructions for assembling a ten-speed bicycle
d. the reason that plants need light to grow

The End of Odysseus's Voyage

TRADITIONAL GREEK LEGEND
Retold by Sally Benson

In this part of the Odyssey, strangers help Odysseus to return home. How do these people compare with others Odysseus has met during his travels?

The land where Odysseus had fallen exhausted was Scheria (sher′ ē ə), the country of the Phaeacians (fē′ ə cē′ ans). These people had originally dwelt very near the Cyclopes. After many quarrels with the savage race, they migrated to another island. They were a peaceful, godlike people, and the gods themselves often appeared among them. Their island was so remote from the wars of the mainland that the Phaeacians had almost forgotten the use of the bow and arrow.

On the night Odysseus swam ashore and while he lay sleeping on a bed of leaves, the daughter of the king of the island had a dream. She dreamed that Athene appeared before her to remind her that her wedding day was not far distant; it would be wise to wash all the family clothes for the great occasion. This was quite a task, as the fountains were far away and all the garments had to be carried to them.

When the princess awoke, she told her parents about her dream. Her father then ordered grooms to harness a wagon to carry the clothes. Her mother, the queen, packed a lunch of food and wine. The princess climbed into the cart, while her lovely attendants followed on foot. They arrived at the riverside, turned the mules out to graze, and unloaded the wagon. They worked with speed and cheerfulness, and in no time at all the clothes were clean and spread on the shore to dry.

Then the girls bathed themselves and sat down beneath a tree for the picnic lunch. When they had eaten, they amused themselves with a game of ball. Athene, who had been watching them, caused the ball thrown by the princess to fall into the water. At that, they all screamed, and the noise awoke Odysseus.

He looked through the bushes and saw a group of maidens. By their dress and actions, he knew the maidens were of high rank. He needed their help badly. When Odysseus stepped out from the thicket, all the young girls screamed again and fled in all directions—all but Nausicaa (nô sē′ kə), the princess.

Odysseus told her his story and begged her for food and fresh clothing. The princess promised him her father's hospitality and, calling back her attendants, scolded them for their foolish fears. "This man," she said, "is an unhappy wanderer. It is our duty to cherish him. Phaeacians have no enemies to fear, and the poor and needy are sent to us by Zeus. Go bring him food and clothing from the wagon. You will find my brother's garments there, washed clean and fresh."

Odysseus bathed and put on the clothes the maidens brought him. When the princess saw him clad in the splendid robes, she whispered to her maidens that she wished the gods would send her such a husband. Turning to Odysseus, she asked him to follow them to the city. "But when we draw near it," she added, "wait in a grove, for I fear the remarks that might be made by the people if they see me return with a gallant stranger."

He agreed to hide in the grove and to follow her to the palace later. After allowing her time to reach the palace, he went his way. As he neared the outskirts of the city, he met a young woman who was carrying a pitcher to the well. It was Athene who had assumed this form. Odysseus asked her to direct him to the palace of the king, and the maiden offered to be his guide. Under the guidance of the goddess and, by her power, enveloped in a cloud that shielded him from sight, Odysseus passed among the busy crowd. He looked with wonder at the harbor, the ships, the forum, and the battlements, until he came to the palace. Here the goddess left him.

Before entering the courtyard of the palace, Odysseus stood and gazed about him. The splendor of the scene astonished him. Bronze walls stretched from the entrance to the interior house. The doors were gold. The doorposts were carved out of silver, and the lintels were silver ornamented with gold. Along the walls were seats covered with scarves of the finest texture, the work of the Phaeacian maidens, and on these seats the princes sat and feasted. Golden statues of graceful youths held lighted torches which shed a soft radiance over everything. Fifty women served in the household. Some were employed to grind the corn, others to wind off the purple wool or ply the loom. For the Phaeacian women as far exceeded all other women in household arts as the mariners of their country did the rest of mankind in the management of ships.

A spacious garden lay outside the court, filled with pear, pomegranate, apple, fig, and olive trees. Neither winter's cold nor summer's drought arrested their growth, and they flourished in constant succession, some budding while others were maturing. In one part of the garden one could see the vines, some in blossom, some loaded with grapes. On the garden's borders, flowers bloomed all year, and the air was sweet with their perfume. In the center of the garden, two fountains poured forth their waters.

Odysseus was filled with admiration. He was not observed by the others because he was still enveloped in the cloud Athene had thrown around him. After feasting his eyes on all the beauty, he went into the hall where the chiefs and senators were assembled. They were pouring an offering to Hermes, whose worship followed the evening meal. Just then, Athene dissolved the cloud that surrounded Odysseus. He walked to the queen's throne, knelt at her feet, and impored her to help him to return to his native country. Then, withdrawing, he seated himself in the manner of supplicants, by the hearthside.

For a time, no one spoke. At last an aged statesman, addressing the king, said, "It is not fit that a stranger who asks our hospitality should be kept waiting in supplicant guise. Let him, therefore, be led to a seat and supplied with food and wine."

The king arose, took Odysseus by the hand, and led him to the table. He dismissed his guests, and Odysseus was left alone with the king and queen. The queen recognized that the clothes he wore were those which her maidens and she herself had made. She asked him from whom he had received these garments. He told them of the wreck of his raft, his escape by swimming, and the help given him by the princess. The royal couple heard his story and promised to furnish him with a ship so that he might return to his native land.

The next day, a ship was prepared, and a crew of stout rowers selected. Then everyone went to the King's palace, where a great banquet had been prepared. After the feast, the young men of the country showed Odysseus their skill in running and wrestling. They challenged him to show what he could do. He arose from his seat, seized a quoit far heavier than any the Phaeacians had thrown, and sent it farther than the farthest throw of theirs.

After the games, they returned to the hall and the herald led in the blind bard Demodocus (dǝ mō' dǝ cus). He took for his theme the story of the Wooden Horse. Apollo inspired him and he sang so feelingly of the terrors and exploits of that eventful time that Odysseus was moved to tears.

When the king saw his grief, he turned to him. "Why are your sorrows awakened at the mention of Troy?" he asked. "Did you lose a father or brother there? Or perhaps a dear friend?"

Odysseus said that he himself had fought at Troy. Then he recounted all the adventures that had befallen him since his departure from that city. The king was so moved by his tale that he proposed that all the chiefs should present Odysseus with a gift. They obeyed and vied with one another in loading the illustrious stranger with costly things.

The next day Odysseus set sail and in a short time arrived at Ithaca, his own land. When the vessel touched the strand, he was asleep, and the mariners, without awaking him, carried him ashore. They laid him on the chest that contained his presents and then sailed away.

Developing Comprehension Skills

1. Describe the setting of Scheria.

2. Name two ways in which the goddess Athene helped Odysseus in the land of Scheria.

3. In what ways were the Phaeacians different from others whom Odysseus had encountered, such as the Cyclopes, the Lotus-Eaters, and the Sirens?

4. Would you want to trade places with Odysseus? Would you want to go through his experiences? Why or why not?

Reading Literature: Greek Legends

1. **Analyzing Plot.** You have read the story of Odysseus's voyage home from the Trojan War. Select five major events from Odysseus's adventures. List them in the order in which they happen. Then find one adventure that causes the next adventure to occur. Write a sentence to explain which adventure is the cause and which adventure is the result. Be sure to use a cause and effect signal word in your sentence.

2. **Contrasting Cultures.** Ancient Phaeacian custom required that all strangers be treated with hospitality. The gods demanded such courteous behavior. This is the main reason that the princess and her parents help the Greek Odysseus. Contrast this ancient custom with what you think would be the attitude of people today. Would you help a stranger as the princess does? Would you feel that you should? What would affect your decision whether or not to help?

3. **Analyzing a Hero.** During his adventures in Scheria, Odysseus behaves in ways that normally would not be considered heroic. At one point, Odysseus begs for food and clothes. At another point, he breaks down in tears. How can Odysseus act in these ways and still be considered a hero? Explain a way that this behavior might be interpreted as strength of character.

The Fate of the Suitors

TRADITIONAL GREEK LEGEND
Retold by Thomas Bulfinch

As you read the story of Odysseus's return home, keep in mind that he had been away for many years. Look for the motives that cause him to act the way he does.

Odysseus had now been away from Ithaca for twenty years. When he awoke he did not recognize his native land. Athene appeared to him in the form of a young shepherd, informed him where he was, and told him the state of things at his palace. Imagining him dead, more than a hundred nobles of Ithaca and of the neighboring islands had been for years suing for the hand of Penelope, Odysseus's wife. They lived in his palace and ordered its people about as if they owned both. To take vengeance upon them, it was important that Odysseus should not be recognized. Athene accordingly changed him into an unsightly beggar, and, as such, he was kindly received by Eumaeus (yo͞o mā′ əs), a faithful servant of his house.

Telemachus (tə lem′ ə kəs), Odysseus's son, was absent in quest of his father. He had gone to the courts of those kings who had returned from the Trojan expedition. While he was away on the search, Athene told him to return home. When he arrived, he sought out Eumaeus to learn something of the state of affairs at the palace. Finding someone with Eumaeus, he treated the stranger courteously and promised him assistance. Eumaeus then went to the palace to inform Penelope privately of her son's arrival. Secrecy and caution were necessary because the suitors were plotting to kill Telemachus.

When Eumaeus had gone, Athene presented herself to Odysseus and told him to make himself known to his son. At the same time she restored his look of vigorous manhood. Telemachus viewed this transformation with astonishment and, at first, thought Odysseus must be more than mortal. Then Odysseus told Telemachus who he was and explained that the disguise had been the idea of Athene.

The father and son planned how they could get the better of the suitors and punish them for their outrages. It was arranged that Telemachus should proceed to the palace and mingle with the suitors. Odysseus

Penelope at Her Loom, 1509, PINTORICCIO. Reproduced by the courtesy of the Trustees, the National Gallery, London.

would go as a beggar for, in those days, beggars were admitted into the halls of chieftains and often treated like guests. Odysseus reminded his son not to show unusual interest in him.

At the palace they found the usual scene of feasting and disorder. The suitors pretended to receive Telemachus with joy at his return. The old beggar was permitted to enter and was provided with a portion from the table. A touching incident occurred as Odysseus entered the courtyard. His old dog remembered him.

As Odysseus sat eating his portion in the hall, the suitors began to insult him. When he protested, one of them raised a chair and

The Return of Odysseus (Homage to Pintoriccio and Benin), 1977, ROMARE BEARDEN.
Collage on masonite, 44" × 56". © The Art Institute of Chicago. All rights reserved.

hit him. Telemachus had hard work to restrain his indignation at seeing his father treated unjustly but, remembering his father's directions, said little.

Penelope had put off a decision to marry again for so long that she could not delay further. Her husband's return could no longer be expected. She therefore consented to submit the question of her choice of husband to a contest of skill among the suitors. The test selected was that of shooting with the bow. Twelve rings were arranged in a line. He whose single arrow was sent through the whole twelve was to have the queen for his prize. A bow that one of his brother heroes had given to Odysseus in former times was brought from the armory and, along with its quiver full of arrows, was laid in the hall. Telemachus had taken care that all other weapons should be removed.

Telemachus endeavored to bend the bow, but found all his efforts fruitless. Modestly confessing that he had attempted a task beyond his strength, he yielded the bow to another. The next contender tried to with no better success and, amidst the laughter and jeers of his companions, gave it up. Another tried it, and another. They rubbed the bow with tallow, but all to no purpose; it would not bend.

Then spoke Odysseus, humbly suggesting that he should be permitted to try. "For," said he, "beggar that I am, I was once a soldier, and there is still some strength in these old limbs of mine." The suitors hooted with derision, but Telemachus spoke up for him and let him try. Odysseus took the bow. With ease he adjusted the cord to its notch, then he sped an arrow unerringly through the rings.

Without allowing the suitors time to express their astonishment, Odysseus said, "Now for another mark!" and aimed directly at one of the most insolent of the suitors. The arrow pierced his throat, and the suitor fell dead. Telemachus, Eumaeus, and another faithful follower, well armed, now sprang to the side of Odysseus. The suitors, in amazement, looked around for arms but found none. Neither was there any way of escape, for Eumaeus had secured the door. Odysseus announced himself as the long-lost chief, whose house they had invaded, whose substance they had squandered, and whose wife and son they had persecuted for ten long years. He told the suitors that he meant to have ample vengeance. All were slain, and Odysseus was left master of his palace and possessor of his kingdom and his wife.

Developing Comprehension Skills

1. How long had Odysseus been away from his home in Ithaca?

2. Name two things that had been happening at Odysseus's palace while he was gone.

3. It was necessary for Odysseus to be disguised when he returned to his palace so that he would not be recognized. Why did Athene choose the disguise of a beggar?

4. When Telemachus returned home, he went directly to Eumaeus for information. What did this action reveal about the role of Eumaeus in Odysseus's household?

5. At the end of the legend, Odysseus killed all of Penelope's suitors. To the ancient Greeks, Odysseus's action was considered heroic. Do you think the slaughter was heroic? Why or why not?

Reading Literature: Greek Legends

1. **Contrasting Social Customs.** Travelers such as Odysseus are received quite differently in Ithaca than in Scheria, the land of the Phaeacians. Make a list to show the differences in the ways that these cultures treat strangers.

2. **Organizing Major Action.** Make a time line to show five important events in "The Fate of the Suitors." Begin with the time Odysseus arrives at Ithaca. End with the time he again becomes master of his palace. Write a complete sentence about each event. Label the five points on the time line.

first event

last event

3. **Supporting Main Ideas.** In telling stories, writers indirectly explain several main ideas, or **themes**, about life. Each of the following statements is a main idea from a story you have read. Events from the stories are also listed. Match each main idea with a supporting detail from the list of events.

Main Ideas:

a. The all-powerful gods control all that happens to people on earth.
b. A hero sometimes may be excused for actions not accepted by normal people.
c. There is more glory in fighting than in living a peaceful life.
d. A person must be willing to die for love.
e. Isolation from the rest of society causes a person to become evil.

Events:

(1) The Trojan War begins so that Menelaus can regain Helen from Paris.

(2) Odysseus is given gifts by the King of Scheria to celebrate his heroic deeds.
(3) The god Hyperion causes a shipwrecking storm after Odysseus's men kill the god's cattle.
(4) Scylla turns into a monster when she refuses love and goes into hiding.
(5) In a fit of rage Odysseus kills all the suitors at his palace.

Developing Vocabulary Skills

Completing Analogies. An **analogy** is a special type of sentence used to compare words. In an analogy, there are two pairs of related words. Each pair is related in the same way. Here are two examples:

a. *Finger* is to *hand* as *toe* is to *foot.*
b. *Day* is to *night* as *dawn* is to *dusk.*

In the first example, the relationship between *finger* and *hand* is that a *finger* is part of a *hand.* In the same way, a *toe* is part of a *foot.*

In the second example, the two words in each pair are opposites.

In an analogy question, you are given the first pair of words and must complete the second pair. To answer the question, you must figure out the relationship between the first two words. Then you must find the missing word that will form the same relationship with the third word given. Here is an example:

One-eyed is to Polyphemus as six-headed is to ——.

Circe   Charybdis   Scylla   Calypso

One-eyed describes a physical appearance of *Polyphemus. Six-headed* describes a physical appearance of the monster *Scylla.* Therefore, *Scylla* is the answer.

The following analogies use words and names you have read in Chapter One selections. Choose the answer that will correctly complete each analogy.

1. Create is to destroy as origin is to ____.
   begin   end   original   start

2. Tetrahedron is to four as octagon is to ____.
   ten   two   six   eight

3. Zeus is to gods as Hera is to ____.
   Muses   Furies   nymphs   goddesses

4. Priam is to Troy as Menelaus is to ____.
   Ida   Athens   Sparta   Ithaca

5. Apollo is to sun as Artemis is to ____.
   Earth   moon   stars   rainbow

6. Hercules is to Hydra as Theseus is to ____.
   Icarus   Scylla   Minotaur   Medusa

Developing Writing Skills

1. **Analyzing Your Definition of a Hero.** Some of Odysseus's behavior would not be considered heroic today. Your definition of a hero depends on your viewpoint on life. Write two paragraphs to describe your standards for a hero. Explain why you would choose those qualities.

   Pre-Writing. Review the personal definition of a hero that you wrote for "Developing Skills in Critical Thinking" on page 65. Add new traits to your definition if you feel they are important. Then, for each heroic quality you have included, consider why it is important to your idea of a hero.

   Writing. Begin with a detailed definition of your idea of a hero. Write one paragraph to state the qualities you selected for a hero. In the second paragraph, explain why you chose each trait.

   Revising. Read your explanation. Check to make sure that you have included at least one reason for each heroic quality.

2. **Describing a Personal Hero.** Review the definition of a hero that you wrote for "Developing Skills in Critical Thinking" on page 65. Write a paragraph about a person who fits your definition.

Developing Skills in Critical Thinking

Classifying. There are many ways to work with information in stories you read. One way is to classify, or group, the stories according to elements. For example, you might classify stories according to the characters: stories about monsters or stories about gods. You might classify stories according to settings: those that take place on earth or those that take place on Olympus. The same story might be classified in more than one group. For example, "The Perils of Odysseus" is about both the monster Scylla and the god Hyperion.

Review the legends you read in this chapter. Think of three different classifications in which to group the legends. Then, decide which stories fit in each of the classifications. Remember that the same story can be placed in more than one group. Make a chart with a heading for each classification. List the titles of the legends in the groups where they belong.

Kyklops

HOMER
Translated by Robert Fitzgerald from
The Odyssey

You have read one version of the story of Cyclops. In this version the name Cyclops is spelled Kyklops, *which is closer to the original Greek word. As you read this selection, decide how it differs from the other version.*

A prodigious man
slept in this cave alone, and took his flocks
to graze afield—remote from all companions,
knowing none but savage ways, a brute
so huge, he seemed no man at all of those
who eat good wheaten bread; but he seemed rather
a shaggy mountain reared in solitude.
We beached there, and I told the crew
to stand by and keep watch over the ship;
as for myself I took my twelve best fighters
and went ahead. . . .

We climbed, then, briskly to the cave. But Kyklops
had gone afield, to pasture his fat sheep,
so we looked round at everything inside. . . .

My men came pressing round me, pleading:

"Why not
take these cheeses, get them stowed, come back,
throw open all the pens, and make a run for it?
We'll drive the kids and lambs aboard. We say
put out again on good salt water!"

Ah,

how sound that was! Yet I refused. I wished
to see the caveman, what he had to offer—
no pretty sight, it turned out, for my friends.

We lit a fire, burnt an offering,
and took some cheese to eat; then sat in silence
around the embers, waiting. When he came
he had a load of dry boughs on his shoulder
to stoke his fire at suppertime. He dumped it
with a great crash into that hollow cave,
and we all scattered fast to the far wall.
Then over the broad cavern floor he ushered
the ewes he meant to milk. He left his rams
and he-goats in the yard outside, and swung
high overhead a slab of solid rock
to close the cave. Two dozen four-wheeled wagons,
with heaving wagon teams, could not have stirred
the tonnage of that rock from where he wedged it
over the doorsill. Next he took his seat
and milked his bleating ewes. . . .

                                        He poked the fire,
heaping on brushwood. In the glare he saw us.

"Strangers," he said, "who are you? And where from?
What brings you here by sea ways—a fair traffic?
Or are you wandering rogues, who cast your lives
like dice, and ravage other folk by sea?"

We felt a pressure on our hearts, in dread
of that deep rumble and that mighty man.
But all the same I spoke up in reply:

"We are from Troy, Akhaians, blown off course
by shifting gales on the Great South Sea;
homeward bound, but taking routes and ways
uncommon; so the will of Zeus would have it. . . .
It was our luck to come here; here we stand,
beholden for your help, or any gifts
you give—as custom is to honor strangers.
We would entreat you, great Sir, have a care

for the gods' courtesy; Zeus will avenge
the unoffending guest.''

He answered this
from his brute chest, unmoved:

"You are a ninny,
or else you come from the other end of nowhere,
telling me, mind the gods! We Kyklopês
care not a whistle for your thundering Zeus
or all the gods in bliss; we have more force by far.
I would not let you go for fear of Zeus—
you or your friends—unless I had a whim to.''

 004

Developing Comprehension Skills

1. Who is the storyteller of this poem, identified as "I"?

2. In the first seven lines of the poem, the narrator gives a detailed description of Kyklops. What three separate words reveal that Kyklops lived by himself?

3. Odysseus's men plead with him to "make a run for it." However, Odysseus chooses to stay and see the caveman. Later in the poem Odysseus says:

    Ah, how sound that was! Yet I refused. I wished to see the caveman, what he had to offer—no pretty sight, it turned out, for my friends.

    What does Odysseus's comment suggest about the outcome of his decision to stay?

4. Do you like this version of the Polyphemus adventure more or less than the version you read earlier? Why?

Reading Literature: Greek Legends

1. **Contrasting Prose and Poetry.** The introductory description of the Cyclopes in the story "The Voyage of Odysseus" states:

    These huge giants had but one eye which was placed in the middle of the forehead. They lived in caves and tended their flocks, eating whatever roots and wild grasses grew on the rocky shores.

    In this description, the storyteller writes in prose, or a story-like style. The sentences are complete sentences. A second line begins only when the writing on the first line reaches the right margin. Sentences are grouped together into paragraphs.

    Contrast the prose description of the Cyclopes to the first seven lines of the poetic description of Kyklops. Homer did not use a prose style. Instead, he wrote the description as a poem. This modern translation reflects this. In poetry ideas are not always presented in complete sentences. The poet breaks ideas into lines for a visual effect. Lines do not always start at the left margin. They do not always end at the right margin. The word position is important to understanding.

The prose and poetry versions of the Cyclops also differ in the effects they create. Consider how you react after reading each version. Which version gives you a more personal feeling about the Cyclops? Which version simply states the events? Can you find any reasons for the difference in the effects of the two versions?

2. **Identifying Emotions and Characters.** Many of the ideas in a poem are only suggested to us by the poet. To understand the total effect of the poem, we must pay attention to the poet's hints. Identify which emotion is suggested by each of the following sets of lines. Also tell which character or characters feel the emotion.

 a. "My men came pressing round me, pleading . . . run for it . . ."
 b. ". . . and we all scattered fast to the far wall."
 c. "We felt a pressure on our hearts, in dread of that deep rumble and that mighty man."
 d. "But all the same I spoke up in reply . . ."

3. **Recognizing the Effect of Imagery.** The poet provides images about Kyklops throughout the poem. List five different phrases that describe the Kyklops's size and power.

4. **Understanding Details.** In the poem, Odysseus states the following:

 "We lit a fire, burnt an offering, and took some cheese to eat."

In the story of Hyperion's cattle on page 78, the narrator also reports that the crew "killed some of the cattle and tried to make amends for their deed by offering a portion of the kill to the gods." Can you explain why the men made offerings to the gods in both of these situations?

Developing Vocabulary Skills

Using Greek Roots. The name Cyclops is based on *kyklos*, the Greek word for "circle." Several English words are based on the Greek root *cyclo* and *cyclos*. (Notice that the English version is spelled with "c" instead of "k.") Explain how each English word listed below is connected to the idea of a circle. Use the dictionary to check word meanings.

cycle   cyclone   bicycle   encyclopedia

Developing Writing Skills

1. **Changing a Poetic Description Into Prose.** The poet does not give one complete description of the setting. Instead, he scatters words and phrases about the setting throughout the poem. Write a paragraph to describe the land where Kyklops lives.

 Pre-Writing. Make a list of all the details used in the poem to describe the setting. Then, organize the details so they make sense. For example, group together all the details about weather.

 Writing. Use the poet's details to write a paragraph in your own words. You may need to add to the poet's ideas. Provide a complete picture of the setting.

 Revising. Find a good listener. Ask the person to listen to you read your description. Tell the person to picture the setting mentally. Then, ask the person to describe the setting to you. The person may interpret a part of the setting in a way that surprises you. Revise any sentence that is not clear.

2. **Keeping a Diary.** Imagine that you were one of Odysseus's men. Select an adventure from "The Odyssey" that you found exciting. Write a personal account of the adventure.

Developing Skills in Speaking and Listening

Interpreting the Mood of a Poem. Choose one of the following sections of "Kyklops" to prepare for reading aloud:

the first eleven lines
the ten lines beginning with: "My men came pressing round me, pleading"
the ten lines beginning with: "We felt pressure on our hearts, a dread"

Before reading your section aloud, you should understand its mood. The mood of a selection is the feeling it gives to the reader or listener. Think about "Kyklops." Does the story make you laugh, or does it put you in a serious mood? Imagine Odysseus narrating the story. What tone of voice would he use? Which parts would he say loudly? which softly?

Practice reading the section of the poem you selected. Try to speak the same way you imagine Odysseus would have spoken. Do not pause at the end of every line. Pause only at punctuation marks. Say all the words clearly.

Using Your Skills in Reading Greek Myths and Legends

The following paragraphs are from a Greek myth about a greedy king named Midas. The god Dionysus had given him the power to change all he touched to gold. Midas soon realized that he could not eat gold. What elements of myths do you find in this excerpt from the tale?

Dionysus felt that the greedy king had learned his lesson and took pity on him. "Go," he said, "to the river Pactolus. There wash away your fault and its punishment."

Midas hurriedly made his way to the source of the river. Obeying the god, he plunged his head and body into the waters. He had scarcely touched the water before the gold-creating power passed into it. The river sands became gold, as they remain to this day.

Using Your Comprehension Skills

Read the following excerpt from a selection in Chapter 2. Then identify at least one detail that it states directly about each of the following: description of a character, time order, cause and effect.

The goddess Frigga walked for miles and miles over the Earth in search of gold for her necklace. At last she came to a statue that stood in a little village. It was made of pure gold.

Frigga cried out with pleasure! Here at last was more than enough gold for her necklace. As the queen of the gods came closer, she saw it was a statue of her husband, Odin. It looked so much like Odin that for a minute she expected it to speak.

Using Your Vocabulary Skills

Read the following sentences. The underlined word in each is used in Chapter 2. Tell what you would use to find its meaning:

word parts   context clues   word origins   the dictionary

1. The only sound in the cave was the <u>gush</u> of the air from the bellows.
2. The monster stirred <u>impatiently</u> in the darkness.
3. Thor rode in a <u>chariot</u>, a two-wheeled vehicle, that was drawn by two goats.
4. Grendel stood on a little <u>knoll</u> one evening.
5. "No armor <u>avails</u> against his claws of steel," Hrothgar said.
6. Beowulf made no effort to <u>retard</u> the hag; he wanted her to move fast.

Using Your Writing Skills

Choose one of the writing assignments below.

1. From among all the gods, goddesses, and heroes you have read about in this chapter, choose your favorite character. Write a description of this character in one to three paragraphs. Your description should concentrate on the qualities that made you choose him or her.
2. Create your own god or goddess, and write a description of him or her. Describe what the god or goddess looks like. Explain what his or her major responsibility is. Provide an example of the sort of action this god or goddess is likely to take. Tell, also, what this character's attitude toward humans is. Your description should be from one to three paragraphs long.

Using Your Skills in Critical Thinking

The list of names below includes gods, goddesses, and other characters from Greek myths and legends. Choose any eight of these characters. Group them in one or two categories of your choice. Then explain your categories and your reasons for selecting those eight.

Athene	Odysseus	Zeus	Hera
Hercules	Prometheus	Circe	Perseus
Pandora	Medusa	Ariadne	Poseidon
Hector	the Minotaur	Polyphemus	Theseus
Penelope	Icarus	Apollo	Helen of Troy
Deucalion	Cerberus	Telemachus	Hades

Norse Myths and Legends

Sea Tragedy, about 1892, ALBERT PINKHAM RYDER.
Oil on canvas, 39.5 × 33.5 cm. Ball State University Art Gallery, Muncie, Indiana.
Permanent loan from the Frank C. Ball Collection, Ball Brothers Foundation.

Reading Literature: Norse Myths and Legends

What Are Norse Myths and Legends?

As you learned in Chapter 1, myths and legends are very old stories. Storytellers first told these stories thousands of years ago. A **myth** explains a mystery of nature, such as how the world came to be. The explanation usually involves gods or godlike beings. The listeners believed in both the characters and the events. A **legend** entertains and instructs. For example, it may show the importance of bravery or of courtesy. A legend usually involves humans, although gods or monsters may also appear. The listeners approved of the lesson and enjoyed the story, but they did not necessarily believe it.

In ancient times, almost every group of people created their own myths and legends. The myths in this chapter were created by the people who lived long ago in Scandinavia and Germany. About 1000 A.D., some of these people in Scandinavia were called the Norse. The myths and legends get their name from those people.

The History of Norse Myths and Legends

As with the Greeks, there were full-time storytellers among the Germanic and Scandinavian people. They recited myths and legends long before the stories were written down. Gradually many separate stories were brought together in two long poems, called *Eddas*. These poems were finally written down in the 1200's. In them we find many Norse myths.

The legend of Beowulf was probably written in the 700's. It was written by a poet living in England, in the language known as Old English. However, it was drawn almost completely from the legends the poet heard as he grew up. These were legends brought to England by the Scandinavians who had settled there. In this poem, the poet described a great warrior and leader. This type of hero had long been a model for the people of the North.

Elements of Norse Myths and Legends

Norse myths and legends have some similarities to the Greek stories. They both concern gods, heroes, and forces of evil. However, there are also strong differences. This is understandable when you think about the two different groups of people.

The Greeks enjoyed a warm, pleasant climate. The people who created the Norse myths, in contrast, lived in a cold, harsh climate. This difference shows in the settings of their myths.

The Greeks had developed a love of music and art, as well as respect for bravery. Many people of the North believed that being a good warrior was the highest possible goal. These beliefs affect their choice of heroes.

Characters. Many types of beings appear in Norse myths. The gods are powerful beings who are generally good, and friendly to humans. The giants are almost as powerful, but evil and against both gods and humans. The dwarfs are small, ugly beings who live underground.

In Norse legends, there are monsters, dragons, and other creatures. The human heroes of these legends are always warriors, shown only in battle. We never learn, for example, whether Beowulf has a wife and family back home, as Odysseus did.

Setting. As in the Greek myths, the setting of Norse myths can be anywhere in the universe. The lands of the gods, of humans, and of giants are described as touching each other.

How To Read Norse Myths and Legends

1. As you read a myth the first time, enjoy it as you would any story. Try to picture the characters in action in their special settings.
2. Read the myth a second time or review it thoughtfully. Look for similarities with Greek myths. Look for differences. Thinking about the characters and events in this way will help you see what is special about each myth.
3. Look for ways in which the major characters are like modern people. Can reading about them help us see ourselves more clearly?

Comprehension Skills: Comparisons and Contrasts

Making Comparisons and Contrasts

The Norse myths and legends in this chapter are similar in some ways to the Greek myths and legends in Chapter 1. They are very different in other ways. You will find it helpful to watch for both similarities and differences. Identifying the similarities between two works of literature is called **making a comparison**. Identifying the differences between them is called **making a contrast**. Some elements that can be compared and contrasted are setting, character, plot, and theme.

For example, the two paragraphs below describe the homes of the gods in the two groups of legends. Can you compare and contrast these two settings? Read both passages. As you read the second, write on a separate paper any similarities or differences that you notice.

OLYMPUS, HOME OF THE GREEK GODS

Zeus chose as his kingdom the very top of a mountain in Thessaly and called it Olympus. Here, with the exception of Poseidon and Hades, all the gods lived. They were shut off from the Earth by a gate of clouds. Each god had a palace of his own.

ASGARD, HOME OF THE NORSE GODS

At the top of the world the gods made a beautiful city for themselves. They called it Asgard. It was filled with gold and silver palaces. Because the gods wanted a road from their shining city down to the Earth, they took fire and water and air and made a wonderful rainbow.

Seeing similarities between works helps you to recognize important themes and techniques. Did you notice these similarities?

Both Asgard and Olympus are homes for gods.
Both Asgard and Olympus are in high places.
Both are connected to Earth.

Seeing differences between works helps you notice the qualities that make each selection special. Can you spot these differences?

Asgard is a city, while Olympus is a kingdom.
Asgard has a rainbow bridge; Olympus has a gate of clouds.
All Norse gods live in Asgard. Two Greek gods live outside Olympus.

Exercises: Making Comparisons and Contrasts

A. Read these passages about monsters in the Greek and the Norse myths. Then answer the questions below about comparison and contrast.

THE CYCLOPS, *from Greek legend*

The Cyclops lived in a cave on an island with rocky shores. He was a huge giant who had but one eye, which was placed in the middle of the forehead. When Odysseus and his men wandered into his cave, he grabbed several of the men, pulled them apart, and ate them.

GRENDEL, *from Norse legend*

Grendel had a shaggy form, resembling a huge, clumsy man. He had fingers like iron claws, rolling eyes, and a hideous countenance, swollen purplish red. Grendel lived in a cave in a lonely, cold region. At night, he attacked the king's hall and ripped apart a man sleeping there.

1. In what ways do the two characters look alike?
2. How do the two look different?
3. How are the characters' homes similar? How are they different?
4. How are their actions similar? How are they different?

B. Read the following summary of a Norse myth. Then review the Greek myth of Pandora. Compare and contrast the two myths. Identify at least one similarity and at least one difference.

Odin, the ruler of the gods, is angered by the destruction of his statue. He doesn't know that his own wife, Frigga, had someone break the statue. She was trying to cover up her theft of gold to make a necklace. In fury, Odin walks out of sight. While he is gone, there is no one to protect the world from evil. Earth is attacked by the frost giants. Asgard is filled with confusion.

Vocabulary Skills: Word Parts

Using Word Parts To Find Meaning

You have seen that many unfamiliar words are based on familiar words. They may look new because extra word parts have been added to the **base word**. A word part added at the beginning of a base word is a **prefix**. A word part added at the end is a **suffix**. The word **affix** can be used for either a prefix or a suffix. Here is an example of a base word with two affixes:

	Prefix	+	**Base Word**	+	**Suffix**
disagreeable =	dis		agree		able

To unlock a word with affixes, first separate the affixes from the base word. In the example, the prefix *dis–* means "not." The suffix *–able* means "having the quality." *Disagreeable* means "not having the quality of agreeing." A disagreeable person is hard to get along with.

It's helpful to know the meanings of common affixes. Then you may be able to figure out unfamiliar words in which you find them. The following charts list several of the affixes used most often.

	Prefix	**Example**
dis–	means "opposite of" or "not."	disappear
il–, im–, in–, ir–	mean "not or opposite of."	illegal, immoderate, inexact, irregular
mis–	means "wrong" or "wrongly."	misdeed, misuse
non–, un–	mean "not."	nonresident, unfold
pre–	means "before."	preview
re–	means "again" or "back."	reappear, repay
sub–	means "under" or "less than."	substandard
super–	means "above" or "greater than."	superstructure, superhero

In this list of suffixes, note that adding a suffix sometimes changes the spelling of the base word. It may also change its part of speech.

	Suffix	Example
–able	means "capable of being" or "having the quality of."	usable, honorable
–er, –or	mean "one who does a certain thing."	winner, conductor
–ful	means "full of" or "having."	graceful, hopeful
–less	means "without."	shapeless
–ly	means "in a certain manner."	surely
–ment	means "the act of" or "the state of being."	movement, contentment
–ness	means "the state of being."	greatness
–ous	means "full of" or "having."	courageous
–ward	means "in the direction of."	westward

Exercises: Using Word Parts To Find Meaning

A. Each word or base word below is from Chapter 2. Write the base word. Identify every prefix or suffix. Then figure out the meaning of the word.

1. unconquerable
2. helplessly
3. harshness
4. subsurface
5. suspenseful
6. spacious
7. thoughtfully
8. re-echo
9. upward
10. supernatural
11. uneven
12. famous

B. In each sentence, find at least one word with a prefix or suffix from the charts. Identify each word part and tell what the word means.

1. Norse myths tell that nonliving things were created first.
2. The god Loki demanded that the dwarfs be respectful toward him.
3. The most skillful dwarf produced marvelous gifts.
4. The travelers found shelter in a cavernous building.
5. They were unprepared for the coldness and wetness in that land.
6. The hero waited impatiently for the monstrous creature to appear.

Norse Myths

Almost every day, you use the name of a god or goddess from Norse myths. Here are the origins of four names of weekdays:

Twi—Tuesday   Odin—Wednesday (Woden's Day)
Thor—Thursday   Freya—Friday

These names entered the English language about 500 A.D., when many Scandinavian people came to England. Read the myths in this section to learn why those people wanted to honor Odin and Thor.

Viking Helmet, about 550–800. History Museum, Stockholm. Courtesy of Giraudon/Art Resource, New York.

The Beginning of a World

TRADITIONAL NORSE MYTH
Retold by Catharine F. Sellew

The Norse story of creation begins with ice. This is a part of nature not included in other creation stories. Why would ice be a natural part of the Norse story? Read to find out how ice is important.

Long, long ago, before there were any days or nights—long before there was any time at all—there was no world, no earth or sky or sea. Only a deep crack yawned in the universe like the mouth of a huge monster. All around were mist and darkness, but deep down in the dark pit of the crack leaped the red tongue of fire.

There, too, a bottomless spring never stopped bubbling and running over. As the water rushed into the cold darkness, it turned into sheets of ice. The great spirit looked down upon this ice and darkness. He saw that nothing grew there. He saw that all was gray and silent. Therefore, he made a tremendous man called a giant and placed him on the ice. He made a huge cow which gave the giant gallons and gallons of milk.

The huge cow used to feed on the salt she found in the ice. One day, while she was licking the salt, her rough tongue came upon a golden hair. She licked and licked and found more golden hairs. Soon she found they were growing on the head of another giant, frozen in the ice. Day after day she kept licking until she got to his shoulders, then his chest, then his waist. Finally he stood before her free from the ice. He was even taller and more handsome than her master. His name was Bure (by o͞or′ə).

That was the beginning of a world of giants. It was a cold world with no sunshine, no blue sky, no green grass.

Some of the giants were evil, and they fought and quarreled with the good giants like Bure. Finally the grandsons of Bure conquered the bad giants and drove them far out into the cold gray twilight at the edge of the universe. It was so cold that their breath turned to ice the minute it passed their lips, and then it fell like icicles on the ground.

Then the children of the good giants made for themselves a new world in which they were to be the gods who ruled over everything.

In the center of the universe they created a green land with rivers and lakes and

mountains. That was the earth. Then they carved a man out of a tall ash tree and a woman out of a graceful elm. The gods gave the man and woman the power to move and think. And they placed them on the earth to start the human race.

At the top of the world, the gods made a beautiful city for themselves. They called it Asgard. It was filled with gold and silver palaces. Because the gods wanted a road from their shining city down to the earth and then beyond to the dark world of the giants, they took fire and water and air and made a wonderful rainbow. The rainbow was so wide and so strong and so long that it stretched like a bridge across the three parts of the universe.

Then they found four very strong and very ugly little men called dwarfs to hold the four corners of the sky on their shoulders. Their names were Nordri, Sudri, Austri, and Westri, which mean North, South, East, and West. The gods filled the sky with sparks that shone when there was no sun or moon nearby. They called them stars.

In this new world there grew a mighty tree that was ever green. It was so tall that its topmost branches shaded the palaces of the gods and its lower branches shaded the earth and the land of the giants. The tree had three roots, one growing in each of the three parts of the world.

The ruler of this new world was All-Father, king of the gods. He was a great warrior. He called himself Odin (ō dēn').

Odin's beautiful gray horse, Sleipner (slāp'nêr), had eight feet and could run faster than the wind. Sleipner carried his master through many fierce battles and on many long and dangerous adventures. When the great All-Father galloped across the rainbow bridge, the thundering of the horse's hoofs echoed from the heavens to the deepest caves of the giants.

Developing Comprehension Skills

1. According to Norse mythology, two things existed before time began. What two things existed in the deep crack in the universe? What were the first two living things to be created?

2. According to the Norse myth, who created the earth? Why was Earth created?

3. In the myth, the gods live in Asgard, above the earth. Humans live on the earth. The bad giants live at the edge of the universe. These parts of the universe are connected in two ways. Can you identify at least one way?

4. What evidence in the myth lets you know that ice was important in the lives of the Norse people?

5. You have read several different myths that explain the creation of mankind. In one Greek creation myth, Prometheus formed a human from a handful of earth. In a second Greek myth, stones are turned into people. In the Norse myth, people are shaped from trees. Which of these three creation stories do you prefer? Explain your opinion.

Reading Literature: Norse Myths

1. **Comparing Characters.** The Norse version of creation included many characters. Where do all the beings rank in the order of the world? Create a list that includes these beings: mankind, the gods of Asgard, the great spirit, and the bad giants. List the most powerful at the top and the least powerful at the bottom.

2. **Explaining Action.** This myth does not state why the great spirit created a living creature. However, details about what the great spirit saw suggest a reason. Review the second

paragraph of the myth. Try to figure out a reason for the creation of the first giant.

3. **Recognizing Symbols.** Storytellers often use objects or colors to represent complicated ideas. You may know that a dove is used to represent peace. The color red often stands for anger. An object or color used to signal an idea is called a **symbol**. A symbol for an idea often gets the attention of the reader better than an explanation of that idea. Symbols make important ideas easier to notice and to remember.

In the Norse creation myth, ice is used as a symbol of death. Wherever there is ice, breathing and movement stop. For example, the giant Bure is freed from the ice and given life only when the cow melts the ice away.

There is also a symbol in the myth that stands for life. This symbol is used to give life to humans. The symbol also supports life in all parts of the universe. Skim through the myth. Find the object that symbolizes life.

4. **Comparing Plots.** Review the Greek story "The Beginning of the World." Compare it to the Norse creation myth. Divide each **plot**, or order of events, into five stages:

Stage 1—There is no world. There is no earth, or sky, or sea.
Stage 2—Two types of gods come into being: kind and cruel. They battle each other for power.
Stage 3—The kind gods win over cruel gods.
Stage 4—The kind gods establish their rule over the world. They also create their own kingdom.
Stage 5—People are created and placed in the world.

Create a chart about the Greek and Norse creation myths. For each story, list the specific events of the five stages of creation.

5. **Identifying Conflict.** The plot of a story always describes a **conflict**, or a struggle between opposing forces. External conflict is one type of conflict. **External conflict** is an outward struggle. The main character fights with other characters, or nature, or supernatural forces. Who is involved in the external conflict in "The Beginning of a World"? What is the struggle about? Who wins?

Developing Vocabulary Skills

Finding Spelling Changes in Base Words. It is easy to add a suffix to some base words. For example, *friend* + *ly* = *friendly*. However, the spelling of some base words changes when a suffix is added. Read the following examples. They present three spelling rules for adding suffixes to base words.

a. When a suffix beginning with a vowel is added to a word ending in silent *e*, the *e* is usually dropped.

change + *ing* = *changing*

Note that the *e* is not dropped when a suffix beginning with a consonant is added.

use + *ful* = *useful*

b. When a suffix is added to a word ending in *y* preceded by a consonant, the *y* is usually changed to an *i*.

lonely + *ness* = *loneliness*

Note that when the *y* is preceded by a vowel, it is not changed.

delay + *ed* = *delayed*

c. Words ending in one consonant preceded

by one vowel double the final consonant before adding *-ing*, *-ed*, or *-er*.

occur + ing = occurring

Note that when two vowels appear in the word, the final consonant is not doubled.

cheat + ed = cheated

Read each of the following sentences about the myth you have just read. On your paper, copy every underlined word. Then write the base word and its endings. If the spelling of the base word has changed, decide which of the spelling rules was used. On your paper, write the letter of the spelling rule.

1. There, too, a <u>bottomless</u> spring never <u>stopped bubbling</u> and <u>running</u> over.

2. The gods wanted a road from their <u>beautiful</u>, <u>shining</u> city down to the earth.

3. Sleipner <u>carried</u> his master on many long and <u>dangerous</u> adventures.

4. The gods <u>carved</u> a man out of a tall ash tree and a woman out of a <u>graceful</u> elm.

Developing Writing Skills

1. **Analyzing Results.** In both the Greek and the Norse myths, the gods played an important role in Creation. Refer to your answer for "Reading Literature: Norse Myths" question 4. Choose either the Greek or Norse creation story. Contrast the universe as it existed in stage 2 with the universe in stage 5. Do you think the actions of the gods made the universe a better place by the end of stage 5? Why or why not? Write a paragraph to explain your opinion.

2. **Describing a Setting.** Setting, or the time and place of the action, is important in "The Beginning of a World." The storyteller gives detailed descriptions of the setting. Choose a setting that you particularly like. Write a paragraph describing the place.

   Pre-Writing. One way to describe a setting is to give details that appeal to the senses: sight, sound, touch, taste, and smell. List the five senses on your paper. Write at least one detail about your setting to appeal to each sense. For example, a detail appealing to the sense of touch might state: "The marble wall was smooth and cold." A detail about color would appeal to sight.

   Writing. Describe the setting you chose in one paragraph. Include the details from your list. Explain what a person in that place can see, hear, touch, taste, and smell.

   Revising. Read your description to another person. Then, ask the person to list from your setting a detail about each of the five senses. Sometimes, a detail for a sense might be hard to recall. Then you need to change that sentence in your paragraph.

Developing Skills in Study and Research

Using the Library Filing System. Suppose you wanted to find more information about the Norse people and their mythology. You could look for books about subjects mentioned in the Norse creation myth. To find the books on the shelves, you would need to understand the library filing system.

The most commonly used library filing system is the Dewey Decimal System. Skim the list of Dewey Decimal categories on page 626 in the Handbook. Decide how each of the following books would be coded. List the number range for each book on your paper. For example, a book of poetry would have an 800–899 number code in the Dewey Decimal System.

a book about Norse mythology
a fictional book about giants
a book about the history of Iceland
a book that explains ice
a book of Scandinavian art

Developing Skills in Speaking and Listening

Reading a Story Aloud. The myths were originally passed along by storytellers. Now that the stories have been written down, it is easy to forget their oral tradition. However, the myths are still entertaining when they are spoken rather than read silently.

Select a section of one of the myths you have read. Choose a section that is several paragraphs long. Prepare to read it aloud to the class. The part you choose may focus on a character or on the setting. Try to have your voice express the mood that the story explains.

Decide which words and ideas to emphasize. Practice an appropriate speed of reading, not too fast or too slow. Be sure you can pronounce all the words. Read through the selection several times so that you are comfortable with it.

When you are ready, present the selection to the class.

How Odin Lost His Eye

TRADITIONAL NORSE MYTH
Retold by Catharine F. Sellew

As you read this myth, pay attention to the details about the Norse god Odin. How does he compare to the Greek idea of a god? In what ways is Odin like Zeus? In what ways is he different?

Once when the world was still very young, Odin sat on his throne in the most beautiful palace in Asgard. His throne was so high that he could see over all three parts of the world from where he sat. On his head he wore a helmet shaped like an eagle. On his shoulders perched two black ravens called Memory and Thought. At his feet crouched two snarling wolves.

The great king gazed thoughtfully down on the earth below him. He had made the green land that stretched out before his eyes. With the help of the other gods, he had made men and women who lived on that earth, and he felt truly like the All-Father he was called.

The fair elves had promised they would help his children of the earth. The elves were the tiny people who lived between heaven and earth. They were so small that they could flit about doing their work unseen. Odin knew that they were the artists who painted the flowers and made the beds for the streams. They took care of all the bees and the butterflies. And it was the elves who brought the gentle rain and sunshine to the earth.

Even the ugly dwarfs, who lived in the heart of the mountains, agreed to help. They forged iron and metals, made tools and weapons. They dug gold and silver and beautiful jewels out of the earth. Sometimes they even cut the grain and ground the flour for the farmers on the earth.

All seemed to be going well. Odin found it hard to think of evil times. But he knew that the frost giants were only waiting for a chance to bring trouble to his children. They were the ones who brought cold and ice to the world and shook the earth in anger. They hated Odin and all the work of the gods.

From high on his lofty throne, Odin looked down beyond the earth deep into the gloomy land of his enemies. He saw dark figures of huge men moving about. They looked like evil shadows. He, the king of the gods, must have more wisdom. It was not enough just to see his enemies. He must know more about them.

So Odin wrapped his tall figure in a blue cloak. Down from his throne he climbed. Down the broad rainbow bridge he strode, and across the green earth till he came to one of the roots of the great ever green tree. There, close by the tree, was a well full of clear water. Its surface was so still it was like a mirror. In it one could see pictures of things that had happened and things that were going to happen.

Beside the well sat an old man. His face was lined with the troubles of the world. His name was Mimir (mē mêr'), which means Memory. No one, not even the great Odin, could see the pictures in the well unless he first drank some of its water. Only Mimir could give the magic drink.

"Aged Mimir," Odin said to the old man, "you who hold the knowledge of the past and future in your magic waters, let me have but one sip. Then I can know enough to protect the men and women of the earth from the hate of the giants."

Mimir looked kindly at Odin, but he did not smile. Although he spoke softly, his voice was so deep it reminded Odin of the distant roar of the ocean.

"The price of one drink from this well is not cheap." Mimir said. "And once you have drunk and gazed into the mirror of life, you may wish you had not. For sorrow and death as well as joy are pictured there. Think again before you ask to drink."

Once the king of the gods had made up his mind, however, nothing could change it. He was not afraid to look upon sorrow and death.

"What is your price?" Odin asked.

"You are great and good, Odin," answered Mimir. "You have worked hard to make the world. Only those who know hard work may drink from my well. Yet, that is not enough. What have you given up that is dear to you? What have you sacrificed? The price of a drink must be a great sacrifice. Are you willing to pay the price?"

What could the king of the gods sacrifice? What was most dear to him? Odin thought of his handsome son, Balder, whom he loved most in the world. To give up his son would be like giving up life. Odin stood silent before Mimir. Indeed that would be a high price!

Then Mimir spoke again. He had read Odin's thoughts.

"No, I am not asking for your dear son. I ask for one of your eyes."

Odin put his hands up to his bright blue eyes. His eyes had taught him what was good and beautiful—what was evil and ugly. Those eyes had also seen his children, the men and women of the earth, struggling against the hate of the giants. One eye was a small sacrifice to win knowledge of how to help them. Without another thought, Odin plucked out one of his blue eyes and handed it to Mimir.

Then Mimir smiled and gave Odin a horn full of the waters of his well. "Drink deeply, brave king, so you may see all that you wish in the mirror of life."

Odin lifted the horn to his lips and drank. Then he knelt by the edge of the well and watched the pictures passing across its still and silent surface. When he stood up again, he sighed, for it was as Mimir had said. He had seen sorrow and death as well as joy. Only the glorious promise at the end gave him courage to go on.

That is how Odin, the great king of the gods, became one-eyed. If you can find Mimir's well, you will see Odin's blue eye resting on the bottom. It is there to remind men and women of the great sacrifice he made for them.

Developing Comprehension Skills

1. According to Norse myths, the gods helped mankind. What other two groups helped mankind?

2. Why did Odin think it was important to look into the future?

3. How did Odin feel about making the sacrifice Mimir demanded?

4. Odin sacrificed an eye for knowledge about the future. What does this action reveal about Odin's personality?

5. Odin decided to learn what would happen in the future. Do you think you would want to know what the future held? Explain why or why not.

Reading Literature: Norse Myths

1. **Understanding Action.** In the myth, Mimir controls the power to see into the future. He requires Odin to make a sacrifice in order to see the future. What lesson does Mimir hope the sacrifice will teach Odin?

   At first, Odin thought Mimir would require him to sacrifice his son. Odin feels that would be a very high price. Then, Mimir asks Odin to sacrifice an eye. Odin agrees quickly. How do you think Odin's previous thoughts about sacrificing his son affect his decision?

2. **Comparing Myths.** To compare two things, you look for what they have that is similar. The Norse god Odin can be compared to the Greek Titan Prometheus. In the myths, they are alike in several ways. They are both powerful beings. Both make a sacrifice for humans. What does Odin sacrifice? Why? Review the Greek myth, "The Beginning of the World." What does Prometheus sacrifice? Why? How are the attitudes of Odin and Prometheus toward mankind the same?

3. **Understanding Conflict.** A struggle that takes place within a character is called **internal conflict**. This type of conflict usually involves a decision that the character must make. Identify the internal conflict that Odin faces in this myth. Can you also find an external conflict that Odin is worried about?

Developing Vocabulary Skills

Identifying Affixes and Base Words. You have learned than an **affix** is a prefix or suffix added to a base word. The letters that form some affixes may also appear as parts of some base words. For example, the letters *r* and *e* are found at the beginning of *reach*. However, the letters *ach* do not form a word. Therefore, the letter combination *re* is part of the word *reach*. It is not a prefix in this case.

For each of the following words, two or three letters are underlined. Tell whether they are an affix (prefix or suffix) or part of the base word. If you are unsure, take the underlined letters off the word. Then decide whether what is left is a word by itself, or not.

1. tremend<u>ous</u>   5. <u>re</u>move

2. <u>un</u>iverse   6. soft<u>ly</u>

3. <u>cu</u>nning   7. <u>di</u>stant

4. <u>mis</u>spell   8. ug<u>ly</u>

Developing Writing Skills

1. **Analyzing Character Traits.** Think of Odin's special strengths. Then review the myth and try to find one weakness that Odin has. Write a paragraph describing both the

strengths and weaknesses of Odin's character. Do you think Odin is a believable character? Why or why not? Include your opinions in the paragraph.

2. **Describing an Event.** Both good and bad events occur in the myths. Think of something good that has happened to you. Write a paragraph to describe the event.

Pre-Writing. What was the good event? List the following details:

Who was involved in the event?

What happened?

When did it occur?

Where were you?

How did it make you feel?

Write a topic sentence that summarizes your reaction to the event.

Writing. Begin the paragraph with the topic sentence you developed. Then state each detail about the event in a complete sentence. Present the information in an order that makes sense.

Revising. Check that every group of words expresses a complete thought. Read each sentence out loud. Does it make sense? If it doesn't, add words to make the ideas or events clear.

Developing Skills in Critical Thinking

Recognizing Slanted Language. A careful reader is aware that words have two kinds of meaning. **Denotations** are the dictionary meanings. **Connotations** are the feelings or ideas the words give. Words with strong positive connotations make you feel in favor of something. Words with strong negative connotations may sway you against something.

For example, the words *slender* and *skinny* are close in meaning. They almost seem to be synonyms. However, *slender* gives a favorable picture of a healthy, graceful person. *Skinny* implies an unfavorable meaning of too thin, too far from average. *Thin* creates a neutral idea, neither positive or negative.

Skim the myth "How Odin Lost His Eye." Find five sentences with words that have strong connotations. The connotations may be either positive or negative. List the five sentences on your paper. Think about how the storyteller swayed your opinion in each sentence. Write the word *Positive* next to those that gave you a favorable impression of a character, action, or setting. Write the word *Negative* next to those that turned you against something in the story. Then, underline the exact word or words that gave you the feeling.

Frigga's Necklace

TRADITIONAL NORSE MYTH
Retold by Catharine F. Sellew

As you read this myth, pay attention to the motives, or reasons, for the characters' actions. Why do Odin and Frigga behave as they do? What do their actions reveal about human nature?

Frigga (frē′gə), the queen of the gods, sat beside Odin on the high throne on the top of the world. She was very beautiful, with white plumes in her hair that waved softly in the breeze. She wore snowy white robes and a wide, golden belt from which hung a ring of keys. She smiled down at the men and women of the earth and watched over their homes and children.

Often she feasted with the other gods and goddesses, but best of all she loved to spin golden thread and weave clouds of glowing colors to put in the sky. Her spinning wheel was set with jewels that sparkled at night. The people of the earth saw them shining in the sky and called them stars.

Frigga was kind and beautiful, but she was also very vain. She could not be happy unless she was the most beautifully dressed goddess in Asgard.

One day she took out her box of jewels and looked at one necklace after another. None of them was quite brilliant enough or quite the right length. None of them really suited her. She wanted a new necklace.

It should be a necklace of pure gold, she decided. It should be made in such a design that everyone—especially her husband, Odin—would wonder at it. So Frigga sent a messenger down to the workshop of the dwarfs. They could make magic things out of metals and jewels that they dug from the heart of the mountains.

Frigga's messenger went to the most skillful of the dwarfs and told him what the queen of the gods wanted. "It must be more beautiful than anything you have ever made," the messenger commanded.

"And all of gold?" asked the dwarf.

"Yes, pure gold. You must not use any other metal."

"But we do not have enough gold for such a necklace," said the dwarf, shaking his head sadly.

"Then dig deeper into the heart of the mountains until you have found enough. This is an order from Frigga! It is the goddess queen who demands it!"

"I know! I know! But we have already made many ornaments of gold for that beautiful lady and the other gods and goddesses. We have only a little gold left. Please explain this to her highness. Tell her I will make a necklace of wondrous beauty. It will be made of all the metals of the earth in a design worthy only of the lovely Frigga!"

When the messenger went back and told Frigga what the most skillful dwarf had said, she was very disappointed. A necklace of many metals would no doubt be beautiful, but for her new gold gown, pure gold was needed. If the dwarfs could not get enough gold, she would find some.

Then the beautiful goddess put on her traveling robes and swept down the rainbow bridge. She walked for miles and miles over the earth in search of gold for her necklace. There were gold rings here. There were gold bracelets there. But they belonged to the men and women of the earth, whom Frigga loved as though they were her own children. She did not wish to take such things from them.

At last she came to a statue that stood in a little village. It was much taller than any man of the earth. It shone so brightly that beams of light came from it and threw a dazzling glow for miles around. It was made of pure gold.

Frigga cried out with pleasure! Here at last was more than enough gold for her necklace. Just a small piece of the statue would be plenty. As the queen of the gods came closer, she saw it was a statue of her husband, Odin. It looked so much like Odin that for a minute she expected it to speak.

But, no, it was only a speechless statue. She broke off a piece of gold just big enough for the necklace. No one would miss it. Even if it were missed, no one would know where it had gone.

The most skillful dwarf turned the stolen piece of gold into a necklace for Frigga. Never had there been such a handsome necklace. It had been hammered and twisted and carved in a way that immediately caught everyone's attention. All the goddesses gazed upon it with envy and wonder. Even Odin praised it.

"It is a thing of rare beauty," he said. "Fit only for my queen to wear." He smiled upon Frigga, and she was very happy.

Now the men and women of the earth had made the statue of the All-Father so that they might worship him. Odin had been very pleased. He had been kind to those faithful men and women, and he had protected them from the evil of the frost giants. In the dark of the night he often walked through the village and smiled upon the simple homes full of sleeping men and women. Even in the dark the gold statue glowed and threw a warm light upon the stones of the street.

It was on such a night that Odin discovered a piece of gold had been taken from his statue. He was very angry!

"What is this?" he shouted. "Who has dared to steal gold from my statue? He shall pay heavily for this. Do not think I am unable to discover the thief!"

Odin's voice rang through the silent village. Dark clouds rolled across the night

and howled, "Thief! Thief!" The giants in the dark cold depths of the earth laughed and shook their fists with joy. Evil was again in the world, and the great Odin was angry.

Now Odin did not smile. He did not seem to notice Frigga or what she wore. He spoke seldom and sat upon his throne scowling down upon the earth. Nothing Frigga said or did could rouse him. She began to be afraid. What would happen if he ever found out she had stolen the gold?

Finally, Odin went back to the statue. He wrote magic verses upon it so that the next morning it would be able to speak and name the thief.

From her throne in Asgard Frigga saw him writing upon the statue. Her face went white with terror. What could she do? Odin might never forgive her. Should she confess? No. His anger would be too terrible to bear. He must never know the truth.

Quickly, while Odin was still on the earth, Frigga fled to the land of the dwarfs. Down the dark, winding underground passages she stumbled. Loose stones slipped under her feet, and several times she almost fell. Down and down she went until she came to the workshop of the most evil dwarf. The most skillful dwarf could not help her this time.

"Help me! Help me!" she begged as the tears ran down her pale cheeks. The evil little dwarf gazed at her in surprise. His face was grimy and red from working. His little green eyes gleamed with cunning, but his heart softened as he looked at the frightened goddess.

sky. A fierce wind howled and tugged at the roofs of the little houses. The men, women, and children pulled their blankets over their heads and trembled with fear.

"The thief shall pay for this!" Odin roared again. The wind picked up his words

"What can I do?" he croaked. "I have no power against the great Odin."

"You must think of something," sobbed Frigga. "The statue will speak my name in the morning. Break the statue! You must break the statue! You can do it!"

"I wouldn't dare," said the dwarf.

"Please! Please!" begged the goddess. Through her tears, the great queen smiled upon the little dwarf. "You are the only living creature who can help me. Is your heart hard and cold like the frost giants'? Will you leave me to face my husband's fearful rage when, by using your great cunning, you can save me? Tell me you are not so cruel! Please destroy the statue!" Again Frigga wept.

"Well," said the dwarf slowly, "perhaps I can help you. I would not do such a thing for anyone else. I shall be taking a great chance."

"Surely you are not afraid to take a chance," Frigga said. She smiled at him and the rosy color came back into her cheeks. "I shall never forget your great kindness." Then she ran back up the dark passages and on up to her throne in Asgard.

The next morning Odin returned to the statue. Alas! It was broken into a million gold pieces scattered upon the ground. There was no longer any statue to speak the name of the thief. Odin stood looking down at the heap of gold with his one blue eye. As Frigga watched him from her throne, her heart stood still with fear, but Odin only stood there silently thinking. She could not see the black rage that darkened his brow.

What was he thinking? Had he guessed now who the thief was? How could he? What was he doing standing there?

Then the great king of the gods turned on his heel. He did not look back. Without looking to the right or to the left, he walked straight ahead until he disappeared from sight.

Days passed. Weeks passed. Months passed. Odin did not return. Frigga sat alone on her high throne. The frost giants laughed with glee. Now who would rule the world and protect the people from evil? They blew cold blasts upon the earth. Storms raged on land and sea. The sun no longer warmed the world. Ice and snow covered everything.

In Asgard all was confusion and sadness. Odin had left the world. His silent anger was worse than any rage Frigga or the other gods and goddesses had ever known.

Frigga remembered the happy days before she had risked so much for the sake of vanity. The necklace no longer seemed beautiful. Because of it, she had brought on all this evil and trouble. She knew that Odin had left the world because evil had been done, even though he might not have learned the name of the thief. She wept and prayed all night and all day for his forgiveness.

Then one day, when they had given up hope of ever seeing Odin again, the great All-Father returned. He smiled upon Frigga and the other gods and goddesses. He looked down upon the dark, cold world. As he gazed, the ice began to melt. The sun began to break through the gray clouds. The plants began to grow. Odin was no longer angry. All was forgiven. The frost giants grumbled and growled, but there was nothing they could do.

Frigga never knew whether Odin had guessed the whole truth, but she never wore the beautiful gold necklace again.

Developing Comprehension Skills

1. Why did Frigga insist on a new necklace of solid gold?

2. How did Odin react when he found out that someone had taken a piece of gold from his statue?

3. What qualities of Frigga's personality are emphasized in this story?

4. In what way does Frigga's attitude toward life change from the beginning of the myth to the end?

5. Which character would you rather rely on in a crisis: Frigga or Odin? Why?

Reading Literature: Norse Myths

1. **Understanding Details of Plot.** Only one dwarf was willing to help Frigga destroy Odin's statue. Why might the dwarf have agreed to such a dangerous task? List three reasons. What details in the story helped you make these inferences?

2. **Contrasting Characters.** Make a list of Frigga's personality traits. Divide your list into two parts: positive traits and negative traits. Include at least five traits in the list. Then make another list for Odin's personality traits. Divide the list in the same way as the list for Frigga. When you are finished, con-

trast the lists for Frigga and Odin. Which character do you think is presented in a more favorable way in the Norse myth?

3. **Understanding Motivation.** Often, characters are forced to act in a certain way to avoid unfavorable results. For example, Frigga decides not to confess her theft of the gold. She has two reasons. First, she might not be forgiven if she tells the truth. Second, she would have to live with Odin's angry temper if she admits her guilt. Odin turns away from the statue and disappears for months. What do you think is Odin's motivation, or reason for action?

4. **Analyzing Plot.** The action of this story begins with Frigga. She wants a new necklace for her new gown. This desire seems harmless. However, the action builds. Soon, Frigga finds herself faced with a major problem. Evil has entered the world. Trace the events of the plot to show the growth of evil. Begin with Frigga's request for a gold necklace. Include both Frigga's and Odin's actions. What happens at the end of the myth? What effect do Odin's actions have?

5. **Identifying Conflict.** Frigga faces several conflicts, or struggles, because of the necklace. Her external conflicts include the search for gold and the argument with the dwarf. Frigga wins these struggles. She also faces at least one internal conflict in this story. Explain an internal conflict that Frigga deals with. How is it settled?

Developing Vocabulary Skills

Adding Affixes to Base Words. Each of the following phrases defines a word. Each phrase also contains a base word from one of the myths you have read. Read the definition and figure out the word being defined. Write the word on your paper by adding a prefix, a suffix, or both to the base word. Sometimes you will need to add two suffixes. Use the affixes, or the prefixes and suffixes, that are listed in the introduction on pages 104 and 105 of this book.

1. in a manner that is filled with thought
2. the opposite of respect
3. one who rules
4. to pay back
5. the state of being cold
6. without help
7. to put in the wrong place
8. not in a patient way

Developing Writing Skills

1. **Writing a Character Analysis.** Think about the way that Frigga behaves in this myth. Look for the motives, or reasons, for her actions. Write a paragraph about whether Frigga's behavior is believable. In other words, does she act in a reasonable way? Explain your opinion. Remember, Frigga lives in unusual circumstances.

   Pre-Writing. Make a list of Frigga's main thoughts and actions in the story. Arrange the list in correct time order. Then divide the list to show the beginning, middle, and end of the story.

   Compare Frigga's behavior during the three parts of the story. Do you see any differences in her behavior? How does she change? Can you find or infer logical reasons for this change?

Writing. Begin with a sentence stating your main idea about Frigga. Then, use sentences to support the topic sentence. Tell about Frigga's main actions. Tell why you think she reacts as she does. Discuss whether or not Frigga changes. Include your opinion of Frigga.

Revising. Form a small group with three or four classmates. The members should take turns reading their paragraphs to the group. Evaluate each paragraph by discussing the following:

Is the topic sentence clear?
Does each detail in the paragraph support the topic sentence?
Is each sentence easy to understand?
Does the order of the sentences in the paragraph make sense?

If the group answers "no" to any question about your paragraph, then revise your writing. Change the part of the paragraph that gives an unclear or wrong idea.

2. **Anticipating Action.** A part of the action in the story, "Frigga's Necklace," is missing. Consider the following points:

What did Odin think about as he stared at the destroyed statue?
Why did Odin leave?
Where did he go?
Why did he decide to return?

Write this part of the story yourself. Make your descriptions clear and detailed.

Developing Skills in Critical Thinking

Recognizing Persuasion Techniques. Frigga was a master at persuading the dwarf to destroy Odin's gold statue. She used five different methods, or techniques, of persuasion:

1. **hero appeal:** to convince her audience that he was the only person who could help.

2. **comparison with an enemy:** to force her audience to prove that he was not like the frost giants.

3. **appeal to basic humanity:** to force her audience to show he really was a good person.

4. **appeal to courage:** to force her audience to prove that he was not a coward.

5. **promise of a favor in return:** to promise her audience payment, of sorts, for his help.

These same persuasion techniques are used today by many people. You can find examples in the field of advertising. Select an advertisement that you have seen or heard for a real product. The ad may be from a newspaper or magazine. It may be a slogan used in television or radio advertisements. Decide which methods of persuasion are used in the ad. There may be one method or several. Try to figure out the audience toward which the ad is directed. Is the ad convincing? If so, why? If not, what would you change about it?

Be ready to discuss your findings and opinions with the class.

Sif's Golden Hair

TRADITIONAL NORSE MYTH
Retold by Catharine F. Sellew

This selection is the beginning of a three-part myth about the fire god Loki. What qualities does Loki show in this part of the story? Do you think his experiences will change his personality?

When the sky grew black and the thunder growled and the lightning flashed, the people of the North used to say that Thor was driving his chariot across the heavens. Thor was one of Odin's sons. When he was only a baby, he lifted and tossed aside ten loads of bearskins. Odin and Frigga knew then that their son was to be one of the heroes of Asgard.

Thor grew up to be the largest and strongest of the gods. He had bright red hair and a bushy red beard that flashed sparks when he was angry. Great muscles bulged in his arms. No wonder he was named the thunder god!

Thor was much too heavy for a horse to carry. He rode in a chariot pulled by two goats called Toothcracker and Toothgnasher. He was forbidden to pass over the rainbow bridge. The bridge had been built so that it would not hold the weight of a giant. The gods were afraid that it would not hold Thor, either, and that the heat from his fiery red hair would destroy it. Thor was forced to drive through rivers of cold mist to join the council of the gods by the fountain at the foot of the ever green tree.

Now Thor had a very beautiful wife called Sif (sēf). One reason for Sif's beauty was her golden hair. It fell in wonderful gleaming waves from the top of her head all the way to the ground, so that she seemed to be covered by a gorgeous golden veil. Thor was very proud of his wife's beautiful hair.

One morning Thor wakened and leaned over to kiss his wife good morning. Alas! Sif's golden hair was gone! Thor rubbed his eyes. He must be dreaming! No, there lay his beautiful wife with all her hair cut off. Her head was white and bare.

"Sif! Sif!" Thor shook his wife awake. "What have you done?"

Sif opened her blue eyes in surprise. She was not used to being so rudely awakened.

"What's the matter?" she murmured.

"Your hair! Where is your hair?"

"My hair?" Sif put her hands up to her head. She felt the roughness where her hair had been cut. "Thor! Thor! What has happened?" Sif hid her head under the bearskin on the bed. "My hair has been cut off! My beauty is gone. I'll be ugly for the rest of my life!"

Thor tried to comfort her, but he was so upset and angry he did not know what to say. Who could have done such a thing? Surely no one in Asgard hated Sif. Yet why should anyone cut off her hair unless it was because of jealous hatred? Maybe it was a poor kind of joke.

A joke! A wicked joke! Thor jumped up from the bed where Sif lay sobbing. "It is that evil Loki who has done this to you!" he cried. "No other in Asgard would want to do this wicked thing."

Loki (lō'kē), the fire god, was a mischief-maker. He loved to make trouble. He liked to see people get excited over things he had done secretly. He was very handsome and looked so cheerful and friendly that usually no one suspected him.

Thor knew better. Out of the door he went, shouting great oaths that echoed like thunder all over the world. Sparks flew from his hair and beard. The earth shook under his angry step.

Odin, the All-Father, heard Thor shouting. When he heard what had happened to Sif's golden hair, he, too, thought of Loki.

"Find him," Odin called after Thor. "And if he did cut off Sif's hair, punish him. But remember to be fair. Do not let your temper control you!"

Loki, far away, heard those words and trembled. Thor's anger was greatly to be

Loki, 1822, HERMANN ERNST FREUND.
The Ny Carlsberg Glyptotek, Copenhagen.

feared, but when the All-Father was angry, too, there was even more reason to be afraid. So he ran away as fast as he could.

Thor soon caught up to him. Loki quickly changed himself into a horse and raced ahead, but this did not fool Thor, who ran close behind. Then Loki turned himself into a fish and leaped into a river. Thor pulled a fish net out of his pocket, and soon Loki was flip-flopping helplessly in it. When Thor's big fist closed around the fish, Loki turned himself back to his real form. He tried to speak and plead forgiveness, but Thor's hands were closing around his throat.

Just in time, Thor remembered Odin's words—"Be fair." Thor did not know, he had only guessed that Loki was guilty. He loosened his iron grip.

"Forgive me," gasped the mischief-maker. "I will get Sif a new head of hair! Let me go, and I will make up for my wrong."

"So you did cut off her hair!" thundered Thor. His hands grabbed again at Loki's throat.

"Stop! Let me go! Unless you allow me to live, Sif will never be beautiful again."

"How soon will you get her a new head of hair?" snapped Thor. "She cannot show herself before the gods and goddesses until she has her hair."

"Before the daylight is gone, Sif will have a new head of hair," promised Loki. "It will be as long and as beautiful as ever."

Thor paused. "Very well," he agreed at last. "But if you do not come back before evening with the golden hair for my dear wife, I will break every bone in your body!"

Then the great thunder god quickly returned to his palace to tell poor Sif of Loki's promise.

Developing Comprehension Skills

1. Give three reasons why Thor was called "the thunder god."

2. What was Odin's warning to Thor?

3. Explain why "the fire god" was a good name for Loki.

4. Do you think Loki should be punished for his cruel joke? Explain your opinion. Would you change your mind if Loki could get Sif a new head of hair?

Reading Literature: Norse Myths

1. **Understanding a Character.** Sif is very upset by the loss of her hair. Why is Sif's hair so important to her? Suppose Sif's hair could not be replaced immediately. How do you think her life would change?

2. **Identifying Values.** Thor is a powerful god in the myth, but he also has human feelings. Thor is motivated by what is important to him. Skim through the myth. Try to find three things in life that Thor values highly.

3. **Analyzing Details of Plot.** Plot can be divided into several sections. In part of the story, action builds and the struggle grows more intense. This is the **rising action**. During the rising action, Thor catches Loki. Why does Thor loosen his grip around Loki's throat the first time? What does this action tell you about Thor's personality?

The action continues. Loki confesses to the crime. Thor grabs Loki's throat again. For what reason does Thor let go of Loki the second time? What does this last action reveal about Thor?

The Magic Gifts

TRADITIONAL NORSE MYTH
Retold by Catharine F. Sellew

Here is the second part of the story about Loki. His mischief has gotten him into trouble. Will he be able to save himself? Or will he just make matters worse?

Loki watched the angry thunder god disappear in the distance. He sighed with relief, and rubbed his swollen throat where Thor's hands had nearly choked him. He must get busy. It was almost noon. There was much to be done before the shadow of night's chariot crossed the sky.

He must find a head of hair as beautiful as the locks he had cut from Sif's head. Loki reached into his pocket. Silky threads of gold spilled out into the light. It was Sif's hair! The sunshine fell on it and flashed back with such brightness that Loki closed his eyes. Then he turned and went into a cave in the side of a mountain. This was the shortest way to the home of the dwarfs.

Loki ran swiftly down the long winding tunnels. Dead leaves rustled under his feet. The air smelled of wet earth. He had to bend his shoulders to keep from hitting his head on the rough ceiling. The dwarfs called out to him as he passed, for Loki was well known in this land of magic. Their green eyes shone in the darkness. How ugly

they are, thought Loki. They were never allowed outside their mountain while day still lit the earth.

A faint light flickered through the darkness, growing brighter and brighter as Loki drew closer. Voices and the clash of metal echoed in the passageway. He could hear the roar of the bellows that blew the flames hotter. At last he came out into a brightly lit cave. In the corners were huge piles of shining metals and glittering jewels. In the center beside the stone hearth and anvil stood a dwarf called Dvalin (dvā′lən). Beads of sweat covered his wrinkled forehead as he worked before the hot fire. He turned when he heard Loki call out.

"Ah, Loki, what mischief are you up to now?" Dvalin asked with a grin.

"I'm in trouble," answered the god.

"Again?" chuckled the dwarf.

"Speak to me with respect," Loki cried angrily. "You forget I am a god."

"I beg your pardon," and Dvalin turned back to his work. He knew this handsome god needed his help. Loki could not put on airs with him. But he rather liked the young mischief-maker just the same.

"You must make me a head of hair as beautiful as this." Loki tossed Sif's locks in a heap on the floor of the cave. In the firelight the hair gleamed like the metal the dwarfs dug from the heart of the mountains. "And it must grow into the head of the goddess and become alive. I must have it before the daylight on the earth is gone."

"You are a devil!" muttered the dwarf. He looked thoughtfully at the mass of hair on the floor and scratched behind his pointed ear.

"Come, come," teased Loki. "Don't tell me your magic can't make a head of hair!" But he was worried. What could he do if Dvalin failed him?

"Well," the dwarf said slowly, "perhaps I can do what you want."

"Good!" cried Loki. He sat down on a three-legged stool and prepared to wait. Dvalin scurried around the cave. He took three handfuls of crushed buttercups, which he had picked in a field by moonlight. He added three cups of dew that sparkled like diamonds, a lump of rich gold metal, and a pinch of magic powder. All these he stirred together in a big black pot. Then he called his helpers to build up the fire. Loki watched lazily, thinking of all that had happened that morning.

"Dvalin," he called suddenly. The dwarf was busy with his work and only nodded his head in answer. "Odin was very angry with me. If I had a wonderful gift for him, he might forget my mischief. Surely you could make the All-Father some useful present with your great magic?"

"You ask a great deal," Dvalin called over his shoulder.

"You will be well repaid. I will make you known as the most skillful dwarf in all the world."

Dvalin smiled. "I'll see what I can do," he said. And he shouted down the passageways for more help. Dwarfs scuttled into the cave from all directions. Some dropped down from the walls where they had been sleeping in the hollows of the rock. Some crept out from behind the pile of jewels that they had been counting. Some came in dragging picks and shovels.

Then what a clamor of voices and ringing metal! The fire blazed brighter. The cave grew hotter and hotter.

As time passed, Loki began to worry again. It was so dark far down under the earth that he could not tell whether the sun was still in the sky.

"Hurry! Hurry!" he called, but the busy dwarfs did not hear him. Already the shadows of night might cover the earth! Already Loki's punishment might have been decided by the gods! The young god jumped to his feet and looked into the tunnel that led to the top of the earth. Of course, all he could see was inky blackness. Then Dvalin called him.

"What do you think of this?" he asked, his face shining with pride. He took the sharp point of a spear from the glowing coals. "Give this to the All-Father. Tell him to fasten it to the end of the branch he cut from the ever green tree. He will then have a spear that will never miss its aim. And any man or god who swears an oath upon its point will never be able to break his word."

"Wonderful! Wonderful!" exclaimed Loki. "But Sif's hair—"

"And look at this," cried Dvalin. He took something small that one of the dwarfs held out to him. When he unfolded it, it looked like a tiny boat. Then the dwarfs took hold of each end and pulled and pulled. It grew larger and larger until it filled half the cave.

"You can make it even larger," explained Dvalin. "It will hold all the gods in Asgard and all their horses. It will sail in the air as well as on water. And yet it can be folded up and put in your pocket." And— whisk—the boat was all rolled up and handed to Loki!

"Marvelous!" gasped Loki. "But the golden hair—" None of these other things would save him if he returned without the golden hair.

"Oh, the golden hair," smiled Dvalin. "You look out for yourself, don't you? No, I haven't forgotten the golden hair." He took an armful of shimmering gold from another dwarf. It was even more wonderful than the hair that Loki had cut from Sif's head. Dvalin had spun it from the magic mixture he had made in the black pot. He assured Loki that the minute it touched Sif's head it would grow just like real hair.

Loki quickly thanked Dvalin and tucked the three magic gifts under his cloak. "Your name will be famous all over the world," he called over his shoulder, and dashed into the dark passageway that led to the top of the earth.

As Loki burst out of the side of the mountain, day was just disappearing into the river of mist. He was not too late. In triumph he entered Thor's palace.

Developing Comprehension Skills

1. Describe the two gifts Dvalin made for Odin.

2. Consider what you know about Loki's behavior and about the dwarfs. Why do you think Loki was well known by the dwarfs?

3. In this part of the story, Loki is worried. Why is he worried? Does he show his fear to Dvalin? How?

4. Loki requested help from someone who was not a god. What does this tell you about Loki's personality? Do you think Loki is a strong or weak character?

Reading Literature: Norse Myths

1. **Identifying a Character's Motives.** Review the myth. Find two reasons Dvalin put so much effort into Loki's projects.

2. **Understanding Purpose.** Do you think the main purpose of this myth was to explain something about nature, to give a moral lesson, or to entertain?

3. **Examining a Setting.** The dwarfs lived in mountain caves. List at least three details that describe the caves. In what ways does this environment fit the dwarfs?

The Dwarfs' Contest

TRADITIONAL NORSE MYTH
Retold by Catharine F. Sellew

This selection is the conclusion of the myth about Loki. Pay close attention to Loki's reaction to the dwarf Brock. In what ways has Loki's personality changed since his trouble with Thor? In what ways is Loki the same?

All the gods were waiting for Loki to return from the land of the dwarfs. It grew so late that they began to fear he would fail to carry out his promise to the thunder god. When they saw him leap out of the mountain with a smile on his face, they knew Sif was to have her new hair. However, would it be as beautiful as the locks Loki had cut?

The last moments of daylight lit the sky. All Asgard watched Loki hold the new hair against poor Sif's head. There it grew fast, a shimmering veil as lovely as ever! Some said it was even more beautiful. Tears of joy rolled down Sif's cheeks, and she ran happily to Thor, her husband.

Then Loki proudly gave the spear and the magic boat to Odin.

"How wonderful!" gasped the gods. "Who made these magic things? How did you persuade a dwarf to make them for you?" Loki was stormed with questions. The gods—even the great All-Father—forgot what a mischief–maker he was.

"The master craftsman," said Loki when the questions had stopped, "is none other than the dwarf Dvalin. I declare him the most clever and skillful of all blacksmiths!"

The gods clapped their hands and shouted Dvalin's name so loudly that the ugly dwarf could hear it deep down in the heart of the mountain. He smiled happily. It was indeed a great reward to have all the gods give him such high praise.

Then the gods heard a harsh cry:

"That's not true! You dare not say that Dvalin is most skillful! Everyone knows my brother, the dwarf Sindri, is the greatest blacksmith! Loki lies! Loki lies!"

There stood an ugly dwarf whom the gods knew to be Brock, brother of the clever Sindri (sin'drē). The sun had set and Brock (brok) had crawled out onto the earth, as the little creatures within the mountains sometimes did after dark.

The gods looked with surprise at the angry dwarf. He was jumping up and down with rage, shaking his fists at Loki. His brows were knitted together in a terrible scowl. His green eyes gleamed with hatred.

"You dare boast of that stupid Dvalin! I will make you pay for the mischief you have

been making ever since you were born!"
screamed Brock. Loki laughed in the
dwarf's face.

"The dwarf who made these magic gifts
could not be stupid. You are jealous."

"That's enough, Loki," Odin spoke up in
his deep voice. He looked kindly at Brock.
"It is true that before this we have said that
your brother, Sindri, was the greatest blacksmith. But Sif's hair and my spear and marvelous boat are the most wonderful magic
we have yet seen."

"Great All-Father," answered Brock
with bowed head, "Sindri will make three

things that you and all the other gods will declare more wonderful than any of those."

"Ha!" laughed Loki. "Wait till old Sindri hears that! You have got him in a fix now! I'll wager my own head that he cannot do such a thing."

Brock smiled, showing his pointed yellow teeth. "Great All-Father, honored gods, you have heard what Loki said?" he asked.

"We have heard," they all answered. And Brock disappeared as quickly as he had come.

Down in the heart of the mountain, Brock went to his brother's workshop. He told him what Loki had said and the wager he had made. Sindri sat for a long time thinking.

"You expect much of me, Brother," he said at last. "Dvalin is not stupid. The things he made are truly wonderful."

"Ah! But you can do better—far, far better!" cried the faithful Brock. "I will gladly blow the fire with the bellows."

"Very well. I will do my best," replied Sindri. "But you must never stop the bellows, not even for a second. The fire must burn at an even heat."

Brock crouched by the fire and worked the bellows. The coals turned from red to yellow and finally to a white heat. Then Sindri threw a lump of gold into the leaping flames and crouched in the darkest corner of the cave. There he muttered secret words to the hidden powers of magic.

Meanwhile a huge horsefly buzzed into the cave. Round and round Brock's head it flew. When he shook his head to try to scare the fly away, it only flew closer and closer. Brock had never seen such a big horsefly. Suddenly it landed on his hand and stung him. It hurt dreadfully—much more than any ordinary horsefly sting—but Brock did not let go of the bellows. He kept the fire at a steady heat even as the bite swelled and turned purple.

At last Sindri stopped muttering and came out of the corner. "You can stop now," he said as he lifted the lump of gold from the fire with a pair of tongs. The shapeless lump had become a huge wild boar with golden bristles!

"The god of sunshine can drive this boar across the sky. Sunshine will flash from its bristles and light the world!" exclaimed Sindri.

"Wonderful! Wonderful!" chuckled Brock as he rubbed his swollen hand. "But we must keep on with our work." He picked up the bellows and turned again to the fire.

Again Sindri tossed a lump of gold onto the fire and went off to his dark corner. Again the huge horsefly buzzed into the cave and around Brock's head. Its buzzing rang in the dwarf's ear and made him feel dizzy. In the bright light of the fire, the fly seemed to be a black spot dancing before Brock's eyes, trying to blind him.

"You must be sent by the devil," Brock shouted angrily. "In fact," he added with a sudden thought, "I wouldn't be surprised if you were that devil Loki!"

At that, the horsefly stung the dwarf cruelly on the cheek. The pain shot across his face and almost stunned him. But Brock held firmly to the bellows and the fire roared. Would Sindri never come back to the fire? Brock gritted his teeth.

Finally Sindri returned. This time he pulled a gold ring from the fire. It was as big as a bracelet, but perfectly plain. Brock was puzzled.

"What is this, Brother?"

"Ah, Brock, you are disappointed. Don't be. This is a magic ring. This you will give to Odin. Every ninth night, eight rings, exactly like this one, will drop from it. It means that Odin will have many beautiful children. It means that there will always be people in the world."

Brock was pleased, but he thought to himself, "These gifts are wonderful, but so are Dvalin's. The third must be even better!" Yet Sindri smiled with satisfaction as

he told Brock to blow up the fire. This time he threw a lump of iron upon the flames.

The fire curled its flaming tongue around the dark metal. It threw snaky shadows on the walls of the cave. The shadow of Brock blowing the bellows seemed to grow on all sides. The only sounds in the cave besides Sindri's low muttering were the crackle of the flames and the *sush* of the air from the bellows.

Had the horsefly gone? Brock was sure now that it had been Loki. Had he given up so soon? Or did he think the gifts were so poor that there was no need to try to ruin Sindri's work? Ah no! The loud buzzing sounded again, and the huge horsefly sped out of the darkness straight at Brock's face, stinging him in the eye.

Brock cried out with pain, but he kept at the bellows. The fire was terribly hot, and the air in the room seemed stifling. Poor Brock could feel the blood flow into his eyes! It ran down his cheek. His head was spinning and he could hardly see, but he must keep the fire hot. He could hear Sindri muttering and muttering. He dared not call to him for fear he would break the spell. He must wipe the sticky blood from his face or soon he would be unable to see at all.

Quickly—ever so quickly—he stopped the bellows just long enough to brush his hand across his face. But it was not quick enough. Sindri rushed from his corner.

"What have you done? Why did you stop? Did I not tell you what would happen? All my work—" He grabbed up the tongs and anxiously pulled the iron from the fire. Then he smiled as he held up a huge hammer with a queer short handle.

"All is well," he said. "The handle is a little short because the fire died down for a moment. But that makes little difference. This you will give to Thor. Only he is strong enough to hurl it. It will destroy the enemies of the gods. And after Thor has thrown it, back it will fly to his hand so that he will never have to go after it."

"Ah, Sindri," smiled Brock. "This gift is the greatest of all. We will have Loki's head for this!" He put the golden boar, the magic ring, and the great hammer on a sledge and dragged them up out of the mountain to present them to the gods.

It was just as Brock had said. The gods were pleased with the wonderful boar. The ring was indeed a thing of magic. But so were Dvalin's gifts. And then Brock, with all his strength, lifted the great hammer and gave it to Thor. It was not a thing of beauty, but what a weapon it was for the gods! That hammer might win the war against the giants. No gift of Dvalin's gave the gods such power.

"Yes, Brock," said Odin, "your brother is a great blacksmith. Because of this hammer he shall be known as the greatest blacksmith in the world!"

"And Loki will pay his bet?" Brock could still feel the pain from the stings of the horsefly.

"Ah," spoke up Loki hastily. "It was all in fun, good Brock."

"It was a wager," answered Brock firmly. "It was made before all the gods."

"That is so," agreed the great All-Father a little sadly, for he did not like to see those in Asgard suffer. However, a god always kept his word.

But Loki laughed. "You may have my head," he said. "I guess it is rightfully yours, but you cannot touch my neck!" How could Brock cut off Loki's head without touching his neck? Clever Loki! Brock stormed with anger, but the gods agreed that what Loki said was true.

"Then, since your head is mine," cried Brock angrily, "I shall get Sindri's needle and sew up your lips so your evil words can no longer make trouble in this world."

When Brock returned with Sindri's needle, Loki had to let him sew those telltale lips together. Then the gods returned to their palaces in Asgard. They were sad that one of them must suffer, but Loki had made an agreement. They knew that he should live up to it.

Developing Comprehension Skills

1. Why was Brock angry with Loki?

2. You have now read three selections about the god Loki. Select the main events of Loki's adventures. Arrange the events in order on a time line. Label each event. Include five to ten happenings.

3. Loki's appearance as a horsefly showed that he had magical powers. Whose powers were greater, those of the dwarfs or those of Loki? Why do you think so?

4. Loki lost the bet with Brock. However, Loki was a god and Brock was only a dwarf. Do you think that a god should have to pay a dwarf? Why or why not?

Reading Literature: Norse Myths

1. **Identifying Climax.** During the rising action of a story, the conflict grows more intense. The most exciting part of the story is called the **climax** or turning point. At this point, the action of the story is at a peak. Usually the main character wins or loses the struggle. In "The Dwarfs' Contest," Loki struggles against Brock. At what point is the conflict settled? Who wins?

2. **Analyzing Character Traits.** You have read about two times that Loki has faced death. Think about the cause of Loki's problems. Was Loki to blame for Thor's anger? Is Loki to blame for his predicament with Brock? What do you think is Loki's main weakness?

3. **Understanding Purpose.** In this myth, the gods do not offer special help to either Loki or Brock. Think about how this affects the outcome of the bet. What important value does this myth present?

Developing Vocabulary Skills

Building Words with Affixes. The following sentences tell about events in the myths you have read. The words in parentheses are also taken from the myths. To make sense in its sentence, each word needs a prefix or a suffix added to it. Refer to the lists of affixes on pages 104 and 105. Add the correct prefix or suffix to each word in parentheses. Some words will need both affixes. You may also need to add such endings as -ed and -s. Remember to make any necessary spelling changes. The new word should complete the sentence. On your paper, write the completed sentence.

1. The gods were _____ that the bridge would not hold Thor. (fear)

2. Sif felt the _____ on her head where her hair had been cut off. (rough)

3. When Thor's big fist closed around the fish, Loki _____ to his real form. (turn)

4. Any excuse Loki made would have been _____. (allow)

5. Dvalin added three _____ of dew that sparkled like diamonds. (cup)

6. Loki's calls went _____ as the busy dwarfs worked on the gifts. (heard)

7. The ugly dwarf, Brock, _____ shook his fists at Loki. (angry)

8. The gods were in _____ with Loki that Brock could not touch Loki's neck. (agree)

Developing Writing Skills

1. **Writing About Theme.** Storytellers of myths often included direct statements to express a theme. The theme of a story is a main idea that the author wanted to express. The fol-

lowing sentences are from the last three Norse myths you have read. Select one of these three sentences that you think expresses a theme of the myths. Write a paragraph explaining the theme. Use examples from the Norse myths to support the idea.

> Do not let your temper control you!
> If I had a wonderful gift for him, he might forget my mischief.
> Loki had made an agreement. The gods knew that he should live up to it.

2. **Writing a Humorous Episode.** The Norse storytellers suggest that humor is part of human nature. Think of something funny that has happened to you. Or make up a funny story that could happen. Write two or three paragraphs to explain the episode.

Pre-Writing. Many humorous episodes are about unpleasant or embarrassing situations. Think about the problem that exists in your tale. Is the problem itself funny or ridiculous? Or is it serious and the way it is handled funny? Will the conflict be solved?

Then, order the events to show how they build to the climax. Is your story full of coincidences? Is there a series of bad luck? How does one event trigger another? What makes the action funny?

Next, think about the characters. What do they look like? How do they act? Are they funny? How?

Finally, describe the setting. Is it strange or normal? Include details about both the place and the time.

Writing. Use first-person point of view. Refer to yourself as "I." Build up to the climax. Suspense will add to the effect of the humor. Be sure to describe the setting and

the characters. You might conclude with a funny comment about your reaction.

Revising. Read your account aloud to someone else. If the person laughs, you have succeeded. Otherwise, have the person suggest changes that would add to the humor. Rewrite those sections.

Developing Skills in Study and Research

Using the Card Catalog. One library resource, called the card catalog, will help you locate books in the library. Review the introduction to the card catalog on page 627 in the Handbook. Using the card catalog, research the following information about Greek and Norse mythology.

1. Locate a title card for one of the following books or stories. Remember that *A*, *An*, and *The* do not count as first words on title cards. On your paper, write the title, call number, author's name, and number of pages.

   Scandanavian Mythology
   Mythology
   "The Odyssey"
   "The Song of Beowulf"
   Words from the Myths
   Voyage to Atlantis

2. Authors are filed alphabetically by last name. Find the author cards for one of the following writers. There will be one card for each book by the author you choose. On your paper, write the title and call number of any book by that author.

Robert Fitzgerald	Catharine F. Sellew
Homer	Thomas Bulfinch
Sally Benson	Olivia E. Coolidge

3. Locate the subject cards for the topic *Folklore*. There will be one card for each book about that subject. Select two books about folklore. On your paper, list the book titles, authors, and call numbers.

Developing Skills in Critical Thinking

Recognizing Accurate Generalizations. A **generalization** is a statement about a group that supposedly is true of all the members of the group. A generalization should be accurate. That is, it should be based on facts. For example, the following statement is an accurate generalization:

Teenagers are usually active people.

The statement is supported by several facts:

Sports are widespread among teenagers.
Teenagers buy many records and tapes.
Over fifty percent of teenagers own bicycles.
Many teenagers have part-time jobs.
Teenagers are in school all day.

A generalization is inaccurate if it is not based on facts. Then it is unfair to the people being described. For example, the following statement is an unfair generalization:

All ninth-graders are disorganized.

This statement may be true of some ninth-graders. You may be able to think of several examples. However, if you think of even one ninth-grader who is organized, then the statement is not accurate. It is then an unfair generalization about all members of the group.

Each of the following statements deals with the myths you have read.

Decide whether each statement is an accurate generalization or an unfair generalization. For each accurate statement, list at least two supporting facts. If you find a fact that disagrees with the statement, write *Unfair Generalization*. Be ready to explain your ideas.

1. The Greek and Norse gods never helped human beings.
2. The goddesses in Norse mythology never act independently.
3. Dwarfs in Norse mythology were ugly and stupid.
4. The good guys always win in Greek myths and legends.
5. Violence was common in ancient Greece.

Viking sword. University Museum of National Antiquities, Oslo, Norway.

Thor's Voyage to the Land of the Giants

TRADITIONAL NORSE MYTH
Retold by Catharine F. Sellew

This selection begins a myth about the land of the frost giants. Thor asks Loki to accompany him there. How has the relationship between Thor and Loki changed? Has Loki changed? Read to find out.

Now that Loki could no longer laugh and joke, Asgard seemed very dull and quiet. The gods missed their lively companion. But they reminded themselves that no mischief had been done since Brock had sewed up Loki's lips. That was indeed a good thing.

Even Thor felt sorry for Loki. Perhaps this would teach the young fire god a lesson. Thor knew that it would not be long before Loki found a way to cut Brock's stitches. Then he would be his merry self again.

That is the way it happened. One morning Loki's laughter rang out in the city of the gods, and he pranced before them. His lips were still thick and swollen, but Brock's stitches were gone!

Since Thor had received Sindri's magic hammer, he had been anxious to go to the land of the giants. He would show those wicked rulers of ice and darkness how great and powerful were the gods! With him he wanted a brave and daring companion. He

thought of Loki, whose punishment seemed to have made him eager to please others. In fact, Loki seemed to have forgotten his love of mischief.

"Will you come with me?" Thor asked him after explaining his plan. "But no mischief, mind you!" he thundered.

"Mischief!" cried Loki. "How can you think of such a thing? Haven't I been punished enough for my jokes? But Asgard is dull these days. I want adventure!"

"Very well," agreed Thor. "See that you don't try any of your old tricks."

They set out on their long journey to the land of the giants. Thor's two strong goats pulled the chariot swiftly through the gates of Asgard. The gods cheered and waved to them as they raced out of sight.

Thor's great hammer was carefully fastened to his magic belt. Whenever he needed extra strength, all he had to do was to pull his belt tighter about his waist. He wore thick gloves to protect his hands from the heat of the hammer. Loki leaned back in his seat while Thor held the reins. He enjoyed the feel of the bright sunshine and the wind whistling through his hair.

Thus they traveled swiftly all day. By the time the sun had disappeared behind black mountains, they had reached the edge of the land of the giants. Before them was a tiny cottage where a poor peasant family lived. They stopped there, and the peasants welcomed the great red-bearded man and his handsome friend.

"We have very little to offer," said the father, "but we are glad to share it with you." The mother set a small cheese and a loaf of barley bread on the table. Loki's eyes twinkled as he looked at Thor. He knew the great thunder god could swallow it all in one gulp and hardly know he'd eaten it! Thor laughed and said that he would provide the meat, whereupon he killed his two goats and added them to the meal. The peasants gasped with wonder.

"Eat all you wish," roared Thor, "but see that you don't break any of the bones. When you have eaten all the meat off them, throw them on the goats' skins over there."

The peasants and their two children ate hungrily and threw aside the bones as Thor had commanded.

Now Loki had been good for so long that he felt he simply must play a joke. One little harmless joke he could chuckle over in the old happy way! In spite of the warning Thor had given him before they set out on their journey, he leaned over and whispered to the peasants' son, "It's a shame, not to taste the good paste in the center of the bone! It is the most delicious part of the goat. Why don't you break a small bone and try it? No one will ever know." He smiled at the boy. As long as the red-bearded man's friend had suggested it, the boy saw no harm in trying it. He did what Loki said. Indeed the marrow was good!

The next morning, when Thor woke, he waved his hammer over the skins upon which the bare bones lay. Up sprang the goats alive again, ready to pull the chariot. But, alas, one of them had a slight limp.

"Someone disobeyed my orders," thundered Thor, angry sparks flying from his red beard. The peasants trembled, for they realized now that their guests were gods. The son, Thialfi (thē al′ fē), fell upon his knees. He told what he had done and begged forgiveness. Thor glared at Loki.

"I should have known I could not trust you!" he muttered. Then he turned to the boy. "Evil thoughts were put into your head," he said kindly, "so you are not altogether to blame. To win forgiveness you and your sister, Roskva (rosk′ və), must come with us and be our servants. We will leave my goats in the care of your father and mother. Come! We must be on our way." And he led them out of the door before the parents could thank him.

All the next day they traveled on foot. Finally they came to a great sea. It was cold and gray. Angry waves pounded against the shore. The gods told the children to follow them and not to be afraid. Then they waded into the rough sea and began to swim.

Rise of the Full Moon, 1937, ARTHUR DOVE. The Phillips Collection, Washington, D.C.

Thialfi and Roskva took a deep breath and followed. Lo! It was as easy to swim as in their quiet pond at home, for they were traveling with gods.

Finally, the swimmers pulled themselves up on a strange shore. The mist over this land was so thick that they could not guess what hour it was, but Thor declared it was time to look for a place to rest for the night. They went ahead very slowly, feeling with their hands and feet. Thialfi cried out as he felt something cold and wet and soft in front of him. When the others came to help, they discovered it was only wet moss on the side of a great boulder.

"Look ahead!" cried the thunder god. He pointed to a dark mass that loomed in the mist. As they came closer, it looked like a strangely shaped house. The doorway filled one side and was wide open. An odd tower went off at a queer angle.

Carefully they tiptoed inside. There was no fire, no hearth upon which to place great logs. The house was quite empty, without furniture, yet it seemed safe enough. At least it was shelter from the wet, cold mist. The travelers threw themselves on the floor and soon fell fast asleep.

After a while Roskva woke with a start. Her teeth were chattering. No, the ground was trembling! The whole strange house was shaking. She could hear a dull rumbling and roaring. Then all was still for a moment, only to begin again as though the whole world were shuddering.

"Thialfi! Thialfi!" Roskva whispered and reached out in the darkness for her brother's hand. Thialfi was sitting up, too. Then Thor and Loki felt their way over to the children. No one knew what was happening. Whatever it was, the strange house did not appear to be tumbling down on top of them. The shaking did not seem to do any harm. Finally, it seemed to stop.

"I saw a small room off this great hall," said Thor. "The three of you finish the night in there. I will guard the doorway till morning." They entered and soon fell asleep.

Next morning Thor's loud laughing woke them. "Well, I found out about the earthquake last night," he chuckled. He grinned down at them while they sat up and rubbed their eyes. "You know what this palace is?"

They shook their heads. Loki jumped to his feet. He was a little ashamed of having been frightened last night, now that Thor seemed to think it all such a joke.

"You've been sleeping in the thumb of a giant's mitten!" Thor drew back his head and roared with good humor. "The giant was sleeping just outside!"

"Oh!" cried Roskva with a little scream.

"The earthquake was his snoring! There's nothing to fear," he added as he saw the white and frightened face of the young girl. "I've been talking to him. He's agreed to show us the way to the gates of the city of the giants. Come along and meet him."

He led them outside. There stood two black boots. Up and up into the mist loomed the figure of the giant. His face was just a gray blur to the gods who stood like dwarfs below him.

"These are my friends," Thor shouted to the giant. "Lead on and we will follow." The giant bent down to pick up his mitten and grinned at them. His mouth looked like a great cavern with a row of white stones. His breath was hot in their faces. Then he started out into the mist. The gods and their servants followed the black heels of his huge boots. They were nearing the end of their journey.

Viking wooden harness collars with bronze decoration, 10th century. Danish National Museum Copenhagen.

Developing Comprehension Skills

1. Why was Thor so anxious to go to the land of the giants?

2. As the peasants presented the small meal, "Loki's eyes twinkled as he looked at Thor." What feeling do you think Loki's twinkling eyes suggested?

3. Why did Loki play a joke on Thialfi?

4. Do you think that Thor was fair in taking Thialfi and his sister with him as punishment for eating the bone? Explain your opinion.

Reading Literature: Norse Myths

1. **Understanding Characters.** Thor commands the peasant children to leave home and travel with him. The parents do not seem to be upset that Thor takes their children. Why do you think the parents show no anger? Is their reaction believable? Why or why not?

2. **Recognizing Character Development.** Characters in a story are like real people in certain ways. An important character changes because of his or her experiences. Select either Thor or Loki. List the qualities you first saw in that character. For example, Thor was introduced as having a thunderous temper. Loki was introduced as a mischievous character. Try to list at least two other qualities for the character you choose. What has happened to the character since he was introduced? What quality about the character has changed? Why?

3. **Analyzing Plot and Conflict.** You have read the first part of the adventure in the land of the frost giants. List three main events that have occurred. What conflicts, or struggles, have been suggested? Name at least two conflicts. Tell whether each conflict is external or internal. Has any conflict reached a climax, or turning point?

The Contest with the Giants

TRADITIONAL NORSE MYTH
Retold by Catharine F. Sellew

This selection concludes the story of Thor's adventure. Thor had wanted to show the frost giants the power and greatness of the gods. In what way does Thor accomplish his goal? Read to learn how he is surprised.

For another whole day Thor and Loki and the two children followed the giant through the land of mist. When night came, the giant lay down upon the ground. He tossed his knapsack over to Thor and told him and his companions to eat all they wanted of the food that was in it. Then he went to sleep.

Thor and Loki pulled and tugged at the straps that tied the sack together. Thialfi and his sister tried to help. All four pulled and pulled. With sticks and stones they tried to pry the knots apart. Then they tried to cut the thick leather, but nothing would rip the tough hide. Finally they gave up and went to bed hungry.

However, even sleep was impossible, for this night the giant's snores were worse than before. The earth trembled constantly while his deep breathing roared in their ears. Thor was terribly angry at such rudeness. He was sure the giant knew they would not be able to open the knapsack of food. Even worse now he was keeping them awake with his snores. Thor, the thunder god, would teach him a lesson! He took his great hammer from his belt and struck the giant on the forehead. The giant stirred slightly and turned over.

"Was that a leaf that fell upon my head?" he murmured and began to snore again. The children and the gods looked at each other in wonder. Could it be that the blow had not even hurt this great creature? Thor ran his hand through his red hair and scowled up at the huge body of the sleeping giant. Once again he raised his hammer and hurled it with all his might at the giant. Again the giant stirred in his sleep.

"A piece of bark must have fallen on my face," he complained.

"Try again!" cried Loki. "Draw in your belt so you can put more strength behind it. Something must have gone wrong before. Perhaps you didn't hit him squarely."

So again Thor threw his hammer at the giant. This time the huge man sat up. "Umph!" he grumbled. "It's late in the night for birds to be dropping twigs from the trees. But I'm sure one just fell on my head. Well, there's still time to get some more sleep." Then he rolled onto his side with a great yawn.

Thor shook his fist at the giant's back. He tried not to show the children how upset he was. Loki shook his head and leaned against a tree, trying to rest in spite of everything. They would need all their strength and more the next morning, if Thor's hammer could not defend them against the giants.

When the next morning finally came, the giant pointed to a road that, he said, would lead them straight to the palace of the king of the giants. Then he left them. Down the road went the two gods and the two children. Suddenly, out of the heavy mist in front of them arose a silvery castle. It was made of great gleaming blocks of ice. The beautiful glittering pillars were icicles, and the roofs of the high towers and halls were of the whitest snow. A cold blast of icy wind whipped around the corners and blew down the road into the faces of the travelers, making their eyes water and their noses sting.

Across the entrance to this magnificent castle was a gate of heavy bars. The travelers were small enough to slip through the spaces between the bars, and thus they entered the castle and stood before the king of the giants. The king was sitting on a throne at the end of a tremendous hall. Other great giants stood around laughing and talking till they saw the strangers enter. Then a dead silence fell on the court.

The king peered down at the little gods and their servants. He stretched his great thick neck to see them over his huge knees, and he leaned forward on his throne of rocks and ice in order to hear what they said. For although Thor and Loki shouted, their voices had to carry a long way before they reached the giant king's ears.

"So you are the great gods I have heard so much about," bellowed the king. "How small you are!" And his laugh rang from the high rafters. It echoed a hundred times throughout the palace hall. "How small! How small! How small!" came from every corner.

"Surely creatures as small as you cannot do all that we are told you do!" All the other giants stood looking at them and grinning.

At this, Loki stepped closer to the king. No one was going to make fun of him!

"We may not be as large as you, but we are far wiser and cleverer. We can do all that you can do—and better than you can do it!"

"What's that?" said the giant. "Speak up. I can't hear you." And the king leaned even further forward on his throne.

"He must be deaf," muttered Thor angrily. He stepped up beside Loki and, in his voice of Thunder, repeated what the other god had said. But, in the land of the giants, the thunder seemed like a far distant grumbling. It wasn't even loud enough to echo from the rafters.

"He must have a cold," the king said to one of his attendants. Then he leaned back on his throne and waved his hand at everyone in the hall. "Well, let us have a contest to prove whether what these gods say is true. What do you wish to do?" he shouted down to Loki. Loki's face still burned red with anger. But his stomach was empty and ached from a day without food. He said he could eat more than any giant right then, and he could eat it twice as fast.

"Very well," said the king. He ordered his cook to match his hunger with Loki's. A long, narrow wooden dish was placed on the floor. It was so long it stretched across the width of the hall. It was full of a hot meat stew. Loki sat at one end of the wooden dish, and the giant cook sat at the other. The delicious smell of the food made the hungry Loki grin and forget the jeering giants. When the king gave the signal, the cook and Loki began to gulp down the food.

Finally Loki reached the center of the long dish and looked up in triumph. But, alas, there sat the cook beside him! The cook had eaten all the bones and his half of the wooden dish!

The giants roared with laughter as they saw the look of surprise and anger on Loki's face. Loki sprang to his feet and went over to Thor.

"There's some strange magic in this," he whispered. "We gods are not so weak. Why, if these giants are so strong, do they fear us when we are in Asgard?"

"I do not understand," said Thor with a dark scowl.

"Well," chuckled the king, "perhaps you can do better at something else."

"My thirst is never satisfied," cried Thor, stepping forward. "In one breath I can drain the largest drinking vessel you have in the palace."

At once a large horn was brought into the hall and handed to Thor. It was filled to the brim with rich brown ale. Thor took it in his strong hands. He threw back his head and drew a deep breath. Then he lifted the great horn to his lips and drank and drank. Great blue veins stood out on his forehead, and his face grew redder and redder until it turned purple, and still he drank. Loki and the peasants looked on with pride. But the giants only smiled.

At last, with a gasp, Thor lowered the horn from his lips. Everyone crowded forward to look into the horn. Lo, the ale had only gone down an inch! It could not be. Thor looked again, but the ale was only a little way from the top.

"Try again," urged the king. "Really good drinkers here can empty it the first time. Moderately thirsty ones take two gulps, whereas small drinkers take all of three." So Thor tried again, and again he barely lowered the line of the ale in the great horn. A third time he did no better. Finally he sat down, defeated.

Then up jumped Thialfi. He challenged any one of the giants in a race. A young giant stood up and they went forth to a great bare field around which they ran like the wind. Thor and Loki were surprised to see Thialfi's grace and speed, but the giant soon overtook him. Once more the gods lost the contest.

Thor refused to give up. With his hand on his hand on his magic belt, he suggested a wrestling match.

"Come," said the giant, "I admire your courage, but look at your size. It is a foolish challenge."

"Do you refuse?" cried Thor angrily.

"Well, no. But I can hardly let anyone stronger than my old nurse here wrestle with you. I shouldn't like to see any real harm come to one of the great gods while on a friendly visit in the land of the giants."

There was nothing for Thor to do but go ahead and wrestle with an old woman. His hair flamed even brighter, and his scowl darkened his face. Such insults were too much to bear! Even so, he tightened his belt and rolled up his sleeves and took his stand. Then the old woman and the great thunder god rolled and struggled, turned and tussled on the floor in the center of the hall until at last Thor was thrown. He had lost the match.

When Thor—still determined to do something successfully—suggested proving his strength by weight lifting, the giants' cat was brought into the room. Indeed it was such a big cat, it looked like a tiger. However, Thor tightened his belt once again with satisfaction. He knew he had lifted far heavier weights than this cat. He bent with a smile over the cat's back and put his arms around its body. Then he heaved with all his might, expecting to toss it to the high rafters. It did not budge! He tugged and pushed and pulled, but the cat did not move!

"There's some strange magic in this," he could hear Loki mutter. Thor agreed, but he was determined to try once more. Taking a deep breath, he gritted his teeth and with a tremendous jerk managed to lift one of the cat's paws from the ground.

A roar of laughter from the giants was Thor's reward.

"Well, well," said the king. "Better luck next time. But after this, perhaps you gods will speak with more respect of us giants. In the morning I will take you to the edge of our land and start you on your way back to Asgard."

There was nothing left for the gods and children to do but rest and prepare for the morning's journey.

The next morning the king of the giants looked at them with a new light in his eyes. As they stood in the cold gray mist at the edge of the sea he said, "Thor and Loki, Thialfi and Roskva, now that you are leaving my kingdom, I have something to tell you. If I had ever guessed what strength and courage you had, I never would have let you enter my palace. For I was the giant whose snores woke you. I was the giant who led you to my own gates."

The giant turned to the red-haired god. "When you, Thor," he continued, "struck at me with your hammer, you hit a mountain instead of my forehead. I feared your hammer. By my magic I placed an invisible mountain between you and me. If you could see the great cracks your hammer made in that mountain, you would know why I fear you."

Then the giant turned to Loki, who stood looking at him with raised eyebrows. "My cook, who ate more and faster than you, was really wild fire, which destroys all. And Thialfi, ran a race with thought, which travels more swiftly than any runner.

"That horn from which you drank, Thor, my friend, was connected with the sea, which nobody can empty. And my nurse was old age, whom none can resist. The cat was in fact the terrible snake that twists itself around the world. When you managed to lift one of its feet, we were terrified for fear you would actually loosen the horrible creature and bring destruction to us all. So you see why I will never again allow such as you to enter the land of the giants. Only by our knowledge of magic can we defeat the gods!"

At this, Thor roared with rage. So Loki had been right! It had not been a fair contest. Thor raised his hammer in anger. But the mist had grown thicker and grayer, and the giant king had disappeared. Though still angry, he lowered his hammer.

"You see!" said Loki with a satisfied smile. But Thor said nothing, for he was staring down at the shore of the sea. Several feet above the place where the waves now washed the sand a dark line marked where the water had been. Thor smiled. He knew now that he had drunk long and well from the great horn. Certainly he had done better than any other god could have done and far better than any giant. He was content at last to return to Asgard where the bright sun shone.

Developing Comprehension Skills

1. What two things did the giant do at the beginning of the myth that irritated Thor?

2. The members of Thor's group challenged the giants to a variety of contests. Each contest emphasized a different skill. Match the characters and the areas in which they competed. Then arrange the competitions in the order they occurred.

   Loki   eating
   Thialfi   speed
   Thor   drinking
               strength
               wrestling

3. At first, Thor was depressed because he had lost every contest. What did he notice that made him feel better?

4. Loki was the first to suspect the giants of magic and trickery. Why is this fitting?

5. Sometimes a strength in a character's personality can turn into a weakness. Do you think that Thor is overly confident? Or is it good that he believes in himself?

Reading Literature: Norse Myths

1. **Understanding a Character.** Thor is upset because his magic hammer has no effect on the giant. Why do you think Thor wants to hide his emotion from the children?

2. **Analyzing the Climax of a Story.** In this myth, Thor struggles against the frost giants. The climax, or turning point, of the story comes at the end. Thor and his friends have lost every contest with the giants. Then, the king of the giants tells Thor the truth about the strengths of the gods. As the story ends, have the giants clearly defeated the gods? Or have the gods won because the giants respect them? Do you think there can be a clear winner in this conflict? Why or why not? Explain your opinion.

3. **Recognizing Theme.** Think about the king of the frost giants and Thor, the leader of the group. What do they have in common? Name the values that they both feel are important. Select one of these values. Think about how the storyteller stresses the value. What theme, or main idea, of the story is based on this value? Write a sentence to state this theme.

Developing Vocabulary Skills

Understanding the Prefixes *In-* and *Im-*. You have learned that the prefix *in-* can mean "not." In some words, it means "in, into." The prefix *im-* also has those meanings. For example, *immature* means "not mature" and *imprint* means "to print into."

The following sentences are about the myths you have read. Each underlined word contains the prefix *in-* or *im-*. Write the meaning of each word on your paper.

1. Odin knew the elves' work was immeasurable.

2. The design imprinted on the necklace would make Frigga happy.

3. The evil face with green eyes looked inhuman.

4. Frigga's ingratitude had brought on all the trouble.

5. The passage into the mountain became impassable.

6. The strong blows of the hammer indented the mountainside.

Developing Writing Skills

1. **Explaining Unmatched Details.** The Norse myths were told from memory. Sometimes later details in the stories do not match descriptions given earlier. Write a paragraph about the inconsistent, or unmatched, details in the Norse myths you have read.

Pre-Writing. Brainstorm with your classmates. Think of examples of inconsistencies in the Norse myths. For example, the land of the frost giants is supposed to be unbearably cold. But when Thor travels there, the coldness of the setting does not affect him or his friends. List the examples you find.

Writing. Develop a paragraph based on your list of information. Begin with a sentence stating that details in myths are often inconsistent. Include at least three examples. You might include your own ideas about why the details differ.

Revising. Ask another person to read your paragraph. Have the person point out each of the three examples you included. If the person has trouble identifying any example, you need to change the wording. Try to make every idea clear.

2. **Writing About Conflict.** In the myth "The Contest with the Giants," Thor and Loki battle with the frost giants. Each competition is part of the external struggle of the gods against the giants. Select one of the competitions Thor and his friends face. Or, make up a competition of your own. Write a one-to-two paragraph description of the details of the conflict. Use words that are clear and lively. Try to explain the feeling, or mood, of the scene.

Developing Skills in Speaking and Listening

Persuading an Audience. Pretend you are Thor. You must convince Loki to join you on the voyage to the land of the giants.

Review the persuasion techniques you studied on page 124. Select one technique. Use it to organize a one-minute speech. Your goal is to convince Loki to make the trip.

Rehearse the speech aloud several times. Use your voice to emphasize the important words and ideas. Remember, you are trying to convince someone to do something. Be forceful.

When you are ready, present the speech.

Norse Legend

Imagine that you and several friends are sitting around a campfire far from the closest town. Night is falling, and the fire casts moving shadows behind you. You hear strange whispers in the bushes beyond the firelight. You begin to feel shivers down your back.

Now you should be ready for the tale of the monster Grendel and the hero who faced him.

The She-Wolf, 1943, JACKSON POLLOCK. Oil, gouache and plaster on canvas. 41⅞" × 67".
Collection, The Museum of Modern Art, New York. Purchase.

The Song of Beowulf

TRADITIONAL NORSE LEGEND
Retold by Olivia E. Coolidge

Legends tell about human heroes who take part in the conflict of good against evil. What qualities do you think make Beowulf the hero in this Norse legend?

The lands of King Hrothgar (rôth'gär), the Dane, lay at the edge of barren moorlands whose wind-swept ridges echoed with the howling of wolves, the moaning of winds, and the rushing of water. Few ranged this desolate country but huntsmen and wandering shepherds, and, of those who had ventured thither, many had never returned. This was the home of the monster, Grendel, who preyed on beasts and men. Some had seen him pass in the moonlight with an aged hag creeping at his heels. They spoke of his shaggy form, resembling a huge, clumsy man, of his fingers like iron claws, of his rolling eyes and hideous countenance, a swollen, angry red.

Down on the coastal plain the great hall of Hrothgar shone like the golden sun. Its high roof was a landmark for chieftains. The paved road leading to its doorway was set with colored stones. Gold shone on the long tables and on the splendid hangings that adorned the walls. The trunk of a whole tree burned in the central hearth, sending its smoke curling up to the high vents in the roof past timbers brightly painted and as yet hardly dimmed by soot. Great tubs of ale stood ready for the feasting. When the torches were lit, the queen herself brought drink to the nobles, while her women served the rest. Shouting and laughter arose, or the minstrel would sing of some hero such as Sigmund, the Volsung, who won the gift of Odin's sword.

Grendel stood on a little knoll at the foot of the hills one evening, staring at the lights in the valley as he listened to the distant sounds of King Hrothgar's feast. Rage and hatred twisted the monster's features. He was waiting until the noises should die and the lights be dimmed. Then he would creep over the pasture and plowland, past the storehouses, up the paved road, and set his great shoulder to the iron-bound doors. He would burst the bars and fall like a savage bear on the sleepers within, as he had often done before. He stirred impatiently in the darkness. There was no moon.

The feasting was late in Hrothgar's hall that night, for guests from Sweden had come. Beowulf, (bā′ə woolf′), the prince of the Geats,[1] had vowed to destroy the horrible monster who was nightly ravaging Hrothgar's hall. The Swedish ship had put in to the harbor that day, and now Beowulf sat in the high seat of honor, while the queen herself brought him his ale horn. "Welcome, brave guest," she said to him. "It is a great deed of valor that you have sworn to do. None of our men can slay this monster who haunts us, so that it is death to sleep in our hall."

"No sword will pierce him," agreed the aged Hrothgar. "No armor can resist his claws of steel. He is far taller than human and stronger than three men. There is no hero in Denmark who can rid us of this fearsome demon."

As Beowulf lifted his horn, the light shone on his armor of linked mail. He tilted his red head back as he drank, then set down the horn and turned to his host with a smile. "If weapons cannot help me, I will slay this monster with my bare hands, or die," said he.

Old Hrothgar looked at the huge young man, wondering at his courage as he replied, "Many a one has sworn over the ale-cup that he would kill Grendel. The floor is red with the blood of these heroes. It seems to me there are no warriors left in Denmark to equal those who have gone. I am old and have seen too much slaughter, yet I will not dissuade you. I think you are far the strongest man that my eyes have ever beheld."

King Hrothgar drank to his guest, and his men hailed Beowulf's men. Red firelight gleamed on bright helmets, on golden cheek guards, on rows of shields, on long spears tipped with iron. Servants bore fresh drink to the tables, while talk and laughter went round. It was late when the king grew weary, but at last he rose. "I shall bid you good night, strangers," he said. "I am old now, but great warriors have served me. I give you my word that no men but my own have ever guarded my hall until now." He motioned to his followers to attend him.

Beowulf took off his sword and stripped himself of his armor, without which his huge back and arms looked almost gigantic. "Spread bedding for my men," he cried to the servants. "They will wait for the monster with their weapons beside them, but I will face him bare-handed as I am."

Men brought out beds and bolsters. Beowulf's followers laid their shields at their heads, their helmets on the bench above them, and their long spears against the wall. Torches were dimmed, and soon the only sounds were heavy breathing or the tossing of restless men.

Out on the hillside the monster stirred as the lights went out. With a rolling gait like a bear on his hind legs, he moved out of the thickets into the pasture land.

Beowulf lay wakeful, listening. Boards creaked now and then, the glowing fire crackled, wind rustled the hangings. Outside, he could hear no noise.

Suddenly with a mighty crash the door burst inward. A shaggy form stood in the

---

1. **Geats** (gēts), early peoples of Southern Sweden.

entrance, filling it from side to side. For a moment Grendel surveyed the hall, which was dimly lighted by the embers of the fire. Then with a snarl he leaped on one man so quickly that none had time to prevent him. The victim gave a loud cry, which was choked almost as soon as it was uttered. Beowulf lay still in his place, for the man had died in an instant. The others too were quiet, waiting for the movement of their chief.

Grendel stood up from his prey and paused once more as his eyes went round the room. Quickly, Beowulf made a slight motion. The monster saw it and leaped across the floor with a single bound to fall on the hero, his iron claws reaching towards his victim's throat.

Beowulf scrambled up on one knee. His hands shot out, caught a hairy arm by the wrist, and twisted it sideways. With a fearful crash the monster pitched headfirst onto the floor. Beowulf leaped on his back, still holding the arm. Grendel kicked out, and a bench went flying. He staggered up and whirled to dash his enemy onto a pillar. Beowulf kicked in his turn, and the fiend went thudding against the wall. Boards cracked, shields clattered to the floor, and a hanging sword fell full upon Grendel's back, glancing off his iron hide as though he wore chain armor. With a howl the monster threw himself to the ground and rolled to throw off his adversary. Beowulf clung the tighter, and the two went over and over, grasping at tables, tearing at hangings, kicking and clawing. Men sprang to Beowulf's aid, but so dark was the room and so wild the struggle that none dared to strike, lest he wound his master.

At last the two rolled into the center of the floor, and Grendel's cheek fell full on the burning coals. With a horrible cry he leaped up and shook the hero from his back, though he could not free his arm. Now Grendel's iron claws might have torn at his enemy if he had thought to use them, but he was bewildered by the pain of the fire and terrified by the might of the grip which held him. He had no idea but that of flight.

Then followed a fierce tug-of-war down the length of the hall to the doorway. There Beowulf braced his foot behind the door jamb and stood immovable, while Grendel, half in the open, pulled with all his strength. Beowulf twisted the arm savagely. The hero pulled mightily until with a rending sound the demon's arm broke clean. He fled moaning into the night, while Beowulf tumbled backward with the grisly trophy pressed close against his breast.

When the sun was up next morning, great bloodstained tracks could be seen marking the path of Grendel's flight. Horsemen followed them rejoicing far into the hills. Hrothgar smiled on the wreck and ruin in his hall as he gave orders to replace the torn hangings, to set up the benches, and renew the iron bands of the doorway.

The feast that night in Hrothgar's hall was more glorious than ever before. To Beowulf the king gave horses, a saddle set with jewels, and a helmet and breastplate inlaid with gold. The queen came forth in state to bring Beowulf drink and to offer her own gifts, a coat of linked mail and a bright jeweled collar. Men drank to the health of Beowulf's followers, and the king bestowed on them rings of gold. The minstrel sang of the heroes of old. When he had ended, those next to him cried, "Sing us tomorrow a song of Beowulf. His deeds must be remembered among us for as long as this hall shall stand."

The evening wore into night. Hrothgar rose and went to his dwelling, but all his men rejoicing dragged their mattresses into the hall. Sleep fell on their eyes, while the hideous hag, the mother of Grendel, brooded over the corpse of her son in her distant lair. At last she arose and crept over the hillsides, down into the pasture land, and across the plain towards the darkened hall.

The iron bands on the door were not yet in place. The watchman slept heavily after the feast, and the hall was wrapped in slumber. Men sat up and grasped for their weapons as the witch wife burst in among them. They were heavy with sleep, however. Before they could stop her, the old hag seized on the nearest man. She choked him with her iron fingers, threw him on her back, and was out of the hall in an instant with her burden. She fled chuckling back to the swamps while men called for torches or struck vainly at shadows, panicked by the sudden uproar.

The face of King Hrothgar was grey and lined in the morning light, for the vanished noble had been his trusty counselor and dearest friend.

"This was no mighty monster," declared one of his warriors. "This was the hag whom men have described as creeping at Grendel's heels. I saw her as she fled through the moonlight with her hair straggling down her back and a withered arm about her prey. She will not surprise us again, and she has not the might of Grendel. She is unlikely to attempt such a raid again."

"That gives me small comfort," said Hrothgar gloomily. "If she returns, we may at least take vengeance for my trusty warrior and friend. But who can seek her out in her lair and destroy her? That is a deed beyond the power of man."

"Where is this lair?" asked Beowulf.

"In the midst of the hills lies a darkened valley in which is a deep, black pool. Frost never melts from the trees overshadowing it. No birds call in their branches, and no sound is heard but the moaning of wind. Huntsmen say that a deer pursued by their dogs will turn to face them and die rather than plunge into that water. Snake-like monsters and strange sea-dragons climb out on the rocks. They can also be seen coiling their pale grey lengths below the surface as they watch for prey. Fire glows at night deep down in the inky depths. There lives the monster."

"Where fire can breathe, there can I," cried Beowulf. "I fear no water dragons. If you will guide me to this pool, I will try the adventure."

A great horse was bridled for Hrothgar, and his warriors pressed behind him in full armor as he rode forth with Beowulf in state. Over the uplands and down steep, narrow pathways the track was still marked by the blood of Grendel and by the footprints of his mother, the hag.

The water tossed and swirled in the desolate pool. The beasts who lived there coiled frantically in the eddies.

Beowulf was clad in his battle armor with a helmet on his head and a great sword by his side. "If I die," said he to Hrothgar, "send the treasures you gave me back to the land of the Geats with my men, and tell the king, my kinsman, of the glory which I have won." He turned to the black water and, before Hrothgar could answer, leaped headlong into the pool.

Foam flew around him as the serpents rushed upon him from all sides, while the great hag swept out of her cave in the darkness to seize him in her arms. Beowulf struggled in the darkness, kicking out at the beasts with his feet, for his coat of mail protected his body, and the hag held him around the arms.

Down swam the hag, while Beowulf made no attempt to be free, lest he retard her, for he knew he must soon come out into the air or drown. Presently she turned up through an underwater passage and broke surface in a cavern, where burned the fire whose reflection shepherds had seen in the depths of the pool.

Beowulf wrenched himself free and reached for his sword. He lifted it high to hew at the fearsome creature. Right where the neck joins the shoulder his blow fell, but the iron hide of the witch wife turned it aside, and the sword bent in his hand. He threw the weapon to the ground and leaped upon her, but she twisted from under him and dragged him down headlong. She fell on him and stabbed him fiercely, but his armor withstood the blow. In another second he had thrown her to one side and sprung to his feet. He cast a swift glance

Beowulf Fighting with Grendel's Mother, 1931.
ROCKWELL KENT. Rare Book and Manuscript Library, Columbia University, New York City.

about him, searching for a heavy rock, when his eye fell upon a huge sword hanging on the wall. Swift as a cat he leaped for the weapon. He had no time to swing, but he stabbed with all his force. The point met her full in the throat as she rushed upon him. She sank down in a welter of blood, and the fight was over.

Beowulf looked about the cave, littered with the bones of countless hideous meals. On a rude bed in one corner lay Grendel's mangled body. Beowulf stared down on the hairy, purple face, the bloodshot eyes, and the grinning teeth. Deliberately he raised the sword and chopped off the head. The magical blade bit through Grendel's neck, but the creature's venomous blood ate the iron away like acid, and the hilt alone was left in his hand.

The people of Hrothgar sat in silence by the edge of the pool. Blood and the bodies of monsters floated to the surface. The eddies smoothed out until the pool was quiet. Then after a long, long time, they saw more blood. "He is dead," said Hrothgar heavily. "All the brave men die in this land."

His own men looked at him in a silent fury, but none offered to dive into the fearsome water. "He is dead indeed," replied an old man. "No one could live under there so long."

Hrothgar rose stiffly from the rock on which he was sitting. "The sun is low, and we should go home," he said.

"We shall wait for our master," replied the leader of the Geats, Beowulf's men.

King Hrothgar slowly climbed onto his horse. "It will be a long wait," said he.

"Beowulf is not like other men," said the Geat. "No hag in a pool can drown him. He will return."

The sun was almost setting when Beowulf came swimming up through the surge untouched by the serpents, Grendel's head gripped in his hand. The Geats shouted loudly as they jumped to their feet and ran down to greet him. They clattered home through the dusk, singing in triumph.

Hrothgar sat in his high seat, but the meat lay untouched before him, and his ale-cup stood neglected by his hand. Beowulf strode proudly into the hall with his men crowding behind him, bearing the jeweled hilt of the magic sword and the dreadful head of Grendel swinging by the hair. The king leaped up to greet him, and the rafters of the great hall trembled with the shout that arose.

Beowulf went his way to his country in Sweden with his dragon ship laden with treasure, and with promises of friendship and lifelong good will. Next night in the hall of Hrothgar, the minstrel had made a new song. From that time the Song of Beowulf was chanted in Denmark until long after the kingdom of Hrothgar had ceased to endure.

Developing Comprehension Skills

1. What did Grendel look like? Include at least three details in your description.

2. Why did Beowulf decide to attack Grendel with only his bare hands?

3. In what two ways was Beowulf rewarded for his heroic deeds?

4. Name two ways in which the legend of Beowulf is different from the myths you have read in this chapter.

5. First, Beowulf destroyed Grendel and saved the kingdom of Hrothgar. Then he searched for and killed Grendel's mother. Do you think Beowulf was right in this second action? Why or why not?

Reading Literature: Norse Legends

1. **Explaining Conflict.** In this legend, external conflict is obvious. Beowulf fights with Grendel. Internal conflict is a character's inner struggle with thoughts and feelings. It is often less obvious. Hrothgar struggles with the idea of violence. He knows men must die if Grendel is to be defeated. He must decide whether to continue the fight. Think of another character in the Norse stories you have read who struggles with an internal problem. What is the conflict? How does the character settle the problem?

2. **Contrasting Characters.** Beowulf and Grendel both show great physical strength. However, Beowulf wins the struggle with Grendel. Name two actions taken by Beowulf during the fight that give him the advantage over Grendel. What do Beowulf's and Grendel's styles of fighting reveal about their characters?

3. **Analyzing Plot.** The plots of the Norse myths you have read tell basic events. In contrast, the plot of the Beowulf legend is more complex. It tells much more than the simple events. The storyteller develops, or builds, the rising action by:

    a. providing rich details in descriptions

    b. presenting a number of conflicts, both internal and external

    c. including a feeling of suspense

    d. revealing the personalities of the characters in the story

   Choose one of the above methods. Find at least two examples of the method in the legend of Beowulf.

4. **Defining the Danish Hero.** Beowulf's struggle with Grendel represents the conflict of good against evil. List the specific actions taken by Beowulf that please Hrothgar. What heroic qualities do these actions show?

Developing Vocabulary Skills

Combining Words to Form Compounds. The Beowulf legend contains many words that are actually word combinations. These are called compounds. For example, the word *huntsmen* is a combination of *hunt* and *men*. Sometimes there is a slight change in spelling. An *s* was added between the two words in *huntsmen*, for example. Sometimes the combined word is spelled with a hyphen, as in *tug-of-war*.

Read the following list of words. In the story, they have been combined to form compounds.

land	way	life
door	long	light
moon	first	head
mark	foot	prints

Each of the following sentences should be completed by a compound word. Combine two words from the list to form the compound. On your paper, write the complete sentence.

1. Grendel stood outside in the _____, looking at Hrothgar's hall.

2. Hrothgar's hall was a _____ to the people of the kingdom.

3. Grendel burst through the _____ of the hall in a surprise attack.

4. The warriors tracked Grendel's _____ to find where he lived.

5. Beowulf dove _____ into the pool of water.

6. Hrothgar and the Danes would feel _____ gratitude toward Beowulf, the hero.

Developing Writing Skills

1. **Analyzing Internal Conflict.** King Hrothgar faces a dilemma. He wants to rid his kingdom of the monster Grendel. However, he does not want to lose any more brave warriors. Review the legend to find specific examples of the King's conflicting thoughts. Then, write a paragraph detailing Hrothgar's internal conflict. Include at least three supporting details from the legend. If Hrothgar solves his conflict, tell how he does so.

2. **Changing Point of View.** King Hrothgar and the Danes see Grendel as a horrible monster. Rewrite a section of the legend to tell the story from Grendel's point of view.

   Pre-Writing. Use your imagination. List ideas on the following questions:

   What does Grendel see and hear as he approaches the hall?

   Why might he feel rage and hatred?

You may think of other ideas. Add them to your notes. Decide exactly which part of the action to rewrite. List the main events of that scene.

Writing. Use first-person point of view Write the story as though you are Grendel. Refer to Grendel with the word *I*. Include the main action. Also include Grendel's feelings and reactions to events.

Revising. Ask another person to read your story about Grendel. Have the person identify Grendel's opinions and feelings. If the person has trouble, you need to change a part of your story.

Developing Skills in Study and Research

Using Maps To Draw Conclusions. Where the Norse people lived affected their myths. Use the library to locate a map of their land.

One book that contains maps is the **atlas**. Locate the atlas section in your library. Select an atlas about Europe. Find a map that shows northern Europe. Answer the following questions based on the map.

1. Locate Denmark, the home of Hrothgar. What countries are near Denmark?

2. Locate Sweden, the home of Beowulf. Explain the route that Beowulf took.

Next, locate an atlas of the world. Use it to answer these questions.

3. Compare the locations of Denmark and Sweden to the location where you live. Is your climate similar to the Norse climate?

4. Name two elements in the legend of Beowulf that are connected to the geographic setting.

Using Your Skills in Reading Norse Myths and Legends

Here is an excerpt from a further adventure of Beowulf. Identify in it at least one detail that is typical of Norse myths and legends.

After the battles with Grendel and his mother, Beowulf returned to his home. There he became ruler of a large territory. After many years, he faced a new danger.

Deep within a cave, a dragon had been guarding its huge treasure. Then a man wandered into the cave by chance and saw a jeweled goblet, among other riches. The man took the goblet and hurried away before the dragon was aware of him.

Soon the dragon realized that someone had stolen his goblet. In fury, he left his cave. He began to terrorize the countryside, breathing fire at homes and people. Word came to Beowulf that his people were being attacked. Immediately he decided to go against the dragon alone.

Using Your Comprehension Skills

Read the following excerpt from a myth you will read in Chapter 3. Then compare and contrast the characters with Prometheus and Epimetheus.

Long, long ago there lived in that region of the world now known as Australia two brothers named Naru and Masa. Now, as it happened, Naru was very clever while his brother was extremely stupid.

One day Naru carved a squid out of wood. It looked so real that he decided to throw it into the sea. Instantly it came alive and swam away.

Using Your Vocabulary Skills

The underlined words in the following sentences are from Chapter 3. For each one, identify the base word and any affix added to it. Then explain how each affix changes the meaning of the base word.

1. The grizzly bear said his neighbor's voice was <u>ridiculous</u>.
2. He said that man should move <u>swiftly</u> but silently.

3. The coyote said these were the <u>stupidest</u> speeches he had ever heard.

4. In this way, the animals <u>disagreed</u> among themselves.

5. Just show me another who is <u>stronger</u> than I!

6. He watched her with bright, <u>unblinking</u> eyes.

7. Shetu put her hand to her mouth in <u>amazement</u>.

8. Her husband would not give up his <u>foolish</u> idea.

Using Your Writing Skills

Choose one of the writing assignments below.

1. Review the Norse myth that tells of the contest with the giants. Is there more than one conflict in this adventure? Describe each conflict you identify. Tell whether the conflict is internal or external. Explain who or what is involved in the conflict. Finally, tell whether the conflict is brought to a conclusion, and how.

   Write a separate paragraph about each conflict you identify.

2. Reread the excerpt about Beowulf's new adventure given in the first exercise in this review. Then write your own version of what happens next. In your story, try to match the tone and attitudes that you found in the Norse myths and legends.

Using Your Skills in Study and Research

Imagine that you have been asked to do research on the Vikings. You are to find out what they thought about the Norse gods, goddesses, heroes, and monsters. You have also been asked to find out how the Vikings presented these characters in their art. You have only fifteen minutes left to do your research in the library. You probably have time to use only one or two resources. Which of these resources will you use first? If you have time, which will you use second? Identify your top two choices and explain the reasons for your choices.

1. the card catalog
2. the catalog for the picture file
3. the *V* volume of the encyclopedia
4. the picture file
5. the index of the encyclopedia
6. the atlas

CHAPTER 3

Myths from Many Lands

Superman, 1952, PHILIP PEARLSTEIN.
Collection of Dorothy Pearlstein. Courtesy of Hirschl
and Adler Modern, New York.

Reading Literature: Myths from Many Lands

Why Are There Myths in Many Lands?

Did the world get rivers from a god's tears? Or did rivers come from the blood of a dead giant? Are they from a creature within a golden egg? The myths of three different countries give these three different explanations. Throughout the world, people explain the same things in different ways. Each group of people has its own myths, or stories that explain how things came to be.

You might wonder why people do not come up with the same explanation. One major reason is that each group bases their explanations on what they see around them. The Norse myth about the beginning of the universe, for example, talked about ice and snow. The Greek version, coming from a warmer land, didn't mention the cold. Another reason is that each explanation includes things or ideas that are important to that group. For example, the Norse depended on trees for protection and warmth. It is not surprising that trees appear in their myth of the creation of humans.

It is interesting to find similarities among myths from different lands. However, it is also important to see differences. Remember that a myth reflects the thinking and the needs of the people who created it.

The History of Myths

There have been myths almost as long as there have been people. Scientists who have studied prehistoric people report this. They believe that the earliest myths began perhaps as long ago as 250,000 B.C.

Myths can be separated into two groups. **Creation myths** tell of the beginnings of gods or the Earth or humans. The American Indian myth in this chapter, for example, describes the creation of humans. **Explanatory myths** explain elements of nature, such as mountains or sunsets. An example is the Nigerian myth in this chapter, which explains thunder. At the same time, this story shows how myths can teach lessons.

There are many theories on how myths develop. One theory says that a myth may be based on a real person or event. For example, myths from many lands tell of a flood covering the world. Perhaps, hundreds of thousands of years ago, there was a tremendous flood. All the groups of people hurt by this flood may have described it in their myths. Another theory is that people create myths to satisfy inner needs. For example, people have always created mighty heroes, like Hercules, to respect. Today's tales of superheroes, such as Superman, have much in common with the ancient myths. They may become the myths of tomorrow.

The Elements of Myths from Many Lands

Plot. Every myth tells a story. The supernatural is part of each story. Myths dramatize happenings that could not actually occur. In the American Indian myth in this chapter, for example, animals talk and model clay.

Setting. The setting of each myth shows the traditional way of life in that country. For example, the Nigerian myth is set in a jungle. The people live by hunting and farming. The Australian myth is set near the sea. The people live by fishing.

Characters. In any myth the main character is either a god, a human or part-human hero, or an animal that acts like a human. Heroes have the traits that the society respects.

How To Read Myths of Many Lands

1. Keep in mind that each myth has been handed down orally. Reading it aloud may bring it alive.
2. Try to find the purpose of each myth. What does it explain? Does it also teach a lesson? How might this myth satisfy people?
3. Compare myths. Notice similarities in such things as purpose, plot, or characters. Look for similarities with Greek and Norse myths.
4. Contrast the myths. Notice different explanations for the same thing. Also notice different settings and different kinds of heroes. What can you guess about the people who created each myth?

Comprehension Skills: Paragraph Organization

Recognizing Different Kinds of Paragraphs

In writing, a basic unit is the paragraph. Each paragraph is made up of one or more sentences. In most good paragraphs, all the sentences are about one idea, called the **main idea**. The way the sentences are arranged depends on the kind of paragraph. On these pages, you will learn about the four basic kinds of paragraphs.

Narrative Paragraphs. A paragraph that tells about an event is a **narrative paragraph**. Its sentences tell the steps in which the event happened. Therefore, they usually follow **time order**. This is also called **chronological order**. Here is an example.

> One day Naru carved a squid out of wood. It looked so real that he decided to throw it into the sea. Instantly it came alive and swam away.

Descriptive Paragraphs. A paragraph that describes a person, object, or scene is a **descriptive paragraph**. Usually, one sentence states what is being described, which is the main idea. This is the **topic sentence**. It often comes first. The rest of the sentences give details about the topic. Usually, the details are arranged as you would notice them. This is called **spatial order**. Here is an example.

> The man went to a corn bin that stood on the edge of the compound. It was made of mud and looked rather like an outsized water-pot. When the man had climbed in through the opening at the top, he found he could see over the edge only by standing on tiptoe.

Persuasive Paragraphs. A paragraph that tries to persuade is a **persuasive paragraph**. The first sentence is usually the topic sentence. It states what the reader should do or believe. The other sentences give reasons. The reasons are usually arranged from most important to least important, or sometimes from least important to most important. This is called **order of importance**.

In this example, the speaker is trying to persuade her husband not to bother another man.

"Keep away from him, for I'm sure he will destroy you! Then what will become of me?"

Explanatory Paragraphs.   A paragraph that explains something is an **explanatory paragraph**. Usually, the first sentence is the topic sentence. The rest of the sentences give details, usually in chronological order or order of importance. Here is an example.

Once upon a time there was a man who believed he was stronger than anyone else in the whole world. He certainly was strong, for whenever he went to the forest to get firewood for his home, he would bring back a load ten times as big as most men could carry. Sometimes, when he found a dead tree lying on the ground, he would toss it onto his head with a mighty heave and carry it home in one piece.

Understanding Paragraphs

Not every paragraph fits the descriptions above. A paragraph might combine narration and description, for example. The topic sentence of the paragraph may come last, or in the middle. Or, like most narrative paragraphs, the paragraph may not have a topic sentence.

However, comparing every paragraph to these descriptions can help you better understand your reading. Keep alert to what each paragraph is doing. State the main idea in your own words. Then see if there is a topic sentence. Can you explain how the sentences are arranged?

Exercise: Understanding Paragraph Organization

Read the following paragraph. Identify the kind of paragraph it is. State its main idea. If it has a topic sentence, identify it. Tell the order in which the sentences are arranged.

The mountain lion was the first to speak. He declared that he should like to see man created, like himself, with a mighty voice wherewith he could frighten all animals. He would also have him covered with hair and with strong talons in his claws.

Vocabulary Skills: Context Clues

Using Context Clues

When you first began to speak, you knew only a few words. You learned new words by paying attention to the way other people used them. In the same natural way, you can learn new words in your reading. You can figure them out by paying attention to the way writers use them. This is called **using context clues**. The words and sentences around a specific word are called the **context** of that word.

Here are some of the most common types of context clues.

Definition or Restatement Clues. Sometimes a writer realizes that a word will be new to readers. To save them the trouble of looking in a dictionary, the writer states the meaning in the context.

The writer may set off the definition as you might see it in the dictionary. For example, the word *squid* is defined in context here:

The squid is a sea animal that has tentacles attached to its head.

More often, the writer will restate the meaning in less exact wording than in a dictionary definition.

Masa carved a barracuda—a large fish that preys on other fish.

A writer can use the following key words and phrases as signals to definition or restatement clues:

is   that is   which is   who is   called   in other words   or

A writer can also use certain punctuation marks as signals:

dashes —   commas ,   parentheses ( )

Examples: The men planted guinea corn, <u>which is</u> a kind of grain.
A kind of grain <u>called</u> guinea corn grows well here.
We planted guinea corn, a kind of grain, last year.
Guinea corn (<u>a</u> kind of grain) grew in the field.

Synonyms. Sometimes a word is used in context with its synonym. A **synonym** is a word that has the same or almost the same meaning. If you recognize the synonym, you can figure out the new word. For example, the synonym *nonsense* indicates the meaning of *folly* in this sentence:

> The mole thought it was folly and nonsense to talk about wings.

At times, synonyms appear in separate sentences. You can usually recognize synonyms because they both refer to the same thing. They are usually the same part of speech. They may appear in the same parts of their sentences. Notice the synonyms in these sentences:

> Shetu's *obstinate* husband argued with her. He was too *headstrong* to listen to the facts.

> The Coyote *envied* the owl. He *was jealous of* his wings.

Exercises: Using Context Clues

A. Each sentence below is about myths in this chapter. Identify the word whose meaning is given in context. State the meaning. Then identify whether you used **definition or restatement** clues or **synonyms**.

1. The Coyote is a trickster, one who deceives others.
2. He called a council. All the animals attended the assembly.
3. The myth is from the Miwok Indians, a tribe of native Americans.
4. The hero of the story is a cuckoo—a bird native to the island.
5. "The Fish" is an Australian creation myth (a story that explains how things came to be).

B. Look for the meaning of each underlined word in context. If there are context clues, state the meaning. If there are not, write **No clues.**

1. The barracuda devoured the <u>herrings</u>. He ate all the small fish.
2. The wind blew them <u>higgledy-piggledy</u>, that is, in total confusion.
3. The woman took a large <u>calabash</u> and put it on her head.
4. Without <u>faltering</u> or hesitating, the child pulled on the rope.
5. The baby was an <u>orphan</u>—a child whose parents have died.

Legend of Creation

MIWOK INDIAN MYTH

This tale is told by the Miwok Indians of northern California. It is an example of a creation myth. As you read this tale, make note of each animal's idea of what traits a man should have. Which animal do you agree with?

After Coyote had finished all the work of making the world and the lower animals, he called a council of the animals to consider the creation of man.

They all sat down in a circle in an open space in the forest. The mountain lion was at the head. On his right sat the grizzly bear, next came the cinnamon bear, and so on according to their rank, the last being the little mouse, which sat at the lion's left.

The mountain lion was the first to speak. He declared that he should like to see man created, like himself, with a mighty voice wherewith he could frighten all animals. He would also have him covered with hair and with strong talons in his claws.

The grizzly bear said it was ridiculous to have such a voice as his neighbor, for he was always roaring with it so that he scared away the very prey that he wished to capture. He thought the man ought to have great strength and be able to move about very swiftly, but silently, and be able to grip his prey without making a noise.

The buck said that in his way of thinking the man would look very foolish unless he had a pair of magnificent antlers on his head to fight with. He also thought it absurd to roar so loudly. He would pay more attention to man's ears and eyes than he would to his throat, for he would have the first like a spider's web and the second like fire.

The mountain sheep solemnly declared he could not see what sense there was in such antlers branching in every direction, only to be caught in the thickets. If the man had horns mostly rolled up, they would be like a stone on each side of his head, giving it weight and enabling him to butt a great deal harder.

When it was the coyote's turn to speak, he declared that all these were the stupidest speeches he had ever heard and that he could hardly keep awake while listening. Every one of them wanted to make man like himself. They might just as well take one of their own cubs and call it a man.

"As for myself," said he, "I know I am not the best animal that can be made, and I can make one better than myself or any other. Of course the man would have to be

Seer, 1950, ADOLPH GOTTLIEB. The Phillips Collection, Washington, D.C.

like me in having four legs, five fingers, and so on. It would be well enough for him to have a voice like the lion, only he need not roar with it all the time."

He admitted that the grizzly bear had some good points, one of which was the shape of his feet, which enabled him to stand erect easily; and he was in favor, therefore, of making man's feet nearly like those of the grizzly. The grizzly was also happy in having no tail, for he had learned from his own experience that a tail was only a harbor for fleas.

Coyote also admitted that the buck's eyes and ears were pretty good, perhaps better than his own. Then there was the fish, which was naked and which he envied because hair was such a burden most of the year. Coyote also wished the man to have claws as long as the eagle's so that he could hold things in them.

But, said he, with all their separate gifts they must acknowledge that there was no animal beside himself that had wit enough to supply the man; so that he should be obliged to make him like himself in that respect also—cunning and crafty.

After the coyote had stopped speaking, the beaver said he had never heard such nonsense in his life. No tail, indeed! He would make man with a broad, flat tail so he could carry mud and sand on it.

The owl said all the animals seemed to have lost their senses, since none of them wanted to give the man wings. "Of what use," said he, "could anyone on earth be to himself without wings?"

The mole said it was perfect folly to talk about wings, for with them the man would be certain to bump his head against the sky. Besides, if he had wings and eyes both, he would get his eyes burnt by flying too near the sun, but without eyes he could burrow in the cool, soft earth and be happy.

Last of all, the little mouse squeaked out that he would make a man with eyes, of course, so he could see what he was eating; but as for burrowing in the ground, that was absurd.

In this way, the animals disagreed among themselves, and the council broke up in a row. Every animal set to work to make an animal according to his own ideas, and, taking a lump of earth, each one commenced molding it like himself except the coyote, who began to make a model such as he had described in the council.

It was so late before they fell to work that nightfall came on before anyone had finished a model, and they all lay down and fell asleep, all except the cunning coyote. He stayed awake and worked hard all night. When all the other animals were asleep, he went around and spoiled their models by putting water on them.

Early the next morning Coyote finished his model and gave it life long before the others could make their new models.

Developing Comprehension Skills

1. The first list below names animals in the legend. The second list includes their ideas about what man should have. Match each animal with its idea for creating man.

   Animals

   mountain lion

   grizzly bear
   buck
   mountain sheep

   coyote

   owl

   mole

   mouse

   Ideas About Man

   a. four legs, no tail, five fingers, voice
   b. antlers to fight with
   c. wings
   d. mighty voice, hair, and talons
   e. ability to burrow in the earth
   f. strength to move swiftly and quietly
   g. rolled horns on the sides of his head
   h. eyes to see what he is eating

2. In the first few paragraphs, the author described the main character and all the supporting characters. In what order were the characters introduced? Why do you think the storyteller chose this order?

3. A topic sentence states the main idea of a piece of writing. Sometimes a storyteller includes a topic sentence. Other times, no topic sentence is stated. Then, the main idea must be inferred or figured out. What is the main idea of this legend? Is it stated in a topic sentence?

4. Native Americans have traditionally believed that humans are closely related to nature. They do not believe that humans are masters of nature. Explain how this creation myth shows that belief. In what major way is this story different from the story of Prometheus? How is this myth different from the Norse creation myth? What do these differences suggest about Indian beliefs?

Reading Literature: Myths

1. **Understanding Setting.** Describe the setting, or time and place, for this legend. Why is this setting appropriate for this myth?

2. **Contrasting Two Descriptions.** The grizzly bear and the lion have different ideas about man. List the traits that each animal thinks a man should have. In your opinion, which animal's ideas would be more valuable for a person? Why?

3. **Explaining a Character.** The lion wants man to have a mighty voice. The grizzly bear thinks great strength is important. The buck selects antlers for man. How does each animal's choice reveal its personality?

4. **Finding Details.** Coyote describes himself as "cunning and crafty." How does he show these characteristics?

Developing Vocabulary Skills

Using Definition and Restatement Clues. Read the following sentences about events in the myth you just read. The underlined words may be unfamiliar to you. The meanings of the words can be figured out by definition or restatement clues. For each underlined word, write:

   a. the meaning
   b. the key words or punctuation marks that signal clues

1. Coyote called a <u>council</u>. That is, he called a meeting of the animals.

2. A <u>buck</u> is a male deer.

3. The grizzly bear's feet enabled him to stand <u>erect</u> (upright).

4. The mole could <u>burrow</u>—dig tunnels—in the earth.

5. Eventually, the meeting ended in a noisy quarrel, called a <u>row</u>.

6. To be <u>cunning</u> is to be clever or crafty.

Developing Writing Skills

1. **Explaining a Symbol.** The animals in the myth sometimes resemble people in what they say and do. What comparisons can you make between the animals and human beings? Write a paragraph to explain how the animals represent, or symbolize, people.

   Pre-Writing. List at least three ways in which the animals in the story are like people. Include their actions, words, and thoughts. Then, number your details in an order that makes them easy to understand. Select the key words you will use in your paragraph to connect the ideas. Use words such as *both, alike,* and *similar* to show the comparison. Think about why the storyteller makes the animals act like people. What idea might the storyteller have wanted to explain about human nature?

   Writing. Begin with a topic sentence to state the main idea. Include the three examples you selected to support this main idea. Be sure to use key words to signal the comparison of animals and people.

   Revising. Read your paragraph to check that it is easy to understand. Circle the key words that show the comparisons. There should be at least three. Then, count the ways in which you explained that animals in the legend act like people. You should have included three examples. If your paragraph meets these requirements, it is a good explanation of the symbols in the myth.

2. **Changing the Effect of a Story.** Rewrite the ending of this Indian legend. How could it have ended differently? You may want to change the plot, the characters, or both. Be sure to think about Coyote's action. In the Indian myth, he created man while the others slept. Will your version of the story be similar or totally different?

Developing Skills in Speaking and Listening

Making a Presentation. Join three or four other students in class to form a small group. Each student should take the part of one of the animals in this myth. Make up a short speech that fits your animal's ideas about creating a human. You may use details from the Indian story or add new ideas of your own. Remember, each animal suggests that a human should have traits like its own.

Practice the presentation with the members of your group. Appoint a narrator to introduce the story. Be sure the narrator also introduces each animal and controls the order of speakers. Limit each speaker to a few minutes of talking.

As you speak, be sure your voice is loud enough for everyone to hear. You may read from your paper. Read slowly enough that your ideas are clear to the listeners.

When your group is ready, make the presentation to your class.

The Story of the Cuckoo

NEW GUINEA MYTH

This myth presents ideas about loyalty and hard work. Would people today agree with the ideas of the storyteller from New Guinea?

Long ago, before men walked the earth, there once was a forest god whose son died and went to the underworld. Calling all the animals together, the forest god asked them to sing songs of praise to his son as long as they were able.

Early in the morning the singing began, and it continued all through the day and long into the night. One by one the animals and birds began to tire, however, and at last the only voice echoing through the forest was the loud, clear tone of the cuckoo. On and on she sang, though trembling with exhaustion, until at last the forest god commanded her to stop.

"You have satisfied me," said the forest god. "Your devotion shall be rewarded. For such excellent service I permit you now and forever to lay your eggs in the nests of all other birds. You shall not spend your energy building nests, nor hatching eggs; that, too, will be the task of the other birds. Their duty shall be to take care of your eggs."

This is the reason why even today the cuckoo does not build a nest nor hatch the eggs of her own young.

Developing Comprehension Skills

1. What fact about cuckoos does this myth explain? What fact about the singing of birds does it explain?

2. Arrange the following events in the order they happened in the story:

> The cuckoo outlasted all the other animals in spite of its exhaustion.
> The forest god's son died and went to the underworld.
> The forest god asked the animals to sing songs of praise.
> The forest god rewarded the cuckoo for its devotion.

3. Compare the forest god with the gods you read about in Chapters 1 and 2. Is the forest god more like the Greek gods or more like the Norse gods? Explain your answer.

4. How would the forest god's reward to the cuckoo affect the other birds?

5. The forest god rewarded the cuckoo in two ways. Do you think the cuckoo deserved such generous rewards? Why or why not?

Reading Literature: Myths

1. **Examining Setting.** What do you learn about the setting? Identify any facts stated directly by the storyteller. Then, tell what else you can figure out about the setting. What details in the story suggest that the setting might be like this?

2. **Recognizing Character Traits.** Which of the following traits describe the cuckoo? For each trait you choose, list two details from the myth that support the description.

exhausted	angry
weak-voiced	devoted
proud	dishonest
shy	jealous

The Fish

AUSTRALIAN MYTH

This Australian myth explains why fish have certain habits. It also teaches a lesson. Look for both elements as you read this Pacific Island tale.

Long, long ago there lived in that region of the world now known as Australia two brothers named Naru and Masa. Now, as it happened, Naru was very clever while his brother was extremely stupid.

One day Naru carved a squid out of wood. It looked so real that he decided to throw it into the sea. Instantly it came alive and swam away. However, to express its gratitude to Naru, from that day on it drove a school of small herrings close to shore so that Naru might catch them easily and have plenty to eat.

After a while, Masa noticed that his brother had more than enough fish to eat for his supper whereas he, Masa, had scarcely any at all. Greatly curious as to how his brother managed to catch so many fish, he decided to question him.

"Where do you find so many fish, brother? Tell me so that I may go there, too."

"Masa, I will tell you a secret," replied Naru. "I carved a squid that looked so real that when I threw it into the water it became alive. Out of gratitude it has been driving the herrings close to shore so that I may easily catch them for my supper."

Thinking for a moment, Naru suggested, "Why don't you carve a fish too? But make sure that it is a squid," he warned with a severe tone in his voice.

Masa went home immediately and sat down to carve a fish. But because he was extremely stupid, he greedily carved a barracuda instead of a squid, as his brother had suggested. As soon as it was finished, he threw the wooden barracuda into the water, and, just like the squid earlier, the barracuda became alive. Immediately it swam toward the herrings and devoured them. Seeing this, Masa began to cry.

"What kind of fish did you carve?" demanded Naru angrily.

"A barracuda," sobbed his brother.

"You fool!" exclaimed Naru in despair. "Now your fish will eat up all the others, and in the end he won't even spare us."

And that is exactly what happened.

Even to this day, barracudas attack fish and people.

Melanesian dance mask in the form of a fish, date unknown.
Museum of Mankind. Reproduced by the courtesy of the trustees of The British Museum, London.

Developing Comprehension Skills

1. Why did Masa carve a barracuda instead of a squid, as his brother told him?

2. What lesson about life did Masa learn at the end of this tale?

3. The myths you have read come from many countries. However, they often present ideas that are similar. Think about the myths that describe the creation of living things. In the myths, humans are made from clay, stones, and trees. In "The Fish," a squid and a barracuda are made from wood. What general statement do the myths seem to make about the origin of living things?

Reading Literature: Myths

1. **Comparing Details.** Compare and contrast the fish created by Naru and the one created by Masa. What were their similarities and differences? What effects did each fish have on the events?

2. **Recognizing Character Traits.** In the myth, Naru is considered clever and Masa stupid. Think about the details the storyteller uses to contrast the characters. Name at least one example of Naru's cleverness and one example of Masa's mistakes.

3. **Understanding Purpose.** Name one time that Naru and Masa act brotherly. Name

something that happens between them that is not brotherly. Why would the storyteller have included both types of behavior?

Developing Vocabulary Skills

Finding Synonym Clues. The following statements contain words from the myths. The meaning of each underlined word can be figured out by finding a synonym clue. Look in the same sentence or a nearby sentence. Look for a word that refers to the same thing as the underlined word. On your paper, write each underlined word and its synonym.

1. The cuckoo was underlined{exhausted}. She was very tired from all the singing.

2. To express its underlined{gratitude} to Naru, the squid drove herrings close to shore. This act of thankfulness made it easy for Naru to catch fish to eat.

3. Naru warned his brother with a strict and underlined{severe} tone in his voice.

4. The barracuda underlined{devoured} the herrings. Masa began to cry when the barracuda ate the smaller fish.

5. Naru yelled out with underlined{despair}. He felt a loss of hope about the whole situation.

Developing Writing Skills

1. **Contrasting Results.** You may or may not agree with the forest god's choice of reward in "The Story of the Cuckoo." Consider a different award that you might give the cuckoo. Write a paragraph. Contrast the award you select to the reward given by the forest god. Include details of how each reward will affect the cuckoo. Also tell how the awards will affect the other animals.

2. **Writing an Explanatory Myth.** "The Story of the Cuckoo" and "The Fish" are both explanatory myths. Each explains the behavior of certain animals. Choose one of your favorite animals. Write a short myth to explain one of its behaviors.

Pre-Writing. List at least five behaviors that are normal for the animal you chose. For example, geese always travel in flocks. Think about how the people of an ancient culture might have explained the animal. Use your imagination. For example, thousands of years ago, geese may have been frightened by a horrible monster. They began to travel together because they were afraid to be alone. Limit your ideas to one of the animal's behaviors.

Writing. Explain the animal's behavior in one to three paragraphs. Begin by describing the setting where the animal lived. Remember to include some realistic details, too. Myths were told to explain nature so they had to appear sensible.

Revising. Read your animal myth to someone else. Ask the person to tell you what fact about the animal the story explains. If the person cannot determine the myth's purpose, or main idea, then you need to revise. Also ask the person to name several believable parts of the story. If this is difficult, your myth is too unrealistic. Add some believable details to your story.

Developing Skills in Study and Research

1. **Using the Card Catalog.** In this chapter, you have read myths from both New Guinea and Australia. The myths explain the behavior of

animals. You can use the library to find animal myths from other countries. Use the following steps to do your research:

a. In the card catalog, locate the subject cards for *Mythology*.

b. Skim through these cards. Try to find cards with the subheading *Animals*.

You may find a card in the *Mythology* group that reads *See* or *See also*. This is a **cross reference card**. It refers you to another subject heading in the catalog that might be helpful. If you find a cross reference card, read its headings. You may find a subject similar to *Animals*, such as *Bears* or *Snakes*. Check the cards for any subject that might include animal myths. Or the cross reference card might list countries that have mythologies. If so, select a country.

c. Find a card with information about an animal myth from a country other than New Guinea or Australia.

d. Copy the book title, author, and call number from the card.

2. **Outlining Information.** Select an animal myth that you have read. Make an **outline**, or organized summary, of it.

The following plan is one type of informal outline. Use it to organize important details from the myth. There might not be information in the myth for a certain section in this outline. Leave out that section in your outline. You may find information in the myth that does not fit any section in the outline. If so, add a section.

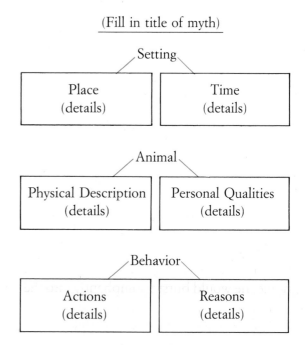

(Fill in title of myth)

Setting

| Place (details) | Time (details) |

Animal

| Physical Description (details) | Personal Qualities (details) |

Behavior

| Actions (details) | Reasons (details) |

The Tale of the Superman

MYTH OF THE HAUSA PEOPLE

This story from Nigeria describes at least three different superman characters. Look for similarities and differences in the characters as you read. Which character seems most like a superman to you?

Once upon a time there was a man who believed he was stronger than anyone else in the whole world. He certainly was strong, for whenever he went to the forest to get firewood for his home, he would bring back a load ten times as big as most men could carry. Sometimes, when he found a dead tree lying on the ground, he would toss it on to his head with a mighty heave and carry it home in one piece. But he was proud, too; and, when he reached home, he would burst triumphantly into the compound, fling the load down on the ground, and call to his wife: "Come and see what your superman has brought you!"

His wife would bend low as she came out of the door of her mud hut, then straighten her back and smile.

"Superman?" she would mock. "If you really saw a superman, you would run away from him. Don't talk to me of supermen! Strong you may be, but superman, no!"

Then the man would get angry and sit down under the cassia tree outside his hut muttering: "It's a lie! I am a superman. Just show me another who is stronger than I.

Then I will believe you when you say I am not a superman."

One day the man's wife, whose name was Shetu, went to draw water. She took a large calabash,[1] put it on her head, and walked along the winding bush path until she came to a well. Now this well was a magic one, and, although Shetu managed to throw the bucket down into the water, she could not pull it up. She hauled and she tugged and she heaved; leaning backwards and digging her heels into the ground, she put her whole weight to the task. She even called upon Allah to help her but all to no avail.

"Alas!" she exclaimed, sinking down on the mud beside the well and wiping the perspiration from her forehead with the hem of her skirt. "Ten men would be needed to raise that bucket from the well today. I must go home without any water."

Sadly she rose to her feet and began the journey back along the dusty path that wound in and out between the forest trees.

---

1. **Calabash.** A container made from the gourd, the fruit of the tropical calabash vine.

Suddenly she saw another woman approaching, and they stopped to exchange greetings.

"Why are you returning from the well with your calabash empty?" asked the stranger. "Has the well dried up?"

"Oh no!" exclaimed Shetu, "I have been struggling for a long time to raise the bucket from the water, but it is too heavy and I am not strong enough. It needs at least ten men to bring it to the top."

The other woman smiled and said: "Do not despair! Come, follow me to the well. I will see that you get your water after all."

Shetu was sure that the woman would not be able to help her, but she decided to follow to prove the truth of her words. As the woman led the way back along the path, Shetu noticed a fine-looking baby tied on her back. He turned his head and stared at her with bright, unblinking eyes for so long that she began to feel uncomfortable under his gaze.

At length they reached the well, and Shetu showed the woman the long rope that stretched far down into the well, with the magic bucket on the end.

"See!" she began, "I threw the bucket down but could not raise it up. I fear you will not be able to help either."

The woman laughed, untied the child from her back, and told him to pull the bucket up from the well. Without faltering, the child seized the rope in his little, fat hands and pulled the bucket up as easily as if it had been a feather on the end of a piece of string.

Shetu put her hand to her mouth in amazement. She could not speak, but the other woman did not seem at all disconcerted and told her child to draw more water. He did it again and again, without any sign of strain.

The two women set to work, washing first themselves and then the clothes they were wearing. These soon dried in the hot sun. Then they filled their calabashes with water and began their homeward journey.

After a little while, they came to a place where another path branched off to the east, and the woman with the baby turned up this new track.

"Where are you going?" asked Shetu.

"Home, of course," replied the other.

"Is your home along that path?" said Shetu. "I did not know that it led to a village. What is your husband's name?"

"My husband's name is Superman," said the stranger, and walking quickly along the narrow track she soon disappeared into the forest.

Shetu was too amazed to speak, but as soon as she got back to her hut she told her husband all that had happened during the day. At first he would not believe her, but soon he realized that she was speaking the truth, and anger welled up in him like bubbles rising in a pot of broth.

"Aha!" he exclaimed. "So there is another man who calls himself a superman, is there? Just let me see him, that's all! I'll soon show him who is the real superman!"

"O no!" begged his wife. "Keep away from him, in Allah's name, for I'm sure he will destroy you, and then what will become of me? If you had seen the strength of his infant son, you would realize that the father must be fifty times as strong."

But nothing she could say would persuade her obstinate husband to give up his foolish idea.

"Early tomorrow morning," he said firmly, "you must take me to the path that leads to this man's house."

The next day the husband got up before dawn and, full of confidence, took his hunting weapons from their hiding place. With a quiver of sharp arrows on his back, his bow in his hand, and his trusty sword slung from his shoulder, he felt ready for anything.

Then he shouted to his terrified wife, "Come along, lazy-bones! Come out of that hut and lead me to the place where this impostor lives! No, wait!" he exclaimed. "First of all take me to this magic well, that I may see the bucket for myself."

The woman picked up her calabash, placed it on her head, and led the way to the well. She was far too worried to realize how foolish it was to take a vessel to a well from which neither of them would be able to draw water; but she hurried along the path, with her husband still shouting at her from the rear. Presently she noticed that there was another figure on the path in front of her, and, when she and her husband reached the well, they found the other woman and her baby son there too.

Shetu's husband ignored them and began to peer down into the well, straining to catch sight of the water at the bottom.

Crowned head of an Oni, 12th–15th Century. Zinc brass from Wunmonije Compound, Ife Museum of Ife Antiquities, Nigeria. Photograph by Dirk Bakker.

"Give me that bucket!" he stormed, and, snatching it from the ground beside the well, he threw it with all his strength down into the dark cavity. They all heard it strike the water with a resounding splash.

"I'll put an end to this nonsense once and for all," he boasted, as he began to haul on the rope. "Ten men, indeed! Watch me pull the bucket up!"

He grunted and groaned, he swore and he sweated, but the bucket would not come up. Frustrated, he leaned further and further into the well, cursing the bucket, the rope, and the water so heartily that he forgot to keep his foot anchored against the rim of the well and all but tumbled in after the bucket. Just in time, the baby boy reached his hand over the cloth that tied him to his mother's back, seized both the rope and the man, and whisked man and bucket safely out of the well with never a word.

The man sat on the ground in dazed surprise, rubbing his head and watching the child, who had clambered down from his mother's back, pull up bucket after bucket of cold, clear water, while his mother filled her water-pot.

Then Shetu turned to him triumphantly. "Now that you have seen what the son of the real superman can do, are you not afraid to meet the superman himself?"

The man had been silently wondering how he could get out of his visit to the real superman's compound; but, since his wife had shamed him by suggesting he would be afraid, he had to put a brave face on things. So he said stubbornly, still rubbing his bruised head, "I am more determined than ever to go and see this so-called superman."

"Right! Then you go alone," said Shetu, and seizing her calabash which the child had filled with water, she placed it on her head and hurried away from the well.

The other woman turned doubtfully to the man. "So you want to see my husband, do you?" she asked. "You'd be far better off if you went home." But he would not listen. Presently the woman fastened her baby on her back again and led the way through the forest.

At last they reached the woman's compound. It looked much the same as any other home. There was nothing to show that it belonged to a superman, so the man's courage began to return.

"My husband, the superman, is away hunting in the forest," explained the woman. "You can hide somewhere until he comes back, and then you can peep out and look at him. But do not let him see you. He eats men like you!"

"Bah!" said the man, "I'm not afraid. There's no need for me to hide."

"What if I tell you that my husband ate a whole elephant for breakfast today, and that he has been known to eat ten elephants at one sitting?" asked the woman. "Are you not then afraid, O foolish little man?"

Then the man let her lead him to a corn bin that stood on the edge of the compound. It was made of mud and looked rather like an outsized water-pot. When the man had climbed in through the opening at the top, he found he could see over the edge only by standing on tiptoe.

"Now, keep quiet if you value your life," admonished the woman as she left him. "I must cook my husband's supper."

Towards evening the man in the corn bin heard a sound like an approaching tornado. A great wind began to shake the forest trees and to lift the thatch from the nearby huts. Then into the clearing around the compound came the master of the house. As he spoke, the air throbbed with the power of his voice, and his feet shook the ground like an earthquake.

"Wife! Wife!" he called. "Have you cooked me my elephant?"

"Indeed I have," replied the woman. "Come and see whether this one is big enough for your supper."

The man in the corn bin cowered with fright. So it was true! There was, after all, another more worthy of the name of Superman. How he did hope with all his heart that the elephant the woman had cooked was big enough. He stood trembling while he heard the superman eating his supper and cracking elephant bones like sticks of sugar cane.

"Allah grant that the elephant is a big one," he murmured again and again between his chattering teeth.

Time passed until, when the sky was dark and night had come, the real superman shouted, "Wife! Wife! I smell the smell of man. Where is he, that I may eat him?"

"Good husband, I am the one whom you can smell," she replied. "There is no one here but me." However, she found it difficult to satisfy her husband that there was no one hidden in the compound. He prowled about, shaking the place with his shouts and heavy footsteps, while the man in the corn bin nearly died of fright.

At last the superman left the compound and began to search in the nearby forest land, roaring all the while, "I smell the smell of a man."

As soon as he was gone, the woman crept over to the corn bin and whispered to the terrified man within, "Oh, why did you not believe me from the first? What a lot of trouble we should both have saved."

"Alas! I am truly sorry," said the foolish man. "But how could I believe such a thing unless I saw it with my own eyes? And how can I escape from this place?"

"Now listen," whispered the woman. "Soon my husband will return for the night. Watch the door of our hut, and, when my husband is fast asleep, I will put my little lamp outside. Then you must make haste and escape and never come back again."

"Thank you! Thank you!" said the man, trembling violently as he felt the wind blow across the compound, announcing the return of the superman.

The hours passed slowly, but the man dared not sleep. Then at last, just before dawn, he saw a tiny flickering light, like a firefly, at the door of the hut. Carefully, he swung himself up on to the rim of the corn bin and let himself down to the ground without a sound. Then he began to run, and how he did run! Never had his feet taken such long strides or his heart beat so quickly. Just when he thought he was safe, he heard the roars of the superman in the distance, and his heart sank. He felt sick with fright.

"I smell the smell of a man," shouted the voice he had learned to dread.

The poor man ran faster and faster, until he came to a field where some men were clearing the ground to make a farm. They stopped in their task of uprooting bushes and felling trees and inquired, "Hey! Where are you going? Who is chasing you, that you run so fast?"

"Someone who calls himself Superman is chasing me," panted the runner. "Can you help me?"

"There are several of us here," replied the men. "Stay with us until this so-called superman catches up, and we'll deal with him."

The man crouched, panting, on the ground, when suddenly a mighty wind rose up, so strong that it lifted all the laborers off the ground and dropped them several yards away.

"Here!" they called in fright. "What's happening to us?"

"It's the superman," exclaimed the terrified fugitive. "He puffs and blows so strongly that a great wind precedes him."

"If that's the case, we are no match for him." said the men, now terrified in their turn. "You'd better keep on running."

Again the man leaped to his feet in fear and began his race. Presently he came to another group of men, who were hoeing up the ground in preparation for planting. They looked at him in amazement.

"Hey! Where are you going? Who is chasing you, that you run so fast?" they shouted.

"Someone who calls himself Superman is chasing me," puffed the man. "Can you help me?"

The men laughed. "There are ten of us here," they said. "Surely we can deal with

your so-called superman. Stay with us until he catches up to you."

The man collapsed gratefully onto a heap of earth and tried to get his breath back. Then the men who were hoeing found themselves blown about by a strong wind, which tumbled them higgledy-piggledy all over their farm.

"Here!" they said. "What's happening?"

"It's that superman," said the man despondently. "He puffs and he blows so strongly that a great wind precedes him."

"In that case, we are no match for such a man," said the men who had been hoeing. "You'd better keep on running." They lay flat on their faces, hoping that the superman would not see them as he passed by.

By now the poor man was nearly dead with fatigue, but with a great effort he managed to drag himself to his feet and continued to run away from the superman, even faster than before. Presently he came to another group of men, who were planting guinea corn seed in a patch of ground already cleared and hoed.

"Hey! Where are you going?" they called in surprise. "Who is chasing you, that you run so fast?"

"Someone who calls himself Superman is chasing me," replied the poor fellow in a weak voice. "Can you help me?"

"Well, there are a dozen or more of us here," replied one of the men. "I don't think a superman would bother us much. Stay with us until he catches up to you."

The man staggered and fell, too exhausted to say more, but after a few moments a mighty wind came. It lifted up the men who were sowing, whirled them round in the air, and cast them to the ground in a heap.

"Here!" they gasped. "What's happening to us?"

"It's that superman," explained the runner in despair, knowing full well what would be the outcome.

"Then you'd better keep on running," said the frightened men, as they dropped their long planting-hoes and handfuls of seed and ran helter-skelter into the forest to hide.

The man thought his end had come, but, rousing himself to make one last effort, he ran on. Suddenly, as he rounded a bend in the path, he saw in the distance what looked like a huge man sitting under a baobab[2] tree, his enormous legs stretched out beside the path.

"I've dodged a wasp, only to run into a hornet," the fleeing man thought, as he tried to hide behind a bush. "But no! nothing can be worse than the fate that will befall me if I stop running."

So he went on his way, with his heart in his mouth.

When he reached the baobab tree, he found that it was indeed a gigantic man sitting there, surrounded by roasted elephants, which he was hungrily eating, and throwing their huge bones away over his shoulder into the forest.

"Stop!" he boomed. "Who is chasing you, that you run so fast?"

___

2. **Baobab tree**. An African tree with a huge trunk.

The exhausted man fell in a heap at the giant's feet and panted, "Someone who calls himself Superman is chasing me. Can you help me?"

"Of course I can," boomed the giant. "I am Giant-of-the-Forest. Stay with me until he catches up to you."

Suddenly the wind made by the puffings and blowings of the superman lifted our poor man from the ground and twirled him round and round in the air. Then he fell down some distance away from the gaint.

"Come back," called Giant-of-the-Forest. "Don't you want me to help you?"

"I couldn't stop myself," explained the man. "It's the breath of that superman."

The giant did not seem at all put out. He laughed kindly and said, "Give me your hand. I will sit on it, and then the breath of this so-called superman cannot blow you away."

There they sat—and the man's arm was almost crushed by the weight of the giant—until Superman came rushing up to them. He was in a fine temper!

"Give me that man," he bellowed to the giant. "He's mine! I want to eat him."

"Come and take him then," said the giant, grinning horribly.

Then Superman leaped at the giant, who rose to his feet and began to fight with him. They leaped, they stamped, they struggled and wrestled, twisting their legs together, each trying to throw the other to the ground. Then, with a mighty leap, they endeavored to loosen each other's grip. So mighty was the leap that they rose together far into the heavens and disappeared from sight.

The man could not believe his luck at first, but he soon came to his senses, slipped quietly into the forest, and began another long race to his home.

When he got back, his wife was delighted to see him, for she had never expected to set eyes on him again. He told her all about his alarming adventures, trying to show himself in the light of a hero. But his wife would have none of it.

"Let that be a lesson to you," she said callously. "Never boast about your achievements again. However strong or clever or rich or powerful you are, there is always somebody more so."

The man had to admit that she was right.

As for the real Superman and the Giant-of-the-Forest, to this day they are still up there wrestling in the heavens. When they are tired, they sit on a cloud to recover their strength, but soon they rise up again and continue to struggle. If you listen carefully, you will sometimes hear them fighting. People may tell you it is thunder, but you will know it is really Superman and Giant-of-the-Forest wrestling high above the clouds.

Developing Comprehension Skills

1. Why did the "would be" Superman in the myth give himself the title?

2. A series of events convinced the "would be" Superman that he was not the strongest person alive. What events gave him that idea? List the events in the order they occurred in the story.

3. At one point in the story, the "would be" Superman said to himself, "I've dodged a wasp, only to run into a hornet." Who was the wasp? Who was the hornet?

4. Which character in the myth do you think deserved to be called Superman? Why? Find details to support your idea.

Reading Literature: Myths

1. **Understanding Conflict.** Shetu's husband becomes involved in an external conflict. He struggles to escape from the giant named Superman. Think about how Shetu's husband entered into this conflict. What personality trait got him into such trouble?

2. **Determining Main Ideas.** The giant named Superman chases and threatens Shetu's husband. The Giant-of-the-Forest tries to help Shetu's husband. Think about the reasons for the behavior of these two supermen. How is the storyteller using the supermen to present ideas about human behavior?

3. **Analyzing Details of Plot.** In this legend, the storyteller introduces various groups of farm workers. Shetu's husband meets these groups as he is fleeing for his life. What effect do these characters have on the plot? Why do you think the storyteller included these characters?

4. **Identifying Setting.** List all the details used by the storyteller to describe the location. Which details affect the action? Which details do you think make the story realistic?

Developing Vocabulary Skills

Identifying Context Clues. Read the following sentences about the Nigerian myth of the Superman. There is a context clue provided to help you figure out the meaning of each underlined word. On your paper, write the meaning of each underlined word. Also write whether you used a **definition or restatement** clue or a **synonym** clue.

1. Shetu and her husband lived in a compound—an enclosed space with buildings inside of it.

2. Shetu would sometimes mock, or imitate, her husband.

3. A calabash is a container made from the fruit of a calabash vine.

4. Shetu's husband carried a quiver of sharp arrows on his back. The container of arrows and his bow were his hunting weapons.

5. To boast is to brag about oneself.

6. The Superman and the giant endeavored to loosen each other's grip. They tried to wrestle free.

Developing Writing Skills

1. **Writing About Main Idea.** One main idea appears often in mythology: All of us have weaknesses we cannot always control. Write a paragraph to support this main idea. Use details from the myths and legends you have read in your textbook.

Pre-Writing. Select two of the following characters: Odysseus, Loki, or Shetu's husband. Think about each character's main weakness. For each character, select a trait from the following list.

pride	determination
stubbornness	quick temper
overconfidence	narrowmindedness
competitiveness	

For each trait, list two instances in which the trait caused the character problems.

Writing. State the main idea in your first sentence. This is your topic sentence. Then write five to seven sentences to support the main idea. Use details about the characters you selected. Finish your paragraph with a concluding sentence. It should somehow review the main idea.

Revising. Ask another person to outline your paragraph. Does the outline include the main idea you tried to write about? Does it mention each of your examples of the main idea? Perhaps the outline is missing some information. Ask the person to recall those parts of your paragraph. If the person cannot remember those ideas, they were not clear. Rewrite those parts of your paragraph.

2. **Imagining a Setting.** "The Tale of the Superman" takes place in Nigeria. However, the storyteller does not provide a very detailed description of the setting. Write a paragraph to provide a clear picture of the setting. You might list the descriptions given by the storyteller, and then add to them. Or, you may make up descriptions of your own. Include details that appeal to each of the five senses: sight, sound, smell, touch, and taste. Be creative, but be sure to include some real-

istic ideas as well. Make your description fit the events of the story.

3. **Writing About Yourself.** In "The Tale of the Superman," Shetu's husband learns a lesson about bragging. Write a paragraph about how you learned a lesson in life. Include details about where and when the events happened. Tell who was involved in the lesson with you. Did the others learn with you? Or did they try to teach the lesson? Explain the events in the order they happened. You might conclude the paragraph with a restatement of the lesson.

Developing Skills in Study and Research

Using the Audio-Visual Catalog. You have read myths and legends from many different countries. Suppose you wanted to find information on those countries that could not be given in books. There is a library resource that might be helpful. The audio-visual catalog is organized like the card catalog for books. However, it lists information on audio-visual materials in the library. These include records, tapes, filmstrips, movies, and other materials that you can listen to or view. Audio-visual material is usually kept in a separate part of the library from books.

Make a list of the countries for which you have read myths and legends. Check the audio-visual catalog to find information on these countries. Select a country other than the United States. For that country, list the titles of at least three films, filmstrips, records, or tapes. Choose titles that might give information about the landscape, the climate, the races of people, their clothing, the types of housing, or the occupations of people in the country.

Superman

JEROME SIEGEL
and JOE SHUSTER

This American comic strip version of the Superman legend first appeared in 1939. Compare Clark Kent with the Superman you read about in the Nigerian myth. What similarities exist?

... RAISE TREMENDOUS WEIGHTS . . .

... RUN FASTER THAN A STREAMLINE TRAIN --

... AND NOTHING LESS THAN A BURSTING SHELL COULD PENETRATE HIS SKIN!

WHAT TH'--? THIS IS THE SIXTH HYPODERMIC NEEDLE I'VE BROKEN ON YOUR SKIN!

TRY AGAIN, DOC!

THE PASSING AWAY OF HIS FOSTER-PARENTS GREATLY GRIEVED CLARK KENT. BUT IT STRENGTHENED A DETERMINATION THAT HAD BEEN GROWING IN HIS MIND.

CLARK DECIDED HE MUST TURN HIS TITANIC STRENGTH INTO CHANNELS THAT WOULD BENEFIT MANKIND • AND SO WAS CREATED--

SUPERMAN

CHAMPION OF THE OPPRESSED. THE PHYSICAL MARVEL WHO HAD SWORN TO DEVOTE HIS EXISTENCE TO HELPING THOSE IN NEED!

Developing Comprehension Skills

1. How and why did Clark Kent get to Earth?

2. Clark Kent had super powers. Name five examples that are given in the cartoon to support this idea.

3. The people at the orphan asylum could not deal with Clark's strength. However, the Kents gave him the guidance he needed. List at least three words that summarize the Kents' personalities.

4. Do you agree with the advice Clark's foster father gave to him? Why or why not?

Reading Literature: Myths

1. **Contrasting Two Characters.** Clark Kent and the Superman from the Nigerian tale both have superhuman traits. Name at least one similarity and one difference in their characteristics. Which Superman do you think is more believable? Or do you think neither is believable? Explain your answer.

2. **Comparing Myths.** The Greek story of Hercules had its beginning long ago. However, it is similar to the modern story of Superman in several ways. Compare the main characters, the major conflict, and the purposes of the two myths. What similarities do you find?

3. **Determining Purpose.** Myths and legends are told to explain nature, to teach lessons about life, and to entertain. Name two purposes of the American superman story.

Developing Vocabulary Skills

Finding the Meaning of an Unfamiliar Word. Each of the following sentences contains a word from this chapter. Sometimes you will be able to figure out the meaning of the underlined word from word parts or context clues. In other sentences, you will not find these helps to discovering word meanings. You would need to use a dictionary.

Try to determine the meaning of each underlined word. If you can figure out the meaning, write the word and the meaning on your paper. Also write the way you found the meaning: **Word Parts** or **Context Clues**. If you cannot figure out the meaning of a word, then just write **Dictionary**.

1. Clark Kent astounded people with his strength. He surprised them with what he could lift.

2. According to the story, Superman became a champion of the oppressed.

3. Coyote thought that many of the animals had absurd, or ridiculous, ideas.

4. Shetu was sometimes callous and insensitive toward her husband.

5. If people are obstinate—that is, stubborn— then it is difficult to get along with them.

6. The child gave Shetu an uncomfortable stare.

Developing Writing Skills

1. **Writing an Analysis.** The comic strip version of the Superman story in your textbook appeared in 1939. Write a paragraph to explain how the cartoon reflects the time period when it was created.

   Pre-Writing. Look carefully at each frame, or section, of the cartoon. What parts of the comic strip seem out of date or old to you? For example, you might notice the car that Superman lifts is not a current model. Try to list at least three other dated parts of the cartoon.

Think about your reaction to the comic strip. Does it bother you that parts of the cartoon seem old? Can you think of a disadvantage to reading out-of-date material? What advantage could dated material give a reader?

Writing. Begin your paragraph with a topic sentence that states your main idea. In the paragraph, give examples of dated elements in the cartoon. Then, explain the advantages or disadvantages you find in reading an older cartoon. You might conclude your paragraph by restating your main idea in a more general way.

Revising. Read your topic sentence aloud. Does it make sense? Is the main idea clear? Then, check to be sure your paragraph includes at least three sentences that support the topic sentence. Are the ideas presented in a logical way? Your paragraph should have unity. That is, the ideas should fit together to explain the topic.

2. **Writing with Imagination.** If you had been born with Clark Kent's powers, how would you use them? Think about the temptations you would face in life. How would you deal with others who wanted you to work for them? Write your ideas in one or two paragraphs. Don't repeat the ideas in the cartoon. Instead, use your imagination.

Developing Skills in Critical Thinking

Understanding a Cartoon. A comic strip is a series of cartoons, or drawings, that tell a humorous or adventurous story. The artist who creates a comic strip works differently than the writer of a story does. The cartoonist relies on eye-catching art to get the reader's attention. The characters' faces, hairstyles, and clothing are important. Size, color, and shape are meaningful. You see the story, much as you view a film. The cartoonist must show the characters, events, and mood. Then he or she uses words to help explain the main ideas.

It is helpful to analyze the special features of any cartoon you read. Try to answer the following questions about the Superman cartoon in your text.

1. What is the first thing your eyes focus on?

2. Can you follow the plot without reading the words? Name one idea in the cartoon that is communicated without words. Name one idea that needs words to make it clear.

3. Artists often use repetition to stress an idea. Find something that is repeated in this cartoon. What idea does it stress?

4. How is action revealed in the cartoon? Does the artist mostly rely on words, drawings, or color?

5. Look at the illustrations of the main character. What do the drawings emphasize?

6. This is a comic strip. Find something funny. Also, find something adventurous.

Using Your Skills in Reading Myths

Read the following portion of a Navajo Indian myth. Then answer these questions. Does it explain how something came to be? If so, what does it explain? Does it teach a lesson? If so, what does it teach? Or does it simply entertain?

In the beginning there was First Man. He was a god who had once been an ear of corn. He and First Woman made the sun, the moon, and the stars out of precious stones. They were planning to arrange the stars in an orderly way in the heavens. However, Coyote, always the trickster, scattered the stars about the sky.

Using Your Comprehension Skills

The following paragraph is from a short story you will read in Chapter 5. Read it carefully. Then tell what kind of paragraph it is: narrative, descriptive, persuasive, or explanatory. Tell how its sentences are organized. If it has a topic sentence, identify which sentence that is. Last, tell what the paragraph is about.

There was now a fine, cold drizzle falling, and the wind had risen from its uncertain puffs into a steady blow. The few people astir in that quarter hurried dismally and silently along with coat collars turned high and pocketed hands. In the door of the hardware store, the man who had come a thousand miles to fill an appointment smoked his cigar and waited.

Using Your Vocabulary Skills

The underlined word in each of the following sentences is used in Chapter 5. For each, identify whether you can determine the meaning of the underlined word from definition or restatement clues, or from synonyms. Then state the meaning of the word.

1. The king wished to rule his country with fair and impartial justice.

2. The young man was a <u>courtier</u>, that is, a person in attendance at the court of a ruler.

3. The people were <u>submerged</u>—covered—in their winter clothes.

4. In his art, this painter <u>distorts</u>, or twists, the shapes of objects.

5. The girl is a <u>prodigy</u>. She is the only person with extraordinary talents whom I have met.

6. There were <u>primroses</u> growing in the yard. A primrose is a perennial plant with variously colored flowers.

Using Your Writing Skills

Choose one of the writing assignments below.

1. Choose one of the myths in this chapter. Review the story, giving particular attention to the supernatural being or beings in the myth. Then compare and contrast the supernatural being or beings with human beings.

2. Write an original myth. Your myth should explain one of the following:
   a. Why birds rise at dawn
   b. Why snowflakes have six points
   c. Why lightning bugs, or fireflies, shine
   d. How the first footrace was held

Using Your Skills in Study and Research

Complete the following partial outline with terms listed below. Choose details related to the given topics.

Terms: Conflict   Theme   Supernatural Beings
           Time   Human Beings   Plot
           Purpose   Monsters   Place

Outline: Story Elements To Be Examined
      I. Setting
         A.
         B.
      II. Characters
         A.
         B.
         C.

CHAPTER 4

How Writers Write

Synchromy in Orange: To Form, 1913–14, MORGAN RUSSELL.
Oil on Canvas 135″ × 121½″, Albright-Knox Art Gallery, Buffalo, New York.
Gift of Seymour H. Knox, 1958.

Using the Process of Writing

"It's impossible to write a good story by carrying a rabbit's foot in your pocket," says writer Isaac Bashevis Singer. Writers work to create good writing. They follow certain stages called the **process of writing**.

pre-writing—a time of planning
writing
revising—a time of rewriting or reworking

Gregory in the Pool, (Paper Pool 4: A, B, D, G), 1978, DAVID HOCKNEY. Printed and published by Tyler Graphics, Ltd.,
© Copyright David Hockney/Tyler Graphics Ltd.

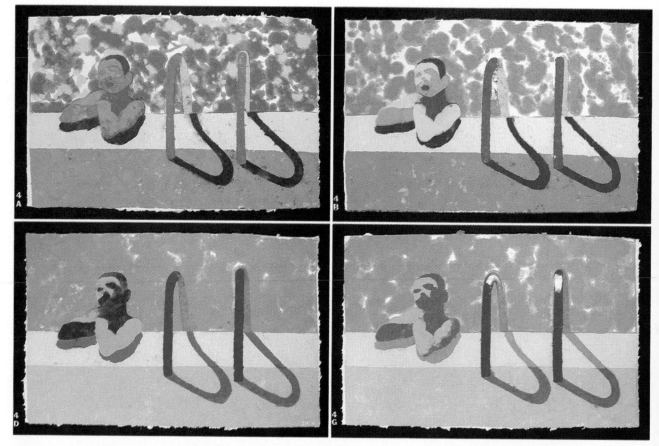

Understanding the Process of Writing

Have you ever seen a statue you liked especially well? You can enjoy looking at a statue without knowing exactly how the artist cut and chiseled the stone. You can admire its smoothness and shape, without being an expert.

Imagine, however, that you tried to carve a statue. You would face the same problems sculptors face. You might try the same techniques. You would begin to see every other statue in a new way. As a sculptor yourself, you would appreciate the skill it takes to make a beautiful statue.

Reading can be compared to seeing a statue. You can enjoy a good poem or story without understanding the skill that went into it. However, understanding what went into it helps you appreciate that poem or story even more.

In this chapter, you will learn how professional writers write. You will learn about the techniques writers use. You will practice ways to make your own writing clear and lively. After all, the best way to learn the process and techniques of writing is by writing.

Pre-Writing

The first stage of writing is pre-writing. Some writers say it is the most important stage. Pre-writing is a time for thinking and planning.

In one sense, pre-writing can include almost everything that a writer experiences. The writer can make use of bits of knowledge and experiences years later. Carol Ryrie Brink, author of *Caddie Woodlawn*, advises young writers to "begin to make your five senses work for you. See, hear, smell, taste, and touch the things around you."

Many writers keep journals where they record interesting ideas, striking details, and colorful events. Isaac Bashevis Singer explains his approach to collecting ideas:

> My stories are all based upon things that have come to me in life without my going out to look for them. The only notes I take are notes on an idea for a story. . . . When such an idea comes to me, I put it down in a little notebook I always carry around.

When you want to begin a specific writing activity, the pre-writing stage prepares you. It includes these steps:

1. Choose and limit a topic. If you are about to write, think about areas that interest you or make you curious. List experiences about which you have strong memories. With these subjects in mind, list specific ideas for topics. Look over the topics and choose a favorite.

Every writer begins with a topic that interests at least one person—the writer. Almost any idea can be considered. Walter Edmonds, author of *Drums Along the Mohawk*, tells how he finds a topic:

> I get ideas from all sorts of sources—old newspapers, books, or letters from readers.

Madeleine L'Engle, author of *A Wrinkle in Time*, explains how she collects ideas:

> My story ideas are somewhat like a big, old-fashioned French stove with several pots on the back keeping warm. As ideas come along, I drop them into the appropriate pot, and, when one book is finished, I pull forward onto the fire whichever pot seems most ready to be written into a book. I get my ideas from everywhere, everybody, and everything.

Kurt Vonnegut gives this important advice: "Find a subject you care about and which you in your heart feel others should care about."

Once you have such a topic, limit it. Make sure the topic is narrow enough to be handled in the form you are using.

2. Decide on a purpose. You need to keep in mind a general goal. What do you want your writing to accomplish? Should it ask questions or answer them? Should it make the reader laugh or get the reader angry about a problem?

What and how you write depend on your purpose.

3. Consider your audience. Some authors write for children, while others gear their writing to adults. Some authors want to reach members of a certain group, such as hockey players or stamp collectors. These writers write in a way that will interest their special audiences.

When you write, think about who your readers will be. For different audiences, you would write differently. For example, in writing for young children, you would use simple words and clear action. For adult readers, you would use a more formal style. Knowing your audience will help you reach that audience.

Nobel Prize-winning writer John Steinbeck thinks of his audience in this way:

> In writing, your audience is one single reader. I have found that sometimes it helps to pick out one person—a real person you know or an imagined person—and write to that one.

4. Gather supporting information. Writers must gather facts. They want their writing to be accurate as well as interesting. Their research includes reading, interviewing, and observing first-hand. If you have been keeping a journal for some time, review it before you begin a specific writing activity. It may already hold descriptions, facts, and phrases that could help you.

Best-selling novelist Irving Wallace gives advice on researching a subject:

> Read all you can about it, interview experts on it, even travel to the sites of the story to guarantee authenticity and get a feel for the background. In my case, this process takes six months to a year.

Writers gather information until they feel thoroughly familiar with their subject. Short story writer Paul Gallico explains how he gets to know his subject:

> I spend two or three days writing character sketches, setting down all and everything I know about each of the characters in the story. Like the iceberg, seven-eighths of this material remains submerged and doesn't show, but the characters have now taken on life for me, and I am able to think and speak and act as they might.

Make a list of questions you need to answer about the topic. Then use all the resources you can to answer these questions.

Don't rely on your memory. As you do your research, take notes.

5. Organize your ideas. At first, organizing ideas is like cleaning a closet. The writer goes through his or her notes and throws away what is not needed. He or she sorts into groups the ideas that should be kept. As you organize your ideas, you may discover that you need more information or more details. If so, go back for more research.

Once you are satisfied with your list of ideas, you should arrange the ideas in order. For example, in stories it's usually best to arrange events in time order. For writing meant to persuade or convince, it's best to arrange reasons either from most important to least important, or from least important to most important.

Best-selling author Stephen King stresses the need for planning and organization:

> All good writing has some kind of underlying structure or framework. It must, no matter how powerful the writing might be. Without a framework, it is as useless as a mass of muscle would be without an underlying structure of bone.

Many writers use outlines of some type to help them organize their material. Jean George, author of *Julie of the Wolves*, compares her outline to "the pencil sketch an artist renders before he starts to paint." Its purpose, she says, "is to get the story into my head before I begin the first draft."

Some writers use a formal outline. Others simply list their ideas in order. Some writers make complete outlines in their heads before they write. However it's done, every writer arranges ideas in a way that makes sense to that writer.

Writing the First Draft

The pre-writing stage ends when a writer begins the first draft. How does an author know when it is time to start writing? "When it becomes more painful not to," playwright Edward Albee answers.

Patricia Highsmith describes a similar feeling:

> I often reach a point beyond which I cannot think, cannot make an outline, and I become impatient to see something on paper, and so I begin.

When you write a first draft, try to follow your outline and your pre-writing notes. However, if a better idea occurs to you, you may choose to change the outline.

Write—and write quickly. At this stage, concentrate on getting ideas onto the paper, not on grammar, spelling, and punctuation. Humorist Stephen Leacock points out what happens if your main concern is to avoid mistakes:

> You can't avoid anything if you are writing nothing. You must write first and "avoid" afterwards. A writer is in no danger of splitting an infinitive if he has no infinitive to split.

After you finish writing your first draft, it is time to take a good look at what you have written. It is time to revise.

Revising

Revising means making changes to improve a piece of writing. Not even famous writers get everything right the first time.

> New ideas and new material are added or rejected, as the case may be. Details are changed or developed further. Most of all, each paragraph, each sentence, each word is worked over and over. This takes a long time. —H.A. and Margaret Rey

> I rewrite and rewrite and rewrite. My record is eight complete different drafts! —Jean George

Most authors agree that when you revise you need to stand back and look at your own work objectively.

> The writer must survey his work critically, coolly, and as though he were a stranger to it. . . . He must be willing to prune, expertly and hard-heartedly. —Eleanor Estes

To revise your writing, review it carefully. Don't be afraid to cut something that does not add to your main idea. Isaac Bashevis Singer says, "The wastepaper basket is a writer's best friend."

The following questions will help you improve your writing.

1. Is your writing interesting? Will it attract readers?
2. Have you stuck to your topic? Do all ideas and details belong in this piece of writing? Are any ideas or details missing?
3. Is your organization logical? Do your ideas flow together smoothly? Are the paragraphs in the clearest possible order? In each paragraph, do all the sentences stick to the main idea?
4. Have you used the most exact, clear words you can find? Does your language match your audience?

Mark up your first draft with your additions and corrections. Draw arrows to show changes in paragraph order or sentence order. Cross out parts that aren't needed. You may find that your pages are becoming crowded with notes. Eleanor Estes says, "At the end of each revision, a manuscript may look like a battered old hive, worked over, torn apart, pinned together, added to, deleted from, words changed and words changed back." If your pages begin to look unreadable, recopy them.

to lecture me again. I said:

"Scat!" ~~and So~~ he darted right ~~back~~ to my knee, put his broad

furry paws on my pants and looked me in the face. I shall never

forget the ~~x~~ fear and ~~xxxxxxxxfxxxxxxxxxxx~~ wonder that I felt *at the*

bravery ~~of~~ *the* Baron Weasel. ~~transferred a feeling to me he avoided~~ *He stood his ground and berated* me. I

could see by the flashing ~~bright lights of~~ his eyes, and the curl

furious at me for trapping him. He couldn't

of his lip that he was ~~terribly indignant. He might just as well~~

talk, but I knew what he meant.

~~have talked to me. And in a way, he did.~~

filled   *absolutely*

Wonder ~~spread over~~ me as I realized he was ~~totally~~ unafraid. *in my presence.*

other   *had been*

No ~~_~~ animal, and I knew quite a few by now, ~~had been~~ so brave, ~~and~~

jumped on   *This surprised and*

Screaming, he ~~darted over me, and this~~ scared me. He leapt ~~to~~ from

my lap to my head, took a mouthful of hair and wrestled ~~with~~ it. *was too frightened to move.*

rose.

~~My~~ goose bumps ~~were detrish bumps, came and I remained~~

I guess he figured I was

~~frozen.~~ A good thing, too, because ~~just as I was about to hit him~~

not going to fight back and   *anger*   *of peace. Still, I*

~~in self defense,~~ his scream changed to a purr~~ring chatter. It was~~

couldn't move.

Presently,

~~a friendly noise and so I sat perfectly still.~~   *royalty*

Down climbed the Baron as stately as ~~royalty~~, and off he marched,

never looking back ~~again.~~ He sunk beneath the leaves like a fish

~~b~~beneath the water, ~~and~~ Not a stem rippled to mark his way.

And so, the Baron and I met for the first time, and it ~~is~~ the

beginning of a harassing, but wonderful friendship.

Frightful had been watching all this. Her feathers were down.

~~her~~ She was skinny with fright. So young and inexperienced she

knew an enemy when she saw one. I picked her up and whispered into

neck

her birdy smelling ~~_~~ feathers.

wild ones

"You ~~all out here~~ know, ~~too much.~~"

Since I couldn't go home,

I decided to spend the day in the marsh down the west side

of the mountain. There were a lot of cattails and frogs there,

~~and my supplies were running low. I kept a lot of frogs in~~

~~the spring for two days.~~

Author Jean Craighead George shows how she corrected a page of her manuscript while
writing the story *My Side of the Mountain*.

Many writers find it helpful to read their work aloud as they revise. Ruth Stiles Gannet uses this procedure:

> Now it is time to read it aloud and listen to how it sounds. Does it read smoothly, with some sense of rhythm? When it doesn't, I rearrange or substitute to avoid awkward word combinations. Have I used too many words or dull words? If so, I cut them out.

Another technique many writers use is seeking the opinion of others. Madeleine L'Engle explains how she gets feedback:

> I don't try ideas on anyone, but I do like to read bits and pieces of manuscript to people—either children or grown-ups, whoever is available.

Finally, many authors find it helpful to set aside their work for a time. When they read it again later, they often notice ways to improve it. Poet Myra Cohn Livingston explains how she gets a fresh viewpoint:

> Searching for the right form to express certain ideas takes time. I try to put poems away, once written, and take them out much later.

Proofreading. A final stage in the revising process is proofreading. Proofreading is a last check on punctuation, grammar, spelling, and capitalization. When you proofread, your goal should be to make your writing clear and correct. Mark your corrections on your final draft.

Making a Final Copy. With the finishing touches completed, you are ready to make a final copy. The final copy of any piece of writing should be neat and readable. Copy your final draft with all of its corrections. Then proofread the final copy.

Practicing the Process of Writing

When you write, use the ideas in this chapter. Refer also to the Process of Writing section of the Handbook in this text. As you develop your own skills, you will come to understand why writers write. You, too, will share in their excitement. Like poet Gabriel Fielding, you may decide that "Writing is a voyage, an odyssey, a discovery because I'm never certain of precisely what I will find."

Using the Sounds of Language

Words are the writer's tools. The good writer chooses words for both their meaning and their sound. In this section, you will learn about the following ways that writers use the sounds of language:

alliteration   rhyme   onomatopoeia
rhythm   assonance

Solo, 1979, ROMARE BEARDEN. Private Collection. Courtesy of Sheldon Ross Gallery, Birmingham, Michigan.

Alliteration

Alliteration is the repetition of a consonant sound at the beginning of words.

Examples: do or die   now or never
            safe and sound   sweet smell of success

Alliteration in Prose.   Alliteration is fun to say and enjoyable to hear. Without knowing it, you probably already use alliteration to call attention to certain words. Many familiar phrases and expressions use alliteration. These include "down in the dumps," "hale and hearty," and "turn the tables." Tongue twisters rely on alliteration: "rubber baby buggy bumpers." Many sayings, such as these, use alliteration:

He who laughs last laughs best.
Time and tide wait for no man.

When writers want to emphasize certain words, they may use alliteration. Notice the ideas that are emphasized by alliteration in these examples:

The deep churned. Something was happening far down in the dim, foggy-green depths.
— Paul Annixter, "Battle in the Depths"

Touch each object you want to touch as if tomorrow your tactile sense would fail.   — Helen Keller, "The Seeing See Little"

There is always something left to love. And if you ain't learned that, you ain't learned nothing.
— Lorraine Hansberry, *A Raisin in the Sun*

Alliteration in Poetry.   Alliteration is one of the poet's most important sound techniques. It makes particular words stand out. It also connects the words that are emphasized. Look for the repeated consonant sounds in this poem:

Then up and spake an old Sailor,
　Had sailed to the Spanish Main,
"I pray thee, put into yonder port,
　For I fear a hurricane."
　　　　　　—Henry W. Longfellow, "The Wreck of the Hesperus"

Often, the sounds and meanings of the words combine to create a mood. Here, repetition of *b* and *t* stresses a feeling of urgency.

Hear the loud alarum bells—
　Brazen bells!
What a tale of terror, now, their turbulency tells!
　　　　　　—Edgar Allan Poe, "The Bells"

What consonant sounds are repeated in the following lines?

Swing low, sweet chariot,
Comin' for to carry me home.
　　　　　　—Traditional Spiritual

Exercises: **Using Alliteration**

A. Identify the alliteration in each of these selections. Tell which consonant sounds are repeated.

1. I saw lingering, late and lightless,
　A single swan, swinging, sleek as a sequin.
　　　　　　—W. R. Rodgers, "The Swan"

2. In hundreds of houses sleepy women woke sleepier children.
　　　　　　—Esther Forbes, *Johnny Tremain*

3. They were women then
　My mama's generation
　Husky of voice—Stout of
　Step　　　　　　—Alice Walker, "Women"

4. Homeless, they have a hundred homes. They flit from furnished room to furnished room, transients forever.
　　　　　　—O. Henry, "The Furnished Room"

B. Find five examples of alliteration in headlines, sayings, or songs.

Rhyme

Rhyme is the repetition of sounds at the ends of words. Rhyme may involve one or more syllables.

Examples: rest alive remember
          best survive September

Rhyme in Prose. Rhyme is not usually used in prose. Some sayings, though, use rhyme. Here are two examples:

Birds of a feather flock together.
A friend in need is a friend indeed.

Rhyme makes sentences memorable and pleasing to the ear. Speakers like to use it to catch their listeners' attention.

Let us have faith that right makes might, and in that faith let us dare to do our duty as we understand it.
—Abraham Lincoln, Address at New York City

Rhyme in Poetry. Rhyme helps to create the musical quality of poetry. Rhyme also emphasizes key words. It may occur within a line.

We'll grind and break and bind and take
And plunder ye and pound ye!
—C. S. Lewis, "Narnian Suite"

Usually, however, rhyme comes at the ends of lines. Sometimes lines that come after one another rhyme.

I saw a star slide down the sky,
Blinding the north as it went by,
Too burning and too quick to hold,
Too lovely to be bought or sold,
Good only to make wishes on
And then forever to be gone.
—Sara Teasdale, "The Falling Star"

Sometimes every other line rhymes, as in this example:

> Go quietly; a dream,
>   When done, should leave no trace
> That it has lived, except a gleam
>   Across the dreamer's face.
>   —Countee Cullen, "If You Should Go"

Notice the pattern of rhyme in this poem.

> They are all gone away,
>   The House is shut and still,
> There is nothing more to say.
>   —E. A. Robinson, "The House on the Hill"

The pattern of rhyme in a poem is its rhyme scheme. You can use letters to show the rhyme scheme. Each line of a poem is given a letter. Lines that rhyme are given the same letter.

> Once when the snow of the year was beginning to fall,   *a*
> We stopped by a mountain pasture to say, "Whose colt?"   *b*
> A little Morgan had one forefoot on the wall,   *a*
> The other curled at his breast. He dipped his head   *c*
> And snorted at us. And then he had to bolt.   *b*
> We heard the miniature thunder where he fled.   *c*
>   —Robert Frost, "The Runaway"

Exercises: Using Rhyme

A. Identify the rhyme scheme of the following stanza of a poem.

> The day is done, and the darkness
>   Falls from the wings of Night,
> As a feather is wafted downward
>   From an eagle in his flight.
>   —Henry W. Longfellow, "The Day Is Done"

B. Identify the rhyme schemes of the Teasdale and Cullen poems above.

C. Write a four-line poem with this rhyme scheme: *a b a b*

Rhythm

Rhythm is the pattern of stressed and unstressed syllables in a sentence or a line of poetry. The pattern is shown by marking syllables with the following symbols:

/   for accented, or stressed syllables
‿   for unaccented, or unstressed syllables

Example: Máry hád a líttle lámb.
Its fléece was whíte as snów.

Rhythm in Prose. Good prose has rhythm. Writers may slow down the rhythm of their prose to describe a calm, quiet scene. They may quicken the rhythm of their writing for fast-paced action. Accented syllables, punctuation, and pauses all slow the rhythm of prose. Here is an example of a slow rhythm that builds tension:

> And then, when my head was well in the room, I undid the lantern cautiously—oh, so cautiously—cautiously (for the hinges creaked)—I undid it just so much that a single, thin ray fell upon the vulture eye.
> —Edgar Allan Poe, "The Tell-Tale Heart"

Here are examples of prose with quick, lively rhythm:

> Jumping, ducking, and breaking through, I ran straight before my nose, till I could run no longer.
> —Robert Louis Stevenson, *Treasure Island*

> The sled started with a bound, and they flew on through the dusk, gathering smoothness and speed as they went, with the hollow night opening out below them and the air singing by like an organ.
> —Edith Wharton, *Ethan Frome*

Rhythm in Poetry. Rhythm helps to create the strong effect of poetry. It may set a mood. Notice how the strong, pounding rhythm in this example echoes the sound of marching troops.

Ŏ whắt ĭs thăt sound thăt sŏ thrĭlls thĕ eár
    Dówn ĭn thĕ vălley drúmmĭng, drúmmĭng?
Ónlў thĕ scárlĕt soldĭers deár,
    Thĕ sóldĭers cómĭng.

> —W. H. Auden, "O What Is That Sound That
> So Thrills the Ear?"

Poets sometimes break their rhythm patterns to emphasize important words. In this poem, note the three heavy beats in the third line.

Whĕn Dánĭel Boóne goĕs bý, ăt nĭght,
Thĕ phántŏm deér arĭse
Ănd áll lóst, wĭld Ámerĭca
Ĭs búrnĭng ĭn theĭr eýes.

> —Rosemary and Stephen Vincent Benét, "Daniel
> Boone"

Exercises: Using Rhythm

A. Read these selections aloud to hear the rhythm. Explain how the rhythm
works with the meaning in each selection. Describe the mood.

1. Where would you be when the white waves roar
   On the tumbling storm-torn sea?
   Tucked inside
   Where it's calm and dry
   Or searching for stars in the furious sky . .
   Whipped by the whine of the gale's wild cry
   Out in the night with me?
   > —Karla Kuskin, "Where Would You Be?"

2. A quarter of an hour passed, and a half, and a whole. I was alert; I kept
   watching the riverbank and the rows of mat huts that crowded to the verge
   of the muck at the bank. I grew weary, tensely waiting for the cook.
   > —John Hersey, *A Single Pebble*

B. Copy the poem in exercise A above. Mark the stressed and unstressed
syllables.

Onomatopoeia

Onomatopoeia is the use of words that sound like what they mean.

Examples: tick-tock, crash, plink, wham, tweet

Onomatopoeia in Prose. Writers use onomatopoeia when they speak of sounds. There are many words that suggest sounds, such as *hum, murmur,* and *splash.* Sometimes writers may also invent words to imitate a sound. You might find words such as *wham, pow,* and *zing* in a comic strip.

Find examples of onomatopoeia in the following selections. It may be helpful to read the sentences aloud.

> I lay in bed, and at the same time I rode that train to Siberia. I heard the clacking of the wheels, the whistle of the locomotive.
> —Isaac Bashevis Singer, "Growing Up"

> From far below came the whimpering of the raccoon kits, and an occasional mournful howl from Wowser.
> —Sterling North, *Rascal*

> The limes were there, the white thorns were there, and the chestnut-trees were there, and their leaves rustled harmoniously when I stopped to listen, but the clink of Joe's hammer was not in the midsummer wind.
> —Charles Dickens, *Great Expectations*

Onomatopoeia in Poetry. Poets use onomatopoeia to create lively effects. Onomatopoeia is a way in which the sound of a poem can echo its meaning. Notice the use of onomatopoeia in these poems:

> Scraw,
> scraw,
> go away!
> Nobody loves the blue jay.
> —Eve Merriam, "Creatures We Can Do Without"

We rush into a rain
That rattles double glass

        —Theodore Roethke, "Night Journey"

The doors are twisted on broken hinges.
Sheets of rain swish through on the wind.

        —Carl Sandburg, "Four Preludes on Playthings
         of the Wind"

I'm sitting in the living room,
When, up above, the Thump of Doom
Resounds. Relax. It's sonic boom.

        —John Updike, "Sonic Boom"

Exercises: **Using Onomatopoeia**

A. Find the example of onomatopoeia in each of the following:

1. From the thick grass at the foot of the bush came a low hiss—a horrid cold sound that made Rikki-Tikki jump back two clear feet.

        —Rudyard Kipling, "Rikki-Tikki-Tavi"

2. The whing of father's racquet and the whack
of brother's bat on cousin's ball

        —Isabella Gardner, "Summer Remembered"

3. You could hear the tinkle of ice in a lemonade pitcher. In a distant kitchen, because of the heat of the day, someone was preparing a cold lunch. Someone was humming under her breath, high and sweet.

        —Ray Bradbury, *The Martian Chronicles*

4. See how he dives
From the rocks with a zoom!

        —William Jay Smith, "Seal"

B. Use onomatopoeia in four sentences to recreate these sounds.

    a school bell   conversation   a car engine   an animal

C. Invent four onomatopoetic words to imitate sounds. Define each word.

D. Find three examples of onomatopoeia in advertisements.

Assonance

> **Assonance** is the repetition of a vowel sound within words.
>
> Examples: fr<u>ee</u> and <u>ea</u>sy   m<u>a</u>ke the gr<u>a</u>de

Assonance in Prose. Prose writers sometimes repeat vowel sounds to reinforce the meaning of words. It also helps to create moods. Here, the long *o* sounds mysterious.

> Poetry is old, ancient, goes far back. It is among the oldest of living things. So old is it that no man knows how and why the first poems came.
> —Carl Sandburg, *Early Moon*

Assonance in Poetry. In poetry, too, assonance stresses words and moods.

> And so, all the night-tide, I lie down by the side
> Of my darling, my darling, my life and my bride
> —Edgar Allan Poe, "Annabel Lee"

Exercises: Using Assonance

A. Find the examples of assonance in these selections.

1. Slow things are beautiful:
   The closing of the day,
   The pause of the wave
   That curves downward to spray

   > —Elizabeth Coatsworth, "Swift Things Are Beautiful"

2. Night came on, and a full moon rose high over the trees into the sky, lighting the land till it lay bathed in ghostly day.

   > —Jack London, *The Call of the Wild*

B. Write three sentences using assonance. Repeat the same vowel sound at least twice in a sentence. Make sure the sound works with the meaning.

Using Figures of Speech

Figures of speech use ordinary words in unusual ways. They force a reader to look at familiar things as if they were new. Writers use figures of speech because they lead readers to think about things and ideas in a fresh way. In this section, you will learn about these figures of speech:

simile   personification
metaphor   hyperbole

Summer (detail), 1573, ARCIMBOLDO. The Louvre, Paris. Courtesy of Scala/Art Resource, New York.

Simile

A **simile** is a comparison between two unlike things. It uses the words *like* or *as*.

Examples: My kitten is as fierce as a tiger.
The snow settled on the roof like a comforting blanket.

Similes in Prose.   A simile is a figure of speech that is often used in prose. Writers use similes to make their meanings clear and memorable. Like other figures of speech, similes put sharp pictures in your mind. Similes can also help to set mood.

Johnny stalked out of the kitchen as stiff-legged as a fighting tom-cat.
—Ester Forbes, *Johnny Tremain*

He was only a little boy, ten years old, with hair like dusty yellow grass and with shy polite grey eyes, and with a mouth that worked when he thought.   —John Steinbeck, *The Red Pony*

The sun rose over Stony Lonesome and hung like a burning balloon in the sky as Danny danced back up the Smokey Creek trail.
—Jim Kjelgaard, *Big Red*

Similes in Poetry.   Similes help poets pack a great deal of feeling into a few words. Frequently, similes paint pictures that appeal to the senses.

In the following selection, a simile compares the future to a flame. The bright, warm image suggests hopefulness.

We have tomorrow
Bright before us
Like a flame.

—Langston Hughes, "Youth"

Try to picture the images the following similes paint.

Eyes like a lake
Where a storm-wind roams
Caught me from under
The rim of a hat.

—Carl Sandburg, "Under a Hat Rim"

The Truth
is quite messy
like
a wind blown room

—William J. Harris, "The Truth is Quite Messy"

Exercises: Using Simile

A. Explain each simile. Tell what things are compared.

1. Like a small grey
   coffee-pot
   sits the squirrel.

   —Humbert Wolfe, "The Grey Squirrel"

2. The stars twinkled down like a million flirting eyes.

   —Maureen Daly, *Sixteen*

3. What happens to a dream deferred?
   Does it dry up
   Like a raisin in the sun?
   Or fester like a sore—
   and then run?
   Does it stink like rotten meat?

   —Langston Hughes, "Dream Deferred"

B. Write similes to complete the following phrases,

1. The sand on my feet feels like _____.
2. The stadium crowd cheered like _____.
3. At rush hour, the cars moved as _____ as _____.
4. The water in the bay was as _____ as _____.

C. Find three examples of similes in advertisements, stories, or poems.

Metaphor

> A **metaphor** is a comparison that states that one thing is another, unlike thing. (A metaphor compares without using *like* or *as*.) It suggests a way in which two things are alike.
>
> Examples: The flowers are a carpet of color.
> The ship plows the sea.

Metaphors in Prose. Writers often use metaphors to describe things or feelings. These descriptions can be more exact than normal speech. The metaphor in the first example describes the clearness and gentleness of the sea.

> We often seemed to be riding under the sky on a billowing mirror; or perhaps the sea was crystal clear and bottomless.
> —Thor Heyerdahl, *The Voyage of Ra*

What does this metaphor emphasize?

> The drive was a ribbon now, a thread of its former self, with gravel surface gone, and choked with grass and moss.
> —Daphne du Maurier, *Rebecca*

In the following example, a dog's muscles are compared to springs. His movements are compared to an explosion.

> He sprang high on his steel-spring muscles in an explosion of happiness, and bounded in circles around her.
> —Dorothy Canfield Fisher, "The Apprentice"

An extended metaphor carries a metaphor to some length. The following extended metaphor compares reading to eating.

> I was hungry enough for literature to want to take down the whole paper at this one meal, but I got only a few bites, and then had to postpone.
> —Mark Twain, *A Connecticut Yankee in King Arthur's Court*

Metaphors in Poetry. A metaphor gives you a fresh way of experiencing ordinary sights and sounds. Notice the comparisons in these poems:

> A soft sea washed around the House
> A sea of summer Air
>
>> —Emily Dickinson, "A Soft Sea Washed Around the House"

> Lumps of mud,
> the toads are jumping
> down the trail in twilight.
>
>> —José Juan Tablada, "Haikus"

Exercises: Using Metaphor

A. Identify each metaphor. Tell what two things are being compared. Explain how they are alike.

1. A house divided against itself cannot stand. I believe this government cannot endure permanently half slave and half free.

   —Abraham Lincoln, Second Lincoln-Douglas Debate

2. Poor Little Abe,
   Left all alone
   Except for Tom,
   Who's a rolling stone,

   —Rosemary and Stephen Vincent Benét, "Nancy Hanks"

3. My heart is what it was before,
     A house where people come and go;
   But it is winter with your love,
     The sashes are beset with snow

   —Edna St. Vincent Millay, "Alms"

4. Maybe you couldn't enjoy your life and put it into the bank, too.

   —Willa Cather, "Neighbor Rosicky"

B. Write metaphors to describe two of the following things:

snake   fire   closet   computer   music   mountains

Personification

> **Personification** is a special form of comparison. Personification gives human characteristics to an object, place, ideas, or animal.
>
> Examples: The motor coughed.
>
> The moon gazed down.

Personification in Prose. Personification is used mainly for special effect. Notice how these examples treat lifeless things as humans.

The old house was the same, droopy and sick.
—Harper Lee, *To Kill a Mockingbird*

It was a clear athletic stream that rushed and ran, and jumped and splashed. —Jean George, *My Side of the Mountain*

Places are personified too, as in these examples:

And for your country, boys, and for the flag, never dream a dream but of serving her as she bids you, though the service may carry you through a thousand hells.
—Edward Everett Hale, "Your Country"

The giant kingdom that was the Reata Ranch lay dozing in the sun, its head in the cloud-wreathed mountains far to the north, its arms flung east and west in careless might.
—Edna Ferber, *Giant*

Personification in Poetry. Personification is used frequently in poetry. In these examples, personification gives life to things made by humans.

In the evening the city
Goes to bed
Hanging lights
About its head.   —Langston Hughes, "City"

The jukebox has a big square face,
A majestic face, softly glowing with red and green and purple lights.
—Kenneth Fearing, "King Juke"

In these examples, elements of nature are given human traits.

There are sunsets who whisper a good-by. . . .
There are sunsets who dance good-by.
—Carl Sandburg, "Sunsets"

Spring brings out her baseball bat, swings it through the air,
Pitches bulbs and apple blossoms, throws them where it's bare,
—Myra Cohn Livingston, *A Circle of Seasons*

Exercises: Using Personification

A. Identify the personification in each example. Tell what is being compared to humans. How is it like humans?

1. Inside the pencil
   crouch words that have never been written
   —W. S. Merwin, "The Unwritten"

2. A great door in the side of the vessel whispered out a breath of oxygen.
   —Ray Bradbury, *The Illustrated Man*

3. The lawnmower
   Grinds its teeth
   Over the grass,
   Spitting out a thick
   Green spray;
   —Valerie Worth, "Lawnmower"

4. The city is so big
   Its bridges quake with fear
   —Richard García, "The City Is So Big"

B. Use personification to describe each of the following objects. How is each thing similar to a human? Does it do anything a human does? Does it look human?

a pencil sharpener   a vacuum cleaner   a skyscraper

Hyperbole

> **Hyperbole** is exaggeration. It puts a picture into the reader's mind. Hyperbole is frequently used in humorous writing.
>
> Example: You could have knocked me over with a feather.

Hyperbole in Prose. Hyperbole is used for emphasis or for humorous effect. With hyperbole, an author makes a point by overstating it.

Hyperbole is common in tall tales. Here is an example:

> At three weeks, Paul Bunyan got his family into a bit of trouble by kicking around his little tootsies and knocking down something like four miles of standing timber.

Hyperbole is often used in descriptions. It emphasizes some qualities of a person or thing by exaggerating them, as in this selection.

> The skin on her face was as thin and drawn as tight as the skin on an onion and her eyes were gray and sharp like the points of two ice-picks.   —Flannery O'Connor, "Parker's Back"

Hyperbole can also be used to describe a person's emotions. In the following selection, a boy is pulling a man up from a deep hole. See how hyperbole is used to describe the boy's thoughts as he struggles.

> It was not a mere man he was holding, but a giant; or a block of granite. The pull was unendurable. The pain unendurable.
> —James Ramsey Ullman, "A Boy and a Man"

What is exaggerated in the following examples?

> There did not seem to be brains enough in the entire nursery, so to speak, to bait a fishhook with.
> —Mark Twain, *A Connecticut Yankee in King Arthur's Court*

People moved slowly then. There was no hurry, for there was nowhere to go, nothing to buy and no money to buy it with, nothing to see outside the boundaries of Maycomb County.

—Harper Lee, *To Kill a Mockingbird*

Hyperbole in Poetry.   Hyperbole is common in humorous poetry. Hyperbole can make a point in a light-hearted way. It can be used to poke fun at someone or something. For example, read this description of a dull town.

It's a slow burg—I spent a couple of weeks there one day.
—Carl Sandburg, "The People, Yes"

This poem uses hyperbole in a description of a young boy.

Why does a boy who's fast as a jet
Take all day—and sometimes two—
To get to school?

—John Ciardi, "Speed Adjustments"

Hyperbole can emphasize a truth by exaggerating it.

Here once the embattled farmers stood
And fired the shot heard round the world.

—Ralph Waldo Emerson, "The Concord Hymn"

Exercises: Using Hyperbole

A. Identify the hyperbole in each example. What is being exaggerated?

1. He runs a mile in nothing flat.
   He can run right out from under his hat
   —John Ciardi, "Speed Adjustments"

2. If I read a book and it makes my whole body so cold no fire can warm me, I know that is poetry.
   —Emily Dickinson, Letter to Col. Thomas Higginson

B. Write your own hyperboles about being loud, cold, and late.

Understanding the Process of Writing

Review the stages in the process of writing: pre-writing, writing, and revising. Then read the following statements by authors. Identify the stage about which each author is commenting.

1. I make no attempt to correct as I go along because I know I must go over the manuscript word for word later. I am busy telling a story and do not want to interrupt it with clerical details.

   —Keith Robertson

2. I discover that I have gotten an idea somewhere. . . . Then over the next six months or a year or two years, it gradually, slowly develops—I think about it occasionally. The characters are forming at that time.

   —Edward Albee

3. With each draft I become more and more concerned with getting the sentence structure and the wording just the way I want it. The story must be paced, and the sentences must read as smoothly and rhythmically as possible.   —Robert M. McClung

Understanding the Sounds of Language

In the following excerpts, find an example of each of these techniques using sound:

alliteration   rhyme   rhythm   onomatopoeia   assonance

Explain how the technique helps the reader understand or appreciate the excerpt.

1. Sling your knuckles on the bottoms of the happy
   tin pans, let your trombones ooze, and go husha-husha-
   hush with the slippery sandpaper.

   —Carl Sandburg, "Jazz Fantasia"

2. He kept his eyes fixed on her, marveling at the way her face changed with each turn of their talk, like a wheat-field under a summer breeze.

    —Edith Wharton, *Ethan Frome*

3. He swings down like the flourish of a pen
Signing a signature in white on white.

    —Robert Francis, "Skier"

4. He solved ten problems in trigonometry. His mind cut neatly through their knots and separated them.

    —John Updike, "A Sense of Shelter"

5. He nested with owl,
And with bear-cub and possum,
And knew all his orchards
Root, tendril, and blossom.

    —Rosemary and Stephen Vincent Benét, "Johnny Appleseed"

6. She had seemed a pale, quiet woman in the house at Paddington, but in court she had flamed out against the sober background, flaunting herself like a tropical flower.

    —Agatha Christie, *Witness for the Prosecution*

7. Speak gently, Spring, and make no sudden sound;
For in my windy valley, yesterday I found
New-born foxes squirming on the ground—
Speak gently.

    —Lew Sarett, "Four Little Foxes"

8. Then, on his back, with his tail lashing and his jaws clicking, the shark plowed over the water as a speedboat does.

    —Ernest Hemingway, *The Old Man and the Sea*

Understanding Figures of Speech

In the above excerpts, find an example of each of the following figures of speech:

simile   metaphor   personification   hyperbole

Explain the effect of each figure of speech.

CHAPTER 5

Short Stories

Reading Literature: Short Stories

What Is a Short Story?

A **short story** is a work of fiction that develops a single idea. It can be read in one sitting. Because the story is brief, each detail counts.

Some short stories are concerned with adventure. Others focus on the workings of people's minds. Some stories are closer to reality than others. In this chapter, for example, "Thank You, M'am" could happen in any town. "The Third Wish," however, is like a fairy tale. Any definition of the short story must cover a wide variety of stories.

The History of the Short Story

The telling of tales is not new. Myths and legends were told more than 10,000 years ago. Over 2,000 years ago, the Bible included stories. Around the 1300's A.D., great storytellers wrote tales in verse.

The modern short story, however, began only in the 1800's. Then writers became interested in developing this form. The American writer Edgar Allan Poe is often called "father of the modern short story." Poe stressed that short story writers must select each detail with great care. Every detail must help create "a certain unique or single effect."

During the 1800's and 1900's, the short story has become one of the most widely read kinds of literature. Great authors from all over the world have contributed to this form. In this book you will find stories by writers from America, Russia, England, and South America.

The Elements of a Short Story

Plot. The action or events of a story make up its plot. Usually the plot shows how a conflict, or struggle, develops and is settled. The conflict and the events of the plot may be **external**. That is, they are outside the main character. They may be **internal**, or within the character. In many stories, the plot follows these steps:

> **Introduction, or Exposition:** This first part tells what the reader needs to know. It states who the characters are. It tells what has happened beforehand, and how the action begins.
> **Rising Action:** In this part, events add complications.
> **Climax:** This is often a turning point in the story. The main character usually makes a decision or changes in some way.
> **Falling Action:** This part shows the effects of the climax.
> **Resolution:** This last part of the story tells how the struggle ends. It suggests how the action will affect the characters.

Characters.   In a short story the reader gets to know only one or two characters well. For example, in the first story of this chapter, we get to understand one character, a princess. Writers make characters seem real in three major ways. They can show the characters' actions, explain their thoughts, and report their words. Each writer should clearly suggest a character's **motivations**, or reasons for acting.

Setting.   In some stories, the time and place of the action are of major importance. It is necessary, for example, for "The Lady, or the Tiger?" to be set in ancient, unfamiliar times. In other stories the setting is less important. "Lather and Nothing Else" might happen in almost any country, in almost any time period.

Suspense.   In any good story, the writer tells just enough to keep the reader wondering what will come next. Often the reader becomes tense or worried about the next events. This is especially true when a character's life is in danger. The writer gradually builds the interest higher and higher. This building-up of interest is called **suspense.**

How To Read a Short Story

1. Choose the right time and place to read the story. You should not be interrupted or distracted. Give yourself a chance to experience and recognize the single effect that the writer is trying to make.
2. As you read the story enjoy the mood it creates. Let the characters excite or annoy you. Try to guess what will happen next.

Comprehension Skills: Inferences

Making Inferences

A writer may give information in a story directly or indirectly. For example, a story might begin with this direct statement:

A girl named Deborah woke up early one morning.

Or, the story might give the same information with this sentence:

The sky was changing from a deep purple to a pale pink as Deborah sleepily opened her eyes and looked out her bedroom window.

In the second example, the writer is depending on the reader to make some connections. The reader should know that when the sky gets lighter, the sun is rising. He or she should know that when a person is sleepy but opening her eyes, she is waking up. The reader can combine this knowledge with the facts in the sentence. By doing so, the reader can figure out what is happening. A reader who is applying his or her knowledge to the facts of a story in this way is **making inferences**.

Writers have many reasons for using indirect statements. First, limiting a story to direct statements would make it boring. Second, a reader would feel insulted to be told everything. Even more important, a writer who counts on the readers to make inferences can say a great deal in a few words. For example, from the second sentence, you could guess that the day was clear. You could guess that the sun was just rising. You could not infer these additional ideas from the first sentence, a direct statement.

In order to understand a short story, it is necessary to make inferences. Here is a sentence from one of the stories in this chapter. What can you infer about the story from the sentence?

His scarfpin was a large diamond, oddly set.

First, you might infer that the character is wealthy or showy. Next, you might guess that the setting is not modern, since men do not wear scarfpins today. So far, you have made inferences about character and setting. From other sentences, you might make inferences about the plot, the mood, or any other element. Like a detective, you should be alert for clues from which you can infer meaning.

Predicting Outcomes

If you know the ingredients in a recipe, you may be able to guess how the dish will taste. Similarly, if you understand the characters in a story, you may be able to predict their next moves. Depending on how carefully you read, you may even be able to predict the ending of a story. As you read each new story, it's fun to pause every so often and predict possible outcomes. Don't expect to be right all of the time, of course. A writer can always introduce a new fact that will affect the plot. If you have made predictions, however, you will more easily identify the new fact. This will help you keep up with the writer.

Exercises: Making Inferences and Predicting Outcomes

A. For each statement below, make one inference about character. If possible, make another inference about setting, mood, or relationships.

1. Laurie said, noticing his father, "Hi, Pop, you old dust mop!"
2. The woman did not ask the boy anything about where he lived, or his folks, or anything else that would embarrass him.
3. If things get too rough, I run. And as anybody can tell you, I'm the fastest thing on two feet.
4. Then he saw how thin and pale she was growing.
5. He came in without a word. When I recognized him I started to shake.

B. In this story, Mr. Peters has just saved a swan tangled in thorn bushes, and the swan has changed into a little man. Read the passage. Then predict whether Mr. Peters will choose reasonable wishes.

"Well, Sir," the little man said threateningly, "I see you know some of the laws of magic. You think that because you have rescued the King of the Forest from a difficulty, you should have some fabulous reward."

"I expect three wishes, no more and no less," answered Mr. Peters, looking at him steadily and with composure.

Vocabulary Skills: Context Clues

Recognizing Different Types of Context Clues

You have learned about definition and restatement clues and about synonyms. Using these context clues, you can often figure out the meanings of new words. There are also other types of context clues.

Comparison Clues. Often an unfamiliar word is used in a comparison with a familiar word. Your knowledge of the familiar word may unlock the meaning of the new one. Here is an example:

The thatch in the roof was as likely to burn as any other straw.

The sentence compares two materials, thatch and straw. The words "as likely as any other straw" show that thatch is straw.

Some phrases that signal comparison clues are _like, as, same_ or _same as, similar to,_ and _other._

Contrast Clues. In a comparison clue, you learn that a new word is like a known word. In a contrast clue, you learn that a new word is different from the known word. Here is an example:

At night the street was pacific, unlike the crowded, noisy chaos it was during the day.

In this contrast, the word _pacific_ is opposed to _crowded, noisy,_ and _chaotic._ From this, you can guess that it means "peaceful."

Some phrases that alert you to contrast clues are the following: _although, but, though, on the other hand, however, yet, unlike, different from, in contrast to, not,_ and _as opposed to._

Examples in Context. You may find an unfamiliar word as an example of a familiar word. In this sentence, for example, you can tell that a _ventriloquist_ is a kind of performer in a show.

At the show we saw magicians, ventriloquists, and other performers.

You may find the familiar words as examples of the unfamiliar word.

> I had several rationalizations for not studying—I had a headache, it was too late, I wouldn't do well on the test anyway.

From these examples of *rationalizations,* you can guess the word means "reasons" or "excuses."

Some key words that point out example clues are *for example, such as, especially, for instance, like, other, such,* and *one kind.*

Inferring Meaning from Context. Not every meaning in context is signaled by key words or punctuation. Many times you must piece together hints in the context. Using the hints, you can make educated guesses, or inferences, about the meaning of word. Read this passage, for example, for clues to the meaning of *solemnized.*

> Immediately after the lady stepped forth, another door opened. From it came a priest followed by a band of dancing maidens. This procession advanced to where the man and the lady stood, and the wedding was promptly solemnized. Then the brass bells rang forth gaily, and the married couple made their way out of the arena.

From the information in the passage, you could infer that *solemnized* means "celebrated" or "made official."

Exercises: Using Different Types of Context Clues

A. Tell what kind of context clue you find in each sentence: definition or restatement, synonym, comparison, contrast, example, or inference.

1. He could make the journey by mulecart, train, or another <u>conveyance</u>.
2. The king issued unreasonable <u>decrees</u>. Nevertheless, everyone had to obey his commands.
3. The policeman examined the <u>vicinity</u>, or area.
4. He was a <u>stalwart</u> fellow, not at all cowardly.
5. Her new <u>sidekicks</u> are just as silly and loud as her old companions.

B. Use the context clues in Exercise A to figure out the meaning of each underlined word.

Great Classic Stories

The four stories in this section have been read and enjoyed for many years. One of them is by O. Henry, an American writer noted for his surprise endings. It is not the only story in the group with an unexpected development at the end. As you read these stories, watch out for the surprise endings. Try, also, to watch for other similarities among stories.

The Flying Carriage, 1913, MARC CHAGALL. Solomon R. Guggenheim Museum, New York. Photograph by Robert E. Mates.

The Lady, or the Tiger?

FRANK R. STOCKTON

The Princess in this story is faced with a difficult conflict. As you read, look for clues that suggest the decision she will make. Would you make the same choice?

In the very olden time, there lived a semibarbaric King. He was a man of strong will who loved authority. At the same time he wished to rule his subjects with fair and impartial justice. Among his notions for doing this was that of building a huge arena—not as a place for entertaining the people with contests of gladiators, but as a great public court. Thus, whenever one of his subjects was charged with a serious crime, the King gave public notice that on an appointed day the fate of the accused person would be decided in the arena.

When all the people had assembled in the galleries, the King, sitting high up on his throne on one side of the arena, gave a signal. Immediately, a door opened beneath him, and the accused subject stepped out into the amphitheater. On the other side of the arena, directly opposite this accused person, were two doors, exactly alike and side by side. It was the duty and the privilege of the person on trial to walk directly to these doors and open one of them. He could open either door he pleased; he was influenced in his choice only by chance.

If he opened one of them, there came out a hungry tiger, the fiercest that could be found, which immediately sprang upon him and tore him to pieces, as a punishment for his guilt. The moment the case of the criminal was thus decided, iron bells were solemnly clanged, and the audience left the arena with bowed heads, mourning greatly that one so young and strong, or so old and respected, should meet so sad a fate.

However, if the accused person opened the other door, there came forth from it a lady, the most suitable to his years and station that His Majesty could select from among his fair subjects. The accused man was immediately married to this lady as a reward for his innocence. It mattered not that he might already possess a wife, or that he might be in love with someone else. The King allowed no such obstacles to stand in the way of the decision of the arena.

Immediately after the lady stepped forth, another door opened beneath the King. From it came a priest followed by a band of dancing maidens blowing joyous tunes on golden horns. This procession advanced to where the innocent man and the lady stood, and the wedding was promptly solemnized. Then the brass bells rang forth gaily, the people shouted glad hurrahs, and the married couple, preceded by children strewing flowers, made their way out of the arena.

This was the King's method of administering justice. Its perfect fairness is obvious. The criminal could not know out of which door the lady would come. He opened the one he pleased, without having the slightest idea whether, in the next instant, he was to be devoured or married. On some occasions the tiger came out of one door, and on some occasions it came out of the other. The accused person was instantly punished if he found himself guilty; and if he proved himself innocent, he was rewarded on the spot, whether he liked it or not. There was no escape from the justice of the King's arena.

This method of administering justice was well liked by the people. When they gathered on the great trial days, they never knew whether they were to witness a bloody slaughter or a hilarious wedding. They enjoyed the element of chance that the plan afforded and thought the trial was entirely fair—for did not the accused person have the whole matter in his own hands?

The King had a daughter with a spirit as proud and determined as his own. As is usual in such cases, she was his darling, the apple of his eye. Among his courtiers was a young man of good family, but not of royal blood, who had dared to fall in love with the Princess. She was well satisfied with her lover, for he was both handsome and brave, and their affair moved on happily until one day the King happened to discover its existence. He did not hesitate in regard to his duty. The unhappy youth was immediately cast into prison, and a day was set aside for his trial in the King's arena.

This, of course, was an especially important occasion; for His Majesty, as well as all the people, was greatly interested in the trial. Never before had such a case occurred—never before had a subject dared to love the daughter of a king. The tiger cages of the kingdom were searched for the most savage beast that could be found. Also, the ranks of maiden beauty throughout the land were carefully surveyed so that the young man might have a fitting bride in case fate did not bring him death instead.

Of course, everyone knew that the youth was guilty of the deed with which he had been charged. He had fallen in love with the Princess; and neither he, she, nor anyone else thought of denying that. The King, however, would not think of allowing any fact of this kind to interfere with the workings of his court of justice.

The appointed day arrived. From far and near the people gathered, thronging the great galleries of the arena. Other crowds, unable to gain admittance, massed themselves against its outside walls. The King and his courtiers were now in their places, directly opposite the twin doors—those fateful doors, so terrible in their similarity!

All was ready. The signal was given. A door beneath the royal party opened, and the lover of the Princess walked into the arena. Tall and fair, his entrance was greeted with a low hum of admiration and anxiety. No wonder the Princess loved him! What a terrible thing for him to be there!

As the youth advanced into the arena, he turned, as the custom was, to bow before the King. However, he did not think at all of the King. His eyes were fixed upon the Princess, who sat to the right of her father.

From the moment that the decree had gone forth that her lover must decide his fate in the King's arena, she had thought of nothing, night or day, but this great event. Having more power, influence, and force of character than anyone who had ever before been interested in such a case, she had done what no other person had done—she had learned the secret of the doors. She knew in which of the two rooms behind those doors stood the cage of the tiger, with its open front. She knew, too, in which room waited the lady. Through these thick doors, heavily curtained with skins on the inside, it was impossible that any noise or suggestion from within should come to the person who should approach to raise the latch of one of the doors. However, gold, and the power of a woman's will, had brought the secret to the Princess.

Not only did she know in which room stood the lady, ready to emerge if her door were opened, but she knew who the lady was. She was one of the fairest and loveliest of the damsels of the court—and the Princess hated her. Often had the Princess seen this fair creature throwing glances of admi-

Tiger, Japanese hanging scroll, 19th Century, DOKOKAN GANKU. The Metropolitan Museum of Art, Rogers Fund, 1936. (36.100.11)

ration at her lover, and sometimes the Princess thought the glances were even returned. Now and then she had seen them talking together. It was for but a moment or two, but much can be said in a brief space. The lady was lovely, but she had dared raise her eyes to the loved one of the Princess. With all the intensity of the half-savage royal blood that flowed in her veins, the

Princess hated the woman who stood behind that silent door.

When her lover turned and looked at her, and his eyes met hers, he saw that she knew behind which door crouched the tiger and behind which door stood the lady. He had expected her to know. He understood her nature and was confident that she would never rest until she had made plain to herself this secret. The moment he looked up, he knew that she had succeeded.

Then it was that his quick and anxious glance asked the question, "Which?" It was as plain to her as if he had shouted it from where he stood. There was not an instant to be lost. The question had been asked in a flash; it must be answered in another.

Her right arm lay on the cushioned parapet before her. She raised her hand and made a quick movement toward the right.

No one but her lover saw her. Every eye but his was fixed on him. He turned, and walked across the empty space. Every heart stopped beating; every breath was held; every eye was fixed upon that man. Without the slightest hesitation he went to the door on the right and opened it.

Now, the point of the story is this: Did the tiger come out of that door, or did the lady?

The more we ponder this question, the harder it is to answer. It requires a difficult study of a human heart. Think of it, reader, not as if the decision depended upon yourself, but upon that hot-blooded, semibarbaric Princess, her soul torn between love, despair, and jealousy. She had lost him, no matter which door he chose. But who should have him?

How often, in her waking hours and in her dreams, had she stared in wild horror and covered her face with her hands as she thought of her lover opening the door on the other side of which waited the cruel fangs of the tiger!

How much oftener had she pictured him at the other door! That picture of his rapturous delight as he opened the door of the lady had caused the Princess to gnash her teeth and tear her hair. Her heart had burned in agony when she had pictured him rushing to meet the woman, when she had heard, in imagination, the glad shouts from the people and the joyous ringing of the bells as the couple was joined in marriage. Every detail of the triumphant scene the Princess had imagined, and each of them had torn her soul with jealous rage.

Would it not be better for him to die at once? And yet, that awful tiger, those shrieks, that blood!

Her decision now had been indicated in an instant, but it had been made after days and nights of anguished thought. She had known that she would be asked, and she had decided what she would answer. Now, without the slightest hesitation, she had moved her hand to the right.

The question of her decision is not an easy one to answer, and it is not for me to presume to set myself up as the one person capable of answering it correctly. So I leave it all with you: Which came out of the opened door—the lady, or the tiger?

Developing Comprehension Skills

1. How did the King's public court work?

2. What happened when the King found out that the young man loved the Princess?

3. The Princess did not like the lady who stood behind one of the doors. How might this feeling have influenced the decision the Princess had to make?

4. What do you think about the King's method of dealing with crime? Did his court really provide justice, that is, fair treatment? Explain the reasons for your opinion.

Reading Literature: Short Stories

1. **Understanding Characterization.** The author of this story does not rely on direct description to tell about the Princess. However, he gives suggestions about her. Then he lets the reader figure out her character traits. Name something you learn about the Princess in each of the following ways:

   her actions
   her thoughts
   others' reactions to her

2. **Explaining Motivation.** A character's reason for acting, or **motivation**, should fit the character. Which door do you think the princess told her lover to open? What in her personality suggests this decision?

3. **Analyzing the Setting.** The time and place, or setting, of a story should support the plot. Think about the specific details of this story's setting. In what ways does the setting seem appropriate for what happens?

4. **Identifying Conflict.** In a short story, there is usually one main conflict, or struggle. This conflict gives suspense or excitement to the story. It determines how the plot unfolds. Read the choices below. Select the main conflict in "The Lady, or the Tiger?" Then explain why you think your choice is correct.

   the lady against the tiger
   the young man against the King
   the young man against the Princess
   the Princess against herself

5. **Analyzing Details of Plot.** In the rising action of "The Lady, or the Tiger?" the author develops suspense. One way he does this is by stopping the action of the story at an exciting part. For example, the action stops when the young man walks into the arena. The author then fills in background details. By interrupting the action, he tries to make you wonder what will happen. Name at least one other place in this story where the author stops the action. Does his method succeed in making you curious about the ending?

Developing Vocabulary Skills

Reviewing Definition or Restatement Clues. Read the following sentences about events in the story. The meanings of the underlined words can be figured out by definition or restatement clues. For each underlined word, write the meaning you get from the context. Also write the key words or punctuation marks provided.

1. The King's system of justice was impartial. That is, it did not take sides.

2. The galleries were the rooms set aside for the public to watch the spectacle.

3. A decree is an official announcement made by a king.

4. In those days, young ladies in the kingdom were called <u>damsels</u>.

5. The King and Princess were <u>semibarbaric</u>, which is half-savage.

6. He wanted to <u>ponder</u> the question before he answered. In other words, he wanted to think about it for a while.

Developing Writing Skills

1. **Comparing and Contrasting Characters.** The author gives many details about the characters of the King and the Princess. Write two paragraphs comparing and contrasting these two characters.

   Pre-Writing. List the following information for each character:

   > physical description
   > background information
   > his or her thoughts
   > the internal conflict faced
   > reason for major action

   You may find information for a topic for one character but not another. You may also find information that does not fit one of these categories. Add it to your list.

   Writing. In your first paragraph, compare the King and the Princess. Tell in what ways they are similar. Give details from the story. Use key words such as *both*, *alike*, and *similarities* to signal the comparison.

   In the second paragraph, contrast the two characters. Tell how they are different. Choose examples from the story that set them apart. Use words such as *opposite*, *more than*, and *less than* to signal the contrast.

   Revising. Ask another person to read your work. Can the person tell you several similarities and several differences between the King and the Princess? If not, you need to revise one of the paragraphs. Also check to be sure your key words sound right. They should tie your ideas together.

2. **Changing the Point of View.** In "The Lady, or the Tiger?" the narrator describes an important action made by the Princess:

   > She raised her hand and made a slight, quick movement toward the right.

   Use this sentence to begin a paragraph, and write an ending for the story. Your ending should be limited to what happens to the young lover. Use the third-person point of view. That is, use *he* and *him* to talk about the young man. However, tell only things that the lover would know. Tell what the young man thinks and feels when he sees the Princess give the signal. Tell what he sees beyond the door he opens. Then tell what this makes him think about the Princess.

Developing Skills in Study and Research

Using the SQ3R Method. It is sometimes difficult to read new material. One study approach that will help you with your reading is called SQ3R. The term **SQ3R** stands for five steps: Survey, Question, Read, Recite, and Review. Read the introduction to SQ3R on page 628 in the Handbook.

In the library, find an encyclopedia article about one of the following topics. Or select an article about another topic that relates to the story you just read.

law	courts
tigers	barbarians

Follow the SQ3R method to read the article. Write down the following information.

1. First, **survey** the article; that is, get a general idea about it. In order to survey, list the title, headings, and subheadings of the article. Write a one-sentence summary stating what you think the article is about.

2. During the **question** step, write down at least three questions that could be asked about the article.

3. As you **read** the article, keep your study questions in mind. Look for information to answer them. When you finish reading, write down two main points from the article.

4. Try to **recite** answers to your questions. That is, explain the answers out loud. Also, write down at least three important pieces of information not in the questions.

5. As a **review**, read the list of headings and subheadings again. Add to the list all the details from the article that you can recall.

6. Think about what you learned in the SQ3R steps. How did it add to or change your idea about "The Lady, or the Tiger?"

Developing Skills in Critical Thinking

Making Inferences. Many important ideas in a short story are never stated directly. However, the author provides clues to help us infer, or figure out, these unstated ideas.

Today in the United States and many other countries, men and women are considered equal. Think about whether this is true of the country pictured in "The Lady, or the Tiger?" Find passages in the story that indicate how the people regarded women. On your paper, list at least three details about the treatment of women. What is the attitude toward women suggested by these details? The author does not directly state this information. You will need to make an inference. Write a sentence to summarize your idea.

A Spark Neglected

LEO TOLSTOY

This story is about a feud between two families. What clues to the outcome does the author provide? Try to predict the end of the story. Read to find out if your guess is correct.

There once lived in Russia a peasant named Ivan Stcherbakof. He was the best worker in the village and had three sons, all able to work; his wife was a thrifty woman, and they had a quiet and hard-working daughter-in-law. They had only one idle mouth to feed, that of Ivan's old father, who had been lying ill on the top of the great brick oven for seven years. Ivan had all he needed, three horses and a colt, a cow with a calf, and fifteen sheep. He and his children might have lived quite comfortably had it not been for a quarrel with his next-door neighbor, Limping Gabriel, the son of Gordey Ivanof.

As long as old Gordey was alive the peasants lived as neighbors should. If the women wanted a sieve or a tub, or the men a sack, they sent to the other house. Such safeguards as locking up barns and sheds or hiding things from one another were never thought of.

When the sons came to be at the head of the families, everything was changed. The trouble all began about a trifle. Ivan's daughter-in-law, Sonia, had a hen that every day laid an egg in the cart. One day the hen flew across into Gabriel's yard and laid her egg there. When Sonia went over, Gabriel's mother asked: "What do you want, young woman?"

"Why, you see, my hen flew across this morning. Didn't she lay an egg here?"

"We never saw anything of it. We collect our own eggs. And we don't go looking for eggs in other people's yards, lass!"

Offended, the young woman answered sharply. The women began abusing each other. Ivan's wife joined in; Gabriel's wife rushed out; then a general uproar commenced. Gabriel, returning from the fields, stopped to take his wife's part. Ivan and his son joined in, and finally Ivan pulled a handful out of Gabriel's beard. Thus the quarrel began, and from this a feud grew.

Ivan's old father tried to persuade them to make peace, saying: "It's stupid, children, picking quarrels about an egg. The children may have taken it—well, what matter? God sends enough for all. And suppose your neighbor did say an unkind word; show her how to say a better one! If

The Harvesters, 16th Century, PIETER BRUEGEL. The Metropolitan Museum of Art, Rogers Fund, 1919. Photograph by Eric Pollitzer. (19.164)

there has been a fight—well, we're all sinners, so make it up. To nurse your anger will be worse for you yourselves."

The younger folk would not listen. Not a day passed without a quarrel, or even a fight. After a time the families began to steal from each other, causing each other to pay fines. Finally, in the seventh year of the quarrel, Sonia accused Gabriel of horse-stealing, and Gabriel hit her such a blow

that she was laid up for a week. Ivan had Gabriel condemned to be flogged. After this humiliation, Gabriel was overheard to mutter: "Very well! He will have my back flogged! That will make it burn; but something of his may burn worse than that!"

Then Ivan's old father spoke up again. "Ah, lad, malice blinds you. Others' sins are before your eyes, but your own are behind your back. He's acted badly? If he were bad but you were good, there would be no strife. If you get a hard word from anyone, keep silent, and his own conscience will accuse him. Forgive him; then life will be easy, and your heart will be light. In the morning make up with Gabriel, and invite him here for tomorrow's holiday. Don't delay; put out the fire before it spreads."

Ivan began to think his father was right; but at this moment the women came into the house, telling of more quarreling. Then Ivan's heart again grew cold, and he gave up the thought of making peace. Late that evening he went the rounds of his farm to see whether anything was in danger. As he reached the far corner of the shed, he saw something flare up for a moment near the plow; he clearly saw a man, crouching down, lighting a bunch of straw he held in his hand. The thatch flared up at the eaves, and, standing beneath them, Gabriel's whole figure was clearly visible.

"Now I'll have him," thought Ivan; and, paying no attention to the fire now blazing furiously, he rushed at Gabriel. The latter fled. Ivan followed and was about to seize him when Gabriel, seizing an oak beam, struck Ivan down and stunned him.

When Ivan came to his senses, Gabriel was no longer there. Ivan saw that his back shed was all ablaze; flames and smoke and bits of burning straw mixed with the smoke were being driven toward his hut. "What is this?" cried Ivan, still half dazed. "Why, all I had to do was just to snatch it out from under the eaves and trample on it! Then the fire would never have gotten started." Be-

fore he could get to the fire, the hut was aflame. Nothing could be done. After Ivan's house, Gabriel's also caught fire. Then, carried by the rising wind, the flames spread to the other side of the street. Half the village was burned down.

Ivan barely managed to save his old father; his family escaped in what clothes they had on; everything else was lost, even the grain in the granaries. Ivan kept repeating, "One need only have pulled it out and trampled on it."

In the morning his old father sent for him. "Who has burned down the village?" began the old man.

"Gabriel, Father. I saw him."

"Ivan, I am dying. You in your turn will have to face death. Now, before God, say whose is the sin."

Only then Ivan came to his senses and understood it all. He answered simply, "Mine, Father." Then he fell on his knees before his father, saying, "Forgive me. I am guilty before you and before God."

The old man cried: "Praise the Lord! Praise the Lord! What must you do now?"

Ivan was weeping.

"I don't know how we are to live now, Father!" he said.

The old man smiled faintly. "If you obey God's will, you'll manage! Mind, Ivan! Don't tell who started the fire! Hide another man's sin, and God will forgive two of yours!" Closing his eyes, the old man sighed, stretched out, and died.

Ivan did not lodge a complaint against Gabriel, and no one knew what had caused the fire. At first Gabriel felt afraid, but after a while he got used to it. The men left off quarreling, and then their families left off also. While rebuilding their huts, both families lived in one. When the village was restored, Ivan and Gabriel built next to each other and lived as good neighbors should. Ivan remembered his old father's command to quench the fire at the first spark. If anyone does him an injury he now tries, not to revenge himself but, rather, to set matters right.

Now Ivan is on his feet again and lives better even than he did before.

Developing Comprehension Skills

1. How did the feud between the two families begin?

2. Only one person tried to stop the quarrel from becoming a feud. Who was that person? In your own words, tell what that person said about the first quarrel.

3. The last event in the feud is the fire set by Gabriel. Earlier in the story, Gabriel's words foreshadow, or hint about, this later action. What does Gabriel say to suggest that a fire might be set?

4. You can infer that the families took each other to court. The author provides clues in two different events. Name at least one of these events.

5. Who was responsible for the feud? Who could have stopped it? Give reasons for your answers.

6. If you were Ivan, would you have told who started the fire? Or would you have followed your father's advice? Why?

Reading Literature: Short Stories

1. **Explaining the Title.** The title of this story has two meanings. One of the "sparks" that is "neglected" is the one that sets fire to Ivan's shed. The other meaning of "A Spark Neglected" does not refer to a fire at all. What do you think this other meaning of the title might be? What character or action is being compared to a neglected spark?

2. **Understanding Characterization.** Ivan is the main character in this story. What kind of person is he? How does he change in the story? How does his personality affect the plot?

3. **Making a Plot Diagram.** A **plot diagram** shows the five parts of the plot of a story. It is drawn to show the climax as the peak of action.

   Copy the plot diagram and the following list of statements onto your paper.

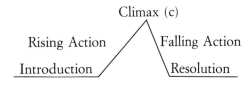

   a. Ivan does not tell anyone that Gabriel started the fire.

   b. Gabriel sets the shed on fire.

   c. Ivan admits his guilt to his dying father.

d. Gabriel and Ivan build homes next to each other and live as good neighbors.

e. The Stcherbakof family lived near the Ivanof family in a Russian village.

Label the diagram with letters to show these five parts of "A Spark Neglected." The correct position of statement *c* has been marked for you. It describes the climax.

4. **Stating the Theme.** The theme of a story is its message to the reader. What is one theme of this story? Give two details from the story that support your answer.

Developing Vocabulary Skills

Reviewing Synonym Clues. Sometimes an unfamiliar word is presented with its synonym in context. You have learned how to look for synonym clues. They can appear in the same sentence as the word, or in a nearby sentence.

The following statements contain words that were used in the story. Figure out the meaning of the underlined words by looking for synonym clues. On your paper, write the synonym for each underlined word.

1. If the men needed a sack, they sent to the other house. They would soon receive the needed bag.

2. The young woman answered sharply because she felt offended and insulted by the comment of her neighbor.

3. The old man tried to prevent the feud. He said, "If there has been a fight between the families, make it up."

4. Ivan had Gabriel condemned to be flogged. After he was whipped, Gabriel plotted revenge against Ivan.

5. If one side is bad and the other side is good,

there will be no strife. It takes two bad wills to create conflict.

6. The fire flared up in the eaves of the shed. There, beneath the overhanging edge of the roof, Ivan saw Gabriel.

7. When the village was restored, the two homes were rebuilt side by side.

8. "I only needed to trample on it! Oh, Why did I not stamp out the fire?"

Developing Writing Skills

1. **Understanding a Character.** Although Ivan is the central character in the story, his father plays an important role. What is the old man's place in the family? What does he say and do in the story? What kind of influence does he have? Write at least one paragraph explaining the role of the old father in "A Spark Neglected."

2. **Writing About an Idea.** In the story, Ivan's father speaks out against revenge several times. His advice turns out to be good. Have you ever been in a position to use the advice he gave? Write two paragraphs showing the truth of the lesson Ivan learned. You might write about an event in your life. Or you might make up an event. Tell the story in the first person, as if it happened to you.

Pre-Writing. Outline the series of events that you experienced or made up. Think about how the situation began. Were you the person mainly responsible? Did anyone try to give you advice? Did you listen? What did you do to make the situation better? Or worse? How did the event finally end? Write down all the details. Then arrange them to show how they built up to the lesson.

Writing. In the first paragraph, write about the events in the order you arranged them. Include all the details about your behavior. In the second paragraph, tell how others reacted. Also tell what you learned.

Revising. Read your paragraphs aloud to someone else. Ask the person to listen for the main idea. It should be easily understood. Otherwise, you need to rewrite the second paragraph. You may also need to rearrange the events in the first paragraph. Each event should build on the one before it.

Developing Skills in Study and Research

Doing Background Reading. The opening paragraph of "A Spark Neglected" tells of life in a different century. The old man sleeps on top of a brick oven. This is certainly nothing like our ovens. To find out more about the oven in the story, you will need to find information about the history and culture of Russia. This type of research is called **background reading**.

Research the oven described in the story. Use the card catalog and the encyclopedia as resources. Try to find out what sort of oven it was. Was it a common part of Russian households? When?

On your paper report the steps you take as you look for the information. If you do research in an encyclopedia, write down the title of the encyclopedia and the volume number, the title of the entry, and the page numbers of each entry you check. If you use the card catalog, write down each subject and subheading that you check. Also write down each book title, call number, author's name, and page number where you look for information.

If you find information about the oven, summarize it on your paper. If you cannot find the information, suggest another way you might look for it on a second try.

After Twenty Years

O. HENRY

Loyalty is an important part of friendship. However, what happens when another important value conflicts with loyalty? Read this story about two friends. Find out how they deal with this question.

The policeman on the beat moved up the avenue impressively. The impressiveness was habitual and not for show, for spectators were few. The time was barely ten o'clock at night, but chilly gusts of wind with a taste of rain in them had well nigh depeopled the streets.

Trying doors as he went, twirling his club with many intricate and artful movements, turning now and then to cast his watchful eye down the pacific thoroughfare, the officer, with his stalwart form and slight swagger, made a fine picture of a guardian of the peace. The vicinity was one that kept early hours. Now and then you might see the lights of a cigar store or of an all-night lunch counter, but the majority of the doors belonged to business places that had long since been closed.

When about midway of a certain block, the policeman suddenly slowed his walk. In the doorway of a darkened hardware store a man leaned, with an unlighted cigar in his mouth. As the policeman walked up to him, the man spoke up quickly.

"It's all right, officer," he said, reassuringly. "I'm just waiting for a friend. It's an appointment made twenty years ago. Sounds a little funny to you, doesn't it? Well, I'll explain, if you'd like to make certain it's all right. About that long ago there used to be a restaurant where this store stands—'Big Joe' Brady's restaurant."

"Until five years ago," said the policeman. "It was torn down then."

The man in the doorway struck a match and lit his cigar. The light showed a pale, square-jawed face with keen eyes, and a little white scar near his right eyebrow. His scarfpin was a large diamond, oddly set.

"Twenty years ago tonight," said the man, "I dined here at 'Big Joe' Brady's with Jimmy Wells, my best chum and the finest chap in the world. He and I were raised here in New York, just like two brothers, together. I was eighteen and Jimmy was twenty. The next morning I was to start for the West to make my fortune. You couldn't have dragged Jimmy out of New York; he thought it was the only place on earth. Well, we agreed that night that we would meet here again exactly twenty years from that date and time, no matter what our conditions might be or from what distance we might have to come. We figured that in twenty years each of us ought to have our destiny worked out and our fortunes made, whatever they were going to be."

"It sounds pretty interesting," said the policeman. "Rather a long time between meets, though, it seems to me. Haven't you heard from your friend since you left?"

"Well, yes, for a time we corresponded," said the other. "But after a year or two we lost track of each other. You see, the West is a pretty big proposition, and I kept hustling around over it pretty lively. But I know Jimmy will meet me here if he's alive, for he always was the truest, stanchest old chap in the world. He'll never forget. I came a thousand miles to stand in this door tonight, and it's worth it if my old partner turns up."

The waiting man pulled out a handsome watch; the lids of it were set with several small diamonds. "Three minutes to ten," he announced. "It was exactly ten o'clock when we parted here at the restaurant door."

"Did pretty well out West, didn't you?" asked the policeman.

"You bet! I hope Jimmy has done half as well. He was a kind of plodder, though, good fellow as he was. I've had to compete with some of the sharpest wits going to get my pile. A man gets in a groove in New York. It takes the West to put a razor-edge on him."

The policeman twirled his club and took a step or two. "I'll be on my way. Hope your friend comes around all right. Going to call time on him sharp?"

"I should say not!" said the other. "I'll give him half an hour at least. If Jimmy is alive on Earth, he'll be here by that time. So long, officer."

"Good-night, sir," said the policeman, passing on along his beat, trying doors as he went.

There was now a fine, cold drizzle falling, and the wind had risen from its uncertain puffs into a steady blow. The few foot passengers astir in that quarter hurried dismally and silently along with coat collars turned high and pocketed hands. In the door of the hardware store the man who had come a thousand miles to fill an appointment, uncertain almost to absurdity, with the friend of his youth, smoked his cigar and waited.

About twenty minutes he waited, and then a tall man in a long overcoat, with collar turned up to his ears, hurried across from the opposite side of the street. He went directly to the waiting man.

"Is that you, Bob?" he asked, doubtfully.

"Is that you, Jimmy Wells?" cried the man in the door.

"Bless my heart!" exclaimed the new arrival, grasping both the other's hands with his own. "It's Bob, sure as fate. I was certain I'd find you here if you were still in existence. Well, well, well!—twenty years is a long time. The old restaurant's gone,

Bob; I wish it had lasted, so we could have had another dinner there. How has the West treated you, old man?"

"It's been bully. It has given me everything I asked it for. You've changed lots, Jimmy. I never thought you were so tall by two or three inches."

"Oh, I grew a bit after I was twenty."

"Doing well in New York, Jimmy?"

"Moderately. I have a position in one of the city departments. Come on, Bob; we'll go around to a place I know of and have a good long talk about old times."

The two men started up the street, arm in arm. The man from the West, his egotism enlarged by success, was beginning to out-

Rainy-Night, 1930, CHARLES BURCHFIELD. San Diego Museum of Art. Gift of Misses Anne R. and Amy Putnam.

line the history of his career. The other, submerged in his overcoat, listened with interest.

At the corner stood a drugstore, brilliant with electric lights. When they came into this glare, each of them turned simultaneously to gaze upon the other's face.

The man from the West stopped suddenly and released his arm.

"You're not Jimmy Wells," he snapped. "Twenty years is a long time, but not long enough to change a man's nose from a Roman to a pug."

"It sometimes changes a good man into a bad one," said the tall man. "You've been under arrest for ten minutes, 'Silky' Bob. Chicago thinks you may have dropped over our way and wires us she wants to have a chat with you. Going quietly, are you?

That's sensible. Now, before we go on to the station here's a note I was asked to hand you. You may read it here at the window. It's from Patrolman Wells."

The man from the West unfolded the little piece of paper handed him. His hand was steady when he began to read, but it trembled a little by the time he had finished. The note was rather short.

Bob:
  I was at the appointed place on time. When you struck the match to light your cigar I saw it was the face of the man wanted in Chicago. Somehow I couldn't do it myself, so I went around and got a plainclothes man to do the job.

Jimmy

Developing Comprehension Skills

1. Why was the man from the West waiting in front of a closed hardware store at night?

2. What kind of job did Jimmy Wells, the man who stayed in New York, have?

3. How did Bob, the man from the West, make a living? Give evidence from the story to explain your answer.

4. Why did Jimmy Wells send a plainclothes man to deal with his friend? What does this action tell you about Jimmy's character and personality?

5. If you were in a situation similar to that of Jimmy Wells in this story, what would you do? Give reasons for your answer.

Reading Literature: Short Stories

1. **Understanding Mood.** You would probably not characterize this as a happy or cheerful story. Read the first paragraph again. Look for descriptions of setting that set the gloomy mood of the story. How do these descriptions fit the events?

2. **Explaining Conflict.** The main conflict in the story takes place inside Jimmy Wells. List the two loyalties Jimmy Wells feels in this story. Explain in your own words why they conflict.

3. **Analyzing the Author's Methods.** "After Twenty Years" contains hints about the ending. However, they are cleverly disguised so that the reader does not easily suspect how the story will turn out.

   Read the following list of quotes from the story. Each is a clue in disguise. For each one, explain how the clue leads to the ending.

a. The man in the doorway struck a match and lit his cigar. The light showed a pale, square-jawed face with keen eyes, and a little white scar near his right eyebrow.

b. "Did pretty well out West, didn't you?" asked the policeman.

c. "Hope your friend comes around all right. Going to call time on him sharp?"

d. "You've changed lots, Jimmy. I never thought you were so tall by two or three inches."

e. "I have a position in one of the city departments."

4. **Understanding Colloquial Expressions.** In "After Twenty Years," the characters use **colloquial expressions**. That is, they use the informal words and phrases of everyday conversation. Jimmy Wells and Silky Bob do not speak formal English. Their conversation is colorful. Their expressions often grow out of their situations.

   It is not always easy to understand colloquial expressions. For example, you may be unfamiliar with the following colloquial expression. In relation to the story, what do you think it means?

   Jimmy was careful not to *spill the beans* when he talked to Bob.

   Review the following quotes from the story. Each uses colloquial expression. Use details from the story to figure out what each passage means. On your paper, write an explanation in your own words.

a. The West is a *pretty* big *proposition*.

b. I've had to compete with some of the *sharpest* wits going to get my *pile*.

c. A man gets in a groove in New York. It takes the West *to put a razor-edge on* him.

d. Going to *call time* on him sharp?

e. It's been *bully*. It has given me everything I asked it for.

Developing Vocabulary Skills

Using Comparison and Contrast Clues. On pages 236, you learned that comparison clues show how a new word is like a familiar word. In this example, the new word is underlined and the familiar word is italicized.

This <u>conflagration</u> is bigger than the *fire* of 1800.

You also learned that contrast clues show how a new word is unlike a familiar one. The following sentence is an example.

The coach was <u>agitated</u> with the call, but he remained *calm* in front of the team.

Read the following sentences about the stories you have read. Figure out the meaning of each underlined word by using a comparison or contrast clue. On your paper, write any key words, the type of clue, and the meaning of each underlined word.

1. The policeman's actions that night were <u>habitual</u>, as regular as any other night on duty.

2. His hand was steady when he began to read, but it <u>trembled</u> when he finished.

3. A <u>trifle</u> started the feud between the families. It was the same as the small incidents that start many quarrels.

4. The <u>malice</u> Ivan felt against Gabriel was like Gabriel's bad feelings toward Ivan.

5. The Princess's lover was not part of the royal family. He was a <u>commoner</u>.

6. The weddings in the arena were <u>hilarious</u>. They were different from serious marriage ceremonies.

Developing Writing Skills

1. **Writing a Character Analysis.** A character's actions should grow out of the character's personality. In the story, Jimmy and Bob must have been good friends. They each kept a twenty-year-old promise to meet. Something even stronger than friendship must have motivated Jimmy to turn in his friend. What motivated Jimmy Wells? Decide whether or not Jimmy Wells's actions fit his personality. Write two paragraphs to explain your ideas.

Pre-Writing. First, try to summarize Jimmy Wells's character traits. Make a list of details given by the author to describe Jimmy Wells.

Next, think about Jimmy's actions in having Bob arrested. Was it a hard decision for Jimmy to turn his old friend over to the police? Did the decision take very long to make? What clues does the author give to suggest the answers?

Writing. In the first paragraph you write, describe Jimmy Wells before his meeting with Bob. Tell what he looks like, how he acts, how he fits in with his surroundings.

In the second paragraph, explain Jimmy's decision to have Bob arrested. Tell why this was a logical action. Show how Jimmy's personality supports the decision he made.

Revising. Read your first paragraph again. Does it present a clear description of Jimmy

Wells? Read the second paragraph. Does the second paragraph agree with the ideas in the first? If not, you need to revise your writing. The ideas should build on one another. The explanation should have unity.

2. **Setting a Mood.** A good writer introduces and then develops the mood, or feeling, of a story. One way to introduce the mood of a story is through the setting. In "After Twenty Years," the time is late at night. The scene is an empty street. There is a cold rain and it is windy. The mood introduced by the author is a gloomy one.

Write a paragraph in which you describe a scene. Tell details of the time and place that will communicate a mood. Choose a mood different from that in the story. Try to set the stage so that a reader can feel the effects of the setting.

Developing Skills in Study and Research

1. **Understanding Types of Newspaper Articles.** In the story, Bob is suspected of becoming rich illegally. If this were a true story, information about his crimes could have been found in the newspaper. Daily newspapers are one source of information about current events.

In a newspaper, there are two main types of articles about events. **Informational** articles, sometimes called news articles, present facts about current events. These articles give information about who, what, when, and where. **Editorial** articles present opinions about current events. These articles often give the writer's ideas about why something happened. Often the name of the writer of an editorial article will be given.

Obtain a copy of a recent newspaper from your city or region. If you cannot find one, use a copy available in the library. You will notice that the newspaper is divided into different sections.

List the title of each section on your paper. Sometimes there will be a letter name for each section as well. For example, Section C in the paper may be Sports. Then, select one section. Skim through that section. Decide how many articles in the section are informational and how many are editorial. Remember, informational articles give only the facts. Editorial articles also include the writer's opinion. Next to the section title on your paper, write *Mostly Informational* or *Mostly Editorial*.

2. **Using the Newspaper.** Skim the sections of a newspaper to find an example of each of the following. For each informational article, write the section name. For each editorial article, write the section name and the writer's name.

   a. an informational article about national or world news
   b. an editorial article about sports
   c. an editorial article about local news
   d. an editorial article about a movie, play, or television show
   e. an informational article about the weather

Charles

SHIRLEY JACKSON

When Laurie starts school, his relationship with his parents changes. Look for clues in the story that support this statement. What does Laurie do to deal with the big change in his life?

The day my son Laurie started kindergarten, he gave up his little-boy clothes and began wearing blue jeans with a belt. I watched him go off that first morning with the older girl next door, looking as though he were going off to a fight.

He came home the same way at lunchtime. "Isn't anybody here?" he yelled. At the table, he knocked over his little sister's milk.

"How was school today?" I asked. "Did you learn anything?"

"I didn't learn nothing," he said.

"Anything," I said. "Didn't learn anything."

"But the teacher spanked a boy," Laurie said, "for being fresh."

"What did he do?" I asked. "Who was it?"

Laurie thought. "It was Charles," he said. "The teacher spanked him and made him stand in the corner. He was really fresh."

"What did he do?" I asked. But Laurie slid off his chair, took a cookie, and left.

The next day, Laurie remarked at lunch, "Charles was bad again today." He grinned. "Today Charles hit the teacher," he said.

"Good heavens," I said. "I suppose he got spanked again?"

"He sure did," Laurie said.

"Why did Charles hit the teacher?" I asked.

"Because she tried to make him color with red crayons. Charles wanted to color with green crayons, so he hit the teacher. She spanked him and said nobody play with Charles, but everybody did."

The third day, Charles bounced a seesaw onto the head of a little girl and made her bleed. The teacher made him stay inside during recess.

On Thursday, Charles had to stand in a corner, because he was pounding his feet on the floor during story time. Friday, Charles could not use the blackboard because he threw chalk.

On Saturday, I talked to my husband about it. "Do you think kindergarten is too disturbing for Laurie?" I asked him. "This Charles boy sounds like a bad influence."

"It will be all right," my husband said. "There are bound to be people like Charles in the world. He might as well meet them now as later."

On Monday, Laurie came home late. "Charles!" he shouted, as he ran up to the house. "Charles was bad again!"

I let him in and helped him take off his coat. "You know what Charles did?" he demanded. "Charles yelled so much that the teacher came in from first grade. She said our teacher had to keep Charles quiet. And so Charles had to stay after school, and all the children stayed to watch him."

"What did he do?" I asked.

"He just sat there," Laurie said, noticing his father. "Hi, Pop, you old dust mop."

"What does this Charles look like?" my husband asked. "What's his last name?"

"He's bigger than me," Laurie said, "and he doesn't wear a jacket."

I could hardly wait for the first Parent-Teacher meeting. I wanted very much to meet Charles's mother. The meeting was still a week away.

On Tuesday, Laurie said, "Our teacher had a friend come to see her in school today."

My husband and I said together, "Was it Charles's mother?"

"Naaah," Laurie said. "It was a man who came and made us do exercises, like this." He jumped off his chair and touched his toes. Then he sat down again. "Charles didn't even do exercises."

"Didn't he want to?" I asked.

"Naah," Laurie said. "Charles was so fresh to the teacher's friend, they wouldn't let him do exercises."

"Fresh again?" I said.

"He kicked the teacher's friend," Laurie said. "The teacher's friend told Charles to touch his toes, and Charles kicked him."

"What do you think they'll do about Charles?" my husband asked.

"I don't know," Laurie said. "Throw him out of school, I guess."

Wednesday and Thursday were routine. Charles yelled during story time and hit a boy in the stomach and made him cry. On Friday, Charles stayed after school again, and so did all the other children.

On Monday of the third week, Laurie came home with another report. "You know what Charles did today?" he demanded. "He told a girl to say a word, and she said it. The teacher washed her mouth out with soap, and Charles laughed."

"What word?" his father asked.

"It's so bad, I'll have to whisper it to you," Laurie said and whispered into my husband's ear.

"Charles told the little girl to say that?" he said, his eyes widening.

"She said it twice," Laurie said. "Charles told her to say it twice."

"What happened to Charles?" my husband asked.

"Nothing," Laurie said. "He was passing out the crayons."

The next day, Charles said the evil word himself three or four times and got his

Family (detail), 1970, PÀBLO PICASSO. Museum Picasso, Paris. Courtesy of Art Resource, New York.

mouth washed out with soap each time. He also threw chalk.

My husband came to the door that night as I was leaving for the Parent-Teacher meeting. "Invite her over after the meeting," he said. "I want to get a look at the mother of that kid."

"I hope she's there," I said.

"She'll be there," my husband said. "How could they hold a Parent-Teacher meeting without Charles's mother?"

At the meeting, I looked over the faces of all the other mothers. None of them looked unhappy enough to be the mother of Charles. No one stood up and apologized for the way her son had been acting. No one mentioned Charles.

After the meeting, I found Laurie's teacher. "I've been so anxious to meet you," I said. "I'm Laurie's mother."

"Oh, yes," she said. "We're all so interested in Laurie."

"He certainly likes kindergarten," I said. "He talks about it all the time."

"He's had some trouble getting used to school," she said, "but he'll be all right."

"Laurie usually adjusts quickly," I said. "I suppose his trouble might be from Charles's influence."

"Charles?" the teacher said.

"Yes," I said, laughing, "You must have your hands full with Charles."

"Charles?" she said. "We don't have any Charles in the kindergarten."

Developing Comprehension Skills

1. What did Laurie think about his first day of school?

2. Laurie comes home from school each day with a list of bad things that Charles has done. What seems to be Laurie's attitude toward Charles and his activities? Give evidence to support your answer.

3. At the end of the story, we find out that there is no Charles in Laurie's class. Who was Laurie talking about when he described Charles's activities?

4. Do you think Laurie was having a normal reaction to kindergarten? Give reasons for your opinion.

Reading Literature: Short Stories

1. **Recognizing Foreshadowing.** In the first paragraph of the story, Laurie's mother sends him off to school in jeans and "looking as though he were going off to a fight." This introduction turns out to be **foreshadowing**. That is, it gives a hint about how Laurie will approach school. What later action or actions does it foreshadow?

2. **Understanding Tone.** The tone of a story is the attitude of the narrator toward the material he or she is presenting. Do you think that the tone of "Charles" is serious or humorous? Give some evidence to support your answer.

3. **Making Inferences About a Character.** The reader learns about Laurie's mother by her reactions to Laurie's stories. However, the author does not reveal how Laurie's mother reacted to the teacher's statement that there was no Charles in class. Tell how you think Laurie's mother felt when she heard that information. Give evidence from the story to show that your opinion about Laurie's mother is probably correct.

4. **Understanding Surprise Endings.** In this chapter you have read four short stories with unexpected endings. "The Lady, or the Tiger?" really has no ending. In "A Spark Neglected," a change in one of the characters causes the story to end differently than the reader may have expected. In "After Twenty Years" and "Charles," the surprise comes from a new piece of information presented at the end. Which of these three types of endings was most surprising to you? Which did you like best? Which did you like least? Give reasons for your answers.

Developing Vocabulary Skills

Using Example Clues. In some example clues, a familiar word may be given as an example of the unfamiliar word. In others, the unfamiliar word is given as an example of a familiar one. A list of key words for example clues is on page 237. The following sentence gives example clues for the word *arachnids*:

> He was afraid of spiders, scorpions, and other arachnids.

Read the following sentences. Each uses a context clue to define a word from the stories you have read. Some sentences use example clues. Others use definition or restatement clues. Decide which type of clue helps you figure out the meaning of each underlined word: *example clue* or *definition or restatement clue*. Write the type of clue, the key word, and the meaning of the word on your paper.

1. During that time, one kind of beating or punishment was <u>flogging</u>.

2. Several <u>obstacles</u> made his journey difficult, especially the bitter cold, the loss of his compass, and the lack of food.

3. To the teacher, schooldays were <u>routine</u>. That is, they did not vary from day to day.

4. Silky Bob's tone of voice revealed excessive pride, <u>egotism</u>, and other boastful feelings.

5. The <u>fiercest</u>, or wildest, tiger would be placed behind one of the doors.

6. The <u>dismal</u>, dreary, and otherwise gloomy nature of the room was obvious.

Developing Writing Skills

1. **Analyzing Plot Structure.** The climax, or peak of action, comes at the very end of this story. The falling action and resolution take place in the reader's mind. The reader must stop and think about the fact that there is no Charles in Laurie's class. He or she must figure out how that fact affects the rest of the story.

   If the falling action and resolution had been written, what would they reveal? Why is the story more effective and more humorous without these parts of the story? Write a paragraph answering these two questions.

2. **Changing the Point of View.** In "Charles," the narrator tells about the thoughts of Laurie's parents. However, the narrator does not reveal much about the teacher's thoughts or Laurie's thoughts. Select one of these characters. Retell part of the story from his or her point of view. Use first-person narration.

   Pre-Writing. Select one episode, or event, from the story. Decide whether to focus on Laurie or on his teacher. List the main action in that part of the story. Include the thoughts of the character you chose. Do not list other characters' thoughts. The ideas you present will be different from those revealed by the writer of the story.

   Writing. Limit your writing to two or three paragraphs about the event. Remember to use first-person point of view. That is, make sure the narrator is in the story. The character will refer to himself or herself as *I* or *me*. Present the thoughts of the character you selected.

   Revising. Ask another person to read your paragraphs. Can the person tell from which character's point of view you wrote? If not, you need to rewrite that section of your story. Reveal only what one character knows.

Developing Skills in Study and Research

Using The Readers' Guide. In the story you have just read, the main character has difficulty adjusting to school. One way to find information about students and education is to read magazines, also called periodicals. There is a library resource that will help you locate information in periodicals. *The Readers' Guide to Periodical Literature* lists the titles of articles in a large number of widely-selling magazines. The *Guide* is published each month and lists articles published during the last month. At the end of every three months, and at the end of the year, the monthly indexes are combined for easier reference.

Find a recent volume of *The Readers' Guide* in the library. Do the following research.

1. Locate the page at the front of the volume that explains the symbols and abbreviations used in *The Readers' Guide*. Write down the meaning for each of the following symbols and abbreviations.

   a. il   c. 6:46–7   e. pors
   b. Sat R   d. Ap   f. F'79

2. Look in *The Readers' Guide* under the subject heading for *Education*. Try to find the title of an article about students' viewpoints of education. If you cannot find one, choose an article on a related topic. Write down the volume and date of *The Readers' Guide* in which you found the entry. Then write down the following information.

   a. the title of the article
   b. the title of the periodical in which the article appears
   c. the volume number and date of that issue of the periodical
   d. the page numbers of the article

Developing Skills in Speaking and Listening

Reading a Dialog. Select one of the following passages. Decide what mood the dialog is meant to express. Then, work with a partner. Prepare to read the dialog aloud. Adjust your speed of reading to sound like a normal conversation. Try to express the mood of the story in your voice.

1. Laurie tells his mother about his first day at school. (page 259)

2. Laurie talks with his mother about his second day at school. (page 259)

3. Laurie tells his parents about Charles staying after school. (page 260)

4. Laurie tells his parents about the visitor who did exercises. (page 260)

5. Laurie tells his father about the girl who said a bad word. (page 261)

Great Modern Stories

All the myths and legends in Chapters 1, 2, and 3 are about super-human or heroic characters. The characters in these modern short stories are much more like normal human beings. Still, each character is remarkable in some way. As you read the stories, look for qualities that make each character unique and memorable.

The Blind Singers, 1913, ROBERT HENRI. Hirshhorn Museum and Sculpture Garden, Smithsonian Institution, Washington, D.C.

Reading Literature: More About Short Stories

More About the Elements of a Short Story

You have learned about three necessary elements in a short story: characters, plot, and setting. You have learned that the way the writer develops the plot creates suspense. Now you will learn more about different types of characters and different types of conflicts. In addition, you will learn about three other elements you will find in every story: narrator, point of view, and theme.

Characters. A short story can have as few as one or two characters. Even when it has more characters, only one or two are important. The important characters are called the **major characters**. Everyone else in the story is a **minor character**. In "After Twenty Years," for example, and in "Charles," there are only two major characters. In "The Lady or the Tiger?," you might say that the only major character is the Princess. Her father and her lover are mentioned only because their actions led to her struggle to make a decision.

If a character changes during the story, he or she is called a **dynamic character**. Gordy in "A Spark Neglected" is an example. If the character does not change, he or she is called a **static character**. An example of this type of character is Gordy's father.

Conflict. Almost every plot involves a conflict, or struggle between two forces. Usually, the introduction in the story lets the reader know what the conflict is. The rising action shows the struggle becoming more and more intense. Often, at the climax, the main character makes a decision or discovery that determines how the conflict will end. The falling action and resolution then show the conflict being settled.

There are several kinds of conflict, and a story may have more than one. The main character may come into conflict with another character, as in "A Spark Neglected." The main character may struggle against the forces of nature or society, as in "All Summer in a Day." These conflicts with forces outside the character are called **external conflicts**. The main character may also experience **internal conflict**, a struggle with opposing feelings. An example is in "Lather and Nothing Else."

Narrator. The person telling the story is called the **narrator**. Often the narrator is a character in the story. Then the reader learns about the narrator from what he or she does in the story. Other times the narrator is outside the story, explaining the events. Then the reader may learn about the narrator from his or her comments on the events.

Point of View. Point of view refers to the way the narrator tells the story. If the narrator is a character in the story, the story is told in the **first-person point of view**. The narrator uses the first-person pronouns *I* and *me*. "Raymond's Run" is an example.

If the narrator is outside the story, the story is told in the **third-person point of view**. The narrator uses the third-person pronouns *he,* *she,* and *they* to talk about the characters. If the narrator can see into all the characters' minds, then the writer has used the **third-person omniscient point of view**. An example is "The Lady, or the Tiger?" If the narrator is limited to understanding only one character's thoughts, then the writer has used the **third-person limited point of view**. For example, in the story "The Weapon," the reader learns of only Graham's thoughts and feelings.

Theme. In every story, a writer expresses some opinion or shows a concern for some topic. For example, in "A Spark Neglected," Tolstoy was arguing against revenge. In "After Twenty Years," O. Henry was concerned about the conflict between friendship and duty. The idea or concern that the writer presents in a short story is its **theme**.

Often a story may have more than one theme. Different readers may see different themes. In "A Spark Neglected," for example, a second important theme is the need to respect older people.

Usually, it is not difficult to identify one or more of the themes of a story. Ask yourself why the writer included the descriptions and events he or she chose. Remember that every detail in a short story is there for a reason. Also, it is helpful to compare and contrast stories. The differences between two stories point out the differences in themes.

A Man Who Had No Eyes

MacKINLAY KANTOR

In this story, there is a chance meeting between two characters. Each quickly forms an impression of the other. As you read, look for how they learn more about each other. Do their first impressions change?

A beggar was coming down the avenue just as Mr. Parsons emerged from his hotel.

He was a blind beggar, carrying the traditional battered cane and thumping his way before him with the cautious, half-furtive effort of the sightless. He was a shaggy, thick-necked fellow; his coat was greasy about the lapels and pockets, and his hand splayed over the cane's crook with a futile sort of clinging. He wore a black pouch slung over his shoulder. Apparently he had something to sell.

The air was rich with spring; the sun was warm and yellowed on the asphalt. Mr. Parsons, standing there in front of his hotel and noting the clack-clack approach of the sightless man, felt a sudden and foolish sort of pity for all blind creatures.

Also, thought Mr. Parsons, he was very glad to be alive. A few years ago he had been little more than a skilled laborer; now he was successful, respected, admired. . . . Insurance. . . . And he had done it alone, unaided, struggling beneath handicaps. . . .

And he was still young. The blue air of spring, fresh from its memories of windy pools and lush shrubbery, could thrill him with eagerness.

He took a step forward just as the tap-tapping blind man passed him by. Quickly the shabby fellow turned.

"Listen, guv'nor. Just a minute of your time."

Mr. Parsons said, "It's late. I have an appointment. Do you want me to give you something?"

"I ain't no beggar, guv'nor. You bet I ain't. I got a handy little article here"—he fumbled until he could press a small object into Mr. Parsons's hand—"that I sell. One buck. Best cigarette lighter made."

Mr. Parsons stood there, somewhat annoyed and embarrassed. He was handsome with his immaculate gray suit and gray hat and walking stick. Of course the man with the cigarette lighters could not see him. . . . "But I don't smoke," he said.

"Listen. I bet you know plenty people who smoke. Nice little present," wheedled the man. "And mister, you wouldn't mind helping a poor guy out?" He clung to Mr. Parsons's sleeve as he waited for the answer.

Mr. Parsons sighed and felt in his vest pocket. He brought out two half dollars and pressed them into the man's hand. "Certainly. I'll help you out. As you say, I can give it to someone. Maybe the elevator boy would—" He hesitated, not wishing to be boorish and inquisitive, even with a blind peddler. "Have you lost your sight entirely?"

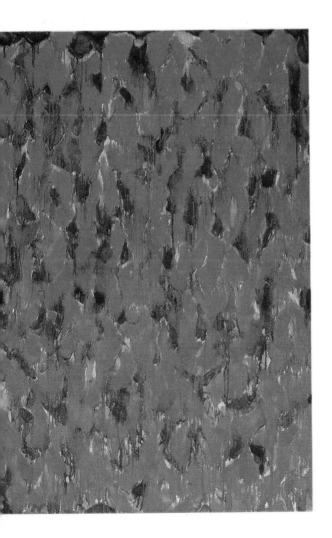

The shabby man pocketed the two half dollars. "Fourteen years, guv'nor." Then he added, with an insane sort of pride, "Westbury, sir. I was one of 'em."

"Westbury," repeated Mr. Parsons. "Ah, yes. The chemical explosion. . . . The papers haven't mentioned it for years. But at the time it was supposed to be one of the greatest disasters in—"

"They've all forgot about it." The fellow shifted his feet wearily. "I tell you, guv'nor, a man who was in it don't forget about it. Last thing I ever saw was C shop going up in one grand smudge and that awful gas pouring in at all the busted windows."

Mr. Parsons coughed, but the blind peddler was caught up with the train of his one dramatic reminiscence. Also, he was thinking that there might be more half dollars in Mr. Parsons's pocket.

"Just think about it, guv'nor. There was a hundred and eight people killed, about two hundred injured, and over fifty of them lost their eyes. Blind as bats—" He groped forward until his dirty hand rested against Mr. Parsons's coat. "I tell you, sir, there wasn't nothing worse than that in the war. If I had lost my eyes in the war, okay. I would have been well took care of. But I was just a workman, working for what was in it. And I got it. You're so right I got it, while the capitalists were making their dough! They was insured, don't worry about that. They—"

Red No. 1, 1953, SAM FRANCIS. Collection of Marie-Hélène and Guy Weill, Scarsdale, New York.

"Insured," repeated his listener. "Yes. That's what I sell—"

"You want to know how I lost my eyes?" cried the man. "Well, here it is!" His words fell with the bitter and studied drama of a story often told, and told for money. "I was there in C shop, last of all the folks rushing out. Out in the air there was a chance, even with buildings exploding right and left. A lot of guys made it safe out the door and got away. And just when I was about there, crawling along between those big vats, a guy behind me grabs my leg. He says, 'Let me past, you—!' Maybe he was nuts. I dunno. I try to forgive him in my heart, guv'nor. But he was bigger than me. He hauls me back and climbs right over me! Tramples me into the dirt. And he gets out, and I lie there with all that poison gas pouring down on all sides of me, and flame and stuff. . . ." He swallowed—a studied sob—and stood dumbly expectant. He could imagine the next words: Tough luck, my man. Awfully tough. Now, I want to—
"That's the story, guv'nor."

The spring wind shrilled past them, damp and quivering.

"Not quite," said Mr. Parsons.

The blind peddler shivered crazily. "Not quite? What do you mean, you—?"

"The story is true," Mr. Parsons said, "except that it was the other way around."

"Other way around?" He croaked unamiably. "Say, guv'nor—"

"I was in C shop," said Mr. Parsons. "It was the other way around. You were the fellow who hauled back on me and climbed over me. You were bigger than I was, Markwardt."

The blind man stood for a long time, swallowing hoarsely. He gulped: "Parsons. By heaven! By heaven! I thought you—" And then he screamed fiendishly: "Yes. Maybe so. Maybe so. But I'm blind! I'm blind, and you've been standing here letting me spout to you, and laughing at me every minute! I'm blind!"

People in the street turned to stare at him.

"You got away, but I'm blind! Do you hear! I'm—"

"Well," said Mr. Parsons, "don't make such a row about it, Markwardt. So am I."

Developing Comprehension Skills

1. Mr. Parsons seems quite satisfied with his life. List at least two reasons he gives for feeling this way.

2. How does Mr. Parsons feel about being stopped by the beggar?

3. At what point in the story do you think Mr. Parsons recognizes the beggar as Mr. Markwardt? How does recognizing the beggar affect Mr. Parson's attitude toward him?

4. Do you feel sympathy for Mr. Markwardt? Why or why not?

Reading Literature: Short Stories

1. **Identifying Characterization.** Write three headings on your paper: *Physical Descriptions*, *Words Describing Actions or Speech*, and *Actions That Took Place Before the Story*. Under each heading make two columns. Label one *Parsons* and the other *Markwardt*. Review the story for details about the characters. Try to list at least two descriptions of each character in each of the three columns.

2. **Inferring the Theme.** A short story reveals a **theme**, or main idea about life. In this story, Parsons and Markwardt have similar handicaps. Think about how each character deals with his blindness. What theme is suggested by their reactions?

3. **Understanding Point of View.** In the story "A Man Who Had No Eyes," the narrator knows more than the characters know. For example, the narrator describes how the characters look. However, neither character in the story knows how the other looks, because both are blind. Suppose the story were told from the viewpoint of one of the characters. What extra information might the reader know? What information would be missing?

Developing Vocabulary Skills

Using Context Clues. Each of the following sentences contains a word from the story that may be unfamiliar to you. Determine the meaning of the underlined word. Use one of these context clues: *definition or restatement, synonym, comparison,* or *contrast*. On your paper, write the type of clue and the meaning of each word.

1. Mr. Parsons walked out the hotel door. Just as he emerged onto the street, a beggar walked by.

2. The man moved furtively, like a person who does not want others to know what he is doing.

3. Her clothing was recently cleaned and had not a speck of dirt or lint on it. In short, it was immaculate.

4. The beggar was shabby, in contrast to the neat appearance of Mr. Parsons.

5. The capitalists—that is, the owners of the factory—were insured.

6. The man had spoken in a friendly way until then, but now his voice took on a clearly unamiable tone.

7. The new clerk was boorish, the same as the other insensitive employees at the store.

Developing Writing Skills

1. **Writing About Unstated Ideas.** Much of what happens in this story is not part of the

outward action. Instead, the story is based on **internal action**—that is, thoughts in the characters' minds. Select either Mr. Parsons or Mr. Markwardt. Write a paragraph explaining the meeting on the sidewalk. Tell about the thoughts going through the character's mind.

Pre-Writing. Review the story. List the outward actions of the character. Also list any thoughts of the character that the narrator directly states.

Based on the information stated in the story, figure out what else the character must be thinking. For example, Mr. Parsons is probably very surprised when Mr. Markwardt mentions Westbury. However, the narrator does not tell you so. Try to imagine what else is going through the character's mind. List these unstated thoughts on your paper. Also list a detail from the story that supports each of your ideas.

Writing. Begin your paragraph with a sentence identifying the character. Then explain the thoughts you think the character has. Try to show how each thought builds on what has come before. Use key words such as *because*, *therefore*, and *as a result*.

Revising. Read your paragraph. Check that your topic sentence is clear. Be sure that you have given at least three examples of the character's unstated thoughts. Do the sentences in your paragraph build on one another? If not, you may need to reorganize them. Or you may need to add key words to signal the relationship of ideas.

2. **Portraying Feelings.** Imagine that you are Mr. Markwardt. How do you feel about having to sell cigarette lighters on the street?

How do you feel about having lost your sight in a factory explosion? How do you feel knowing that no one remembers the tragedy? Do you feel better or worse after meeting Mr. Parsons again? Write one or two paragraphs expressing your reactions. Try to write in the same way that Mr. Markwardt talked.

Developing Skills in Critical Thinking

Identifying Facts in an Argument. In this story Mr. Markwardt tries to persuade Mr. Parsons to give him money. Mr. Parsons, however, realizes that Mr. Markwardt's argument is not based on fact.

A **fact** is a statement that can be proven. Here is an example:

MacKinlay Kantor wrote the story, "A Man Who Had No Eyes."

A fact differs from an opinion, which explains a personal view. What word makes the following statement an opinion?

"A Man Who Had No Eyes" is a sad story.

A fact also differs from a statement that appeals to emotion:

You would be proud to be a man like Mr. Parsons.

A good argument is built on facts, not opinions or appeals to emotions.

Advertisements are arguments that attempt to convince you to buy products. Find a magazine or newspaper advertisement for a product. Read the ad carefully. What reasons does it give for buying the product? How many of the reasons are facts?

Thank You, M'am

LANGSTON HUGHES

This story begins with a crime. Do you think the victim does the right things? As you read, think about how you would react in this situation.

She was a large woman with a large purse that had everything in it but a hammer and nails. It had a long strap, and she carried it slung across her shoulder. It was about eleven o'clock at night, dark, and she was walking alone, when a boy ran up behind her and tried to snatch her purse. The strap broke with the sudden single tug the boy gave it from behind. But the boy's weight and the weight of the purse combined caused him to lose his balance. Instead of taking off full blast as he had hoped, the boy fell on his back on the sidewalk and his legs flew up. The large woman simply turned around and kicked him right square in his blue-jeaned sitter. Then she reached down, picked the boy up by his shirt front, and shook him until his teeth rattled.

After that the woman said, "Pick up my pocketbook, boy, and give it here."

She still held him tightly. But she bent down enough to permit him to stoop and pick up her purse. Then she said, "Now ain't you ashamed of yourself?"

Firmly gripped by his shirt front, the boy said, "Yes'm."

The woman said, "What did you want to do it for?"

The boy said, "I didn't aim to."

She said, "You a lie!"

By that time two or three people passed, stopped, turned to look, and some stood watching.

"If I turn you loose, will you run?" asked the woman.

"Yes'm," said the boy.

"Then I won't turn you loose," said the woman. She did not release him.

"Lady, I'm sorry," whispered the boy.

"Um-hum. Your face is dirty. I got a mind to wash your face. Ain't you got nobody home to tell you to wash your face?"

"No'm," said the boy.

"Then it will get washed this evening," said the large woman, starting up the street, dragging the frightened boy behind her.

He looked as if he were fourteen or fifteen, frail and willow-wild, in tennis shoes and blue jeans.

The woman said, "You ought to be my son. I would teach you right from wrong. Least I can do right now is to wash your face. Are you hungry?"

"No'm," said the being-dragged boy. "I just want you to turn me loose."

"Was I bothering you when I turned that corner?" asked the woman.

"No'm."

"But you put yourself in contact with me," said the woman. "If you think that that contact is not going to last awhile, you got another thought coming. When I get through with you, sir, you are going to remember Mrs. Luella Bates Washington Jones."

Sweat popped out on the boy's face, and he began to struggle. Mrs. Jones stopped, jerked him around in front of her, put a half nelson[1] about his neck, and continued to drag him up the street. When she got to her door, she dragged the boy inside, down a hall, and into a large kitchenette-furnished room at the rear of the house. She switched on the light and left the door open. The boy could hear other roomers laughing and talking in the large house. Some of their doors were open, too, so he knew that he and the woman were not alone. The woman still had him by the neck in the middle of her room.

She said, "What is your name?"

"Roger," answered the boy.

"Then, Roger, you go to that sink and wash your face," said the woman, where-

---

1. **half nelson**, a wrestling hold

upon she turned him loose—at last. Roger looked at the door—looked at the woman—looked at the door—and went to the sink.

"Let the water run until it gets warm," she said. "Here's a clean towel."

"You gonna take me to jail?" asked the boy, bending over the sink.

"Not with that face; I would not take you nowhere," said the woman. "Here I am trying to get home to cook me a bite to eat, and you snatch my pocketbook! Maybe you ain't been to your supper either, late as it be. Have you?"

"There's nobody home at my house," said the boy.

"Then we'll eat," said the woman. "I believe you're hungry—or been hungry—to try to snatch my pocketbook!"

"I want a pair of blue suede shoes," said the boy.

"Well, you didn't have to snatch my pocketbook to get some suede shoes," said Mrs. Luella Bates Washington Jones. "You could of asked me."

"M'am?"

The water dripping from his face, the boy looked at her. There was a long pause. A very long pause. After he had dried his face, and, not knowing what else to do, dried it again, the boy turned around, wondering what next. The door was open. He could make a dash for it down the hall. He could run, run, run, run!

The woman was sitting on the day bed. After a while she said, "I were young once and I wanted things I could not get."

There was another long pause. The boy's mouth opened. Then he frowned, not knowing he frowned.

The woman said, "Um-hum! You thought I was going to say 'but,' didn't you? You thought I was going to say, 'but I didn't snatch people's pocketbooks.' Well, I wasn't going to say that." Pause. Silence. "I have done things, too, which I would not tell you, son—neither tell God, if He didn't

Black Manhattan, 1969, ROMARE BEARDEN. Collection of Mr. and Mrs. Theodore Kheel, New York.

already know. Everybody's got something in common. So you set down while I fix us something to eat. You might run that comb through your hair so you will look presentable."

In another corner of the room, behind a screen, was a gas plate and an icebox. Mrs. Jones got up and went behind the screen. The woman did not watch the boy to see if he was going to run now, nor did she watch her purse, which she left behind her on the day bed. But the boy took care to sit on the far side of the room, away from the purse, where he thought she could easily see him out of the corner of her eye if she wanted to. He did not trust the woman not to trust him. And he did not want to be mistrusted now.

"Do you need somebody to go to the store," asked the boy, "maybe to get some milk or something?"

"Don't believe I do," said the woman, "unless you just want sweet milk yourself. I was going to make cocoa out of this canned milk I got here."

"That will be fine," said the boy.

She heated some lima beans and ham she had in the icebox, made the cocoa, and set the table. The woman did not ask the boy anything about where he lived, or his folks, or anything else that would embarrass him. Instead, as they ate, she told him about her job in a hotel beauty shop that stayed open late, what the work was like, and how all kinds of women came in and out, blondes, redheads, and Spanish. Then she cut him a half of her ten-cent cake.

"Eat some more, son," she said.

When they were finished eating, she got up and said, "Now here, take this ten dollars and buy yourself some blue suede shoes. Next time, do not make the mistake of latching onto my pocketbook nor nobody else's—because shoes got by devilish ways will burn your feet. I got to get my rest now. But from here on in, son, I hope you will behave yourself."

She led him down the hall to the front door and opened it. "Good night! Behave yourself, boy!" she said, looking out into the street as he went down the steps.

The boy wanted to say something other than, "Thank you, m'am," to Mrs. Luella Bates Washington Jones; but although his lips moved, he couldn't even say that as he turned at the foot of the barren stoop and looked up at the large woman in the door. Then she shut the door.

Developing Comprehension Skills

1. What argument did Mrs. Jones give Roger for dragging him down the street to her house?

2. The way Mrs. Jones treated Roger at first made him feel frightened. What did she say that changed his fright to surprise?

3. Mrs. Jones told Roger, "When I get through with you, sir, you are going to remember Mrs. Luella Bates Washington Jones." When you were reading the story for the first time, what did you think Mrs. Jones would do to make Roger remember her? What did Roger think Mrs. Jones was planning to do to make him remember her? What evidence from the story supports your answer?

4. How do you know that Roger ended up respecting Mrs. Jones?

5. Do you think Roger was a bad person? Why or why not?

Reading Literature: Short Stories

1. **Tracing Character Development.** What type of person does Roger seem to be in the first several paragraphs of the story? In what ways does he change by the end of the story? Give specific examples. In your opinion, what causes the changes?

2. **Analyzing a Character.** Think about the character of Mrs. Jones in "Thank You, M'am." Someone has just tried to steal her purse. Does she act the way you would expect? What type of person is she? Describe her qualities. Use evidence from the story to support your statements.

3. **Diagraming the Plot.** The climax of a story involves a change in the action or attitude of a major character. Draw a plot diagram on your paper. Refer to page 249 if you have forgotten the form. Label the following points on the diagram.

> **Introduction:** Mrs. Jones is described as a large woman with a large purse.
> **Rising Action:** Mrs. Jones catches a purse-snatcher.
> **Falling Action:** At the door, Mrs. Jones says "Good night" and tells Roger to behave himself.
> **Resolution:** Roger leaves, unable to say "Thank you."

The climax of the story has not been identified for you. Decide what action or attitude changes in the story. Choose one of the following sentences to identify the climax. Then write the sentence on your diagram to label the climax.

> Roger tries to pull away.
> Roger sees the open door but stays in the room anyway.
> Roger and Mrs. Jones eat dinner.

4. **Understanding Setting.** The setting of this story is important to the plot. For instance, we know that the events take place in a city. Reread the description of Mrs. Jones's apartment. What is her apartment like? Do you think Mrs. Jones is wealthy? How does that affect Roger's reaction to her generosity? Find another part of the setting in this story that affects the plot.

5. **Stating the Theme.** "Thank You, M'am" makes use of irony. **Irony** is the contrast between what is expected and what really happens. You might have expected the theme of this story to reveal that "crime

doesn't pay." In this story, however, it almost seems as if the opposite is true. The writer uses irony to make us think harder about the theme. What do you think is the theme, or main idea about life, in this story?

Developing Vocabulary Skills

Determining Word Meaning. The meaning of an unfamiliar word cannot always be figured out by using context clues or word parts. You must then turn to the dictionary. Each of the following sentences is drawn from the story. Try to determine the meaning of the underlined word from context clues or word parts. If you can, write on your paper *Context Clues*, *Word Parts*, or *Both*. Then write the meaning of the word. If there are no clues, write *Dictionary*.

1. The boy's weight and the weight of the purse <u>combined</u> caused him to lose his balance.

2. "Then, Roger, you go to that sink and wash your face," said the woman, <u>whereupon</u> she turned him loose—at last.

3. "I want a pair of blue <u>suede</u> shoes," said the boy.

4. He did not trust the woman not to trust him. And he did not want to be <u>mistrusted</u> now.

5. "You might run that comb through your hair so you will look <u>presentable</u>."

6. He turned at the foot of the <u>barren</u> stoop and looked up at the large woman in the door.

Developing Writing Skills

1. **Explaining an Opinion.** Think about the way Mrs. Jones treated Roger. Do you think she did the right things? Or should Roger have been punished? Is he likely to snatch anyone else's purse? Why or why not? Write one to two paragraphs giving your opinion of Mrs. Jones's actions.

2. **Writing a Dialog.** In "Thank You, M'am," the reader learns about the character Mrs. Jones from what she says. For example, in the conversation on page 274, we learn that Mrs. Jones is a caring person. She is concerned that Roger has not eaten supper. Dialog, or conversation, is one way to show character. Select one of the following situations, or make up one of your own. Write a dialog between yourself and a friend that fits the situation. Let your statements show what kind of person you are. If you like, you may pretend to be different from your real self.

   a. someone asks you for help on a school assignment

   b. someone tries to give you a kitten or puppy

   c. someone asks your opinion about a movie, book, or record album

   d. someone is upset and you try to calm the person down

   Pre-Writing. First, make a rough outline of the main points of the conversation. Decide whether both speakers will talk the same amount or whether one will say more. Think about what qualities the conversation will reveal about each person. For example, the dialog may show that one person is stubborn and the other flexible.

   Then, review the section of a grammar book that explains the rules for using quotation marks in dialog. Be sure to check the position of commas, end marks, and quotation marks. Remember that a new paragraph begins each time the speaker changes.

Writing. Begin the dialog with a statement or question from the other person. Then write your response. Use *I* and *me* to refer to yourself. Throughout the dialog, switch back and forth between the speakers. Include only words that the people would actually speak. End the conversation with a clear conclusion.

Revising. Find two people to read the dialog aloud. Listen carefully as they read. Make note of any part of the conversation that does not sound smooth and natural. Change any section of the dialog that sounds awkward.

Developing Skills in Study and Research

Outlining Information. You collect information in many situations. For example, you might take notes for a school report or for a project. Notes are most useful when they are organized. One way to organize notes is to put them into an outline form. **Outlining** is a way of organizing information according to main ideas and supporting details.

The form of an outline clearly shows main topics, subtopics, and details. Examine the following example of the pattern used in a formal outline. Notice how numerals and letters are used. Notice how the parts are indented.

TITLE
I. Main topic
  A. Subtopic
    1. Detail relating to A
    2. Second detail relating to A
  B. New subtopic
II. Main topic

Imagine that you are preparing to write a comparison of the characters in "Thank You, M'am." Here are the main topics and some subtopics for an outline for that comparison. Complete the outline with more subtopics and with details.

I. Roger
  A. What he does
  B. What he thinks
II. Mrs. Jones

Raymond's Run

TONI CADE BAMBARA

Listen to Squeaky as she tells this story. What do you learn about her from the way she talks? Decide whether you would want to have her as a friend.

I don't have much work to do around the house like some girls. My mother does that. And I don't have to earn my pocket money by hustling; George runs errands for the big boys and sells Christmas cards. And anything else that's got to get done, my father does. All I have to do in life is mind my brother Raymond, which is enough.

Sometimes I slip and say my "little" brother Raymond. But, as any fool can see, he's much bigger and he's older too. But a lot of people call him my little brother cause he needs looking after cause he's not quite right. And a lot of smart mouths got lots to say about that too, especially when George was minding him. But now, if anybody has anything to say to Raymond, anything to say about his big head,[1] they have to come by me. And I don't play the dozens[2] or believe in standing around with somebody in my face doing a lot of talking. I much rather just knock you down and take my chances even if I am a little girl with skinny arms and a squeaky voice, which is how I got the name Squeaky. And if things get too rough, I run. And as anybody can tell you, I'm the fastest thing on two feet.

There is no track meet that I don't win the first place medal. I used to win the twenty-yard dash when I was a little kid in kindergarten. Nowadays, its the fifty-yard dash. And tomorrow I'm subject to run the quarter-meter relay all by myself and come in first, second, and third. The big kids call me Mercury[3] cause I'm the swiftest thing in the neighborhood. Everybody knows that—except two people who know better, my father and me. He can beat me to Amsterdam Avenue with me having a two fire-hydrant headstart and him running with his hands in his pockets and whistling. But that's private information. Cause can

---

1. **big head,** a result of Raymond's physical problem, hydrocephalus (hi'drə sef'ə ləs), which causes fluid to accumulate within the skull, resulting in an enlargement of the head
2. **play the dozens,** to trade insults in a joking way
3. **Mercury,** Roman name for the Greek god Hermes; see page 9

you imagine some thirty-five-year-old man stuffing himself into shorts to race little kids? So as far as everyone's concerned, I'm the fastest and that goes for Gretchen, too, who has put out the tale that she is going to win the first-place medal this year. Ridiculous. In the second place, she's got short legs. In the third place, she's got freckles. In the first place, no one can beat me and that's all there is to it.

I'm standing on the corner admiring the weather and about to take a stroll down Broadway so I can practice my breathing exercises, and I've got Raymond walking on the inside close to the buildings, cause he's subject to fits of fantasy and starts thinking he's a circus performer and that the curb is a tightrope strung high in the air. And sometimes after a rain he likes to step down off his tightrope right into the gutter and slosh around getting his shoes and cuffs wet. Then I get hit when I come home. Or sometimes if you don't watch him he'll dash across traffic to the island in the middle of Broadway and give the pigeons a fit. Then I have to go behind him apologizing to all the old people sitting around trying to get some sun, and getting all upset with the pigeons fluttering around them, scattering their newspapers and upsetting the waxpaper lunches in their laps. So I keep Raymond on the inside of me, and he plays like he's driving a stage coach which is O.K. by me so long as he doesn't run me over or interrupt my breathing exercises, which I have to do on account of I'm serious about my running, and I don't care who knows it.

Now some people like to act like things come easy to them, won't let on that they practice. Not me. I'll high-prance down 34th Street like a rodeo pony to keep my knees strong even if it does get my mother uptight so that she walks ahead like she's not with me, don't know me, is all by herself on a shopping trip, and I am somebody else's crazy child. Now you take Cynthia Procter for instance. She's just the opposite. If there's a test tomorrow, she'll say something like, "Oh, I guess I'll play handball this afternoon and watch television tonight," just to let you know she ain't thinking about the test. Or like last week when she won the spelling bee for the millionth time, "A good thing you got 'receive,' Squeaky, cause I would have got it wrong. I completely forgot about the spelling bee." And she'll clutch the lace on her blouse like it was a narrow escape. Oh, brother. But of course when I pass her house on my early morning trots around the block, she is practicing the scales on the piano over and over and over and over. Then in music class she always lets herself get bumped around so she falls accidentally on purpose onto the piano stool and is so surprised to find herself sitting there that she decides just for fun to try out the ole keys. And what do you know—Chopin's waltzes just spring out of her fingertips and she's the most surprised thing in the world. A regular prodigy. I could kill people like that. I stay up all night studying the words for the spelling bee. And you can see me any time of day practicing running. I never walk if I can trot, and shame on Raymond if he can't keep up. But of course he does, cause if he hangs back someone's liable to walk up to him and get smart, or take his allowance from him, or ask him where he got that great big pumpkin head. People are so stupid sometimes.

So I'm strolling down Broadway breathing out and breathing in on counts of seven, which is my lucky number, and here comes Gretchen and her sidekicks: Mary Louise, who used to be a friend of mine when she first moved to Harlem from Baltimore and got beat up by everybody till I took up for

Sunny Side of the Street, 1950, PHILIP EVERGOOD. Collection of the Corcoran Gallery of Art, Washington, D.C. Museum Purchase, Anna E. Clark Fund.

her on account of her mother and my mother used to sing in the same choir when they were young girls, but people ain't grateful, so now she hangs out with the new girl Gretchen and talks about me like a dog; and Rosie, who is as fat as I am skinny and has a big mouth where Raymond is concerned and is too stupid to know that there is not a big deal of difference between herself and Raymond and that she can't afford to throw stones. So they are steady coming up Broadway and I see right away that it's going to be one of those Dodge City scenes cause the street ain't that big and they're close to the buildings just as we are. First I think I'll step into the candy store and look over the new comics and let them pass. But that's chicken and I've got a reputation to consider. So then I think I'll just walk straight on through them or even over them if necessary. But as they get to me, they slow down. I'm ready to fight, cause like I said I don't feature a whole lot of chit-chat, I much prefer to just knock you down right from the jump and save everybody a lotta precious time.

"You signing up for the May Day races?" smiles Mary Louise, only it's not a smile at all. A dumb question like that doesn't deserve an answer. Besides, there's just me and Gretchen standing there really, so no use wasting my breath talking to shadows.

"I don't think you're going to win this time," says Rosie, trying to signify with her hands on her hips all salty, completely forgetting that I have whupped her behind many times for less salt than that.

"I always win cause I'm the best," I say straight at Gretchen who is, as far as I'm concerned, the only one talking in this ventriloquist-dummy routine. Gretchen smiles, but it's not a smile, and I'm thinking that girls never really smile at each other because they don't know how and don't want to know how and there's probably no one to teach us how, cause grown-up girls don't know either. Then they all look at Raymond who has just brought his mule team to a standstill. And they're about to see what trouble they can get into through him.

"What grade you in now, Raymond?"

"You got anything to say to my brother, you say it to me, Mary Louise Williams of Raggedy Town, Baltimore."

"What are you, his mother?" sasses Rosie.

"That's right, Fatso. And the next word out of anybody and I'll be their mother too." So they just stand there and Gretchen shifts from one leg to the other and so do they. Then Gretchen puts her hands on her hips and is about to say something with her freckle-face self but doesn't. Then she walks around me looking me up and down but keeps walking up Broadway, and her sidekicks follow her. So me and Raymond smile at each other and he says, "Gidyap" to his team and I continue with my breathing exercises, strolling down Broadway toward the ice man on 145th with not a care in the world cause I am Miss Quicksilver herself.

I take my time getting to the park on May Day because the track meet is the last thing on the program. The biggest thing on the program is the May Pole dancing, which I can do without, thank you, even if my mother thinks it's a shame I don't take part and act like a girl for a change. You'd think my mother'd be grateful not to have to make me a white organdy dress with a big satin sash and buy me new white baby-doll shoes that can't be taken out of the box till the big day. You'd think she'd be glad her daughter ain't out there prancing around a May Pole getting the new clothes all dirty and sweaty and trying to act like a fairy or a flower or whatever you're supposed to be when you should be trying to be yourself, whatever that is, which is, as far as I'm concerned, a poor black girl who really can't afford to buy shoes and a new dress you only wear once a lifetime cause it won't fit next year.

I was once a strawberry in a Hansel and Gretel pageant when I was in nursery school and didn't have no better sense than to dance on tiptoe with my arms in a circle over my head doing umbrella steps and being a perfect fool just so my mother and father could come dressed up and clap. You'd think they'd know better than to encourage that kind of nonsense. I am not a strawberry. I do not dance on my toes. I run. That is what I am all about. So I always come late to the May Day program, just in time to get my number pinned on and lay in the grass until they announce the fifty-yard dash.

I put Raymond in the little swings, which is a tight squeeze this year and will be impossible next year. Then I look around for Mr. Pearson, who pins the numbers on. I'm really looking for Gretchen if you want to know the truth, but she's not around. The park is jam-packed. Parents in hats and corsages and breast-pocket handkerchiefs peeking up. Kids in white dresses and light-blue suits. The parkees unfolding chairs and chasing the rowdy kids from Lenox Avenue as if they had no right to be there. The big guys with their caps on backwards, leaning against the fence swirling the basketballs on the tips of their fingers, waiting for all these crazy people to clear out of the park so they can play. Most of the kids in my class are carrying bass drums and glockenspiels and flutes. You'd think they'd put in a few bongos or something for real like that.

Then here comes Mr. Pearson with his clipboard and his cards and pencils and whistles and safety pins and fifty million other things he's always dropping all over the place with his clumsy self. He sticks out in a crowd because he's on stilts. We used to call him Jack and the Beanstalk to get him mad. But I'm the only one that can out-run him and get away, and I'm too grown up for that silliness now.

"Well, Squeaky," he says, checking my name off the list and handing me number seven and two pins. And I'm thinking he's got no right to call me Squeaky, if I can't call him Beanstalk.

"Hazel Elizabeth Deborah Parker," I correct him and tell him to write it down on his board.

"Well, Hazel Elizabeth Deborah Parker, going to give someone else a break this year?" I squint at him real hard to see if he is seriously thinking I should lose the race on purpose just to give someone else a break. "Only six girls running this time," he continues, shaking his head sadly like it's my fault all of New York didn't turn out in sneakers. "That new girl should give you a run for your money." He looks around the park for Gretchen like a periscope in a submarine movie. "Wouldn't it be a nice gesture if you were . . . to ahhh. . . ."

I give him such a look he couldn't finish putting that idea into words. Grownups got a lot of nerve sometimes. I pin number seven to myself and stomp away, I'm so burnt. And I go straight for the track and stretch out on the grass while the band winds up with "Oh, the Monkey Wrapped His Tail Around the Flag Pole," which my teacher calls by some other name. The man on the loudspeaker is calling everyone over to the track and I'm on my back looking at the sky, trying to pretend I'm in the country, but I can't, because even grass in the city feels hard as sidewalk, and there's just no pretending you are anywhere but in a "concrete jungle," as my grandfather says.

The twenty-yard dash takes all of two minutes cause most of the little kids don't know no better than to run off the track or run the wrong way or run smack into the fence and fall down and cry. One little kid, though, has got the good sense to run straight for the white ribbon up ahead so he wins. Then the second-graders line up for the thirty-yard dash and I don't even bother to turn my head to watch because Raphael Perez always wins. He wins before he even begins by psyching the runners, telling them they're going to trip on their shoelaces and fall on their faces or lose their shorts or something, which he doesn't really have to do since he is very fast, almost as fast as I am. After that is the forty-yard dash, which I use to run when I was in the first grade. Raymond is hollering from the swings cause he knows I'm about to do my thing cause the man on the loudspeaker has just announced the fifty-yard dash, although he might as well be giving a recipe for angel food cake cause you can hardly make out what he's sayin' for the static. I get up and slip off my sweat pants and then I see Gretchen standing at the starting line, kicking her legs out like a pro. Then as I get into place I see that ole Raymond is on line on the other side of the fence, bending down with his fingers on the ground just like he knew what he was doing. I was going to yell at him but then I didn't. It burns up your energy to holler.

Every time, just before I take off in a race, I always feel like I'm in a dream, the kind of dream you have when you're sick with fever and feel all hot and weightless. I dream I'm flying over a sandy beach in the early morning sun, kissing the leaves of the trees as I fly by. And there's always the smell of apples, just like in the country when I was little and used to think I was a choo-choo train, running through the fields of corn and chugging up the hill to the orchard. And all the time I'm dreaming this, I get lighter and lighter until I'm flying over the beach again, getting blown through the sky like a feather that weighs nothing at all. But once I spread my fingers in the dirt and crouch over for the Get on Your Mark, the dream goes and I am solid again and am telling myself, Squeaky, you must win, you must win, you are the fastest thing in the world, you can even beat your father up Amsterdam if you really try. And then I feel my weight coming back just behind my knees and the pistol shot explodes in my blood and I am off and weightless again, flying past the other runners, my arms pumping up and down and the whole world is quiet except for the crunch as I zoom over the gravel in the track. I glance to my left and there is no one. To the right, a blurred Gretchen, who's got her chin jutting out as if it would win the race all by itself. And on the other side of the fence is Raymond with his arms down to his side and the palms tucked up behind him, running in his very own style, and it's the first time I ever saw that and I almost stop to watch my brother Raymond on his first run. But the white ribbon is bouncing toward me and I tear past it, racing into the distance till my feet with a mind of their own start digging up footfuls of dirt and brake me short. Then all the kids standing on the side pile on me, banging me on the back and slapping my head with their May Day programs, for I have won again and everybody on 151st Street can walk tall for another year.

"In the first place . . ." the man on the loudspeaker is clear as a bell now. But then he pauses and the loudspeaker starts to whine. Then static. And I lean down to catch my breath and here comes Gretchen walking back, for she's overshot the finish line too, huffing and puffing with her hands on her hips taking it slow, breathing in steady time like a real pro and I sort of like her a little for the first time. "In first place . . ." and then three or four voices get all mixed up on the loudspeaker and I dig my sneaker into the grass and stare at Gretchen who's staring back, we both wondering just who did win. I can hear old Beanstalk arguing with the man on the loudspeaker and then a few others running their mouths about what the stopwatches say. Then I hear Raymond yanking at the fence to call me and I wave to shush him, but he keeps rattling the fence like a gorilla in a cage like in them gorilla movies, but then like a dancer or something he starts climbing up nice and easy but very fast. And it occurs to me, watching how smoothly he climbs hand over hand and remembering how he looked running with his arms down to his side and with the wind pulling his mouth back and his teeth showing and all, it occurred to me that Raymond would make a very fine runner. Doesn't he always keep up with me on my trots? And he surely knows how to breathe in counts of seven cause he's always doing it at the dinner table, which drives my brother George up the wall. And I'm smiling to beat the band cause if I've lost this race, or if me and Gretchen tied, or even if

I've won, I can always retire as a runner and begin a whole new career as a coach with Raymond as my champion. After all, with a little more study I can beat Cynthia and her phony self at the spelling bee. And if I bugged my mother, I could get piano lessons and become a star. And I have a big rep as the baddest thing around. And I've got a roomful of ribbons and medals and awards. But what has Raymond got to call his own?

So I stand there with my new plans, laughing out loud by this time as Raymond jumps down from the fence and runs over with his teeth showing and his arms down to the side, which no one before him has quite mastered as a running style. And by the time he comes over I'm jumping up and down so glad to see him—my brother Raymond, a great runner in the family tradition. But of course everyone thinks I'm jumping up and down because the men on the loudspeaker have finally gotten themselves together and compared notes and are announcing "In first place—Miss Hazel Elizabeth Deborah Parker." (Dig that.) "In second place—Miss Gretchen P. Lewis." And I look over at Gretchen wondering what the "P" stands for. And I smile. Cause she's good, no doubt about it. Maybe she'd like to help me coach Raymond; she obviously is serious about running, as any fool can see. And she nods to congratulate me and then she smiles. And I smile. We stand there with this big smile of respect between us. It's about as real a smile as girls can do for each other, considering we don't practice real smiling every day, you know, cause maybe we too busy being flowers or fairies or strawberries instead of something honest and worthy of respect . . . you know . . . like being people.

Developing Comprehension Skills

1. In the story, Squeaky tells the reader about herself. What does she have to do for her family?

2. What is Squeaky's attitude toward people who poke fun at Raymond? What actions does she take toward these people?

3. Squeaky loves to run. List at least five different sentences from the story that suggest her attitude toward running.

4. At the end of the story, Squeaky begins to like Gretchen. Why? What is your opinion of Squeaky? Would you want her to be your friend? Why or why not?

Reading Literature: Short Stories

1. **Understanding Setting.** Where does this story take place? List three clues that tell you. Why is the setting important to the events of this story?

2. **Analyzing a Character.** What does Squeaky think a person should be doing instead of May Pole dancing? This statement sums up an important quality about Squeaky. Give examples from the story showing that Squeaky's actions live up to her words.

3. **Identifying Conflicts.** There are several conflicts in this story. List all the conflicts that you can find. Which do you think is the main conflict? How does it relate to the title?

4. **Stating the Theme.** Through Squeaky's character, the author is saying something about growing up as a girl in modern society. Reread the last two sentences of the story. What theme do you think they express?

Developing Vocabulary Skills

Explaining Informal Expressions. This story is written in the first-person point of view. It is written to sound like the real speech of a young girl. Squeaky's speech contains many colorful expressions that are nonstandard English.

The following list gives examples of some of Squeaky's expressions. Use context clues to figure out what each statement means.

1. from the jump   (page 283, paragraph 1)

2. she hangs out   (page 283, paragraph 1)

3. the parkees   (page 284, paragraph 3)

4. I'm so burnt   (page 285, paragraph 2)

5. cause he's on stilts   (page 284, paragraph 4)

Developing Writing Skills

1. **Comparing Two Characters.** The authors of "Thank You, M'am" and "Raymond's Run" both focus on a young person's viewpoint. Compare the characters Roger and Squeaky.

Write two paragraphs explaining how they are alike and what they learn.

Pre-Writing. Make two lists on your paper: one for Roger and one for Squeaky. Select details from the story to explain the following ideas.

a. At the beginning of the story, what things are important to the character?

b. What attitude does the character have toward others?

c. How does the character feel about himself or herself?

d. What does the character learn about life? From whom?

Writing. In your first paragraph, tell how Roger and Squeaky are alike. Include at least three details from your lists. Use key words such as *similar*, *both*, and *comparison* to tell how the two characters relate.

In the second paragraph, explain what Roger and Squeaky learn about life. Again, include details from your lists. Conclude with a sentence that summarizes the comparison of the two characters.

Revising. Proofread your writing. Make sure each group of words expresses a complete thought. Check to see that you used several key words to signal the comparisons. Make sure the ideas in your second paragraph build on the details in the first paragraph.

2. **Creating an Original Character.** In this story we learn about Squeaky from her own thoughts as she narrates. We also see her actions toward other characters, and we hear several of her conversations.

Create a character with your own imagination. Write a paragraph describing the character. Include a physical description. Also tell how the character behaves. Tell what the character thinks of himself or herself. Explain the character's attitudes toward others.

Developing Skills in Study and Research

Refining a Research Topic. You may want to learn more about running, or track and field events, after you have read "Raymond's Run." One resource to check for information is an encyclopedia. Another is *The Readers' Guide to Periodical Literature.*

Track and field is a broad, or general, topic. Therefore, each library resource will list many subheadings about it. Each resource will also suggest other closely related topics, called cross references, to research. You could not possibly research the entire topic of track and field. For a broad topic such as this one, you will need to limit your research to a specific area.

Using either an encyclopedia index or *The Readers' Guide*, look up the subject Track and Field. Read through the list of articles. Also check the articles listed under the cross reference topics suggested. Use the information you find to answer the following questions.

1. Suppose as an assignment your teacher asked you to write a report about running. What specific topics within the general subject of track and field might you select? List five possible report ideas.

2. Choose one of the report topics you suggested. Select at least three articles that you think would provide information about the topic. Write down the article titles. For encyclopedia articles, list the encyclopedia, the volume number, and page numbers. For periodical articles, list the magazine title, volume number, date, and page numbers.

Developing Skills in Speaking and Listening

Reading Orally. One of the elements of this story that makes it so successful is the language the writer uses. Squeaky sounds like a real person. Choose a section of the story that you particularly like. Limit yourself to one or two paragraphs. Practice reading the selection the way you think Squeaky would have said it. Read through the selection enough times that you are comfortable with it. Practice a reading speed that seems like normal conversation. Do not rush through the selection.

When you are ready, read the selection aloud to a group. Try to make eye contact with people in your audience. It will help make them feel that you are Squeaky talking to them. Be sure to speak loudly and clearly. Try to make your voice fit Squeaky's personality.

Lather and Nothing Else

HERNANDO TÉLLEZ

Imagine that the man destroying your country is suddenly in your power. What would you do? Read to find out how the speaker in this story answers the question.

He came in without a word. I was stropping my best razor. And when I recognized him I started to shake. But he did not notice. To cover my nervousness, I went on honing the razor. I tried the edge with the tip of my thumb and took another look at it against the light.

Meanwhile, he was taking off his cartridge-studded belt with the pistol holster suspended from it. He put it on a hook in the wardrobe and hung his cap above it. Then he turned full around toward me and, loosening his tie, remarked: "It's hot as the devil. I want a shave." With that he took his seat.

I estimated he had a four days' growth of beard. The four days he had been gone on the last foray after our men. His face looked burnt, tanned by the sun.

I started to work carefully on the shaving soap. I scraped some slices from the cake, dropped them into the mug, then added a little lukewarm water, and stirred with the brush. The lather soon began to rise.

"The fellows in the troop must have just about as much beard as I." I went on stirring up lather. "But we did very well, you know. We caught the leaders. Some of them were brought back dead, others are still alive. But they'll all be dead soon."

"How many did you take?" I asked.

"Fourteen. We had to go pretty far in to find them. But now they're paying for it. And not one will escape; not a single one."

He leaned back in the chair when he saw the brush in my hand, full of lather. I had not yet put the sheet on him. I was certainly flustered. Taking a sheet from the drawer, I tied it around my customer's neck.

He went on talking. He evidently took it for granted I was on the side of the existing regime.

"The people must have gotten a scare with what happened the other day," he said.

"Yes," I replied, as I finished tying the knot against his nape, which smelt of sweat.

"Good show, wasn't it?"

"Very good," I answered, turning my attention now to the brush. The man closed his eyes wearily and awaited the cool caress of the lather.

I had never had him so close before. The day he ordered the people to file through the schoolyard to look upon the four rebels hanging there, my path had crossed his briefly. But the sight of those mutilated bodies kept me from paying attention to the face of the man who had been directing it all and whom I now had in my hands.

It was not a disagreeable face, certainly. And the beard, which aged him a bit, was not unbecoming. His name was Torres. Captain Torres.

I started to lay on the first coat of lather. He kept his eyes closed.

"I would love to catch a nap," he said, "but there's a lot to be done this evening."

I lifted the brush and asked, with pretended indifference: "A firing party?"

"Something of the sort," he replied, "but slower."

"All of them?"

"No, just a few."

I went on lathering his face. My hands began to tremble again. The man could not be aware of this, which was lucky for me. But I wished he had not come in. Probably many of our men had seen him enter the shop. And with the enemy in my house I felt a certain responsibility.

I would have to shave his beard just like any other, carefully, neatly, just as though he were a good customer, taking heed that not a single pore should emit a drop of blood. Seeing to it that the blade did not slip in the small whorls. Taking care that the skin was left clean, soft, shining, so that when I passed the back of my hand over it

not a single hair should be felt. Yes. I was secretly a revolutionary, but at the same time I was a conscientious barber, proud of the way I did my job. And that four-day beard presented a challenge.

I took up the razor, opened the handle wide, releasing the blade, and started to work, downward from one sideburn. The blade responded to perfection. The hair was tough and hard; not very long, but thick. Little by little the skin began to show through. The razor gave out its usual sound as it gathered up layers of soap mixed with bits of hair. I paused to wipe it clean, and, taking up the strop once more, went about improving its edge, for I am a painstaking barber.

The man, who had kept his eyes closed, now opened them, put a hand out from under the sheet, felt of the part of his face that was emerging from the lather, and said to me: "Come at six o'clock this evening to the school."

"Will it be like the other day?" I asked, stiff with horror.

"It may be even better," he replied.

"What are you planning to do?"

"I'm not sure yet. But we'll have a good time."

Once more he leaned back and shut his eyes. I came closer, the razor on high.

"Are you going to punish all of them?" I timidly ventured.

"Yes, all of them."

The lather was drying on his face. I must hurry. Through the mirror, I took a look at the street. It appeared about as usual: there was the grocery shop with two or three customers. Then I glanced at the clock: two-thirty.

The razor kept descending. Now from the other sideburn downward. It was a blue beard, a thick one. He should let it grow like some poets, or some priests. It would suit him well. Many people would not recognize him. And that would be a good thing for him, I thought, as I went gently over all the throat line. At this point you really had to handle your blade skillfully, because the hair, while scantier, tended to fall into small whorls. It was a curly beard. The pores might open, minutely, in this area and let out a tiny drop of blood. A good barber like myself stakes his reputation on not permit-

ting that to happen to any of his customers.

And this was indeed a special customer. How many of ours had he sent to their death? How many had he mutilated? It was best not to think about it. Torres did not know I was his enemy. Neither he nor the others knew it. It was a secret shared by very few, just because that made it possible for me to inform the revolutionaries about Torres' activities in the town and what he planned to do every time he went on one of his raids to hunt down rebels. So it was going to be very difficult to explain how it was that I had him in my hands and then let him go in peace, alive, clean-shaven.

His beard had now almost entirely disappeared. He looked younger, several years younger than when he had come in. I suppose that always happens to men who enter and leave barbershops. Under the strokes of my razor Torres was rejuvenated; yes, because I am a good barber, the best in this town, and I say this in all modesty.

A little more lather here under the chin, on the Adam's apple, right near the great vein. How hot it is! Torres must be sweating just as I am. But he is not afraid. He is a tranquil man, who is not even giving thought to what he will do to his prisoners this evening. I, on the other hand, polishing his skin with this razor, avoiding the drawing of blood, careful with every stroke—I cannot keep my thoughts in order.

Confound the hour he entered my shop! I am a revolutionary but not a murderer. And it would be so easy to kill him. He deserves it. Or does he? No, damn it! No

one deserves the sacrifice others make in becoming assassins. What is to be gained by it? Nothing. Others and still others keep coming, and the first kill the second, and then these kill the next, and so on until everything becomes a sea of blood. I could cut his throat, so, swish, swish! He would not even have time to moan, and with his eyes shut he would not even see the shine of the razor or the gleam in my eye.

I'm shaking like a regular murderer. From his throat a stream of blood would flow on the sheet, over the chair, down on my hands, onto the floor. I would have to close the door. The blood would go flowing, along the floor, warm, indelible, not to be stanched, until it reached the street, like a small scarlet river.

I'm sure that with a good strong blow, a deep cut, he would feel no pain. He would not suffer at all. And what would I do then with the body? Where would I hide it? I would have to flee, leave all this behind, take shelter far away, very far away. But they would follow until they caught up with me. "The murderer of Captain Torres. He slit his throat while he was shaving him. What a cowardly thing to do!"

And others would say: "The avenger of our people. A name to remember"—my name here. "He was the town barber. No one knew he was fighting for our cause."

And so, which will it be? Murderer or hero? My fate hangs on the edge of this razor blade. I can turn my wrist slightly, put a bit more pressure on the blade, let it sink in. The skin will yield like silk, like rubber, like the strop. There is nothing more tender than a man's skin, and the blood is always there, ready to burst forth. A razor like this cannot fail. It is the best one I have.

But I don't want to be a murderer. No, sir. You came in to be shaved. And I do my work honorably. I don't want to stain my hands with blood. Just with lather, and nothing else. You are an executioner; I am only a barber. Each one to his job. That's it. Each one to his job.

The chin was now clean, polished, soft. The man got up and looked at himself in the glass. He ran his hand over the skin and felt its freshness, its newness.

"Thanks," he said. He walked to the wardrobe for his belt, his pistol, and his cap. I must have been very pale, and I felt my shirt soaked with sweat. Torres finished adjusting his belt buckle, straightened his gun in its holster, and, smoothing his hair mechanically, put on his cap. From his trousers pocket he took some coins to pay for the shave. And he started toward the door. On the threshold, he stopped for a moment, and, turning toward me, he said:

"They told me you would kill me. I came to find out if it was true. But it's not easy to kill. I know what I'm talking about."

Developing Comprehension Skills

1. Was the barber in the story on the side of the group in power, or was he on the side of the revolutionaries? On which side was his customer?

2. What was going to happen to the people who had been captured?

3. Why was the barber nervous and sweating while he shaved his customer?

4. Were many of the people in the town revolutionaries? Give evidence from the story to support your opinion.

5. Do you think the barber made the right decision at the end of the story? Give reasons for your answer.

Reading Literature: Short Stories

1. **Identifying the Conflict.** External conflict can be a struggle between two people or between people and the forces of nature. Internal conflict occurs within a person. What is the main conflict in this story? Which type of conflict is it? The barber resolves the conflict. What does he finally decide to do?

2. **Understanding the Title.** This story is called "Lather and Nothing Else." What could the something "else" refer to? Explain how you think the title relates to the main conflict in the story.

3. **Appreciating the Use of Detail.** The author uses vivid description in this story. For example, he gives very clear descriptions of the shaving process. The descriptions are so detailed that the reader can almost see and feel the shave. Think about how descriptions relate to the events of the story. How do the details make the story more enjoyable? How do they add to the suspense?

4. **Understanding Irony.** Irony occurs when something happens that is the opposite of what we expect. How is the ending of this story ironic? If the barber had known at the beginning of the story what the customer tells him at the end, would the conflict have been the same? Explain your answer.

Developing Vocabulary Skills

Using Series Clues. Sometimes a writer uses a series of words to suggest the meaning of an unfamiliar word. The unfamiliar word is used in a series along with familiar words. This is called a **series** clue. Here is an example.

Gabriel does not like to eat beets, asparagus, or *okra.*

The writer relies on your knowledge about beets and asparagus. You know that they are vegetables. Therefore, you can assume that *okra* is also a vegetable.

Each of the following sentences contains a word from "Lather and Nothing Else." Find the context clue in each sentence. It may be a series clue or one of the others you have learned. Figure out the meaning of each underlined word. List the words and their meanings.

1. Before he sat down, Torres put his holster, pistol, and cartridges in the wardrobe.

2. Many people in the town thought Torres was an executioner and a murderer.

3. The barber used the razor, the strop, the brush, and the mug of lather.

4. He shaved the captain's sideburns, chin, and nape.

5. The barber dreamed he would be called the <u>avenger</u>, the hero, the brave one.

6. Torres stopped on the <u>threshold</u> for a moment to say something to the barber. Then he swung the door open and went out into the street.

Developing Writing Skills

1. **Organizing an Argument.** There are several ways to interpret this story. Do you think the barber was a hero or a traitor? Write a paragraph stating your opinion. Use examples from the story to support what you think.

2. **Changing the Point of View.** The story is told in the first person, giving only the feelings of the barber. Retell the story from the point of view of Torres, the customer.

   Pre-Writing. List everything you know about Torres from the story. Include details about what he looks like, how he acts in the barbershop, what he thinks about the government, and what he does to his enemies. In retelling the story, you may want to use only this information. Or you may want to add new details. Use your imagination. Then consider what Torres thinks about the barber. Does Torres know the barber is an enemy? How does this affect the way Torres acts in the barbershop? Does Torres look down on the barber? Or does he respect him? In your version of the story, will Torres fight the barber? Or will he come and go peacefully?

   Writing. Have Torres narrate the events. Use *I* to refer to Torres. Write about what happens. Be sure to include Torres's thoughts. However, do not include thoughts of the barber. Make use of detailed description as the writer of the original story did. For instance, you might choose to describe how the shave felt, what the barber's hands looked like, or what sounds you heard.

   Revising. Read through your story. If you find the name *Torres*, rewrite the sentence. Torres is narrating and should call himself *I*. You should find references to the barber. If not, add sentences to identify the barber. Be sure your version of the story makes Torres's thoughts clear.

Developing Skills in Speaking and Listening

Using Nonverbal Communication. The barber's hands begin to tremble several times during the story. The movements of his hands indicate that he is nervous. Sometimes people communicate as effectively nonverbally as they do with words.

Nonverbal communication refers to all the motions and facial expressions that suggest certain meanings. For example, when you shrug your shoulders you are indicating that you don't know something. Wrinkling your nose is a sign that you dislike something.

Some gestures are less obvious than others. For example, a twinkle in a person's eyes might indicate excitement. Lack of movement might indicate fear.

For the next several days, pay close attention to the people around you. Observe yourself, your family, and your friends. Watch their movements and their facial expressions. Make a list of the ways you notice people communicating without words.

The Third Wish

JOAN AIKEN

Three wishes are granted to the main character in this story. He is warned that the wishes may bring unhappiness. As you read, decide whether the warning is accurate.

Once there was a man who was driving in his car at dusk on a spring evening through part of the forest of Savernake. His name was Mr. Peters. The primroses were just beginning, but the trees were still bare and it was cold; the birds had stopped singing an hour ago.

As Mr. Peters entered a straight, empty stretch of road he seemed to hear a faint crying, and a struggling and thrashing, as if somebody was in trouble far away in the trees. He left his car and climbed the mossy bank beside the road. Beyond the bank was an open slope of beech trees leading down to thorn bushes through which he saw the gleam of water. He stood a moment, waiting to try and discover where the noise was coming from, and presently heard a rustling and some strange cries in a voice that was almost human—and yet there was something too hoarse about it at one time and too clear and sweet at another. Mr. Peters ran down the hill, and, as he neared the bushes, he saw something white among them that was trying to extricate itself; coming closer he found that it was a swan that had become entangled in the thorns growing on the bank of the canal.

The bird struggled all the more frantically as he approached, looking at him with hate in its yellow eyes, and when he took hold of it to free it, hissed at him, pecked him, and thrashed dangerously with its wings, which were powerful enough to break his arm. Nevertheless, he managed to release it from the thorns, and carrying it tightly with one arm, holding the snaky head well away with the other hand (for he did not wish his eyes pecked out), he took it to the verge of the canal and dropped it in.

The swan instantly assumed great dignity and sailed out to the middle of the water, where it put itself to rights with much dabbling and preening, smoothing its feathers with little showers of drops. Mr. Peters waited, to make sure that it was all right and had suffered no damage in its struggles. Presently the swan, when it was satisfied with its appearance, floated in to the bank once more, and in a moment, instead of the great white bird, there was a little man all in green with a golden crown and long beard, standing by the water. He had fierce, glittering eyes and looked by no means friendly.

"Well, Sir," he said threateningly, "I see you are presumptuous enough to know some of the laws of magic. You think that because you have rescued—by pure good fortune—the King of the Forest from a difficulty, you should have some fabulous reward."

"I expect three wishes, no more and no less," answered Mr. Peters, looking at him steadily and with composure.

"Three wishes, he wants, the clever man! Well, I have yet to hear of the human being who made any good use of his three wishes—they mostly end up worse off than they started. Take three wishes then —" he flung three dead leaves in the air "— don't blame me if you spend the last wish in undoing the work of the other two."

Mr. Peters caught the leaves and put two of them carefully in his notecase. When he looked up, the swan was sailing about in the middle of the water again, flicking the drops angrily down its long neck.

Mr. Peters stood for some minutes reflecting on how he should use his reward. He knew very well that the gift of three magic wishes was one that brought trouble more often than not, and he had no intention of being like the forester who first wished by mistake for a sausage, and then in a rage wished it on the end of his wife's nose, and then had to use his last wish in getting it off again. Mr. Peters had most of the things that he wanted and was very content with his life. The only thing that troubled him was that he was a little lonely and had no companion for his old age. He decided to use his first wish and to keep the other two in case of an emergency. Taking a thorn he pricked his tongue with it, to remind himself not to utter rash wishes aloud. Then, holding the third leaf and gazing round him at the dusky undergrowth, the primroses, great beeches, and the blue-green water of the canal, he said:

"I wish I had a wife as beautiful as the forest."

A tremendous quacking and splashing broke out on the surface of the water. He thought that it was the swan laughing at him. Taking no notice, he made his way through the darkening woods to his car, wrapped himself up in the rug, and went to sleep.

When he awoke, it was morning and the birds were beginning to call. Coming along the track towards him was the most beautiful creature he had ever seen, with eyes as blue-green as the canal, hair as dusky as the bushes, and skin as white as the feathers of swans.

"Are you the wife that I wished for?" asked Mr. Peters.

"Yes I am," she replied. "My name is Leita."

She stepped into the car beside him and they drove off to the church on the outskirts of the forest, where they were married. Then he took her to his house in a remote and lovely valley and showed her all his treasures—the bees in their white hives,

Summer, 1890, FRANK WESTON BENSON.
National Museum of American Art. Smithsonian Institution,
Washington, D.C., Gift of John Gellatly.

the Jersey cows, the hyacinths, the silver candlesticks, the blue cups, the luster bowl for putting primroses in. She admired everything, but what pleased her most was the river that ran by the foot of his garden.

"Do swans come up here?" she asked.

"Yes, I have often seen swans there on the river," he told her, and she smiled.

Leita made him a good wife. She was gentle and friendly, busied herself about the house and garden, polished the bowls, milked the cows, and mended his socks. As time went on, however, Mr. Peters began to

feel that she was not happy. She seemed restless, wandered much in the garden, and sometimes, when he came back from the fields, he would find the house empty. She would only return after half an hour or so with no explanation of where she had been. On these occasions, she was always especially tender and would put out his slippers to warm and cook his favorite dish—Welsh rarebit with wild strawberries—for supper.

One evening, he was returning home along the river path when he saw Leita in front of him, down by the water. A swan had sailed up to the verge, and she had her arms round its neck and the swan's head rested against her cheek. She was weeping, and, as he came nearer, he saw that tears were rolling, too, from the swan's eyes.

"Leita, what is it?" he asked, troubled.

"This is my sister," she answered. "I can't bear being separated from her."

Now he understood that Leita was really a swan from the forest, and this made him very sad because when a human being marries a bird it always leads to sorrow.

"I could use my second wish to give your sister human shape, so that she could be a companion to you," he suggested.

"No, no," she cried, "I couldn't ask that of her."

"Is it so very hard to be a human being?" asked Mr. Peters sadly.

"Very, very hard," she answered.

"Don't you love me at all, Leita?"

"Yes, I do, I do love you," she said, and there were tears in her eyes again. "But I miss the old life in the forest, the cool grass and the mist rising off the river at sunrise, and the feel of the water sliding over my feathers as my sister and I drifted along the stream."

"Then shall I use my second wish to turn you back into a swan again?" he asked, and his tongue pricked to remind him of the old king's words, and his heart swelled with grief inside him.

"Who would darn your socks and cook your meals and see to the hens?"

"I'd do it myself, as I did before I married you," he said, trying to sound cheerful.

She shook her head. "No, I could not be as unkind to you as that. I am partly a swan, but I am also partly a human being now. I will stay with you."

Poor Mr. Peters was very distressed on his wife's account and did his best to make her life happier, taking her for drives in the car, finding beautiful music for her to listen to on the radio, buying clothes for her and even suggesting a trip round the world. She said no to that; she would prefer to stay in their own house near the river.

He noticed that she spent more and more time baking wonderful cakes—jam puffs, petits fours, éclairs, and meringues. One day he saw her take a basketful down to the river, and he guessed that she was giving them to her sister.

He built a seat for her by the river, and the two sisters spent hours together there, communicating in some wordless manner. For a time he thought that all would be well, but then he saw how thin and pale Leita was growing.

One night when he had been late doing the accounts, he came up to bed and found her weeping in her sleep and calling: "Rhea! Rhea! I can't understand what you say! Oh, wait for me, take me with you!"

Then he knew that it was hopeless and she would never be happy as a human. He kissed her goodbye, then took another leaf from his notecase, blew it out of the window, and used up his second wish.

Next moment, instead of Leita there was a sleeping swan lying across the bed with its head under its wing. He carried it out of the house and down to the brink of the river. Then he said "Leita! Leita!" to waken her and gently put her into the water. She gazed round her in astonishment for a moment, and then came up to him and rested her head lightly against his hand; next instant, she was flying away over the trees towards the heart of the forest.

He heard a harsh laugh behind him and, turning round saw the old king looking at him with a malicious expression.

"Well, my friend! You don't seem to have managed so wonderfully with your first two wishes, do you? What will you do with the last? Turn yourself into a swan? Or turn Leita back into a girl?"

"I shall do neither," said Mr. Peters calmly. "Human beings and swans are better in their own shapes."

For all that he looked sadly over towards the forest where Leita had flown, and he walked slowly back to his empty house.

The next day, he saw two swans swimming at the bottom of the garden, and one

Home of the Heron, 1893, GEORGE INNESS. Oil on canvas, 30″ × 45″. Edward B. Butler Collection.

of them wore the gold chain he had given Leita after their marriage; she came up and rubbed her head against his hand.

Mr. Peters and his two swans came to be well known in that part of the country; people used to say that he talked to the swans and they understood him as well as his neighbors. Many people were a little frightened of him. There was a story that once when thieves tried to break into his house they were set upon by two huge white birds that carried them off bodily and dropped them in the river.

As Mr. Peters grew old, everyone wondered at his contentment. Even when he was bent with rheumatism he would not think of moving to a drier spot, but went slowly about his work, milking the cows and collecting the honey and eggs, with the two swans always somewhere close at hand.

Sometimes people who knew his story would say to him:

"Mr. Peters, why don't you wish for another wife?"

"Not likely," he would answer serenely. "Two wishes were enough for me, I reckon.

I've learned that even if your wishes are granted they don't always better you. I'll stay faithful to Leita."

One autumn night, passers-by along the road heard the mournful sound of two swans singing. All night the song went on, sweet and harsh, sharp and clear. In the morning Mr. Peters was found peacefully dead in his bed with a smile of great happiness on his face. In between his hands, which lay clasped to his breast, were a withered leaf and a white feather.

Developing Comprehension Skills

1. Why did Mr. Peters earn a reward? Was the reward given in a grateful way?

2. Mr. Peters's first wish was granted. Did it make him happy? Give a reason for your answer.

3. Review the section of the story about the fairy tale of the forester. How was Mr. Peters's second wish like the forester's third wish? How was it different?

4. What was Mr. Peters's reason for deciding not to use his third wish?

5. Do you think Mr. Peters used his wishes wisely? Give reasons for your answer.

Reading Literature: Short Stories

1. **Understanding Mood.** The author of this story chose her words very carefully. She created a mood, or feeling, of peacefulness and beauty. She also gave the story a sense of mystery. Reread some of the passages that describe the forest, Leita, and Mr. Peters's farm. List in one column words that suggest the peacefulness and beauty. In another column list words that help give the idea of mystery. Include details about things you would see and hear. If you were to make this story into a movie, what music would you choose for the opening scene? Either state the title of the piece or name of the musician, or describe how the music would sound.

2. **Identifying Foreshadowing.** The term **foreshadowing** means giving hints in a story about what is going to happen. When Mr. Peters finds his wife crying with a swan, he realizes that his wish may not be successful. Even earlier in the story, the reader was given several hints that the outcome might not be a happy one. Name two of these hints. Tell why they made you suspect that Mr. Peters's wish might not make him happy.

3. **Diagraming the Plot.** This story has a plot that follows the typical pattern. First comes the introduction, which sets up the story. Next there is a period of rising action. During this time the reader begins to expect something dramatic to happen. Third, the climax occurs. There is a major change in action or in the attitude of a character. Fourth is the falling action, the events that occur after the climax. Last, the resolution ends the story. Usually, the result of the climax is explained.

   Draw a plot diagram for this story. Use the diagram on page 249 for reference. Include the five parts of a plot. Label each point on the diagram with a description of the action during that part of the story.

4. **Explaining the Title.** Remember what the forester in the fairy tale found out about wishes. What did Mr. Peters find out? Identify the sentence spoken by Mr. Peters that directly states a theme of this story. Explain why you think the writer called this story "The Third Wish."

Developing Vocabulary Skills

Identifying Antonyms. You learned that a word can be used in context with its synonym. Sometimes a word is used in context with its antonym. **Antonyms** are words that have opposite meanings. For example, *neat* is an antonym for *messy*, and *joyful* is an antonym for *sad*. Match each word in the first column with the correct antonym in the second column.

frantically	clear
content	hold
confusing	calmly
release	unhappy

Developing Writing Skills

1. **Explaining the Believability of a Story.** Much of the action in "The Third Wish" is complete fantasy, or make-believe. Certain events in the story could not happen in the real world. For instance, people in the story turn into birds and birds turn into people. Yet something about the story makes us accept the plot. By the end, we can even find ways to compare the story with the real world. Write an explanation of the story showing how the author mixes fantasy with reality.

Pre-Writing. List all the elements of fantasy that you can find in the story. It might help to compare this story to fairy tales you might know. Then make a separate list of ways in which the story is like the real world. Choose events that could possibly happen in reality. Look for characters that seem like real people in certain ways.

Writing. You need to write two paragraphs. In the first, explain what makes the story seem make-believe. Give at least three examples. In the second paragraph, compare the story to the real world. Again, try to include three examples.

Revising. Read the first paragraph you wrote. Be sure it gives examples only of fantasy. Then check that the second paragraph includes only actions and feelings possible in the real world. Have you used one or more key words to lead the reader from the first paragraph to the second? If not, add a word or phrase such as *although, on the other hand,* or *nevertheless.*

2. **Setting a Mood.** One of the things that makes this story enjoyable to read is the author's skill in setting the mood. The mood is peaceful and lovely, but at the same time it is a little scary and suspenseful.

Select a mood, or feeling, that you find easy to imagine. Write the first one or two paragraphs of a story that could create that mood. Use descriptive words to set the mood you want readers to feel.

To be effective, you must first decide what your story will be about. How will the mood you are trying to achieve fit the plot? Then think of sights, sounds, and feelings that help make the mood clear. Choose words to make those ideas seem alive. You do not need to write an entire story. Write only the introduction.

Developing Skills in Critical Thinking

Organizing Ideas in an Argument. You have learned that an argument must be supported by reasons and facts. The reasons and facts must be presented in a logical order. The most effective order is to build the argument from the weakest point to the strongest point. This is called organizing in order of importance. This method will leave the audience with the most powerful reason fresh in their minds. Practice organizing ideas by doing the following exercises.

1. Arrange the following ideas by order of importance. Write them on your paper in the order that you think is best.
   Argument
   Running is an excellent way for a person to stay physically fit.

   Reasons
   a. It doesn't cost anything.
   b. Almost anyone can find time to run on a regular basis.
   c. Running will probably remain a popular outdoor activity.
   d. It is good exercise for the heart, lungs, and muscles.
   e. Running doesn't require special ability.

2. Select one of the following arguments. Think of at least five reasons that support the argument. List the reasons on your paper in order of importance. Start with the least important and build to the most important reason.
   a. There is no need to use violence in settling a dispute.
   b. Obeying the law is more important than keeping a friend.
   c. Competition is a natural human need.
   d. It is often necessary to hide your emotions from others.

Science Fiction Stories

The three stories that follow are science fiction. **Science fiction** is fiction based on scientific facts or theories. The setting of a science fiction story is often in the future. Often it is on another planet or in a different dimension of time. The setting may seem unfamiliar. Yet the writer creates that unfamiliar setting to comment on very familiar problems in our present world.

Painting for Young People, 1943, MAX ERNST. Private Collection.

All Summer in a Day

RAY BRADBURY

Have you ever thought about living on another planet? Do you think life would be a great adventure? Would people behave differently there than on Earth? Read this story to find out one writer's opinion.

"Ready?"

"Ready."

"Now?"

"Soon."

"Do the scientists really know? Will it happen today, will it?"

"Look, look; see for yourself!"

The children pressed to each other like so many roses, so many weeds, intermixed, anxiously peering out for a look at the hidden sun.

It rained.

It had been raining for seven years; thousands upon thousands of days compounded and filled from one end to the other with rain, with the drum and gush of water, with the sweet crystal fall of showers and the concussion of storms so heavy they were tidal waves come over the islands. A thousand forests had been crushed under the rain and grown up a thousand times to be crushed again. This was the way life was forever on the planet Venus, and this was the schoolroom of the children of the rocket men and women who had come to a raining world to set up civilization and live out their lives.

"It's stopping! It's stopping!"

"Yes, yes!"

Margot stood apart from them, from these children who could never remember a time when there wasn't rain and rain and rain. They were all nine years old, and, if there had been a day, seven years ago, when the sun came out for an hour and showed its face to the stunned world, they could not recall. Sometimes at night she heard them stir, in remembrance, and she knew they were dreaming and remembering gold or a yellow crayon or a coin large enough to buy the world with. She knew they thought they remembered a warmness, like a blushing in the face, in the body, in the arms and legs and trembling hands. Then they always awoke to the tatting drum, the endless shaking down of clear bead necklaces upon the roof, the walk, the gardens, the forests, and their dreams were gone.

All day yesterday they had read in class about the sun. About how like a lemon it was, and how hot. And they had written small stories or essays or poems about it:

I think the sun is a flower,
That blooms for just one hour.

That was Margot's poem, read in a quiet voice and in the still classroom while the rain was falling outside.

"Aw, you didn't write that!" protested one of the boys.

"I did," said Margot. "I did."

"William!" said the teacher.

That was yesterday. Now the rain was slackening, and the children were crushed before the great thick windows.

"Where's teacher?"

"She'll be back."

"She'd better hurry or we'll miss it!"

They turned on themselves, like a feverish wheel, all tumbling spokes.

Margot stood alone. She was a very frail girl who looked as if she had been lost in the rain for years and the rain had washed out the blue from her eyes and the red from her mouth and the yellow from her hair. She was an old photograph dusted from an album, whitened away, and if she spoke at all her voice would be a ghost. Now she stood, separate, staring at the rain and the loud wet world beyond the huge glass.

"What're you looking at?" demanded William.

Margot said nothing.

"Speak when you're spoken to." He gave her a shove. But she did not move; rather she let herself be moved only by him and nothing else.

They edged away from her; they would not look at her. She felt them go away. This was because she would play no games with them in the echoing tunnels of the underground city. If they tagged her and ran, she stood blinking after them and did not follow. When the class sang songs about happiness and life and games, her lips barely moved. Only when they sang about the sun and the summer did her lips move as she watched the drenched windows.

Then of course, the biggest crime of all was that she had come here only five years ago from Earth, and she remembered the sun and the way the sun was and the sky was when she was four in Ohio. And they, they had been on Venus all their lives, and they had been only two years old when last the sun came out and had long since forgotten the color and heat of it and the way it really was. But Margot remembered.

"It's like a penny," she said once, eyes closed.

"No, it's not!" the children cried.

"It's like a fire," she said, "in the stove."

"You're lying, you don't remember!" cried the children.

But she remembered and stood quietly apart from all of them and watched the patterning windows. And once, a month ago, she had refused to shower in the school shower rooms, and clutched her hands to her ears and over her head, screaming the water mustn't touch her head. So after that, dimly, dimly, she sensed it, she was different, and they knew her difference and kept away.

There was talk that her father and mother were taking her back to Earth next year; it seemed vital to her that they do so, though it would mean the loss of thousands of dollars to her family. The children hated her for all these reasons of big and little consequence. They hated her pale snow face, her waiting silence, her thinness, and possible future.

"Get away!" The boy gave her another push. "What're you waiting for?"

Then, for the first time, she turned and looked at him. What she was waiting for was in her eyes.

"Well, don't wait around here!" cried the boy savagely. "You won't see nothing!"

Her lips moved.

"Nothing!" he cried. "It was all a joke, wasn't it?" He turned to the other children. "Nothing's happening today. Is it?"

They all blinked at him and then, understanding, laughed and shook their heads. "Nothing, nothing!"

"Oh, but," Margot whispered, her eyes helpless. "But this is the day, the scientists predict, they say, they know, the sun . . ."

"All a joke!" said the boy, and seized her roughly. "Hey, everyone, let's put her in a closet before teacher comes!"

"No," said Margot, falling back.

They surged about her, caught her up and bore her, protesting, and then pleading, and then crying, back into a tunnel, a room, a closet, where they slammed and locked the door. They stood looking at the door and saw it tremble from her beating and throwing herself against it. They heard her muffled cries. Then, smiling, they turned and went out and back down the tunnel to the classroom, just as the teacher arrived.

"Ready, children?" She glanced at her watch.

"Yes!" said everyone.

"Are we all here?"

"Yes!"

The rain slackened still more.

They crowded to the huge door.

The rain stopped.

It was as if, in the midst of a film concerning an avalanche, a tornado, a hurricane, a volcanic eruption, something had, first, gone wrong with the sound apparatus, thus muffling and finally cutting off all noise, all of the blasts and repercussions and thunders, and then, second, ripped the film from the projector and inserted in its place a peaceful tropical slide which did not move or tremble. The world ground to a standstill. The silence was so immense and unbelievable that you felt your ears had been stuffed or you had lost your hearing altogether. The children put their hands to their ears. They stood apart. The door slid back and the smell of the silent, waiting world came in to them.

The sun came out.

It was flaming bronze, and it was very large. The sky around it was a blazing blue tile color. And the jungle burned with sunlight as the children, released from their spell, rushed out, yelling into the springtime.

Red Sun, 1935, ARTHUR DOVE. The Phillips Collection, Washington, D.C.

"Now, don't go too far," called the teacher after them. "You've only two hours. You wouldn't want to get caught out!"

But they were running and turning their faces up to the sky and feeling the sun on their cheeks like a warm iron; they were taking off their jackets and letting the sun burn their arms.

"Oh, it's better than the sun lamps."

"Much, much better!"

They stopped running and stood in the great jungle that covered Venus, that grew and never stopped growing, tumultuously, even as you watched it. It was a nest of octopi, clustering up great arms of fleshlike weed, wavering, flowering in this brief spring. It was the color of rubber and ash, this jungle, from the many years without sun. It was the color of stones and white cheeses and ink, and it was the color of the moon.

The children lay out, laughing, on the jungle mattress, and heard it sigh and squeak under them, resilient and alive. They ran among the trees, they slipped and fell, they pushed each other, they played hide-and-seek and tag, but most of all they squinted at the sun until tears ran down their faces. They put their hands up to that yellowness and that amazing blueness and they breathed of fresh, fresh air and listened and listened to the silence that suspended them in a blessed sea of no sound and no motion. They looked at everything and savored everything. Then wildly, like animals escaped from their caves, they ran and ran in shouting circles. They ran for an hour and did not stop running.

And then—

In the midst of their running one of the girls wailed.

Everyone stopped.

The girl, standing in the open, held out her hand.

"Oh, look, look," she said, trembling.

They came slowly to look at her opened palm.

In the center of it, cupped and huge, was a single raindrop.

She began to cry, looking at it.

They glanced quietly at the sky.

"Oh. Oh."

A few cold drops fell on their noses and their cheeks and their mouths. The sun faded behind a stir of mist. A wind blew cool around them. They turned and started to walk back toward the underground house, their hands at their sides, their smiles vanishing away.

A boom of thunder startled them, and like leaves before a new hurricane, they tumbled upon each other and ran. Lightning struck ten miles away, five miles away,

a mile, a half mile. The sky darkened into midnight in a flash.

They stood in the doorway of the underground for a moment until it was raining hard. Then they closed the door and heard the gigantic sound of the rain falling in tons and avalanches, everywhere and forever.

"Will it be seven more years?"

"Yes. Seven."

Then one of them gave a little cry.

"Margot!"

"What?"

"She's still in the closet where we locked her."

"Margot."

They stood as if someone had driven them, like so many stakes, into the floor. They looked at each other and then looked away. They glanced out at the world that was raining now and raining and raining steadily. They could not meet each other's glances. Their faces were solemn and pale. They looked at their hands and feet, their faces down.

"Margot."

One of the girls said, "Well . . . ?"

No one moved.

"Go on," whispered the girl.

They walked slowly down the hall in the sound of cold rain. They turned through the doorway to the room in the sound of the storm and thunder, lightning on their faces, blue and terrible. They walked over to the closet door slowly and stood by it.

Behind the closet door was only silence.

They unlocked the door, even more slowly, and let Margot out.

Developing Comprehension Skills

1. Why were the children living on Venus? How long had they lived there? How long had Margot lived on Venus?

2. In what ways did Margot behave differently from most of the children?

3. Margot was very sad about living on Venus. What reasons did she have for feeling so sad? Can you suggest any reasons why the other children did not try to help her?

4. At the end of the story, the other children seemed sincerely sorry for having locked up Margot. Why do you suppose their attitudes changed after they had experienced the sunshine?

5. Would you rather be Margot or one of the other children? Why?

Reading Literature: Short Stories

1. **Finding the Exposition.** The first several paragraphs of this story are its **exposition**, or introduction. What background information is given about the setting in these paragraphs? What introductory facts are told about Margot? What background is given about the other children? Why does a reader need to know this information before reading the rest of the story?

2. **Recognizing Science Fiction.** What parts of "All Summer in a Day" would seem unrealistic in today's world? What parts of the story seem realistic to you?

3. **Understanding Author's Purpose.** Think about Margot's reaction in moving to Venus. Think about the way the other children treat her. What comment about people do you think the writer is making in this story?

Developing Vocabulary Skills

Recognizing Connotations of Words. One way a writer creates mood is by using words with strong connotations. The **connotation** of a word is its emotional meaning. *Lively, exciting,* and *bright* have positive, happy connotations. *Gloomy, tiring,* and *grey* have negative, dreary connotations.

Make two lists on your paper: one for "All Summer in a Day" and one for "The Third Wish." The following words appear in those stories. The words with positive connotations create a joyful mood in "The Third Wish." Those with negative connotations create a dreary mood in "All Summer in a Day." Decide the connotation of each word. Then write it in the correct list.

glittering	pale
darkened	beautiful
sweet	crushed
fortune	rain
storms	gentle

Developing Writing Skills

1. **Evaluating the Plot.** It is not likely that a whole classroom of children would behave as they do in the story. One or more of them would probably have refused to lock Margot up. Or perhaps someone would have gone to release her or to tell the teacher.

   If the action of everyone locking Margot away seems unrealistic, why did the writer include it? Why did he show the entire group behaving in one way? Write a paragraph explaining your opinion.

2. **Writing a Description.** In the story, the writer compares Margot to an old photograph. He also compares her voice to a

ghost. Direct comparison of two things is called **metaphor**. In a metaphor, the writer does not say that something is like another thing. The writer says that something is another thing:

She was an old photograph. . . .

Choose a person who you know. Write a description of that person, using a metaphor in your description.

Pre-Writing. Make a list of all the things you recall about the person. Concentrate on what the person looks like. Include the person's physical traits and the expressions the person uses.

In a second list, note the most important qualities you know of the person. Do any of the physical traits strongly compare or contrast with the qualities? For example, is the person very frail physically but always fearless and determined?

Review both lists. Then try to summarize the main feeling you get about the person you are describing. Think of an object that gives you a similar feeling. Write a one-sentence metaphor that compares the person to the object.

Writing. Limit your writing to one paragraph in length. Select words that will create a clear picture about the person. Include words about colors and motions. Be especially careful to note any physical traits that show or conflict with personal characteristics. In your paragraph, be sure to include the metaphor you wrote.

Revising. Find someone else who knows the person you described. Ask this person to read the description. If the person cannot identify your subject, ask which details are confusing or inaccurate. Is there an important idea that you left out of the description? Does the metaphor suggest the appropriate comparison? Does it reveal the person's most important quality?

Developing Skills in Study and Research

Taking Notes. In doing any research, it is helpful to take notes on the information you find. If research notes are to be useful, they must be organized. One way to organize notes is to use index cards. Write each main piece of information on a separate index card. For example, in researching Venus, you would list information about climate on one card. Information about plant life would be listed on a different card. Identify the subtopics—such as climate and plant life—at the tops of the cards, as titles. Keep a written record of the source of information at the bottom of each card. For an example, see the Handbook on Reading and Writing, page 629.

Practice using the index card system. Research the planet Venus. Use any resources available in your library, such as an encyclopedia, the card catalog for nonfiction books, *The Readers' Guide* for magazines, and atlases for maps. Find at least three facts about Venus. Take notes on index cards, or on separate sheets of paper. Use a new card or piece of paper for each fact.

From the facts you find, decide whether "All Summer in a Day" is based on facts. Be prepared to explain your opinion to the class.

The Weapon

FREDRIC BROWN

There are several weapons in this story. As you read, decide which weapon the title refers to. Who controls that weapon?

The room was quiet in the dimness of early evening. Dr. James Graham, key scientist of a very important project, sat in his favorite chair, thinking. It was so still that he could hear the turning of pages in the next room as his son leafed through a picture book.

Often Graham did his best work, his most creative thinking, under these circumstances, sitting alone in an unlighted room in his own apartment after the day's regular work, but tonight his mind would not work constructively. Mostly he thought about his mentally arrested son—his only son—in the next room. The thoughts were loving thoughts, not the bitter anguish he had felt years ago when he had first learned of the boy's condition. The boy was happy; wasn't that the main thing? To how many men is given a child who will always be a child, who will not grow up to leave him? Certainly that was rationalization, but what is wrong with rationalization when—the doorbell rang.

Graham rose and turned on lights in the almost-dark room before he went through the hallway to the door. He was not annoyed; tonight, at this moment, almost any interruption to his thoughts was welcome.

He opened the door. A stranger stood there. He said, "Dr. Graham? My name is Niemand. I'd like to talk to you. May I come in a moment?"

Graham looked at him. He was a small man, nondescript, obviously harmless—possibly a reporter or an insurance agent.

However, it didn't matter what he was. Graham found himself saying, "Of course. Come in, Mr. Niemand." A few minutes of conversation, he justified himself by thinking, might divert his thoughts and clear his mind.

"Sit down," he said, in the living room. "Care for a cup of coffee?"

Niemand said, "No thank you." He sat in the chair. Graham sat on the sofa.

The small man interlocked his fingers; he leaned forward. He said, "Dr. Graham, you

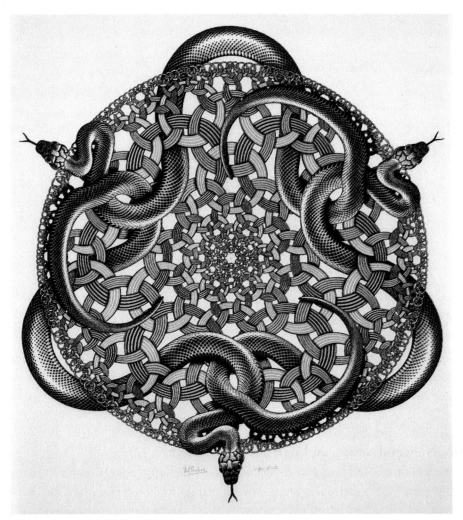

Ring Snakes, 1969, M. C. ESCHER. National Gallery of Art, Washington, D.C. Cornelius Van S. Roosevelt Collection 1982.

are the man whose scientific work is more likely than that of any other man to end the human race's chance for survival.''

A crackpot, Graham thought. Too late now he realized that he should have asked the man's business before admitting him. It would be an embarrassing interview—he disliked being rude, yet only rudeness was effective.

"Dr. Graham, the weapon on which you are working—"

The visitor stopped and turned his head as the door that led to a bedroom opened and a boy of fifteen came in. The boy didn't notice Niemand; he ran to Graham.

"Daddy, will you read to me now?" The boy of fifteen laughed the sweet laughter of a child of four.

Graham put an arm around the boy. He looked at his visitor, wondering whether he had known about the boy. From the lack of surprise on Niemand's face, Graham felt sure he had known.

"Harry"—Graham's voice was warm with affection—"Daddy's busy. Just for a little while. Go back to your room; I'll come and read to you soon."

" 'Chicken Little?' You'll read me 'Chicken Little?' "

"If you wish. Now run along. Wait, Harry, this is Mr. Niemand."

The boy smiled bashfully at the visitor. Niemand said, "Hi, Harry," and smiled back at him, holding out his hand. Graham, watching, was sure now that Niemand had known: the smile and the gesture were for the boy's mental age, not his physical one.

The boy took Niemand's hand. For a moment it seemed that he was going to climb into Niemand's lap, and Graham pulled him back gently. He said, "Go to your room now, Harry."

The boy skipped back into his bedroom, not closing the door.

Niemand's eyes met Graham's, and he said, "I like him," with obvious sincerity. He added, "I hope that what you're going to read to him will always be true."

Graham didn't understand. Niemand said, " 'Chicken Little', I mean. It's a fine story—but may 'Chicken Little' always be wrong about the sky falling down."

Graham suddenly had liked Niemand when Niemand had shown liking for the boy. Now he remembered that he must

close the interview quickly. He rose.

He said, "I fear you're wasting your time and mine, Mr. Niemand. I know all the arguments, everything you can say I've heard a thousand times. Possibly there is truth in what you believe, but it does not concern me. I'm a scientist, and only a scientist. Yes, it is public knowledge that I am working on a weapon, a rather ultimate one. But, for me personally, that is only a by-product of the fact that I am advancing science. I have thought it through, and I have found that that is my only concern."

"But, Dr. Graham, is humanity ready for an ultimate weapon?"

Graham frowned. "I have told you my point of view, Mr. Niemand."

Niemand rose slowly from the chair. He said, "Very well, if you do not choose to discuss it, I'll say no more." He passed a hand across his forehead. "I'll leave, Dr. Graham. I wonder, though . . . may I change my mind about the coffee you offered me?"

Graham's irritation faded. He said, "Certainly. Cream and sugar?"

"Please."

Graham went into the kitchen. He got the coffee, cream, and sugar.

When he returned to the living room, Niemand was just leaving the boy's bedroom. He heard Niemand's, "Good night, Harry," and Harry's happy, "Night, Mr. Niemand."

Graham poured the coffee. Later, Niemand declined a second cup and started to leave.

Hand with Reflecting Sphere, 1935, M. C. ESCHER.
National Gallery of Art, Washington, D.C. Rosenwald Collection, 1960.

Niemand said, "I took the liberty of bringing a small gift to your son, doctor. I gave it to him while you were getting the coffee for us. I hope you'll forgive me."

"Of course. Thank you. Good night."

Graham closed the door; he walked through the living room into Harry's room. He said, "All right, Harry. Now I'll read to—"

There was sudden sweat on his forehead, but he forced his face and his voice to be calm as he stepped to the side of the bed. "May I see that, Harry?" When he had it safely, his hands shook as he examined it.

He thought, only a madman would give a loaded revolver to a retarded child.

Developing Comprehension Skills

1. How did Dr. Graham feel about his son?

2. How did Dr. Graham feel about working on a weapon that could destroy the world? Use your own words in your answer.

3. What did Neimand think of Dr. Graham's work on the weapon?

4. Do you think that Mr. Neimand planned all along to give Harry the gun? Use information you find in the story to support your answer.

5. Why do you think Mr. Neimand gave Harry the loaded gun?

6. What is your opinion of Dr. Graham?

Reading Literature: Short Stories

1. **Finding the Introduction and Rising Action.** The last two paragraphs of "The Weapon" contain the climax, the falling action, and the resolution. The rest of the story is the introduction and rising action. Review the story to separate these two parts of the plot. On your paper, list at least two details from each of these parts. Then identify the climax, one detail of the falling action, and the resolution of the story.

2. **Understanding Conflict.** The main conflict in this story is external. It is between Dr. Graham and Mr. Neimand. The story seems to imply that there also should be a conflict inside the main character. What conflict would this be?

3. **Identifying Comparisons.** The last sentence of the story reads, "only a madman would give a loaded revolver to a retarded child." The sentence has a double meaning. First, it

suggests that Mr. Neimand is a madman. He just gave a loaded gun to Harry. It also suggests there is another madman. Who is this other madman? What "loaded revolver" is he trying to give someone?

4. **Appreciating a Minor Character.** Harry says nothing important and does nothing important in the story. However, he is a significant character because of his relationship with his father. Name at least two times in the story that the doctor thinks about his son. How does Harry indirectly affect his father's actions? How does Neimand use Harry to make his point?

5. **Determining Author's Purpose.** Science fiction writers often use their stories to present opinions about today's world. What message about our technology is the writer trying to express in this story?

Developing Vocabulary Skills

Using Synonym and Antonym Clues. Some sentences provide an **antonym** clue. They give a familiar word that is the opposite of an unfamiliar word. The following sentences use words from "The Weapon." Each sentence contains a synonym or antonym clue. Use the clue given to write a definition of each underlined word.

1. Harry, Graham's son, was mentally arrested. Graham found it difficult, yet rewarding, to live with a retarded child.

2. The visitor would interrupt him. A few minutes of conversation might divert his thoughts and clear his mind for work.

3. Graham was working on an ultimate weapon. But Neimand wondered if society could handle the greatest possible weapon.

4. He requested Mr. Neimand to leave. Mr. Neimand accepted the dismissal politely.

5. When Graham opened the bedroom door, anxiety overtook him. But he forced his face and voice to express a calmness until he had retrieved the gun from his son.

Developing Writing Skills

1. **Writing an Argument.** It is easy to state a personal opinion. However, it is often difficult to support an opinion. Select one of the following opinions about scientists presented in this story:

> Mr. Neimand thinks that scientists should be held responsible for the effect of their work on the world.

> Dr. Graham does not feel that scientists should worry about future uses or effects of their work.

Write an organized argument to defend your opinion.

Pre-Writing. Prepare reasons to use in writing your argument. List all the points you can think of to support your opinion. Draw ideas from the story and from current news. Take notes on facts that support each statement you list.

Number the statements in your list by order of importance. Start with the least important and build to the most important point.

Writing. Develop an organized argument. Start with a sentence stating your opinion on the subject of scientists' responsibilities. Present your reasons in order of importance. Use key words or phrases to introduce each reason.

Two types of key words help make an argument clear. Some key words help state the reasons or facts. These include: *because, so, since, if, therefore,* and *as a result.*

Other key words help to put the reasons or facts in order of importance. These include: *the first reason, second, more important, most important,* and *finally.*

Revising. Read your argument to a group. Ask the group members to evaluate your argument. Then change any part of your argument that they do not find convincing.

2. **Creating a Setting.** You have read eleven stories in this chapter. Each story has a setting that fits the action. In some stories, such as "The Third Wish," the setting is very detailed and a part of the action. In other stories, the setting is only a background and is not described in detail. This is true in the story "Raymond's Run."

Create your own setting for a story. Then write a paragraph describing the setting. Identify the time period—the past, present, or future. Tell about the place. Include details that appeal to several of the five senses. Try to make your setting express a mood.

Developing Skills in Critical Thinking

Classifying Science Fiction. Science fiction is a special type of story. Read the introduction on page 305. Then write your own definition of science fiction. As part of your definition, include a list of elements, or characteristics, common to science fiction stories. You may use details from the stories in your textbook as examples. You also may use details from other science fiction works.

The Assassin

ROBERT SILVERBERG

Everyone is fascinated by the idea of time travel. Why does this character want to go back in time? Read to find out how he affects history.

The time was drawing near, Walter Bigelow thought. Just a few more adjustments, and his great ambition would be fulfilled.

He stepped back from the Time Distorter and studied the complex network of wires and tubes with an expert's practiced eye. TWENTY YEARS, he thought. Twenty years of working and scrimping, of pouring money into the machine that stood before him on the workbench. Twenty years, to save Abraham Lincoln's life.

Now he was almost ready.

Bigelow had conceived his grand idea when still young, newly out of college. He had stumbled across a volume of history and had read of Abraham Lincoln and his struggle to save the Union.

Bigelow was a tall, spare, rawboned man standing better than six feet four—and with a shock he discovered that he bore an amazing resemblance to a young portrait of the Great Emancipator. That was when his identification with Lincoln began.

He read every Lincoln biography he could find, steeped himself in log-cabin legends and the texts of the Lincoln-Douglas debates. Gradually, he became consumed with bitterness because an assassin's hand had struck Lincoln down at the height of his triumph.

"Awful shame, great man like that," he mumbled into his glass one night in a bar.

"What's that?" a sallow man at his left asked. "Someone die?"

"Yes," Bigelow said. "I'm talking about Lincoln. Awful shame."

The other chuckled. "Better get yourself a new newspaper, pal. Lincoln's been dead for a century. Still mourning?"

Bigelow turned, his gaunt face alive with anger. "Yes! Yes—why shouldn't I mourn? A great man like Lincoln—"

"Sure, sure," the other said placatingly. "I'll buy that. He was a great president, chum—but he's been dead for a hundred years. One hundred. You can't bring him back to life, you know."

"Maybe I can," Bigelow said suddenly— and the great idea was born.

It took eight years of physics and math before Bigelow had developed a workable time-travel theory. Seven more years passed before the first working model stood complete.

He tested it by stepping within its field, allowing himself to be cast back ten years. A few well-placed bets, and he had enough cash to continue. Ten years was not enough. Lincoln had been assassinated in 1865— Friday, April 14, 1865. Bigelow needed a machine that could move at least one hundred twenty years into the past.

It took time. Five more years.

He reached out, adjusted a capacitor, pinched off an unnecessary length of copper wire. It was ready. After twenty years, he was ready at last.

Bigelow took the morning bus to Washington, D.C. The Time Distorter would not affect space, and it was much more efficient to make the journey from Chicago to Washington in 1979 by monobus in a little over an hour, than in 1865 by mulecart or some such conveyance, possibly taking a day. Now that he was so close to success, he was too impatient to allow any such delay as that.

The Time Distorter was cradled in a small black box on his lap; he spent the hour of the bus ride listening to its gentle humming and ticking, letting the sound soothe him and ease his nervousness.

There was really no need to be nervous, he thought. Even if he failed in his first attempt at blocking Lincoln's assassination, he had an infinity of time to keep trying again.

He could return to his own time and make the jump again, over and over. There were a hundred different ways he could use to prevent Lincoln from entering the fatal theater on the night of April 14. A sudden phone call—no, there were no telephones yet. A message of some kind. He could burn down the theater the morning of the play. He could find John Wilkes Booth and kill him before he could make his fateful speech of defiance and fire the fatal bullet. He could—

Well, it didn't matter. He was going to succeed the first time. Lincoln was a man of sense; he wouldn't willingly go to his death having been warned.

A warm glow of pleasure spread over Bigelow as he dreamed of the consequences of his act. Lincoln alive, going on to complete his second term, President until 1869. The weak, ineffectual Andrew Johnson would remain Vice-President, where he belonged. The south would be rebuilt sanely and welcomed back into the Union; there would be no era of carpetbaggers, no series of governmental scandals and no dreary post-war era.

"Washington!"

Moving almost in a dream, Bigelow left the bus and stepped out into the crowded capitol streets. It was a warm summer day; soon, he thought, it would be a coolish April evening, back in 1865. . . .

He headed for the poor part of town, away from the fine white buildings and gleaming domes. Huddling in a dark alley on the south side, he undid the fastenings of the box that covered the Time Distorter.

He glanced around, saw that no one was near. Then, swiftly, he depressed the lever.

The world swirled around him, vanished.

Then, suddenly, it took shape again.

He was in an open field now; the morning air was cool but pleasant, and in the distance he could see a few of the buildings that made the nation's capitol famous. There was no Lincoln Memorial, of course, and the bright needle of Washington's Monument did not thrust into the sky. Nevertheless, the familiar Capitol dome looked much as it always had, and he could make out the White House further away.

Bigelow refastened the cover of the Distorter and tucked the box under his arm. It clicked quietly, reminding him over and over again of the fact that he was in the year 1865 — the morning of the day John Wilkes Booth put a bullet through the brain of Abraham Lincoln.

Time passed slowly for Bigelow. He made his way toward the center of town and spent the day in downtown Washington, hungrily drinking in the gossip. Abe Lincoln's name was on everyone's tongue.

The dread War had ended just five days before with Lee's surrender at Appomattox. Lincoln was in his hour of triumph. It was Friday. The people were still discussing the speech he had made the Tuesday before.

"He said he's going to make an announcement," someone said. "Abe's going to tell the Southerners what kind of program he's going to put into effort for them."

"Wonder what's on his mind?" someone else asked.

"No matter what it is, I'll bet he makes the South like what he says."

He had never delivered that speech, Bigelow thought. The South had been doomed to a generation of hardship and exploitation by the victorious North that had left unhealing scars.

The day passed. President Lincoln was to attend the Ford Theatre that night, to see a production of a play called "Our American Cousin."

Bigelow knew what the history books said. Lincoln had had an apprehensive dream the night before: he was sailing on a ship of a peculiar build, being borne on it with great speed toward a dark and undefined shore. Like Caesar on the Ides of March, he had been warned—and, like Caesar, he would go unheeding to his death.

Bigelow would see that that never happened.

History recorded that Lincoln attended the performance, that he seemed to be enjoying the play, and that shortly after ten that evening, a wild-eyed man would enter Lincoln's box, fire once, and leap to the stage, shouting, "Sic semper tyrannis!"

The man would be the crazed actor John Wilkes Booth. He would snag a spur in the drapery as he dropped to the stage, and would break his leg—but nevertheless he would vanish into the wings, make his way through the theater he knew so well, mount a horse waiting at the stage door. Some days later he would be dead.

As for President Lincoln, he would slump forward in his box. The audience would be too stunned to move for a moment—but there was nothing that could be done. Lincoln would die the next morning without recovering consciousness.

"Now he belongs to the ages," Secretary of State Stanton would say.

No! Bigelow thought. It would not happen. It would not happen. . . .

Evening approached. Bigelow, crouching in an alley across the street from the theater, watched the carriages arriving for the performance that night. Feeling oddly out of place in his twentieth-century clothing, he watched the finely-dressed ladies and gentlemen descending from their coaches. Everyone in Washington knew the President would be at the theater that night, and they were determined to look their best.

Bigelow waited. Finally, a handsome carriage appeared, and several others made way for it. He tensed, knowing who was within.

A woman of regal bearing descended first—Mary Todd Lincoln, the President's wife. Then Lincoln appeared.

For some reason, the President paused at the street-corner and looked around. His eyes came to rest on the dark alley where Bigelow crouched invisibly, and Bigelow stared at the face he knew almost as well as his own: the graying beard, the tired, old,

wrinkled face, the weary eyes of Abe Lincoln.

Then he rose and began to run.

"Mr. President! Mr. President!"

He realized he must have been an outlandish figure, dashing across the street in his strange costume with the Time Distorter clutched under one arm. He drew close to Lincoln.

"Sir, don't go to the theater tonight! If you do—"

A hand suddenly wrapped itself around his mouth. President Lincoln smiled pityingly and turned away, walking on down the street toward the theater. Other hands seized Bigelow, dragged him away. Blue-clad arms. Union soldiers. The President's bodyguard.

"You don't understand!" Bigelow yelled. He bit at the hand that held him, and got a fierce kick in return. "Let go of me! Let go!"

There were four of them, earnest-looking as they went about their duties. They held Bigelow, pummelled him angrily. One of them reached down for the Distorter.

In terror Bigelow saw that his attempt to save Lincoln had been a complete failure, that he would have to return to his own time and try all over again. He attempted to switch on the Distorter, but before he could open the cover rough hands had pulled it from him.

"Give me that!" He fought frantically, but they held him. One of the men in blue uniforms took the Distorter, looked at it curiously, finally held it up to his ear.

His eyes widened. "It's ticking! It's a bomb!"

"No!" Bigelow shouted, and then watched in utter horror as the soldier, holding the Distorter at arm's length, ran across the street and hurled the supposed bomb as far up the alley as he possibly could.

There was no explosion—only the sound of delicate machinery shattering.

Bigelow watched numbly as the four men seized his arms again.

"Throw a bomb, will you? Come on, fellow—we'll show you what happens to guys who want to assassinate the President!"

Further down the street, the gaunt figure of Abe Lincoln was just going into the theater. No one gave Bigelow a chance to explain.

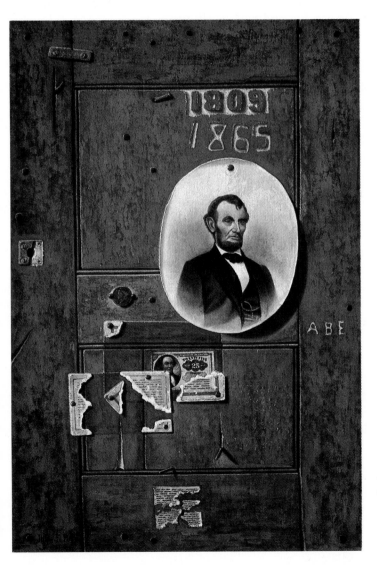

Reminiscences of 1865, painted after 1900, JOHN F. PETO. The Minneapolis Institute of Arts.

Developing Comprehension Skills

1. In your own words describe the purpose of the Time Distorter.

2. What did Bigelow do to prepare for his trip backwards in time?

3. Why did Bigelow want to prevent Lincoln's assassination?

4. What made Bigelow seem dangerous to the president's bodyguard?

5. Suppose you had been able to speak to Bigelow before he tried to warn the President. What advice would you have given him?

Reading Literature: Short Stories

1. **Recognizing Science Fiction.** Name several elements in the story that make it science fiction. When do you think this story was written? Give evidence from the story to support your opinion.

2. **Understanding Characterization.** The character Bigelow is more than just a good scientist and an admirer of Lincoln. He appears to be extreme and unreasonable. Review the beginning of the story. Find two details about Bigelow that indicate he may be abnormal in his admiration of Lincoln. Why do you think the author developed the character this way?

3. **Diagraming the Plot.** Draw a plot diagram to illustrate the five parts of the story. Include one detail of the introduction, two details of the rising action, a clear statement of the climax, one detail of the falling action, and an explanation of the resolution.

4. **Understanding Irony.** "The Assassin" contains **irony**. That is, the events turn out in a way opposite to what you expected. What did Bigelow expect to happen if he did not achieve his goal immediately? What really happens? What idea does the ending express about machines controlling history?

Developing Vocabulary Skills

Reviewing Ways To Find Word Meaning. You have learned many ways to determine the meaning of an unfamiliar word. Sometimes it is helpful to look at **word parts**—the prefix, suffix, and base word. Other times there may be **context clues** to the meaning. Still other times you need to check a **dictionary** for the meaning of a word.

Read the following sentences about the story "The Assassin." Try to use word parts or context clues to find the meaning of each underlined word. Write the word and its meaning on your paper. Also write which method you used to determine the meaning: *Word Parts* or *Context Clues*. If there are no clues to the meaning, write *Dictionary*.

1. Bigelow had developed a workable time-travel theory, or scientific idea.

2. President Lincoln was known to many people as an emancipator.

3. Bigelow refastened the cover of the Time Distorter after he had pressed the button.

4. The Time Distorter provided Bigelow with an infinity of chances. If he failed, he could return to his own time and make the jump again, over and over, as many times as he needed.

5. Bigelow wanted to prevent the weak and ineffectual Andrew Johnson from becoming the next president.

6. The humming of the box soothed Bigelow and eased his <u>nervousness</u>.

7. Lincoln had an <u>apprehensive</u> dream the night before the performance.

8. The soldier ran across the street and <u>hurled</u> the supposed bomb as far up the alley as he could possibly throw it.

Developing Writing Skills

1. **Comparing Two Characters.** In both "The Weapon" and "The Assassin" the main character is a scientist who has worked on a brilliant invention. Write a two-paragraph comparison of these characters. You might choose to write about one or more of the following issues. Or you may choose your own topics of comparison.

    a. the scientists' attitudes toward their own inventions
    b. the purposes of the inventions
    c. the scientists' plans for the use of the inventions
    d. the behaviors of the scientists
    e. the conflicts the scientists face

2. **Creating a Plot.** You have studied the five parts of a plot. In this chapter, you have read stories with many different plots. You have created your own characters and settings. (See pages 288 and 318.) Use your knowledge and your imagination to create a plot. Write two detailed outlines that explain the events of your story.

    Pre-Writing. Determine the main character. You will not need to describe the character fully, but you will need to think about the character's actions in the plot. What will be the main conflict? With whom or what will the character struggle? Will there be a clear winner of the conflict? What will happen after the conflict ends?

    Write notes on the actions you want to include. Also, imagine the setting. It may be part of the action, or it may be only background. Add details about the setting to your writing notes.

    Decide whether you will use suspense in the building of the plot. Also think about the ending of the story. Will there be a surprise? Will the actions tie together? Will you leave the reader with a question?

    Writing. You will be writing two outlines. For the first, fill in the following outline form. Include details describing these parts of your story.

    I. Setting
    II. Characters
    III. Conflict

    Write a second outline about the main action of the story. Separate the events into three parts: Beginning, Middle, and End. Put details from the introduction in the Beginning section. Events of rising action should go into the Middle section. Decide whether to put the Climax in the Middle or End. Falling action and the resolution should be listed under the End section. Use complete sentences in the outline to explain the events of the story.

    Revising. Check each of your two outlines. Be sure that the details fit the headings under which they appear. Check that the headings and details are listed in an order that makes sense. Skim each outline one more time. Have you left out an important idea? Your outlines should present a clear summary of the plot you created.

Using Your Skills in Reading Short Stories

The following paragraph is from "The Dinner Party," a short story by Mona Gardner. The story is set in India, at a party given by a British couple for their friends. Read the paragraph. Then point out at least three phrases in the paragraph that build up suspense.

The American does not join in the argument but watches the other guests. As he looks, he sees a strange expression come over the face of the hostess. She is staring straight ahead, her muscles contracting slightly. With a slight gesture, she summons the native boy standing behind her chair and whispers to him. The boy's eyes widen, and he quickly leaves the room.

Using Your Comprehension Skills

Here is part of a poem by May Swenson which you will read in Chapter 6. Read these lines and decide what on Earth they are talking about.

A tourist came in from Orbitville,
parked in the air, and said:

The creatures of this star
are made of metal and glass.

They have four eyes.
The two in back are red.

Using Your Vocabulary Skills

In each of the following sentences, there is a context clue. The clue gives the meaning of a word you will come across in Chapter 6. For each sentence, identify the word whose meaning is given. Then state the meaning of the word in your own words. Last, identify which kind of clue you found: definition or restatement, synonym, comparison, contrast, example, series, or inference.

1. At this bank you can get francs, rubles, pesos, or <u>pounds</u> for your dollar.

2. The pitchfork <u>pierced</u> the clumps of soil as sharply as a knife cutting butter.

3. Scouts were sent to find a good place for a <u>bivouac</u>. A bivouac is an area where troops can rest or assemble.

4. Two trails <u>diverge</u> from this one about a mile north. Where the two branch off, take the one on the left.

5. Unlike her sister, who follows rules and cooperates with her teachers, Jenny is a <u>rebel</u>.

Using Your Writing Skills

Choose one of the writing assignments below.

1. Choose any two stories from this chapter. Compare and contrast their settings. Point out how the setting influences the events in each story. Write from one to four paragraphs.

2. Here are the elements of a new story. Make up details to fit these elements, and write two or three paragraphs of the introduction for your story. Include as much information about characters, setting, and plot as you can in those paragraphs. Choose whatever mood you wish.

> **Setting:** a store near your school
> **Characters:** a clerk in the store and a mysterious stranger
> **Conflict:** the stranger wants to buy things that are not available in any store

Using Your Skills in Critical Thinking

Develop an argument for or against this statement: Scientists should seriously investigate the possibilities of time travel. State your opinion. Then list at least three reasons to support your opinion. Arrange them in order from weakest to strongest.

CHAPTER **6**

Violet, Black, Orange, Yellow on White and Red,
1949, MARK ROTHKO, Solomon R. Guggenheim Museum,
New York. Gift, Elaine and Werner Dannheisser and the
Dannheisser Foundation, 1978. © Estate of Mark Rothko.

Reading Literature: Poetry

What Is Poetry?

Poetry is difficult to define. More than any other type of writing, it involves our feelings. It takes many forms and has many purposes.

Here is one definition of poetry: It is language that says more than ordinary language, and says it more intensely than ordinary language. It uses figures of speech. Each figure of speech suggests several meanings with only a few words. Poetry uses many words with strong connotations. These words appeal to the reader's emotions. The language of poetry is strong.

Here is another definition of poetry: It is literature that fits language into a rhythm or pattern. Often, a poem is arranged in lines and the lines are arranged in stanzas. However, not all poems are arranged into lines and stanzas. Usually, a poem has a definite, regular rhythm. Still, not all poems fit their words into a regular rhythm.

Whatever form a poem takes, it makes you see in a new way.

The History of Poetry

Poetry is one of the oldest forms of literature. You will recall that, in ancient times, myths were told in poem form. Wandering poets carried them from place to place. They sang or chanted the poems to their audiences. Before poems were ever written down, they were part of the oral tradition in literature.

Even after most poetry was written, sung poetry has remained popular. A ballad, for example, is a kind of folk poetry. It tells a story in song. Early settlers in America brought ballads with them and soon created new ones. These were some of the earliest literature in North America. You may be familiar with such ballads as "The Ballad of John Henry," "Casey Jones," and "Sweet Betsy from Pike."

Poetry has been sung and written throughout history, all over the world.

The Elements of Poetry

Shape. Poems are usually written in lines. The lines are grouped in stanzas. The beginning of a new line or stanza does not have to be the beginning of a new sentence. In fact, many poems, especially modern poems, do not use sentences at all.

In many poems, a regular pattern of rhythm and rhyme is repeated in every stanza. In some poems, the shape that the words form on the paper suggests a picture. These poems are called **concrete poems**.

Language. A poet chooses words very carefully for exact meanings and for the feelings they suggest. In addition, almost every poem has one or more figures of speech. Yet, the words are chosen not only for meaning, but for sound, as well. Rhythm is an important part of every poem. Many poems use alliteration, rhyme, and other sound effects, also.

Speaker. Even though a poem uses *I* and *me,* the speaker is not necessarily the poet. Often the poet invents a separate character. The reader must imagine that character saying the poem.

Theme. The theme of a poem is the writer's main idea or concern. Sometimes a poem describes how an object looks. Its theme is the desire to describe the object. Other times a poet may make a serious statement about how people should behave.

Mood. Mood is the emotion you feel reading a poem. Some poems are sad, others are joyful, and still others are angry. The main purpose of some poems is to set a mood.

How To Read a Poem

1. Let yourself get involved in the poem. When it describes something, try to see, hear, smell, taste, and feel that thing.
2. Read the poem aloud to hear its sound. Often the sound of a poem suggests or stresses its meaning.
3. Make sure that you understand every word in a poem. Pay particular attention to figures of speech.
4. Identify the speaker. It could make all the difference.

Comprehension Skills: Figurative Language

Recognizing Literal Language

You have probably read or heard someone make a comment similar to this one:

The store was literally bursting with shoppers!

In this case, the person is not using the word *literally* in its true meaning. *Literal* means "exact" or "not exaggerated." By pretending that the statement is not exaggerated, the person stresses the fullness of the store.

Literal language is language that means exactly what is said. Most of the time, we use literal language.

Recognizing Figurative Language

The opposite of literal language is figurative language. **Figurative language** is language that means more than what it says on the surface. It usually gives us a feeling about its subject. For example, one poet writes about the "song of the truck." She does not mean that a truck can actually sing. Rather, she is speaking figuratively. She is referring to road noises as music. By using the word *song,* and suggesting music, she brings joyful feelings to mind.

Poets use figurative language almost as frequently as literal language. When you read poetry, you must be conscious of the difference. Otherwise, a poem may make no sense at all.

For example, can you explain these lines from "The Storyteller"?

He talked, and as he talked
Wallpaper came alive.

Of course, the poet is not using literal language. He doesn't mean that the wallpaper literally jumped off the walls. Rather, he is using figurative language. This exaggeration suggests the power of the storyteller.

Sometimes the literal meaning of a line does not make sense, and only the figurative meaning does. At other times, both literal and figurative meanings make sense. As you read poetry, you must be alert for statements with both literal and figurative meanings.

Recognizing Symbols

Sometimes a writer uses something physical, like an object or color, to stand for an idea. The thing that stands for something else is called a **symbol**. You are familiar with some symbols in everyday life. For example, in street signs, the color red is a symbol of danger.

In writing, a symbol is a type of figurative language. If a writer repeatedly refers to one object, you might suspect that it may be a symbol. Decide whether it might stand for something besides itself.

Exercises: Understanding Figurative Language

A. Read these lines from poems. Identify the meaning you think fits best.

1. I hear America singing, the varied carols I hear.
   a. I am aware of all the activities that make America special.
   b. I am listening to a very large chorus.
   c. It sounds as if everyone is singing today.

2. We can . . . leave behind us
   Footprints on the sands of time.
   a. We can make impressions as we walk on sand.
   b. The beach is a good place to understand time.
   c. Our lives can affect others in years to come.

B. Read these lines from poems. Then tell in your own words what the figurative language in each means.

1. When dreams go
   Life is a barren field.

2. I'd wake and hear the cold splintering, breaking

3. Out of my blood and my brain
   I make my own interior weather,
   my own sun and rain.

Vocabulary Skills: Origins of English Words

Recognizing the Origins of English Words

Why do we use the word *mother* to describe a woman who has a child? Why don't we use *glemp*? Where do English words come from?

People who have studied the English language have discovered several important ways in which words have become part of the language. Even now, the language continues to grow. Knowing about the ways words enter the language may help you figure out some words.

The English Language.   English began with a prehistoric language called Indo-European. Several other languages came from this same source. For example, from the Indo-European base *mater* we get the German *Mutter,* French *mère,* Spanish *madre,* and English *mother.* The first settlers of the island that is now Great Britain spoke one form of Indo-European.

For over a thousand years, that island was the scene of many battles. One nation after another invaded the island. Some of the invaders stayed and became part of the English people. Others returned to their homelands. All left behind words that became part of the English language. Great numbers of words entered English from Latin, Greek, early Germanic languages, and French. Gradually, the language developed. What we call Modern English had formed by about 1500 A.D.

Borrowed Words.   The process of borrowing words from other languages continues today. Here are just a few of the words that English has taken from other languages in recent times:

Spanish–ranch, chile, sombrero, canyon, plaza, fiesta, tornado
African–canary, jazz, gumbo
Persian–lilac, paradise, spinach
American Indian–hickory, hominy, skunk, moccasin
Arabic–algebra, magazine
Chinese–catsup, silk

Words from Names. New words may be based on the name of a person or place. For example, *herculean,* which means "having great strength," comes from the Greek myth about Hercules. *Pasteurize* is a more recent addition. It comes from the name of the scientist, Louis Pasteur.

Clipped Words. Some new words are shortened forms of existing words. *Cab,* for instance, was clipped from *cabriolet.*

Combined Words. Words may be put together from two existing words or word parts. *Safeguard,* for example, is a compound combining two complete words. *Brunch* is a blend of two words, *breakfast* and *lunch. Microcomputer* combines the Greek prefix *micro-,* meaning "small," with *computer.*

Words from Sounds. Words can imitate sounds. Such words are called **echoic.** Examples include *lull, chirp, creak,* and *hush.*

Exercises: Recognizing Word Origins

A. Mars was the Roman god of war. *Mercury* was the Roman name for Hermes, winged messenger of the gods. Recall what you learned about the Titans in Chapter 1. Now figure out the meaning of each underlined word below.

1. The earthquake caused a *titanic* landslide.
2. Andrea is fun to be with, but she has a *mercurial* temper.
3. After fiery speeches by their leaders, the citizens' mood became *martial.*

B. The following words were added to English in three different ways. Use the clues that you see and hear in the words. Separate the words into three groups: *Words from Names, Combined Words,* and *Words from Sounds.*

howl	telegraph	shrill	pompadour	television
zeppelin	telecast	mackintosh	roadhog	roar
boycott	cardigan	telescope	meow	splash

C. What short word has been formed by clipping from each word below?

fanatic   omnibus   advertisement   examination

Observations

Have you ever tried to write a word upside down? Have you tried to copy a word while looking at its reflection in a mirror? If you have, you know that the word suddenly looks new and strange. You must look at it more carefully than you ever have before. In these poems, the poets try to have the same effect on us. They make familiar things look new.

Urban Freeways, 1981, WAYNE THIEBAUD. Private Collection. The Allan Stone Gallery, New York.

To Look at Any Thing

JOHN MOFFITT

The speaker in this poem makes a suggestion about how we can understand our world. Read to find what that suggestion is. Do you agree with the speaker?

To look at any thing,
If you would know that thing,
You must look at it long:
To look at this green and say
'I have seen spring in these
Woods,' will not do—you must
Be the thing you see:
You must be the dark snakes of
Stems and ferny plumes of leaves,
You must enter in
To the small silences between
The leaves,
You must take your time
And touch the very peace
They issue from.

Developing Comprehension Skills

1. What does the speaker say we must do to understand something thoroughly?

2. The poem uses the woods as an example of something you might want to know. Suppose you are trying to understand a person. How can you "be the thing (or person) you see"?

3. Do you think that the advice in the poem is easy to practice? Is it a good idea to "be" everything you see?

Reading Literature: Poetry

1. **Understanding Metaphor.** A metaphor compares two unlike things. This poem compares leaves with plumes, which are feathers. "Ferny plumes of leaves" helps you imagine one kind of leaves. Another metaphor in this poem is "dark snakes of stems." What kind of stems does this metaphor help you imagine?

2. **Understanding Alliteration.** This poem stresses certain words by using alliteration, the repetition of beginning sounds. Reread the first four lines. Listen for the *l* sound. Then find at least two other examples of alliteration.

   In each example, which words are stressed by alliteration? Can you think of a reason for stressing these words?

I Hear America Singing

WALT WHITMAN

Much of Walt Whitman's poetry is about common people. As you read the following poem, see if you can identify his feelings for America and her people.

I HEAR AMERICA SINGING, the varied carols I hear;
Those of mechanics—each one singing his, as it should be, blithe
    and strong;
The carpenter singing his, as he measures his plank or beam,
The mason singing his, as he makes ready for work, or leaves off
    work;
The boatman singing what belongs to him in his boat—the
    deckhand singing on the steamboat deck;
The shoemaker singing as he sits on his bench—the hatter singing as
    he stands;
The wood-cutter's song—the ploughboy's, on his way in the
    morning, or at the noon intermission, or at sundown;
The delicious singing of the mother—or the young wife at work
    —or the girl sewing or washing—Each singing what belongs to
    her, and to none else;
The day what belongs to the day—At night, the party of young
    fellows, robust, friendly,
Singing, with open mouths, their strong melodious songs.

Susan Comforting the Baby (No. 1), about 1881, MARY CASSATT.
Columbus Museum of Art, Ohio. Bequest of Frederick W. Schumacher.

Developing Comprehension Skills

1. In three places, the poet leaves out a word. Reread the first two lines. What word is understood after *his* in these lines? Identify the other two places where this same word is missing.

2. A carol is defined as a "song, especially of joy." List the various people who are described as singing carols.

3. The poet says that each person has his or her own song. What might he mean?

4. The poet lists people according to their jobs. This suggests that the job a person does becomes part of the person's "song." Do you agree or disagree? Give a reason.

Reading Literature: Poetry

Understanding Figurative Language. This poem talks about people singing carols, or joyful songs. However, could some people be singing sad songs? Would that change the idea of the poem? Why or why not?

Song of the Truck

DORIS FRANKEL

This poem appeals to the sense of hearing and also to a feeling of motion. As you read it, think of what makes the "song" this poet writes about.

This is the song that the truck drivers hear
In the grinding of brake and the shifting of gear,
From the noise of the wheel and the clarion horn,
From the freight and the weight—
                    a song has been born:
Mohair and cotton and textiles and silk,
Chickens and onions and apples and milk,
Rubber and clothing and coffee and tires,
Harness and hay and molasses and wires,
Petroleum, vinegar, furniture, eggs,
Race horses, stoves, and containers and kegs,
Chemicals, cantaloupes, canned goods and seeds—
Song of the cargo America needs!
Song of the wheels in the well-traveled grooves—
Coastline to coastline—
            America moves!

Developing Comprehension Skills

1. The poem mentions four actual sounds the truck drivers hear. Identify them.

2. Most of the cargo items mentioned in the poem do not make any sound. How can they be part of a "song"? What do you think the poet means by "song"?

3. Compare the main idea, or theme, of this poem to the main idea of "I Hear America Singing." How are they alike?

Reading Literature: Poetry

1. **Recognizing a Pattern of Rhyme.** "Song of the Truck" is the first poem in this chapter that uses rhyme. The poem is written in seven rhyming couplets. Examine the poem. Also examine the term *couplet*. Then explain the term *rhyming couplet*.

2. **Appreciating Rhythm.** The pattern of accented syllables creates a regular rhythm.

> This is the song that the truck drivers
> hear.

How does the use of this strong rhythm fit the idea of the poem?

3. **Identifying Patterns and Rhymes.** Poets can create end rhymes, that is, those made at the end of lines. Rhymes also can be internal, made by words rhyming within one line. Rhythm can be achieved by creating patterns with accented and unaccented syllables, or by repeating words and phrases. In "Song of the Truck," find one internal rhyme and three repetitions.

4. **Recognizing Mood.** Reread the poem. What feelings do you get from it? Explain your answer.

5. **Comparing Poems.** In one way, "Song of the Truck" is like "I Hear America Singing." They both use the word *song* to describe something special and exciting about a person or activity. Which poem uses the term in a more general way? Which limits the term?

Which of the two poems creates a more modern picture? How does it do so?

Unfolding Bud

NAOSHI KORIYAMA

This entire poem presents one comparison. The poet describes two very different things in almost the same way. As you read the poem, try to see what the poet sees.

One is amazed
By a water-lily bud
Unfolding
With each passing day,
Taking on a richer color
And new dimensions.

One is not amazed,
At a first glance,
By a poem,
Which is as tight-closed
As a tiny bud.

Yet one is surprised
To see the poem
Gradually unfolding,
Revealing its rich inner self,
As one reads it
Again
And over again.

Pink Lily with Dragonfly, 1981, JOSEPH RAFFAEL.
Van Straaten Gallery, Chicago.

Developing Comprehension Skills

1. What two things are compared in this poem?

2. What causes a water-lily to take on "richer color" and "new dimensions"?

3. In what way can a poem "gradually unfold"?

4. Is the comparison between a bud and a poem a new idea to you? If so, do you think it will affect the way you read poems in the future? Explain your answer.

Reading Literature: Poetry

1. **Recognizing Theme.** In any piece of writing, a writer usually expresses one of his or her concerns. Sometimes the writer makes a general statement about that topic. As you remember, such a statement is called the **theme** of the selection.

   In this poem, the writer is concerned about what poetry is. What general statement does he make about the topic? State the theme in your own words.

2. **Recognizing Structure.** A poet can show the **structure,** or organization, of a poem in several ways. The same poem can use more than one of these. One way is through the use of repetition, as in "I Hear America Singing." Another way is through the use of rhyme, as in "Song of the Truck." A third way is through the use of stanzas. The stanzas may be all the same length or of different lengths.

   "Unfolding Bud" uses two of these ways of showing the organization of a poem. Which two does it use? Point out words or ideas in the poem to support your answer.

3. **Identifying Levels of Meaning.** The speaker in this poem describes both the water-lily and the poem with the same words. In the description of the water-lily, the words *tight-closed* and *unfolding* are used in a **literal** sense. That is, the words are used with their usual meaning. We do not have to use any imagination to understand what the speaker means.

   However, in the description of the poem, the words are used in a **figurative** sense. That is, they are used in an unexpected way. We must use imagination to figure out what the speaker has in mind.

   Think about the word *song* in "Song of the Truck." Is it used in its literal sense or in a figurative sense? In "I Hear America Singing," is the word *singing* used literally or figuratively?

Developing Vocabulary Skills

Recognizing Borrowed Words. In "Song of the Truck," there is a list of items carried by the trucks. The names of many of these items are borrowed from other languages. Try to match the correct word from the poem with each word history described below.

1. This word came from the French word *fourniture*. It means movable articles in a house.

2. This word came from the Latin word *textilis*, which means "woven."

3. This word for a popular beverage was taken from the Turkish word *kahve*. In turn *kahve* came from the Arabic *qahwa*.

4. *Chickens* is a word that was used in Old English, before 1100 A.D. However, the hard-shelled food that chickens produce was

once called *ey*. After 1100, that name was dropped and this Scandinavian word was used for the same product.

5. This name for several kinds of syrup came from the Portuguese word *melaco*. That was based on *mel*, the Latin word for honey.

6. This word names a fabric that is made from the fleece of an Angora goat. The word came originally from an Arabian word, *mukhayyar*.

Developing Writing Skills

1. **Explaining an Opinion.** You have now read four poems. Which of them do you think had the most effect on you? Which helped you most to see a familiar thing in a new way? Which will you remember best? Write a paragraph explaining which poem meant the most to you.

    Pre-Writing. On your paper, write a phrase or sentence that explains a comparison the poem used. List anything else about the poem that took your attention or made you think. This could include rhymes, alliteration, rhythm, the tone of voice the speaker used, or the ideas in the poem. Decide which part of the poem you will remember most clearly. Number your notes in order of importance.

    Writing. Begin your paragraph by telling the name of the poem and suggesting how it affected you. For example, you might write a topic sentence like this:

    "Unfolding Bud" helped me realize that it takes time to understand a poem.

    Then explain what the poet did in this poem that caused it to give this effect to you. Refer to your notes.

Revising. Reread your paragraph. Did your explanation support your topic sentence? Did you point out specific words or lines in the poem that were meaningful to you? Are your reasons for remembering the poem listed in the order of importance? Mark any corrections on your first draft. Make a clean copy.

2. **Comparing and Contrasting Poems.** Choose one of these sets of poems: "To Look at Any Thing" and "Unfolding Bud," or "I Hear America Singing" and "Song of the Truck." Can you find ways the two poems are alike? In what ways are they different? You may consider rhyme, rhythm, theme, the senses to which they appeal, or any other quality you choose. Write a paragraph in which you compare their similarities and contrast their differences.

3. **Using Your Senses.** In "To Look at Any Thing," the speaker advises you to look at a thing long and to "be" the thing you see. Choose one object that is close at hand, which you can look at and touch. You should like the object well enough to want to "be" it. Examine the object closely. Then write a description of it. Give details that appeal to sight, sound, and touch. If possible, include details that appeal to smell and taste, also. Your description should be exact enough to let your reader "be" the thing you describe.

Developing Skills in Speaking and Listening

Interpreting a Poem Orally. For this activity, work with three classmates. Each member of the group should choose a different poem from among the four that have been read. Then each group member will prepare his or her poem and read it for the others in the group. Here are some suggestions for preparing, reading, and listening to these poems.

1. **Choosing the Poem.** Three of the poems in this section use a conversational rhythm. Those poems are "To Look at Any Thing," "I Hear America Singing," and "Unfolding Bud." When you read these poems aloud, you must pause where there are commas, periods, or other breaks in the ideas. You do not automatically pause at the end of each line. You must think about the meaning of the words as you read them. Then you can put stress on the words that are most important.

   The fourth poem, "Song of the Truck," has a strong, regular rhythm. In addition, it uses a list in which all the items are about the same length. This can easily lead to a singsong reading. To avoid that problem when you read the poem aloud, you must make some choices. Which words in the first four lines and the last four lines are more important and deserve more stress? Which words in the list do you want to emphasize? Which parts of the list should go faster? Which should go slower?

2. **Preparing the Poem.** After you have chosen your poem, read it aloud to yourself at least two times. Put stress on the important words. Pause where a pause makes sense. Listen to yourself, both for the meaning of the words and the sounds. Make sure that you are pronouncing every word correctly. Make sure that you are not reading too quickly and losing words.

3. **Presenting the Poem.** When you read your poem to your group, try to keep in mind the things you practiced. Also, try to make your voice loud enough for everyone in the group to hear.

4. **Listening to a Poem.** When another member of the group reads a poem, keep your book closed. Concentrate on what the reader is saying. Be able to tell the reader whether you could understand the words and the ideas. Let the reader know whether his or her voice was at the right speed and volume.

Fueled

MARCIE HANS

This poem examines two things that seem to be very unlike one another. The poet, however, finds similarities between them. As you read, look for comparisons and contrasts.

Fueled
by a million
man-made
wings of fire—
the rocket tore a tunnel
through the sky—
and everybody cheered.
Fueled
only by a thought from God—
the seedling
urged its way
through the thickness of black—
and as it pierced
the heavy ceiling of the soil—
and launched itself
up into outer space—
no
one
even
clapped.

Developing Comprehension Skills

1. What two objects are compared in this poem?

2. What two events are compared? How do people react to each event?

3. The poet says that the rocket is fueled "by a million man-made wings of fire." What does she mean by that?

4. Reread the last four lines of the poem. Do you suppose the writer wants people to clap every time a seedling sprouts? Can you think of the real reason she had for writing those lines?

Reading Literature: Poetry

1. **Understanding Metaphor.** "Fueled" uses several metaphors. Explain each of these comparisons:

    tore a tunnel through the sky
    ceiling of the soil

    In addition, the whole poem builds up another comparison. As you may remember, a long metaphor like this one is called an *extended metaphor.* Explain the extended metaphor in this poem.

2. **Identifying Structure.** The poem is printed as one stanza. However, it is made up of two sentences. The ideas in the poem are separated into two parts, according to the sentences. What word alerts the reader to this separation of ideas?

3. **Understanding Alliteration.** Alliteration can add emphasis to some phrases. For example, The alliteration in "a million man-made wings" stresses the fact that humans made the rocket. Alliteration can also bring together words that the writer wants the reader to connect. In the second part of the poem, the sound of *s* at the beginning of the word connects words spread across seven lines. Identify those words.

4. **Recognizing Rhythm.** Both sentences in the poem describe action. Which sentence uses more words to tell about the action? Does using more words speed up or slow down the feeling of movement in the sentence?

    At one point the writer forces the reader to slow down and think about the idea in the words. Where do you find this happening? What method does the poet use to achieve that effect?

Steam Shovel

CHARLES MALAM

In this poem we see another comparison between an object in nature and one made by humans. Here, however, the speaker points out only similarities. As you read, try to picture a combination of the two things.

The dinosaurs are not all dead.
I saw one raise its iron head
To watch me walking down the road
Beyond our house today.
Its jaws were dripping with a load
Of earth and grass that it had cropped.
It must have heard me where I stopped,
Snorted white steam my way,
And stretched its long neck out to see,
And chewed, and grinned quite amiably.

Developing Comprehension Skills

1. What two things does the poem compare?

2. Can you find three ways in which the things are similar?

3. You have read three extended metaphors: "Unfolding Bud," "Fueled," and "Steam Shovel." Which two poems do you think are more alike? How are they alike? What makes the third poem different?

Reading Literature: Poetry

1. **Appreciating Condensed Language.** Two words in line 2 tell what is needed to understand the metaphor. What are they?

2. **Identifying Rhyme Scheme.** This poem uses an unusual pattern of rhyme, or **rhyme scheme**. You can show the rhyme scheme by writing a letter for each line of the poem. Use the same letter for lines that rhyme. Here is the rhyme scheme for the first three lines of this poem:

    The dinosaurs are not all dead   *a*
    I saw one raise its iron head   *a*
    To watch me walking down the road   *b*

   On your paper, write out the rhyme scheme for all ten lines of "Steam Shovel." How does the pattern of rhyme help to signal the end of the poem?

Macavity:
The Mystery Cat

This poem is about a most extraordinary cat! His crimes are many, but he always evades the law. As you read, look for qualities that make this cat almost believable.

T.S. ELIOT

Macavity's a Mystery Cat: he's called the Hidden Paw—
For he's the master criminal who can defy the Law.
He's the bafflement of Scotland Yard, the Flying Squad's despair:
For when they reach the scene of crime—*Macavity's not there*!

Macavity, Macavity, there's no one like Macavity,
He's broken every human law, he breaks the law of gravity.
His powers of levitation would make a fakir stare,
And when you reach the scene of crime—*Macavity's not there*!
You may seek him in the basement, you may look up in the air—
But I tell you once and once again, *Macavity's not there*!

Macavity's a ginger cat, he's very tall and thin;
You would know him if you saw him, for his eyes are sunken in.
His brow is deeply lined with thought, his head is highly domed;
His coat is dusty from neglect, his whiskers are uncombed.
He sways his head from side to side, with movements like a snake;
And when you think he's half asleep, he's always wide awake.

Macavity, Macavity, there's no one like Macavity,
For he's a fiend in feline shape, a monster of depravity.
You may meet him in a by-street, you may see him in the square—
But when a crime's discovered, then *Macavity's not there*!

He's outwardly respectable. (They say he cheats at cards.)
And his footprints are not found in any file in Scotland Yard's.
And when the larder's looted, or the jewel-case is rifled,
Or when the milk is missing, or another Peke's been stifled,
Or the greenhouse glass is broken, and the trellis past repair—
Ay, there's the wonder of the thing! *Macavity's not there!*

And when the Foreign Office find a Treaty's gone astray,
Or the Admiralty lose some plans and drawings by the way,
There may be a scrap of paper in the hall or on the stair—
But it's useless to investigate—*Macavity's not there!*
And when the loss has been disclosed, the Secret Service say:
'It *must* have been Macavity!'—but he's a mile away.
You'll be sure to find him resting, or a-licking of his thumbs,
Or engaged in doing complicated long division sums.

Macavity, Macavity, there's no one like Macavity,
There never was a Cat of such deceitfulness and suavity.
He always has an alibi, and one or two to spare:
At whatever time the deed took place—MACAVITY WASN'T THERE!
And they say that all the Cats whose wicked deeds are widely known
(I might mention Mungojerrie, I might mention Griddlebone)
Are nothing more than agents for the Cat who all the time
Just controls their operations: the Napoleon of Crime!

Developing Comprehension Skills

1. Identify at least three of the crimes Macavity is charged with. Which lines accuse him of these crimes?

2. Macavity is said to have powers of levitation. That is, he has the ability to rise in the air. If you have seen a cat take a sudden high jump, you might agree that cats have that ability. Explain how other details in the description in stanza 2 might fit a real cat.

3. The poem mentions Scotland Yard, the Foreign Office, and the Admiralty. What is Macavity's homeland?

4. What do you consider the funniest part of "Macavity: The Mystery Cat"? Explain why you chose those lines.

Reading Literature: Poetry

1. **Recognizing Personification.** In **personification**, a nonhuman thing is spoken of as if it were human. Identify at least five lines which describe Macavity as if he were human.

2. **Appreciating Repetition.** What line is repeated several times in the poem? Why do you think this repetition occurs? How does it help the poem?

3. **Recognizing Tone.** The attitude the writer shows in a selection is called the **tone**. Which of these words best describes the tone of this poem: *serious, playful, frightened, angry*? Give a reason for your answer.

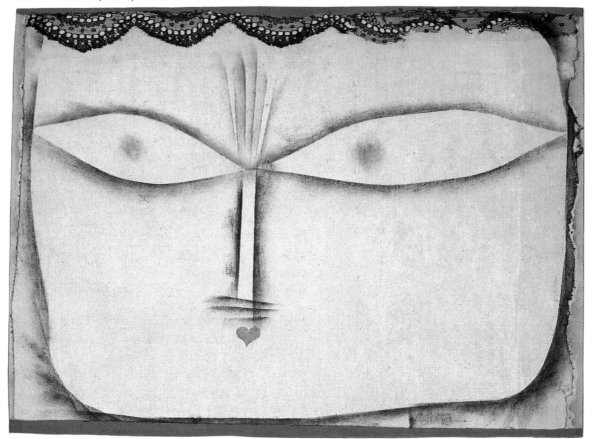

Idol for Housecats, 1924, PAUL KLÉE. Norton Simon Museum of Art, Pasadena, California, Blue Four Collection.

Crossing

PHILIP BOOTH

Most of us have experienced waiting at a train crossing. Does this poem give an accurate picture of what the waiting is like?

STOP LOOK LISTEN
  as gate stripes swing down,
    count the cars hauling distance
     upgrade through town:
      warning whistle, bellclang,
       engine eating steam,
        engineer waving,
         a fast-freight dream:
          B&M boxcar,
           boxcar again,
            Frisco gondola,
eight-nine-ten,
  Erie and Wabash,
   Seaboard, U.P.,
    Pennsy tankcar,
twenty-two, three,
  Phoebe Snow, B&O,
thirty-four, five,
  Santa Fe cattle
   shipped alive,
    red cars, yellow cars,
     orange cars, black,
      Youngstown steel
     down to Mobile
      on Rock Island track,

fifty-nine, sixty,
  hoppers of coke,
   Anaconda copper,
   hotbox smoke,
eighty-eight,
  red-ball freight,
   Rio Grande,
    Nickel Plate,
     Hiawatha,
      Lackawanna,
     rolling fast
     and loose,
ninety-seven,
 coal car,
  boxcar,
   CABOOSE!

Rolling Power, 1939, CHARLES SHEELER. Smith College Museum of Art, Northampton Massachusetts. Purchased 1940.

Developing Comprehension Skills

1. The train in this poem is very long. How many cars does it contain?

2. Have you ever seen a sign with the words "Stop, Look, and Listen"? Where does the poem suggest the sign might be?

3. Names like *B&O*, *Frisco*, and *Erie and Wabash* are mentioned in the list of cars. What is the meaning of these names?

4. "Crossing" appeals to both sight and sound. Name two details that suggest what the speaker sees.

5. Does this poem give you the feeling of waiting at a crossing? Give a reason for your opinion.

Reading Literature: Poetry

1. **Appreciating Form.** Sometimes a poet uses the shape of a poem to add to the reader's experience of it. From the shape of "Crossing," tell whether the train is coming from the speaker's left or from the right. How can you tell?

2. **Appreciating Sounds.** This is a poem in which sound is very important. Find at least one example of each of the following:

   a. alliteration   (the repetition of beginning sounds)

   b. assonance   (repetition of vowel sounds)

   c. onomatopoeia   (the use of words that suggest sounds)

3. **Recognizing Rhyme.** Most of the lines of this poem follow a regular *abcb* rhyme scheme:

B&M boxcar,	*a*
boxcar again,	*b*
Frisco gondola,	*c*
eight-nine-ten	*b*

However, the poet had a special shape in mind for this poem. In order to create that shape, he made two exceptions to this rhyme pattern. For example, here the usual third line has become two lines:

red cars, yellow cars,	*a*
orange cars, black,	*b*
Youngstown steel	*c*
down to Mobile	*c*
on Rock Island track	*b*

Find all the regular four-line rhyme patterns. Identify the rhyming words at the ends of the *b* lines. Then identify the second exception to the pattern. Into how many lines does the poet break the usual four lines?

4. **Understanding Purpose.** Some purposes for writing poems include the following:

to express a mood
to describe an experience
to present an opinion
to give advice

Why do you suppose the poet wrote this poem?

Developing Vocabulary Skills

Reviewing Context Clues. You know that you can often find the meaning of an unfamiliar word in the context in which that word appears.

You have learned how to use the following context clues: definition or restatement clues, synonyms, comparison clues, contrast clues, example clues.

The underlined words in the following sentences are from poems in this section. Read the sentences for each word. Tell what kind of context clues you find. Then tell the meaning of the word that you learn from the context.

1. A fakir, an Islamic or Hindu holy man, is often a magician, as well.

2. The thief looted the safe. He stole jewels, cash, and valuable papers.

3. Macavity is never impolite. Everyone is impressed with his suavity.

4. Most people do not believe in levitation—the ability of a nonflying object to float in the air.

5. She wore her hair cropped, or cut close to the head.

6. When things get broken, my little brother always has an alibi, that is, an excuse to prove he was somewhere else.

7. A trellis, or a frame of crossed strips of wood or metal, is often found in a garden, with vines on it.

8. The workers unloaded many freight cars, such as hoppers and gondolas.

Developing Writing Skills

1. **Examining Tone.** When you were reading "Macavity: The Mystery Cat," what feeling did you think the poet had about Macavity? Was the writer serious? Did he fear Macavity? Did he like or dislike cats? How did he want the reader to feel about the subject of the poem? How can you tell?

Write a paragraph explaining the tone the writer used in "Macavity." If you prefer, you may write about the tone in "Fueled," "Steam Shovel," or "Crossing." Use words or lines from the poem to support your statements.

2. **Writing an Extended Metaphor.** In an extended metaphor, the writer compares two unlike things. He or she points out several matches between the two things. The two things, the writer says, are the same in these ways. You have read several examples of extended metaphors: "Unfolding Bud," "Fueled," and "Steam Shovel." In this activity, you will write one of your own.

Pre-Writing. List at least six machines you have used today. They could include such things as toasters, bicycles, wheel chairs, radios, pencil sharpeners, or computers.

After each item, list several details that tell what the object looks like or what it does. Think about shapes, colors, speeds, and sounds. If you have ever felt that the object has a personality of its own, add that to you list of details.

Next, review each machine on your list. Is there any living thing that it reminds you of? Do the shapes, colors, or actions of the machine suggest the shapes, colors, or actions of an animal or plant or person? Make a note of each way the two things are alike.

Then, choose the machine that has the most matches with a living thing. Circle the notes on your list that show those similarities, or make a new list.

Writing. Describe the machine you chose as if it were the animal, plant, or person it reminds you of. You may write a paragraph or a poem. Include several details from your list.

Revising. Examine the verbs in your description. Is each verb exact? Is it a verb that people normally use to tell what living things do? If you used verbs such as *is* or *seems*, change such verbs to stronger ones.

Also, check whether you used words such as *like*, *as*, or *the same as*. Try to take such words out. Remember, you are not saying that the machine seems like a living creature. You are saying that it is a living creature.

Developing Skills in Study and Research

Using a Thesaurus. A **thesaurus** is a reference book that lists words with their synonyms, antonyms, and related words. It may explain the slight differences in meanings among the words grouped together. Find a thesaurus, perhaps in your school library. Use the directions in the thesaurus to find listings for three of the words below. For each of the three words, write on your paper at least four related words you find in the thesaurus listing.

clap	launch	urge	stretch
defy	meet	find	break
swing	wave	eat	listen

Child on Top of a Greenhouse

THEODORE ROETHKE

Almost everyone likes a bird's-eye view of the world now and then. In this poem, a child climbs to the highest place available for a good view. As you read, try to decide whether the child regrets the climb.

The wind billowing out the seat of my britches,
My feet crackling splinters of glass and dried putty,
The half-grown chrysanthemums staring up like accusers,
Up through the streaked glass, flashing with sunlight,
A few white clouds all rushing eastward,
A line of elms plunging and tossing like horses,
And everyone, everyone pointing up and shouting!

Developing Comprehension Skills

1. Identify in the poem at least one sharply defined detail that appeals to the sense of sight. Identify a detail that appeals to the sense of sound, and another that appeals to the sense of touch.

2. In the speaker's description, is the wind strong, or just a breeze? How do you know?

3. The speaker says that the chrysanthemums are "staring up like accusers." The flowers can't actually give an opinion. The speaker must be transferring someone else's opinion to the chrysanthemums. Who do you think is accusing the child of wrongdoing? What details in the poem make this suggestion?

4. The poet has presented a clear, exciting picture of what it might feel like at the top of a greenhouse. Is he saying that the child's act is acceptable or good? Give a reason for your opinion.

Reading Literature: Poetry

1. **Understanding Point of View.** Who is the speaker in this poem? How do you know?

2. **Recognizing the Mood of the Speaker.** The speaker never makes a direct statement about feeling afraid or daring, thrilled or guilty, or having some combination of feelings. The reader must guess the speaker's mood from what he or she says. One way to figure out the child's mood is to examine the details he or she notices.

The speaker first reports the feeling of wind, then the sounds made by his or her feet, and then the view below those feet. The sunlight catches the child's attention next. After that the child sees the clouds and their motion, the trees and their motions, and finally the people on the ground and their actions.

From the order in which the child notices things, does it seem as if the people on the ground are important to him or her? Does the child seem worried about the people's reaction? Or is the child simply aware of the people as he or she is of the clouds and trees?

Next, look at the action words the speaker uses: *billowing, crackling, staring, flashing, rushing, plunging, tossing, pointing,* and *shouting.* How many of them show strong, exciting action? Do any of them suggest guilt or fear?

Think about these clues. Then state what you think is the mood of the speaker.

3. **Identifying Techniques.** The poet more than once uses **assonance**, the repetition of vowel sounds. For example, the short *i* sound appears three times in line 1, in *wind, billowing,* and *britches.* Find another example of assonance in the poem.

Identify the two similes. For each, tell what is being compared to what.

Central Park Tourney

MILDRED WESTON

A tourney (or tournament) is a trial or contest. Participants must demonstrate great skill and a mastery of their sport. What tournament is described in this poem? Is it a real contest?

Cars
In the Park
With long spear lights
Ride at each other
Like armored knights;
Rush,
Miss the mark,
Pierce the dark,
Dash by!
Another two
Try.

Staged
In the Park
From dusk
To dawn,
The tourney goes on:
Rush,
Miss the mark,
Pierce the dark,
Dash by!
Another two
Try.

Developing Comprehension Skills

1. Who is participating in the tourney?

2. What time of day is it? How do you know?

3. What do you think these lines mean: "Rush, Miss the mark, Pierce the dark, Dash by!"? In your own words, explain the action they describe.

4. What do the last two lines mean? Who are the other two? What do they try?

5. In a jousting tournament, two mounted knights would rush at each other, aiming spears at one another. The one who could knock the other off his horse won the joust. What is happening in this joust? Why is the image of knights a good one? Is it funny or frightening or both? Explain your answer.

Shakespeare at Dusk, 1935, EDWARD HOPPER. Collection of Mr. and Mrs. Carl D. Lobell, New York.

Reading Literature: Poetry

1. **Understanding Figurative Language.** The first stanza includes both a simile and a metaphor. Identify each of them.

2. **Recognizing Connotations.** The word *staged* suggests that an activity is planned and perhaps rehearsed ahead of time. It suggests that the participants in the activity are trying to have a certain effect, such as making people laugh or cry. How does the use of *staged* affect the meaning of the poem?

3. **Identifying Tone.** Is the writer serious, thoughtful, amused, excited, worried? Can you suggest a better description of the poet's attitude?

4. **Appreciating Repetition.** Six lines are repeated in stanza 2. How does this repetition reinforce the meaning of the poem?

   At least three other poems you have read in this chapter also used repetition to give shape and to stress meaning. Can you name two of those other poems?

Apartment House

GERALD RAFTERY

Have you seen many large apartment houses or high-rises? Perhaps you are living in one now. As you read this poem about such buildings, try to decide whether the poet likes or dislikes them.

A filing-cabinet of human lives
Where people swarm like bees in tunneled hives,
Each to his own cell in the towered comb,
Identical and cramped—we call it home.

Land of Lincoln, 1978, ROGER BROWN. Courtesy of Phyllis Kind Gallery. New York and Chicago. Photograph by William H. Bengtson.

Developing Comprehension Skills

1. To what does this poem compare people?

2. In one metaphor, the speaker says that the apartment house is a filing cabinet. Explain how that comparison fits.

3. In a second metaphor, the speaker calls the apartment house a beehive with cells. What fact about apartment living suggests this?

4. Comparing a place where people live with places where there are just objects or insects makes the apartment house seem unfit for humans. Is this what the poet is trying to say? Or is there a reason to think otherwise?

Reading Literature: Poetry

1. **Understanding Theme.** Think about your answer to question 4 above. Then state what you think is the theme, or main idea, of this poem.

2. **Identifying Rhyme Scheme.** Write out the rhyme scheme of this poem. Use letters to stand for lines that rhyme.

3. **Appreciating Rhythm.** Three of the four lines in this poem have four strong beats. The fourth has five strong beats. Find the line with five beats. Why did the poet squeeze more beats into that line? How does the extra beat fit in with the meaning of the line?

4. **Recognizing Irony.** The contrast between what is expected and what occurs is called **irony**. Find an example of irony in this poem.

Southbound on the Freeway

MAY SWENSON

The myths you have read in Chapters 1, 2, and 3 all said that humans were special creations of gods or godlike beings. What does this poem say about us?

A tourist came in from Orbitville,
parked in the air, and said:

The creatures of this star
are made of metal and glass.

Through the transparent parts
you can see their guts.

Their feet are round and roll
on diagrams or long

measuring tapes, dark
with white lines.

They have four eyes.
The two in back are red.

Sometimes you can see a five-eyed
one, with a red eye turning

on the top of his head.

He must be special—

the others respect him
and go slow

when he passes, winding
among them from behind.

They all hiss as they glide,
like inches, down the marked

tapes. Those soft shapes,
shadowy inside

the hard bodies—are they
their guts or their brains?

Developing Comprehension Skills

1. What does the visitor to Earth describe? What does this visitor think they are?

2. Explain what each of these phrases actually refers to:

   a. diagrams or long measuring tapes.
   b. four eyes
   c. transparent parts
   d. a five-eyed one
   e. soft shapes

3. What comment about humans is the poet making with these lines?

   > Those soft shapes,
   > shadowy inside
   > the hard bodies—are they
   > their guts or their brains?

4. Do you think this poem is funny? Explain your answer.

Reading Literature: Poetry

1. **Appreciating Imagery.** Think of all the things on Earth that a visitor from space might see. Why did the poet have the visitor notice cars?

2. **Understanding Irony.** What is ironic about the visitor thinking that cars are the dominant life form on Earth? Do we humans ever act as if we think that way?

3. **Becoming Aware of Point of View.** This poem lets us look at ourselves from the outside. It points out that even when someone has some of the facts right, he or she does not always have the whole truth. Identify one of the correct statements that the visitor makes about our actions. Can you suggest a reason why the visitor misinterpreted this fact?

Developing Vocabulary Skills

Spelling Compound Words Correctly. Some compounds are written without any break between the two words that have been combined. Examples are *sundown* and *nothing*. Other compounds are written with a hyphen. An example is *man-made*. Still other compounds are written as if they were separate words, such as *steam shovel*.

Because there are three ways of writing compounds, it is not always easy to tell which way a compound should be written. Another difficulty is that, over many years, spellings sometimes change in English. Poets, too, sometimes use hyphens for special effects. Often, the only way you can be sure of the correct spelling is by checking a dictionary.

Use the poet's spellings as you write down the following compounds.

1. Examine "I Hear America Singing," "Crossing," and "Child on Top of a Greenhouse." Find ten closed compounds, that is, compounds spelled as one word.

2. Examine "Unfolding Bud," "Macavity," and "Southbound on the Freeway." Find two compounds written with hyphens.

3. Examine "Song of the Truck." Find one open compound, that is, a compound written as two separate words.

Developing Writing Skills

1. **Explaining a Symbol.** Both "Central Park Tourney" and "Southbound on the Freeway" use cars in describing part of modern life. Because the cars represent something about the way we live, they are a **symbol** of modern living. Each poem uses the symbol

in a particular way. Choose one of the poems. Write a paragraph explaining what the cars in that poem symbolize about modern life.

Pre-Writing. Reread both poems. On your paper, note ideas about what the symbol suggests. What are the cars doing? How is that like what people do? Does it seem that the cars have feelings? Are those feelings common in people?

Choose the poem you feel says more about modern life. Decide whether the cars symbolize something good or bad, or simply represent a fact.

Then look at your notes critically. Some of them are more usable than others. Put a check mark next to each idea you want to include in your paragraph. Then number the checked ideas in the order of their importance.

Writing. Begin your paragraph by telling which poem you are basing your answer on. Then explain the ideas in your notes, using complete sentences. Try to end with a summary of your ideas.

Revising. Reread your paragraph, looking for words that connect ideas. Did you use *and's* at the beginnings of sentences? If so, omit them and see if the paragraph still makes sense. Did you use words like *because, for this reason,* and *in this way*? If not, would they help? Make any changes that are needed to show the connections between ideas more clearly.

2. **Writing a Description.** In "Child on Top of a Greenhouse," the poet described the scene and the child's feelings in less than sixty words arranged in seven lines. Choose a set-

ting; go there, if possible, to take notes on what you see. Then write a very short description of the place. Your description may have from sixty to eighty words. The words may be arranged in seven or eight lines of poetry, or they may be written as prose. Include details that will give the reader a suggestion of how you feel about the place.

3. **Keeping a Journal.** Many poets find it helpful to keep a journal. There, they record any ideas that they think might be good topics for poems. They jot down similes, metaphors, and other figurative language that occurs to them. They insert descriptions of people, things, and scenes that are particularly memorable. They keep the journal only for their own information. Later, they refer to these notes for ideas or good phrases to use in the writing that they will show others.

If you are not already keeping a journal, begin one now. Any writing in your journal is for you alone. You do not have to worry about such things as spelling and grammar. However, you will find that correct spelling, grammar, and punctuation will keep your ideas clear. You may want to take time to make your writing correct. Whenever you put an idea, a phrase, or a description into your journal, make sure that it will be understandable in months to come. Then, when you look through the journal for help, you can use these notes.

Developing Skills in Speaking and Listening

Reading for Rhythm. When you read some poems aloud, the most important effect to concentrate on is the rhythm or tempo. Three poems of this type are "Macavity: The Mystery Cat," "Crossing," and "Central Park Tourney." Select one of these poems and prepare to read it for a group.

Review the suggestions for preparing a poem listed in the Speaking and Listening exercise on pages 344 and 345. Follow these guidelines.

1. "Macavity": Choose any two stanzas to read aloud. In reading this poem, let your voice get soft and loud, fast and slow. This not only avoids monotony, it also brings out the suspense, drama, and humor in the poem.

2. "Crossing": Decide whether the train will move fast throughout the entire poem, or whether it will slow down at one or more points. Then, as you read, let the changing speeds of your voice suggest the different speeds of the train.

3. "Central Park Tourney": Notice that the first five lines in each stanza should run together without a break. The last six lines in each stanza should sound choppy.

Developing Skills in Critical Thinking

Recognizing Faulty Logic. In "Southbound on the Freeway," the alien visitor observed some facts correctly. For example, cars are made of metal and glass, they do roll, and most cars do go slow when a car with a red light on top is nearby. However, the visitor used these accurate observations to jump to some illogical conclusions.

Here are several statements on which the alien tourist based his or her conclusions. Can you find the error in each of them? Can the statement be changed to be more logical? Can you suggest better guidelines for the alien to use in the future?

1. If something moves, it is alive.

2. If a thing is too small to be seen clearly, it is unimportant.

3. If an unfamiliar thing is like a familiar thing in one way, the two things are alike in many ways.

For a Dead Kitten

SARA HENDERSON HAY

In this poem, the speaker is saddened by the death of a pet. However, her questions show that her sadness is only part of her problem. Read to find out what puzzles her.

Put the rubber mouse away,
Pick the spools up from the floor,
What was velvet-shod, and gay,
Will not want them any more.

What was warm, is strangely cold,
Whence dissolved the little breath?
How could this small body hold
So immense a thing as Death?

Developing Comprehension Skills

1. What was the purpose of the rubber mouse and the spools?

2. *Shod* means "wearing shoes." Why is the kitten described as "velvet-shod"? What does the term suggest?

3. The speaker's first question is "Whence dissolved the little breath?" Tell in your own words what she wants to know.

4. Why is the word *Death* in the last line capitalized?

5. Is the speaker afraid of death? Does she show anger? What is her attitude toward death?

Reading Literature: Poetry

1. **Examining Language.** The poet stresses the theme by the words she chooses. For example, *whence* is a formal word. It lets you know how serious the speaker is.

   There are two sets of opposites: *warm* and *cold*, *small* and *immense*. There are also contradictory phrases: since it isn't solid, "breath" cannot "dissolve"; and nothing can "hold" death. How do these contradictions stress the mood of the poem?

2. **Identifying Theme.** What is the poet saying about death? State the theme in your own words.

The High School Band

REED WHITTEMORE

You will understand this poem best if you hear every word. If you can, read it aloud. Otherwise, listen to it with your mind's ear. Think about how the sounds make the ideas clear.

On warm days in September the high
    school band
Is up with the birds and marches along
    our street,
Boom, boom,
To a field where it goes boom boom until
    eight forty-five
When it marches, as in the old rhyme,
    back, boom boom,
To its study halls, leaving our street
Empty except for the leaves that descend,
    to no drum,
And lie still.
In September
A great many high school bands beat a
    great many drums,
And the silences after their partings are
    very deep.

Autumn Leaves No. 2, 1927, GEORGIA O'KEEFFE.
Private Collection. Courtesy of Kennedy Galleries, New York.

Developing Comprehension Skills

1. When and where does the band practice?

2. What is the only noticeable happening on the street after the band goes into the school?

3. Whose point of view does this poem give?

4. The poet connects the coming of the band with the rising of birds. He connects the departure of the band with the falling of leaves. In this way, he suggests that there is something general, like a law of nature, in the band's comings and goings. What happens in nature during fall? Combine that information with the events in the poem. State what you think the poem is saying about life in general.

Reading Literature: Poetry

1. **Identifying Sensory Images.** To which sense does this poem appeal most strongly? Identify two passages that appeal to that sense.

2. **Recognizing Onomatopoeia.** What echoic word appears in this poem? Where do you find it? Which band instrument does it imitate?

3. **Appreciating Rhythm.** The ideas in this poem develop in two parts. The first eight lines present a sharp image of the street where the band practices. The last three lines use that experience to make a general statement. The change in topic is brought out not only in the meanings of the words. It is also brought out in their rhythms.

Read over the first seven lines, to the word "Empty." The rhythm of the words imitates the beat of the band music. As you read the words, you can easily imagine the sound of the band's drum.

In lines 7 and 8 the tempo changes, just as the topic starts to change.

On your paper, copy the last three lines, beginning with "In September." Leave space between the lines for accents. Draw an accent (/) over every syllable that you feel should be stressed. How does the number of stressed syllables affect the speed with which you say the lines? How does the speed relate to the meaning of the lines?

Nine Triads

LILLIAN MORRISON

Here, the poet presents three times three, or nine, groups of thoughts. Further, each group is a triad, or group of three. Try to determine how all nine triads are related. Can you suggest why the poet used three's?

Three grand arcs:
    the lift of the pole vaulter over the bar
    the golf ball's flight to the green
    the home run into the bleachers

Three pleasurable curves:
    the ice skater's figure eight
    the long cast of the fisherman
    the arched back of the gymnast

Three swishes that lift the heart:
    the basketball's spin through the net
    the skier's swoop down the snowpacked hill
    the diver's entry into the water

Three glides of satisfaction:
    the ice hockey forward's, after the goal
    the swimmer's turn at the end of the pool
    the finish of the bobsled run

Three swift arrivals to admire:
    the completed pass
    the arrow into the bull's-eye
    the sprinter at the tape

The Footballer, 1961, PABLO PICASSO.
Museum Picasso, Paris. Courtesy of Art Resource, New York.

Three shots requiring skill:
　　the slapshot
　　the shot-put
　　the putt-out

Three carriers of suspense:
　　the place kick for a field goal
　　the rim shot
　　three balls and two strikes

Three vital sounds:
　　the hunter's horn
　　the starter's gun
　　the bell for the end of the round

Three excellent wishes:
　　to move the body with grace
　　to fly without a machine
　　to outrun time

Developing Comprehension Skills

1. Identify a line in the poem that refers to each sport listed below:

   a. baseball　　d. swimming　　g. skiing
   b. football　　 e. archery　　 h. skating
   c. hockey　　　 f. running　　　i. golf

   Can you identify any other sports?

2. How are all the triads related?

3. Which two triads appeal to the sense of hearing? To what sense do the others appeal?

4. Which is your favorite triad? Why? Is it the poet's selection of details that affects your choice? Or do your own feelings about particular sports influence your choice of a favorite triad?

   Should your own feelings be part of your reaction to poetry?

Reading Literature: Poetry

1. **Identifying Repetition.** This poem obviously uses repetition of the word *three*. Is repetition used in any other ways? Explain your answer.

2. **Understanding Theme.** It could be said that this poem celebrates something. What do you think that is?

3. **Appreciating Rhythm.** The rhythm in this poem is not very regular. It varies a bit from stanza to stanza to fit the topic. Compare the rhythm in stanzas 1 and 6. How do the stanzas differ in rhythm and in topic?

4. **Recognizing Poetry.** This selection looks like many other lists. However, several features set it off from other lists. One is the use of rhythm. Another is the combination of details to produce a certain effect. What is the feeling you get reading this poem, especially its last three lines?

Developing Vocabulary Skills

Recognizing Word Origins. Each underlined word in the following sentences originated in one of these four ways:

words from names   borrowed words
words from sounds   combined words

Use context clues, pronunciation clues, and spelling clues to identify any words from names, words from sounds, and combined words. Any word that does not fit into one of these three categories is a borrowed word. On your paper, write what you believe is the source of each underlined word.

1. The warning bell at the train crossing <u>clanged</u> loudly.

2. <u>Cantaloupes</u> were first grown in Europe on the estate known as Cantalupo, near Rome.

3. Randall is training for the <u>pole vault</u>.

4. Just listen to that fire <u>crackle</u>!

5. Jennifer's arrow pierced the <u>bull's-eye</u>.

6. The <u>caboose</u> is the last car on the train.

7. The cat's tail <u>swished</u> through the air.

8. How long ago was the game of <u>basketball</u> invented?

Developing Writing Skills

1. **Analyzing Patterns of Organization.** These are some of the patterns of organization used in the poems of this section:

   a. patterns of rhyme
   b. stanza form
   c. development of ideas
   d. lists
   e. repetition

   Choose one of these methods of organization. Write a paragraph that explains what the method is. In the paragraph, give two examples from the poems in this section, "Observations." If you need to quote lines from the poem, remember to use quotation marks correctly and to copy the words of the poem exactly.

2. **Writing a Poem with a List.** Three of the poems in this section featured lists. Review the techniques used in "I Hear America Singing," "Song of the Truck," and "Nine Triads." Choose a topic that interests you. Then write a poem of at least twelve lines that uses a list.

   Pre-Writing. First review the three poems that use lists. Notice the changes in rhythm, the alliteration, the rhyme, and other uses of sound. Then note three or more possible topics. After each topic, note as many examples or items for the list as you can think of. Compare your lists. Choose the topic about which you know the most and have the best ideas. If you like, choose a funny topic.

Next, decide in what order to arrange your list items. Number them on your note paper.

Writing. The first line or two of your poem should explain what the topic is. The rest of the poem should be the list itself. The end of the poem should complete the list or summarize it, so that the reader will know when the poem is done.

Revising. Either read the poem to a friend or ask the friend to read it. The reader should be able to state what the main idea is and why the list is in the poem. If necessary, add words or lines to make this clear.

Developing Skills in Critical Thinking

Classifying Poems. In this section, the poems have been grouped, or classified, according to the theme of *Observations*. There are other ways to group the same poems. For example, rhymed poems could have been separated from unrhymed poems. Poems about nature could have been separated from poems about people. Choose your own system of classifying the poems you have read in this section. List the titles of your categories. Under each category title, list the titles of the poems that fit in the category. Use at least three categories. Be sure to find a category for each poem.

Human Relationships

Emotions can bring people together or drive them apart. In the following poems, the writers examine several important emotions, such as love, loneliness, and courage. See if you have ever had the same feelings that these poets describe.

Ada and Vincent in the Car, 1972, ALEX KATZ. Joseph Hirshhorn Foundation. Courtesy of Marlborough Gallery, Inc., New York.

More About the Elements of Poetry

You have learned that poets choose their words carefully for meaning, feeling, and sound. You have seen that they arrange the words to create a pattern of sounds. At the same time, they arrange the words to show the organization of ideas. Here are some concerns that help a poet select the best words.

Sensory Images.   In poetry, sensory images help the reader see or hear or feel things. Sensory images, also called **imagery**, are details that appeal to the senses. An apple, for example, might be described as "juicy and tart." The words "juicy and tart" appeal to your sense of taste. "The rolling rumble and crash" of thunder, on the other hand, appeals to your sense of hearing. Imagery may appeal to any of your senses.

Here are examples of imagery from the poems you have read:

Sight
a ginger cat, very tall and thin
streaked glass, flashing with sunlight

Hearing
strong melodious songs
crackling splinters of glass and dried putty

Touch
soft shapes . . . inside the hard bodies

While all writing uses imagery, poetry is especially rich in this kind of language. Poets try to give the most exact details possible. Then their readers can imagine the experience more accurately.

Rhythm.   Poetry usually has a regular beat. The pattern of stressed and unstressed syllables in the lines of a poem is called its **rhythm**. There are many possible patterns of rhythm.

For example, the stressed syllables could come one after another. Examine this example. Then read the second line.

/ ⌣ ⌣ / ⌣ /
. . . marches along our street,

/ /
Boom, boom

Or, the stressed syllables could alternate with one or with several unstressed syllables. Examine and read the first line of the example.

⌣ / ⌣ / ⌣ / ⌣ / ⌣ / ⌣ / ⌣ /
Macavity's a Mystery Cat: he's called the hidden Paw—

Types of Rhythm. There might be only one or two stressed syllables in a line. Or, there could be as many as seven or more.

In this example, every unstressed syllable is followed by a stressed syllable. You hear the beat sounding like ta-DUM, ta-DUM, ta-DUM. This kind of meter is called **iambic**. If the stressed syllable came first, the meter would be **trochaic**, as here:

/ ⌣ / ⌣ / ⌣ / ⌣
Tell me not in mournful numbers

These are just a few of the possible rhythm patterns a poem can use. Once a poet chooses a rhythm, he or she finds words that fit both the meaning and the chosen rhythm.

Rhyme. Rhyme is the repetition of the same sound at the ends of lines. This kind of rhyme is called **end rhyme**.

eighty-eight,
red-ball freight

Rhyme may also occur within a line. This is called **internal rhyme**.

Phoebe Snow, B & O

When a poet is writing a poem with rhyme, he or she often tries to think of words with many rhymes. One of these words may make sense at the end of one line. Then there are several possible rhymes for the ends of other lines. That makes it easier to find a word with the meaning the poet wants. Many poets enjoy the challenge of finding rhymes.

Ingratitude

WILLIAM SHAKESPEARE
From "As You Like It."

The English language has changed a bit since this poem was written, but winter weather has not. Read to find out if the feelings expressed by the speaker may still be felt today.

Blow, blow, thou winter wind,
Thou art not so unkind
   As man's ingratitude;
Thy tooth is not so keen
Because thou art not seen,
   Although thy breath be rude.

Freeze, freeze, thou bitter sky,
Thou dost not bite so nigh
   As benefits forgot;
Though thou the waters warp,
Thy sting is not so sharp
   As friend remembered not.

Cloud Study, 1821, JOHN CONSTABLE.
Yale Center for British Art, Paul Mellon Collection, New Haven, Connecticut.

Developing Comprehension Skills

1. To *warp* means "to bend or twist out of shape." Explain how wind can warp water.

2. Explain each of these passages:

   > Thy tooth is not so keen
   > Because thou art not seen
   >
   > Thou dost not bite so nigh
   > As benefits forgot
   >
   > Thy sting is not so sharp
   > As friend remembered not.

   Are they different complaints, or simply different ways of making the same point? If so, what is that point?

3. Why is the speaker talking to the wind and sky rather than to a person?

4. On a scale of 1 to 10, with 1 being "old-fashioned" and 10 being "modern," how would you rate this poem? Give a reason for your rating. You may base your rating on theme, language, form, mood, or any other element that you consider important.

Reading Literature: Poetry

1. **Identifying Onomatopoeia.** Reread the first line. What sound is repeated in several words? How does that sound suggest what the words describe?

2. **Identifying the Rhyme Scheme.** At the time this poem was written, many words were pronounced differently. Perhaps the words *wind* and *kind* were closer in ending sounds than they are today. The same may be true of *warp* and *sharp*. Today the words do not rhyme even though they look as if they should. They are examples of **visual rhyme**.

   Counting the two visual rhymes as if they were real rhymes, write the rhyme scheme of this poem.

3. **Recognizing Sound Patterns.** The poem "Ingratitude" is a song in one of William Shakespeare's plays. The play-goers would have heard the words being sung. They would not have a chance to go back and read the words over to make sure they understood them. Therefore, Shakespeare wanted to warn his listeners before starting each new idea. He used an attention-getting device at the beginning of each group of three lines. What is that device?

4. **Understanding Figurative Language.** Explain what the speaker means when he says that the wind has teeth and breath. How can the sky be said to bite? What does the speaker tell us about his feelings through these images?

Never Seek To Tell Thy Love

WILLIAM BLAKE

Is the speaker in this poem any happier than the speaker in "Ingratitude"? Read the poem to find out.

Never seek to tell thy love,
Love that never told can be:
For the gentle wind does move
Silently, invisibly.

I told my love, I told my love,
I told her all my heart,
Trembling, cold, in ghastly fears,
Ah! she doth depart.

Soon as she was gone from me,
A traveller came by,
Silently, invisibly:
He took her with a sigh.

Developing Comprehension Skills

1. The words in line 2 are in an unusual order for the sake of rhyme and rhythm. Restate lines 1 and 2 in more modern words and a more natural order.

2. Of what did the speaker's love have "ghastly fears"? Why did she leave the speaker?

3. After the speaker's love left him, another man won her. What words suggest that the traveler won the woman without seeming to make any effort?

4. Because of losing his loved one, the speaker makes a general rule. Do you agree with his warning never to express your love? Will keeping your love a secret improve a relationship?

Reading Literature: Poetry

1. **Understanding Reasoning.** At first, it may seem difficult to understand the speaker's thinking. He says that you should not tell your love because the wind moves silently. There does not appear to be a connection between the two ideas.

   However, the speaker is using the wind as a model to be followed. The wind, the speaker says, is silent; therefore, you should be silent. The wind shows you how to get what you want. Can you suggest a reason for his using the wind as a model?

2. **Appreciating Repetition.** The poet uses repetition to help make certain ideas clear. In stanza 2, the phrase "I told my love" or "I told her" appears three times. How does this repetition help you to see why the woman was frightened away?

3. **Understanding Tone.** Compare the tone of the speaker in "Ingratitude" with the tone of the speaker in this poem. Which of these words could you use for one or both of them? How would you describe the differences between the speakers?

sad	depressed	angry
hurt	bitter	lonely

When I Was One-and-Twenty

A. E. HOUSMAN

Like the two preceding poems, this poem uses a few unfamiliar words. For example, it refers to units of English money—pounds, guineas, and crowns. Read to find out if its ideas are also unfamiliar.

When I was one-and-twenty
  I heard a wise man say,
"Give crowns and pounds and guineas
  But not your heart away;
Give pearls away and rubies
  But keep your fancy free."
But I was one-and-twenty,
  No use to talk to me.

When I was one-and-twenty
  I heard him say again,
"The heart out of the bosom
  Was never given in vain;
'Tis paid with sighs a plenty
  And sold for endless rue."
And I am two-and-twenty,
  And oh, 'tis true, 'tis true.

Giant Magnolias, 1885–95, MARTIN JOHNSON HEADE. Courtesy of R.W. Norton Art Gallery, Shreveport, Louisiana.

Developing Comprehension Skills

1. In the first stanza, what did the wise man advise the speaker to do?

2. The word *rue* means "regret." Explain what the wise man meant when he said that a heart is "sold for endless rue."

3. Stanza 1 tells about when the speaker was twenty-one and ignored the wise man's advice. How old is the speaker at the end of stanza 2? How has he changed his mind? What do you suppose happened to cause him to change his mind?

4. Have you ever heard other people give the same advice as the wise man, although in different words? Would you give that advice yourself? Why or why not?

Reading Literature: Poetry

1. **Recognizing Tone.** Do you think the writer intended the poem to be serious or light-hearted? Before you answer, examine the following elements of the poem.

   a. **Language:** Is every idea expressed in a sentence? Or does the poet also use informal, casual expression?

   b. **Rhythm:** Is there a moderate or stately tempo? Or does the rhythm seem light and fast-moving?

   c. **Rhyme:** Is the rhyme scheme complicated or simple?

   d. **Development of Ideas:** Is there a logical development of ideas? Or does the speaker lead you to expect one thing and then deliver something different?

2. **Appreciating Humor.** The poet uses the phrase "I was one-and-twenty" three times in the poem. What is humorous about the statement "I am two-and-twenty," in the second from the last line?

3. **Identifying Rhythm.** Copy only the first stanza of this poem, leaving space between the lines. Mark every stressed syllable with an accent, ´. Mark every unstressed syllable with this mark: ˘. You will find that in almost every case, there is one unstressed syllable before every stressed syllable. This pattern, ˘´, is called an **iambic** rhythm. Examine the number of stressed syllables per line. Match this poem with the correct iambic rhythm listed below.

   a. iambic monometer—one strong beat per line
   b. iambic dimeter—two strong beats
   c. iambic trimeter—three strong beats
   d. iambic tetrameter—four strong beats
   e. iambic pentameter—five strong beats

Faces

SARA TEASDALE

Have you ever wondered about the lives of people you see on the street? Read to find out what this speaker finds in the faces of strangers.

People that I meet and pass
    In the city's broken roar,
Faces that I lose so soon
    And never found before,

Do you know how much you tell
    In the meeting of our eyes,
How ashamed I am, and sad
    To have pierced your poor disguise?

Secrets rushing without sound
    Crying from your hiding places—
Let me go, I cannot bear
    The sorrow of the passing faces.

—People in the restless street,
    Can it be, oh, can it be
In the meeting of our eyes
    That you know as much of me?

Office Girls, 1936, RAPHAEL SOYER. Oil. 26" × 24".
Collection of Whitney Museum of American Art. Purchase.

Developing Comprehension Skills

1. In stanza 1, what is meant by "the city's broken roar"?

2. Why does the speaker say that the strangers are wearing disguises? What would they need to disguise?

3. Why does the speaker feel sorry for other people? What worry does she have for herself? What is the theme of this poem? That is, what general topic concerns the poet?

4. Are most people trying to hide problems from others? Or is it possible that the speaker is thinking so much about her own problems that she assumes everyone feels as sad as she does? Explain your opinion.

Reading Literature: Poetry

1. **Understanding Sensory Images.** In stanza 1 we find the phrase "the city's broken roar." From that we know that the poet is thinking of the low, rumbling sound of the city traffic. In addition, it tells us that she does not feel comfortable in the city, because she describes it as if it were a wild beast.

   Think about each of these images from the poem. Explain what the speaker sees or hears, or thinks she sees or hears. Then tell what you think her feelings about the subject are. Point out words with strong connotations—that is, related feelings—that make you think as you do.

   a. Secrets rushing without sound
      Crying
   b. People in the restless street
   c. . . . the meeting of our eyes

2. **Identifying Rhyme Scheme.** Using letters of the alphabet, show the rhyme scheme for this entire poem. Does every stanza have a different pattern or the same pattern?

Developing Vocabulary Skills

Recognizing Older Words. William Shakespeare lived from 1564 to 1616; William Blake lived from 1757 to 1827. The English of their times was quite different from the English of today. Their poems use some words that are no longer common. Even modern poets like A.E. Housman sometimes use old-fashioned words for the rhyme or rhythm. You should be able to recognize some of the more common old-fashioned words.

In the first column below are words from the first three poems in this section. Match each word with its modern form listed in the second column.

1. thy   a. near
2. thou   b. do
3. dost   c. your
4. 'tis   d. are
5. art   e. it is
6. nigh   f. you

Developing Writing Skills

1. **Giving an Opinion.** Each of the first four poems in this section presented either a sad or bitter view of life. Do you agree with the view of any of the four? Is it possible that you might agree at certain times, for example, when you yourself feel sad? Choose one of the poems. Write from one to three paragraphs discussing its outlook on life. Tell whether you think the view of life expressed in the poem is a fair statement. Would you be satisfied with this view all of your life? Tell why or why not.

2. **Presenting a Mood.** Sara Teasdale's poem "Faces" gives a picture of a city street through the eyes of a sad person. Write an original poem that shows a city street or country road through the eyes of a happy, optimistic person. Your poem does not have to rhyme. It should be at least twelve lines long.

Pre-Writing. Copy "Faces," leaving two or three lines of space between every two lines. Then go through the poem circling every word with sad or otherwise upsetting connotations, such as *broken*, *roar*, and *never*. In the space above each circled word, write a word with opposite connotations. The new word may be opposite in meaning, if you like, but it need not be.

When you are finished, read through the poem, with your corrections. Parts of it will not make much sense. Find the parts that do make sense, and build on them. You may want to add more details about what the speaker sees or hears. Drop the parts that don't make sense or try to correct them. You may want to improve the rhyme or rhythm. Keep in mind that the mood is the element you are most interested in. Make sure it is clearly cheerful.

Writing. Read over your version of "Faces." Decide whether you want to smooth it over or start fresh. If you want to keep it, copy your version. Leave out any part that does not make sense, and add any new lines or words that make the setting or the mood clearer. If you decide to start over, use as many of the words with cheerful connotations as possible.

Revising. Read your poem one more time. Is it at least twelve lines long? If you want it

to rhyme, is the rhyme scheme regular? If you want it to have a regular rhythm, is there a clear pattern of stressed and unstressed syllables? Does it present details about a street scene that a happy person would notice? Most importantly, does it present an optimistic mood? If your answer to any question is *no*, try once more to improve the poem.

Developing Skills in Study and Research

Choosing and Limiting a Topic. Frequently when you begin to research a topic for a report, you have no idea how much material you will find. If you find too little, you may not be able to write an interesting report. If you find too much, you or your reader will not be able to make sense of it. Therefore it is important to do a little research before you settle on your final topic. If you must make your topic larger or smaller, this early research may give you ideas of how to do it.

Choose one of the four poets whose work has appeared in this section: William Shakespeare, William Blake, A.E. Housman, and Sara Teasdale. Look up your poet in at least four of the following sources:

the card catalog
the *Readers' Guide to Periodical Literature*
an encyclopedia
a biographical dictionary, if your library has one
two or more poetry anthologies

Take brief notes about each of your sources. Describe how much material you found in the source. Is it enough for a short report of about five paragraphs? Is it too much?

After taking notes on the four sources, evaluate what you have learned. If the topic of an entire life is too large, what more limited topic within that person's life sounds good? Make a list of five possible topics.

Developing Skills in Speaking and Listening

Reading To Show a Character. In each poem of this section, the speaker is a definite character with a definite attitude. To read any one of these poems well, you must become that character. Choose one of the four poems and prepare to read it to a group.

To begin preparations, think about what tone of voice each of these speakers would use. Once you decide whether the character is angry, sad, jealous, or feeling some other emotion, you can decide which words get stressed. See pages 344 and 345 for further suggestions on preparing to read poetry. After you have read your poem, ask members of your audience to identify the mood you were trying to show.

The Storyteller

MARK VAN DOREN

"The Storyteller" describes the power a good speaker can have on his or her audience. As you read, watch for the images this poet uses to illustrate that power.

He talked, and as he talked
Wallpaper came alive;
Suddenly ghosts walked,
And four doors were five;

Calendars ran backward,
And maps had mouths;
Ships went tackward
In a great drowse;

Trains climbed trees
And soon dipped down
Like honey of bees
On the cold brick town.

He had wakened a worm
In the world's brain,
And nothing stood firm
Until day again.

Developing Comprehension Skills

1. List three impossible things this storyteller can make his listeners believe.

2. What kinds of stories was this man telling? Give a reason for your answer.

3. What might be meant by these lines?
   He had wakened a worm
   In the world's brain

4. Examine the painting on the opposite page. Compare what the painter does to what the storyteller in this poem does. In what ways are a good storyteller and a good artist alike?

Reading Literature: Poetry

1. **Identifying Rhyme Scheme.** Write the rhyme scheme for all four stanzas of this poem. Does each stanza use a different pattern or the same pattern?

2. **Identifying Alliteration and Assonance.** Find an example of alliteration, and one of assonance, in each of the four stanzas.

3. **Recognizing Other Uses of Sound.** In order to make any vowel sound, you must shape your mouth in a certain way. Usually, you do this automatically. A poet, however, some-

Disintegration of the Persistence of Memory, 1952–54, SALVADOR DALI.
Oil on canvas. The Salvador Dali Museum, St. Petersburg, Florida, U.S.A.

times stresses words by the movements they require you to make in your mouth. A good example of this is in the line "soon dipped down," in stanza 3. Slowly shape your mouth to make these vowel sounds in this order:

the $\overline{oo}$ sound in *soon*
the *i* sound in *dipped*
the *ou* sound in *down*

Did you feel your tongue going further and further back in your mouth? The movement of your tongue emphasizes the movement described in the words.

Other times the poet uses these automatic movements to slow down or speed up your reading. Reread the poem, feeling the changes in your mouth. Find another phrase where you notice those changes.

4. **Understanding Uses of Sound.** Why do you suppose the poet paid so much attention to the sounds in this poem?

Mother to Son

LANGSTON HUGHES

A poet uses only the words that will express the right meaning or mood, that will have the right effect. As you read, decide why this poet used black dialect. Why is it essential to the meaning of the poem?

Well, son, I'll tell you:
Life for me ain't been no crystal stair.
It's had tacks in it,
And splinters,
And boards torn up,
And places with no carpet on the floor—
Bare.
But all the time
I'se been a-climbin' on,
And reachin' landin's,
And turnin' corners,
And sometimes goin' in the dark
Where there ain't been no light.
So boy, don't you turn back.
Don't set you down on the steps
'Cause you finds it's kinder hard.
Don't you fall now—
For I'se still goin', honey,
I'se still climbin',
And life for me ain't been no crystal stair.

Hard in Slack, 1927, WASSILY KANDINSKY.
The Hilla von Rebay Foundation, Solomon R. Guggenheim
Museum, New York.

Developing Comprehension Skills

1. What two things is the speaker comparing?

2. In what way can life have "tacks in it, And splinters, And boards torn up"? Explain what kinds of experiences you think fit this description.

3. The speaker talks about "reachin' landin's, And turnin' corners." Is she referring to good or bad experiences? Why do you think so?

4. Do you think this woman would be a good mother? Would it be easy to be her child?

Reading Literature: Poetry

1. **Examining Structure.** This poem is printed as one stanza. However, in it are three separate groups of lines. Each group of lines develops one idea, using repetition and another technique that you have not studied before.

   The first seven lines form the first group. Like a well written paragraph, the group begins with a topic sentence: "Life for me ain't been no crystal stair." Lines 3 through 7 give four details, repeating the word *and* three times:

   a. tacks
   b. And splinters
   c. And boards torn up
   d. And places with no carpet on the floor—Bare.

   Notice how each added detail is longer than the one before. How does this build-up add interest to what the speaker says?

   Identify the lines that form the second group. What words and word form are repeated in this section? Where do you find a build-up of details?

   Identify the third group of lines. What words are repeated? What sentence pattern is repeated and built up?

   How does the poet use repetition to pull together the beginning and ending of the poem?

2. **Understanding the Speaker.** Although she does not tell any specific facts about herself, you learn a great deal about the speaker. In your own words, tell what sort of life she has had. Also, describe her. What are her strengths? How do you know? How does the language in the poem help you to understand what she is like?

Lament

EDNA ST. VINCENT MILLAY

A lament is defined as an expression of grief or sorrow. How does this mother express her grief?

Listen, children:
Your father is dead.
From his old coats
I'll make you little jackets;
I'll make you little trousers
From his old pants.
There'll be in his pockets
Things he used to put there,
Keys and pennies
Covered with tobacco;
Dan shall have the pennies
To save in his bank;
Anne shall have the keys
To make a pretty noise with.
Life must go on,
And the dead be forgotten;
Life must go on,
Though good men die;
Anne, eat your breakfast;
Dan, take your medicine;
Life must go on;
I forget just why.

Developing Comprehension Skills

1. Who are the characters in this poem? How are they related? Who has died?

2. Are the children older or younger than ten years old? What clues in the poem give you the answer?

3. The speaker uses a very matter-of-fact approach as she tells the children of their father's death. Then she turns her attention to pennies and keys. What is the reason for her strange behavior? Which two lines explain her feelings?

4. Is this woman's reaction to her husband's death believable? Might a person respond to a death in the family this way? Give a reason for your answer.

Reading Literature: Poetry

1. **Understanding the Speaker.** As the poem begins, the speaker's factual statements make you think that she is in control. She seems to be making sense, although in an unnaturally cold way.

   However, the language of the poem quickly gives hints that she is putting up a front. Look for examples of repetition of single words and of sentence patterns. Are the words and phrases she repeats of strong interest? Or is she saying them just to have something to say? Look for repetition of a whole sentence. Why does she repeat this sentence?

   Another clue to her mood is the pattern in which she repeats words. Examine this list. See if you can add another example to it.

   > line 3: old coats
   > line 4: little jackets
   > line 5: little trousers
   > line 6: old pants
   > line 9: Keys and pennies
   > line 11: pennies
   > line 13: keys

   What does the woman's habit of going back and forth with words suggest about her thinking?

2. **Recognizing Rhyme.** Not counting the repeated sentence, in this poem there is only one pair of lines that rhyme. Identify those lines. Why do you think the poet used rhyme at that point? What is its effect on the meaning and the mood?

3. **Identifying the Theme.** What do you think is the theme, or main concern, of this poem? You may state the theme as a complete sentence or a phrase.

Those Winter Sundays

ROBERT HAYDEN

This speaker remembers when houses were heated by coal furnaces. Every night the fire was banked, or covered. Every morning more coal had to be put on the fire. Read to find out why the speaker thinks of this now.

Sundays too my father got up early
and put his clothes on in the blueblack cold,
then with cracked hands that ached
from labor in the weekday weather made
banked fires blaze. No one ever thanked him.

I'd wake and hear the cold splintering, breaking.
When the rooms were warm, he'd call,
and slowly I would rise and dress,
fearing the chronic angers of that house,

Speaking indifferently to him,
who had driven out the cold
and polished my good shoes as well.
What did I know, what did I know
of love's austere and lonely offices?

1950—A No. 2, 1950. CLYFFORD STILL. Hirshhorn Museum and Sculpture Garden, Smithsonian Institution, Washington, D.C.

Developing Comprehension Skills

1. What did the father do on Sunday mornings? At the time, what did the speaker think about this action?

2. Now, what does the speaker think about his father's actions? What does he think about his own actions?

3. What might have happened since the speaker's childhood that affected his thinking?

4. This poem describes a person regretting past actions and lack of awareness. Do you think that many people experience such regrets? Do you think reading this poem would make them feel better or worse about themselves?

Reading Literature: Poetry

1. **Understanding Figurative Language.** Explain what the poet means by these descriptions of the cold:

   a. the blueblack cold
   b. I'd hear the cold splintering, breaking

   What do these descriptions tell you of the speaker's feelings about the cold?

2. **Inferring Meaning.** In stanza 2, the speaker refers to the "chronic angers of that house." What does the phrase tell you about the members of the family?

3. **Comparing Characters.** In what ways is the father in this poem like the mother in "Mother to Son"?

4. **Identifying Uses of Sound.** Reread the phrases below. Identify which use of sound you find in each: alliteration, assonance, strong movement in shaping vowels. More than one technique may occur in the same phrase.

   a. the blueblack cold
   b. cracked hands that ached from labor in the weekday weather
   c. When the rooms were warm, he'd call
   d. what did I know of love's austere and lonely offices?

Developing Vocabulary Skills

Recognizing Related Words. Often there are different English words that are based on the same Latin or Greek word or word part. If you know what that word or word part means, you can often figure out several words.

The words *petroleum* and *chronic* have appeared in poems in this chapter. Read the following word parts from Greek and Latin. Use them and the context clues in the sentences below to figure out the meanings of *petroleum, chronic,* and the other underlined words.

petro-	rock
chrono-	time
syn-	with, together
ana-	not, without
-logy	the study of
-oleum	oil
-meter	instrument for measuring

1. Every ship carries a <u>chronometer</u> to use in checking its position.

2. Several hundred feet down the drillers discovered <u>petroleum</u>.

3. Chris has a <u>chronic</u> complaint about the food in the cafeteria.

4. Arrange the events in <u>chronological</u> order.

5. In her science class, Mina became interested in <u>petrology</u>.

6. The two swimmers are doing <u>synchronized</u> movements.

7. After lying in chemicals for hundreds of years, the logs became <u>petrified</u>.

8. In the movie, the Greek warrior was wearing a wristwatch. The audience laughed at the <u>anachronism</u>.

Developing Writing Skills

1. **Comparing and Contrasting Speakers.** Choose two of the speakers in these four poems: "The Storyteller," "Mother to Son," "Lament," and "Those Winter Sundays." Write four paragraphs comparing and contrasting the speakers.

Pre-Writing. Reread each of the poems, paying special attention to what you learn about the speaker. Take notes. Then compare your notes. Choose two speakers who have strong similarities or strong differences or both.

After choosing your poems, read them again critically. Look for additional likenesses and differences. Add them to your notes.

Next, organize your notes. Group all the similarities in one place, and number them in the order of importance. Do the same for differences. Try to find one main idea that connects all the ideas in each group.

Writing. In your first paragraph, explain which speakers you are writing about. Use the second paragraph to discuss the similarities. Explain the differences in the third paragraph. Last, summarize the main ideas of paragraphs 2 and 3 in the final paragraph.

Revising. Make sure that each paragraph sticks to one topic: introduction in paragraph 1, development of comparisons in paragraph 2, development of contrasts in paragraph 3, and summary in paragraph 4. Move any sentence that does not belong where it is.

2. **Using Alliteration.** Choose an activity you do every day. Describe it in a paragraph of at least eight sentences or a poem of at least eight lines. Use strong, exact verbs and adjectives. Use alliteration in three or more places.

Developing Skills in Speaking and Listening

Interpreting a Speaker. Review the four poems in this section. Choose your favorite and prepare to read it for a group. Review the suggestions on page 345 for help in preparing the poem. Concentrate on making the speaker a real person. Let the character become natural to you, so that your face, voice, and gestures are all like the speaker's.

Piñones

LEROY QUINTANA

Piñones are a kind of nut, sometimes called the pine nut. To this speaker, do they have any special meaning? Read the poem to find out.

when i was young
we would sit by
an old firewood stove
watching my grandmother make candy,
listening to the stories
my grandparents would tell
about "the old days"
          and eat piñones

now we belong
to a supersonic age
and have college degrees.
we sit around color t.v. sets
watching the super bowl
listening to howard cosell,
stories of rioting, war, inflation
          and eat piñones

Developing Comprehension Skills

1. List three details the speaker tells about his youth.

2. List three details the speaker tells about his present life. Identify a detail that answers both this question and the one above.

3. Does the speaker feel his life has changed in any basic way? Explain your answer.

4. Is the speaker saying that life was better in the old days? Is he saying that life is better now? Do you agree with what he is saying? Why or why not?

Reading Literature: Poetry

1. **Identifying Theme.** Refer to your answer for question 4, above. In your own words, state the theme of this poem. Explain how the title of the poem hints at the theme.

2. **Using Punctuation Clues to Meaning.** In this poem, there are no capital letters. At the end of each stanza, where a sentence ends, there is no period. Think about the purposes of capital letters and periods. Can you suggest why this poet chose not to use them? What might he be trying to avoid?

3. **Examining Structure.** This poem relates stanzas 1 and 2 by using comparison and contrast. Almost every statement in stanza 1 has a related statement in stanza 2. For example, stanza 1 talks about "when I was young." Stanza 2 contrasts that with today, when "we belong to a supersonic age and have college degrees." Identify two more sets of contrasting details, and one comparison.

4. **Identifying Mood.** How would you describe the mood of this poem, that is, the feeling it gives you? How does this poem about a family compare in mood with any one of these other poems about families: "Mother to Son," "Lament," "Those Winter Sundays"?

Eviction

LUCILLE CLIFTON

"Southbound on the Freeway" presents a picture of life on Earth as seen by a tourist from outer space. What does this poem have in common with that one? Read to find an important similarity.

What I remember about that day
is boxes stacked across the walk
and couch springs curling through the air
and drawers and tables balanced on the curb
and us, hollering,
leaping up and around
happy to have a playground;

nothing about the empty rooms
nothing about the emptied family

Developing Comprehension Skills

1. What happened on the day the speaker describes? Around what was she playing?

2. About how old was the speaker at the time? How can you tell?

3. Make a general statement about point of view that would fit both this poem and "Southbound on the Freeway." (If you need to review that poem, it is on page 362.)

Reading Literature: Poetry

1. **Examining Form.** How many stanzas do you find in this poem?

   Which of these methods does the poet use to show the organization, or structure, of the poem? Explain how the method is used.

   > rhyme
   > a specific pattern of rhythm
   > repetition of words or patterns of words

2. **Making Inferences.** The most likely reason for this eviction was that the family couldn't pay the rent. One detail given by the speaker suggests that the family didn't have much money. Identify that detail.

3. **Recognizing Mood.** Verbs are often the most powerful group of words in setting a mood. Examine the verbs and forms of verbs in stanza 1: *remember, is, stacked, curling, balanced, hollering, leaping.* The last five all suggest actions you can picture. How does this affect the mood of stanza 1?

   Next, examine the verbs and forms of verbs in stanza 2: *emptied.* You can picture how a box might be emptied. Can you picture how a family might be emptied? How does this stress the meaning of the poem? How does it affect the mood of stanza 2?

4. **Noting Punctuation Clues.** According to usual rules of punctuation, there should be a comma after the second from the last line. There should be a period after the last line. Why do you suppose the poet left out those punctuation marks?

Window of a Deserted House, 1917,
CHARLES BURCHFIELD.
Private Collection. Kennedy Galleries, New York.

Outwitted

EDWIN MARKHAM

A circle is a closed curve. That means that it has no breaks through which anything can come in or out. If you are outside someone else's circle, how can you join him or her? Read to find one solution to this question.

He drew a circle that shut me out—
Heretic, rebel, a thing to flout.
But Love and I had the wit to win;
We drew a circle that took him in!

Coal, 1962, KENNETH NOLAND. Private Collection. Courtesy of André Emmerich Gallery, New York.

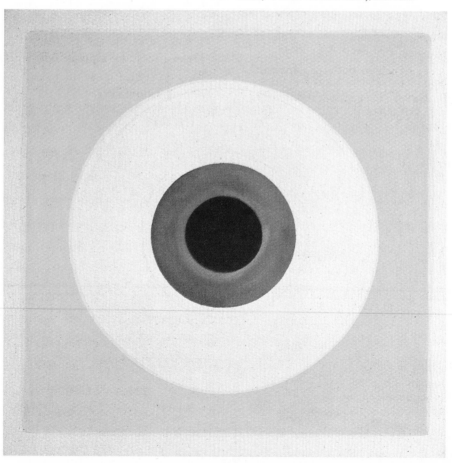

Developing Comprehension Skills

1. In your own words, tell what situation is described in the first two lines of the poem.

2. Who is the "Heretic, rebel, a thing to flout"? Explain one of these names.

3. What do the last two lines mean in terms of day-to-day living? Give an example of a way the speaker could prove that his circle included the other person.

4. Who would be helped more if the advice in the poem were put into practice: the person inside the first circle or the speaker in the larger circle?

Reading Literature: Poetry

1. **Identifying Figures of Speech.** Find an example of personification in this poem. What is spoken of as a living person?

   Find a metaphor in the poem. What physical thing is being compared to an emotional or social situation?

2. **Understanding the Theme.** In your own words, tell the main idea of this poem.

3. **Examining Rhyme and Rhythm.** What is the rhyme scheme of "Outwitted"? What is the term for this arrangement of rhyming lines?

   Here is the rhythm pattern of the first line of the poem. Two other lines have exactly the same pattern. Identify those two lines.

   / ◡ ◡ / ◡ ◡ / ◡ /
   He drew a circle that shut me out

Developing Vocabulary Skills

Recognizing Ways Words Enter the Language. Each word listed below is from a poem in this chapter. It came into being in one of these ways:

    clipping   imitating sounds
    borrowing

Match each numbered word below with one of the descriptions. On your paper, write the word, the letter identifying its description, and the way in which the word came to be.

1. boom   3. fancy   5. circle
2. chemist   4. holler   6. tobacco

  a. This word comes from *alchemist*, a kind of medieval scientist who tried to turn other metals into gold.

  b. This word is related to *hollo, hallo, holla,* and *hullo,* all of which sound like shouts.

  c. This word means to make a deep, rumbling sound, or it is the sound itself.

  d. This word comes from an Arawak Indian word for a pipe for smoking, or the roll of leaves smoked.

  e. This word came from the Latin word for *ring*. We also use the original Latin spelling in our word *circus*.

  f. This word comes from *fantasy*.

Developing Writing Skills

1. **Evaluating a Theme.** The general theme for this section has been "Human Relationships." What are some of the particular relationships discussed in these poems? Write at least three paragraphs discussing how completely the poems present the range of human relationships.

   Pre-Writing. Review the eleven poems in this section. Write the titles on eleven slips of paper. On each slip, write one or more themes of that poem. Then compare the slips. Group those that seem to discuss the same type of relationship.

Next, decide in which order you will discuss each group. For example, you might choose to start with unpleasant feelings and work up to pleasant ones.

Last, decide what you think of the range of human relationships presented here. Was it a wide range? Was each type of relationship important enough to be discussed in poetry? Decide on a main idea that will summarize the relationships you have examined.

Writing. In your first paragraph, state your main idea. Also suggest the organization you will use to explain your idea. The last paragraph should summarize the main idea. The number of paragraphs you will need in the body, or middle, of your paper depends on the number of different relationships you found. Refer to specific poems.

Revising. Ask someone to read your evaluation. Can the reader restate your main idea in his or her own words? Can he or she identify at least two different relationships, and tell which poem or poems illustrate each of those relationships?

If not, try to determine what the problem is. Is your main idea not supported by the details? Or are the examples of different relationships mixed up together? Or are grammar, spelling, and punctuation mistakes making your ideas hard to understand? Revise your work as necessary.

2. **Expressing a Mood in Poetry.** Choose a feeling you might have about another person—love, disgust, friendship, or rivalry, for example. List as many words as you can think of that suggest that feeling. Then write a six- or eight-line poem about that feeling. Use in the poem as many of the words with strong connotations as you can.

Psalms of Life

People have always wondered about the most puzzling question of all: What is the purpose of life? Each of the poems in this section gives a clue. Each poet shares his or her personal answer. Together, the poems are songs of life and its endless possibilities. They may help you, too, to find your own answers to the question.

Rooms by the Sea, 1951, EDWARD HOPPER. Yale University Art Gallery, New Haven, Connecticut. Bequest of Stephen Carlton Clark, B.A. 1903.

A Psalm of Life

HENRY WADSWORTH
LONGFELLOW

In this poem, "numbers" refers to the accents in poetry and to poetry in general. Does this poet like depressing poems? Does he approve of depressing people? Read to find out what kind of people he admires.

Tell me not, in mournful numbers,
  Life is but an empty dream! —
For the soul is dead that slumbers,
  And things are not what they seem.

Life is real! Life is earnest!
  And the grave is not its goal;
Dust thou art, to dust returnest,
  Was not spoken of the soul.

Not enjoyment, and not sorrow,
  Is our destined end or way;
But to act, that each to-morrow
  Find us farther than to-day.

Art is long, and Time is fleeting,
  And our hearts, though stout and brave,
Still, like muffled drums, are beating
  Funeral marches to the grave.

In the world's broad field of battle,
  In the bivouac of Life,
Be not like dumb, driven cattle!
  Be a hero in the strife!

Ashville, 1949, WILLEM de KOONING. The Phillips Collection, Washington, D.C.

Developing Comprehension Skills

1. Rearrange the words of line 3 in a more natural order. Then restate the idea in your own words.

2. The speaker says that the grave is not our goal. Then what is, according to stanzas 2 and 3?

3. In what lines does the speaker point out that we must die? How does he believe we should live?

4. Can you suggest reasons why this poem has become famous and loved?

Reading Literature: Poetry

1. **Understanding Organization.** What idea does each stanza develop? Are there cause and effect relationships among the ideas?

   Identify the rhyme scheme and an example of alliteration in each stanza.

2. **Identifying Simile.** Find two similes. In each, what two things are compared?

3. **Recognizing Mood.** Reread the poem, listening especially for the rhythm. Then tell what feeling you get from the poem.

Footprints

HENRY WADSWORTH LONGFELLOW

Here is a second poem by the writer of "A Psalm of Life." What similarities do you find in the poems? As you read, look for Longfellow's advice.

Lives of great men all remind us
   We can make our lives sublime,
And, departing, leave behind us
   Footprints on the sands of time;

Footprints that perhaps another,
   Sailing o'er life's solemn main,
A forlorn and shipwrecked brother,
   Seeing, shall take heart again.

Let us, then, be up and doing,
   With a heart for any fate;
Still achieving, still pursuing,
   Learn to labor and to wait.

Developing Comprehension Skills

1. What proof does the poet offer that we can make our lives sublime, or noble?

2. In stanza 1, the speaker says that we can leave "Footprints in the sands of time." What sorts of things can we leave behind us to show we have been on Earth?

3. In stanza 2, the word *main* refers to the ocean. In what sense are we all "Sailing o'er life's solemn main"?

4. Explain the metaphor about the shipwreck in stanza 2.

5. You may have heard this expression: "It's not whether you win or lose; it's how you play the game." Think about the two poems by Longfellow that you have read. Do you believe the poet would have agreed with that expression? Why or why not?

Reading Literature: Poetry

1. **Appreciating Figurative Language.** The idea that we can leave "footprints" behind us is encouraging. However, the speaker does not promise that our lives will have an effect forever. How does the metaphor suggest that the effects of our lives may be limited?

   Even though the memory of our lives may be limited, it may do good. Which words of the metaphor tell us that?

2. **Understanding Rhythm.** In reading this poem, it would be easy to fall into a sing-song pattern. Most of the words fit into a pattern of alternating stressed and unstressed syllables. Even when you speak the poem in your mind, you would want to avoid reading the poem in such a lifeless way.

   Think of the message the words express. Decide which words are important to the message. These words should be given the most stress, more than other stressed syllables that are not as important. Also, identify the places where there is a change in the ideas or a pause in developing them. These places do not always fall at the ends of lines. As you read, pause at these places.

   Think about the ideas in stanza 1. Then compare the two words for each line listed below. Which word deserves more stress?

   line 1: great, men
   line 2: our, lives
   line 3: leave, behind
   line 4: on, sands

   Decide, also, where there are breaks between ideas in the first stanza. After which words would you pause?

3. **Identifying Mood.** How would you describe your feelings after reading this poem? Would any of these words fit: *cheerful, determined, confident?* Explain your answer.

Miracles

WALT WHITMAN

The first line of this poem grabs your attention with alliteration. What else does the poet say should grab your attention? Read to discover where he finds miracles.

Why, who makes much of a miracle?
As to me I know of nothing else but miracles,
Whether I walk the streets of Manhattan,
Or dart my sight over the roofs of houses toward the sky,
Or wade with naked feet along the beach just in the edge of the
      water,
Or stand under the trees in the woods,
Or talk by day with any one I love . . .
Or sit at table at dinner with the rest,
Or look at strangers opposite me riding in the car.
Or watch honey-bees busy around the hive of a summer forenoon,
Or animals feeding in the fields,
Or birds, or the wonderfulness of the sundown, or of stars shining so
    quiet and bright,
Or the exquisite delicate thin curve of the new moon in spring;
These with the rest, one and all, are to me miracles,
The whole referring, yet each distinct and in its place.

To me every hour of the light and dark is a miracle,
Every cubic inch of space is a miracle,
Every square yard of the surface of the earth is spread with the same,
Every foot of the interior swarms with the same.

To me the sea is a continual miracle,
The fishes that swim—the rocks—the motion of the waves—the
    ships with men in them,
What stranger miracles are there?

Return to the Beginning: In Memory of Ginger, 1981, JOSEPH RAFFAEL. Nancy Hoffman Gallery, New York.

Developing Comprehension Skills

1. List any five of the "miracles" the speaker names. To which of our five senses does each miracle appeal?

2. How does the speaker define *miracle*?

3. Do you agree with his definition of a miracle? Why or why not?

Reading Literature: Poetry

1. **Understanding Theme.** The first line of this poem suggests that the speaker is rejecting miracles. Does the rest of the poem support that idea? What is the theme?

   Why did the poet use that opening question? Why did he use the ending question?

2. **Identifying Rhythm.** Does this poem use a regular rhythm or an irregular, conversa-

tional one? How does the rhythm reinforce the theme?

3. **Recognizing Structure.** The poet uses the device of a list to hold together the long first stanza. He avoids monotony, however, by listing first verbs and then nouns. After the word "Whether," how many verbs does he list? How many nouns?

   He also avoids monotony by varying the amount of detail about each item. Sometimes he builds on a basic pattern, adding more and more detail in each line. Identify two or three lines that show this contrast in length and amount of detail.

   To connect all three stanzas, the writer uses repetition. What phrase is found near the beginning of each stanza? Can you find other examples of repetition of words?

Developing Vocabulary Skills

Completing Analogies. In an **analogy**, two pairs of words are compared. Each pair is related in the same way. Here is an example:

> Breakfast is to morning as dinner is to evening.

Breakfast is a meal eaten, usually, in the morning, while dinner is a meal eaten, usually, in the evening.

In an analogy question, one of the four words is missing. You must figure out how the two words in one pair are related. Then you can supply the missing word in the other pair.

Complete the following analogies involving words from this chapter.

1. Steamboat is to water as _____ is to rails.
2. Woman is to heroine as _____ is to hero.
3. Ceiling is to over as floor is to _____.
4. Canine is to dogs as feline is to _____.
5. Engine is to beginning as caboose is to _____.
6. Nine is to baseball as five is to _____.
7. Lament is to sorrow as carol is to _____.
8. Slumber is to sleep as labor is to _____.

Developing Writing Skills

1. **Writing About a Hero or Heroine.** In "Footprints," the poet says that

> Lives of great men all remind us
> We can make our lives sublime.

Which great man or woman would you choose to remind you of how great you could become? Choose the person whom you would model yourself after. The person does not have to be famous, but must have some special quality. Write one or more paragraphs explaining which person you would choose, and why.

2. **Describing a Miracle.** In "Miracles," the poet lists numerous daily events that he finds extraordinary and miraculous. Choose an event that you consider particularly remarkable. It may be an event on Whitman's list, or your own choice. Describe the event in such a way that anyone else would see something remarkable about it. Give exact details. Be sure to include words with strong favorable connotations.

3. **Writing a Poem with Rhyme.** Choose a topic that excites or encourages you. Write an eight-line poem about the topic, using regular rhythm and a pattern of rhyme.

Pre-Writing. List several possible topics. For each, write at least ten words that relate to the topic. Do not worry yet whether all the words will fit into the poem; just brainstorm ideas.

Next, look at your lists. By now, you should have a feeling for or against each topic. Choose the topic you feel most positive about.

Now, take a closer look at your list of words. Can you think of any rhymes for the words? Write as many rhymes as you can come up with. Add more words to the list, and write rhymes for them, also. When you have ten or twelve good rhymes, try to think of sentences that could use those words to say something about the topic.

When you think of a sentence that makes sense and uses a rhyme, write it out. Mark its rhythm pattern. Move words around or replace them until you get a regular rhythm pattern. Now decide whether you are satisfied with the rhyme pattern. If you want to change it, play with making the sentence longer or shorter. Continue to rearrange words until you find a rhyme scheme and a rhythm pattern that feels comfortable for the topic.

Writing. Using the patterns of rhyme and rhythm that you have decided on, write your poem. You may use the trial sentences you started with, or you may begin anew. Your list of rhyming words may be useful to you, but if those words are not enough, add more rhymes to your list. Make sure your poem makes sense.

Revising. Read your poem aloud, preferably to a friend. Is the rhyme scheme clear? Is the rhythm regular? Is the tempo right for the topic, or does the poem move too slow or too fast? You may need to change the whole rhythm, or you may need to change only a word or two. Read and revise the poem several more times until you are satisfied.

Developing Skills in Speaking and Listening

1. **Listening for Alliteration.** In "Miracles," the poet used a conversational tone and made the poem sound like everyday speech. Sometimes everyday speech sounds like poetry. For the next day or so, listen carefully to what you hear in normal conversations. Listen particularly for alliteration. When you hear alliteration used for emphasis in conver-sation, make a note of it. Be ready to explain when you heard it, and whether you think the speaker consciously used it for effect.

2. **Presenting a Poem Chorally.** When a group works together to present a poem, the interpretation is called a **choral** presentation, because the group works as a chorus. Poems that use lists are especially good for choral presentations. Parts of the poem can be read by the group altogether. Other parts—particularly the lists—can be broken up, and the parts can be assigned to individual speakers. The variety in voices keeps the list interesting to hear. When a poem is interpreted this way, the trickiest part is keeping the rhythm steady as one person and then another speaks.

Work with a group to present one of these poems that use lists: "I Hear America Singing," "Song of the Truck," "Nine Triads," and "Miracles." Decide among yourselves how to break up the parts of the list so that each person has about the same number of lines. Decide which lines at the beginning and end would sound good said as a group. Then practice reading the poem together. Remember to put stress on the important words, and to go faster or slower only when the meaning calls for it. Each person must listen and be ready to come in on his or her lines.

When you feel your group is ready, make arrangements to present your poem to the rest of the class. Speak loudly and clearly. Afterwards, ask your audience their opinion of the presentation.

Lineage

MARGARET WALKER

People whose ancestors were royalty or famous figures in history are proud to trace their lineage. Were this speaker's ancestors royal or famous? Is she proud of them? Read to find out.

My grandmothers were strong.
They followed plows and bent to toil.
They moved through fields sowing seed.
They touched earth and grain grew.
They were full of sturdiness and singing.
My grandmothers were strong.

My grandmothers are full of memories
Smelling of soap and onions and wet clay
With veins rolling roughly over quick hands
They have many clean words to say.
My grandmothers were strong.
Why am I not as they?

Woodbury County, Iowa, 1936, RUSSELL LEE. Library of Congress.

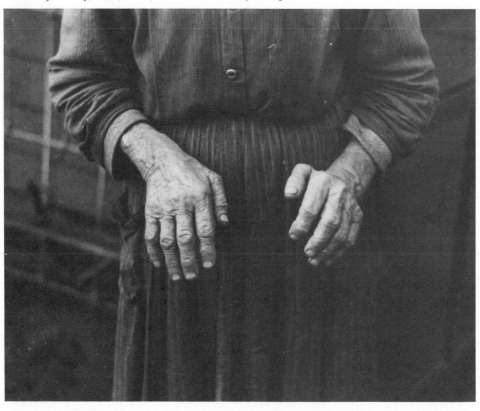

Developing Comprehension Skills

1. Name some of the activities in which the speaker's grandmothers took part.

2. The speaker describes her grandmothers as having "many clean words to say." What does she mean by this?

3. What is the speaker's opinion of her grandmothers? What is her opinion of herself?

4. Do you suppose that when the grandmothers were plowing, sowing, cleaning, and cooking, they thought of themselves as strong? What encouragement could you give the speaker?

Reading Literature: Poetry

1. **Appreciating Repetition.** Can you find repetition of sentence patterns and of whole sentences? What effect does this repetition have on the organization of the poem? What effect does it have on the mood?

2. **Making Inferences.** In the following lines, the poet uses one or two words to suggest a range of activities. To what do "soap" and "onions" and "wet clay" refer?

> My grandmothers are full of memories
> Smelling of soap and onions and wet clay

3. **Identifying Uses of Sound.** Find at least three examples of alliteration in this poem. Find two examples of assonance. Identify where the poet uses rhyme.

4. **Comparing and Contrasting Poems.** Review the poem "Footprints," on page 406. The form, language, and mood of that poem differ strongly from the form, language, and mood of "Lineage." The themes of the two poems, however, are related. How is this speaker reacting to her grandmothers' "footprints"? Is she reacting in the way the speaker of "Footprints" expected?

As you read this poem, try to picture the images it describes.

Dreams

LANGSTON HUGHES

Hold fast to dreams
For if dreams die
Life is a broken-winged bird
That cannot fly.

Hold fast to dreams
For when dreams go
Life is a barren field
Frozen with snow.

Developing Comprehension Skills

1. To what two things does the poem compare life?

2. What does the speaker mean by *dreams*?

3. In your own words, state the theme, or main idea, of this poem. Do you agree with it? Why or why not?

Reading Literature: Poetry

1. **Identifying Rhyme.** What pattern of rhyme do you find in this poem? Write the rhyme scheme for the first stanza. Is the pattern in the second stanza the same?

2. **Recognizing Alliteration and Assonance.** Besides using rhyme, the poet links the

Point of Tranquility, 1958, MORRIS LOUIS. The Hirshhorn Museum and Sculpture Garden, Smithsonian Institution, Washington, D.C.

words of the poem by using alliteration and assonance. Find two examples of each. Can you suggest reasons why the poet stresses those words or lines?

3. **Understanding Metaphor.** Why does the poet give two metaphors to describe life without dreams? How are they different?

4. **Recognizing Mood.** The poem concentrates on what life is like without dreams. What is the mood of the poem?

Now examine the painting that appears above. What do you feel is the mood of the painting? Does it suggest life with or without dreams?

Thumbprint

EVE MERRIAM

Listen to yourself as you read this peom, at least in your mind. What three words do you find yourself stressing?

In the heel of my thumb
are whorls, whirls, wheels
in a unique design:
mine alone.
What a treasure to own!
My own flesh, my own feelings.
No other, however grand or base,
can ever contain the same.
My signature,
thumbing the pages of my time.
My universe key,
my singularity.
Impress, implant,
I am myself,
of all my atom parts I am the sum.
And out of my blood and my brain
I make my own interior weather,
my own sun and rain.
Imprint my mark upon the world,
whatever I shall become.

Developing Comprehension Skills

1. What is the "treasure" of which the speaker is proud?

2. To the speaker, what does her thumbprint represent?

3. Explain these lines in your own words:
   I make my own interior weather,
   my own sun and rain.

4. Should the speaker be proud of herself? Is it important to recognize that each person is an individual? Give a reason for your answer.

Reading Literature: Poetry

1. **Recognizing Mood.** Identify all the times that the speaker uses each of these words: *my, own, mine, I.* It might seem that the speaker is bragging and would become annoying. However, of what is the speaker bragging? How are the speaker and reader alike? For whom is the speaker bragging? What mood, then, do you get from reading the poem?

2. **Identifying Theme.** What is the theme of this poem?

3. **Understanding Figures of Speech.** What image do you get from each of the passages below? What idea does each metaphor suggest to you?

   My signature,
   thumbing the pages of my time
   My universe key
   Imprint my mark upon the world

4. **Recognizing Rhyme.** The rhymes in these lines pop up in unexpected places, adding to the fun of the poem. For example, reread lines 1 through 5. Find the rhymes for *design* and *alone.*

   In the rest of the poem, can you find the rhymes for *singularity* and *brain*? Can you find two rhymes for *thumb*?

5. **Appreciating Uses of Sound.** This poem uses alliteration and assonance frequently. In addition, it also uses repetition of consonant sounds in the middle of words. For example, look at "whorls, whirls, wheels."

   Identify at least two examples each of alliteration, assonance, and repetition of consonant sounds in the middle of words.

to be nobody-but-yourself

e. e. cummings

"Thumbprint" told us to take delight in being individuals. What warning does this poem give to individuals?

to be nobody-but-yourself in a world
which is doing its best, night and day,
to make you everybody else—means to
fight the hardest battle which any
human being can fight, and never stop
fighting.

Developing Comprehension Skills

1. According to the speaker, what is the world trying to do to you?

2. Why do you suppose the poem shows "nobody-but-yourself" as one word?

3. Why does the speaker say that being yourself is a battle? Do you agree? Why or why not?

Reading Literature: Poetry

1. **Understanding the Form.** All the lines of this poem make up one sentence. According to the rules of punctuation, only a period is needed at the end of the sentence. However, this poet was noted for his unusual use of capitalization and punctuation. Besides adding hyphens in the term "nobody-but-yourself," he has added a dash in the middle of line 3, and a comma before the *and*. How do these punctuation marks help the reader understand the sentence?

   The word "fighting" is on a line by itself. How does that arrangement help the reader find the theme of the poem?

2. **Recognizing Repetition.** This poem uses a conversational tone, no rhyme, and little alliteration. However, it stresses the most im-

portant ideas by using repetition. What word appears twice in one form and a third time with a different ending?

3. **Understanding Theme.** What warning does this poem give? State it in your own words.

Developing Vocabulary Skills

Recognizing Related Words. Many words in English are related to each other. Some of them entered the language as separate words. However, these separate words were all based on one word from Greek or Latin or another language. Others entered the language in one form but have become several forms since then. We may have combined some of these words in compounds. We may have added prefixes or suffixes to the words.

Sometimes you can find a common base in a group of words. You may know the meaning of some of the words in the group. Then you can use that common base, along with context clues, to figure out an unfamiliar word in the group.

In each group below, there is one word from this chapter. Three of the words come from the same base word. The fourth is not related. On your paper, write the three related words.

1. ingratitude, gratify, gravity, grateful
2. melodious, melody, melodic, melancholy
3. grace, grackle, gracious, graceful
4. singularity, single, sign, singular
5. gradually, graded, gradations, grating
6. difference, diffuse, differ, indifferent
7. destined, dusty, destination, destiny
8. medicine, medical, medium, medicinal

Developing Writing Skills

1. **Writing a Definition.** Both "Thumbprint" and "to be nobody-but-yourself" discussed the idea of being an individual. What do you think it means to be an individual? What are the qualities of a person who is truly his or her own person? Write one or more paragraphs defining and describing your view of an individual.

Pre-Writing. Think about what the poems said about individuality. Also, consider what makes some people stand out, in a good sense. List qualities of these people that are different from most of us. In a few words, suggest one or two problems that most of us face. Jot down your ideas of how an individual might face those problems. Then review your notes. Choose the most important characteristics, or qualities, you have listed. Arrange them in an order that makes sense to you.

Writing. Begin by explaining that an individual is a special sort of person. Then describe what makes an individual special. Explain how an individual can be identified. Use the ideas in your notes, and follow the order you decided on in pre-writing. However, if you discover a better way of presenting ideas, change your plan to the better way.

Revising. First, check the organization of your ideas. If you have more than one paragraph, do the sentences in each paragraph belong together? Is every idea based on the idea before it? Is every idea stated clearly?

Next, look at the language you used. Is every word the most specific word? Are the verbs strong?

Last, check the grammar, spelling, punctuation, and legibility of your writing. Make sure there are no careless mistakes that lie between your reader and your ideas.

Mark any corrections on your draft. Make a clean copy.

2. **Explaining an Opinion.** "Lineage" talked of the importance of strength of character. "Dreams" talked of the importance of hopes for the future. Is strength more important than hope, or less important? Or are the two qualities both necessary? Write at least one paragraph explaining your opinion and your reasons for the opinion.

3. **Giving Advice in Poem Form.** Write a poem of at least four lines, giving advice on some topic. The poem may use rhyme or not, as you choose. It may have regular or irregular rhythm. Use alliteration, assonance, and at least one metaphor or simile in your poem.

Developing Skills in Critical Thinking

Categorizing. The poems in this chapter have been placed in large groups according to general themes. How else could you group them? You might choose to group poems that use rhyme separately from poems that do not. You might group all poems with metaphors, or those with extended metaphors.

Decide on three different methods of categorizing, or grouping, the poems in this chapter. Using each of your methods, list which poems would fall into each group. Be ready to explain why you chose the categories you chose.

The Road Not Taken

ROBERT FROST

This poem begins with a choice. As you read the speaker's comments about making that choice, try to decide why he considers that decision important.

Two roads diverged in a yellow wood,
And sorry I could not travel both
And be one traveler, long I stood
And looked down one as far as I could
To where it bent in the undergrowth;

Then took the other, as just as fair,
And having perhaps the better claim,
Because it was grassy and wanted wear;
Though as for that, the passing there
Had worn them really about the same,

And both that morning equally lay
In leaves no step had trodden black.
Oh, I kept the first for another day!
Yet knowing how way leads on to way,
I doubted if I should ever come back.

I shall be telling this with a sigh
Somewhere ages and ages hence:
Two roads diverged in a wood, and I—
I took the one less traveled by,
And that has made all the difference.

Developing Comprehension Skills

1. Find the traveler's reason for choosing one road. State it in your words.

2. In what way is choosing a path in the woods like making any other choice in life? Review the details about the speaker's choice. Tell how one of the details could fit a choice you might make.

3. The speaker says that choosing the road less traveled by "has made all the difference." Is he exaggerating? Can one choice affect a person's whole life? Explain your opinion.

Reading Literature: Poetry

1. **Making Inferences.** Imagine that this speaker is the poet himself. In what sense does a poet take a road "less traveled by"?

2. **Identifying Rhyme Scheme.** Write the rhyme scheme for the first stanza. Do all the stanzas follow that pattern?

Stopping by Woods on a Snowy Evening

ROBERT FROST

This poem, like "The Road Not Taken," is by Robert Frost. As you read it, listen for Frost's conversational tone. Watch for details that will let you hear and feel and see what the speaker experiences.

Whose woods these are I think I know.
His house is in the village though;
He will not see me stopping here
To watch his woods fill up with snow.

My little horse must think it queer
To stop without a farmhouse near
Between the woods and frozen lake
The darkest evening of the year.

He gives his harness bells a shake
To ask if there is some mistake.
The only other sound's the sweep
Of easy wind and downy flake.

The woods are lovely, dark and deep,
But I have promises to keep,
And miles to go before I sleep,
And miles to go before I sleep.

Developing Comprehension Skills

1. How is the speaker traveling?

2. Where has the speaker stopped? Why?

3. Which of these words best describes the speaker's feelings about stopping:

    pleased   guilty   self-conscious

    Explain your answer.

4. Why does the speaker resume his journey?

5. What point is the speaker making about what we should do with our lives? Do you agree that each of us has "promises to keep"? What promises might these be?

Reading Literature: Poetry

1. **Identifying Rhyme Scheme.** Write the rhyme scheme for this entire poem, not just the first stanza. What is unusual about this rhyme scheme?

2. **Understanding Symbolism.** Both "The Road Not Taken" and this poem are by Robert Frost. As in the first poem you read, the

Winter Harmony, 1890–1900, JOHN H. TWACHTMAN. National Gallery of Art, Washington; Gift of the Avalon Foundation, 1964.

woods here may stand for life itself. If so, what might the traveler's pause to enjoy the view stand for? What might be meant by the traveler's decision to keep his promises before resting?

3. **Appreciating Repetition.** Keep in mind your answers for questions 1 and 2 in this section. Can you suggest two reasons why the poet repeated the last line?

4. **Recognizing Imagery.** Identify at least four details about the setting. To which sense does each detail appeal?

How do the sounds of the words in this passage stress the meaning of the words?

The only other sound's the sweep
Of easy wind and downy flake.

5. **Understanding Mood.** How would you describe the mood of this poem?

Requiem

ROBERT LOUIS STEVENSON

The word requiem comes from a Latin word for "rest." In English, it is the name of a prayer or service for the dead. Why is the word a satisfying title for this poem?

Under the wide and starry sky
   Dig the grave and let me lie,
Glad did I live and gladly die,
   And I laid me down with a will.

This be the verse you grave for me:
   Here he lies where he longed to be,
Home is the sailor, home from sea,
   And the hunter home from the hill.

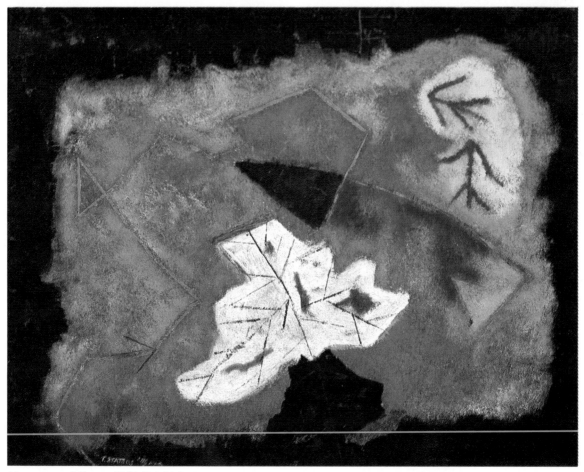

Movement of Plants, 1945, THEODOROS STAMOS. Munson-Williams-Proctor Institute, Utica, New York. Edward W. Root bequest.

Developing Comprehension Skills

1. The speaker is dictating a verse. Where is the verse to be engraved for him?

2. How would you describe the speaker's attitude toward death?

3. Is this attitude a healthy one? Is it a common one? Explain both answers.

Reading Literature: Poetry

1. **Identifying Uses of Sound.** Write the rhyme scheme of this entire poem. Which sounds do you hear most often at the ends of the rhyming words?

   How many examples of alliteration can you find in the poem?

2. **Appreciating Sounds.** The vowels and certain consonants, including *l*, *m*, and *w*, take

very little effort to form. How many words in this poem feature one or more of those consonants? What sounds do you notice in the rhymes? What effect do these sounds have on the mood of the poem?

3. **Recognizing Metaphor.** Explain the last two lines. What does the poet suggest by these images of homecoming? Again, what is the effect on the mood?

Developing Vocabulary Skills

Reviewing Word Origins. Identify the way in which each of the following underlined words came into the English language.

> borrowing
> making a word from a name
> clipping
> combining words or word parts
> imitating a sound

1. Undergrowth refers to shrubs or small trees growing under or among tall trees.

2. The word admiral started with an Arabian phrase, *amir al*, which means "chief of."

3. Mum is an easy-to-spell version of chrysanthemum.

4. One word that describes a sharp, sudden sound is slap.

5. The Norse gods Odin and Thor are honored in our names for two days of the week, Wednesday and Thursday.

Developing Writing Skills

1. **Evaluating a Technique.** Throughout this chapter, you have noticed that many poets use repetition for various effects. Write five short paragraphs explaining different uses of repetition. Your first paragraph should be an introduction that tells what you intend to discuss. The second, third, and fourth paragraphs should present three different effects of repetition, or discuss its use in three different poems. The fifth paragraph should summarize the body paragraphs.

2. **Using Your Journal.** Near the beginning of this chapter, it was suggested that you keep a journal of thoughts and opinions. Use some of the entries in your journal to write a poem on any topic you like. The poem must use at least two of the following techniques:

metaphor	rhyme
simile	regular rhythm
personification	alliteration
hyperbole	assonance

Pre-Writing. Review the notes in your journal. Do any of them already use techniques listed in the question? If not, could one of the ideas or observations be changed a little to make use of the technique? On a separate sheet, jot down your ideas. Which topics lead you to think most creatively? Choose one of them for the topic of your poem. Reread the list of techniques above. Have you written an example of each? In your poem, try to use as many of the techniques as you can.

Writing. Select the best of your notes. Beginning with them, write your poem.

Revising. Ask a friend to read and comment on your poem. Did it give a sharp image of something? Did it use at least two of the techniques listed? If not, try to add what is missing. Then rewrite a clean copy.

Developing Skills in Study and Research

Making Use of Reference Books. Use the card catalog in your library to find several anthologies of modern poetry. Use the tables of contents or indexes in the anthologies to find five or six poems by Robert Frost. Of those poems, choose one that you like and can explain. On your paper, identify the title of the poem, the source book in which you found it, and the page on which it appears. Then write notes on any techniques you have studied that are used in this poem.

Developing Skills in Critical Thinking

Recognizing Necessary Features. Literature can be classified according to type. Prose and poetry are two main types of literature. You have read selections from both categories. Think about how you recognize the difference between prose and poetry. What important features do you consider in classifying works of literature? For example, you might look at the organization of the writing or at the way the writer uses language. Make a list of what you think are the meaningful differences between prose and poetry.

Using Your Skills in Reading Poetry

Read the following stanzas from the poem "The Challenge of Thor," by Henry Wadsworth Longfellow. Then follow the directions below.

I am the God Thor,	Here amid icebergs
I am the War God,	Rule I the nations;
I am the Thunderer!	This is my hammer,
Here in my Northland,	Miolner the mighty;
My fastness and fortress,	Giants and sorcerers
Reign I forever!	cannot withstand it!

1. Identify the speaker.
2. Identify which of these sound techniques the stanzas use.

   rhyme   rhythm   alliteration   repetition of words or phrases

3. Explain how the sound techniques stress the meaning of the stanzas.

Using Your Comprehension Skills

Here is a paragraph from a selection you will read in Chapter 7. Read it, watching for the author's tone. Identify at least one example of figurative language. Tell what you believe is the author's purpose in using figurative language rather than literal language.

"Punch, brothers, punch with care!
Punch in the presence of the passenjare!"

I came across these jingling rhymes in a newspaper, a little while ago, and read them a couple of times. They took instant and entire possession of me. All through breakfast they went waltzing through my brain; and when, at last, I rolled up my napkin, I could not tell whether I had eaten anything or not. I had carefully laid out my day's work the day before. I took up my pen, but all I could get it to say was "Punch in the presence of the passenjare." I fought hard for an hour, but it was useless. My head kept humming.

Using Your Vocabulary Skills

Each underlined word below is used in Chapter 7. Tell how each entered the English language: by borrowing, from a name, from clipping a longer word or term, from combining words, or from a sound.

1. The word jingle suggests the clinking sound it means.

2. Straggle, meaning "to stray from course," joins *stray*, meaning "wander," and *draggle*, "to hang trailing."

3. The bowie knife was named in honor of one of the heroes of the Alamo, Jim Bowie.

4. Both gentle and Gentile have their sources in a Latin word, *gentilis,* meaning "belonging to a people."

5. Anyone making a parachute jump should check the chute carefully ahead of time.

Using Your Writing Skills

Choose one of the following assignments.

1. Choose any poem in this chapter. Analyze the poem thoroughly. Discuss its use of these figures of speech: simile, metaphor, personification, hyperbole. Also, discuss its use of these sound techniques: rhyme, rhythm, alliteration, assonance, onomatopoeia. Discuss also its use of sensory images, its theme, and its mood.

2. Write either a paragraph or a poem, with or without rhyme, that includes the following: at least one sensory image, at least one simile or metaphor, and at least one instance of alliteration.

Using Your Skills in Critical Thinking

Imagine that you have been asked to write a single paragraph about poetry. Find ways of limiting the broad topic to a subtopic you can manage in one paragraph. Use the elements of poetry or other information discussed in this chapter. For example, one step might be to separate poems with regular rhythm patterns from poems with conversational rhythms. Show at least four steps in breaking down the topic of *poetry*.

Nonfiction

Quill in Inkwell, Book and Candle, 1899, JOHN PETO.
Private Collection. Courtesy of Kennedy Galleries, New York.

Reading Literature: Nonfiction

What Is Nonfiction?

In fiction, such as myths and short stories, the subject matter is imaginary. In nonfiction, the subject matter is factual. The writer of nonfiction writes about actual people, places, and things.

There are two basic approaches to the subject matter. The writer can try to report facts with as few personal opinions as possible. Or, the writer can present his or her personal opinions about some facts. Often, nonfiction writing falls somewhere between these two approaches. It is impossible to leave out opinions altogether. After all, the writer must begin by deciding which facts to include. These decisions are opinions. A careful reader must keep this in mind when reading nonfiction.

Here are the forms of nonfiction in the first part of this chapter:

A **diary** is the day-by-day record a person keeps of his or her own activities and thoughts. It is meant for the writer alone.

An **autobiography** is the story of a person's own life. Usually, the writer wants to share what he or she learned from the events.

A **biography** is the story of another person's life. The writer bases the report on records of what the person did and said.

A **personal recollection**, like an autobiography, is written about a person's own life. However, it concentrates on one event.

The History of Nonfiction

As long as writing has existed, nonfiction has existed. The kinds of nonfiction, though, have changed and developed over the years.

The first biographies, for example, were written to glorify heroes or leaders. These accounts told only the subject's good acts. By the 1800's, however, biographers were beginning to include the subject's weaknesses, also. The first great modern biography was by James Boswell, an English writer. He wrote *The Life of Johnson* about his friend Samuel

Johnson, writer of one of the earliest English dictionaries. Modern biographies try to be true to the subject's personality and history. They usually are researched carefully and try to be objective.

The Elements of Nonfiction

Characters, Plot, and Setting. Like fiction, nonfiction has characters, plot, and setting. However, these elements are real, not made up. The main character in an autobiography or biography is called the **subject**. The subject's words, thoughts, and actions are presented.

Purpose. Different types of nonfiction have different purposes. Biographies and autobiographies, for example, have the purpose of informing the reader. They use explanatory, descriptive, and narrative paragraphs. (See pages 166 and 167 for a discussion of types of paragraphs.) Other types of nonfiction, such as newspaper editorials, are intended to win readers over to a certain opinion. They use persuasive paragraphs. Sometimes a piece of writing combines purposes. In his diary, for example, Davy Crockett both explains and persuades.

Tone. The writer's attitude toward his or her subject matter is called **tone**. A writer's tone may be sympathetic, as in "We'll Always Sing His Songs." It may be bitter, as in "The First Day of the War." It may be comic, hopeful, solemn, or anything the writer likes.

How To Read Nonfiction

1. As you read, try to separate facts from opinions. Keep in mind that the writer has chosen facts that present a certain picture of the subject. Think about what might be missing as well as what is there.
2. Think about the writer's purpose. What is he or she trying to explain? Or is the writer trying to win you over to his or her opinion of an action or a person? You can appreciate how well a writer says something, even when you don't agree. In fact, this ability is an important quality of a critical reader.
3. Be aware of the writer's tone. Frequently a writer reveals much about himself or herself by the tone he or she uses. This is especially important in autobiographical writing.

Comprehension Skills: Fact and Opinion

Distinguishing Between Fact and Opinion

One purpose of nonfiction is to inform. Therefore, it often contains many facts. A **fact** is a statement that can be proved. From reading nonfiction selections, you can learn many facts. However, a nonfiction selection is tricky to read. One reason is that some of its statements may be facts, but not all of them. In addition, there may be important facts left out. Further, the way that the selection presents its facts may make them hard to identify or use. You must read carefully.

Identifying Opinions. Most nonfiction presents both facts and opinions. An **opinion** is a statement that cannot be proved true. Note the difference between these two sentences:

My cousin wrote me a letter.

My cousin wrote me a boring letter.

The first sentence is a fact. Another person could verify, or show the truth of, that sentence. The second sentence, however, is an opinion. The word *boring* shows what the speaker thinks of the letter. Another person might disagree with that judgment.

What happens if you recognize opinions? For one thing, you understand the writer better. More importantly, you get to choose whether to agree or disagree. You do not blindly accept someone else's decisions.

Judging Opinions. Every writer must have opinions. Opinions help the writer put the facts together in some meaningful way. Without opinions, a piece of writing would have no organization. The reader's job is to identify the opinions and decide which are worth accepting.

One guideline for making that choice is seeing how closely the opinion matches the facts. Does the writer support each opinion with facts? Can you think of other facts that do not support the opinion?

Another guideline is considering the qualifications of the writer. That is, you decide whether the writer is likely to know what he or she is talking about. You might trust a scientist writing about science.

A third guideline is considering the writer's purpose. You know, for example, that the purpose of an ad is to sell something. This should make you cautious about accepting any statement in an ad.

Recognizing Slanted Writing. Slanted writing is one-sided and biased. The writer has a definite opinion. However, he or she pretends to be impartial and fair to both sides. A reader who is not careful might think that the selection is telling the truth.

In slanted writing, the writer gives only the facts that agree with his or her opinion. Other important facts are ignored. Also, the writer uses words with strong connotations. The favored opinion is discussed with positive words. The opposite view gets negative words.

A third technique of slanted writing is faulty generalizing. **Generalizing** means making a general statement based on a few facts. A faulty generalization is an inaccurate statement based on facts.

Exercises: Recognizing Fact, Opinion, and Slanted Writing

A. Identify each statement as fact or opinion.

1. China, India, the Soviet Union, and the United States have a total population of 1,790,000,000.

2. It was a wonderful thing, that bank account of Mama's.

3. She became the only black woman bank president in the country.

B. Read this passage and answer the following questions.

Foster was finally reduced to the pitiful condition of the nameless poor on the Bowery. After three years of this privation, Foster died in Bellevue Hospital, reminding us of his warmth and sweetness with his last words, "Dear Friends and Gentle Hearts."

1. Identify at least one fact in the passage.

2. Identify at least one of the author's opinions shown in the passage.

3. List at least three words in the passage with strong connotations.

4. State what you think the writer wants the reader to believe.

Vocabulary Skills: The Dictionary

Using a Dictionary

As you know, there are several ways to figure out the meaning of an unfamiliar word. Your first reaction should be to look at the word itself for familiar word parts. Next, you should examine the context for clues. Third, you could see whether word origins such as clipping or combining might help you. Last, you would turn to a dictionary or glossary.

A **dictionary** is an entire book that gives information about the spelling, meanings, and sources of words. The words are listed in alphabetical order. A dictionary for students lists all the words that you would likely come across in your reading for school or enjoyment. A **glossary** is a much shorter dictionary. It appears within another book, as at the back of this text. It lists only words from the book.

You should be familiar with the following features of each entry.

Entry Word. Each word listed is printed in boldface, or heavy, letters. The breaks between syllables are indicated by spacing, dashes, or dots. Here is an example: **glo·ry**. The entry word tells you the correct spelling and where to break the word when it won't fit on a line.

Respelling. The respelling of the word appears next, usually in parentheses. It uses symbols that show how to pronounce the word.

glo·ry (glôr′ ē)

In the dictionary, the symbols are explained in a key at the front and on every page or every second page. The symbols in this example are explained in the Glossary Key, on page 633. Boldface accent marks show which syllable gets most stress when you say the word. A lighter accent mark indicates a syllable with a lighter stress.

Part of Speech. Each entry word is used as at least one part of speech. The meanings in an entry are grouped by part of speech. The part of speech used most often is usually listed first. Notice in this example the additional information given about the part of speech:

glo·ry (glôr′ ē) **n.,** *pl.* **-ries**

The **n.** stands for "noun." The *pl.* stands for "plural." The **-ries** shows that the plural form of the noun *glory* is spelled *glories.*

To find the right meaning of a word, you need not read all the meanings in the entry. First determine the part of speech of the word in its sentence. Then look for that part of speech in the entry.

Word Origin.   Some dictionaries give the word origin after the part of speech. Others give it at the end of the entry. It is usually set off by brackets. The abbreviations and symbols inside the brackets tell how the word came into English. The abbreviations and symbols are explained, usually, at the front of the dictionary.

glo·ry (glôr′ ē) **n.,** *pl.* **-ries** [<OFr. <L. *gloria*]

The example shows that *glory* came from Old French, which took it from Latin. In Latin it was spelled *gloria.*

Definitions.   The entry may list many definitions, or meanings, grouped by parts of speech. First find the part of speech you need. Then search for the meaning that fits best in the sentence you have read.

Exercise: **Using a Dictionary**

Use this dictionary entry to answer the questions below.

ap·pe·tite (ap′ ə tīt′) **n.** [<M.E. & OFr. <L. *appetitus*] **1.** a desire for food or for a specific food **2.** any strong desire or craving [an *appetite* for learning]

1. How is *appetite* divided into syllables?
2. Which syllable is given the most stress?
3. From which language did Middle English and Old French take this word?
4. Tell which definition is used in this sentence:
   The adventurers had an appetite for excitement.

 Diaries

Most **diaries** are written for personal reasons. They are not intended for publication. Sometimes, however, someone other than the writer has an opportunity to read a diary. Once in a great while, that reader believes that everyone should have a chance to read the diary. Here are excerpts from two such diaries. As you read them, decide why their publishers wanted to share them with you.

Anne Frank. 1941. © 1984 by ANNE FRANK-Fonds/COSMOPRESS, Genève

The Life of Davy Crockett by Himself

DAVY CROCKETT

From the first entry in this diary to the last, Davy Crockett shows a fearless attitude towards his enemies. As you read, look for passages that reveal this attitude.

February 19, 1836. San Antonio

. . . We are all in high spirits, though we were rather short of provisions, for men who have appetites that could digest anything but oppression; but no matter, we have a prospect of soon getting our bellies full of fighting, and that is victuals and drink to a patriot any day. We had a little sort of convivial party last evening. Just about a dozen of us set to work most patriotically, to see whether we could not get rid of that curse of the land, whisky, and we made considerable progress; but my poor friend, Thimblerig, got sewed up just about as tight as the eyelet-hole in a lady's corset, and a little tighter too, I reckon; for when he went to bed he called for a bootjack,[1] which was brought to him, and he bent down on his hands and knees, and very gravely pulled off his hat with it, for the darned critter didn't know his head from his heels. But this wasn't all the folly he committed; he pulled off his coat and laid it on the bed, and then hung himself over the back of a chair. . . . Seeing the poor fellow completely used up, I carried him to bed.

February 22

The Mexicans, about sixteen hundred strong, with their President Santa Anna at their head, aided by Generals Almonte, Cos, Sesma, and Castrillon, are within two leagues of Bexar.[2] . . . Some of the scouts came in and brought reports that Santa Anna had been endeavoring to excite the Indians to hostilities against the Texans, but so far without effect. The Comanches, in particular, entertain such hatred for the Mexicans, and at the same time hold them in such contempt, that they would rather turn their tomahawks against them and drive them from the land, than lend a helping hand. We are up and doing and as lively as Dutch cheese in the dog days.[3] . . .

February 23

Early this morning the enemy came in sight, marching in regular order and displaying their strength to the greatest advan-

---

1. **bootjack**, a device that helps pull off a boot
2. **Bexar**, now the city of San Antonio
3. **dog days**, the hot, uncomfortable days in summer when the Dog Star rises and sets with the sun

David Crockett, 1834, ALBERT NEWSAM.
National Portrait Gallery, Washington, D.C.

We have had a large national flag made; it is composed of thirteen stripes, red and white, alternately, on a blue ground, with a large white star of five points, in the centre, and between the points the letters TEXAS. As soon as all our little band, about one hundred and fifty in number, had entered and secured the fortress in the best possible manner, we set about raising our flag on the battlements.

The enemy marched into Bexar, and took possession of the town, a blood-red flag flying at their head, to indicate that we need not expect quarters if we should fall into their clutches. In the afternoon a messenger was sent from the enemy to Colonel Travis, demanding an unconditional and absolute surrender of the garrison, threatening to put every man to the sword in case of refusal. The only answer he received was a cannon shot, so the messenger left us with a flea in his ear, and the Mexicans commenced firing grenades at us, but without doing any mischief. . . .

February 24

Very early this morning the enemy commenced a new battery on the banks of the river, about three hundred and fifty yards from the fort, and by afternoon they amused themselves by firing at us from that quarter. Our Indian scout came in this evening, and with him a reinforcement of thirty men from Gonzales, who are just in the nick of time to reap a harvest of glory; but there is some prospect of sweating blood before we gather it in. . . .

tage, in order to strike us with terror. But that was no go; they'll find that they have to do with men who will never lay down their arms as long as they can stand on their legs. We held a short council of war, and, finding that we should be completely surrounded and overwhelmed by numbers if we remained in the town, we concluded to withdraw to the fortress of Alamo and defend it to the last extremity. We accordingly filed off, in good order, having some days before placed all the surplus provisions, arms, and ammunition in the fortress.

The firing commenced early this morning, but we haven't lost a single man, and our outworks have sustained no injury. Our sharpshooters have brought down a considerable number of stragglers at a long shot. . . . The enemy have been busy during the night, and have thrown up two batteries on the opposite side of the river. The battalion of Matamoras is posted there, and cavalry occupy the hills in the east and on the road to Gonzales. They are determined to surround us, and cut us off from reinforcement, or the possiblity of escape by a sortie. Well, there's one thing they cannot prevent; we'll still go ahead, and sell our lives at a high price.

February 26

Colonel Bowie has been taken sick from over-exertion and exposure. He did not leave his bed today until twelve o'clock. He is worth a dozen common men in a situation like ours. . . .

February 27

The cannonading began early this morning, and ten bombs were thrown into the fort, but fortunately exploded without doing any mischief. So far it has been a sort of tempest in a teapot, not unlike a pitched battle in the Hall of Congress, where the parties array their forces, make fearful demonstrations on both sides, and then fire away with loud-sounding speeches, which contain about as much meaning as the report of a howitzer charged with a blank cartridge. Provisions are becoming scarce, and the enemy are endeavoring to cut off our water. If they attempt to stop our grog in that manner, let them look out, for we shall become too wrathy for our shirts to hold us. We are not prepared to submit to an exercise of that nature, and they'll find it out. This discovery has created considerable excitement in the fort.

February 28

Last night our hunters brought in some corn, and had a brush with a scout from the enemy beyond gunshot of the fort. They put the scout to flight and got in without injury. They bring accounts that the settlers are flying in all quarters, in dismay, leaving their possessions to the mercy of the ruthless invader, who is literally engaged in a war of extermination more brutal than the untutored savage of the desert could be guilty of. Slaughter is indiscriminate, sparing neither sex, age, nor condition. Buildings have been burnt down, farms laid waste, and Santa Anna appears determined to verify his threat and convert the blooming paradise into a howling wilderness. For just one fair crack at that rascal, even at a hundred yards' distance, I would bargain to break my Betsey[3] and never pull trigger again. My name's not Crockett if I wouldn't get glory enough to appease my stomach for the remainder of my life. . . .

The enemy, somewhat emboldened, draws nigher to the fort. So much the bet-

---

3. **Betsey**, frontier name for a gun

ter. There was a move in General Sesma's division toward evening.

February 29

Before daybreak, we saw General Sesma leave his camp, with a large body of cavalry and infantry, and move off in the direction of Goliad. We think that he must have received news of Colonel Fanning's coming to our relief. We are all in high spirits at the prospect of being able to give the rascals a fair shake on the plain. This business of being shut up makes a man wolfish. I had a little sport this morning before breakfast. The enemy had planted a piece of ordnance within gunshot of the fort during the night, and the first thing in the morning they commenced a brisk cannonade, point blank, against the spot where I was snoring. I turned out pretty smart and mounted the rampart. The gun was charged again, a fellow stepped forth to touch her off, but before he could apply the match, I let him have it, and he keeled over. A second stepped up, snatched the match from the hand of the dying man . . . the next instant the Mexican was stretched on the earth beside the first. A third came up to the cannon, my companion handed me another gun, and I fixed him off in like manner. A fourth, then a fifth, seized the match, who both met with the same fate, and then the whole party gave it up as a bad job, and hurried off to the camp, leaving the cannon ready charged where they had planted it. I came down, took my bitters, and went to breakfast. Thimblerig told me that the place

from which I had been firing was one of the snuggest stands in the whole fort, for he never failed picking off two or three stragglers before breakfast, when perched up there. . . .

March 1

The enemy's forces have been increasing in numbers daily, notwithstanding they have already lost about three hundred men in the several assaults they have made upon us. I neglected to mention in the proper place that, when the enemy came in sight, we had but three bushels of corn in the garrison but have since found eighty bushels in a deserted house. Colonel Bowie's illness still continues, but he manages to crawl from his bed every day, that his comrades may see him. His presence alone is a tower of strength. The enemy becomes more daring as his numbers increase.

March 2

This day the delegates meet in general convention at the town of Washington (Texas), to frame our [Texan] Declaration of Independence. That the sacred instrument may never be trampled on by the children of those who have freely shed their blood to establish it, is the sincere wish of David Crockett. Universal independence is an almighty idea, far too extensive for some brains to comprehend. . . .

March 3

We have given over all hopes of receiving assistance from Goliad or Refugio. Colonel

Travis harangued the garrison, and concluded by exhorting them, in case the enemy should carry to fort, to fight to the last gasp and render their victory even more serious to them than to us. This was followed by three cheers.

March 4

Shells have been falling into the fort like hail during the day, but without effect. . . .

March 5

Pop, pop, pop! Bom, bom, bom! throughout the day. No time for memorandums now. Go ahead! Liberty and independence forever!

Here ends Colonel David Crockett's manuscript. Before the sun set again he was dead, as were all of his comrades of the Alamo.

Developing Comprehension Skills

1. Davy Crockett's diary presents some historical information. Who are Crockett and the others fighting against? Why? Find your answers in the diary.

2. The diary is also subjective; that is, it presents Crockett's opinions. Identify two personal feelings that the writer included in the diary.

3. What type of man do you think Davy Crockett was? What parts of his diary lead you to this answer?

4. Most diaries are not written for publication. Why do you think Davy Crockett kept a diary?

5. Would you have liked living the adventures that Crockett experienced? Explain why or why not.

Reading Literature: Diaries

1. **Examining Imagery.** One important part of Crockett's style is his colorful language. He used lively words in his descriptions of people and events. Select two of the following passages from the diary. Explain the meaning of each passage in your own words. You may refer to a dictionary.

   a. The messenger left the Texans with a flea in his ear.

   b. The thirty men from Gonzales were just in the nick of time to reap a harvest of glory.

   c. For a few days, the situation seemed like a tempest in a teapot.

   d. The troops looked forward to the prospect of being able to give the rascals a fair shake on the plain.

   e. Colonel Bowie's presence was a tower of strength to the men.

   f. The men were up and doing and as lively as Dutch cheese in the dog days.

2. **Understanding Contrasts.** Review the story about Thimblerig in the first diary entry. Why do you think Crockett includes this humorous scene? How does it contrast to the main subject that he writes about?

3. **Analyzing Tone.** Crockett's **tone**, or attitude toward his subject matter, is one of enthusiasm for an independent Texas. Select three passages where his choice of words suggests this enthusiasm.

4. **Recognizing Slanted Writing.** In his diary, Davy Crockett explains his view of events. It is natural that he also mentions his opinions. Read the following passage from the diary. Find at least three words with strong connotations, or emotional meanings. What does Crockett believe about his enemy?

   Last night our hunters brought in some corn, and had a brush with a scout from the enemy beyond gunshot of the fort. They put the scout to flight and got in without injury. They bring accounts that the settlers are flying in all quarters, in dismay, leaving their possessions to the mercy of the ruthless invader, who is literally engaged in a war of extermination more brutal than the untutored savage of the desert could be guilty of.

Developing Vocabulary Skills

1. **Using a Pronunciation Key.** A dictionary tells you how to pronounce a word by giving a respelling of the word. The **respelling** uses

letters and symbols to stand for the sounds of each syllable in the spoken word. For example, the respelling of *legend* is (lej′ nd).

How do you find out what each letter and symbol stands for? You must refer to the pronunciation key of that dictionary. The **pronunciation key** lists the symbols that are used in the respellings. For each symbol, the key shows a sample word that uses that sound. These sample words are called **key words**. You already know how to pronounce them. For example, look at the pronunciation key in the glossary of your textbook. Find the symbol ə, called *schwa*. The key tells you that ə is pronounced like the *a* in *alive*.

Find each of the following words from the diary in the glossary of your textbook.

a. assault
b. commence
c. victuals
d. rampart
e. ordnance

Look at the respelling of each word. Match each part of the respelling with a key word in the pronunciation key. For example, the re-spelling for *sortie* is (sôr′ tē). The key words that match the respelling are *corn,* for the ô sound, and *equal,* for the ē sound. Write each word, its respelling, and its key words on your paper.

2. **Using Accent Marks.** The respelling also includes **accent marks**. These explain which syllable to stress when you say the word. A heavy accent mark is called the **primary accent**. If a word has more than two syllables, it may have more than one accent. The lighter accent mark is called the **secondary accent**. The word *indiscriminate* has two accents: (in′ dis krim′ ə nit).

Add the accent marks to the respellings you wrote down for the words in question 1. Then try to say each word by using the accent marks, respelling, and key words.

Developing Writing Skills

1. **Writing a News Article.** A news article in a newspaper and a news report on the radio or television share a special approach to reporting facts. They always give the most important facts first, in order to catch the reader's or listener's attention. They give less important facts later, in case the article or report is too long and must be cut short. Sometimes this means that events are told out of order. However, in that case the writer must provide time-order clues, such as the following.

> *Before* the robbery, the manager had taken the day's receipts to the bank.

> *After* the robber was arrested, police reported that he had a long criminal record.

Pretend that you are a newspaper reporter. Write a one-page report about the defeat of the Texans at the Alamo. You will be presenting only facts, not opinions. Decide whether to report all the events or to focus on one event. If you include all the events, arrange them by time order. If you focus on one event, begin with the most important details and end with the least important. Write one to three paragraphs.

2. **Describing a Place.** Suppose that Davy Crockett's diary was going to be made into a film. It would be important for the film-maker to understand the setting and the

mood. Imagine what the Texans' camp was like. Write a one-paragraph description of the camp. Use words that suggest the feeling of the place.

Pre-Writing. Think about the mood, or emotional feeling, you want to create. Then make lists of nouns, adjectives, verbs, and adverbs you could use to suggest that mood.

Next, make a list of all the objects that you imagine are part of the scene.

Decide how you will present the information about the setting. Will you begin by describing the most important object? Will you start with the least important object and build to the most important? Will you describe objects in the order that your eye follows in looking around a room? On your paper, number your details or put them into an outline form.

Writing. Follow your pre-writing notes as you write your description. Use words and phrases that make the arrangement of objects in the setting clear. Remember that you want your description to express the mood of the setting. Select words from your lists to create the specific mood.

Revising. Read your description carefully. Ask yourself the following questions.

a. Do the words give the reader a good picture of the Texans' camp?

b. Is the topic sentence interesting?

c. Are the details arranged in a way that makes sense?

d. Do the words help create the mood I had in mind?

Change any part of your description that does not present a clear picture.

Developing Skills in Critical Thinking

Recognizing Subjective Statements. A nonfiction selection often mixes facts and opinions. The writer may not identify which is which. One reason for this is that the writer may not realize that some of his or her statements are opinions. The writer may think of them as facts. He or she is looking at an event or an idea subjectively, that is, with a personal view. The writer assumes that everyone else will agree with his or her understanding of the events. A reader must be alert to such statements in order not to confuse them with facts.

For example, reread the entry in Davy Crockett's diary for February 22, 1836. What reasons does he give for the Indians' refusal to fight with the Mexicans? Can you tell whether this is a fact? What other reasons might the Indians have had?

Review the entries for February 29, March 1, and March 2. Find the following phrases in context. Explain how each phrase is subjective.

1. a little sport

2. The enemy becomes more daring as his numbers increase.

3. sacred instrument

The Diary of a Young Girl

ANNE FRANK

During World War II, Germany invaded Holland. Jewish people were sent to concentration camps, where many were killed. This diary was written by a Jewish girl living in Holland. Would you react as she did?

Saturday, 20 June, 1942

It's an odd idea for someone like me to keep a diary; not only because I have never done so before, but because it seems to me that neither I—nor for that matter anyone else—will be interested in the unbosomings of a thirteen-year-old schoolgirl. Still, what does that matter? I want to write, but more than that, I want to bring out all kinds of things that lie buried deep in my heart.

Let me put it more clearly, since no one will believe that a girl of thirteen feels herself quite alone in the world, nor is it so. I have darling parents and a sister of sixteen. I know about thirty people whom one might call friends—I have strings of boy friends, anxious to catch a glimpse of me and who, failing that, peep at me through mirrors in class. I have relations, aunts and uncles, who are darlings too, a good home, no—I don't seem to lack anything. But it's the same with all my friends, just fun and joking, nothing more. I can never bring myself to talk of anything outside the common round. I don't want to set down a series of bald facts like most people do, but I want this diary itself to be my friend, and I shall call my friend Kitty. I will start by sketching in brief the story of my life.

My father was thirty-six when he married my mother, who was then twenty-five. My sister Margot was born in 1926 in Frankfort-on-Main, I followed on June 12, 1929, and, as we are Jewish, we emigrated to Holland in 1933.

The rest of our family, however, felt the impact of Hitler's anti-Jewish laws, so life was filled with anxiety. In 1938 after the pogroms, my two uncles (my mother's brothers) escaped to the U.S.A. My old grandmother came to us; she was then seventy-three. After May 1940 good times rapidly fled: first the war, then the capitulation, followed by the arrival of the Germans, which is when the sufferings of us Jews really began. Anti-Jewish decrees followed each other in quick succession. Jews

Anne (right) playing with her friend. © 1984 by ANNE FRANK-Fonds/ COSMOPRESS, Genève.

must wear a yellow star.[1] Jews must hand in their bicycles. Jews are banned from trams and are forbidden to drive. Jews are only allowed to do their shopping between three and five o'clock and then only in shops which bear the placard "Jewish shop." Jews must be indoors by eight o'clock and cannot even sit in their own gardens after that hour. Jews are forbidden to visit theaters, cinemas, and other places of entertainment. Jews may not take part in public sports.

Swimming baths, tennis courts, hockey fields, and other sports grounds are all prohibited to them. Jews may not visit Christians. Jews must go to Jewish schools, and many more restrictions of a similar kind.

So we could not do this and were forbidden to do that. But life went on in spite of it all. . . . Our freedom was strictly limited. Yet things were still bearable.

Granny died in January 1942; no one will ever know how much she is present in my thoughts and how much I love her still.

Yours, Anne

---

1. **yellow star**. This refers to the Star of David, the universal symbol of Judaism. It is made from two triangles interwoven to form a six-pointed star. In the countries they dominated, the Nazis forced all Jews to wear the star for easy identification.

Dear Kitty,

Our examination results were announced in the Jewish Theater last Friday. I couldn't have hoped for better. They were certainly pleased at home, although over the question of marks my parents are quite different than most. They don't care a bit whether my reports are good or bad as long as I'm well and happy, and not too cheeky: then the rest will come by itself. I am just the opposite. I don't want to be a bad pupil.

When we walked across our little square together a few days ago, Daddy began to talk of us going into hiding. I asked him why on earth he was beginning to talk of that already. "Yes, Anne," he said, "you know that we have been taking food, clothes, furniture to other people for more than a year now. We don't want our belongings to be seized by the Germans, but we certainly don't want to fall into their clutches ourselves. So we shall disappear of our own accord and not wait until they come and fetch us."

"But, Daddy, when would it be?" He spoke so seriously that I grew extremely anxious.

"Don't you worry about it, we shall arrange everything. Make the most of your carefree young life while you can." That was all. Oh, may the fulfillment of these somber words remain far distant yet!

Yours, Anne

Dear Kitty,

Years seem to have passed between Sunday and now. So much has happened, it is just as if the whole world had turned upside down. But I am still alive, Kitty, and that is the main thing, Daddy says.

Yes, I'm still alive, indeed, but don't ask where or how. You wouldn't understand a word, so I will begin by telling you what happened on Sunday afternoon.

At three o'clock, someone rang the front doorbell. I was lying lazily reading a book on the veranda in the sunshine, so I didn't hear it. A bit later, Margot appeared at the kitchen door looking very excited. "The S.S. have sent a call-up notice for Daddy," she whispered. "Mummy has gone to see Mr. Van Daan already." (Van Daan is a friend who works with Daddy in the business.) It was a great shock to me, a call-up; everyone knows what that means. I picture concentration camps and lonely cells— should we allow him to be doomed to this? "Of course he won't go," declared Margot, while we waited together. "Mummy has gone to the Van Daans to discuss whether we should move into our hiding place tomorrow. The Van Daans are going with us, so we shall be seven in all." Silence. We couldn't talk anymore, thinking about Daddy, who, little knowing what was going on, was visiting some old people in the Jewish Hospital; waiting for Mummy, the heat and suspense, all made us very overawed and silent.

Suddenly the bell rang again. We heard Mummy and Mr. Van Daan downstairs, talking; then they came in and closed the door behind them. Each time the bell went, Margot or I had to creep softly down to see if it was Daddy, not opening the door to anyone else.

Margot and I were sent out of the room. Van Daan wanted to talk to Mummy alone. When we were alone together in our bedroom, Margot told me that the call-up was not for Daddy, but for her. I was more frightened than ever and began to cry. Margot is sixteen; would they really take girls of that age away alone? But thank goodness she won't go, Mummy said so herself. That must be what Daddy meant when he talked about us going into hiding.

Into hiding—where would we go, in a town or the country, in a house or a cottage, when, how, were . . . ?

These were questions I was not allowed to ask, but I couldn't get them out of my mind. Margot and I began to pack some of our most vital belongings into a school satchel. The first thing I put in was this diary.

At five o'clock Daddy finally arrived. Then silence fell on the house; not one of us felt like eating anything, it was still hot and everything was very strange. At eleven o'clock our friends Miep and Henk Van Santen arrived. Shoes, stockings, books, and underclothes disappeared into Miep's bag and Henk's deep pockets, and at eleven-thirty they too disappeared. I was dog-tired and although I knew that it would be my last night in my own bed, I fell asleep immediately and didn't wake up until Mummy called me at five-thirty the next morning. Luckily it was not so hot as Sunday; warm rain fell steadily all day.

Margot filled her satchel with schoolbooks, fetched her bicycle, and rode off behind Miep into the unknown, as far as I was concerned. You see I still didn't know where our secret hiding place was to be. At seven-thirty the door closed behind us.

Continued tomorrow.
Yours, Anne

Thursday, 9 July, 1942

Dear Kitty,

So we walked in the pouring rain, Daddy, Mummy, and I, each with a school satchel and shopping bag filled to the brim with all kinds of things thrown together anyhow. We got sympathetic looks from people on their way to work.

Only when we were on the road did Mummy and Daddy begin to tell me bits and pieces about the plan. For months, as many of our goods and chattels and necessities of life as possible had been sent away, and they were sufficiently ready for us to have gone into hiding of our own accord on July 16. The plan had had to be speeded up ten days because of the call-up, so our quarters would not be so well organized, but we had to make the best of it. The hiding place itself would be in the building where Daddy had his office.

There is a large warehouse on the ground level. The company offices are on the next floor above the warehouse. On the second floor, the front of the building is all store-rooms. The right-hand door off the landing leads to our "Secret Annex." No one would ever guess that there would be so many rooms hidden behind that plain gray door. There's a little step in front of the door and then you are inside.

There is a steep staircase immediately opposite the entrance. On the left a tiny passage brings you into our family's bed-sitting room. Next door is a smaller room study and bedroom for the two young ladies of the family. On the right a little room without windows containing the washbasin and a small W.C. compartment, with another door leading to Margot's and my room.

If you go up the next flight of stairs and open the door, you are simply amazed that there could be such a big, light room in such an old house by the canal. There is a gas stove in this room (thanks to the fact that it was used as a laboratory) and a sink. This is now the kitchen for the Van Daan couple, besides being general living room, dining room, and scullery.

A tiny little corridor room will become Peter Van Daan's apartment. Then, just as on the lower landing, there is a large attic. So there you are, I've introduced you to the whole of our beautiful "Secret Annex."

Yours, Anne

The "Secret Annex." Culver Pictures, New York.

Saturday, 11 July, 1942

Dear Kitty,

I expect you will be interested to hear what it feels like to "disappear"; well, all I can say is that I don't know myself yet. I don't think I shall ever feel really at home in this house, but that does not mean that I loathe it here, it is more like being on vaca-

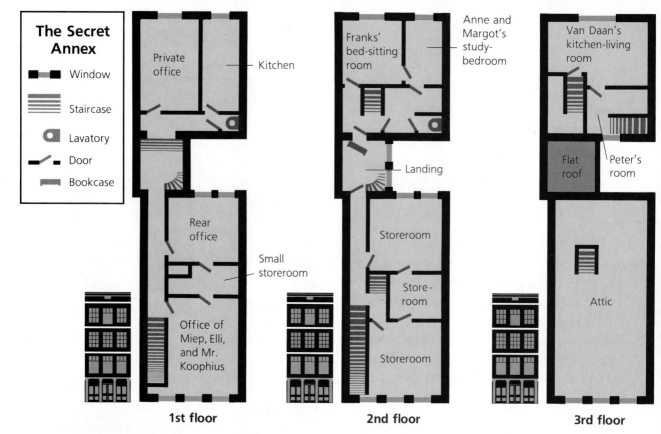

Floor plan of the Secret Annex.

tion in a very peculiar boardinghouse. Rather a mad idea, perhaps, but that is how it strikes me. The "Secret Annex" is an ideal hiding place. Although it leans to one side and is damp, you'd never find such a comfortable hiding place anywhere in Amsterdam, no, perhaps not even in the whole of Holland. Our little room looked very bare at first with nothing on the walls; but, thanks to Daddy who had brought my film-star collection and picture postcards on beforehand, and with the aid of paste pot and brush, I have transformed the walls into one gigantic picture.

There are some large business premises on the right of us, and on the left a furniture workshop; there is no one there after working hours but, even so, sounds could travel through the walls. I am looking for Tuesday when the Van Daans arrive; it will be much more fun and not so quiet.

It is the silence that frightens me so in the evenings and at night. I wish like anything that one of our protectors could sleep here at night. I can't tell you how oppressive it is never to be able to go outdoors. Also I'm very afraid that we shall be discovered and be shot. That is not exactly a pleasant prospect. We have to whisper and tread lightly during the day, otherwise the people in the warehouse might hear us.

Someone is calling me.

Yours, Anne

Friday, 14 August, 1942

Dear Kitty,

I have deserted you for a whole month, but honestly, there is so little news here that I can't find amusing things to tell you every day. The Van Daans arrived on July 13. At nine-thirty in the morning (we were still having breakfast) Peter arrived, the Van Daans' son, not sixteen yet, a rather soft, shy, gawky youth; can't expect much from his company. He brought his cat (Mouschi).

Yours, Anne

Thursday, 25 March, 1943

Dear Kitty,

Yesterday Mummy, Daddy, Margot, and I were sitting pleasantly together when suddenly Peter came in and whispered something in Daddy's ear. I heard something about "a barrel fallen over in the warehouse" and "someone fumbling about at the door." Margot had heard it too; but when Daddy and Peter went off immediately, she tried to calm me down a bit, because I was naturally as white as a sheet and very jittery.

The three of us waited in suspense. A minute or two later Mrs. Van Daan came upstairs; she'd been listening to the wireless in the private office. She told us that Daddy had asked her to turn off the wireless and go softly upstairs. But you know what that's like; if you want to be extra quiet, then each step of the old stairs creaks twice as loudly. Five minutes later Daddy and Peter appeared again, white to the roots of their hair.

They had hidden themselves under the stairs and waited, with no result at first. But suddenly, they heard two loud bumps, just as if two doors were banged here in the house. We all went up in stockinged feet to the Van Daans on the next floor. Mr. Van Daan had a bad cold and had already gone to bed, so we all drew up closely around his bed and whispered our suspicions to him.

Each time Mr. Van Daan coughed loudly, Mrs. Van Daan and I were so scared that we thought we were going to have a fit. That went on until one of us got the bright idea of giving him some codeine, which soothed the cough at once. Again we waited and waited, but we heard no more. Finally we all came to the conclusion that the thieves had taken to their heels when they heard footsteps in the house, which was otherwise so silent.

So we all went to bed; but none of us could get to sleep.

Yours, Anne

Tuesday, 18 May, 1943

Dear Kitty,

I witnessed a terrific air battle between German and British planes. Unfortunately, a couple of the Allies had to jump from burning machines.

All university students are compelled to sign that they approve of the New Order. Eighty per cent have refused to go against their consciences. Naturally they had to bear the consequences. All the students who do not sign have to go to a labor camp in Germany. What will be left of the youth of the country if they have all got to do hard labor in Germany?

Yours, Anne

Monday evening, 8 November, 1943

Dear Kitty,

If you were to read my pile of letters one after another, you would be struck by the many different moods in which they are written. It annoys me that I am so dependent on the atmosphere here, but I'm certainly not the only one—we all find it the same. If I read a book that impresses me, I have to take myself firmly in hand, before I mix with other people; otherwise they would think my mind rather queer. At the moment, as you've probably noticed, I'm going through a spell of being depressed. I really couldn't tell you why it is, but I believe it's just because I'm a coward, and that's what I keep bumping up against.

This evening, while Elli was still here, there was a long, loud, penetrating ring at the door. I turned white at once, got a tummy-ache and heart palpitations, all from fear. At night, when I'm in bed, I see myself alone in a dungeon, without Mummy and Daddy. Sometimes I wander by the roadside, or our "Secret Annex" is on fire, or they come and take us away at night. I see everything as if it is actually taking place, and this gives me the feeling that it may all happen to me very soon! Miep often says she envies us for possessing such tranquility here. That may be true, but she is not thinking about all our fears. I simply can't imagine that the world will ever be normal for us again. I do talk about "after the war," but then it is only a castle in the air, something that will never really happen. If I think back to our old house, my girl friends, the fun at school, it is just as if another person lived it all, not me.

I see the eight of us with our "Secret Annex" as if we were a little piece of blue heaven, surrounded by heavy black rain clouds. The round, clearly defined spot where we stand is still safe, but the clouds gather more closely about us and the circle which separates us from the approaching danger closes more and more tightly. Now we are so surrounded by danger and darkness that we bump against each other, as we search desperately for a means of escape. We all look down below, where people are fighting each other, we look above, where it is quiet and beautiful, and meanwhile we are cut off by the great dark mass, which will not let us go upwards, but which stands before us as an impenetrable wall; it tries to crush us, but cannot do so yet. I can only cry and implore: "Oh, if only the black circle could recede and open the way for us!"

Yours, Anne

Thursday, 6 January, 1944

Dear Kitty,

My longing to talk to someone became so intense that somehow or other I took it into my head to choose Peter.

Sometimes if I've been upstairs in Peter's room during the day, it always struck me as being very snug. But because Peter is so retiring and would never turn anyone out who became a nuisance, I never dared stay long, because I was afraid he might think me a bore. I tried to think of an excuse to stay in his room and get him talking, without it being too noticeable, and my chance came yesterday. Peter has a mania for crossword puzzles at the moment and hardly does anything else. I helped him with them and we soon sat opposite each other at his little table, he on the chair and I on the divan.

It gave me a strange feeling each time I looked into his deep blue eyes, and he sat there with that mysterious laugh playing round his lips. I was able to read his inward thoughts. I could see on his face that look of helplessness and uncertainty as to how to behave, and, at the same time, a trace of his sense of manhood. I noticed his shy manner

and it made me feel very gentle; I couldn't refrain from meeting those dark eyes again and again, and with my whole heart I almost beseeched him: oh, tell me, what is going on inside you, oh, can't you look beyond this ridiculous chatter?

But the evening passed and nothing happened.

Yours, Anne

Friday, 7 January, 1944

Dear Kitty,

I saw my face in the mirror and it looks quite different. My eyes look so clear and deep, and my cheeks are pink—which they haven't been for weeks—my mouth is much softer; I look as if I am happy, and yet there is something so sad in my expression and my smile slips away from my lips as soon as it has come.

Yours, Anne

Saturday, 12 February, 1944

Dear Kitty,

The sun is shining, the sky is a deep blue, there is a lovely breeze and I'm longing—so longing—for everything. To talk, for freedom, for friends, to be alone. And I do so long to cry! I feel as if I'm going to burst, and I know that it would get better with crying; but I can't, I'm restless, I go from one room to the other, breathe through the crack of a closed window, feel my heart beating, as if it is saying, "Can't you satisfy my longings at last?"

I believe that it's spring within me, I feel that spring is awakening, I feel it in my whole body and soul. It is an effort to behave normally, I feel utterly confused, don't know what to read, what to write, what to do, I only know that I am longing . . . !

Yours, Anne

Sunday, 13 February, 1944

Dear Kitty,

Since Saturday a lot has changed for me. It came about like this. I longed—and am still longing—but . . . now something has happened, which has made it a little, just a little, less.

To my great joy—I will be quite honest about it—already this morning I noticed that Peter kept looking at me all the time. Not in the ordinary way, I don't know how, I just can't explain.

I used to think that Peter was in love with Margot, but yesterday I had the feeling that it is not so. I made a special effort not to look at him too much, because whenever I did, he kept on looking too and then—yes, then—it gave me a lovely feeling inside, but which I mustn't feel too often.

I desperately want to be alone. Daddy has noticed that I'm not quite my usual self, but I really can't tell him everything.

Yours, Anne

Anne Frank. Culver Pictures, Inc., New York.

Friday, 18 February, 1944

Dear Kitty,

Whenever I go upstairs now, I keep on hoping that I shall see "him." Because my life now has an object, and I have something to look forward to, everything has become more pleasant.

At least the object of my feelings is always there, and I needn't be afraid of rivals, except Margot. Don't think I'm in love, because I'm not, but I do have the feeling all the time that something fine can grow up between us, something that gives confidence and friendship. If I get half a chance,

I go up to him now. It's not like it used to be when he didn't know how to begin. It's just the opposite—he's still talking when I'm half out of the room.

Mummy doesn't like it much, and always says I'll be a nuisance and that I must leave him in peace. Honestly, doesn't she realize that I've got some intuition? She looks at me so strangely every time I go into Peter's little room. If I come downstairs from there, she asks me where I've been. I simply can't bear it, and think it's horrible.

Yours, Anne

Saturday, 19 February, 1944

Dear Kitty,

It is Saturday again and that really speaks for itself.

The morning was quiet. I helped a bit upstairs, but I didn't have more than a few fleeting words with "him." At half past two, when everyone had gone to their own rooms, either to sleep or to read, I went to the private office, with my blanket and everything, to sit at the desk and read or write. It was not long before it all became too much for me, my head drooped to my arm, and I sobbed my heart out. The tears streamed down my cheeks, and I felt desperately unhappy. Oh, if only "he" had come to comfort me. It was four o'clock by the time I went upstairs again.

Suddenly I felt the tears coming back and I hurried to the lavatory, quickly grabbing a pocket mirror as I passed. There I sat then, fully dressed, while the tears made dark spots on the red of my apron, and I felt very wretched.

This is what was going through my mind. Oh, I'll never reach Peter like this. Who knows, perhaps he doesn't like me at all and doesn't need anyone to confide in. Perhaps he only thinks about me in a casual sort of way. I shall have to go on alone once more, without friendship and without Peter. Perhaps soon I'll be without hope, without comfort, or anything to look forward to again.

However, a little later fresh hope and anticipation seemed to return, even though the tears were still streaming down my cheeks.

Yours, Anne

Wednesday, 23 February, 1944

Dear Kitty,

It's lovely weather outside and I've quite perked up since yesterday. Nearly every morning I go to the attic where Peter works to blow the stuffy air out of my lungs. From my favorite spot on the floor I look up at the blue sky and the bare chestnut tree, on whose branches little raindrops shine, appearing like silver, and at the seagulls and other birds as they glide on the wind.

He stood with his head against a thick beam, and I sat down. We breathed the fresh air, looked outside, and both felt that the spell should not be broken by words. We remained like this for a long time, and when he had to go up to the loft to chop wood, I knew that he was a nice fellow. He climbed the ladder, and I followed; then he chopped wood for about a quarter of an hour, during which time we still remained silent. I watched him from where I stood. He was obviously doing his best to show off his strength. But I looked out of the open window too, over a large area of Amsterdam, over all the roofs and on to the horizon, which was such a pale blue that it was hard to see the dividing line. "As long as this exists," I thought, "and I may live to see it, this sunshine, the cloudless skies, while this lasts, I cannot be unhappy."

Oh, who knows, perhaps it won't be long before I can share this overwhelming feeling of bliss with someone who feels the way I do about it.

Yours, Anne

Tuesday, 7 March, 1944

Dear Kitty,

If I think now of my life in 1942, it all seems so unreal. It was quite a different Anne who enjoyed that heavenly existence from the Anne who has grown wise within these walls. Yes, it was a heavenly life. Boy friends at every turn, about twenty friends and acquaintances of my own age, the darling of nearly all the teachers, spoiled from top to toe by Mummy and Daddy, lots of sweets, enough pocket money, what more could one want?

Now I look back at that Anne as an amusing, but very superficial girl, who has nothing to do with the Anne of today.

What is left of this girl? Oh, don't worry, I haven't forgotten how to laugh or to answer back readily. I'm just as good, if not better, at criticizing people, and I can still flirt if . . . I wish. That's not it though.

Now I think seriously about life and what I have to do. One period of my life is over forever. The carefree school days are gone, never to return.

I don't even long for them any more; I have outgrown them, I can't just only enjoy myself as my serious side is always there.

I look upon my life up till the New Year, as it were, through a powerful magnifying glass. The sunny life at home, then coming here in 1942, the sudden change, the quarrels, the bickerings. I couldn't understand it, I was taken by surprise, and the only way I could keep up some bearing was by being impertinent.

The first half of 1943: my fits of crying, the loneliness, how I slowly began to see all my faults and shortcomings, which are so great and which seemed much greater then. During the day I deliberately talked about anything and everything that was farthest from my thoughts. Alone I had to face the difficult task of changing myself.

Things improved slightly in the second half of the year. I became a young woman and was treated more like a grownup. I started to think, and write stories, and came to the conclusion that the others no longer had the right to throw me about like an

India-rubber ball. I wanted to change in accordance with my own desires.

At the beginning of the New Year: the second great change, my dream. . . . And with it I discovered my longing, not for a girl friend, but for a boy friend. I also discovered my inward happiness and my defensive armor of superficiality and gaiety. In due time, I quieted down and discovered my boundless desire for all that is beautiful and good.

And in the evening, when I lie in bed and end my prayers with the words, "I thank you, God, for all that is good and dear and beautiful," I am filled with joy.

I don't think then of all the misery, but of the beauty that still remains. This is one of the things that Mummy and I are so entirely different about. Her counsel when one feels melancholy is: "Think of all the misery in the world and be thankful that you are not sharing in it!" My advice is: "Go outside, to the fields, enjoy nature and the sunshine, go out and try to recapture happiness in yourself and in God. Think of all the beauty that's still in and around you and be happy!"

I don't see how Mummy's idea can be right, because then how are you supposed to behave if you go through the misery yourself? Then you are lost. On the contrary, I've found that there is always some beauty left—in nature, sunshine, freedom, in yourself; these can all help you. Look at these things, then you find yourself again, and God, and then you regain your balance.

And whoever is happy will make others happy too. He who has courage and faith will never perish in misery.

Yours, Anne

The clocktower as seen out the window from the Secret Annex. © 1984 by ANNE FRANK-Fonds/COSMOPRESS, Genève.

Friday, 17 March, 1944

Dear Kitty,

Margot and I are treated as children over outward things, and we are much older than most girls of our age inwardly.

Although I'm only fourteen, I know quite well what I want, I know who is right and who is wrong, I have my opinions, my own ideas and principles, and although it may sound pretty mad from an adolescent, I feel more of a person than a child. I feel quite independent of anyone.

I know that I can discuss things and argue better than Mummy, I know I'm not so prejudiced, I don't exaggerate so much, I am more precise and adroit and because of this—you may laugh—I feel superior to her over a great many things. If I love anyone, above all I must have admiration for them, admiration and respect. Everything would be all right if only I had Peter, for I do admire him in many ways. He is such a nice, good-looking boy!

Yours, Anne

Sunday, 19 March, 1944

Dear Kitty,

Yesterday was a great day for me. I had decided to talk things out with Peter. After the dishes were done, I stood by the window in his parents' room awhile for the look of things, but it wasn't long before I went to Peter. He was standing on the left side of the open window, I went and stood on the right side, and we talked. It was much easier to talk beside the open window in semidarkness than in bright light, and I believe Peter felt the same.

We told each other so much, so very very much, that I can't repeat it all, but it was lovely; the most wonderful evening I have ever had in the "Secret Annex."

We talked about how we neither of us confide in our parents, and how his parents would have loved to have his confidence, but that he didn't wish it. How I cry my heart out in bed, and he goes up into the loft and swears. How glad he is that my parents have children here, and that I'm glad he is here. That I understand his reserve now and his relationship with his parents, and how I would love to be able to help him.

"You always do help me," he said, "How?" I asked, very surprised. "By your cheerfulness." That was certainly the loveliest thing he said. It was wonderful, he must have grown to love me as a friend, and that is enough for the time being. I am so grateful and happy, I just can't find the words. I must apologize, Kitty, that my style is not up to standard today.

I have just written down what came into my head. I have the feeling now that Peter and I share a secret. If he looks at me with those eyes that laugh and wink, then it's just as if a little light goes on inside me. I hope it will remain like this and that we may have many, many more glorious times together!

Your grateful, happy Anne

Tuesday, 11 April, 1944

Dear Kitty,

I am becoming still more independent of my parents. Young as I am, I face life with more courage than Mummy; my feeling for justice is immovable, and truer than hers. I know what I want, I have a goal, an opinion, I have a religion and love. Let me be myself and then I am satisfied. I know that I'm a woman, a woman with inward strength and plenty of courage.

If God lets me live, I shall attain more than Mummy ever has done, I shall not remain insignificant, I shall work in the world and for mankind!

And now I know that and foremost I shall require courage and cheerfulness!

Yours, Anne

Wednesday, 3 May, 1944

Dear Kitty,

Why do some people have to starve, while there are surpluses rotting in other parts of the world? Oh, why are people so crazy?

I don't believe that the big men, the politicians and the capitalists alone, are guilty of the war. Oh no, the little man is just as guilty, otherwise the peoples of the world would have risen in revolt long ago! There's in people simply an urge to destroy, an urge to kill, to murder and rage, and until all mankind, without exception, undergoes a great change, wars will be waged, everything that has been built up, cultivated, and grown will be destroyed and disfigured, after which mankind will have to begin all over again.

I have often been downcast, but never in despair; I regard our hiding as a dangerous adventure, romantic and interesting at the same time. In my diary I treat all the privations as amusing. I have made up my mind now to lead a different life from other girls and, later on, different from ordinary housewives. My start has been so very full of interest, and that is the sole reason why I have to laugh at the humorous side of the most dangerous moments.

I am young and strong and am living a great adventure. I can't grumble the whole day long. I have been given a lot, a happy nature, a great deal of cheerfulness and strength. Every day I feel that I am developing inwardly, that the liberation is drawing nearer and how beautiful nature is, how good the people are about me, how interesting this adventure is! Why, then, should I be in despair?

Yours, Anne

Sunday, 26 May, 1944

Dear Kitty,

This evening at eight o'clock I had to go to the downstairs lavatory all alone; there was no one down there, as everyone was listening to the radio; I wanted to be brave, but it was difficult. I always feel much safer here upstairs then alone downstairs in that large, silent house; alone with the mysterious muffled noises from upstairs and the tooting of motor horns in the street. I have to hurry for I start to quiver if I begin thinking about the situation.

Again and again I ask myself, would it not have been better for us all if we had not gone into hiding, and if we were dead now and not going through all this misery, especially as we shouldn't be running our protectors into danger any more. But we all recoil from this thought too, for we still love life; we haven't yet forgotten the voice of nature. We still hope, hope about everything. I hope something will happen soon now, shooting if need be—nothing can crush us *more* than this restlessness. Let the end come, even if it is hard; then at least we shall know whether we are finally going to win through or go under.

Yours, Anne

Saturday, 15 July, 1944

Dear Kitty,

How is it that Daddy was never any support to me in my struggle? Why did he completely miss the mark when he wanted to offer me a helping hand? Daddy tried the wrong methods, he always talked to me as child who was going through difficult phases. It sounds crazy because Daddy's the only one who has always taken me into his confidence, and no one but Daddy has given me the feeling that I'm sensible. But there's one thing he's omitted: you see, he hasn't realized that for me the fight to get on top was more important than all else. I didn't want to hear about "symptoms of your age," or "other girls," or "it wears off by itself"; I didn't want to be treated as a girl-like-all-others, but as Anne-on-her-own-merits.

Yet this was not my greatest disappointment; no, I ponder far more over Peter than Daddy. I know very well that I conquered him; he did not conquer me. I created an image of him in my mind, pictured him as a quiet, sensitive, lovable boy, who needed affection and friendship. I needed a living person to whom I could pour out my heart; I wanted a friend who'd help to put me on the right road. I achieved what I wanted, and slowly but surely, I drew him towards me. Finally, when I had made him feel friendly, it automatically developed into an intimacy which, on second thought, I don't think I ought to have allowed.

We talked about the most private things, and yet up till now we have never touched on those things that filled, and still fill, my heart and soul.

"For in its innermost depths youth is lonelier than old age." I read this saying in some book, and I've always remembered it and found it to be true. Is it true then that grownups have a more difficult time here than we do? No. I know it isn't. Older people have formed their opinions about everything and don't waver before they act. It's twice as hard for us young ones to hold our ground, and maintain our opinions, in a time when all ideals are being shattered and destroyed, when people are showing their worst side and do not know whether to believe in truth and right and God.

Anyone who claims that the older ones have a more difficult time here certainly doesn't realize to what extent our problems weigh down on us, problems for which we are probably much too young, but which thrust themselves upon us continually, until, after a long time, we think we've found a solution, but the solution doesn't seem able to resist the facts which reduce it to nothing again. That's the difficulty in these times: ideals, dreams, and cherished hopes rise within us, only to meet the horrible truth and be shattered.

It's really a wonder that I haven't dropped all my ideals, because they seem so absurd and impossible to carry out. Yet I keep them, because I still believe that people are really good at heart. I simply can't build up my hopes on a foundation consisting of confusion, misery, and death. I see the world gradually being turned into a wilderness, I hear the ever approaching thunder, which will destroy us too, I can feel the sufferings of millions and yet, if I look up into the heavens, I think that it will all come right, that this cruelty too will end, and that peace and tranquillity will return again.

Yours, Anne

Tuesday, 1 August, 1944

Dear Kitty,

I've already told you before that I have as it were, a dual personality. One half embodies my exuberant cheerfulness, making fun of everything, my high-spiritedness, and above all, the way I take everything lightly. This side is usually lying in wait and pushes away the other, which is much better, deeper and purer. You must realize that no one knows Anne's better side and that's why most people find me so insufferable.

I'm awfully scared that everyone who knows me as I always am will discover that I have another side, a finer and better side. I'm afraid they'll laugh at me, think I'm ridiculous and sentimental, not take me seriously. I'm used to not being taken seriously, but it's only the "lighthearted" Anne that's used to it and can bear it; the "deeper" Anne is too frail for it. Sometimes, if I really compel the good Anne to take the stage for a quarter of an hour, she simply shrivels up as soon as she has to speak, and lets Anne number one take over, and before I realize it, she had disappeared.

Therefore, the nice Anne is never present in company, has not appeared one single time so far, but almost always predominates when we're alone. I know exactly how I'd like to be, how I am too . . . inside. But, alas, I'm only like that for myself. And perhaps that's why, no, I'm sure it's the reason why I say I've got a happy nature within and why other people think I've got a happy nature without. I am guided by the pure Anne within, but outside I'm nothing but a frolicsome little goat who's broken loose.

As I've already said, I never utter my real feelings about anything and that's how I've acquired the name of chaser-after-boys, flirt, know-all, reader of love stories. The cheerful Anne laughs about it, gives cheeky answers, shrugs her shoulders indifferently, behaves as if she doesn't care, but, oh my, the quiet Anne's reactions are just the op-

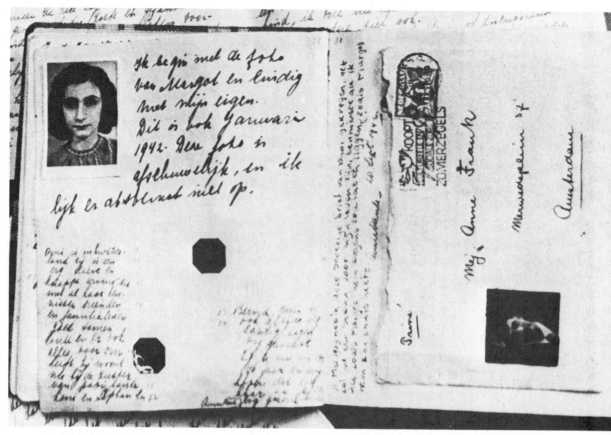

Anne Frank's diary. UPI/Bettmann, New York.

posite. If I'm to be quite honest, then I must admit that it does hurt me, that I try terribly hard to change myself, but that I'm always fighting against a more powerful enemy.

A voice sobs within me: "There you are, that's what's become of you: you're uncharitable, you look supercilious and peevish, people dislike you, and all because you won't listen to the advice given you by your own better half." Oh, I would like to listen, but it doesn't work; if I'm quiet and serious, everyone thinks it's a new comedy and then I have to get out of it by turning it into a joke, not to mention my own family, who are sure to think I'm ill, make me swallow pills for headaches and nerves, and criticize me for being in a bad mood. I can't keep that up: if I'm watched to that extent, I start by getting snappy, then unhappy, and finally I twist my heart round again, so that the bad is on the outside and the good is on the inside and keep on trying to find a way of becoming what I would so like to be, and what I could be, if . . . there weren't any other people living in the world.

Yours, Anne

Anne's diary ends here. On August 4, 1944, the police made a raid on the "Secret Annex." All the occupants, together with their protectors, Kraler and Koophuis, were arrested and sent to German and Dutch Concentration Camps.

The "Secret Annex" was plundered by the Gestapo.[1] Among a pile of old books and newspapers that they left lying on the floor, friends found Anne's diary.

In March 1945, three months before her sixteenth birthday and two months before the liberation of Holland, Anne died in the concentration camp of Bergen-Belsen.

Of all the occupants of the "Secret Annex," Anne's father alone returned. Kraler and Koophuis, who withstood the hardships of the Dutch camp, were able to go home.

---

1. **Gestapo.** Secret police in Nazi Germany

Developing Comprehension Skills

1. In her first diary entry, Anne explained her reasons for keeping a diary. What were these reasons?

2. Anne included historical information in her diary. Name two facts that she told about life in Holland in the early 1940's.

3. A diary includes the personal opinions of the writer. What feelings did Anne have about her mother? What was Anne's opinion of her father?

4. In the diary entry dated Monday, 8 November, 1943, Anne stated that she was a coward. Why did she think so?

5. Would you have wanted Anne Frank as a friend? Why or why not?

Reading Literature: Diaries

1. **Tracing Character Change.** There are several minor characters that are important in Anne's diary. One of them is Peter Van Daan. At first, Anne's attitude toward Peter is not very positive. However, her attitude changes as time passes. How does Anne's view of Peter change? Why? Is Anne aware of any of the reasons you mention? What details in the diary make this suggestion?

2. **Understanding Character.** In the last entry, Anne describes herself as being two different people. What details does she give about her two personalities? Do you think most people see contrasts in their characters? Give reasons for your answer.

3. **Inferring Theme.** At the beginning of her diary, Anne says, "I want to bring out all kinds of things that lie buried deep in my heart." Reread the diary entry for 7 March, 1944. In this entry, Anne tries to explain her outlook on life. In your own words, write what you think Anne meant to be the theme of her diary.

4. **Evaluating the Role of Nonfiction.** In Anne's diary we can find information about the history of the time. However, Anne did not present only factual information. Her diary also gives her personal opinions. What made her better qualified than the average teenager to express opinions on some topics? Do you think we can trust her judgments? Explain your answers.

5. **Determining Mood.** Select two passages in the diary that you think express two different moods. On your paper, identify the date and the first and last sentences of each passage. Write a sentence identifying the mood that each passage brings to the reader. Then list the words or phrases in the passage that create the mood. Look for words with strong connotations, or emotional meanings.

Developing Vocabulary Skills

Determining Correct Pronunciation. Some dictionary entry words may be used as more than one part of speech. For example, sometimes the same word can be used as a noun or a verb. Some of these words are pronounced differently when they are used as different parts of speech. In the following example, each respelling is accented on a different syllable. The correct pronunciation depends on the way the word is used.

> The strange *object* (ob′ jikt) landed in our neighbor's yard.
> Jessica will *object* (əb jekt′) to the plan.

The following sentences use words from selections you have read. First decide if the underlined word is used as a noun, a verb, or an adjective. Then locate the word in a dictionary. On your paper, write the word, its part of speech in the sentence, and the correct respelling.

1. The family felt the <u>impact</u> of Hitler's anti-Jewish laws.

2. Anne's diary reveals that her grandmother was <u>present</u> in her thoughts.

3. They heard a sound downstairs and a <u>minute</u> or two later the wireless radio had to be turned off.

4. Anne thought that in the Secret Annex they were <u>separate</u> from all the outside dangers of the war.

5. Peter became the <u>object</u> of Anne's thoughts and feelings.

6. Because they were in hiding, Anne's parents could not <u>permit</u> her to go outside onto the streets.

Developing Writing Skills

1. **Making Comparisons and Contrasts.** Both Davy Crockett and Anne Frank experienced war in their lives. One volunteered to be part of war; the other had no choice. Compare and contrast how they wrote about war in their diaries. Write four paragraphs about the similarities and differences you find.

   Pre-Writing. Make two lists: one for Anne Frank and one for Davy Crockett. On each list, include at least three subtopics. *Facts, Opinions,* and *Tone* are three possible subtopics you could use. First, review each diary for details about your first subtopic. List the information you find.

   Next, skim each diary two more times. Each time look for words or statements that give details about one of the subtopics. Add these notes to your lists.

   Then look over your lists. Are there any general statements you can make about the two writers? Can you find any obvious similarities or any sharp differences? Perhaps you will want to look at the diaries once more to find the exact wording.

   Now choose the subtopics you will discuss in your composition. You should use from one to three. Circle the details you plan to use.

Finally, outline your ideas. Use the following general plan.

Writing. In your first paragraph, state the general idea of your composition.

In the second paragraph, discuss the ways in which the diaries are alike. Use the details for the subtopics you chose. Use your notes for information.

In the third paragraph, contrast the differences in the diaries.

In the fourth paragraph, summarize your discussion. Pull all the ideas together.

Revising. Read your paragraphs aloud. Listen for any phrase or sentence that does not sound right. You may need to change some words. The ideas should flow smoothly from one sentence to another. The ideas should be clear.

2. **Writing a Diary.** If you have not already done so, begin a personal diary. Make daily entries for at least three weeks. Comment on the events of your life. Describe things that interest you. Discuss your opinions. These entries are for your information only.

At the end of three weeks, review your entries. Select three to share with others. Revise them as you like, to make them understandable to others. Then make a clean copy of those three entries.

Developing Skills in Study and Research

Researching Historical Background. You have learned how to use the resources of a library to find facts. Choose either of the two diaries. Write at least three questions about the diary that cannot be answered by the diary. For each question, list at least two ways of locating an answer. Then use your school or local library to answer your questions. Report both the answers and the sources you used. For each source, note the title, volume number or issue date, and page numbers of the article or chapter that you used.

Autobiographies

A diary is written in fragments. It tells of events just after they have happened. An **autobiography**, in contrast, is a connected story of an entire life. Writers of autobiographies have taken the time to think about the people and events in their lives. They have looked for the most important influences that shaped them as persons. They write their accounts to share with us what they have learned. What strong influence do you see in each of these selections from autobiographies?

Self Portrait, 1930–35, WILLIAM H. JOHNSON. National Museum of American Art, Washington, D.C., Gift of the Harmon Foundation.

The Washwoman

ISAAC BASHEVIS SINGER

In this excerpt from his autobiography, Isaac Singer describes an old washwoman who washed clothes for his family. As you read, keep this question in mind: Why was this old woman so important to Singer?

The author of this memoir was a child in a Jewish family living in Warsaw, Poland, before World War I. His father was a rabbi; the family was religious.

The family spoke Yiddish, not Polish, in the home. Yiddish is a language that developed in Central Europe over hundreds of years. Originally it came from Medieval German. It had grown by borrowing from Hebrew, Russian, Polish, English, and any other language that the Jews had come in contact with.

The Jews were separated from most other Poles because of their religion and their language. In addition, there were laws that restricted Jews from living outside the ghetto or from owning land. Because of this, Jews had little contact with people outside of the Jewish community.

Our home had little contact with Gentiles. The only person who was not Jewish in the building was the janitor. Fridays he would come for a tip. He stood at the door, took off his hat, and my mother gave him six groschen. Besides the janitor there were also the Gentile washwomen who came to the house to fetch our laundry. My story is about one of these.

She was a small woman, old and wrinkled. When she started washing for us, she was already past seventy. Most Jewish women of her age were sickly, weak, broken in body. All the old women in our street had bent backs and leaned on sticks when they walked. But this washwoman, small and thin as she was, possessed a strength that came from generations of peasant forebears. Mother would count out to her a bundle of laundry that had accumulated over several weeks. She would lift the unwieldy pack, load it on her narrow shoulders, and carry it the long way home. She lived on Krochmalna Street too, but at the other end, near the Wola section. It must have been a walk of an hour and a half.

She would bring the laundry back about two weeks later. My mother had never been so pleased with any washwoman. Every piece of linen sparkled like polished silver. Every piece was neatly ironed. Yet she charged no more than the others. She was a real find. Mother always had her money ready because it was too far for the old woman to come a second time.

Laundering was not easy in those days. The old woman had no faucet where she lived but had to bring in the water from a pump. For the linens to come out so clean, they had to be scrubbed thoroughly in a washtub, rinsed with washing soda, soaked, boiled in an enormous pot, starched, then ironed. Every piece was handled ten times or more. And the drying! It could not be done outside because thieves would steal the laundry. The wrung-out wash had to be carried up to the attic and hung on clotheslines. In the winter it would become as brittle as glass and almost break when touched. Also there was always a to-do with other housewives and washwomen who wanted the attic clotheslines for their own use. Only God knows all the old woman had to endure each time she did a wash!

She could have begged at the church door or entered a home for the penniless and aged. However there was in her a certain pride and love of labor. The old woman did not want to become a burden, and so she bore her burden.

My mother spoke a little Polish, and the old woman would talk with her about many things. She had a son who was rich. I no longer remember what sort of business he had. He was ashamed of his mother, the washwoman, and never came to see her. Nor did he ever give her a groschen. The old woman told this without rancor. One day the son was married. It seemed that he had made a good match. The wedding took place in a church. The son had not invited the old mother to his wedding, but she went to the church and waited at the steps to see her son lead the "young lady" to the altar.

The story of the faithless son left a deep impression on my mother. She talked about it for weeks and months. It was an affront not only to the old woman but to the entire institution of motherhood. Mother would argue, "Nu,[1] does it pay to make sacrifices for children? The mother uses up her last strength, and he does not even know the meaning of loyalty."

Thus she would drop dark hints to the effect that she was not certain of her own children: Who knows what they would do some day? This, however, did not prevent her from dedicating her life to us. If there was any delicacy in the house, she would put it aside for the children and invent all sorts of excuses and reasons why she herself did not want to taste it. She knew charms that went back to ancient times, and she used expressions she had inherited from generations of devoted mothers and grandmothers. If one of the children complained of a pain, she would say, "May I be your ransom, and may you outlive my bones!" Or she would say, "May I be the atonement

---

1. **Nu**, a Yiddish exclamation meaning, loosely "So this is the way things are?"

for the least of your fingernails." When we ate she used to say, "Health and marrow in your bones!"

To return to the washwoman. That winter was a harsh one. We were in the grip of a bitter cold. No matter how much we heated our stove, the windows were covered with frostwork and decorated with icicles. The newspapers reported that people were dying of the cold. Coal became dear. The winter had become so severe that parents stopped sending children to cheder,[2] and even the Polish schools were closed.

On one such day the washwoman, now nearly eighty years old, came to our house. A good deal of laundry had accumulated during the past weeks. Mother gave her a pot of tea to warm herself, as well as some bread. The old woman sat on a kitchen chair trembling and shaking, and warmed her hands against the teapot. Her fingers were gnarled from work, and perhaps from arthritis too. Her fingernails were strangely white. These hands spoke of stubbornness, of the will to work not only as one's strength permits but beyond the limits of one's power.

Mother counted and wrote down the laundry list: men's undershirts, long-legged drawers, bloomers, petticoats, shifts, featherbed covers, pillowcases, sheets, and the men's fringed garments. Yes, the Gentile woman washed these holy garments as well.

---

2. **cheder**, Jewish religious school that prepares children for their religious responsibilities

The bundle was big, bigger than usual. When the woman placed it on her shoulders, it covered her completely. At first she swayed, as though she were about to fall under the load. But an inner obstinacy seemed to call out: No, you may not fall. A donkey may permit himself to fall under his burden, but not a human being, the crown of creation.

It was fearful to watch the old woman staggering out with the enormous pack, out into the frost, where the snow was dry as salt and the air was filled with dusty white whirlwinds, like goblins dancing in the cold. Would the old woman ever reach Wola? She disappeared, and Mother sighed and prayed for her.

Usually the woman brought back the wash after two or, at the most, three weeks. This time three weeks passed, then four and five, and nothing was heard of the old woman. We remained without linens. The cold had become even more intense. The telephone wires were now as thick as ropes. The branches of the trees looked like glass. So much snow had fallen that the streets had become uneven, and sleds were able to glide down many streets as on the slopes of a hill. Kind-hearted people lit fires in the streets for vagrants to warm themselves and roast potatoes in, if they had any to roast.

For us the washwoman's absence was a catastrophe. We needed the laundry. We did not even know the woman's address. It seemed certain that she had collapsed, died. Mother declared she had had a premoni-

The Laundress, 1903,
EVERETT SHINN. Collection
of Mr. and Mrs. Melvin Frank.

tion, as the old woman left our house that last time, that we would never see our things again. She found some old torn shirts and washed and mended them. We mourned, both for the laundry and for the old, toil-worn woman who had grown close to us through the years she had served us so faithfully.

More than two months passed. The frost had subsided, and then a new frost had come, a new wave of cold. One evening, while Mother was sitting near the kerosene lamp mending a shirt, the door opened and a small puff of steam, followed by a gigantic bundle, entered. Under the bundle tottered the old woman, her face as white as a linen sheet. A few wisps of white hair straggled out from beneath her shawl. Mother uttered a half-choked cry. It was as though a corpse had entered the room. I ran toward the old woman and helped her unload her pack. She was even thinner now, more bent. Her face had become more gaunt, and her head shook from side to side as though she were saying no. She could not utter a clear word, but mumbled something with her sunken mouth and pale lips.

After the old woman had recovered somewhat, she told us that she had been ill, very ill. Just what her illness was, I cannot remember. She had been so sick that someone had called a doctor, and the doctor had sent for a priest. Someone had informed the son, and he had contributed money for a coffin and for the funeral. However, the Almighty had not yet wanted to take this pain-racked soul to Himself. She began to feel better, she became well, and, as soon as she was able to stand on her feet once more, she resumed her washing. Not just ours, but the wash of several other families too.

"I could not rest easy in my bed because of the wash," the old woman explained. "The wash would not let me die."

"With the help of God you will live to be a hundred and twenty," said my mother, as a benediction.

"God forbid! What good would such a long life be? The work becomes harder and harder . . . my strength is leaving me . . . I do not want to be a burden on anyone!" The old woman muttered and crossed herself, and raised her eyes toward heaven.

Fortunately, there was some money in the house, and Mother counted out what she owed. I had a strange feeling: the coins in the old woman's washed-out hands seem to become as worn and clean and pious as she herself was. She blew on the coins and tied them in a kerchief. Then she left, promising to return in a few weeks for a new load of wash.

She never came back. The wash she had returned was her last effort on this earth. She had been driven by an indomitable will to return the property to its rightful owners, to fulfill the task she had undertaken.

Now at last her body, which had long been no more than a shard supported only by the force of honesty and duty, had fallen. Her soul passed into those spheres where all holy souls meet, regardless of the roles they played on this earth, in whatever tongue, of whatever creed. I cannot imagine paradise without this Gentile washwoman. I cannot even conceive of a world where there is no recompense for such effort.

Developing Comprehension Skills

1. List at least four details that describe the washwoman's job.

2. Read the following statements from "The Washwoman." Determine if each is a fact or the writer's opinion. Remember, a fact can be proven.

   a. Fridays the janitor would come for a tip. He remained standing at the door, took off his hat, and my mother gave him six groschen.

   b. There was in the old washwoman a certain pride and love of labor.

   c. My mother spoke a little Polish.

   d. The old woman had a rich son.

   e. Her body had long been no more than a shard supported only by the force of honesty and duty.

3. Why do you think the washwoman made such a strong impression on the writer?

4. What differences did the writer see between his own mother and the washwoman?

5. You have read part of Isaac Bashevis Singer's autobiography. Based on what you have read, describe what kind of person you think Mr. Singer is.

Reading Literature: Autobiography

1. **Finding Facts in Nonfiction.** It is important to understand the setting, customs, and traditions that Singer writes about. Only then can we appreciate the personal feelings he describes. Name at least two facts you learn about the life of a Jewish family in Poland before World War I.

2. **Explaining Figurative Language.** Singer writes in a colorful style. His choice of words helps the reader imagine the story. In your own words, explain the meaning of each of these passages from "The Washwoman."

   a. Every piece of linen sparkled like polished silver.

   b. The streets were in the grip of a bitter cold.

   c. These hands spoke of stubbornness, of the will to work.

   d. The air was filled with dusty white whirlwinds, like goblins dancing in the cold.

   e. The inner obstinacy seemed to call out.

3. **Understanding a Minor Character.** This story concentrates on the old washwoman. However, Singer also includes information about his own mother. Find two passages in which Singer tells something about his mother. Decide if these are statements of fact or opinion. Then, in your own words, explain Singer's thoughts about his mother.

4. **Analyzing Purpose in an Autobiography.** An autobiography tells about the writer's own life. The writer is the main character. However, in this selection from Isaac Bashevis Singer's autobiography, the washwoman seems to be the main character. The writer is describing the washwoman in order to explain something about himself. What do you think Singer is saying about himself?

Developing Vocabulary Skills

Choosing the Correct Dictionary Meaning. Several words in the selections you have read have more than one meaning listed in the dictionary. Find the underlined word from each of these sentences in a dictionary. On your paper, write the word and the meaning that best fits the context of each sentence.

1. One day the son was married. It seemed that he had made a good <u>match.</u>

2. The story of the faithless son left a deep <u>impression</u> on my mother.

3. If there was any <u>delicacy</u> in the house, she would put it aside and invent all sorts of reasons why she herself did not want to taste it.

4. The hunters brought in some corn and had a <u>brush</u> with an enemy scout.

5. Anne had to hurry for she would <u>quiver</u> if she began thinking about the situation.

6. Older people have formed their opinions and don't <u>waver</u> before they act.

Developing Writing Skills

1. **Analyzing the Writer's Message.** In the last sentence of this selection, Singer says, "I cannot even conceive of a world where there is no recompense for such effort." The word *conceive* means "imagine," and *recompense* means "reward." Write one paragraph explaining what you think Singer meant by that last sentence. Use details from the story to support your idea.

2. **Writing about a Memorable Person.** Think of one person from your early childhood who made a lasting impression on you. Write a character sketch of at least three paragraphs describing this person.

   Pre-Writing. What do you see in your mind when you think about this special person? Make a list of details and ideas. Include words telling what the person looked like and what the person did. Think of several adjectives that describe the person. Are there any metaphors or similes that will help others understand what the person was like? Add these to your list.

   Writing. Limit your writing to memories of one particular event. Use words and ideas from your list to describe the person and his or her effect on you.

   Revising. Find someone who is not familiar with your subject. Ask this person to read your character sketch. Have the reader summarize the impression your writing gave about the person. Was this the effect you had in mind? If not, find out which part of the sketch gives the wrong idea. Revise that section of your writing.

Developing Skills in Speaking and Listening

Introducing a Guest Speaker. Imagine that your class has invited Isaac Bashevis Singer, Anne Frank, and Davy Crockett to speak at your school. You are given the job of introducing one of the guests. Select information from the selection by that writer and from the writer's biography in the Handbook. You may want to write down some notes. Prepare a short introductory speech that you would give. Practice delivering it. Then present the introduction to a small group. Be sure to speak loudly enough for everyone to hear. Use your voice to give the audience the feeling that you admire the author and his or her writing.

Langston Terrace

ELOISE GREENFIELD *and*
LESSIE JONES LITTLE

This selection is part of an autobiography. In it a woman writes about her childhood home. Look for the feelings she expresses about her home. Does your definition of "home" agree with hers?

I fell in love with Langston Terrace the very first time I saw it. Our family had been living in two rooms of a three-story house when Mama and Daddy saw the newspaper article telling of the plans to build it. It was going to be a low-rent housing project in northeast Washington, and it would be named in honor of John Mercer Langston, the famous black lawyer, educator, and congressman.

So many people needed housing and wanted to live there, many more than there would be room for. They were all filling out applications, hoping to be one of the 274 families chosen. My parents filled out one, too.

I didn't want to move. I knew our house was crowded—there were eleven of us, six adults and five children—but I didn't want to leave my friends. I didn't want to go to a strange place and be the new person in a neighborhood and a school where most of the other children already knew each other. I was eight years old, and I had been to three schools. We had moved five times since we'd been in Washington, each time trying to get more space and a better place to live. But rent was so high so we'd always lived in a house with relatives and friends and shared the rent.

One of the people in our big household was Lillie, Daddy's cousin and Mama's best friend. She and her husband also applied for a place in the new project. During the months that it was being built, Lillie and Mama would sometimes walk fifteen blocks just to stand and watch the workmen digging holes and laying bricks. They'd just stand there watching and wishing. And at home, that was all they could talk about. "When we get our new place. . . ." "If we get our new place. . . ."

Lillie got her good news first. I can still see her and Mama standing at the bottom of the hall steps, hugging and laughing and crying, happy for Lillie, then sitting on the steps, worrying and wishing again for Mama.

Finally, one evening, a woman came to the house with our good news, and Mama and Daddy went over and picked out the house they wanted. We moved on my ninth birthday. Wilbur, Gerald, and I went to school that morning from one house, and, when Daddy came to pick us up, he took us home to another one. All the furniture had been moved while we were in school.

Langston Terrace was a lovely birthday present. It was built on a hill, a group of tan brick houses and apartments with a playground as its center. The red mud surrounding the concrete walks had not yet been covered with black soil and grass seed, and the holes that would soon be homes for young trees were filled with rainwater. But it still looked beautiful to me.

We had a whole house all to ourselves. Upstairs and downstairs. Two bedrooms, and the living room would be my bedroom at night. Best of all, I wasn't the only new person. Everybody was new to this new little community. By the time school opened in the fall, we had gotten used to each other and had made friends with other children in the neighborhood, too.

I guess most of the parents thought of the new place as an in-between place. They were glad to be there, but their dream was to save enough to pay for a house that would be their own. Saving was hard, though, and slow, because each time somebody in a family got a raise on the job, it had to be reported to the manager of the project. Then the rent would be raised, too. Most people stayed years longer than they had planned to, but they didn't let that stop them from enjoying life.

They formed a resident council to look into any neighborhood problems that might come up. They started a choral group and presented music and poetry programs on Sunday evenings in the social room or on the playground. On weekends, they played horseshoes and softball and other games. They had a reading club that met once a week at the Langston branch of the public library, after it opened in the basement of one of the apartment buildings.

The library was very close to my house. I could leave by my back door and be there in two minutes. The playground was right in front of my house, and after my sister Vedie was born and we moved a few doors down to a three-bedroom house, I could just look out of my bedroom window to see if any of my friends were out playing.

There were so many games to play and things to do. We played hide-and-seek at the lamppost, paddle tennis and shuffleboard, dodge ball and jacks. We danced in fireplug showers, jumped rope to rhymes, played "Bouncy, Bouncy, Bally," swinging one leg over a bouncing ball, played baseball on a nearby field, had parties in the social room, and bus trips to the beach. In the playroom, we played Ping-Pong and pool, learned to sew and embroider and crochet.

For us, Langston Terrace wasn't an in-between place. It was a growing-up place, a good growing-up place with neighbors who cared, family, friends, and a lot of fun.

Life was good. Not perfect, but good. We knew about problems, heard about them, saw them, lived through some hard ones ourselves; but our community wrapped itself around us and put itself between us and the hard knocks, to cushion the blows.

It's been many years since I moved away, but every once in a long while I go back just to look at things and remember. The large stone animals that decorated the playground are still there: a walrus, a hippo, a frog, and two horses. They've started to crack now, but I remember when they first came to live with us. They were friends, to climb on, to lean against, or to gather around in the evening. You could sit on the frog's head and look out over the city at the tall trees and rooftops.

Nowadays, whenever I run into old friends, mostly at a funeral or maybe a wedding, after we've talked about how we've been and what we've been doing, and how our children are, we always end up talking about our childtime in our old neighborhood. Then somebody will say, "One of these days we ought to have a Langston reunion." That's what we always called it, just "Langston," without the "Terrace." I guess because it sounded more homey. And that's what Langston was. It was home.

Developing Comprehension Skills

1. When she first heard the idea, the writer had mixed feelings about moving to Langston Terrace. What advantages did she see? What disadvantages was she worried about?

2. How did the writer feel when her family actually moved to Langston Terrace? What made her feel this way?

3. The writer explains that Langston Terrace gave her a good feeling. Find three words with positive, or happy, connotations that she uses to describe Langston Terrace.

4. Explain what the writer means by this sentence: "Our community wrapped itself around us and put itself between us and the hard knocks to cushion the blows."

5. What qualities do you think make a place a home?

Reading Literature: Autobiography

1. **Identifying Tone.** The first sentence of "Langston Terrace" expresses the writer's attitude toward the subject. Write a sentence explaining the tone in your own words. Find at least three words or phrases the writer uses to suggest the tone.

2. **Learning About Human Experience.** Literature can tell you how people lived in a certain time and place. It can tell what they hoped for and what problems they faced. This selection tells about the families that moved into Langston Terrace. The writer, recalling her childhood, says that Langston Terrace was thought of as an "in-between place" by many families. Explain what you think this means. Give reasons from the selection to support your answers.

3. **Making Inferences About Character.** The writer does not directly describe herself in this selection. What can you infer about her personality? What do you think her relations with her family were like? How do you think she got along with other people? Did she have many friends? Be sure to support your inferences with details from the selection.

4. **Understanding Theme.** In this selection, the writer does not describe the appearance of Langston Terrace so much as the feeling of the community. Why was the community so important to her? What do you believe she is saying about families, about neighborhoods, and about what is important in growing up?

Developing Vocabulary Skills

Determining Word Meanings. You have learned three methods for determining the meaning of an unfamiliar word:

    a. using the meanings of word parts—the prefixes, suffixes, and base words
    b. using context clues
    c. using a dictionary

Read the following passages from the selections you have read. Figure out the meaning of each underlined word. On your paper, write the word and its meaning. Also write which of the three methods you used to find the meaning.

1. We also learned to sew and embroider and crochet.

2. One of these days we ought to have a Langston reunion.

3. They formed a resident council to look into any neighborhood problems that might come up.

4. They started a choral group and presented music and poetry programs on Sunday evenings in the social room or on the playground.

5. Anne did not like the restlessness of being in hiding.

6. The winter had become so severe that parents stopped sending children to cheder, and even the Polish schools were closed.

7. We have had a large national flag made; it is composed of thirteen stripes, red and white, alternately, on a blue ground, with a large white star of five points in the center.

8. The old woman told the story of her son without rancor.

Developing Writing Skills

1. **Summarizing the Writer's Opinion.** The writer of "Langston Terrace" presented many details explaining how she thought children should grow up. Write two paragraphs summarizing the writer's positive opinions of Langston Terrace.

    Pre-Writing. There are many reasons that the writer liked Langston Terrace. Review the selection to collect these details. Sort them into two lists on your paper. One list should include the physical parts of setting. The other list should include family and community behaviors.

    Develop an outline to organize the details in your lists. It will have two major categories: parts of the setting and people's behaviors. Decide the best order to use in arranging the information.

    Writing. In the first paragraph, summarize the reasons the writer liked the setting of

Langston Terrace. In the second paragraph, explain what the writer liked about the ways Langston people behaved. Follow the structure of your outline.

Revising. Take a good look at your writing. Are the writer's opinions about Langston as clear as you can make them? Is there a topic sentence in each paragraph? Are the details you use clearly organized? Look for specific words and phrases that do not read smoothly. Rewrite these parts of your paragraphs.

2. **Writing a Remembrance.** Think about a place that was important to you when you were younger. It might have been your home, a place in your neighborhood, a secret hiding place, or a park. The place might still be important to you now. Write your memories of that place in two to four paragraphs. Provide details that will let your reader know why the place was important to you.

Developing Skills in Study and Research

Interviewing a Person. Sometimes research involves looking for facts or ideas that are written down somewhere. Research can also mean learning from living people about things that may not be written down. One important way of getting information is by **interviewing**, or questioning a person about his or her background and experiences.

Select an adult whom you know. Plan to interview this person. You will be looking for information about one or both of these topics: a person who influenced the adult's life, or an important place in his or her life. You should ask the adult to give his or her childhood memories of the person or place.

To prepare for the interview, draw up a list of questions to ask the person. Think of what you want to find out. Try to think of questions that may help the person remember better. List questions that encourage the person to give more details about the remembrance.

In scheduling the interview, plan to sit and talk for at least half an hour with the person. If the person's memory is good, you may find that the interview will take even longer. Bring a pad or notebook with you. Write down the main ideas the person tells you. Do not try to record every word. You may ask the person to pause for a moment while you record your notes.

When the interview is over, read through your notes. Add any words necessary to complete the ideas. Turn in your interview notes to your teacher.

Biographies

A good **biography** presents a person's character fairly. It reports the events of his or her life accurately. In order to accomplish these goals, a writer must learn all he or she can about the subject. The biographer uses interviews, letters, diaries, and any other writing by or about the subject. The biographies in this section describe two people who struggled to be recognized for their talents. As you read, see how the writers used the facts to develop a picture of each subject.

Music, 1933–59, PHILIP EVERGOOD. Courtesy of Aca Galleries, New York.

We'll Always Sing His Songs

CARL CARMER

Almost everyone in the United States has heard songs by Stephen Foster. Almost everyone has heard his name. Yet, during his life, Foster was an unknown. What kept him from fame? As you read, look for reasons.

"Thirty-eight cents," the attendant at New York's Bellevue Hospital called out, to complete the record sheet on the man who had just died.

"Thirty-eight cents. I've got it down. Find anything else in his pockets?"

"Not a thing, except some note here."

"What's it say?"

"Ah, nothin'. Just 'Dear Friends and Gentle Hearts.'"

"Yup, a dreamer. Like so many of those poor fellows they bring in here from the Bowery."

"He's better off dead. "Well—got the name right? Stephen Foster, with the 'ph,' not 'v'. And make sure you make it 1864. It's past New Year's, you know."

This was the paradoxical end of a man whose incomparable success still continues. He gave, and still gives, great pleasure to many Americans. Since 1848, just about every American has heard, whistled, or sung his beloved songs. No, despite his miserable death, Stephen Foster did not fail.

Stephen Collins Foster was born near Pittsburgh in 1826—on July 4, appropriately enough. He grew to be a shy and gentle child, staying much to himself. He was happiest when he could sit beside his mother while she played and sang her favorite hymns.

Throughout his childhood, little attention was paid to Stephen's fondness for music. However, when as an adolescent he began to occupy himself with making up tunes and setting them down on paper, his parents were seriously concerned. In the 1840's, while American pioneers were still moving westward, music was regarded as the province of women. A man had greater jobs to do.

It was decided, therefore, that Stephen would go out to Cincinnati, where his older brother Dunning Foster had already set himself up in business.

"You will be his bookkeeper," said Mr. Foster to Stephen. "And I've written him not to show you any favors. Perhaps this job

Stephen Foster. The Bettmann Archive, Inc., New York.

Hall—and Stephen knew that minstrels were always on the lookout for new songs. Modestly, Stephen placed before him the last song he had written.

"It's a comic song," said Stephen, "If you like it, I'd be grateful if you tried it out on the audience."

Roark did like the song, and he and his company of blackface minstrels introduced it the following Saturday afternoon. It was "Oh! Susanna," now one of our song classics. It caught on, and in a few months the whole country was singing it. Only a few people knew that it had been written by Stephen Collins Foster.

That didn't bother Stephen very much. He had proved to himself that he could write a song that people throughout the country would sing with pleasure. That meant, too, that he might even make money someday as a song writer, a particularly important consideration, for he was about to marry lovely Jane MacDowell.

To make it possible to marry Jane, Stephen stuck to his bookkeeping and saved enough money for the wedding and the honeymoon. At last he and his Jeannie were off together, newlyweds, sailing down the Mississippi for New Orleans. As they sailed, the beauty of the wide river, its green banks, its brilliant birds, the sounds of the shrill boat whistles and the churning paddle wheels, the chants of the stevedores rolling the great bales of cotton all fused in his mind into haunting melodies.

"What would you think, Jeannie, if I didn't go back to work for my brother?"

in Cincinnati will give you a start toward a business of your own. Think of the West, Stephen. Young fellows like you are going out there every day and becoming men of wealth and power."

Stephen Foster turned out to be a good bookkeeper and his brother wrote encouraging reports about him to their parents. Dunning did not know, however, that in his brother's mind figures kept turning into the notes of melodies and that it was only with the greatest effort that he was able to make his account books balance.

Then, one evening Stephen called secretly on William Roark. Roark, a minstrel, was performing that week at Melodeon asked Stephen. "If instead, I settled down seriously to composing songs? 'Susanna' would have made a lot of money for me if I'd handled it right. And I know I can write other songs just as good. And I know that at least I could make a living."

"I want you to do exactly what you want most to do," said Jane, "and I'm sure that you will succeed."

Stephen did not go back to bookkeeping upon his return from New Orleans. Instead, he made the rounds of the music publishers, trying to sell them a song he had composed on his honeymoon. When no publisher would buy it, Stephen took it to E. P. Christy, a well-known minstrel singer.

"Why, this is a great song!" exclaimed Christy. "It's a really good tune. But I see

you have crossed out the title. Doesn't it have a name yet?"

"When I showed it to the publishers," said Stephen, "it was called 'Way Down Upon the Suwannee River.' But they said nobody had ever heard of that river, so I think I'll call the song 'Old Folks at Home.'"

"And what do you want from me?" asked Christy.

"You're a famous man," said Stephen. "And I think if you put your name on the song as if you had written it and then took it back to the publishers Firth and Pond— well, I think they'd publish it. And you could make some arrangement with me."

It was agreed that Christy would pay Foster fifteen dollars as an advance and two cents a copy thereafter for every copy sold—that is, if the firm of Firth and Pond published the song.

Stephen was right. With Christy's name on it, the music publishers were eager to issue a song that they had previously rejected when Stephen submitted it. They hurried it through the press and it caught on instantly. Soon it was as popular as "Oh! Susanna," but the use of Christy's name turned out to be the beginning of disaster for Stephen Foster.

He continued to compose beautiful songs—"My Old Kentucky Home," "Massa's in de Cold, Cold Ground," "Old Dog Tray," "Nelly Was a Lady"—and many others. But because the authorship of "Old Folks at Home" was credited to Christy, the publishers regarded Foster as an unestablished composer. They paid him mere pittances for his work. When he ventured to claim authorship of "Old Folks at Home" and "Oh! Susanna," the marching song of the Forty-Niners on their way to California, the publishers looked at him as if he were mad.

Jane tried to remain cheerful and encouraging, but there was a child now, a girl. It was decided that Jane should go back to her family for a while so that the child could be properly cared for. With the last of his money, Stephen took the train for New York. Surely, in that great city, his talent would be recognized.

This was not to be. A few new songs appeared, but they brought little money. Foster was finally reduced to the pitiful condition of the nameless poor on the Bowery. After three years of this privation, Foster died in Bellevue Hospital, reminding us of his warmth and sweetness with his last words, "Dear Friends and Gentle Hearts."

Stephen Foster song sheets. The Foster T. Hall Collection, the University of Pittsburgh.

Developing Comprehension Skills

1. How did Stephen Foster's interest in music begin?

2. In the 1840's, what was society's attitude toward music as a career?

3. The author outlined four periods in Foster's life: childhood, adolescence, married life, and his last three years. Summarize the main events of Foster's life during each period.

4. Do you think Stephen Foster made the right choice when he decided not to return to his bookkeeping job? Why or why not?

Reading Literature: Biography

1. **Analyzing a Biography.** A biography provides detailed information about a character. The writer of this biography tells you directly many facts about Stephen Foster. List at least four of them.

   The writer also suggests other ideas. For example, Foster's determination is suggested by his efforts in New York. Identify at least two other ideas that the writer suggests but does not state directly.

   What information did the writer leave out? List three questions about Foster that you would like answered.

2. **Recognizing the Writer's Opinion.** The writer wanted the reader to have a good impression of Stephen Foster. Scan the biography for words used to describe Foster. Which of them have positive connotations, or emotional meanings? List at least five of these words.

   Do you get one general idea from these five words? What opinion or opinions do you believe the writer had toward Foster?

3. **Recognizing Unity of Structure.** The plan or framework of a piece of writing is called **structure**. In this selection, the writer carefully connects the beginning of the story with the end. Reread the first and last paragraphs. What details does the writer use to connect these parts of the biography?

4. **Using Nonfiction To Learn About a Culture.** Read the following passage drawn from the selection.

   > In the 1840's, while American pioneers were still moving westward, music was regarded as the province of women. A man had greater jobs to do.

   From this passage you can learn about the culture in which Stephen Foster grew up. There was a separation of jobs between men and women. What do you think were some of the "greater jobs" men were supposed to do? How does the writer suggest this?

Developing Vocabulary Skills

Completing Analogies. You have learned that an analogy consists of two pairs of words related in the same way. Here is an example:

Dawn is to sunrise as dusk is to sunset.

In each pair, the first term names a time, and the second term names an event that occurs at that time. Sunrise occurs at dawn; sunset occurs at dusk. Other possible relationships in an analogy include synonyms and antonyms.

Each of the following analogies uses a word from a selection you have read. Choose the word that will complete each relationship.

1. Author is to writer as minstrel is to ___.

   reader   singer   banker

2. Raise is to lower as fuse is to ____.
   separate   stop   mix

3. Paint is to picture as compose is to ____.
   song   building   hand

4. Hesitate is to pause as venture is to ____.
   read   copy   risk

5. Pride is to shame as courage is to ____.
   affection   fear   sound

Developing Writing Skills

1. **Writing a Plan for a Report.** You have learned that a biography tells facts about a person's life. It may also include the biographer's opinions. Select a famous person whom you would like to know more about. Write a paragraph explaining exactly what types of information you would hope to find by reading biographies about the person. Be detailed in your explanation.

2. **Writing a Biography.** Suppose someone wanted to write a biography of your life thus far. What details about your life do you think the writer would present? What events would be the most important? Write a three-paragraph account of your life. Present your ideas as a biographer would tell them. Use the third-person point of view.

   Pre-Writing. Outline the most important events in your life. Include details from your childhood and from your life today. Be sure to arrange them in correct time order. Next, make a list of the personality traits you think you show. Select the trait that best summarizes your personality. Then choose two or three events from your outline that are good examples of your personality. Last, decide how to organize your biography. You may arrange the details in the three paragraphs in time order, or you may decide to present them in order of importance.

   Writing. Remember to write in the third-person point of view. Pretend that someone else is telling the story of your life. Refer to yourself as *he* or *she.* Include the several important events you chose. Also make sure the biography suggests your strongest personality trait.

   Revising. Ask someone who knows you to read the biography. Does the person feel it gives an accurate description? If not, you may need to change the details or the general personality trait you chose.

Developing Skills in Study and Research

Taking Research Notes. If you have done the first activity for Developing Writing Skills, you have chosen a subject for a biographical report. If not, choose a subject now.

Now you are ready to find research materials on your subject. Your main source for materials will be your school or public library. You may use the card catalog, *The Readers' Guide to Periodical Literature,* the microfilm resources, and the reference room in your search. Look up information according to the subject's last name. If you choose, you may also conduct an interview with an expert on your subject. You should have at least three different sources.

Take notes on your research. Write them on index cards or on notebook paper. Use a new card or sheet of paper for each topic. Be sure to write only what you will need for your report. Write in your own words. Include the source information at the bottom of each card. See page 629 in the Handbook for examples.

Banker Maggie Walker

OLIVE W. BURT

Maggie Walker faced many obstacles to achieve her goals in life. What were some of these obstacles? What made her able to deal with them? Read this selection to find out.

Wrapped in an old, patched quilt, ten-year-old Maggie Mitchell sat up in bed. With the stub of a pencil and a bit of yellow paper, she was doing her arithmetic problems for school. Maggie enjoyed working with numbers.

She looked across the room to where her mother was bent over a wooden tub. Mrs. Mitchell was scrubbing a shirt on the corrugated wooden washboard. As she straightened up to wring out the garment, her eyes met Maggie's. "Feeling better, child?"

Maggie nodded. "Pain's all gone now, Ma. And I haven't coughed for a long time."

Her mother tossed the shirt into a basket filled with other laundry. "I'll just get these on the line," she said, "so they'll be dry before dark." She lifted the basket and went out. Left alone, Maggie put down her homework, slid down onto the pillow and closed her eyes. Soon she was asleep.

She didn't hear her mother come back into the room, but she was awakened later by a sharp knock on the door. Mrs. Mitchell dried her hands on her apron as she crossed the room and opened the door. A tall, neatly dressed man stood there. He was the collector for the Independent Order of St. Luke, and he had come to get the ten cents a week that Mrs. Mitchell managed to save. She went to a shelf above the scrubbed pine table and took down a small bowl. From it she took two nickels and a small, dog-eared notebook which she handed to the collector. He put the money in his pocket and wrote in the book.

"You've done very well, Mrs. Mitchell," he said as he handed back the book. "Never missed a week. You'll be glad some day when you need the money for something special."

Maggie's mother looked at the little book and sighed. "It's mighty hard sometimes. And it takes so long!" She put the book back into the bowl.

"I know," the man said. "But keep up the good work, and I'll see you next week." He turned toward Maggie and waved. Then he left.

The St. Luke Bank.
Valentine Museum,
Richmond, Virginia.

Maggie closed her eyes again. She was not sleeping now; she was thinking. Every week, no matter what—whether she had lots of washing to do or none at all—her mother always had ten cents for the collector. The money was being kept safe in the St. Luke bank, and, if they ever needed it, they could get it.

The St. Luke bank—the Independent Order of St. Luke—had been started by a group of black men in Richmond. When they saw that the black people lacked social clubs and a place to turn to for business advice, they decided to provide these services. St. Luke's was a bank, an insurance company, and a social club combined into one organization. It was the first business undertaking to benefit the freed blacks in the United States. Although it was planned to help men only, when Maggie's father died, the directors of the company permitted Mrs. Mitchell to continue with her husband's account.

Maggie Mitchell was born in Richmond, Virginia, on July 15, 1867. Since her father had died, her mother supported the two of them by taking in washing. Maggie helped as much as she could, but her mother wanted her to get an education rather than to do odd jobs for pennies.

Maggie studied hard and worked hard, and every week she saved some of the money she earned. When she was sixteen, she graduated from the Richmond Normal and Colored School. She was now considered ready to leave school and go to work, but the jobs open to blacks, especially black women, were those that required hard work and earned little pay. Maggie thought of the possibilities. She could do laundering, as her mother did. She could get a job as a servant in some white family's home. She could leave the city and do field work on a nearby farm. For Maggie, there was one other choice. At sixteen, she was considered educated enough to teach black children.

None of these things appealed to Maggie. All of her teachers had spoken of her knack with numbers. They had suggested that she find a way to use this skill after she left school. And that was what she aimed to do.

Walking along the street one day, her mind busy with such thoughts, she almost bumped into the St. Luke's man who had collected money from her mother for so many years. "You trying to knock me down, Maggie?" he joked, and was about to go on his way.

"Wait a minute, please!" Maggie called out. "I want to ask you something."

He stopped, and she began to explain her problem. "Are there any jobs for me?" she asked.

He frowned and shook his head. "Not for women. If you were a man you might get work in the bank down the street, or maybe in a store. But no one hires women for work like that. They just don't think any woman can do that sort of thing."

"But I'm good with numbers, better than any boy in my classes. What about St. Luke's? Don't they use bookkeepers?"

The man laughed. "Of course they do. But there aren't any females working there."

"Well, I'm going down there this very minute and ask for a job!" She turned and quickly walked down the street to the office of the Independent Order of St. Luke.

Maggie was not surprised to find the outer office filled with men. They sat about in small groups chatting, playing checkers. She paid little attention to the men, but glanced around until she saw the door marked "Private Office." She knocked sharply, and when a voice called, "Come on in!" she entered, closing the door behind her.

Mr. Simpson, director of the Order, looked up from the work on his desk and was surprised to see Maggie. Not that she was a stranger to him. He had known her father, had helped her mother over bad times, and had watched Maggie grow up, but he did not rise or ask her to sit down. "Why, Maggie Mitchell! What are you doing here?" he said.

Maggie came straight to the point. She told him that she had finished school, was very good with numbers, and would like to come to work at St. Luke. The old man was surprised and amused. He had never thought of hiring a girl, and he did not think the board of directors, who ran the business, would like it.

Maggie found it was no use to argue with him. He was friendly and kind, but he didn't seem to understand. Finally, he said, "You get a job in some other office or get some experience somehow. There are business schools, aren't there? Go to one. When you've had some experience, know something about business, you can come back, and I'll see what I can do for you."

Maggie unhappily thanked him and left the office. Business school was out of the question. It cost too much. So in the end, she accepted a job teaching second grade in a school for black children. Her salary was twenty dollars a month. After buying a few clothes for herself, and giving her mother some money to help with food, she still had some money left over. Maggie used most of it to buy books, crayons, and other things that were not provided for the students by the school. Each month she managed to save some money for business school, but at that rate, it would be years before she could realize her dream.

When Maggie was nineteen, she married Armstead Walker, a young businessman of Richmond. In time they had two sons, Russell, born in 1890, and Melvin, born in 1897. Maggie had become a tall, stately woman with clear, dark eyes and a kind expression. Her voice was low and rich, and she was an excellent speaker. She was enthusiastic about any project she undertook, and she had the energy to carry it out. All this made it possible for her to care for her family and yet continue teaching. She hadn't lost sight of her goal and was saving every cent possible toward the business education she was determined to have. For a time, she attended night school. Then finally she gave up teaching altogether, and spent full time at Richmond Business College. By the time Melvin was two years old, Maggie had her degree in business. With her diploma in hand, she went to the St. Luke office again and applied for work.

Meanwhile, Mr. Simpson had died. Another man now ran the office, and Maggie saw at once that he didn't know anything about running a business. The office was cluttered and dirty. Stacks of papers overflowed the chairs. Even the man's desk was a mess, covered with papers, empty mugs, ash trays, and a spitoon. He listened to Maggie and sighed.

"I do need help here, as you can see. But a woman! If I can't handle the work, how can I expect a woman to?"

Maggie had been prepared for a struggle, but she was determined to get a job at St. Luke's one way or another. Now she had a plan.

"I can at least keep house!" she said. "The first thing I'd do would be to clean up this office!"

The man's face brightened. "That's more like it. You're hired. You'll get eight dollars a month!"

Maggie gulped. That was twelve dollars a month less than she had been earning, but the job was what she wanted—a chance to show what she could do. She'd clean that office, but that wouldn't be all!

For a while, that was all she was permitted to do. But gradually, she began taking over other duties when her boss was out to lunch or in a board meeting. She collected dues in such a pleasant way that folks came in when they knew she was there. Then she took over the bookkeeping and checked applications for loans.

The more Maggie learned about St. Luke's the more she realized it was poorly run. The rent the Order was paying was much too high. There was no reserve fund, though having money set aside for emergencies was the very thing the Order was urging people to do. The money that came in was not wisely invested, and much was lost through careless handling. In fact, St. Luke was on the verge of bankruptcy. The director and his board of six men had no idea how matters stood.

Maggie knew something must be done at once. If the Order went bankrupt, the hundreds of members would lose all their hard-earned savings. How could she change things? The men on the board would not welcome suggestions from a newcomer, especially a woman. She would have to move slowly but tactfully. She waited until her "newness" had somewhat worn off and asked for permission to attend a board meeting.

The Director hesitated. However, when Maggie told him that she had found things in the books that the board should know about, he was startled. He hadn't the faintest idea what was in the company's books, so he obtained the board's permission for Maggie to attend a meeting.

Maggie listened to the rambling reports, and the useless suggestions made by these men. She managed to look interested and to smile approval, and gradually their attitude toward her warmed. When she thought the time was right, she started with the simplest problem: Why didn't they purchase the building in which they had their offices instead of renting space? She had figures to show them how much they would save in a year. The men sat up and listened.

The board did not follow Maggie's suggestion immediately. However, before too long she learned that the building had been purchased. She was ready now to suggest that they install a new system of bookkeeping. This took a bit longer, because the men could not see any advantage to this. In time, however, they gave Maggie free rein to try it out. So it was with her other suggested improvements. Moving slowly and carefully, she got the business organized with the best and newest equipment. She was promoted from clerk to secretary, then to executive secretary with the right to meet regularly with the board and to suggest improvements. Her salary was raised with each promotion.

However, Maggie was not content with just getting the Order working well. She wanted to see it prosper. She wanted it to reach thousands of people instead of hundreds. Also, she wanted it to employ more women, especially black women. When she was in charge of interviewing and hiring employees, she chose women whenever possible. Once they were working, she encouraged them to save a part of their salary each week. To get them started, Maggie promised that as soon as a woman had saved fifty dollars, she would lend her whatever amount she still needed to make the first payment on a home, shop, or a training course. She did not limit their choices. If a woman was talented at sewing, she was helped to open a dressmaking shop. If she liked baking, then a pastry shop was suggested. The study of medicine, law, engineering, or construction was also encouraged.

At that time it was not always possible for a woman to get into the business or career of her choice. People in the early 1900's would not accept the fact that women might be very good at jobs generally considered for men only. But Maggie did her best. She once hired a cleaning woman, only to discover that the woman was really interested in business. Maggie urged the woman to save one dollar a week toward a business course. When she had enough money, she went to school at night and worked during the day. When she finished with her course, she became a bookkeeper. With a good paying job, the woman was later able to own her own home, and continue to save money. "That's what one dollar a week will do!" Maggie would tell people.

In the thirty-five years that Maggie worked for the Order of St. Luke, membership grew from 3,000 to more than 100,000, a large part of them women. Maggie had helped many to buy their own homes and businesses. She once figured that St. Luke had helped more than 700 black families become home owners.

Maggie wanted to help children, too. She knew that the younger they started saving, the easier it would be when they grew up. The black children were workers. They took odd jobs as soon as they were able. Maggie opened a penny bank that would accept any deposit, no matter how small. She went into the schools to explain to the children what a savings account could do for them. She told stories of successful business people, some of whom they knew, who had got their start by saving a little regularly. Soon more than 20,000 black children had accounts in the St. Luke Penny Savings Bank.

In 1911, when a new state law required that banks must be separated from organizations like the Independent Order of St. Luke, Maggie had to make some changes. With the help of her son Russell, a talented accountant, she reorganized the bank. She called the new bank the St. Luke Bank and Trust Company. That name and association had meant so much to her that she wanted to keep the name in her new venture. She was made the first president of this new institution, and so became the only black woman bank president in the country. Under Maggie's direction, it became one of the most successful banks in Richmond.

Though she was active in business, Maggie always had time for civic and social projects. She raised money for schools for black girls and served on the board of directors of the National Training School for Girls at Lincoln Heights, in Washington, D.C. She edited St. Luke's *Herald* for more than thirty years, and she founded several organizations for black women of her city. One of them was the Richmond Council of Women, whose members were dedicated to improving the lives of underprivileged citizens, especially women and girls. This group agitated for better working conditions, higher pay, and wider employment opportunities, in order to help raise the standard of living of thousands of black women and their families.

Maggie Walker's service to her city was recognized when Richmond gave a dinner in her honor. Hundreds of people came to express their gratitude to the woman who had helped them in the struggle to improve the quality of their lives. Among the tributes was one by Governor Lee Trinkle, who declared that "the State of Virginia could never pay its debt to Mrs. Walker for what she had done for the black citizens of Richmond."

Maggie was at the height of success when tragedy struck the family. Coming home late one night, her husband was mistaken for a burglar and shot by one of their sons. It was an accident, and the youth was declared innocent by the court. But afterwards Maggie aged rapidly. Then she had a fall from which she never fully recovered. She spent her last years in a wheelchair and died December 15, 1934.

As a tribute to the memory of Maggie Walker, the St. Luke Bank and Trust Company established a ten-thousand dollar educational fund to help young people who want a college education.

Portrait of Maggie Walker, 1925. Valentine Museum, Richmond, Virginia. Photograph by Scurlock.

Developing Comprehension Skills

1. What was the Independent Order of St. Luke?

2. When Maggie applied for the job of book-keeper, she was turned down. What inaccurate generalization did the two different directors of St. Luke's make? How did Maggie prove them wrong?

3. Tell what you learn about Maggie from each of these facts.
   a. She hired women employees whenever possible.
   b. She opened a penny bank for children.
   c. She founded an organization dedicated to improving the lives of the poor.

4. Was Maggie's ability with numbers her most important talent? Was that the basis of her success? Explain your answer.

Reading Literature: Biography

1. **Analyzing a Character.** In this biography, the writer creates a clear picture of Maggie Walker's character. Read each of the following passages from the biography. Explain in your own words the quality about Maggie that each passage describes.
   a. Maggie studied hard and worked hard, and every week she saved some of the money she earned.
   b. "But I'm good with numbers, better than any boy in my classes. What about St. Luke's? Don't they use bookkeepers?"
   c. However, Maggie was not content with just getting the Order working well. She wanted to see it prosper.
   d. Though she was active in business, Maggie always had time for civic and social projects.

2. **Identifying Details about History.** What information do you learn from this selection about the lives of the newly freed blacks shortly after the Civil War? What do you learn about the roles played by women, especially black women?

3. **Examining the Theme.** One theme of this biography concerns the strength of Maggie Walker's character. There is another theme. What advice would Maggie Walker give to a young person growing up today?

Developing Vocabulary Skills

Reviewing Multiple Meanings. Read the following sentences about the selections you have read. Each underlined word can be used as more than one part of speech. Each word will be listed in the dictionary with more than one meaning. Decide the part of speech of each word as it is used in the sentence. Then find the word in a dictionary. Choose the meaning that best fits the context of the sentence.

1. Santa Anna had been trying to excite the Indians against the Texans, but had not had an effect.

2. Maggie's gradual approach slowly effected improvements in the way the Order of St. Luke did business.

3. The men brought an account that the settlers were fleeing from the invader.

4. She went into the schools to explain a savings account to the children.

5. Anne told Peter that she understood his reserve and the relationship he had with his parents.

6. Some families had no reserve fund set aside for emergencies.

Developing Writing Skills

1. **Outlining a Factual Report.** For this activity, you will use notes to develop an outline for a five-paragraph report about a famous person. You may have completed the Study and Research exercise about note-taking on page 487. If not, you should complete the steps of that exercise before doing this activity.

   Pre-Writing. The first step in making an outline for your report is to organize your notes. Read over the research notes you took about your subject. You will notice that the information falls under certain key topics. For example, you may find notes on the person's early life, mid-life, and later life. Sort your notes into groups. Each group should be made of notes dealing with one of the key topics. Limit yourself to three topics. Put any notes that do not fit into these three groups in a separate pile. You will use them later.

   After you have grouped your notes, read through each group. Put the notes in each group into an order that makes sense. The important details under each major topic must explain or describe that topic. The lesser details under an important detail must explain or describe that important detail.

   Writing. Factual reports are a type of nonfiction. The information for a report is usually organized into three sections: the introduction; the body, composed of the main topics; and the conclusion. You probably do not have research information for the introduction and the conclusion. However, you do have notes for the body. Each group of your notes represents a major topic in the outline. You should have three main topics. Use the following form to write your outline.

Insert more *Important details* and *Lesser details* where you have enough information to do so.

    I. Introduction
   II. First major topic
      A. Important detail
      B. Important detail
        1. Lesser detail
        2. Lesser detail
  III. Second major topic
  IV. Third major topic
   V. Conclusion

   Revising. When you have finished your outline, read it over. Does any information seem to be out of order? Are any of the ideas unrelated to the rest of the outline? Make any changes you think you need. Next, turn in your outline to your teacher.

2. **Describing a Scene.** In this selection the narrator describes a scene that made a strong impression on Maggie as a young girl. The narrator describes her mother doing laundry and the collector from the Order of St. Luke visiting their home. Choose a scene from your childhood that made an impression on you. Write a paragraph describing the scene. Include details about the setting and important people. Try to reveal the mood.

Developing Skills in Critical Thinking

Evaluating Opinions. The writer of "Banker Maggie Walker" clearly admires her subject. Find at least three statements that show her favorable opinion. How can you determine whether her opinion is a reasonable one? What facts does the writer provide to support her opinion?

Personal Recollections

Which incidents from your past stand out in your memory? Certain personal experiences help to shape you as a person. They may have held special sorrow, joy, pride, or fear. The following **personal recollections** report two such experiences. Reading them, you may feel as if you had been through the experiences yourself. The understanding you gain from reading about other people's lives may help to shape your own.

Enigmatic Combat, 1936–37, ARSHILE GORKY. Oil on canvas 35¾" × 48" (90.8 × 121.9 cm.)
San Francisco Museum of Modern Art. Gift of Jeanne Reynal.

Mama and Her Bank Account

KATHRYN FORBES

For Kathryn Forbes's mother, as for Maggie Walker's, a bank account was important to a family's well-being. How did Mama protect her account? Read to find out how the account protected her family as well.

For as long as I could remember, the small cottage on Castro Street had been home. The familiar background was there: Mama, Papa, my only brother, Nels. There was my sister Christine, closest to me in age, yet ever secret and withdrawn—and the littlest sister, Dagmar.

There, too, came the Aunts, Mama's four sisters. Aunt Jenny, who was the oldest and the bossiest; Aunt Sigrid; Aunt Marta; and our maiden aunt, Trina.

The Aunts' old bachelor uncle, my Great-uncle Chris—the "black Norwegian"—came with his great impatience, his shouting and stamping. And brought mystery and excitement to our humdrum days.

But the first awareness was of Mama.

I remember that every Saturday night Mama would sit down by the scrubbed kitchen table and with much wrinkling of usually placid brows count out the money Papa had brought home in the little envelope.

There would be various stacks.

"For the landlord," Mama would say, piling up the big silver pieces.

"For the grocer." Another group of coins.

"For Katrin's shoes to be half-soled." And Mama would count out the little silver.

"Teacher says this week I'll need a notebook." That would be Christine or Nels or I.

Mama would solemnly detach a nickel or a dime and set it aside.

We would watch the diminishing pile with breathless interest.

At last, Papa would ask, "Is all?"

When Mama nodded, we could relax a little and reach for schoolbooks and homework. For Mama would look up and then smile. "Is good," she'd murmur. "We do not have to go to the Bank."

It was a wonderful thing, that Bank Account of Mama's. We were all so proud of it. It gave us such warm, secure feeling. No one else we knew had money in a big bank downtown.

I remember when the Jensens down the street were put out because they couldn't pay their rent. We children watched the big, strange men carry out the furniture and took furtive notice of poor Mrs. Jensen's shamed tears. I was choked with sudden fear. This, then, happened to people who did not have the stack of coins marked "Landlord." Might this, could this, violence happen to us?

I clutched Christine's hands. "We have a Bank Account," she reassured me calmly, and suddenly I could breathe again.

When Nels graduated from grammar school he wanted to go on to high. "Is good," Mama said, and Papa nodded approvingly.

"It will cost a little money," Nels said.

Eagerly we brought up chairs and gathered around the table. I took down the gaily painted box that Aunt Sigrid had sent us from Norway one Christmas and laid it carefully in front of Mama.

This was the "Little Bank." Not to be confused, you understand, with the Big Bank downtown. The Little Bank was used for sudden emergencies, such as the time Christine broke her arm and had to be taken to a doctor, or when Dagmar got croup and Papa had to go to the drugstore for medicine to put into the steam kettle.

Nels had it all written out neatly. So much for carfare, for clothes, for notebooks and supplies. Mama looked at the figures for a long time. Then she counted out the money in the Little Bank. There was not enough.

She pursed her lips. "We do not," she reminded us gently, "want to have to go to the Bank."

We all shook our heads.

"I will work in Dillon's grocery after school," Nels volunteered.

Mama gave him a bright smile and laboriously wrote down a sum and added and subtracted. Papa did it in his head. He was very quick on arithmetic. "Is not enough," he said. Then he took his pipe out of his mouth and looked at it for a long time. "I give up tobacco," he said suddenly.

Mama reached across the table and touched Papa's sleeve, but she didn't say anything. Just wrote down another figure.

"I will mind the Elvington children every Friday night," I said. "Christine can help me."

"Is good," Mama said.

We all felt very good. We had passed another milestone without having to go downtown and draw money out of Mama's Bank Account. The Little Bank was sufficient for the present.

So many things, I remember, came out of the Little Bank that year. Christine's costume for the school play, Dagmar's tonsil operation, my Girl Scout uniform. Always, in the background, was the comforting knowledge that should our efforts fail, we still had the Bank to depend upon.

Even when the strike came, Mama would not let us worry unduly. We all worked together so that the momentous trip downtown could be postponed. It was almost like a game.

During that time, Mama "helped out" at Kruper's bakery for a big sack of only slightly stale bread and coffee cake. As Mama said, fresh bread was not too good for a person and, if you put the coffee cake into the hot oven, it was nearly as nice as when first baked.

Papa washed bottles at the Castro Creamery every night, and they gave him three quarts of fresh milk and all the sour milk he could carry away. Mama made fine cheese.

The day the strike was over and Papa went back to work, I saw Mama stand a little straighter, as if to get a kink out of her back.

She looked around at us proudly. "Is good," she smiled. "See? We did not have to go down to the Bank."

That was twenty years ago.

Last year I sold my first story. When the check came, I hurried over to Mama's and put the long green slip of paper in her lap. "For you," I said, "to put in your Bank Account."

I noticed for the first time how old Mama and Papa looked. Papa seemed shorter now, and Mama's wheaten braids were sheened with silver.

Mama fingered the check and looked at Papa. "Is good," she said, and her eyes were proud.

"Tomorrow," I told her, "you must take it down to the Bank."

"You will go with me, Katrin?"

"That won't be necessary, Mama. See? I've endorsed the check to you. Just hand it to the teller, he'll deposit it to your account."

Mama looked at me. "Is no account," she said. "In all my life, I never been inside a Bank."

And when I didn't—couldn't—answer, Mama said earnestly: "Is not good for little ones to be afraid—to not feel secure."

Developing Comprehension Skills

1. What did Katrin's family do on Saturday nights?

2. Explain the "Little Bank." Name one time that the family used it.

3. What did the Big Bank downtown mean to the young Katrin and her sister Christine?

4. What impression does the writer as an adult have of her mother? Identify three or more words or phrases with strong connotations that support your answer.

5. Do you think it was right for Katrin's mother to tell the children about the bank account? Why or why not?

Reading Literature: Personal Recollections

1. **Describing a Character.** The writer describes Mama by telling her words and actions. Using your own words, describe the character of Mama. Support your description with details from the story.

2. **Recognizing the Family as a Character.** Usually the characters in a story are individual people. However, in this story, the family unit is described as a character. What is this family like? What does the writer do to give the reader a feeling for the family as a group?

3. **Analyzing Language.** There are several clues in the story that suggest Mama and Papa are not living in the same country in which they were born. The narrator speaks of Uncle Chris, the "black Norwegian." The names of the children and aunts—Sigrid, Nels, Marta—seem to be Scandinavian. The way that Mama and Papa speak also suggests that English is not their first language. List at least two statements made by either Mama or Papa that do not follow the rules of grammar. Rewrite each statement in the way that you would say it.

4. **Identifying the Theme.** When people write recollections, they write of events that have special meaning to them. In discussing these events, writers express important ideas, attitudes, or themes about their lives. What do you think is the theme of this recollection?

5. **Recognizing Irony.** You have learned that irony is a contrast between what is expected and what actually happens. What is the irony at the end of this selection? How is the irony related to the theme?

Developing Vocabulary Skills

Identifying Word Origins. Many English words are based on words in other languages. Most dictionaries include information on the origin, or source, of each word.

The following English words are from "Mama and Her Bank Account." Locate the origin for each word in the dictionary. On your paper, write the word and the language or languages of its origin. Refer to the beginning of the dictionary for an explanation of the abbreviations used.

1. secure
2. labor
3. diminish
4. placid
5. sufficient
6. furtive

Developing Writing Skills

1. **Writing an Introductory Paragraph.** You have selected a subject, taken research notes, and organized your notes into an outline. (See the previous writing exercises on pages 487 and 495, and the research exercise on page 487.) It is time to begin writing your report on a famous person.

   The first part of your report is the introductory paragraph. It has two jobs. First, the introductory paragraph should identify the subject of your report. Second, it should catch the reader's interest.

   Using your research notes and outline, write an introductory paragraph for your report. Select one of the following methods to write the opening sentence. Then add details about your subject that are interesting and informative.

   a. Describe an event in the subject's life.
   b. Use a quotation that is related to the life of the subject.
   c. Briefly describe the physical appearance of the subject.
   d. Ask the reader a question.

2. **Imagining a Situation.** Katrin's mother behaved in a certain way so her children would not be upset or worried. Parents often act to protect their children. Imagine yourself as a

parent. What sort of situation might cause you to take action to protect your children? Write an account of at least two paragraphs describing such a situation.

Pre-Writing. Imagine the situation. Think about how it would make you feel as a parent. Make a list of adjectives you might use in describing the situation. In a separate list, write down notes about the main events. What is the problem? What actions do you take as a parent? Decide how to present this information. You will need to create the feeling of tension or nervousness that the situation causes. You could arrange events in time order or in order of importance.

Writing. First, describe the situation. Present the events in an order that adds to the mood. Second, describe your actions.

Use words from your list to reveal the emotion of the situation.

Revising. Read your paragraphs carefully. Is the situation clearly described? Have you used words that help express the mood? Have you arranged the details in order?

Developing Skills in Speaking and Listening

Interpreting a Narrative. Work with a partner to prepare an oral reading of "Mama and Her Bank Account." One person should read the words of the narrator. The other person should read the words said by other members in the family. Try to make your voices express the feelings in the story, such as "solemnly," "reassured," "proudly," and "earnestly."

Untitled, about 1936, ARSHILE GORKY. Oil on canvas with superimposed ink drawing, 15½" × 23½".
Collection Christopher C. Schwabacher, New York. Courtesy of the Solomon R. Guggenheim Museum, New York.

The First Day of the War

MAIA WOJCIECHOWSKA

To Davy Crockett, war was a chance to change the world. To Anne Frank, it was a time of finding one's self. What does the outbreak of war mean to twelve-year-old Maia? Read to find out.

It started like the best of all mornings. I woke up from a dream to the sound of the plane.

He would often come early in the morning, and I always knew he would not land before I got out of bed and ran outside. While waiting, he would make lazy circles in the sky. As I rushed out, there would always be an unasked question in my mind: did he love fear more than freedom or freedom more than fear? For he always did something frightening that might end his freedom: rolls and spins and that horrible, inevitable climb into the infinity of the sky. Each time I saw him go vertically away from me, I thought he wouldn't want to come down.

But he always did. And that descent, straight down, the nose of the plane an arrow shooting the earth, falling, gaining in loudness as he lost altitude, made me catch my breath and forced my eyes to close. Would he straighten up in time? Would a wing catch a treetop as it once did? But he was immortal. The plane might lose a wing or even burn, but nothing would happen to him. Not to my hero, my flying knight, my father.

Even as I raced against the landing plane, trying to reach it before he cut the engine, hoping that he would have time to take me up, trying not to be blown down by the great gusts of wind from the propeller blades, even as I climbed up to the cockpit, I was afraid. Afraid that he would be alone, unreachable, private in that world of his where I couldn't even be a trespasser. Even flying with him, beside him, even then he was still a fugitive from me.

Today was different. The sound of the plane was gone by the time I rushed outside. Then I heard another. Not just one but several planes were flying overhead. Next to me was my newest possession, one he had not yet seen—a Doberman puppy. The dog had no name yet. He was brand new, and I loved him. Yesterday, when I got him, he had run away from the vet who was going to trim his ears and cut his tail to a stump. The litter of five submitted yappingly to the operation, but not he. He tore himself away from me, and I chased him through a swamp, across what I was afraid was a bed of quicksand, wanting to catch him and yet also wanting him to get away. Now his black glistening body, for he had fallen into a puddle, was jumping over weeds and disappearing into the tall grass.

Now there was another plane. I looked up, but it wasn't his—it did not have white and red squared under the wings. The plane dipped down and flew low, parallel with my running dog. It slid down even lower, and there was a sound—a sound I didn't understand, a sound I had never heard before. As my dog leaped up, I saw him for a brief moment over the grass, shadowed by the plane's wing. Then the plane rose and flew away.

I stood in that field not moving, waiting for my dog to continue running in that sunlit place, which was at the edge of my summer world, but I couldn't see him anywhere. And there were no sounds—not one single sound since that sound that I was now beginning to understand. As I started to walk forward, I already knew what I would see, and knowing was evil and I wanted to take back what I knew.

I did not bury my dog. I did not touch him. I turned away from him because he did not move. He would never have a name.

I climbed a tree and sat there, trying not to think of anything, trying not to hate. But trying did no good and I hated—everything I knew and everything that I didn't understand. I hated everyone, especially those who now were making noises inside my house. I hated the car that had pulled in front of the house and its running, sputtering engine. And most of all I hated my mother's voice calling my name and the slamming of the doors. And I hated the summer for having so suddenly ended.

When I got tired of hating, I came down off the tree and swore to myself that nobody would ever know what had happened to my dog. I promised not to say anything to anyone, not until I understood why and who had done it. Not until I found a way of paying them back. Not until after I killed the one who had killed him.

A man I never liked, a friend of my mother's, was yelling at me that I was lucky I wasn't being left behind. I stuck my tongue out at him when he turned his back and told my mother there was no time to pack anything. He pulled her and pushed me toward the car, where my brothers were already seated, both of them sleepy and angry. I didn't dare protest against this kidnapping of my person because I was afraid that if I opened my mouth, I'd cry.

I remembered from way back that every time I felt hurt, I had to do something mean, as if being mean could in itself cure the hurt. I took away a roll my little brother Krzys was eating and threw it out of the car window. And when he, aged six, began to cry, I placed my hand over his mouth. He knew better than to struggle against me. But I could feel his tears on my hand, for he was crying over his loss while I couldn't cry over mine. I consoled myself with the thought that I have a devil inside me and that I would go straight to hell when I die.

The car was taking me away from the field where my dog was lying dead and would be eaten by buzzards before noon. There was a loud argument in the car about the war. Zbyszek, my fourteen-year-old brother, was insisting that we were certainly going to win and especially because he planned to enlist in the Polish Air Force. The man at the wheel was of the opinion that Poland had no chance to defend itself against Germany. And my mother, pulling on a pair of white gloves, expressed her disbelief that the war should have started at such an inconvenient time. We were going to go back to France next week. And I began to laugh. I laughed loud and hard because at twelve I was glad my country was at war with people who shot down dogs.

I realized it would be hard to find him, the one who actually did kill my dog. Maybe I could advertise. "Wanted: The German pilot who shot down a Doberman pup on September 1, 1939. Important reward." He'd answer the ad and I'd be ready for him. I had stolen a book from a Paris bookstore about medieval tortures. It was behind in the house, but I remembered most of them. He would be a long time dying. Water dripping first, then bamboo spikes, or better still nails, rusty and long, under the fingernails. Hot coals and scalding water. I could pull out his hair by the handfuls, or maybe I could even build a rack or a pendulum. What would be nicest of all would be to have him die behind a horse and be dragged around for miles, face down, across fields stubby with weeds, coarse with stones. Or maybe I could find a mad dog and let him be bitten to death. That would be poetic justice.

We were in a sixth-floor apartment in Warsaw. The view from here was fantastic. It was too good to be true. People down below on the street were running in circles; cars, buses, and trolleys were piling up, being abandoned; furniture and suitcases were all over the sidewalks. And in the distance there were several fires. The sirens went on again—I was getting used to their shrieks—and all activities stopped as the sound of the planes came into the apartment through the windows I flung open.

"Why did he leave us here?" My mother kept repeating the question, although my brother had told her several times that the reason her friend locked us in this place was that he wanted to steal from us. Especially the new car, the one my father had just brought into Poland from France—a splendid new, custom-made Delage. I hated to listen to them, so I leaned farther out of the window and was glad when the bombs began to fall. I grabbed Krzys by the hand and dragged him to the window, and we began to imitate the sounds of the bomb. First the plane's engine, then the whistle of the falling bomb, and then its great triumphant explosion. "BOOM!" We laughed like crazy, and Mother suddenly realized we were in "mortal danger" and ordered us to hide under the sofa. I accused her of "sudden senility," which had recently become my favorite expression of disdain, and explained as haughtily as possible that if we were going to be hit, I'd feel much safer falling down six floors than having a sofa come on my head.

"We should be in a shelter," she answered with little logic since she'd tried the door several times and found it locked. Her friend assured us we'd be safe here. She always had a hard time coming to grips with reality and a harder time distrusting people or seeing herself being taken advantage of.

But I couldn't be bothered with her now. The view out of the window was fascinating. Houses collapsed, churches crumbled. Someone, maybe God Himself, had started the biggest game in the world, and I couldn't wait to get involved.

While Zbyszek attacked the door, trying to break it down, I invented a game for Krzys. We broke everything we could get our hands on, and what we couldn't break, we threw out of the window. My mother was carrying on a semihysterical monolog and didn't even notice when the house across the street, almost as tall as the one we were in, was hit directly, collapsed in slow motion and in a great cloud of dust as we were flung down by the explosion. There was broken glass all over the floor now, and the bookcase had fallen not two feet away from my mother. Krzys began to cry, and I hit him because I didn't want to give the Germans the satisfaction of making any of us cry. For suddenly I knew something

else—I knew about wars. It started with the killing of dogs, but then it all became a matter of pride, of winning over fear.

The door opened, and the man who had locked us in was back telling us that he had seen my father. I tried to hear every word he said about him, but Zbyszek was yelling at him accusations of thievery and my mother was asking silly questions about danger from bombs. I pieced together the information about my father: he had been ordered to go to London and Paris to ask for reinforcements for the Polish Air Force. He had taken a plane and was piloting it himself. We were to get a train, go through Rumania to France, where we were to join him because he was ordered not to come back to Poland.

My father had done it again—abandoned us, freed himself from us! Not even a war could stop him from flying away. I hit my fist against the doorframe and wished everyone dead so that I could cry in peace over this news, over life's inhumanity to me.

How many times have I cried over my father without anyone's knowing about it? Each birthday and each name day because he was never there. And whenever it rained. I cried for him inside the dark movie houses when I watched sad films and over books that were not even sad. Only once—how old was I, nine or eight?—I cried in front of him. I had torn up a dress my mother had made for me. A horrid taffeta dress, loud with noises, full of ribbons and bows and laced petticoats. I had hated being a girl and wished to have nothing to do with dresses like that. I tore it off, tore it apart, threw it at her, and went to hide my anger over her attempts to brand me a girl. He had found me in the garden on a swing. He had his belt in his hands, and he hit me with it half a dozen times. Not hard, but he hit me. For the first and only time. And I had cried. Then he talked to me, for the first time about being cruel to my mother and thoughtless. And I cried. Not because he had hit me. Not because of what he said. Not because of what I was, and I was cruel and thoughtless. I cried because he did not know this firsthand but had learned it just then—from his wife.

He didn't know anything about me. He didn't know that I had always wanted to be a boy because being a boy would have made

Untitled (Prime Ordeal), 1945, ROBERTO MATTA ECHAURREN, Collection of the Museum of Contemporary Art. Gift of Mr. and Mrs. Joseph P. Shapiro.

me closer to being like him when I grew up. He did not know about the time Zbyszek's friends had tied me to a tombstone and left me overnight in the cemetery. He didn't know that once the same boys tied me up to a tree, built a pile of sticks under my feet, and dared me to scream as they lit it. He did not know that I told them that not only would I not scream, but also that I would, if they untied my hands, light the fire myself so that they would not get into trouble. He did not know that I had been scared the time he finally allowed me to parachute jump from an airplane, and that I had been lying to him that day, for I had changed my mind and didn't want to jump. He did not know that for a moment, before the chute opened, I wished that God would not let me die before I told my father that I loved him more than life. He didn't know my hates or my longings or my loves, or the fact that I could not fall asleep without reading to myself under the covers. He didn't know that I was jealous of everyone he had time for. He didn't know that I always wanted him to be proud of me. He didn't know my dog had been killed that morning. He didn't know he shouldn't have left us.

Developing Comprehension Skills

1. What forced Maia and her family to flee from their home?

2. Name two facts about Maia's father.

3. Maia twice mentions laughing on the day the war began. The first time, she explains, it was from gladness that her country was "at war with people who shot down dogs." She gave no reason for the second time, during the bombing. Can you suggest a reason?

4. Is Maia's description of her mother subjective or objective? How do you know?

5. At the end of "The First Day of the War," do you like or dislike Maia? Why?

Reading Literature: Personal Recollections

1. **Analyzing Word Choice.** In the first three paragraphs of the story, Maia does not identify her father. She refers to her father as *he*. Explain the conflicting emotions that this word choice suggests.

2. **Recognizing Style of Writing.** An important part of Wojciechowska's writing style is her use of repetition. She often repeats key words and phrases. For example, in one paragraph about her father, the narrator begins sentences with the following phrases:

   > How many times have I cried over my father. . . .
   > I cried for him inside. . . .
   > I cried in front of him. . . .
   > I cried because he did not know this first-hand. . . .

   This repetition of the phrase "I cried" brings out the intensity of her feelings and her lack

of control over the situation. Select another passage from the selection that shows the writer's use of repetition. Write the repeated words and phrases on your paper. Decide what the effect of the repetition is. Then explain why you think the writer repeated the words and phrases.

3. **Identifying Tone.** The writer's attitude toward the subject—the tone—is suggested by the words the writer chooses. In this selection, what do you think is the narrator's attitude, or tone, toward the war? List at least three words or phrases from the selection that express this tone.

4. **Explaining the Theme.** In "The First Day of the War," the writer presents ideas about hero worship, war, anger, and fear of death. Which topic do you think the writer feels is most important? Write a sentence expressing what you think is the theme of this story.

Developing Vocabulary Skills

Reviewing Word Origins. You have learned many ways in which words in the English language have developed. Some English words are clipped, or shortened, versions of longer words. Other English words have been developed from the name of a person or place.

Some of the following words were used in the selections you have read. Others are based on names from the selections. List the words on your paper. Look up each word in a dictionary. Next to each word, write the longer word or the name from which the word came.

1. vet
2. bloomers
3. bowie knife
4. Saturday
5. plane
6. pup

Developing Writing Skills

1. **Writing the Body of a Report.** You have already written an introductory paragraph to your report on a famous person. (See Developing Writing Skills on page 501.) Now, use your outline to write the three-paragraph body of your report.

   Pre-Writing. Review the outline and introductory paragraph you wrote for your report. You may decide to make some changes in your outline. You may add or delete information or change the organization of the information. Be sure that the information still relates to the three major ideas you selected earlier. Check that the order of information makes sense.

   Writing. The body of the report contains three paragraphs. Write one paragraph for each major idea in your outline. You should be able to use each statement marked by Roman numerals on your outline in a topic sentence of a paragraph. Use the details of your outline in supporting sentences in the paragraphs. Add words or sentences to connect the ideas and to show their relationships. Write everything except the concluding paragraph of your report.

   Revising. When you have finished writing the body of your report, read it carefully. Ask yourself the following questions. Rewrite any weak parts of the body.

   a. Does each paragraph tell about one idea?

   b. Have I arranged the paragraphs and ideas within them logically?

   c. Have I used words and phrases that lead the reader from one idea to the next?

   d. Have I followed the outline?

2. **Describing a Favorite Activity.** Maia's father loved to fly. Is there an activity that you have such enthusiasm about? Or is there some activity that you wish you had the skill for? Perhaps you have a love of hiking, sailing, skiing, or cycling. Write one or more paragraphs describing an activity you enjoy or want to learn. In your writing, explain the technical details of the activity. Also include words and phrases that reveal your emotion about the activity.

Developing Skills in Critical Thinking

Recognizing Slanted Writing. All writers use slanted writing to try to persuade their readers. Slanted writing is not necessarily bad. It is the reader's job to be aware of how the writer's slant is affecting his or her reactions to the information being presented.

Practice determining a writer's slant. Find three brief passages from a newspaper or magazine: one that uses positive connotations, one that uses negative connotations, and one that includes only neutral statements. Underline the phrases in each passage that suggest the writer's approach to the subject.

Humorous Sketches

Humor delights because of its unexpectedness. Humor often surprises the reader with its contrasts or its exaggerations. Humor may have a serious point, too, about human weaknesses. However, the serious point is usually buried under more than a few laughs. Here are two **humorous sketches** that are examples of humorous essays at their best.

Golconde, 1953, RENÉ MAGRITTE. Private Collection.

Reading Literature: Different Types of Nonfiction

What Is an Essay?

You have learned that there are several types of nonfiction. You have read several types, including autobiography, biography, and diaries. The broadest category of nonfiction is the essay. An **essay** is a short composition that discusses a topic. Essays can be a few sentences long. They can be many pages long. They can be serious, meant to teach or inform. They can be humorous, meant to amuse. They can be based on fact or on imagination. It is hard to say what they can or cannot do.

Since essays include so many kinds of writing, it is helpful to break them into smaller groups. The most useful way to classify essays is to separate them into formal essays and informal essays. **Informal essays** reflect a writer's feelings and personality. Their organization may seem like that of a friendly conversation. **Formal essays** examine a topic in a thorough, logical manner. They are serious and tightly organized.

Informal essays that discuss the writer's personal experiences are like other autobiographical writing. The selections in this chapter called "personal recollections" might also be called informal essays. The writers discuss feelings and ideas as much as events.

In this section, all the selections are different types of essays. The humorous sketches are informal essays, telling about exaggerated or imaginary personal experiences. The articles are formal essays. They are objective in tone and full of facts. The sayings and proverbs are miniature informal essays. Each one presents one person's view of life, stated briefly and imaginatively. Many people accepted this view and kept the proverb alive in oral tradition for hundreds of years.

The History of the Essay

The essay had its beginnings in the proverb, a wise comment on life. In the early 1500's, collecting proverbs was popular. A French writer named Michel de Montaigne was the first person to write his own proverbs. Unlike the one-sentence proverbs in this chapter, his proverbs were conversational discussions of various topics. They were the first informal essays.

Later in the 16th century, the British writer Francis Bacon wrote the first essays in English. His essays were formal essays. They were logical, precise, and impersonal. In the 18th century, essays were very popular features in newspapers. Two well-known British essayists were Joseph Addison and Richard Steele, who wrote in *The Spectator.*

The writing of formal and informal essays has remained popular. Now they appear in newspapers, magazines, and in published collections. They are also presented on television.

More About the Elements of Nonfiction

Formal essays do not have characters, setting, or plot. Informal essays often do. Another element often found in informal essays, but not in formal ones, is humor. In both types of essays, structure and style are important. Here are discussions of humor, structure, and style.

Humor. Humorous writing is writing that is funny or amusing. When he or she exaggerates, a writer or comedian makes a small, everyday difficulty sound like an impossible problem. You will find this technique in "Learning To Drive." When a writer uses irony, he or she contrasts what is expected, or normal, with what is said or done. Another kind of irony is saying the opposite of what is meant. Both kinds of irony are in Mark Twain's writing.

Structure. The organization of a piece of writing is called its **structure**. The structure of myths, legends, short stories, and stories of people's lives usually depends on time order. The structure of essays, however, is usually logical. That is, the writer decides how to build one idea on another. The writer must show connections between ideas.

Style. The way a writer uses language is called that writer's **style**. Every writer has an individual style. It includes his or her choice of words. It refers to the length of sentences and their arrangement. Use of humor and figures of speech is part of style, also.

Punch, Brothers, Punch

MARK TWAIN

This selection begins almost like a personal recollection. When do you realize it is something different? As you read Mark Twain's tale, note how each development becomes more absurd than the one before.

Will the reader please cast his eye over the following lines, and see if anything harmful can be discovered in them?

Conductor, when you receive a fare,
Punch in the presence of the passenjare!
A blue trip slip for an eight-cent fare,
A buff trip slip for a six-cent fare,
A pink trip slip for a three-cent fare,
Punch in the presence of the passenjare!

CHORUS
Punch, brothers! Punch with care!
Punch in the presence of the passenjare!

I came across these jingling rhymes in a newspaper, a little while ago, and read them a couple of times. They took instant and entire possession of me. All through breakfast they went waltzing through my brain; and when, at last, I rolled up my napkin, I could not tell whether I had eaten anything or not. I had carefully laid out my day's work the day before—a thrilling tragedy in the novel that I am writing. I went to my den to begin my deed of blood. I took up my pen, but all I could get it to say was, "Punch in the presence of the passenjare." I fought hard for an hour, but it was useless. My head kept humming, "A blue trip slip for an eight-cent fare, a buff trip slip for a six-cent fare," and so on and so on, without peace or respite. The day's work was ruined—I could see that plainly enough. I gave up and drifted downtown, and presently discovered that my feet were keeping time to that relentless jingle. When I could stand it no longer, I altered my step. It did no good; those rhymes accommodated themselves to the new step and went on harassing me just as before. I returned home, and suffered all the afternoon; suffered all through an unconscious and unrefreshing dinner; suffered, and cried, and jingled all through the evening; went to bed and rolled, tossed, and jingled right along, the same as ever; got up at midnight, frantic, and tried to read; but there was nothing visible upon the whirling page except

"Punch! Punch in the presence of the passenjare." By sunrise I was out of my mind, and everybody marveled and was distressed at the idiotic burden of my ravings— "Punch! Oh, punch! Punch in the presence of the passenjare!"

Two days later, on Saturday morning, I arose, a tottering wreck, and went forth to fulfill an engagement with a valued friend, the Rev. Mr. ——, to walk to the Talcott Tower, ten miles distant. He stared at me but asked no questions. We started. Mr. —— talked, talked, talked—as is his wont. I said nothing; I heard nothing.

At the end of a mile, Mr. —— said, "Mark, are you sick? I never saw a man look so haggard and worn and absent-minded. Say something, do!"

Drearily, without enthusiasm, I said: "Punch, brothers, punch with care! Punch in the presence of the passenjare!"

My friend eyed me blankly, looked perplexed, then said, "I do not think I get your drift, Mark. There does not seem to be any relevancy in what you have said, certainly nothing sad; and yet—maybe it was the way you said the words—I never heard anything that sounded so pathetic—

But I heard no more. I was already far away with my pitiless, heart-breaking "blue trip slip for an eight-cent fare, buff trip slip for a six-cent fare, pink trip slip for a three-cent fare; punch in the presence of the passenjare." I do not know what occurred during the other nine miles. However, all of a sudden Mr. —— laid his hand on my shoulder and shouted:

"Oh, wake up! Wake up! Wake up! Don't sleep all day! Here we are at the Tower, man! I have talked myself deaf and dumb and blind and never got a response. Just look at this magnificent autumn landscape! Look at it! Look at it! Feast your eyes on it! You have traveled; you have seen boasted landscapes elsewhere. Come, now, deliver an honest opinion. What do you say to this?"

I sighed wearily, and murmured, "A buff trip slip for a six-cent fare, a pink trip slip for a three-cent fare, punch in the presence of the passenjare."

Rev. Mr. —— stood there, very grave, full of concern, apparently, and looked long at me. Then he said, "Mark, there is something about this that I cannot understand. Those are about the same words you said before; there does not seem to be anything in them, and yet they nearly break my heart when you say them. Punch in the—how is it they go?"

I began at the beginning and repeated all the lines.

My friend's face lighted with interest. He said, "Why, what a captivating jingle it is! It is almost music. It flows along so nicely. I have nearly caught the rhymes myself. Say them over just once more, and then I'll have them, sure."

I said them over. Then Mr. —— said them. He made one little mistake, which I corrected. The next time and the next he got them right. Now a great burden seemed to tumble from my shoulders. That torturing jingle departed out of my brain, and a grateful sense of rest and peace descended upon me. I was light-hearted enough to sing; and I did sing for half an hour, straight along, as we went jogging homeward. Then my freed tongue found blessed speech again, and the pent talk of many a weary hour began to gush and flow. It flowed on and on, joyously, jubilantly, until the fountain was empty and dry.

As I wrung my friend's hand at parting, I said, "Haven't we had a royal good time! But now I remember, you haven't said a word for two hours. Come, come, out with something!"

The Rev. Mr. ——— turned a lack-lustre eye upon me, drew a deep sigh, and said, without animation, without apparent consciousness, "Punch, brothers, punch with care! Punch in the presence of the passenjare!"

A pang shot through me as I said to myself, "Poor fellow, poor fellow! He has got it, now."

I did not see Mr. ——— for two or three days after that. Then, on Tuesday evening, he staggered into my presence and sank dejectedly into a seat. He was pale, worn; he was a wreck. He lifted his faded eyes to my face and said:

"Ah, Mark, it was a ruinous investment that I made in those heartless rhymes. They have ridden me like a nightmare, day and night, hour after hour, to this very moment. Since I saw you, I have suffered the torments of the lost. Saturday evening I had a sudden call, by telegraph, and took the night train for Boston. The occasion was the death of a valued old friend who had requested that I should preach his funeral sermon. I took my seat in the cars and set myself to framing the discourse. But I never got beyond the opening paragraph; for then the train started and the car-wheels began their 'clack, clack—clack-clack-clack! clack-clack—clack-clack-clack!' and right away those odious rhymes fitted themselves to that accompaniment.

"For an hour I sat there and set a syllable of those rhymes to every separate and distinct clack the car-wheels made. Why, I was as tired, then, as if I had been chopping wood all day. My skull was splitting with headache. It seemed to me that I must go mad if I sat there any longer; so I undressed and went to bed. I stretched myself out in my berth, and—well, you know what the result was. The thing went right along, just the same. 'Clack-clack-clack, a blue trip slip, clack-clack-clack, for an eight-cent fare; clack-clack-clack, a buff trip slip, clack-clack-clack, for a six-cent fare, and so on, and so on, and so on—punch in the presence of the passenjare!'

"Sleep? Not a single wink! I was almost a lunatic when I got to Boston. Don't ask me about the funeral. I did the best I could, but every solemn individual sentence was meshed and tangled and woven in and out with 'Punch, brothers, punch with care, punch in the presence of the passenjare.' And the most distressing thing was that my delivery dropped into the undulating rhythm of those pulsing rhymes, and I could actually catch absent-minded people

Orion, 1956–62, VICTOR VASARELY. Hirshhorn Museum and Sculpture Garden, Smithsonian Institution, Washington, D.C. © S.P.A.D.E.M., Paris/V.A.G.A., New York, 1984. Photograph by Lee Stalsworth.

nodding time to the swing of it with their stupid heads. And, Mark, you may believe it or not, but, before I got through, the entire assemblage were placidly bobbing their heads in solemn unison, mourners, undertaker, and all.

"The moment I had finished, I fled to the anteroom in a state bordering on frenzy. Of course it would be my luck to find a sorrowing and aged maiden aunt of the deceased there, who had arrived from Springfield too late to get into the church.

"She began to sob, and said, 'Oh, oh, he is gone, he is gone, and I didn't see him before he died!'

" 'Yes!' I said, 'he is gone, he is gone, he is gone—oh, will this suffering never cease!'

" 'You loved him, then! Oh, you too loved him!'

" 'Loved him! Loved who?'

" 'Why, my poor George! my poor, dear nephew!'

" 'Oh—him! Yes—oh, yes, yes. Certainly—certainly.   Punch—punch—oh, this misery will kill me!'

" 'Bless you! bless you, sir, for these sweet words! I, too, suffer in this dear loss. Were you present during his last moments?'

" 'Yes. I—whose last moments?'

" 'His. The dear departed's.'

" 'Yes! Oh, yes—yes—yes! I suppose so, I think so, I don't know! Oh, certainly—I was there—I was there!'

" 'Oh, what a privilege! what a precious privilege! And his last words—oh, tell me, tell me his last words! What did he say?'

" 'He said—he said—oh, my head, my head, my head! He said—he said—he never said anything but Punch, punch, punch in the presence of the passenjare! Oh, leave me, madam! In the name of all that is generous, leave me to my madness, my misery, my despair!—a buff trip slip for a six-cent fare, a pink trip slip for a three-cent fare—endu-rance can no fur-ther go!—PUNCH, punch, punch in the presence of the passenjare!' "

My friend's hopeless eyes rested upon mine a pregnant minute, and then he said impressively, "Mark, you do not say anything. You do not offer me any hope. But, ah me, it is just as well—it is just as well. You could not do me any good. The time has long gone by when words could comfort me. Something tells me that my tongue is doomed to wag forever to the jigger of that remorseless jingle. There—there it is coming on me again: a blue trip slip for an eight-cent fare, a buff trip slip for a—"

Thus murmuring faint and fainter, my friend sank into a peaceful trance and forgot his sufferings in a blessed respite.

How did I finally save him from an asylum? I took him to a neighboring university and made him discharge the burden of his persecuting rhymes into the eager ears of the poor, unthinking students. How is it with *them,* now? The result is too sad to tell. Why did I write this article? It was for a worthy, even a noble, purpose. It was to warn you, reader, if you should come across those merciless rhymes, to avoid them— avoid them as you would a pestilence!

Developing Comprehension Skills

1. How did the jingle affect the narrator? How did he empty his mind of the jingle?

2. What do the lines of the jingle mean?

3. In the article, Rev. Mr. _____ spoke in a disordered way to the maiden aunt. How did the aunt interpret his behavior? Is her reaction at least slightly believable?

4. At the end of "Punch, Brothers, Punch," the narrator states why he wrote the article. He claims he wanted to warn the readers to avoid the jingle. How do you know this statement is untrue? What do you think his purpose really was?

5. Humor is a very subjective topic. That is, what is funny to one person may not be funny at all to another person. Did you find "Punch, Brothers, Punch" funny? What parts did you enjoy most?

Reading Literature: Humorous Sketches

1. **Recognizing Use of Imagery.** In describing the lines of the jingle, Twain writes, "All through breakfast they went waltzing through my brain." Identify two other passages in the sketch that contain colorful expressions. Then explain the meaning of each passage in your own words.

2. **Analyzing Humor.** There are two ways to add comedy to a situation. The writer or comedian may use **irony** to give an unexpected twist. The writer or comedian may also use **exaggeration** to emphasize the ridiculous side of human nature. Which method does Twain use in this selection? Or does he use both? Explain your answer.

3. **Appreciating Language.** Read the entire jingle aloud several times. As the narrator admits, the jingle has no important meaning. However, the jingle is easy to say and hard to forget. Twain uses the following methods to create this effect: rhyme, repetition, alliteration, and rhythm. If necessary, refer to the Handbook to review these terms. Write down parts of the jingle that are an example of each of the first three methods. Then copy four lines of the jingle and show the rhythm of the words with these marks: / for stressed syllables and ⌣ for unstressed syllables.

4. **Identifying Slanted Writing.** Writers use words with emotional meanings to sway your opinions. Find the words that the narrator uses at the end of this selection to describe students. Do these words have positive or negative connotations? What does Twain's opinion of students appear to be?

Developing Vocabulary Skills

Working with Homographs. Some words are entered in the dictionary more than once. These entry words are called **homographs**. They are different words that are spelled the same way. They usually have different origins. They may or may not have the same pronunciation. They always have different meanings. For example, locate the word *pound* in the glossary of this textbook. Notice the three separate entries. Each entry is numbered. Each has a different meaning. These are homographs.

Each of the following underlined words is a homograph. Locate each of these words in the dictionary. Be sure to read all the definitions of each word. On your paper, write the definition that best fits the sentence.

1. The jingle tended to <u>lead</u> the narrator away from his work.

2. When he tried to write, the narrator's <u>pen</u> would write only the jingle.

3. A blue trip <u>slip</u> indicated an eight-cent fare.

4. The jingle was the only <u>strand</u> of thought in the narrator's mind.

5. The narrator's friend gave him a <u>grave</u> look of concern.

Developing Writing Skills

1. **Writing a Conclusion.** If you have not answered the first writing question for both "Mama and Her Bank Account" (page 501) and "The First Day of the War" (page 510), do so now. In order to do this exercise, you need to have written the introduction and body of a biographical report.

   The conclusion of a report draws the ideas together and ends the report in a logical way. Review the introduction and body of your report. Also skim through your notes, including unused notes. Then write a concluding paragraph summarizing the major topics about the subject.

2. **Describing a Reaction.** The narrator in this selection could not get the jingle out of his mind. Have you ever been unable to get something off your mind, no matter how hard you tried? Or can you imagine what it would be like? Write a three paragraph description of your reaction to such a problem.

   Pre-Writing. Decide if your reaction to the problem will be humorous or serious. Make a list of strong adjectives to describe the events and lively verbs to describe your actions. Choose words to reveal the tone.

Then group the details into categories. You might group together events that happened at the same time. You might group details of sight separate from those of sound. Each category will become a paragraph. Decide how to arrange the paragraphs.

Writing. Using your notes, write the description. Be sure to express a tone, concerning the problem. Write about only one group of details in each paragraph.

Revising. Read your description aloud. Are the details presented in a clear order? Does the description make sense? Have you used words that let the reader see, hear, smell, taste, or touch the details? Is the tone you wanted to express obvious?

Developing Skills in Speaking and Listening

1. **Presenting a Paper.** If you have written the introduction, body, and conclusion for a biographical report (see Developing Writing skills, above), prepare to read it to a group. Read your report to yourself several times to become comfortable with it. Practice using a strong voice and stressing each main idea. When you are ready, present your paper.

2. **Listening to a Presentation.** With a small group, listen carefully to your classmate's presentation of a biographical report. Are the main topics about the subject clear? Are details given for each main idea? Are facts about the subject presented in a logical order? What information has the writer omitted that would be helpful? Be prepared to ask the speaker questions about these points. Also be prepared to let the speaker know which parts of the report you liked best.

Learning To Drive

BILLY ROSE

For some people, learning to drive can be a tense experience. How does Billy Rose react to his lessons? Has he written this account to provide guidance for others? Read to find the answers.

On the way back from Mt. Kisco, my wife said, "I wish you'd learn how to drive. Every time you want something, somebody's got to stop what he's doing and chauffeur you into the village."

"Okay," I said, "if you'll play teacher."

Next morning I crawled into the car beside my wife. "Just turn this jigger over," she began, "push in this dingus, pull out this doohickey, step on this wingdoodle, press down on this thingamabob, and you're all set to go."

"What's this gizmo?" I asked.

"The hand brake," she said. "You throw it on quickly in case of emergency."

"What happens if it doesn't work?"

"Hit something cheap," advised my spouse.

A moment later the car went hiccuping down the road. Then for a mile it went smooth as you please. A feeling of confidence came over me, the same feeling all new drivers get just before the lights go out. I pressed down on the gas.

"The pistons seem to be knocking," I said professionally.

"Pistons nothing," said my mate. "Those are my knees."

Everything went fine until we got to the traffic light in the village. I forgot to press the hickey-madoodle on the gilhooley, and the car stalled. The lights changed from green to red, and from red back to green. A cop came over.

"What's the matter?" he asked. "Haven't we got any colors you like?"

After switching the radio on and off, I suddenly pressed the right thing. In the order of the way it happened, I grazed the cop, skidded through the safety zone, clipped the fender on a bus, and came to rest with my bumper against a fire plug. The cop stalked over. He took a handkerchief out of his pocket and dropped it in front of the car.

"Lookit, Gene Autry," he said. "I wanna see you do that all over again, and this time pick up the handkerchief with your teeth."

My wife gave him the big smile. "He's learning to drive," she said.

"No kidding!" said the cop. "How long is this class going to last? Some other drivers would like to use this road when Sonny Boy gets through with it."

"What did I do wrong?" I asked.

"Didn't you hear my whistle? Didn't you see my signal?" he demanded.

I shook my head.

The cop sighed. "I'd better go home. I don't seem to be doing much good around here."

I threw the car into reverse and backed away from the fire plug.

"If you're going to drive much," yelled the cop, "I'd have the car painted red on one side and blue on the other, so the witnesses will contradict one another."

"What kind of cops do they have in Mt. Kisco?" I asked my wife as we headed for home.

"I wouldn't know," she deadpanned. "Maybe he's Milton Berle's brother."

There are two stone posts flanking the drive which leads up to my house. I got past them without a scratch—also without the rear bumper. That did it.

Since then, I've never been behind a wheel. When we go driving, I sit in the back seat and read the Burma Shave signs. The only concession I've made to the Automotive Age is to learn how to fold a road map.

Driver's Seat, 1938, JACOB KAINEN. National Museum of American Art, Smithsonian Institution. Gift of Jacob Kainen.

Developing Comprehension Skills

1. Why was the narrator going to learn to drive?

2. How would you describe the type of instructions the narrator's wife gave him?

3. For what reasons do you think the narrator decided to give up learning to drive?

4. Would you say that the events described in this essay are totally impossible? Or is there anything believable about the situation? Explain your answer.

Reading Literature: Humorous Sketches

1. **Contrasting Tones.** In this selection, the narrator and the policeman express different attitudes toward the subject. What is the narrator's attitude about learning to drive? What words does the narrator say to suggest this tone? What is the policeman's tone? What words suggest this attitude?

2. **Appreciating Verbal Irony.** Sometimes the words and phrases people use can have a double meaning. This is called **verbal irony**. On the surface, the words mean one thing, usually something positive. But they are used by the speaker to mean the opposite, usually something negative. For example, the following sentence seems to be a compliment.

   Wow, you must have studied hard!

   However, suppose a classmate said the sentence to you as he saw a failing grade on your test paper. The meaning he had in mind would not be a compliment.

   Much of the humor in this selection is created by phrases with double meanings.

Explain the verbal irony—both the positive and negative meanings—in each of the following passages.
   a. "Haven't we got any colors you like?"
   b. "Those are my knees."
   c. "How long is this class going to last?"
   d. "I don't seem to be doing much good around here."

3. **Comparing Humorous Sketches.** The writers of "Punch, Brothers, Punch" and "Learning To Drive" create humor in similar ways. Compare the following parts of each humorous sketch: colorful word choice, use of exaggeration, and use of irony. Give details from the selections to support your ideas.

4. **Understanding Humor.** You know that one purpose of humor is to entertain. Another purpose of humor is to stress a serious point. In "Learning To Drive," what serious idea might the writer be trying to express?

Developing Vocabulary Skills

Understanding Allusion. In order to make an explanation clearer, a writer or speaker sometimes makes an **allusion**. That is, he or she makes a reference to a person, thing, idea, or situation that is similar to the one being discussed.

You may or may not be familiar with the references a writer or speaker makes. Sometimes, references might be about a different time period. Other times, references might deal with subjects you know little about. However, you should be able to figure out the general idea of each allusion. Look for clues in the context of the passage.

For example, in this selection you may not be familiar with Gene Autry. However, you can infer that Gene Autry is a person because the policeman calls the narrator by that name. You might infer that Gene Autry has something to do with spectacular motions—similar to the narrator's driving. You also might infer that Gene Autry does tricks—such as picking up a handkerchief with his teeth.

Explain what you think each of the following allusions refers to. Use the context clues in the selection.

    a. Milton Berle
    b. Burma Shave signs

Developing Writing Skills

1. **Writing About Tone.** Although the topic of "Learning To Drive" is serious, the tone used by the writer is humorous. Write an essay of one or more paragraphs explaining how the writer develops a humorous tone.

    Pre-Writing. Skim the story. Which of the following parts contribute to the humor: setting, narrator's words, narrator's thoughts, wife's words, policeman's words, action? On your paper, list any specific examples of humor that you find. Then arrange the examples in order of importance.

    Writing. Begin your essay with a clear topic sentence or a short introductory paragraph. Present at least three examples of how the writer develops the humor in the selection. End the essay with a concluding sentence or short concluding paragraph that restates the main idea.

    Revising. Ask another person to read your paragraph. Can the person identify three ways in which the writer of "Learning To Drive" creates a humorous tone? If not, a part of your essay must be confusing. Rewrite that section in order to provide clear examples.

2. **Writing a Humorous Story.** The narrator of "Learning To Drive" presents the ridiculous side of an event. He exaggerates details and tries to entertain the reader. Think about a humorous event that you experienced, or make up an event. Write a humorous account of the story. You may use colorful language, exaggeration, or irony to develop the humor.

Developing Skills in Study and Research

Using the Thesaurus. A **thesaurus** is a book that lists groups of synonyms. The words in each group have different connotations, or emotional meanings. You use a thesaurus when you need to find a word to express your exact meaning.

Review the first draft of the biographical report you wrote. If you have not written the report, use another piece of your writing for this exercise. Skim the report or other writing to locate five descriptive words. List them on a separate paper. Next to each word, write a brief explanation of the connotation, or feeling, you want the word to express. Then locate each word in a thesaurus. Select a synonym listed in the thesaurus that expresses the connotation more exactly than your original word. Revise your writing to include the new words.

Articles

Informal essays are written from an author's personal experience or about an author's own ideas. **Articles**, however are formal essays. They are not drawn from personal experiences. The author of an article gathers facts by reading, observation, and talking with experts. In fact, the author of an article may be an expert on the subject himself or herself. People turn to articles when they want information.

Subway— 14th Street (detail), 1930, REGINALD MARSH. Hunter Museum of Art, Chattanooga, Tennessee.

People

ISAAC ASIMOV

This next selection is a chapter from a book. In it, Isaac Asimov points out some notable facts and figures about world population. As you read, see if you can identify a general message Asimov may be leading toward in his book.

Take a look around you. What do you see?

You can see almost anything, depending on where you are. You might see a mountain with snow on top, or just snow, or a camel, or a palm tree, or a lot of automobiles, or the ocean or the inside of a building. The one thing you are very likely to see, though, wherever you are, is other people.

If you are at home, you might see your mother and father, or your sisters and brothers, if you have any. If you are outside, you might see nobody at all, but it's more likely you'll see a few people, anyway. If you are in a city, you will probably see a great many people.

If you are at a bullfight, a baseball game or some great public celebration, you will see many thousands of people crowded so closely together you will see almost nothing else.

When you see a great many people in such a crowd, does it ever make you wonder how many people there may be in the whole world, altogether? Actually, nobody knows exactly, for it is difficult to count all those people. Some nations take a "census" every once in a while. When they do that, they count the number of people within their borders and get other information as well.

The first nation to do this in modern times was the United States. It took its first census in 1790 and has continued to take another one every ten years since then. Great Britain and France each started census-taking in 1801. Most of the nations on Earth take censuses now, but they don't all do it very accurately and sometimes certain nations wait a long time between censuses. About twenty nations have never taken a census at all.

Still, suppose we start with the United States, which has a good record when it comes to taking censuses. According to the census taken in 1980, the number of people in the United States as of April 1, 1980, was

226,504,825. That sounds very accurate, but actually it is quite possible that not everybody was counted. Even in the United States, which uses the most modern methods for counting people, some were probably missed (or maybe some people were counted twice).

Even so, we can make an "estimate" by taking a reasonable figure based on everything we know, without trying to make it too exact. We can say that the number of people in the United States (its "population") was about 235,664,000 in 1984.

If we add in the censuses that other nations have taken, and make estimates for what has happened since those censuses were taken—and if we do our best to figure out reasonable populations for those nations that don't take censuses—we can get a figure for the total world population. The best estimate that we can make is that in 1984 the total world population was 4,715,000,000. That's four billion seven hundred and fifteen million people. The total number of people in the world is about twenty times as many as the total number of people in the United States.

If you look at a map of the world or, better yet, at a globe, you will see that the United States spreads out over more of the world than most other nations do. It has a large "area"; so it's no wonder it has a lot of people in it.

Just the same, the United States is not the most populous nation in the world; that is, it does not have the most people. It is actually the fourth most populous nation. Three other nations, also large in area, are more populous.

The most populous nation in the world is China. It doesn't take censuses as often as the United States, so there is some argument as to just how many people there are in China. A reasonable estimate is that China now has a population of about 1,036,600,000. This is more than four times as many people as the United States has. More than one-fifth of all the people in the world live in China.

The second most populous nation is India, with 723,533,000 people. Then comes the Soviet Union with 274,992,000.

These four giant nations, China, India, the Soviet Union and the United States, have a total population of 2,270,789,000. This is more than half of all the people in the world. The other half is divided up among about 150 nations, some of which are very small. There is one tiny nation called Nauru that occupies a small island in the Pacific Ocean. It has a total population of only 7,000.

Of course it isn't at all surprising that a huge nation like China should contain more people than a tiny nation like Nauru. It will make more sense if we figure out some way of talking about population that takes area into account, also.

One way to do this is to imagine all the people in the world spread out evenly. Then we can calculate how many people there are in a particular bit of area. Instead of saying how many people there are altogether, we can talk about so many people in every bit of area of such and such a size. We call that the "population density."

For a particular bit of area suppose we use a "square kilometer": that is, a square with each side one kilometer long. If you walk briskly, you can probably walk one kilometer in fifteen minutes. That means you can walk all around the border of one square kilometer in an hour, or a little less. You see, then, that one square kilometer isn't a very big patch of land. In fact, the surface of the whole Earth has an area of about 510,000,000 square kilometers.

Of course, about 70 percent of Earth's area is covered by ocean. People don't live on the ocean, except when they're on ships for a while, so we shouldn't count it as living area. That still leaves 150,000,000 square kilometers of land in the world.

Suppose we can imagine that the 4,715,000,000 people on Earth are spread out evenly over all the 150,000,000 square kilometers of land. In that case, there will be about thirty-two people on every square kilometer of land. We can say then that the average population density on Earth right now is "thirty-two per square kilometer."

If we're going to do a lot of talking about population density, it might be convenient, and save writing time, to use a shorthand way of saying "people per square kilometer." One way of doing that is to use the following abbreviation: $/km^2$. Then we can say that the average population density on Earth right now is $32/km^2$. That abbreviation still means that there are thirty-two people on every square kilometer of land

surface, and you should still read it as "thirty-two people per square kilometer."

Let's look at the world's average population density another way. Suppose you are 160 centimeters (5 feet, 3 inches) tall and are standing on a large piece of very flat land. In every direction you see the horizon, the line where the land seems to meet the sky. From the height of your eyes, you see the horizon at a distance of about 4½ kilometers.

That means that as you turn around you can see a circle of land that is about sixty-five square kilometers in area. In all that space you could see, on the average, about two thousand people. (Naturally, many of them would be inside houses.)

That is what you would see on the average, but you know that it's not what you would really see. There are places where you would see far fewer than two thousand people and places where you would see far more than two thousand people. The point is that the world's population is not spread out evenly.

Suppose you were standing somewhere on the large icy continent of Antarctica. You would not see anybody. Although Antarctica has an area of 14,000,000 square kilometers, it is so cold and unpleasant that no people live there at all. Occasionally, some scientists come to Antarctica for some weeks or months in order to study it, but that doesn't count. This means that Antarctica, which includes nearly 1/10 of all the land area in the world, has an average density of population of $0/km^2$.

Fifth Avenue and Forty-Second Street, 1933, JOHN MARIN. The Phillips Collection, Washington, D.C.

On the other hand, consider the little European nation of The Netherlands. It has an area of 32,600 square kilometers. It is only 1/450 as large as Antarctica, but it has a population of about 14,490,000. Its average density of population (if its people were spread out evenly over its area) would be 445/km². This density is fourteen times the world average.

Now let's consider the population densities of the four giant nations of the world.

China has an area of 9,561,000 square kilometers. As far as area is concerned, it is the third largest nation in the world. China takes up 1/16 of all the land area of the world. If its 1,036,600,000 people were spread out evenly over its area, there would be 108 people in every square kilometer. China's average population density is 108/km². This is over three times the world average, but it is only a quarter the average population density of The Netherlands.

India has fewer people than China, but it has a considerably smaller area, too. India is only 3,268,000 square kilometers in area. There is so much less space in which to imagine its population spread over evenly that, although the Indian population is smaller than the Chinese, there are more Indians in each square kilometer of India than there are Chinese in each square kilometer of China. The average population density of India is 221/km². This is twice that of China, but is still less than half that of The Netherlands.

The Soviet Union is the largest nation in the world in area. It takes up 22,274,900 square kilometers, or about 1/7 of all the land area in the world. Its 274,992,000 people have so much room that the average population density of the Soviet Union is only 12/km². This is less than half the world average.

The United States is almost as large in area as China. The United States has an area of 9,363,000 square kilometers, but it has only a quarter of China's population. The average population density of the United States is about 25/km², which is just a little under the world average.

Just as some nations have a denser population than other nations, so within each nation there are regions that are more densely populated than other regions. Suppose we consider the United States, for instance, which is made up of fifty different states. The largest state, Alaska, has an area of 1,510,000 square kilometers. It includes 1/6 of all the land in the United States.

However, it has the smallest population of any state in the United States—400,481.

The average population density in Alaska is only 0.26/km². (Does this sound as though there is only about 1/4 of a person in every square kilometer? You don't have to imagine people divided into fourths. What 0.26 /km² means is that there is, on the average, one person in Alaska for every four square kilometers of land.)

What about Rhode Island, which is the smallest of the fifty states? Its area is only 3,140 square kilometers, but its population is 947,154, or 2½ times the population of Alaska. The average population density in Rhode Island is 302/km², which is nearly 1,160 times as high as that of Alaska. Rhode Island is more densely populated than India, but is less densely populated than The Netherlands.

People are most crowded in cities, of course. New York City has an area of 950 square kilometers. It is nearly 1/3 as large as the state of Rhode Island in area, but its population is 7,071,030, which is 7.5 times as great as that of Rhode Island. The average population density of New York City is 7,500/km², 300 times as great as that of the United States as a whole. It is 17 times as densely populated as The Netherlands.

Even in New York City, there are differences in density. The city is made up of five boroughs, and the one with the smallest population is Richmond. Richmond has a population of 352,121 people and an area of 192 square kilometers. The average population density of Richmond is 1,834/km², about a quarter of that of New York City as a whole.

Compare this with the borough of Manhattan, which has the smallest area of any of the five boroughs. The area of Manhattan is 81 square kilometers, but it has a population of 1,510,000. This means that the average population density of Manhattan is $18,642/km^2$, which is more than twice that of New York City as a whole. Manhattan is 42 times as densely populated as The Netherlands.

Every nation in the world has areas that are thinly populated and other areas that are more thickly populated. In the Soviet Union, the large Asian section known as Siberia has an average population density of only $3/km^2$. The average population density of the Ukraine in the southwestern part of the Soviet Union is $82/km^2$, which is 27 times as great as that of Siberia. In China, its westernmost province of Sinkiang has an average population density of only $8/km^2$, while its coastal province of Kiangsu has one of $600/km^2$, which is 75 times as great.

You can see, then, that though there are a great many people on Earth, they are very unevenly distributed. There are vast areas such as Antarctica, Alaska, and Siberia, where there are very few people. Most of the people in the world are crowded into a small part of the land area.

Does this mean that there is plenty of room for people to spread into? Perhaps not. The empty places are empty because they are very cold, very dry, or very mountainous. People don't live in large numbers in Siberia or Alaska or Greenland or the Sahara Desert or Sinkiang or Antarctica, because it isn't very pleasant to live there. In fact, you might wonder if the various parts of the world aren't holding just about as many people as they can hold.

That's an interesting question. It is, perhaps, just about the most important question that is facing the world today. Does the world hold as many people as it can hold, or is there room for more?

In order to answer this question, it is not enough to know how many people there are in the world right now. It would help to know how many people there were in the world in past ages. We have to know whether the number of people in the world has always been about the same, or whether it has been changing. If it has been changing, we have to know how it has been changing.

Once we learn that, we might be able to estimate what the population will be like in the future. Then, perhaps, we can figure out where the world stands as far as population is concerned.

Developing Comprehension Skills

1. Explain the term *population density*.

2. List the four most populous nations and the total population of each. Which of the four giant nations of the world is most crowded?

3. Most of the article "People" is objective. It mainly presents factual information. However, Asimov also includes several subjective, or personal, ideas that cannot be proven. Decide whether each of the following is a statement of fact or personal opinion.

   a. The United States took its first census in 1790.

   b. China does not take censuses as often as the United States.

   c. Antarctica is cold and unpleasant.

   d. Whether the world has room for more people is the most important question facing society today.

4. Is it important for you to know facts about the population of the world? Why or why not?

Reading Literature: Articles

1. **Recognizing Structure.** Asimov begins his essay with a question: "What do you see?" Throughout the article, he answers the question by presenting details about people. How does Asimov end the article? How does the conclusion tie the essay together?

2. **Determining the Organization of Ideas.** Review the section of the article about population density. Begin with paragraph 9 on page 527. End with paragraph 3 on page 531. In this section, does Asimov begin with the general idea and then give detailed examples? Or does he start with facts and details and then build up to the main point? Why do you think he organizes the information about population density in this way?

3. **Identifying Main Ideas.** In the essay, Asimov presents many facts about people. Summarize the information by listing the three or four main ideas of the article.

4. **Analyzing Tone.** Select from the following list the word that best describes the tone of the essay. Then find at least three direct statements from the essay that are examples of this tone.

   humorous   objective
   persuasive   angry

Developing Vocabulary Skills

Inferring Word Meaning. You have studied several types of context clues. **Definition or restatement** clues directly state the meaning of an unfamiliar word. **Comparison** and **contrast** clues tell what the unfamiliar word is like or unlike. **Synonym** and **antonym** clues suggest words that mean the same as or the opposite of the unfamiliar word.

Sometimes the context does not give obvious clues to the meaning of an unfamiliar word. However, the general idea of the whole paragraph can suggest the meaning. Whenever you use the main idea to figure out a word, you infer the meaning of the word. Here is an example.

He was an *avid* science fiction reader. Every spare moment he spent researching books about space travel. He had read all the latest scientific thrillers.

From the main idea, you can conclude that *avid* means "eager and enthusiastic."

Each of the following passages uses a word from a selection you have read. Determine the meaning of the underlined word by using one of the following methods: **definition or restatement** clue, **comparison** clue, **contrast** clue, **synonym** clue, **antonym** clue, or **inference from main idea**. On your paper, write the word, its meaning, and the method you used.

1. At a great public celebration there are always many thousands of people. Because of the crowds that attend, each <u>festivity</u> has to be carefully planned.

2. How many people are there in the whole world? No one knows the exact number. However, some nations occasionally take a <u>census</u>. They count the number of people within their borders. Other information also is collected.

3. The U.S. census reported that there were 226,504,825 people living in the United States as of April 1, 1980. This statement sounds very <u>accurate</u>, but the total is probably wrong by several thousand.

4. In every direction you could see the <u>horizon</u>, the line where land seems to meet the sky.

5. The United States is not the most <u>populous</u> nation in the world; that is, it does not have the most people.

6. His <u>calculation</u> was similar to my estimate.

7. Antarctica is so <u>sparsely</u> populated that it makes Siberia seem densely populated.

8. Suppose the people on Earth were spread out evenly. There would be thirty-two people on every square kilometer of land. The average <u>population density</u> on Earth would then be thirty-two per square kilometer.

Developing Writing Skills

1. **Writing a Final Draft.** You have written the first draft of a five-paragraph biographical report. You have also read your report to a group whose members have provided you with questions to help you make revisions. (If you have not completed these stages of report writing, see pages 495, 501, 510, and 520.) Review the first draft of your report. Make any necessary changes and write the final version.

   Pre-Writing. Carefully read the report. You might find a word, phrase, or sentence that does not give a clear idea. If so, make a new word choice or add key words to show the relationship of ideas. If you find a detail that is unrelated to its paragraph, plan to drop it. Think about whether you have omitted an important piece of information about the person. Decide where the detail would best fit. Check the order of the ideas in your report.

   Writing. Rewrite those parts of your report where you need to add or delete words or change the order of ideas. Be sure that each sentence and paragraph builds on the one before it.

   Revising. Proofread the final copy of the report. First, check your facts. Make sure names, dates, places, and other pieces of information are correct. Use your note cards to help you do this. Then, check your writing. Be sure you have used complete sentences. Check for correct capitalization, punctuation, and spelling. Once you have proofread your report and are satisfied that it has no errors, turn in your final, clean copy to your teacher.

2. **Imagining a Future Place.** In the essay "People," Asimov discusses ideas about future populations. Imagine what the place where you live will be like one hundred years from now. Will it be crowded, or will there hardly be any people? Will the landscape be the same? What will the climate be? What sort of buildings would you see? Write one to three paragraphs describing this future setting. Use words that appeal to the senses. Try to make all the details clear.

Developing Skills in Study and Research

Using Graphs. Sometimes the information about a topic has many different facts and numbers in it. Detailed factual information often can be arranged more clearly in a graphic, or artistic, way than in a paragraph. A **graph** is a type of diagram that shows the relationships of facts.

Examine the following graph. Using the information on the graph, decide if the statements below the graph are true or false.

1980 Population (in millions)

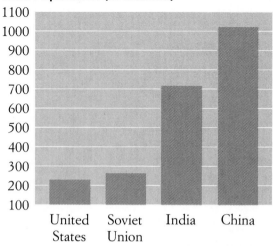

1. There are approximately 235 million people in the United States.

2. There are more people in China than in the Soviet Union and the United States combined.

3. There are fewer people in India than in the United States and Soviet Union combined.

How Smart Are Dolphins?

RUSSELL FREEDMAN

Like "People," this article has a strong logical organization. As you read, watch for the development of its arguments. You should be able to identify about eight separate stages in the answer to the question.

Malia was smart. She learned quickly, mastering many tricks after two or three lessons. She seemed to enjoy performing for audiences at Sea Life Park in Hawaii. She was so clever that her trainers, Karen Pryor and Ingrid Kang, decided to try something new.

Pryor and Kang felt that Malia's act had become too slick and polished. The dolphin knew her routines perfectly. She never made mistakes. There were no surprises. To make Malia's act more lively and interesting, Pryor and Kang decided to show their audiences how a dolphin is trained. They would teach Malia a brand-new trick at each show. When she learned the trick, she would be rewarded with a fish.

In the following days, Malia learned one new trick after another. She was rewarded only for learning something new, not for performing her old tricks. After fourteen shows, the dolphin had learned fourteen new tricks. Pryor and Kang were running out of new tricks to teach her. At one show, they couldn't come up with anything new.

Malia solved the problem herself. She began to perform new stunts she made up herself. She swam on her back with her tail in the air. She threw herself into the air backward and made an arching leap upside down. She jumped from the water and spun like a top in mid-air.

Malia had not been taught these tricks and had never performed them before. She had apparently figured out on her own that she would not be rewarded for performing old tricks. She could earn her reward only by doing something new. She seemed to realize that it didn't matter what she did, as long as she hadn't done it before.

In show after show, Malia came up with new and astonishing stunts. She performed tricks on her own that her trainers never would have imagined. The dolphin appeared to understand the abstract principle that only novelty would win a reward. She seemed to be thinking, not just learning tricks in an automatic way.

Karen Pryor later described Malia's behavior in her book, *Lads Before the Wind*: "Sometimes she was very excited when she saw us in the mornings. Ingrid and I had the unscientific feeling that she sat in her holding tank all night thinking up stuff and rushed into the first show with an air of: 'Wait till you see this one.'"

Inspired by Malia's remarkable behavior, her trainers decided to try the same thing with another dolphin, Hou. They wanted to see if Hou would also catch on to the idea that only novelty would be rewarded. This time they would keep a careful record of everything that happened.

It took a while for Hou to understand what the trainers wanted, but she did catch on. Like Malia, she began to make up and perform one new trick after another.

When humans display this kind of learning, we often call it "imagination" or "creativity." It appeared that such creativity could show up in a dolphin as well. Karen Pryor reported on these experiments in a scientific paper entitled, "The Creative Porpoise."

It seemed that Malia and Hou had performed a feat of intelligence highly unusual in any animal. Did the experiments really prove that?

Karen Pryor tried a similar experiment with pigeons. The pigeons were put through the same kind of training as the dolphins. Surprisingly, they responded in the same way. They learned that they would be rewarded only for doing something new, something they hadn't learned to do before. The pigeons invented such tricks as lying on their backs, standing with both feet on one wing, and hovering two inches above the floor. Pigeons are not considered mental giants, but in this case they seemed as "creative" as the dolphins.

Karen Pryor concluded that the experiments did not, after all, show how smart dolphins are. Given the same kind of training, pigeons were capable of learning the same lesson—that only new behavior would be rewarded. Apparently, the dol-

Dusky dolphins. Photo Researchers, Inc., New York.
© Photograph by Wm. Curtsinger.

phins' feat did not require super-intelligence.

These experiments show how difficult it is to understand the intelligence of a creature different from ourselves. We can test an animal, but we don't always know how to interpret the results.

It's hard enough to measure the intelligence of our fellow humans. It is even more difficult to compare the intelligence of different animals, because their brains work in different ways. Each creature responds to the world around it in its own special way.

Humans live in a world of sight. We learn by seeing. Our eyes tell us a great deal of what we know about the world. A dog, on the other hand, lives in a world of smells. It gets most of its information through its nose, not its eyes. If a dog could design an intelligence test for humans, it might ask a human to follow a scent-trail through a forest. The dog in charge of this test would probably conclude that we are very stupid creatures indeed.

Dolphins live in a world of sound. Sounds tell them most of what they need to know about their underwater world. While it is not possible to see very far under water, sounds travel clearly through the water. Dolphins stay in touch with each other by sending sounds through the water. They also scan the waters around them by means of echo-location. They send out high-frequency sounds, just as bats do. The sounds bounce off objects, and the echoes bring back information about the size of the object, its shape, its texture, and its dis-

tance. By means of echo-location, a dolphin can identify a shark that is too far away to be seen.

Dolphins have much keener hearing than humans. They pick up sounds that we can't hear at all. A dolphin's acoustic nerve, which sends information to the brain, is three to four times bigger than the same nerve in humans. And a dolphin has a much larger part of its brain devoted to hearing than a human has.

Because each creature has a different kind of brain and lives in a special world of its own, it is very tricky to compare animals by means of intelligence tests. A test that is fair to one animal might not be fair to another. In general, however, intelligence is closely linked to learning ability. An animal's intelligence depends, in part, on how fast it can learn, how much it can learn, and how long it can remember.

Anyone who has ever worked with dolphins agrees that they are very intelligent. They learn quickly, they have long memories, and they seem capable of reasoning. They exchange a wide variety of underwater sounds, which they apparently use to send each other messages. Dolphins also have large, complex brains. Some scientists suspect that dolphins are more intelligent than any other animal. The question is: how smart are they?

We can gain a rough idea of an animal's intelligence by looking at its brain. As a rule, smarter animals have bigger and more complex brains, but a giant brain doesn't always mean a giant intelligence.

The biggest brains on this planet belong to whales and elephants. A sperm whale has a brain that weighs about 9,000 grams, nearly 20 pounds. That's the largest brain that has ever existed on earth. An elephant's brain weighs about 6,000 grams. A bottlenosed dolphin, a member of the whale family, has a brain of about 1,600 grams. The human brain is somewhat smaller, averaging about 1,400 grams.

Although whales and elephants have the biggest brains, they don't seem to be the smartest animals on earth. Brain size is important, but the size of the brain compared to the size of the body also is important. By that reckoning, humans are the brainiest creatures on earth.

The brain of an average man accounts for about two percent of his body weight. We might say that each pound of human brain is in charge of about 50 pounds of body. On this scale, dolphins rank next to humans. While a dolphin's brain is bigger than a human's, a dolphin's body also is bigger. Each pound of dolphin brain is in charge of about 85 pounds of dolphin body. Each pound of elephant's brain, in comparison, must handle about 1,000 pounds of body. Much of the elephant's big brain is involved in managing the functions of its huge body. An elephant is smart, but it doesn't have as many brain cells left over for learning as a dolphin or a human.

Next to humans, then, dolphins have the biggest brains for their size. They also have extremely complex brains—another sign of intelligence. In some ways, the dolphin brain is even more intricate and complex than the human brain. However, it is also quite different. The human brain is longer than it is wide. A dolphin's brain is wider than it is long, and it is quite high. The part of the dolphin brain that receives and analyzes sounds appears to be much larger and more complex than in humans. There are other important differences, too. We have barely begun to understand the workings of the human brain, and we know much less about the dolphin brain. So it's difficult to compare them. There is no question, however, that the dolphin has the brain of a highly intelligent animal.

Another way to judge the dolphin's intelligence is by its behavior. We know surprisingly little about the behavior of dolphins in the wild. Because they live in the ocean and move rapidly over long distances, human observers have not been able to spend more than brief moments with them. It is extremely difficult to approach a group of dolphins in a boat and stay with them long enough to study their behavior. The animals are visible briefly as they surface to breathe. Then they are lost to view as they move on under the water.

We do know that dolphins travel together in groups of about twenty or more individuals. At certain times of the year, many of these groups come together to form large herds that may number thousands of dolphins.

Dolphins have been seen to cooperate with each other in a number of ways. They often work together when they hunt for food. A group of dolphins will spread out in underwater formation and advance toward a school of anchovies. They herd the anchovies up toward the ocean surface, where they close in to feed on them.

Dolphins also have been seen to aid and protect members of their group. A shark that tries to attack a dolphin may find itself surrounded by other dolphins. One by one, the dolphins charge the shark at high speed, battering it to death with their hard beaks.

If a dolphin is ill or injured and can't rise to the surface for air, other dolphins rush over and take turns lifting the injured animal to the surface, so it can breathe.

These appear to be intelligent acts. Yet many other animals cooperate in similar ways. Lions and wolves are experts at cooperative hunting. Animals as different as elephants, baboons, and musk oxen cooperate to save a member of their own group who is in danger. In fact, ants cooperate in the same ways when they hunt and when they defend their nests and young from enemies. What seems to be intelligent behavior often turns out to be purely instinctive. We just don't know enough about wild dolphins to draw conclusions about their intelligence.

The best evidence for dolphins' intelligence comes from their behavior in captivity. Bottlenosed dolphins are famous as star performers in seaquariums. They can master a wide variety of complex tricks and stunts. They catch on quickly and often learn a trick simply by watching other dolphins perform it. Trainers say that they learn faster than any other animal.

A standard laboratory test shows just how quickly they can learn. An animal can be trained to push a lever in order to earn a reward. It takes hundreds of trials for a rhesus monkey to learn to do this. Dolphins catch on in about 20 trials.

Besides being quick learners, dolphins are talented mimics—another sign of intelligence. Sometimes they can watch an action only once and then repeat it. One dolphin watched a diver use a mechanical scraper to clean an observation window in its tank. When given the scraper, the dolphin used it just as the diver had.

The dolphin's powers of imitation were once demonstrated by Malia and Hou, the two "creative" dolphins who taught themselves new tricks at Sea Life Park in Hawaii. Malia and Hou lived in separate holding tanks off the main tank where they gave shows for the public. Each dolphin had been trained separately and each performed a different set of tricks.

One day a mix-up occurred. The dolphins were accidentally switched and put in the wrong holding tanks. When it was time for Malia to enter the main tank and begin her routine, Hou appeared instead. The woman who was conducting the show that day didn't realize what had happened. She began to give Malia's cues to Hou. The dolphin seemed upset, but she went ahead and performed all of Malia's tricks. Her performance wasn't perfect, but it was good enough to fool the audience.

When it was Malia's turn to come out and perform, she made it through all of

Hou's tricks. The two dolphins had learned each other's routines simply by watching.

With their keen hearing, dolphins also are experts at imitating sounds. Some researchers say that not only can they imitate the human voice, but they can actually learn the meaning of certain words.

Dolphins seem to send each other messages by means of underwater sounds. To the human ear, dolphin sounds resemble whistles, clicks, blats, mews, yelps, wails, creaks, and squeaks. When dolphins are placed in separate tanks linked by a sound system, they will whistle back and forth as long as they can hear each other. Some researchers believe that these sounds may represent a complex pattern of speech, and that dolphins actually talk to each other by means of their own language.

Do dolphins really communicate in sophisticated ways? Scientists have conducted a number of experiments in attempts to find out.

Jarvis Bastian, a psychologist at the University of California at Davis, tried to determine if one dolphin can send specific information to another. Bastian trained two dolphins named Buzz and Doris to push underwater levers. By pushing the correct lever, they would earn their reward, a tasty fish. If they saw a flashing signal light, they had to push the lever on the left. If they saw a steady light, they had to push the lever on the right.

This is an easy lesson for dolphins. Buzz and Doris both learned it quickly. Then they were placed in a large tank divided by a curtain. They could hear but not see each

Spotted dolphins, Hawaii. Photo Researchers, Inc., New York. © Photograph by Wm. Curtsinger.

other. The signal light was on Doris's side of the tank. The two levers were on Buzz's side. If Buzz pushed the correct lever with his beak, both dolphins would get a fish. Only Doris could see the signal light. Would she be able to tell Buzz which lever to push?

Before long, Doris was sounding off when the light went on, and Buzz was picking the correct lever nine times out of ten. At first the researchers could not figure out how Doris was telling Buzz which lever to push. They finally realized that Doris was making clicking sounds when she saw the steady light, but she was keeping quiet when she saw the flashing light. Did this mean that Doris was deliberately sending information to Buzz?

Buzz was removed from his side of the tank. Doris was tested again with the signal light. She continued to click when she saw a steady light, even though she knew that Buzz wasn't there to push the lever.

Doris had learned to make clicking sounds to earn a reward when the steady light went on. Buzz had learned by trial and error what the clicking sounds meant. The two dolphins were not really communicating however. Buzz could have learned the same thing if the researchers had beeped a horn as a signal to push the lever on the right. Here was another example of how hard it is to set up a test and interpret the results correctly.

Despite years of study, researchers have never come up with convincing evidence that dolphins have a complex language. Although dolphins exchange many sounds, we have no idea what those sounds mean. As one scientist put it, "It's a bit like a man from outer space tapping into the Bell System center trying to make sense of all the beeps and switching."

Some scientists suggest that dolphins may communicate in a way that is unlike anything we can imagine. By sending out high-frequency sounds, a dolphin apparently can "see" into an object under the water. The sounds that bounce back from the object tell the dolphin about its size, shape, texture, and distance. From the return echo, for instance, a dolphin can tell the difference between a sheet of aluminum and a sheet of copper when both are painted the same color.

One dolphin may be able to describe an underwater object to another by re-creating the sounds that bounce back from that object. Instead of "saying" a single word that stands for "shark," for example, the dolphin would repeat the sounds that bounce back from the shark. It would create a sound-picture of the shark, which it could pass along to other dolphins, telling them how big it is, how far away it is, and possibly even what kind of shark it is.

At the moment, that is an unproven theory. The sounds exchanged by dolphins remain an unsolved mystery.

The dolphin's mind remains a mystery, too. While everyone agrees that dolphins are smart, they don't agree on how smart they really are. Karen Pryor, who trained many dolphins at Sea Life Park, once guessed that dolphins rank in intelligence somewhere between dogs and chimpanzees. John Lilly, a devoted student of dolphins who has written many books about them, believes that they may be as intelligent as humans. "It is possible that their intelligence is comparable to ours," says Lilly, "but in a strange fashion."

Other scientists aren't too sure. According to them, we just don't have enough evidence to understand the dolphin mind or to judge the dolphin's intelligence.

Developing Comprehension Skills

1. What did Malia and Hou do that seemed creative to their trainers?

2. Why is it difficult to compare the intelligence of different animals?

3. The writer discusses dolphins' behavior both in the wild and in captivity. He states that "The best evidence for dolphins' intelligence comes from their behavior in captivity." Is this statement a fact or an opinion? What information about dolphins led the writer to this statement?

4. What reasons do you have to trust Pryor's opinions about dolphins?

5. This article presents factual information about dolphins. Would you rather read a nonfiction selection such as this, or a fictional story about dolphins? Why?

Reading Literature: Articles

1. **Determining Facts.** This article presents information about dolphins. Most of the statements are factual, but some report theories or possible interpretations. List five facts from the article.

2. **Explaining the Main Idea.** Reread the final paragraphs of the article. What conclusion does the writer draw in answer to the question: How smart are dolphins?

3. **Analyzing the Title.** Why do you think the writer wrote the title in the form of a question? How does this title relate to the rest of the essay?

Developing Vocabulary Skills

Reviewing Ways To Define Words. You have studied three ways to figure out the meaning of an unfamiliar word. One way is to use **context clues**. A second way is to use **word parts**—base words and affixes. A third way is to use a **dictionary**.

The following sentences use words from the selections you have read. Select the best way to figure out the meaning of each underlined word. On your paper, write the word, its meaning, and the method you used to determine the meaning.

1. A dolphin's <u>acoustic nerve</u>, which is the nerve that sends sound information to the brain, is well developed.

2. Pryor and Kang felt that Malia's act had become too polished. The dolphin knew her routines perfectly. She never made mistakes.

3. Anne recalled the quarrels and bickering in her family.

4. Jews were forbidden to visit the opera, the cinema, and other places of entertainment.

5. Stephen and Jane heard the stevedores.

6. Davy Crockett wrote that a man could become wolfish in certain situations.

Developing Writing Skills

1. **Summarizing Factual Information.** The writer of this selection poses the question, "How smart are dolphins?" Write an answer to the question, using facts from the selection. Limit your answer to three paragraphs in length.

   Pre-Writing. Skim the essay. Make a list of the ways that scientists use to measure animal intelligence. For each, find an example about Malia or Hou that shows the degree of the dolphin's intelligence. Arrange these facts in order of importance.

   Writing. Begin with a clear topic sentence. You may write the topic sentence as a question if you wish. Then include details to explain the main idea. Present the evidence in a logical order that leads to a conclusion.

   Revising. Check to be sure that your answer has a topic sentence, at least three supporting details, and a conclusion. Does your report need transitional words; that is, words that show changes in ideas? If so, add words, such as *also* and *furthermore*, to lead the reader from one idea to the next.

2. **Imagining a Dialog.** The article suggests that dolphins communicate with one another. Suppose that animals were able to talk to humans. What do you think they might say? Choose an animal that you are familiar with. Write a dialog between the animal and a human being, perhaps yourself.

Sayings and Proverbs

A **saying** or **proverb** is usually only a sentence long. However, that sentence states an important fact about life. It may give worthwhile advice about how to behave. Besides teaching, it amuses us by the clever way it is stated. For all these reasons, proverbs stay in our memories. As you read the following selections, compare and contrast the proverbs. Which ones do you think will stay in your memory the longest?

The Peasant Dance, 1568, PIETER BRUEGEL. Kunsthistorisches Museum, Vienna. Courtesy of M. Kavaler/Art Resource, New York.

Proverbs from Many Lands

TRADITIONAL SAYINGS

As you read these proverbs, can you find some common concerns? Can you identify proverbs from different countries that say basically the same thing?

Ecuadorian: It is one thing to cackle and another to lay an egg.

Italian: He gives twice who gives quickly.

Turkish: No matter how far you have gone on a wrong road, turn back.

American: The bad worker blames his tools.

American: Never buy a pig in a poke.

Hebrew: Whoever lies down with a dog will get up with fleas.

French: As you have made your bed, so you must lie in it.

Bulgarian: Gentle words open iron gates.

Hungarian: A quarrel with a friend is like pepper in the food—it makes the friendship stronger.

American: A bird in the hand is worth two in the bush.

Lebanese: A penny in the pocket is worth ten outside of it.

American: A stitch in time saves nine.

Norwegian: A lazy man works twice.

German: Never put off till tomorrow what you can do today.

American: Make hay while the sun shines.

English: Strike while the iron is hot.

Japanese: Make haste about it if it is a good thing.

Fruit Gathering. Cuna Indian mola. Courtesy of Ann Parker.

American: You can't unscramble eggs.

English: There's no use crying over spilt milk.

American: Don't count your chickens before they are hatched.

Irish: Don't bless the fish until you land it.

American: You can't have your cake and eat it too.

English: If you want the hen's egg, you must put up with her cackling.

American: The leopard never changes its spots.

Mongolian: A wolf remains a wolf even if it has not devoured your sheep.

American: A friend in need is a friend indeed.

Russian: You cannot buy a friend with money.

Developing Comprehension Skills

1. According to the Hungarian proverb, what does a quarrel do to a friendship?

2. Many of the proverbs refer to food or animals. Why do you suppose these subjects were chosen to present facts about life?

3. What do you think the term *iron gates* means in the Bulgarian proverb?

4. The Norwegian proverb says that "A lazy man works twice." How is this possible?

5. Which proverb do you think gives the most valuable advice? Explain your answer.

Reading Literature: Sayings and Proverbs

1. **Inferring Theme.** The following proverbs all express a similar idea about behavior. Write one sentence to summarize the theme of the proverbs.

   a. Strike while the iron is hot.
   b. A lazy man works twice.
   c. Make hay while the sun shines.
   d. Never put off till tomorrow what you can do today.

2. **Identifying Tone.** Many of the proverbs have been written with similar tones, such as good-natured, preachy, or serious. Select several proverbs that you feel have the same tone. Describe the tone in your own words. Give examples from the proverbs.

3. **Explaining Symbols.** In some of the proverbs there is a **symbol**. One of the words or phrases is used to represent some other, more general idea. In the following proverb, "spilt milk" is a symbol for situations that you can't do anything about.

   There's no use crying over spilt milk.

   Select one of the following proverbs. In your own words, explain what the underlined symbol represents.

   a. The bad worker blames his <u>tools</u>.
   b. The leopard never changes its <u>spots</u>.
   c. No matter how far you have <u>gone</u> on a wrong <u>road</u>, turn back.

Chinese Proverbs

TRADITIONAL SAYINGS

The people of China have traditionally respected the wisdom gained by age and experience. How can you guess that these proverbs are not very recent?

Water and words are easy to pour, but impossible to recover.

Looking for fish? Do not climb a tree.

O eggs, never fight with stones!

A teacher can open the door, but the pupil must go through by himself.

Every day cannot be a Feast of Lanterns.

The stream far away cannot extinguish the fires nearby.

Patience and the mulberry leaf become a silk gown.

Talk does not cook rice.

To forget one's ancestors is to be a brook without a source, a tree without roots.

All the flowers of all the tomorrows are in the seeds of today.

Developing Comprehension Skills

1. In one Chinese proverb, a person who forgets ancestors is compared to two things. Name those two things.

2. What idea about education is implied in the Chinese proverb about teachers and pupils?

3. Which Chinese proverb do you like best? Why?

Reading Literature: Sayings and Proverbs

1. **Inferring Meaning.** Select any three of the Chinese proverbs. For each proverb, write one sentence explaining the main idea in your own words.

2. **Appreciating Details of Setting.** Review the Chinese proverbs. List any details you find that reveal something about the country of China.

3. **Understanding Main Ideas.** Some proverbs contain details about a specific country or society. However, the main ideas of the proverbs apply to all countries and societies. From the last two selections, choose two proverbs from two different countries. Explain how the main ideas of these proverbs apply to all persons.

Embroidery detail on woman's informal jacket, Ch'ing Dynasty, 19th Century, The Metropolitan Museum of Art, Anonymous Gift, 1946. (46.133.7)

African Proverbs

TRADITIONAL SAYINGS

As you read these proverbs, compare and contrast them to others you have read. Can you find some details that show their origin?

Wood already touched by fire is not hard to set alight.

Do not call the forest that shelters you a jungle.

No one tests the depth of a river with both feet.

He who is bitten by a snake fears a lizard.

He who asks questions cannot avoid the answers.

Those who are absent are always wrong.

There is no cure that does not cost.

Cross the river in a crowd and the crocodile won't eat you.

When the mouse laughs at the cat, there is a hole nearby.

If you climb a tree, you must climb down the same tree.

Two crocodiles, Ashanti brass goldweight, Africa.
The Field Museum of Natural History, Chicago.

Developing Comprehension Skills

1. Why should a person cross the river in a crowd, according to the African saying?

2. In the second African proverb, what connotation does *jungle* have?

3. Find one African proverb in which animals are used to represent people. Explain what you think the proverb suggests about human behavior.

4. Do you think that the proverbs you have read mostly show that people around the world are similar or different? Explain your answer?

Reading Literature: Sayings and Proverbs

1. **Making Inferences About a Culture.** Skim through the African proverbs. What details do the proverbs suggest about the country of Africa? What do the proverbs tell about the ways of life of its people?

2. **Comparing Proverbs.** What similar ideas do you find in the following Chinese and African sayings?

> To forget one's ancestors is to be a brook without a source, a tree without roots.

> Do not call the forest that shelters you a jungle.

3. **Appreciating Imagery.** Most of the proverbs you have read use colorful language. Select two proverbs that you think will be hard for you to forget because of their interesting images. Copy each proverb onto your paper. Then write a translation of each proverb in your own words.

Developing Vocabulary Skills

Defining Idioms. Some phrases mean something different from what they appear to say. These special expressions are called idioms. For example, *break off* means "to stop suddenly." Idioms are listed in the dictionary under an important word in the phrase. They are shown in dark type at the end of dictionary entries.

The following phrases are idioms taken from the proverbs you have read. Try to find each idiom in a dictionary. On your paper, write the idiom and its meaning. If you cannot locate the dictionary definition for any idiom, write your own definition. For clues, review the proverb in which the idiom appears.

> a stitch in time
> make hay
> a pig in a poke

Developing Writing Skills

1. **Comparing Literature.** Many proverbs you have read can be related to characters from selections in this text. Write a paragraph explaining why you think one specific proverb fits a certain character. Support your idea with details from the selections.

2. **Imagining an Author.** Each proverb reveals values that were important to its author. Write a paragraph describing your idea of the person who wrote your favorite proverb.

Developing Skills in Critical Thinking

Classifying Pieces of Literature. The proverbs can be classified by subjects and themes. Think of at least three different categories into which they could be divided. List at least five proverbs for each category.

CHAPTER **7** **R**eview

Using Your Skills in Reading Nonfiction

Each of the two-page introductions entitled Reading Literature is a piece of nonfiction writing. Select any one of the Reading Literature lessons in Chapters 1 through 7. Reread the lesson you choose. Then discuss these elements of nonfiction shown in the lesson: type of nonfiction, purpose, tone, and structure or organization.

Using Your Comprehension Skills

Here are two speeches from "Sherlock Holmes and the Stockbroker's Clerk," which you will read in Chapter 8. Read the speeches. Identify at least two facts and at least two opinions.

> **Holmes.** It is a case, Watson, that may prove to have something in it. There are certainly some very unusual features. And I shall be glad of the chance to hear the story again, so that I may review some of the particulars for myself.

> **Pycroft.** Well, then. I used to be a clerk in a stockbroking firm. I'd been with it five years and was doing very well, when the firm was forced to close. They gave me very good recommendations, but that didn't help the fact that I was out of work. And so I began to look around.

Using Your Vocabulary Skills

Read these sentences from Chapter 8. Tell how you would figure out the meaning of the underlined word: by word parts, by context clues, by word origins, or by the dictionary. Explain your answer. If you can determine the meaning of the word without a dictionary, tell its meaning.

1. After telling my bride about the errand I was about to undertake, I donned my greatcoat and went out the door.
2. I shall be glad of the chance to hear the story again, so that I may review some of the particulars for myself.

3. I was living in a small boarding house in an out-of-the-way corner of London. It was more economical, you know, and my funds were somewhat <u>depleted</u> by my long siege of unemployment.

4. I stood for a moment with my heart in my boots, wondering whether the whole thing was an elaborate <u>hoax</u>, when someone suddenly addressed me.

5. Don't be <u>disheartened</u> by humble appearances.

Using Your Writing Skills

Choose one of the following assignments.

1. Choose one of the following pairs of selections from this chapter. Compare and contrast them in regard to theme, tone, structure, and style. In discussing style, you may consider figures of speech, sensory images, repetition of words and phrases, or other elements.
   a. "The Diary of a Young Girl" and "The First Day of the War"
   b. "The Life of Davy Crockett" and "Punch, Brothers, Punch"
   c. "Banker Maggie Walker" and "Mama and Her Bank Account"
   d. "Learning To Drive" and "People"

2. Write a personal essay of at least two paragraphs on any topic you like. On your paper, identify the tone you wish to express, such as angry, cheerful, or thoughtful. Then copy your essay on the paper.

Using Your Skills in Critical Thinking

Of the following statements, decide which are objective and which are subjective. Remember, an objective statement does not contain opinions. A subjective statement expresses a personal view. Explain your answers.

1. There are too many people in the world.

2. The number of people in the world is constantly growing.

3. China has a higher population density than the United States.

4. The United States ought to increase its population to match China's.

5. It is important to know about such topics as world population.

CHAPTER **8**

Statue of Liberty, 1983, ROBERT RAUSCHENBERG.
Published by New York Graphic Society, Ltd., Greenwich, Connecticut.

Reading Literature: Drama

What Is Drama?

Drama is writing that is meant to be performed. Drama relies on the characters' words and actions to tell a story. A story written in drama form is called a **play**.

Some plays are intended to be acted out on a stage, in front of an audience. Others are written for film or television. Still others are written for radio. Both plays in this chapter are radio plays.

The History of Drama

By 500 B.C., plays were part of Greek religious ceremonies. These dramas were either tragedies or comedies. A **tragedy** usually ended with the death or punishment of the major character. A **comedy** often made fun of current events. Both types of plays used a character called the **chorus**. The chorus was actually a group of actors speaking as one voice.

From about 300 A.D. to about 900 A.D., drama was not popular. Then people started writing and performing plays about Bible stories. Gradually the topics of plays grew broader. By the 1500's, there were new tragedies and comedies and new types of plays. The greatest playwright of this time was William Shakespeare of England.

Later drama developed new forms. In the 1700's, for example, people enjoyed the type of play called **comedy of manners**. These plays poked fun at upper-class society. In the 1800's, audiences asked for **melodrama**. Melodramas usually involved thoroughly evil villains threatening unbelievably good characters. Plays of the 1900's became more realistic. Characters began to act and sound more like real people.

The Elements of Drama

A play has many of the same elements as a short story. We learn about these elements mainly through the characters' words and actions.

Plays follow certain ways of doing things. These set ways of doing things are called **conventions**. For example, a written play always shows the character's name and then his or her words.

Watson. You never cease to amaze me, Holmes. It's incredible!

Characters. The language the character uses often suggests what the character is like. It is important to note such clues that explain why a character acts as he or she does. The reasons are called **motivation**.

Plot. The events of a play are separated into scenes. Each **scene** has a different setting, either in time or place. Usually the events are shown in the order they happen. Sometimes, however, one scene may be followed by another scene showing an earlier action. This second scene is called a **flashback**. In a long play, scenes are grouped in **acts**.

Stage Directions. Stage directions are the writer's instructions for performing the play. They tell actors how to move or deliver lines. They also describe the stage set, costumes, and props. The stage directions for a radio play describe sound effects and music. In the written version of a play, stage directions are often printed in italics.

Dialog and Asides. Conversation between two or more characters is called **dialog**. Sometimes a character speaks directly to the audience. Such a comment is an **aside**. The other characters do not hear it.

Narrator. A **narrator** is a character who introduces or comments on the action. In "Sherlock Holmes and the Stockbroker's Clerk," for example, Dr. Watson acts as narrator. In "Grandpa and the Statue," both the Announcer and Young Monaghan are narrators.

How To Read a Play

1. As you read a play, imagine that you are directing it. Try to picture the production. Imagine how the stage would look.
2. Read the play aloud, if possible. Imagine the sound effects.
3. Read all stage directions carefully. Try to picture the looks, movements, and tone of voice of each character.
4. At all times, keep track of which character is speaking.

Comprehension Skills: Evaluations

Making Evaluations

Imagine that you and three friends go to a restaurant. It would be unusual for all four of you to order exactly the same things. What each person orders depends on personal taste. In the same way, choosing favorite poems or stories or plays depends on personal taste. There is no single piece of writing that is the best for everyone at all times.

Still, there are many points on which different people agree. If you and your friends want a complete dinner, you will not go to a hot dog stand. A hot dog stand might provide a quick snack. However, the four of you would agree that you have a different meal in mind. Your dinner has to have certain qualities that are not available at a stand.

Similarly, when people talk about good literature, they can come to certain agreements. Everyone agrees that good literature has certain qualities that are not found in every piece of writing.

A thoughtful reader recognizes the qualities of the materials he or she is reading. It is important to make judgments, or **evaluations**, about what you read. You now know a great deal about good literature. You have read many examples of it. You have studied its qualities. You have an idea of what most people consider important in good literature. As you choose your own reading materials, you should apply what you know. It is up to you to decide whether the things you read have the qualities of greatness.

Establishing Standards

A fair evaluation of any writing is as objective as possible. That is, the evaluation is not based on emotions. It is not overly personal. Many people should be able to agree with the evaluation and the reasons behind it. To say "This play is no good because I don't like it" is not an objective evaluation. To say "The characters in this play do not sound like any people I know" is a more objective statement.

In evaluating a piece of writing, you should consider its elements one by one. The elements that you would look at include characters, setting, plot, mood, theme, figures of speech, sound techniques, and other uses of language. You can make a fairly objective statement about each element. Next, you can decide how important each element is to the whole. Your final evaluation will consider the whole selection.

Author's Purpose.   An important element in any type of writing is the author's purpose. First you must determine what the purpose is. Then you can determine if the author achieves that purpose. For example, one purpose of a detective play is to create suspense. As you read a detective play, watch for such things as the following: clues that make you wonder, characters that seem mysterious, situations that build tension, solutions that are postponed. Then you can evaluate how successfully the author creates suspense.

Pay attention to your emotional reaction to a selection. You may recognize that a play is meant to create suspense. If you feel no excitement as you read it, you would suspect that the play did not achieve its purpose. At that point, you would search for reasons for your reaction. You should be able to explain why you feel as you do.

Exercises: **Making Evaluations**

A.   Read the following statements. Identify which are objective statements. Be able to explain your decisions.

1. The language of this character sounds like that of a real person.
2. The writer uses repetition of phrases to stress important ideas.
3. Everyone will love this play.
4. The theme of this play is boring.
5. Words with connotations of mystery help to set the mood of the play.

B.   In one type of writing, one element may be more important than others. For each type listed below, choose the more important element.

1. Short story: well developed characters, imaginative figures of speech
2. Article: strong mood, clear organization of ideas
3. Poem: effective uses of sound, appropriate setting

Vocabulary Skills: Levels of Language

Recognizing Levels of Language

What do you notice about the following sentences?

1. A break of ten minutes between the acts has been scheduled.
2. Remember to break up that long speech with a pause or two.
3. She breaks up the audience every night with her jokes.
4. That actor got his big break in *The Spectator*.
5. We'll break the set right after tonight's performance.

Each sentence uses the word *break*. Each one uses it with a different meaning. Several of these meanings are in the dictionary. Others are not. We will examine which meanings you will be likely to find. This variety in meanings shows the importance of looking at the context. It also shows the importance of recognizing the kind, or **level**, of language being used.

In general, there are two levels of English: standard and nonstandard. **Standard English** is language that is understood and accepted everywhere English is spoken. **Nonstandard English** is language that is not understood or accepted everywhere English is spoken. On each level there are different kinds of language.

When you read a formal essay, you can be sure that standard English is being used. When you read other types of literature, however, you must be aware of the level and kind of language the writer uses. This will help you determine the meanings of new words that you find.

Standard English

Standard English can be either formal or informal.

Formal standard English is language that is appropriate for serious or formal situations. It is the language of business letters and public speeches. In the sample sentences above, only the first sentence has the tone of formal English.

Informal standard English is language that is used in everyday speech. It follows the same rules of grammar as formal English, but is not as stiff. For an example, see the second of the sample sentences. Informal English also uses some words or meanings that are not used in formal English, called **colloquialisms**. Of the sample sentences, the third uses *break* in a colloquial sense.

Nonstandard English

Nonstandard English includes language that doesn't follow traditional rules of grammar. For example, the word *ain't* is considered nonstandard. Dialects, which follow their own special rules of grammar, are considered nonstandard. Two more types of nonstandard English are slang and jargon.

Slang. New words or words with new meanings are included in **slang**. Usually, only a few people use a new word. Or, the word may be used for only a short time. If most people begin using the word, and continue to use it over many years, it is no longer slang. It becomes standard English. Sample sentence 4 uses *break* in a new sense. This meaning is not in most dictionaries. Until we see whether this meaning stays in the language, we would consider it slang.

Jargon. The special words or special meanings used by a certain group make up the **jargon** of that group. Sample sentence 5 uses *break* with a meaning that is clear to people in show business. *Break the set* means to take down the scenery.

Exercise: Recognizing Levels of Language

Classify each word group as formal, informal, or nonstandard.

1. this here Frenchman
2. It's all broke!
3. the jig was up
4. I trust that Mrs. Watson has entirely recovered?
5. fade in
6. Gee, it's nice, ain't it?
7. Sherlock Holmes, you old dog!
8. off mike
9. Yeh, it made him feel good. Savin' money. Two and a half cents.
10. I am truly delighted.

Sherlock Holmes and the Stockbroker's Clerk

ARTHUR CONAN DOYLE

One of the most famous of all detectives is Sherlock Holmes. He is noted for his ability to use apparently meaningless details to determine valuable facts. As you read, try to spot the same details he does.

CHARACTERS

Dr. Watson
Sherlock Holmes
Hall Pycroft
Arthur Pinner } *played by*
Harry Pinner } *a single actor*

Porter
Newsboy
Sound-Effects Person
Music-Effects Person

ACT ONE

Watson (*narrating*). Most men, when they get married, retire from the world for a little while, and allow their lives to become circumscribed by the four walls of their homes. But most men do not have an intimate acquaintance with the master detective, Sherlock Holmes. Therefore, I cannot admit to much surprise when, three weeks after my wedding, the bell of my town house door was rung, and I opened it to find my good friend, Sherlock Holmes.

Sound. *Doorbell, followed by a brief pause, then sound of door being opened.*

Holmes. My dear Watson, I am truly delighted to see you.

Watson (*merrily*). Sherlock Holmes, you old dog! Come in, come in!

Holmes. I trust that Mrs. Watson has entirely recovered from all the little excitements connected with our adventure of the Sign of Four?

Watson. Thank you, we are both well.

Holmes. And I hope that the cares of your medical practice, coupled with the joys of marriage, have not served to dampen the interest you used to take in our little deductive problems.

Watson. On the contrary, it was only last night that I was discussing them with Mrs. Watson. That sad business of Pondicherry Lodge, for instance—and the curious mystery of the Beryl Coronet. I wouldn't mind seeing another case like that one.

Holmes. Then you don't consider your collection closed?

Watson. Not at all. I should wish nothing better than to have many more such experiences.

Holmes. Today, for example? Even though you have not been well lately?

Watson *(taken aback).* How did you ever know that, Holmes?

Holmes. You know my methods, my dear Watson. I deduced it.

Watson. But from what?

Holmes. From your slippers.

Watson. How on earth—?

Holmes. Your slippers are new. You could not have had them more than a few weeks—bought them for your wedding trip, I'd say. And yet the soles of them are slightly scorched. For a moment I thought they might have been wet and then burned in the drying. But near the instep there is a small disc of paper with the shopkeeper's marks on it. The damp would of course have removed this. You had, then, been sitting with your feet outstretched to the fire, which a man would hardly do in the middle of June if he were in full health.

Watson. You never cease to amaze me, Holmes. It's incredible!

Holmes. On the contrary, my dear Watson, it's elementary. I am afraid that I rather give myself away when I explain. Results without reasons are so much more impressive. But come, let us get to the business at hand. I have a case in Birmingham today. Will you come?

Watson. Certainly. What is the case?

Holmes. My client will tell it all to you on the train on our way down. Can you come at once?

Watson. In an instant. Let me just get my coat on and have a word with my wife.

Holmes. Very good. I shall meet you outside your door. I have some instructions for the cab driver, and I wish to take advantage of a few extra minutes in the sun.

Music. *Light theme, in and under. Out.*

Watson *(narrating).* After telling my bride about the errand I was about to undertake, I donned my greatcoat and went out the door, to find Holmes standing on my step, breathing in the fresh June air.

Sound. *Door closing.*

Holmes. Ah, here you are, Watson. I have been looking around. I see your neighbor is a doctor, too.

Watson. Yes, he bought an old practice just as I did. As a matter of fact, both our practices are of the same age. They have been here ever since the houses were built.

Holmes. Ah! Then you got hold of the better of the two.

Watson. I think I did. But how did you know?

Holmes. By the steps, my boy. Yours are worn three inches deeper than his. But we chat too long. My client is in the cab waiting for us. Come along and I'll introduce you.

Watson. With pleasure, Holmes.

Sound. *Cab door being slammed.*

Holmes. Dr. Watson, I should like to present to you a most interesting young man—Mr. Hall Pycroft.

Music. *Light theme, in and under. Out.*

Watson *(narrating).* The man whom I found myself facing was a well-built, fresh-complexioned young fellow, with a frank, honest face. He wore a neat suit of sober black, which made him look like what he was—a smart young city man, probably employed somewhere as a junior clerk. It was not until we were all in a first-class railway carriage and well

started upon our journey to Birmingham, however, that I was able to learn what trouble had driven him to Sherlock Holmes.

Sound. *Railroad wheels in softly in background and out.*

Holmes. We have a clear run here of seventy minutes. I want you, Mr. Pycroft, to tell Dr. Watson your very interesting experience, exactly as you told it to me.

Pycroft *(a pleasant-sounding young man).* With pleasure, Mr. Holmes.

Holmes. It is a case, Watson, that may prove to have something in it. There are certainly some very unusual features. And I shall be glad of the chance to hear the story again, so that I may review some of the particulars for myself.

Pycroft. Well, then. I used to be a clerk in a stockbroking firm. I'd been with it five years and was doing very well, when the firm was forced to close. They gave me very good recommendations, but that didn't help the fact that I was out of work. And so I began to look around. At last I saw a vacancy advertised at Mawson & Williams.

Watson. The firm on Lombard Street? It's the richest in London.

Pycroft. So it is, and I knew there'd be many, many applicants for the post. But, even though I had little chance of getting it, I sent in my letter of application. And, believe it or not, back came a letter saying that, if I would appear the next Monday, I might take over my new duties at once. The pay was better than I had been earning before, and the duties were the same. You couldn't have found a happier man in London than I was when I got that position.

Watson. I can well believe it.

Pycroft. But now I come to the strange part of the business. I was living in a small boarding house in an out-of-the-way corner of London. It was more economical, you know, and my funds were somewhat depleted by my long siege of unemployment. I was sitting over my poor supper, thinking about my luck *(Fading)* when the hall-porter brought in a card.

Sound. *Knock on door, door being opened.*

Porter. Mr. Pycroft? There's a gentleman downstairs to see you, sir. Sent up this card.

Pycroft. A gentleman to see me? But nobody knows I live here. Let me see the card. Hmm. "Arthur Pinner, Financial Agent." I don't know him. But still— why not? Show him up.

Porter. Very good, sir.

Pycroft *(musing).* I wonder how on earth the fellow knows me. What does he want of me? And how did he find me?

Porter *(off mike, announcing).* Mr. Arthur Pinner, sir.

Pinner (*a sly, older man, fading on*). Mr. Hall Pycroft, I believe?

Pycroft. Yes, sir. Please come in.

Sound. *Door closing.*

Pinner. You were lately engaged at Coxon & Woodhouse's and are now to be on the staff of Mawson's?

Pycroft. Quite so. You seem to know a great deal about me, sir.

Pinner. Well, the fact is that I have heard some really extraordinary stories about your financial ability. You remember Parker, who used to be manager at Coxon's? He can never praise you enough. Among your strong points, I believe, is a good memory, is it not?

Pycroft. It's pretty fair, I must admit.

Pinner. You don't mind if I test you on that point, do you? I'm sure you read the stock quotations each day. What is the price of Ayrshires?

Pycroft (*promptly*). A hundred and six and a quarter to a hundred and five and seven-eighths.

Pinner. And New Zealand Consolidated?

Pycroft. A hundred and four.

Pinner. British Broken Hills.

Pycroft. Seven to seven-and-six.

Pinner. Wonderful! This quite fits in with all I have heard. My boy, you are much too good to be a clerk at Mawson's.

Pycroft. I am very glad to have a position at Mawson's.

Pinner. Oh, pooh, man, you should be doing far better. Now I'll tell you how it is with me. What I have to offer is little enough for a man of your ability, but compared to Mawson's offer, it's a fortune. When do you start at Mawson's?

Pycroft. On Monday.

Pinner (*laughing*). I'll wager you'll never go there at all. By Monday you will be the business manager of the Franco-Midland Hardware Company, Limited, with a hundred and thirty-four branches all over France, not counting one in Brussels and one in San Remo.

Pycroft. But—I've never heard of it!

Pinner. I daresay you haven't. It has been kept very quiet, because we don't want the word to get around until we have already started our operations in England. The competition, you know. Now, my brother, Harry Pinner, is managing director. He has asked me to find a good business manager. I've heard a good deal about you and have decided that you're the man for me—although we're prepared to offer you only five hundred pounds a year to start.

Pycroft (*amazed*). Five—five hundred pounds! But that's four times what Mawson's giving me.

Pinner. You're worth more, my boy. What do you say to my offer?

Pycroft. It's quite handsome, indeed, Mr. Pinner. But I must be frank. Mawson may not pay so handsomely, but it is a safe, secure company. I know so little about your company.

Pinner. Smart, smart. You are the very man for us. You are not to be talked over. I like that. Now, to answer your question, here's a hundred pounds for you, as an advance against your salary. That's security, isn't it?

Pycroft (*firmly*). You have just hired yourself a business manager, Mr. Pinner. When shall I take over my duties?

Pinner. Be in Birmingham tomorrow at one. I have a note in my pocket that you will take to my brother, Harry Pinner. You will find him at this address, where the temporary offices of the company are located. He will explain your duties.

Pycroft. Really, sir, I hardly know how to express my gratitude.

Pinner. Not at all, my boy. But there are one or two small things — mere formalities — that must be arranged. You have a bit of paper beside you there. Kindly write upon it: "I am perfectly willing to act as the business manager of the Franco-Midland Hardware Company, Limited, at a minimum salary of five hundred pounds."

Sound. *Pen writing on paper.*

Pycroft (*slowly*). "Minimum–salary, five–hundred–pounds." There you are.

Pinner. And one last thing. What do you intend to do about Mawson's?

Pycroft. I declare, I'd forgotten about them. I'll write and resign.

Pinner. Precisely what I don't want you to do. I had a row with Mawson's manager over you. I told him I was interested in you, and he was quite offensive, said that as he had hired you first, you'd no right to consider any other offer, no matter how much to your advantage. As a matter of fact, do you know what he said about you? "We picked Pycroft out of the gutter, and he's too grateful to us not to come to work here, no matter what you pay."

Pycroft. The impudence!

Pinner. Those were his very words. Don't you think it would serve him right to give him no notice at all?

Pycroft. Imagine his talking about me like that — when I've never set eyes on him in my life. I shall certainly not write if you would rather I didn't.

Pinner. Good! That's a promise! Well, Mr. Pycroft, I'm delighted with our business transaction. We have a good man in you. Now don't forget to be in Birmingham tomorrow at one o'clock sharp, and present this letter to my brother. He'll be expecting you. I must be off now, but we shall meet again.

Pycroft. Thank you, Mr. Pinner. I'm eternally grateful, you can be sure.

Pinner. Never you mind. I'm the one who is grateful. Goodbye now, and good luck. *(fading)* May you have all the fortune that you deserve!

Music. *Lively theme, up and out.*

Watson. And was that the entire interview before you took your new position?

Pycroft. That is just about all that passed between us, as near as I can remember. You can imagine, Dr. Watson, how pleased I was at such an extraordinary bit of luck. I sat up half the night thinking about it, and the next day I was off to Birmingham. After settling in a hotel, I made my way straight to the address that had been given me.

Watson. And what sort of offices did you find?

Pycroft. That was the first thing that startled me. When I got to the building, I looked for the company name on the directory-board in the lobby, but it was not to be found.

Watson. How curious!

Pycroft. I stood for a moment with my heart in my boots, wondering whether the whole thing was an elaborate hoax, when someone suddenly addressed me. I looked up, and there before me was a man very like the chap I had seen the night before. He was the same size, with the same voice, but he was clean-shaven, and his hair was of a lighter color. Clear-

ly, the men were brothers. *(fading)* If it hadn't been for the hair, one might have said they were twins.

Harry *(fading on)*. Are you Mr. Hall Pycroft?

Pycroft. Yes, sir, I am.

Harry. I was expecting you, but you are a trifle before your time. I had a note from my brother this morning in which he sings your praises!

Pycroft. I was just looking for the offices when you came.

Harry. We have not put our name up yet, for we only secured these temporary premises last week. *(fading)* Come up with me, and we'll talk the whole thing over.

Music. *Mysterious theme, in and under.*

Pycroft. I followed him to the top of a lofty staircase, and there, right under the roof, were two empty, dusty little rooms, uncurtained and uncarpeted. I had imagined a great office with shining tables and rows of clerks, such as I was used to, and I daresay I rather stared at the two rickety

chairs and one little table that, with a ledger, made up the whole furniture.

Music. *Out.*

Harry *(jovially)*. Come, Mr. Pycroft, don't be disheartened by humble appearances. Rome was not built in a day, and we have lots of money behind us, though we don't make much of a show with it. Pray sit down. From what my brother has written me of you, I know that you are the man we want. You may consider yourself definitely engaged.

Pycroft. What are my duties going to be, Mr. Pinner?

Harry. You will eventually manage the great depot in Paris, which will pour a flood of English crockery into the shops of a hundred and thirty-four agents in France. The purchases will be completed in a week. Meanwhile, you will remain here in Birmingham and make yourself useful.

Pycroft. How?

Harry. Here is a directory of Paris, with the trades listed after the names of the people. I want you to take it home with you and mark off all the hardware sellers, with their addresses. It would be of the greatest use to me to have them.

Pycroft. But surely, sir, there are classified lists available?

Harry. Not reliable ones. Their system is different from ours. Stick at it, and let me have the lists by Monday at twelve. If you continue to show zeal and intelligence, you will find us a good company. Good day, Mr. Pycroft.

Music. *In and under. Fades out.*

Pycroft. Well, gentlemen, what was I to think? The dingy offices—the lack of furniture—the absence of the company name upon the directory-board—all of these gave rise to my suspicions. And yet, Mr. Pinner had offered a good explanation for everything. Even the task he had set me to seemed reasonable, and so I gave it a try. All Sunday I was kept hard at work, and yet by Monday I had got only as far as the letter *H.* I went round to Mr. Pinner, found him in the same dismantled room, and was told to keep at it until Wednesday. On Wednesday it was still unfinished, so I hammered away until Friday—that is, yesterday. *(fading)* Then I brought it round to Mr. Harry Pinner. *(pause)*

Harry *(fading on).* Thank you very much, Mr. Pycroft. I fear that I underrated the difficulty of the task. This list will be of very material assistance to me.

Pycroft. It took some time.

Harry. And now I want you to make a list of the furniture shops, for they all sell crockery.

Pycroft. Very good, sir, if that is what you want.

Harry. And you can come up tomorrow evening at seven, and let me know how you are getting on. But don't overwork yourself, my boy. A couple of hours at a music hall in the evening would do you a world of good. *(laughs evilly)* Yes, yes, Mr. Pycroft. Take your time. *(fading)* There's no hurry. By all means, take your time.

Music. *Mysterious theme. Up and out.*

Pycroft. And that, Dr. Watson, is the whole story.

Watson. And you think that there is some mystery in the business? It all sounds perfectly legitimate and straightforward to me.

Holmes. But that is because Mr. Pycroft neglected to tell you one interesting thing that he observed—a thing of a most peculiar nature.

Pycroft. By George, I did leave that out.

Watson. What is it, man?

Pycroft. As Mr. Harry Pinner discharged me last evening, he laughed as I told you. And I saw that his second tooth upon the left-hand side had been very badly filled with gold.

Watson. And is that all? That doesn't sound like much to me.

Pycroft. You are quite right, Dr. Watson. There's much more to it. When I was speaking to the other chap in London—

Mr. Arthur Pinner—I happened to notice that his same tooth was filled in the identical fashion. Of course you expect that two brothers will resemble each other, but not that they will have the same tooth filled in the same way. And then it suddenly occurred to me that the only differences in their appearances were such things as might be quickly altered with a razor and with dye. The things that can't be quickly changed—the voice, the figure, the teeth, the eyes—those were the same.

Holmes. An excellent observation, you will agree, Watson.

Watson. But if both men were the same, what is the meaning of it? Why had he sent you from London to Birmingham? Why had he gone there early to meet you? And why had he written a letter from himself to himself?

Pycroft. Those are the very questions I asked myself, Dr. Watson. And because I could not answer them, I went to the one man in all of England who could help me find the answers. That is precisely why I have called upon your good friend, Sherlock Holmes.

Music. *In, under, and out.*

Developing Comprehension Skills

1. How did Holmes learn that Watson had not been well lately?

2. List from four to six events that led Pycroft to Holmes. Begin with his losing his job at the stockbroking firm.

3. Contrast the characters of Holmes and Watson. Point out at least two differences.

4. At the end of this part of the play, the characters suspect that Pycroft has been the victim of a hoax. They are puzzled as to the reason. Can you suggest at least one possible reason why Pinner has hired Pycroft?

Reading Literature: Drama

1. **Appreciating Characters.** Sherlock Holmes is considered the central character in this play. However, the play would not be possible without Watson. One important role that Watson fills is that of narrator. What other purpose does he serve? How is his role important for the audience?

2. **Understanding Dialog.** Holmes and Watson are both members of the British upper class of the late 1800's. To show this, the writer has them use formal English. Their sentences are often long, with several ideas related in one sentence. Reread the last sentence on page 562, column 1, beginning with "Therefore." In your own words, state three facts it tells.

3. **Recognizing Setting.** Details about the setting are given in the dialog. Identify at least three facts you learn about the setting.

Sherlock Holmes and the Stockbroker's Clerk

ARTHUR CONAN DOYLE

You now have all the facts that Holmes has. Can you put them together in the same way he can? Continue to match wits with the great detective.

ACT TWO

Watson (*narrating*). I confess that I found Mr. Pycroft's story interesting, but it was not until he mentioned the detail of the gold tooth that I perceived the mystery in the affair. Now, however, I could understand why Holmes had shown such enthusiasm for the case. The train had pulled into Birmingham Station just as Pycroft finished his narrative, and the three of us climbed down onto the platform. Both the young stockbroker's clerk and I turned upon Holmes with eager anticipation, anxious to know how he intended to proceed with the business.

Holmes (*delightedly*). Rather fine, Watson, is it not? There are points in it that please me. I think you will agree with me that an interview with Mr. Arthur Harry Pinner—for we must call him by both names until we discover who he really is—in the temporary offices of the Franco-Midland Hardware Company, Limited, would be a rather interesting experience for both of us.

Watson. But how can we manage it without his suspecting who we are?

Pycroft. Oh, easily enough. You can pretend to be two friends of mine who are in need of jobs. What could be more natural than that I should bring you both around to the managing director of my company?

Holmes. Quite so, quite so. I should like to have a look at the gentleman and see if I can make anything of his little game. I cannot help but wonder, Mr. Pycroft, what it is about you that should have attracted him.

Watson. Shall we go right over to the offices now?

Pycroft. There is no use in that. He comes there only to see me, apparently, for the place is deserted up to the very hour he names.

Holmes. That certainly suggests mischief.

Pycroft (*suddenly*). I say! We are in luck. There he is ahead of us—the very man!

Watson. Which one? Where?

Pycroft. That one there, with his head lowered. He must have come down on the same train as we did.

Holmes. He's probably on his way to keep his appointment with you now, Mr. Pycroft. At least we will not be disappointed. I find myself quite anxious to have a good, long look at Mr. Arthur Harry Pinner.

Music. *Mysterious theme, in, under and out.*

Watson (*narrating*). The man Pycroft had pointed to was a smallish, well-dressed fellow, who seemed quite intent upon his own thoughts, for he never once looked up but went bustling along the streets with firm determination. Following him at a short distance, Holmes, Pycroft, and I never lost sight of him, and soon we found ourselves walking down the street of the company's offices. At the corner, there was a young urchin selling newspapers. (*pause*)

Newsboy (*off mike*). All the London papers here! Get your evening papers!

Harry (*off mike*). Here, boy. A *Standard*—and be quick about it! (*pause*)

Watson (*narrating*). Pinner threw the boy a coin, and, clutching his newspaper tightly, he bustled off into the company's building, a worried look on his face. Following Pycroft's lead, we entered the same doorway and after climbing five flights of stairs, found ourselves outside a half-opened door, at which our client tapped. We entered a bare, unfurnished room such as had been described to us. At the single table sat the man whom we had seen in the street, with his evening paper spread in front of him. As he looked up, I saw an expression of grief, torment, and horror. His brow glistened with perspiration, his cheeks were dead white, his eyes glazed. He looked at his clerk as though he did not recognize him, so preoccupied was he with his own terrible thoughts.

Pycroft. You look ill, Mr. Pinner!

Harry (*abstractedly, almost wildly*). Yes, I—I am not very well. Who are these gentlemen?

Pycroft. They are friends of mine, who are in need of work. I thought you might be able to make use of their experience in your enterprise.

Harry. Yes—yes—possibly, quite possibly. But I cannot talk about it now—I—please, please, leave me alone for a little bit. I—I must be alone.

Pycroft. You forget, Mr. Pinner, that I am here by appointment.

Harry. Appointment? Yes—yes, of course. I beg your pardon. You may wait here. You may all wait here. I must just slip away—if you will excuse me, I must go into the next room, only—only for a moment. *(fading)* Excuse me—just for a moment. I—I must be alone—just for a moment.

Sound. *Door closing, off mike.*

Holmes. Is he trying to give us the slip?

Pycroft. It's impossible. There's no door in that second room except the one he entered by. It's an inside room—not so much as a window in it.

Holmes. Is it furnished?

Pycroft. It wasn't yesterday.

Watson. Then what on earth can he be doing in there? Probably went in merely to recover his composure. He did seem awfully upset. I say—do you suppose he suspects we are detectives? Is that what's upset him?

Holmes. No. He was already upset when we came in.

Sound. *Moans off mike.*

Pycroft. What's that?

Holmes. It's Pinner. See what he's up to.

Sound. *Footsteps running, then door being opened.*

Pycroft. Good grief!

Holmes. He's—he's hanged himself. How is he, Watson?

Watson. Dead, by Jove. He's made a good job of it. Dead as a doornail.

Holmes *(regretfully).* I suppose we ought to call the police in. And yet I confess that I'd like to give them a complete case when they come.

Pycroft. It's a blessed mystery to me. Whatever did he want to bring me all the way up here for, when he—

Holmes *(interrupting).* Pooh! All that is clear enough. It is just this last sudden move that has me confused.

Watson *(incredulous).* You understand the rest, then? I must confess that I am out of my depth.

Holmes. Surely if you consider the events at first, they can only point to one conclusion. The whole thing hinges upon two points. The first is that he made Pycroft write a declaration by which he entered the services of this preposterous company. Do you not see how very suggestive it is?

Watson. No, I'm afraid I don't.

Holmes. Why did they want him to do it? It's not a usual business practice, you know. The only reason is that they were anxious to obtain a specimen of our young friend's handwriting.

Pycroft. But why should they need my handwriting?

Holmes. There can be only one adequate reason. Someone wished to learn to imitate it. And for the explanation of why, we must consider the second point: that you were specifically requested not to resign your position at Mawson's but to leave the manager there under the expectation that Mr. Hall Pycroft, whom he had never seen, was about to enter the office upon the next Monday morning.

Pycroft. Of course! What a blind fool I've been!

Holmes. Suppose that someone turned up in your place, writing in a hand identical to that in which your letter of application was written. How easy it would be for him to pass himself off as you. Of course, it was of the utmost importance to persuade you to accept the fake job offer, for it was essential that an impostor go to Mawson's in your place. That is why you were given the magnificent sum of a hundred pounds in advance; they wanted to make sure of you. And, of course, they very cleverly arranged for you to leave London, so that there would be no chance of your showing up at Mawson's on any pretext.

Pycroft. But why should this man pretend to have been his brother?

Holmes. That is pretty clear, also. There are evidently only two of them in on the scheme—whatever scheme it is. The other is impersonating you at the office. This one acted as your engager and then found that it was wiser to pretend to be your Birmingham employer as well, rather than admit a third person into the plot. He changed his appearance and passed himself off as his own brother. But for the happy accident of the gold tooth, he would have succeeded.

Pycroft. But what scheme were they working? Why should one of them want to gain entrance to Mawson's under false pretenses?

Watson. And why should the other hang himself the minute we walk into the room?

Holmes. That is what I do not yet understand. *(suddenly)* The paper! Of course! I should have thought of it before. The secret must lie there.

Pycroft. Here is the newspaper Pinner was reading. What do you make of it?

Sound. *Rustling newspaper pages.*

Holmes. It's an early edition of the *Evening Standard.* Let me see. Hmm . . . hmm. Aha, here it is. Look at this, Watson, and tell us what you think.

Watson. Ah! Listen to the headline of this story. "Murder at Mawson & Williams. Gigantic Robbery Attempted. Capture of the Criminal."

Pycroft. I begin to understand.

Holmes. By pretending to be you, the criminal managed to gain access to the safe. I gather from the newspaper article that he was discovered by a guard, whom he killed. But fortunately, the police caught him in time. And this fellow, when he learned that the jig was up, decided to kill himself.

Watson. Yes, Holmes, listen to this. "The criminal is lodged in Holloway Gaol.[1] His brother, however, who usually works with him, has not appeared in this job as far as we can presently ascertain, although the police are making energetic inquiries as to his whereabouts."

Holmes. Well, we may save the police some little trouble in that direction.

Pycroft. It's ironic, isn't it? To think that this fellow really had a brother in London after all!

Watson. I must congratulate you, Holmes, on your splendid deductions.

Holmes. You could have done the same, Watson.

Watson. I disagree. You have pieced the thing together with uncanny skill. I don't know how you do it. It's amazing!

Holmes. On the contrary. It's elementary, my dear Watson. Elementary!

Music. *Full to finish.*

---

1. **Gaol** (jāl) British spelling of *jail*

Developing Comprehension Skills

1. Why had Pinner hired Pycroft?

2. When Holmes, Watson, and Pycroft spoke with Pinner, Pinner excused himself from the room. Holmes immediately asked, "Is he trying to give us the slip?" What behavior of Pinner led Holmes to expect such an action?

3. Reread the last two speeches on page 576. With whom do you agree, Watson or Holmes? Explain your answer.

Reading Literature: Drama

1. **Understanding Conflict.** What is the main conflict in the play? Is it internal or external?

2. **Appreciating the Narrator.** The action of this play begins in London, at Watson's home. Then there is a flashback to events in Pycroft's life. The action resumes in Birmingham. How does the use of the narrator pull all these parts together? Point out where Watson speaks as narrator rather than as a character in the play.

3. **Examining the Plot.** In a mystery, it is important that the facts be introduced gradually. This allows the audience to think about the evidence just as the characters do. Write a brief summary of this play, scene by scene. Identify what the audience learns about Pinner's scheme in each scene.

4. **Identifying Minor Characters.** Although he never appears onstage, Pinner's real brother plays a part in the action. What is his role in the mystery? What becomes of him? How is this information presented to the audience?

5. **Evaluating the Form.** Review the different settings of this play. In what way is this play better suited for presentation on radio rather than for the stage?

Developing Vocabulary Skills

Recognizing Formal and Informal Standard English. The dialog in "Sherlock Holmes and the Stockbroker's Clerk" includes several instances of informal standard English. Read the following sentences from the play. If the sentence contains informal standard English, write the word or phrase that makes it informal. Explain any special meanings that the words or phrases have. If the sentence is in formal standard English, write *Formal* on your paper.

1. Stick at it, and let me have the lists by Monday at twelve.

2. I wonder how on earth the fellow knows me.

3. It all sounds perfectly legitimate and straightforward to me.

4. By George, I did leave that out.

5. You forget, Mr. Pinner, that I am here by appointment.

6. Is he trying to give us the slip?

7. Dead, by Jove. He's made a good job of it. Dead as a doornail.

8. You never cease to amaze me, Holmes.

Developing Writing Skills

1. **Analyzing Transitions.** The play you have just read has several short scenes set in different places and times. Therefore, it is important that the audience be given adequate notice of any change, or **transition**, in setting and of the new time and place. Write from one to three paragraphs explaining how the playwright accomplishes this. Point out any

special techniques possible in a play, and especially in a radio play, that he uses for smooth transitions.

2. **Writing a Mystery.** In literature, a **parody** is an imitation of a certain selection or of a type of writing. Often, it is funny. It uses the same techniques as the original, but not with the same serious purpose.

Write your own mystery. It should be a parody of a Sherlock Holmes mystery. The plot should involve Sherlock Holmes and Dr. Watson with a fairy tale or folk tale situation. For example, Sherlock Holmes could take on a case of home invasion reported by the Three Bears.

Pre-Writing. First, select the fairy tale or folk tale you will use. List the titles of several possibilities. Under each title, note the crime and any details in the original story that could be presented as clues. Jot down any ideas you have about how Sherlock Holmes could proceed in his investigation. Then choose the plot that you think you can do the most with.

Next, write a brief outline of the original story. Circle each step that should be presented as a separate scene. Make a separate list of the characters. Begin with Holmes and Watson. Add any characters from the original story that you will keep. For each character, decide on a special way of talking or some habit that will make him or her easy to identify.

List your scenes. For each scene, note what facts will be introduced. Be careful to include every necessary fact, but leave something unclear so that Holmes can have a final speech in which he solves the mystery. Also, make a note of the characters involved in each scene.

Writing. Keeping your outline of scenes before you, write your play. Use the conventions you have learned about, including narrator, dialog, asides, and stage directions. Try to make each character speak a little differently, in order to set him or her off from the others.

Revising. Review your play. Are the facts of the case introduced gradually? Are all the necessary facts given? Does Holmes have a good explanation of his method of deduction? Is the dialog clearly labeled as to speaker? Are the stage directions set off from dialog? Make any necessary improvements.

Developing Skills in Speaking and Listening

Presenting Dialog. Work with a partner to present one of these scenes from "Sherlock Holmes and the Stockbroker's Clerk": the conversation between Holmes and Watson on pages 562 and 563, or the conversation between Pinner and Pycroft on pages 566 to 568. You and your partner should try to make each character as different as possible from the other. Practice reading the lines with meaning. Then present your scene to a small group. Ask members of your audience to report the differences that they hear.

Grandpa and the Statue

ARTHUR MILLER

In this play, the major character is an old man with strong opinions. As you read, compare Grandpa to Sherlock Holmes. Which character seems more real to you? Look in the play for reasons for your decision.

CHARACTERS

Characters in the present time of the play:

Announcer
August
Young Monaghan (Män'ə han)—*a soldier*

Characters from the past, heard in the flashback scenes which Young Monaghan remembers:

Sheean (Shē'ən)
Monaghan—*Grandfather of Young Monaghan*
Child Monaghan—*Young Monaghan himself, as a child*

George ⎫
Charley ⎪
Jack ⎬ *neighborhood children, Child Monaghan's friends*
Mike ⎪
Joe ⎭

Alf ⎫
Girl ⎬ *passengers on the Statue of Liberty boat*
Young Man ⎭

Veteran—*visitor to the Statue*
Sound-Effects Person
Megaphone Voice
Music-Effects Person

Statue of Liberty, New York City.

A Postcard of the Statue of Liberty, about 1910.
National Park Service; Statue of Liberty National Monument

ACT ONE

Music. Theme.

Announcer. The scene is the fourth floor of a giant army hospital overlooking New York Harbor. A young man sitting in a wheelchair is looking out a window—just looking. After a while another young man in another wheel chair rolls over to him and they both look.

Music. Out.

August. You want to play some checkers with me, Monaghan?

Monaghan. Not right now.

August. Okay *(slight pause).* You don't want to go feeling blue, Monaghan.

Monaghan. I'm not blue.

August. All you do most days is sit here looking out this window.

Monaghan. What do you want me to do, jump rope?

August. No, but what do you get out of it?

Monaghan. It's a beautiful view. Some companies make millions of dollars just printing that view on postcards.

August. Yeh, but nobody keeps looking at a postcard six, seven hours a day.

Monaghan. I come from around here. It reminds me of things. My young days.

August. That's right, you're Brooklyn, aren't you?

Monaghan. My house is only about a mile away.

August. That so. Tell me, are you looking at just the water all the time? I'm curious. I don't get a kick out of this view.

Monaghan. There's the Statue of Liberty out there. Don't you see it?

August. Oh, that's it. Yeh, that's nice to look at.

Monaghan. I like it. Reminds me of a lot of laughs.

August. Laughs? The Statue of Liberty?

Monaghan. Yeh, my grandfather. He got all twisted up with the Statue of Liberty.

August *(laughs a little).* That so? What happened to him?

Monaghan. Well. My grandfather was the stingiest man in Brooklyn. "Mercyless" Monaghan, they used to call him. He even used to save umbrella handles.

August. What for?

Monaghan. Just couldn't stand seeing anything go to waste. After a big windstorm there'd be a lot of broken umbrellas laying around in the streets.

August. Yeh?

Monaghan. He'd go around picking them up. In our house the closets were always full of umbrella handles. My grandma used to say that he would go across the Brooklyn Bridge on the trolley just because he could come back on the same nickel. See, if you stayed on the trolley they'd let you come back for the same nickel.

August. What'd he do, just go over and come back?

Monaghan. Yeh, it made him feel good. Savin' money. Two and a half cents.

August. So how'd he get twisted up with the Statue of Liberty?

Monaghan. Well, way back in 1887, around there, they were living on Butler Street. Butler Street, Brooklyn, practically runs right down to the river. One day he's sitting on the front porch, reading a paper he borrowed from the neighbors, when along comes this man Jack Sheean who lived up the block.

Music. *Sneak into above speech, then bridge, then out.*

Sheean (*slight brogue*). A good afternoon to you, Monaghan.

Monaghan (*grandfather*). How're you today, Sheean, how're ya?

Sheean. Fair, fair. And how's Mrs. Monaghan these days?

Monaghan. Warm. Same as everybody else in summer.

Sheean. I've come to talk to you about the fund, Monaghan.

Monaghan. What fund is that?

Sheean. The Statue of Liberty fund.

Monaghan. Oh, that.

Sheean. It's time we come to grips with the subject, Monaghan.

Monaghan. I'm not interested, Sheean.

Sheean. Now hold up on that a minute. Let me tell you the facts. This here Frenchman has gone and built a fine Statue of Liberty. It costs the Lord knows how many millions to build. All they're askin' us to do is contribute enough to put up a base for the statue to stand on.

Monaghan. I'm not . . . !

Sheean. Before you answer me. People all over the whole United States are puttin' in for it. Butler Street is doin' the same. We'd like to hang up a flag on the corner saying—"Butler Street, Brooklyn, is one hundred percent behind the Statue of Liberty." And Butler Street *is* a hundred percent subscribed except for you. Now will you give us a dime, Monaghan? One dime and we can put up the flag. Now what do you say to that?

Monaghan. I'm not throwin' me good money away for somethin' I don't even know exists.

Sheean. Now what do you mean by that?

Monaghan. Have you seen this statue?

Sheean. No, but it's in a warehouse. And as soon as we get the money to build the

Construction of the Statue of Liberty in Paris. From *New York: Photographs 1850–1950,* the Amaryllis Press, New York.

pedestal, they'll take it and put it up on that island in the river, and all the boats comin' in from the old country will see it there, and it'll raise the hearts of the poor immigrants to see such a fine sight on their first look at this country.

Monaghan. And how do I know it's in this here warehouse at all?

Sheean. You read your paper, don't you? It's been in all the papers for the past year.

Monaghan. Ha, the papers! Last year I read in the paper that they were about to pave Butler Street and take out all the holes. Turn around and look at Butler Street, Mr. Sheean.

Sheean. All right. I'll do this: I'll take you to the warehouse and show you the statue. Will you give a dime then?

Monaghan. Well . . . I'm not sayin' I would, and I'm not sayin' I wouldn't. But I'd be more likely if I saw the thing large as life, I would.

Sheean *(peeved)*. All right, then. Come along.

Music. *Up and down and out.*

Sound. *Footsteps, in warehouse . . . echo . . . they come to a halt.*

Sheean. Now then. Do you see the Statue of Liberty or don't you see it?

Monaghan. I see it all right, but it's all broke!

Sheean. Broke! They brought it from France on a boat. They had to take it apart, didn't they?

Monaghan. You got a secondhand statue, that's what you got, and I'm not payin' for new when they've shipped us something that's all smashed to pieces.

Sheean. Now just a minute, just a minute. Visualize what I'm about to tell you, Monaghan, get the picture of it. When this statue is put together it's going to stand ten stories high. Could they get a thing ten stories high into a four-story building such as this is? Use your good sense, now Monaghan.

Monaghan. What's that over there?

Sheean. Where?

Monaghan. That tablet there in her hand. What's it say? July Eye Vee (IV) MDCCLXXVI . . . what . . . what's all that?

Sheean. That means July 4, 1776. It's in Roman numbers. Very high class.

Monaghan. What's the good of it? If they're going to put a sign on her they ought to put it: Welcome All. That's it. Welcome All.

Sheean. They decided July 4, 1776, and July 4, 1776, it's going to be!

Monaghan. All right, then let them get their dime from somebody else!

Sheean. Monaghan!

Monaghan. No, sir! I'll tell you something. I didn't think there was a statue but there is. She's all broke, it's true, but she's here and maybe they can get her together. But even if they do, will you tell me what sort of a welcome to immigrants it'll be, to have a gigantic thing like that in the middle of the river and in her hand a July Eye Vee MCDVC . . . whatever it is?

Sheean. That's the date the country was made!

Monaghan. The divil with the date! A man comin' in from the sea wants a place to stay, not a date. When I come from the old country, I git off at the dock and there's a feller says to me, "Would you care for a room for the night?" "I would that," I sez, and he sez, "All right then, follow me." He takes me to a rooming house. I no sooner sign me name on the register—which I was able to do even at that time—when I look around and the feller is gone clear away and took my valise[1] in the bargain. A statue anyway

---

1. **valise** (və lēs′), suitcase.

can't move off so fast, but if she's going to welcome let her say welcome, not this MCDC. . . .

Sheean. All right, then, Monaghan. But all I can say is, you've laid a disgrace on the name of Butler Street. I'll put the dime in for ya.

Monaghan. Don't connect me with it! It's a swindle, is all it is. In the first place, it's broke; in the second place, if they do put it up, it'll come down with the first high wind that strikes it.

Sheean. The engineers say it'll last forever!

Monaghan. And I say it'll topple into the river in a high wind! Look at the inside of her. She's all hollow!

Sheean. I've heard everything now, Monaghan. Just about everything. Goodbye.

Monaghan. What do you mean, goodbye? How am I to get back to Butler Street from here?

Sheean. You've got legs to walk.

Monaghan. I'll remind you that I come on the trolley.

Sheean. And I'll remind you that I paid your fare and I'm not repeating the kindness.

Monaghan. Sheean? You've stranded me!

Music. *Up and down.*

Young Monaghan. That was Grandpa. That's why I have to laugh every time I look at the statue now.

August. Did he ever put the dime in?

Young Monaghan. Well—in a way. What happened was this: His daughters got married and finally my mom . . . put me out on Butler Street. I got to be pretty attached to Grandpa. He'd even give me an umbrella handle and make a sword out of it for me. Naturally, I wasn't very old before he began working on me about the statue.

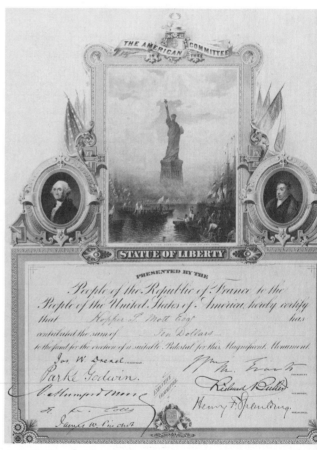

Contribution certificate for the Pedestal Fund, 1883.
Courtesy of the New York Historical Society.

Developing Comprehension Skills

1. What is Grandfather Monaghan's nickname? Why was he given this nickname?

2. Why is Grandpa reluctant to contribute to the Statue of Liberty fund? List two reasons that he states. What do you think his real reason is?

3. Grandpa first raises the objection that he doubts the existence of the statue, so his friend Sheean takes him to the warehouse where the pieces are stored. There Grandpa objects that the statue is broken. Sheean replies as follows:

    > When this statue is put together it's going to stand ten stories high. Could they get a thing ten stories high into a four-story building such as this? Use your good sense, now, Monaghan.

    Next, Grandpa objects to the sign he sees on the statue. Here is Sheean's answer:

    > They decided July 4, 1776, and July 4, 1776, it's going to be!

Do you think that Sheean used a good approach to get Grandpa to contribute? Which things that he said or did were effective methods of persuasion? Which were ineffective?

Reading Literature: Drama

1. **Understanding a Radio Play.** The announcer has only one speech in this play. As the play begins, the announcer sets the scene. Then, the announcer no longer appears, although the scene changes several times. Locate and examine at least two scene changes. Identify two techniques the playwright uses to let the audience know the scene is changing.

2. **Recognizing Humor.** Point out at least one instance in which humor is used in this play. Which character or characters are somewhat comic?

3. **Identifying Author's Tone.** Does the playwright like the characters in this play? What makes you think as you do? Point out evidence in the play.

Grandpa and the Statue

ARTHUR MILLER

So far in this play, the mood has been light. As you read further, think about these questions: Was the play written only to amuse? What other purpose might have been in the playwright's mind?

ACT TWO

Sound. *High wind.*

Child Monaghan (*softly, as though Grandpa is in bed*). Grampa?

Monaghan (*awakened*). Heh? What are you doin' up?

Child Monaghan. Ssssh! Listen!

Sound. *Wind rising up and fading. Rising higher and fading.*

Monaghan (*gleefully*). Aaaaaaaah! Yes, yes. This'll do it, boy. This'll do it! First thing in the morning we'll go down to the docks, and I'll bet you me life that Mr. Sheean's statue is smashed down and layin' on the bottom of the bay. Go to sleep now, we'll have a look first thing.

Music. *Up and down.*

Sound. *Footsteps.*

Child Monaghan. If it fell down, all the people will get their dimes back, won't they Grampa? Slow down, I can't walk so fast.

Monaghan. Not only will they get their dimes back, but Mr. Sheean and the whole crew that engineered the collection are going to rot in jail. Now mark my words. Here, now, we'll take a short cut around this shed. . . .

Sound. *Footsteps continue a moment, then gradually . . . disappointedly they come to a halt.*

Child Monaghan. She's . . . she's still standing, Grampa.

Monaghan. She is that. (*uncomprehending*) I don't understand it. That was a terrible wind last night. Terrible.

Child Monaghan. Maybe she's weaker though. Heh?

Monaghan. Why . . . sure, that must be it. I'll wager she's hangin' by a thread. (*realizing*) Of course! That's why they put her out there in the water so when she falls down she won't be flattening out a lot of poor innocent people. Hey—feel that?

Child Monaghan. The wind! It's starting to blow again!

Monaghan. Sure, and look at the sky blackening over!

Sound. *Wind rising.*

Monaghan. Feel it comin' up! Take your last look at the statue, boy. If I don't mistake me eyes she's tilting toward Jersey already!

Music. *Up and down.*

Young Monaghan. It was getting embarrassing for me on the block. I kept promising the other kids that when the next wind came the statue would come down. We even had a game. Four or five kids would stand in a semicircle around one kid who was the statue. The statue kid had to stand on his heels and look right in our eyes. Then we'd all take a deep breath and blow in his face. He'd fall down like a stick of wood. They all believed me and Grampa . . . until one day. We were standing around throwing rocks at an old milk can. . . .

Sound. *Banging of rocks against milk can.*

George. What're you doin'?

Child Monaghan. What do we look like we're doin'?

George. I'm going someplace tomorrow.

Charley. I know, church. Watch out, I'm throwin'.

Sound. *Can being hit*

George. I mean after church.

Jack. Where?

George. My old man's going to take me out on the Statue of Liberty boat.

Sound. *Banging against can abruptly stops.*

Child Monaghan. You're not going out on the statue, though, are you?

George. Sure, that's where we're going.

Child Monaghan. But you're liable to get killed. Supposing there's a high wind tomorrow?

George. My old man says that statue couldn't fall down if all the wind in the world and John L. Sullivan[1] hit it at the same time.

Child Monaghan. Is that so?

George. Yeh, that's so. My old man says that the only reason your grandfather's saying that it's going to fall down is that he's ashamed he didn't put a dime in for the pedestal.

Child Monaghan. Is that so?

George. Yeh, that's so.

Child Monaghan. Well, you tell your old man that if he gets killed tomorrow not to come around to my grandfather and say he didn't warn him!

---

1. **John L. Sullivan,** world heavyweight boxing champion in the 1880's

Jack. Hey, George, would your father take me along?

George. I'll ask him, maybe he—

Child Monaghan. What, are you crazy, Jack?

Mike. Ask him if he'd take me too, will ya, George?

Child Monaghan. Mike, what's the matter with you?

Joe. Me too, George, I'll ask my mother for money.

Child Monaghan. Joe! Didn't you hear what my grampa said?

Joe. Well . . . I don't really believe that any more.

Child Monaghan. You don't be. . . .

Mike. Me neither.

Jack. I don't really think your grampa knows what he's talkin' about.

Child Monaghan. He don't, heh? *(ready to weep)* Okay . . . Okay. *(bursting out)* I just hope that wind blows tomorrow, boy! I just hope that wind blows!

Music. *Up and down.*

Sound. *Creaking of a rocking chair.*

Child Monaghan. Grampa . . . ?

Monaghan. Huh?

Child Monaghan. Can you stop rocking for a minute?

Sound. *Rocking stops.*

Child Monaghan. Can you put down your paper?

Sound. *Rustle of paper.*

Child Monaghan. I—I read the weather report for tomorrow.

Monaghan. The weather report . . . .

Child Monaghan. Yeh. It says fair and cool.

Monaghan. What of it?

Child Monaghan. I was wondering. Supposing you and me we went on a boat tomorrow. You know, I see the water every day when I go down to the docks to play, but I never sat on it. I mean in a boat.

Monaghan. Oh. Well, we might take the ferry on the Jersey side.

Child Monaghan. Yeh, but there's nothing to see in Jersey.

Monaghan. You can't possibly go to Europe tomorrow.

Child Monaghan. No, but couldn't we go toward the ocean? Just . . . toward it?

Monaghan. Toward it. What—what is it on your mind, boy? What is it now?

Child Monaghan. Well, I . . .

Monaghan. Oh, you want to take the Staten Island ferry. Sure, that's in the direction of the sea.

Child Monaghan. No, Grampa, not the Staten Island ferry.

Monaghan. You don't mean—*(breaks off)* Boy!

Child Monaghan. All the kids are going tomorrow with Georgie's old man.

Monaghan. You don't believe me any more.

Child Monaghan. I do, Grampa, but . . .

Monaghan. You don't. If you did you'd stay clear of the Statue of Liberty for love of your life!

Child Monaghan. But, Grampa, when is it going to fall down? All I do is wait and wait.

Monaghan *(with some uncertainty)*. You've got to have faith.

Child Monaghan. But every kid in my class went to see it and now the ones that didn't are going tomorrow. And they all keep talking about it and all I do . . . Well, I can't keep telling them it's a swindle. I—I wish we could see it, Grampa. It don't cost so much to go.

Monaghan. As long as you put it that way I'll have to admit I'm a bit curious meself as to how it's managed to stand upright so long. Tell you what I'll do. Barrin' wind, we'll chance it tomorrow!

Child Monaghan. Oh, Gramp!

Monaghan. But! If anyone should ask you where we went you'll say—Staten Island. Are y' on?

Child Monaghan. Okay, sure. Staten Island.

Monaghan *(secretively)*. We'll take the early boat, then. Mum's the word, now. For if old man Sheean hears that I went out there I'll have no peace from the thief the rest of m'life.

Music. *Up and down.*

Sound. *Boat whistles.*

Child Monaghan. Gee, it's nice ridin' on a boat, ain't it, Gramp?

Monaghan. Never said there was anything wrong with the boat. Boat's all right. You're sure now that Georgie's father is takin' the kids in the afternoon?

Child Monaghan. Yeh, that's when they're going. Gee, look at those two sea gulls. Whee!—look at them swoop! They caught a fish!

Monaghan. What I can't understand is what all these people see in that statue that they'll keep a boat like this full makin' the trip, year in year out. To hear the newspapers talk, if the statue was gone, we'd be at war with the nation that stole her the followin' mornin' early. All it is, is a big high pile of French copper.

Child Monaghan. The teacher says it shows us that we got liberty.

Monaghan. Bah! If you've got liberty, you don't need a statue to tell you you got it; and if you haven't got liberty, no statue's going to do you any good tellin' you you got it. It was a criminal waste of the people's money. *(quietly)* And just to prove it

Grandpa and the Statue   589

A 1900 photograph of the Staten Island Ferry passing the Statue of Liberty. Staten Island Historical Society, Staten Island.

to you I'll ask this feller sitting right over there what he sees in it. You'll see what a madness the whole thing was. Say, mister?

Alf. Hey?

Monaghan. I beg your pardon. I'm a little strange here, and curious. Could you please tell me why you're going to the Statue of Liberty?

Alf. Me? Well, I tell ya. I always wanted to take an ocean voyage. This is a pretty big boat—bigger than the ferries—so on Sundays, sometimes, I take the trip. It's better than nothing.

Monaghan. Thank you. *(to the child)* So much for the great meaning of that statue, me boy. We'll talk to this lady standing at the rail. I just want you to understand why I didn't give Sheean me dime. Madam, would you be good enough to . . . Oh pardon me. *(to child)* Better pass her by, she don't look so good. We'll ask that girl there. Young lady, if you'll pardon the curiosity of an old man . . . could you tell me in a few good words what it is about that statue that brings you out here?

Girl. What statue?

Monaghan. Why, the Statue of Liberty up 'head. We're coming up to it.

Girl. Statue of Liberty! Is this the Statue of Liberty boat?

Monaghan. Well, what'd you think it was?

Girl. Oh, my! I'm supposed to be on the Staten Island ferry! Where's the ticket man? *(going away)* Ticket man! Where's the ticket man?

Child Monaghan. Gee whiz, nobody seems to want to see the statue.

Monaghan. Just to prove it, let's see this fellow sitting on this bench here. Young man, say . . .

Young Man. I can tell you in one word. For four days I haven't had a minute's peace. My kids are screaming, my wife is yelling, upstairs they play the piano all day long. The only place I can find that's quiet is a statue. That statue is my sweetheart. Every Sunday I beat it out to the island and sit next to her, and she don't talk.

Child Monaghan. I guess you were right, Grampa. Nobody seems to think it means anything.

Monaghan. Not only doesn't mean anything, but if they'd used the money to build an honest roomin' house on that island, the immigrants would have a place to spend the night, their valises wouldn't get robbed, and they—

Megaphone Voice. *Please keep your seats while the boat is docking. Statue of Liberty—all out in five minutes!*

Child Monaghan. Look, Gramp—look down there, Gramp! There's a peanut stand! Could I have some?

Monaghan. I feel the wind comin' up. I don't think we dare take the time.

Music. *Up and down.*

Child Monaghan. Sssssseuuuuuww! Look how far you can see! Look at that ship way out in the ocean!

Monaghan. It is, it's quite a view. Don't let go of me hand now.

Child Monaghan. I betcha we could almost see California.

Monaghan. It's probably that grove of trees way out over there. They do say it's beyond Jersey.

Child Monaghan. Feels funny. We're standing right inside her head. Is that what you meant . . . July IV, MCD . . . ?

Monaghan. That's it. That tablet in her hand. Now shouldn't they have put Welcome All on it instead of that foreign language? Say! Do you feel her rockin'?

Child Monaghan. Yeah, she's moving a little bit. Listen, the wind!

Sound. *Whistling of wind.*

Monaghan. We better get down, come on! This way!

Child Monaghan. No, the stairs are this way! Come on!

Sound. *Running in echo. Then quick stop.*

Monaghan. No, I told you they're the other way! Come!

Veteran (*calm, quiet voice*). Don't get excited, pop. She'll stand.

Monaghan. She's swayin' awful.

Veteran. That's all right. I been up here thirty, forty times. She gives with the wind, flexible. Enjoy the view, go on.

Monaghan. Did you say you've been up here forty times?

Veteran. About that many.

Monaghan. What do you find here that's so interesting?

Veteran. It calms my nerves.

Monaghan. Ah. It seems to me it would make you more nervous than you were.

Veteran. No, not me. It kinda means something to me.

Monaghan. Might I ask what?

Veteran. Well . . . I was in the Philippine War . . . back in '98. Left my brother back there.

Monaghan. Oh, yes. Sorry I am to hear it. Young man, I suppose, eh?

Veteran. Yeh. We were both young. This is his birthday today.

Monaghan. Oh, I understand.

Veteran. Yeh, this statue is about the only stone he's got. In my mind I feel it is, anyway. This statue kinda looks like what we believe. You know what I mean?

Monaghan. Looks like what we believe . . . I . . . I never thought of it that way. I . . . I see what you mean. It does look that way. (*angrily*) See now, boy? If Sheean had put it that way I'd a give him me dime. (*hurt*) Now, why do you suppose he didn't tell me that! Come down now. I'm sorry, sir, we've got to get out of here.

Music. *Up and down.*

Sound. *Footsteps under.*

Hurry now, I want to get out of here. I feel terrible. That Sheean, that fool. Why didn't he tell me that? You'd think . . . .

Child Monaghan. What does this say?

Sound. *Footsteps halt.*

Monaghan. Why, it's just a tablet, I suppose. I'll try it with me spectacles, just a minute. Why, it's a poem, I believe. . . . "Give me your tired, your poor, your huddled masses yearning to breathe free, the wretched refuse of your teeming shore. Send these, the homeless, tempest-tost to me, I lift . . . my lamp beside . . . the golden door!" Oh, dear. (*ready to weep*) It had Welcome All on it all the time. Why didn't Sheean tell me? I'd a given him a quarter! Boy . . . go over there and here's a nickel and buy yourself a bag of them peanuts.

Child Monaghan (*astonished*). Gramp!

Monaghan. Go on now. I want to study this a minute. And be sure the man gives you full count.

Child Monaghan. I'll be right back.

Sound. *Footsteps running away.*

Monaghan *(to himself).* "Give me your tired, your poor, your huddled masses."

Music. *Swells from a sneak to full, then under to background.*

Young Monaghan. I ran over and got my peanuts and stood there cracking them open, looking around. And I happened to glance over to Grampa. He had his nose right up to that bronze tablet, reading it. And then he reached into his pocket and kinda spied around over his eyeglasses to see if anybody was looking, and then he took out a coin and stuck it in a crack of cement over the tablet.

Sound. *Coin falling onto concrete.*

Young Monaghan. It fell out and before he could pick it up I got a look at it. It was a half a buck. He picked it up and pressed it into the crack so it stuck. And then he came over to me and we went home.

Music. *Change to stronger, more forceful theme.*

Young Monaghan. That's why, when I look at her now through this window, I remember that time and that poem, and she really seems to say, "Whoever you are, wherever you come from, Welcome All. Welcome Home."

Music. *Flare up to finish.*

Aerial view of the Statue of Liberty, 1920. From *New York: Photographs 1850–1950*, the Amaryllis Press, New York.

Developing Comprehension Skills

1. How does Grandpa Monaghan "work on" Child Monaghan about the statue?

2. What explanation does Grandpa offer for the statue's being placed on an island in the ocean?

3. Why is Child Monaghan embarrassed in front of his friends? Would you feel that way in his place?

4. Do you think that Grandpa's conviction that the Statue of Liberty will blow over is authentic? Or does he just say this to justify his stingy behavior?

5. Child Monaghan reports that his teacher said the statue shows "that we got liberty." At first, Grandpa refuses to accept this idea. What causes him to change his mind?

Reading Literature: Drama

1. **Recognizing Structure.** Young Monaghan is the element of this play that unifies all the parts. Identify the different scenes in which Young Monaghan appears. How does this character pull the play together?

2. **Appreciating Setting.** Although many locations are shown in the course of this play, the first setting is most important in determining the writer's purpose. Where is the first scene set? How does it help to make the purpose of the play clear? What do you think the purpose is?

3. **Determining Theme.** A major theme of this play is patriotism. What do you think the writer is saying about patriotism?

4. **Identifying Conflict.** Grandpa Monaghan experiences internal and external conflict. Explain each conflict he faces. How is each conflict resolved?

5. **Evaluating Techniques.** The characters in this play frequently use nonstandard English. Is this an effective technique? Why or why not?

Developing Vocabulary Skills

Understanding Nonstandard English. The following sentences from "Grandpa and the Statue" are examples of nonstandard English. Rewrite each in standard English.

1. I'm not throwin' me good money away for somethin' I don't even know exists.

2. It's a swindle, is all it is.

3. Supposing you and me we went on a boat tomorrow.

4. It don't cost so much to go.

5. Gee, it's nice ridin' on a boat, ain't it, Gramp?

6. I betcha we could almost see California.

7. Every Sunday I beat it out to the island and sit next to her, and she don't talk.

8. This statue kinda looks like what we believe.

Developing Writing Skills

1. **Writing an Essay.** In the play you just read, Grandpa feels that the most important message about the United States is that it welcomes all sorts of people. What do you feel is the best quality of this country? Write an essay of at least three paragraphs to answer that question, with reasons for your choice.

   Pre-Writing. If possible, have a brainstorming session with classmates or with members of your family. List every good quality you or your companions can think of. Do not make any judgments at this time. Then, by yourself, think about the items on your list. See whether some of the qualities work together or can be included in one, more general statement about the United States. Choose the quality that you want to discuss.

Next, decide whether you want to write a formal essay or an informal essay. If you choose a formal essay, make an outline that follows this pattern:

I. State the quality you feel is best.
II. Explain the quality.
III. Give reasons for your choice, from least important to most important.
IV. Summarize your opinions.

If your essay will be informal, decide on your own, personal outline.

Writing. Write your essay, being careful to select the most exact words you can to present your ideas clearly. If putting your ideas on paper helps to make them clearer to yourself, you may find it necessary to revise your outline and begin writing again.

Revising. Review your essay. Make sure it includes the ideas listed in the pre-writing outline, even if they are in a different order. Then proofread your writing. If necessary, make a clean copy.

2. **Writing Effective Dialog.** Write a single scene for a story of your choice. Let the dialog alone explain who the characters are, what the setting is, and what conflict the characters face.

Developing Skills in Study and Research

Studying a Play. Imagine that you were going to direct this play. Scene by scene, list the emotions you want your audience to feel. Explain how you will lead them to these feelings. Some techniques you might list include speaking speed of the actors, volume of voices, tone of voices, and use of background music.

Restoration of the Statue of Liberty, 1984.
Stock Boston. ©Photograph by Ulrike Welsch.

Using Your Skills in Reading Drama

The following scene begins a dramatic version of the myth of Pandora. Read the scene. Then answer the following questions:

1. Who is the narrator? Does the narrator take part in the action?
2. What do you learn about the setting?
3. Identify one line of dialog, an aside, and a stage direction.
4. What do you learn about the characters? State at least three details.

Pandora. My earliest memories are of a large room filled with light. I was surrounded by beings much like me but far more beautiful.

Zeus. Our creation is complete. What gifts shall we bestow upon her?

Aphrodite. I can give her beauty. Considering the problems it has made here on Olympus, it should mess up human life wonderfully.

Apollo. You are being unkind, Aphrodite. We were asked to give gifts, not evils. I shall offer her the love of music.

Aphrodite. Don't lecture me, Apollo. You agreed to this plan, too.

Pandora. I didn't understand what plan Aphrodite meant, but why should I care? I was enjoying myself. With every gift the gods and goddesses gave me, I felt myself grow more beautiful and intelligent. At last one god limped forward, carrying an exquisite box of gold.

Zeus. Pandora, please accept this box which Hephaestos has fashioned. It is our gift for Man, whom you shall marry. Hermes will now guide you to Earth, where you will meet Man. Please present this to him. We must ask you not to open the box; it is for Man alone.

Pandora *(to the audience).* Can you imagine that! Twenty minutes old, and I would be married soon! *(to Zeus)* I thank you, mighty Zeus. And I thank all these great and kind gods and goddesses. I will remember your kindness always.

Using Your Comprehension Skills

Skim the table of contents for this book to review the selections you have read. Then, for each purpose listed below, choose one selection that you believe fulfills the purpose well.

1. To amuse the reader and make the reader laugh.
2. To bring out a feeling of dread or worry in the reader.
3. To make the reader think about how to get along with family members.
4. To help the reader see himself or herself more clearly as an individual.

Using Your Vocabulary Skills

Reread the scene from the play about Pandora. Identify which characters use formal standard English. Identify which characters use informal standard English. Point out at least one phrase that indicates the difference between these levels of language.

Using Your Writing Skills

1. Choose one of the two plays in this chapter. Write from one to three paragraphs explaining how the playwright informed the audience about the setting. Refer to various techniques used for different scenes.
2. Use the scene on page 596 as the introduction and write one or more additional scenes of the play about Pandora. Follow the plot of the story on pages 18 to 20.

Using Your Skills in Study and Research

Identify which of the following activities are effective for reading, understanding, and remembering a selection.

1. Reading in a quiet place
2. Taking notes
3. Stopping at every unfamiliar word to look it up in the dictionary
4. Discussing your reading with others
5. Comparing and contrasting selections
6. Skipping sections that seem confusing or difficult

Handbook for Reading and Writing

Literary Terms

Alliteration. The repetition of consonant sounds at the beginnings of words is called alliteration. The repeated sounds usually occur in several words in a series. Alliteration gives a musical quality to prose, poetry, or everyday speech.

> Fueled
> by a <u>m</u>illion
> <u>m</u>an-<u>m</u>ade
> wings of fire   ("Fueled," page 346)

For more about alliteration, see pages 210 and 211.

Article. An article is a serious, formal essay intended to inform or persuade. It is written from a background of compiling and organizing facts.

For more on articles, see page 525.

Assonance. The repetition of vowel sounds within words is called assonance. This repetition can create a desired mood or give a musical quality to prose or poetry. Note the feeling of space and distance created by the repetition of the *o* sound below.

> the lift of the pole vaulter over the bar
> the golf ball's flight to the green
> the home run into the bleachers
> ("Nine Triads," page 369)

For more on assonance, see page 218.

Autobiography. An autobiography is a true story that a person writes about his or her own life. It is usually written long after the events, when the person has had time to judge their importance. An example of an autobiography is "The Washwoman," by Isaac Bashevis Singer (pages 469 to 473).

For more about autobiography, see page 468.

Biography. A biography is a true account of a person's life, based on fact. It is written by someone other than the subject. The writer usually tries to include both the achievements and the weaknesses of a subject. "Banker Maggie Walker" (pages 488 to 494) is an example of a biography.

For more about biography, see page 481.

Character. Every person (or animal) who takes part in the action of a story, poem, or play is called a character. The most important character or characters are called the major characters. Everyone else in the selection is called a minor character. In the short story "Raymond's Run" (pages 280 to 287), Squeaky is the major character, while Raymond and Gretchen are minor characters.

For more about characters, see pages 3, 233, and 266. See also *Character Trait*.

Character Trait. A quality that a character exhibits is called a character trait. It can be indicated by the character's statements, actions, or thoughts. In "The Lady, or the Tiger?" (pages 239 to 242), the Princess exhibits the character trait of jealousy.

For more on character traits, see pages 72 and 243. See also *Character.*

Chronological Order. See *Time Order.*

Climax. The climax of a story usually involves an important event, decision, or discovery. It is the turning point of the story. In "A Spark Neglected" (page 246), the climax comes when Ivan realizes that he could have prevented the fire if he had been less interested in revenge.

For more about climax, see pages 136 and 233. See also *Plot.*

Comparison. A comparison shows how two different things have something in common. Writers often use comparison to make things clearer for the reader.

> I get lighter and lighter until I'm flying over the beach again, getting blown through the sky like a feather that weighs nothing at all. ("Raymond's Run," page 286)

See also *Contrast, Metaphor, Simile.*

Conflict. The struggle a character faces in a story is called the conflict. How the character faces the conflict creates the tension and suspense in the story. The conflict may be within a character, between two or more characters, or between a character and another force such as nature.

For more about conflict, see pages 47 and 266. See also *External Conflict, Internal Conflict,* and *Plot.*

Contrast. A contrast shows how different two things are. Here, contrast is used to show how two doors that look alike can be very different.

> If he opened one of them, there came out a hungry tiger, the fiercest that could be found, which immediately sprang upon him and tore him to pieces. . . . If the accused person opened the other door, there came forth from it a lady, the most suitable to his years and station that His Majesty could select. ("The Lady, or the Tiger?," page 239)

For more about contrast, see pages 102 and 103. See also *Comparison.*

Description. In a description, details are given to help the reader understand a character, setting, or action. A description may give sensory images. It may provide details appealing to sight, hearing, or other senses.

> Instead of the great white bird, there was a little man all in green with a golden crown and long beard, standing by the water. He had fierce glittering eyes and looked by no means friendly.
> ("The Third Wish," page 297)

For more about description, see page 4. See also *Direct Description* and *Indirect Description.*

Dialog. Conversation between characters in a story or play is called dialog. In the written form of a story, the exact words are set off by quotation marks. In plays, no quotation marks are used.

> "Is that you, Bob?" he asked doubtfully.
> "Is that you, Jimmy Wells?" cried the man in the door.
> ("After Twenty Years," page 253)

For more on dialog, see page 557.

Diary. A diary is a written daily record that a person makes of his or her own thoughts and activities. "The Life of Davy Crockett by Himself" is an example of a diary.

For more about diaries, see page 438.

Direct Description. A direct description is a statement of how a character looks or acts. It differs from indirect descriptions, in which the reader infers the characters appearance or action.

> The man in the doorway struck a match and lit his cigar. The light showed a pale, square-jawed face with keen eyes, and a little white scar near his right eyebrow. His scarf pin was a large diamond, oddly set. ("After Twenty Years," page 252)

For more about direct description, see page 4. See also *Description* and *Indirect Description.*

Drama. Writing that is meant to be performed by actors and actresses before an audience is called a drama, or play. It is told through the dialog and actions of its characters. It is a form of fiction that uses characters, setting, plot, dialog, and sometimes a narrator. Stage directions are usually included in a written drama. A cast of characters is usually listed at its beginning. The events of a play are shown in scenes, which change whenever the time or place changes. Several scenes may be included in one act. "Grandpa and the Statue" (pages 579 to 593) is an example of a play.

For more about drama, see pages 556 and 557. See also *Stage Directions.*

Essay. A type of nonfiction in which the writer develops ideas about a topic is called an essay. Informal essays reflect a writer's opinions, feelings, and personality. They are often humorous. Formal essays examine a topic in a thorough, logical way. They are well organized and usually serious. Often, a writer's opinion is not as obviously stated in a formal essay as in an informal essay.

For more about essay, see pages 512 and 513. See also *Nonfiction.*

External Conflict. A struggle occurring between two characters, or between a character and a force such as nature, is called an external conflict. In "The Assassin" (pages 319 to 323), one external conflict is between Bigelow and the force of history, or Fate. A second conflict is between Bigelow and the Union soldiers who were protecting Lincoln.

For more about external conflict, see pages 64 and 266. See also *Conflict, Internal Conflict,* and *Plot.*

Falling Action. Falling action is the part of the plot following the climax, in which the story draws to a conclusion. In "Lather and Nothing Else" (page 290), the climax occurs when the barber decides he cannot be a murderer. In the falling action, Torres reveals he knew about the barber's struggle.

For more on falling action, see page 233. See also *Plot* and *Climax.*

Fiction. Fiction is a type of writing in which the writer uses his or her imagination to create the characters, setting, and plot. Some types of fiction are short stories, legends, and drama. An example of fiction is "A Spark Neglected" (pages 246 to 249).

For more on fiction, see page 232.

Figurative Language. A way of speaking or writing that looks at familiar things in a creative, new way is called figurative language. Some kinds of figurative language are called figures of speech. Four common figures of speech are the following:

Metaphor	The locomotive is a roaring dragon.
Simile	The locomotive sputtered like a whale.
Personification	The locomotive flexed its muscles for a race.
Hyperbole	It took a year for the locomotive to arrive.

For more about Figurative Language, see pages 219 to 227. See also *Hyperbole, Metaphor, Personification,* and *Simile.*

Humor. Writing that amuses the reader has the quality of humor. A certain setting, characterization, or use of words can suggest humor. In "Learning To Drive" (page 521) the policeman asks the following questions when Billy Rose's car stalls at a traffic light: "What's the matter? Haven't we got any colors you like?"

For more about humor, see pages 511 and 513.

Humorous Sketch. A brief piece of humorous writing is called a humorous sketch. An example of this is "Punch, Brothers, Punch" (pages 514 to 518).

Hyperbole. An obvious exaggeration is called hyperbole. It is often used to stress a certain image. In "Raymond's Run" (page 281), Squeaky states that Cynthia "won the spelling bee for the millionth time."

For more about hyperbole, see pages 226 and 227. See also *Figurative Language.*

Imagery. Imagery is language that makes an object or experience so real that we can imagine it with our senses. Sensory images are created with details that help us see, feel, smell, hear, or taste things.

He was a shaggy, thick-necked fellow; his coat was greasy about the lapels and pockets, and his hand splayed over the cane's crook with a futile sort of clinging. ("A Man Who Had No Eyes," page 268)

For more on imagery, see page 374. See also *Figurative Language.*

Indirect Description. Indirect description is the opposite of direct description. The writer does not state directly how a character looks or acts. Instead, the writer leads you to understand a character by what that character says or does. In the following excerpt from "Lather and Nothing Else," you can tell that the character was afraid.

> He came in without a word. I was stropping my best razor. And when I recognized him I started to shake. But he did not notice. (page 290)

See also *Description, Direct Description.*

Internal Conflict. A struggle within a character is called internal conflict. This conflict usually involves a decision the character must make. For example, in "The Third Wish" (pages 297 to 302) Mr. Peters must decide whether or not to have Leita return to her former life.

For more about internal conflict, see pages 64 and 267. See also *Conflict, External Conflict, Plot.*

Introduction. The first part of the plot is called the introduction. It provides the reader with information about characters and setting that is needed to understand the plot.

> In the very olden time, there lived a semi-barbaric King. He was a man of strong will who loved authority. At the same time he wished to rule his subjects with fair and impartial justice. ("The Lady, or the Tiger?," page 239)

For more about the introduction, see page 233. See also *Plot.*

Irony. The contrast between what is expected, or what appears to be true, and what actually happens or exists is called irony. For example, in "The Weapon" (pages 313 to 316) Graham shows concern for his son's personal safety, but he fails to see that his work endangers the boy and the rest of the world as well.

For more about irony, see page 361.

Legend. A legend is a story about notable men and women of the past. Legends often combine fact and fiction. They indicate the values and ideals of the people who told the stories. An example of a legend is "The Trojan War" (pages 60 to 63).

For more about legends, see pages 56, 57, and 100.

Metaphor. A metaphor is a figure of speech comparing two unlike things that have something in common. The comparison is made without the use of *like* or *as,* as in a simile. In the following example, the sun is compared to a flower.

> I think the sun is a flower,
> That blooms for just one hour.
> ("All Summer In a Day," page 307)

For more about metaphor, see pages 222 and 223. See also *Simile* and *Figurative Language.*

Mood. The mood of a selection is the feeling you get as you read it. A writer sets the mood by his or her choice of words, images, and figures of speech. The mood of "Those Winter Sundays" (page 392) is one of melancholy. Other possible moods are cheerfulness and bitterness.

For more about mood, see page 331.

Myth. A myth is a story created to answer basic questions about the world, such as how the world began. It is very old and has been passed on orally over many generations. Every nation has its own myths. An example of a myth is "Pandora, the First Woman" (pages 18 to 20).

For more about myths, see pages 2, 3, 100, 101, 164, and 165.

Narrator. A narrator is the person who tells a story. A narrator may be either a first-person narrator or a third-person narrator. A first-person narrator is usually a character in the story, as in "Charles" (pages 259 to 261). The third-person narrator tells the story from outside the story, as in "The Third Wish" (pages 297 to 301).

There are two types of third-person narrators. A narrator who knows how all the characters think and feel is *omniscient.* The narrator in "The Lady, or the Tiger?" (pages 239 to 242) is omniscient. The narrator who tells only what one character thinks and feels is *limited,* as in "Thank You, M'am" (pages 273 to 276).

For more about narrator, see pages 267 and 557. See also *Point of View.*

Nonfiction. Writing that is based on fact is called nonfiction. It tells about real people, actual places, and true events. An example of nonfiction is "The Diary of a Young Girl" (pages 447 to 465).

For more about nonfiction, see pages 432, 433, 512, and 513.

Onomatopoeia. The use of words that sound like what they are describing is called onomatopoeia.

Here comes Gretchen walking back, for she's overshot the finish line too, *huffing* and *puffing* with her hands on her hips. ("Raymond's Run," page 286)

For more about onomatopoeia, see pages 216 and 217.

Personal Recollection. A personal recollection is similar to an autobiography in that it is written about a person's own life. However, it is generally about one event. "The First Day of the War" (pages 503 to 508) is an example of a personal recollection.

For more about personal recollection, see page 497.

Personification. A figure of speech in which human qualities are given to animals, objects, or ideas is personification.

The mountain lion declared that he should like to see man created like himself. ("Legend of Creation," page 170)

For more about personification, see page 224. See also *Figurative Language.*

Play. See *Drama*.

Plot. The plot is the sequence of events in a story. One event logically follows the next. Usually, each thing that happens is a result of what comes before it. The parts of the plot are the introduction, the rising action, the climax, the falling action, and the resolution.

For more about plot, see pages 232, 233, and 557. See also *Introduction, Rising Action, Climax, Falling Action, Resolution*.

Poetry. Poetry is a type of writing in which the words are arranged in lines rather than in sentences. The sounds of the words and their arrangement are important. The lines are arranged in groups called stanzas. "Thumbprint" (page 416) has one stanza of twenty lines. "Miracles" (page 408) has three stanzas of varying lengths. Sometimes the words of a poem are arranged in such a way that they suggest a picture. These are *concrete poems*.

For more on poetry, see pages 330, 331, 374, and 375. See also *Rhyme, Rhyme Scheme, Rhythm,* and *Stanza*.

Point of View. The way in which a narrator tells a story is called the point of view. There are different points of view, including first-person and third-person. In the first person, the narrator uses "I" and "me." In the third person, the narrator uses "he, she, it." "Raymond's Run" (pages 280 to 287) is told from a first-person point of view. "A Spark Neglected" (pages 246 to 249) is told from a third-person point of view.

For more about point of view, see page 267. See also *Narrator*.

Proverb. A saying, or proverb, states a popular opinion about life, generally in one sentence. Proverbs are usually stated in clever ways that are easy to remember.

For more on proverbs, see page 544.

Purpose. The author must decide what he or she wants the writing to do before beginning the process of writing. The purpose, or reason for writing, may be to amuse, inform, persuade, or express feelings.

For more on purpose, see page 433.

Repetition. When a writer repeats a word or group of words in a selection, he or she is using repetition. Writers often repeat a word or phrase to give special emphasis to a thought or action.

Macavity, Macavity, there's no one like
Macavity.
("Macavity: The Mystery Cat," page 349)

For more on repetition, see page 359.

Resolution. The last part of the plot is the resolution. It ties up the loose ends of a story. In "After Twenty Years" (pages 252 to 255), the resolution occurs when Bob reads the letter handed to him by the policeman.

For more about resolution, see page 233. See also *Plot*.

Rhyme. Rhyme is the repetition of sounds at the ends of words. Rhyming words usually come at the ends of lines in poetry. The rhyming words below are *hear* and *gear*.

> This is the song that the truck drivers hear
> In the grinding of brake and the shifting of
> gear. ("Song of the Truck," page 340)

For more about rhyme, see pages 212, 213, and 375. See also *Rhyme Scheme*.

Rhyme Scheme. A rhyme scheme is the pattern of rhyme in a poem. A different letter of the alphabet stands for each different rhyming ending.

> He talked, and as he talked   *a*
> Wallpaper came alive;   *b*
> Suddenly ghosts walked,   *a*
> And four doors were five;   *b*
> ("The Storyteller," page 386)

For more about rhyme scheme, see pages 213 and 348. See also *Rhyme*.

Rhythm. Rhythm is the pattern of accented and unaccented syllables in poetry. The accented or stressed syllables may be marked with $/$, while the unaccented or light syllables may be marked with $\smile$.

> The dinosaurs are not all dead.
> I saw one raise its iron head
> To watch me walking down the road
> Beyond our house today.
> ("Steam Shovel," page 348)

For more about rhythm, see page 214.

Rising Action. The second part of the plot is the rising action. In this part, it becomes evident that the characters face a problem, or conflict. In "Charles" (pages 259 to 261), the rising action occurs as Laurie each day reports on his day at school.

For more about rising action, see page 233. See also *Plot*.

Sequence. Events or ideas may be arranged in more than one sequence, or order. A writer can tell events in chronological sequence, or time order. Events may be arranged according to cause-and-effect relationships, or in a logical sequence. Details of description may be listed in the order they would be noticed, or in natural order.

For more on sequence of ideas in a paragraph, see page 166. See also *Time Order*.

Sensory Image. See *Imagery*.

Setting. The setting of a story is the time and place in which the events occur. In some stories, setting is more important than in others. The amount of detail given about the setting varies from story to story.

> The room was quiet in the dimness of early evening. Dr. James Graham, key scientist of a very important project, sat in his favorite chair, thinking. It was so still that he could hear the turning of pages in the next room as his son leafed through a picture book.
> ("The Weapon," page 313)

For more about setting, see pages 3 and 233.

Short Story. A short story is a work of fiction that can be read at one sitting. It usually tells about one major character and one major action. "Raymond's Run" (pages 280 to 287) is an example of a short story.

For more about the short story, see pages 232, 233, 266, and 267. See also *Fiction*.

Simile. A simile compares two unlike things, using the word *like* or *as*. The simile points out some quality the two things have in common. In "Central Park Tourney" (page 358), cars are compared to knights.

> Cars
> In the Park
> With long spear lights
> Ride at each other
> Like armored knights;

For more about simile, see pages 220 and 221. See also *Metaphor* and *Figurative Language*.

Stage Directions. Stage directions guide the actors in their performance of a play. The directions may tell the actors how to speak the words or what background sounds are needed. They are provided in the written form of a play, usually set off by italic print or parentheses, or both. In "Grandpa and the Statue" (page 579), the following stage directions may be found: *slight pause, laughs a little, peeved, and softly, as though Grandpa is in bed.*

For more about stage directions, see page 557.

Stanza. A group of lines in a poem is called a stanza. Stanzas, like paragraphs in prose, often show the organization of ideas in a poem. There is usually a space between two stanzas of a poem. An example of a poem with several stanzas is "Unfolding Bud" (page 342).

For more about stanza, see page 331.

Theme. The theme of the selection is the writer's main idea or concern in that selection. In "A Man Who Had No Eyes" (pages 268 to 270), for example, the writer is concerned with the different reactions people can have to difficulties. A second theme is that self pity can destroy a person.

For more about theme, see pages 267 and 331.

Time Order. Time order refers to the progression of events according to time. Most events in a story are also related in other ways, such as cause and effect. It is important to recognize which event comes first. This often explains how it causes the next event. For example, in "The Assassin" (pages 319 to 323), Walter Bigelow first had to invent his time distorter before he could go back in time.

For more on time order, see page 4.

Tone. The author's attitude toward what is being said in a story or poem is the tone. For example, in "Charles" (pages 259 to 261) the author's tone is humorous.

For more about tone, see page 433.

Summary of Comprehension Skills

Cause and Effect. Events are often related by cause and effect. One event causes another event. The second event is the effect of the first event.

Certain clue words tell the reader to look for cause and effect relationships. Among these clue words are: *because, so that, since, in order that,* and *if—then.*

For more about cause and effect, see page 5.

Chronological Order. See *Paragraph Organization.*

Comparison and Contrast. Finding similarities between two works of literature is called making comparisons. Finding the differences between selections is called making contrasts. Some elements that can be compared and contrasted are character, setting, plot, and theme.

For more about comparison and contrast, see pages 102 and 103.

Direct Statement. Understanding what the writer states directly is the key to reading well. The writer often provides a direct description of a character.

> Barbara was a tall blonde, with curls framing her face.

The writer also tries to make the time order clear, sometimes using clue words such as *first, then,* or *later.*

> Judy first read over the entire test. Then she began to answer all of the questions. Later, when she had time, she checked the entire test.

Cause and effect may also be noted in a direct statement. One event causes a later event. The following words signal a cause and effect relationship: *because, since, as a result, so . . . that,* and *if . . . then.*

> Since Bob did not bring his lunch to school, he bought lunch at the cafeteria.

For more about direct statement, see page 4.

Evaluations. After you have read a selection, you should be able to make a judgment or evaluation, about it. A fair evaluation is as objective as possible. It is based on established standards of good writing. When you evaluate a piece of writing, you should consider its elements one at a time. Elements to look at include characters, setting, plot, mood, theme, figures of speech, and sound techniques.

For more about evaluations, see pages 558 and 559.

Fact and Opinion. Facts and opinions are often combined. Facts are statements that can be proved. Opinions express only the writer's beliefs. They are statements that cannot be proved.

Writers often present facts that lead the reader to accept their opinions, as in the example below. The opinion is underlined. Following the opinion are two sentences that state facts.

> <u>Hawaii is the most beautiful of our fifty states.</u> Its islands have both rugged mountains and wide beaches. Many parts of Hawaii are covered with lush, green forests.

For more about separating fact and opinion, see pages 434 and 435.

Figurative Language. Figurative language is a way of speaking or writing that helps you look at familiar things in new ways. Figurative language means more than what it says on the surface.

For example, if someone tells you that you see the world through rose-colored glasses, it does not mean that you always see the color rose. It means that you see things in a positive way.

A writer may use something physical, such as an object or a color, to stand for an idea. That writer is using a symbol. For example, yellow is a symbol for caution.

The opposite of figurative language is literal language. Literal language means exactly what it says.

For more about figurative language, see pages 332 and 333.

Inferences. A logical guess based on given evidence is called an inference. Often a reader is expected to make inferences as he or she reads a selection. One must infer what the writer has not stated from what he or she has said. For example, you may read a sentence such as the following:

> The woman brushed dust off her clothes and climbed stiffly down from the stagecoach.

From the information given, you can infer that the setting is in the past, when stagecoaches were used. The woman has probably completed a long journey.

For more about inferences, see page 234.

Literal Language. See *Figurative Language*.

Main Idea. See *Paragraph Organization*.

Outcomes. When a reader makes a reasonable guess about what will happen next in a story, he or she is predicting an outcome. Some outcomes are easy to predict and others are more difficult.

When you predict outcomes, use the clues that the writer gives you. Consider any information about the characters, the plot, and the setting. Use your personal knowledge and experience to judge what people do in similar situations.

For more about predicting outcomes, see page 235.

Paragraph Organization. There are four basic kinds of paragraphs. To understand a paragraph, it is necessary to recognize the sequence, or the order in which the information is presented. A *narrative paragraph* tells about a series of events. The sentences are usually arranged in the order in which the events happen. Therefore, the sequence they follow is time order or chronological order.

Sometimes events are connected solely by chronological order. Usually, however, the first event must take place before the second event may occur. Here is an example from "After Twenty Years":

> The man in the doorway struck a match and lit his cigar. (page 252)

For more about recognizing time order, see page 166.

A *descriptive paragraph* describes a person, an object, or a scene. Detail sentences are usually arranged in the order or sequence in which you would notice the details. This is called spatial order. In "A Man Who Had No Eyes," the writer describes things as you would see them.

> He was a shaggy, thick-necked fellow; his coat was greasy about the lapels and pockets, and his hand splayed over the cane's crook with a futile sort of clinging. He wore a black pouch slung over his shoulder. (page 268)

A *persuasive paragraph* tries to persuade the reader. Sentences are arranged in a logical sequence. The writer's argument must make sense to the reader. Usually a persuasive paragraph is logically arranged with reasons presented in the order of importance to the writer. The reasons explain why the reader should think or behave in a certain way.

Many newspaper advertisements are examples of persuasive writing.

An *explanatory paragraph* explains something. After the topic sentence, the other sentences give details, usually in chronological order or order of importance.

> Karen Pryor tried a similar experiment with pigeons. The pigeons were put through the same kind of training as the dolphins. Surprisingly, they responded in the same way. They learned that they would be rewarded only for doing something new, something they hadn't learned to do before. The pigeons invented such tricks as lying on their backs, standing with both feet on one wing, and hovering two inches above the floor. ("How Smart are Dolphins?," page 536)

For more about paragraph organization, see pages 166 and 167.

Purpose. A writer decides what he or she wants the writing to accomplish before beginning to write. The purpose of a piece can be to entertain, to inform, to express feelings, to persuade, or to make readers laugh. The writer often chooses his or her topic or organization after considering the purpose of the writing. Treatment of elements such as plot, character, and setting also depend on the author's purpose.

For more about author's purpose, see pages 433 and 557.

Sequence. See *Paragraph Organization.*

Slanted Writing. Some writing appears to tell nothing but facts, but it is actually presenting the writer's opinions. This is called slanted writing. This type of writing can be biased and one-sided. The writer gives only the facts that agree with his or her personal opinion and ignores other facts. The writer may also use words with strong connotations or may use faulty generalizations.

For more about slanted writing, see page 435.

Symbols. See *Figurative Language.*

Time Order. See *Paragraph Organization.*

Word Choice. A writer's choice of words depends on many factors. A writer considers all of the following when he or she chooses a word: the mood of the piece of writing, the writer's tone, the writer's personal style, and the setting. Characters must sound as if they fit in the time and place described. For example, if the story takes place in ancient Greece, the characters might refer to chariots or bows and arrows.

For more about word choice, see page 366.

Summary of Vocabulary Skills

1. Word Parts

Some words are made by combining word parts. When you know the meanings of the word parts, you can discover the meaning of the whole word. Two kinds of word parts are base words and affixes. Two kinds of affixes are prefixes and suffixes.

Base Word. A word to which other word parts are added is called a base word. For example, the base word in *recover* is *cover*. The base word in *powerful* is *power*.

Prefix. A prefix is a word part added to the beginning of a base word. When you add a prefix to a base word, you change the meaning of the word.

Prefix	+	Base Word	=	New Word
mis-	+	spell	=	misspell

For a list of frequently used prefixes, see page 104.

Suffix. A suffix is a word part added to the end of a base word. The new word that is created has a different meaning from the base word alone.

Base Word	+	Suffix	=	New Word
home	+	-less	=	homeless

For a list of frequently used suffixes, see page 105.

You must make spelling changes before you can add suffixes to some words.

1. When a suffix beginning with a vowel is added to a word ending in silent *e*, the *e* is usually dropped.

leave + -ing = leaving

The *e* is not dropped when a suffix beginning with a consonant is added.

time + -ly = timely

2. When a suffix is added to a word ending in *y* preceded by a consonant, the *y* is usually changed to an *i*.

beauty + -ful = beautiful

When *y* is preceded by a vowel, the base word does not change.

joy + -ful = joyful

3. Double the final consonant when adding *-ing*, *-ed*, or *-er* to a one-syllable word that ends in one consonant preceded by one vowel.

skip + -ed = skipped

When two vowels precede the final consonant in a one-syllable word, the final consonant is not doubled.

dream + -ing = dreaming

2. Context Clues

Clues to the meaning of a new word can often be found in context. Context refers to the sentences and paragraphs that surround the word. Look for the following context clues as you read:

Antonyms. An antonym, or opposite, may be used as a clue to the meaning of a word. The antonym may be in the same sentence or in a nearby sentence. It often appears in the same position in the sentence as the new word.

> The Gettysburg Address is well-known for its brevity. Other speeches are famous for their great length.

Brevity is the opposite of "great length."

For more about antonyms, see page 303.

Comparison and Contrast Clues. Writers often compare one idea with another. Sometimes an unfamiliar word may be used in one part of the comparison. Then the other part of the comparison may give you a clue to the meaning of the word. Comparison clues use such clue words as *also, as, similar to, both, than,* and *in addition.*

> Before the tryouts for the play, Beth felt anxious. Other students felt just as nervous.

The comparison tells you that *anxious* means "nervous."

Writers also show how certain things are opposites by using contrast. A contrast clue tells what the new word is not. Some key words in contrast clues are *although, however, yet, on the other hand,* and *different from.*

> Sean is usually loquacious. However, today he has been very quiet.

From this example, *Loquacious* must mean the opposite of "quiet."

For more about comparison and contrast clues, see pages 236 and 237.

Definition or Restatement. The most direct clues to the meaning of a word are definition and restatement.

When definition is used, the meaning of a word is stated directly.

> A somnambulist is a person who walks in his sleep.

When restatement is used, the unfamiliar word is restated in a different way.

> Jeffrey is a somnambulist. That is, he walks in his sleep.

The following key words and punctuation tell you to look for a definition or restatement: *is, who is, which is, that is, in other words, or,* dashes, commas, and parentheses.

For more about definition and restatement clues, see page 168.

Example Clues. In an example clue, a new word is related to a group of familiar words.

The new word may be an example of a familiar term. Sometimes, familiar terms are examples of the new word.

The following key words signal an example clue: *for example*, *an example*, *one kind*, *some types*, *for instance*, and *such as*.

> The class examined one-celled animals, such as the amoeba, under the microscope.

For more about example clues, see pages 236 and 237.

Inference Clues. Writers sometimes leave clues about the meaning of unfamiliar words in different parts of the sentence. For example, clues to a new word in the subject can often be found in the predicate.

> The old lyre made harp-like music.

From this sentence, you can guess that a lyre is a musical instrument.

Sometimes the sentence in which a new word appears has no clues to its meaning. However, it may be possible to find clues to the meaning somewhere else in the same paragraph.

> Michael had never played polo before. The other three players on his team showed him how to drive the little ball through the other team's goal with the long-handled mallet. The hard part was being on horseback.

Context clues tell you that polo must be a game played on horseback by two teams with four members each. The object of the game is to hit a ball through the opponent's goal with a mallet.

Sometimes the main idea of a paragraph will give you a clue about the meaning of a new word. In this example are several clues that help you guess the meaning of the underlined word.

> Tom was described by his friends as indefatigable. He worked long hours, but never seemed tired. He took disappointments in stride. He always found the energy to begin new projects with enthusiasm.

The main idea of the paragraph tells you that *indefatigable* means "tireless."

For more about inferring meanings from context, see page 237.

Synonyms. A word that means the same or nearly the same as another word is called a synonym. Sometimes a word is used in the same sentence or paragraph as its synonym. The writer counts on you to understand either the word or its synonym.

> The blastoff made a terrific din. Its noise could be heard across the desert.

For more on synonyms, see page 169.

Words in a Series. Sometimes a new word may be part of a series of familiar words. If you know the meaning of one of the words, you can guess the meaning of the unknown word. In the following example, you can guess that a *torte* is a type of pastry.

> The bakery sells tortes, cakes, and pies.

For more about words in a series, see page 295.

3. Word Origins

Words in the English language come from many different sources. One ancient source is thought to be a prehistoric language called Indo-European. The first settlers of the island now called Great Britain spoke a form of Indo-European. However, in the centuries since that time, the English language has changed. Words have become part of the language in the following ways:

Borrowed Words. Throughout its history, the English language has taken words from other languages. Many words came from the French, Spanish, Italian, Latin, and Greek languages, as well as others.

Clipped Words. New words are often made by shortening existing words. For example, *math* was clipped from *mathematics*. *Gymnasium* was shortened to make the word *gym*.

Combined Words. Two words may be combined to form one new word. An example is *lifeguard*.

Words from Names. Some words are based on the name of a person or a place. For example, Braille, a system of printing for the blind using a pattern of raised dots, comes from the name of Louis Braille. Braille was a French teacher who invented the system.

Word Parts. Many Greek and Latin word parts are used as prefixes and suffixes in English words. If you know the meaning of the Greek and Latin word parts, you can figure out the meaning of the whole word. For example, the Greek prefix *auto-* means "self." The word part *graph* means "to write." Together, these word parts make the word *autograph*, which is another word for a person's signature.

Words from Sounds. Some words imitate sounds. These words are called echoic words. Some examples are *cluck*, *hoot*, and *zoom*.

For more about word origins, see pages 334 and 335.

4. Reference Books: The Dictionary, Glossary, and Thesaurus

A **dictionary** is an alphabetical listing of words and their meanings. If context clues and word parts do not give enough information to allow you to understand an unfamiliar word, you can use a dictionary.

Some words have more than one meaning. The dictionary lists all the meanings of each word. To choose the right meaning for your particular use, test each definition in the sentence in which you found the word.

A **glossary** can be found in the back of some nonfiction books. Like the dictionary, it is an alphabetical listing of words and their meanings. However, the words a glossary defines are limited to the new or unfamiliar words in the book. The definition of a word in the glossary is often limited to the way it is used in a particular selection.

A **thesaurus** lists words with other words of similar meanings, and sometimes with opposites. The thesaurus usually gives some explanation of the differences. You use a thesaurus when you need to find the exact word for your meaning.

For more about the dictionary, see pages 436 and 437; the glossary, page 485; and the thesaurus, page 355.

See also *The Dictionary* and *The Thesaurus* under Guidelines for Study and Research.

5. Levels of Language

Standard English is English that is accepted and understood everywhere English is spoken. Standard English may be formal or informal. Formal standard English is used in serious or formal situations, such as in business letters, classroom assignments, and speeches. Informal standard English is used in everyday conversation. It follows all the rules of grammar, just as formal English does, but it sounds more natural. It also uses some words or meanings called colloquialisms, words not used in formal English.

Nonstandard English includes language that does not follow the traditional rules of grammar. Words such as *ain't* and local dialects are considered nonstandard.

Slang is a type of nonstandard English. It includes new words or words with new meanings. Some slang words are used for only a short time.

Jargon is a type of nonstandard English that includes special words or special meanings. These are used by a certain group of people, such as people who work in a particular business.

For more about recognizing the levels of language, see pages 580 and 581.

Guidelines for the Process of Writing

When writers write, they follow certain steps. Each time you write, you should follow the same steps. Together, these steps are called the process of writing.

The process of writing has three stages: **pre-writing**, **writing**, and **revising**.

Stage 1: Pre-Writing

In pre-writing, you prepare to write. During this stage you think, plan, do your research, and organize. Below are the five steps of pre-writing.

1. Choose and limit a topic. Make a list of ideas that are interesting to you. Think about what you could say about each topic. Choose the topic that seems most interesting. Then make a list of things you could write about that topic. Limit the items on your list to match the expected length of your writing.

For example, a student was asked to write a paragraph about Greek myths. She thought about the myths she had read. She listed several possible topics concerning myths. Then she circled the one she thought was most interesting.

setting   creation of humans
mood   role of gods in human life

2. Decide on your purpose. Decide what you want to do with the topic. Would you like to explain it, describe it, or criticize it? Do you want to teach your readers or persuade them to do something? Or are you trying to amuse them? Your purpose will determine how you write about your subject.

The student writing about myths decided that, to her, the most interesting idea was the role of the gods in human life. She decided to write a paragraph comparing the role of the gods in "The Beginning of the World" and "The Flood."

3. Decide on your audience. Decide for whom you are writing. You will then be better able to choose your level of language. For example, students reading a story might enjoy informal language. When they read a textbook, they might want a more formal step-by-step approach.

4. Gather supporting information. List what you know about the topic. Decide whether you need more information. If so, you may need to use reference sources, such as encyclopedias.

The student writing about myths reread both of her selections. She wrote notes on every part that had to do with how the gods affected human life.

"The Beginning of the World"
Prometheus was a god.
He shaped a human form from clay.
He put the seed of life in it.
The first man was alive.
Prometheus gave fire to humans.

"The Flood"
Two humans were left alive after a flood.
Goddess Themis told them to throw stones.
Stones turned into more humans.

5. Organize your ideas. Review your list of details and information. Some details will be useful in your writing. Cross out the ones that you will not be using.

Choose a logical order for your details. You may decide to use time order, if you are writing a story. For a description, you may list details in the order you would notice them. Make an outline, or plan, showing the order in which you will present your ideas.

Here is the student's outline for her paragraph. She has written out and underlined her main idea. This will help her keep her sentences on the subject.

Comparison of Myths
Main Idea: Greek myths tell how humans depended on the gods to keep them alive.

Important details:
A. Prometheus, a god, created first human
   1. Used clay
   2. Put seed of life in the human
B. Themis, a goddess, helped humans survive after the flood
   1. Two humans were left alive.
   2. They threw stones.
   3. Stones turned into people.

Stage 2: Writing a First Draft

You should now be ready to put your ideas down on paper. At this stage, don't concentrate on getting everything done perfectly. That will come later. For now, keep your purpose and audience in mind. Follow your outline as much as possible. Remember that you may change your outline if better ideas come to you as you write.

This is how the student in the example wrote the first draft of her comparison.

First Draft

```
Some myths says humans are alive because of kind gods. The god
Prometheus made the first human from clay he put the seed of
life into the first man. Another myth tells about how the
godess Themis after a great flood helped humans. She told them
to throw some stones so the stones turned into other humans
Greek Myths tell how pepole needed the help of kind gods.
```

Stage 3: Revising

Revising means making changes in your writing to improve it. Read what you have written. Ask yourself these questions.

1. Is the writing interesting? Will others want to read it?
2. Did you stick to your topic? Are there any unnecessary details? Should any other details be added?
3. Is the organization easy to follow? Do ideas flow together smoothly?
4. Is every group of words a sentence? Is every word the best word?

Mark any corrections and notes on your first draft. It is not unusual to make corrections to your corrections. You may need to write several drafts before you are satisfied with your work.

Proofreading. Your writing should be correct as well as clear and interesting. Reread what you have written. Check for any errors in capitalization, punctuation, grammar, and spelling. Correct your errors. Use the symbols at the top of page 621.

Look at the sample draft that is being revised. Notice how the writer has improved the piece by crossing out unnecessary words, by adding precise words, and by moving ideas around. The writer has also corrected errors in capitalization, punctuation, grammar, and spelling. To do this, she used proofreading symbols. First study this draft, then compare it with the final draft on page 621. Note how the changes that were marked here have been carried out in the final copy.

Revised Draft

A Greek
~~Some~~ myths says humans are alive because the gods were of kind ~~gods~~. ~~The god~~ In one myth,
a god named formed a the of the earth.
Prometheus ~~made the first~~ human from clay he put the seed of
the human shape and made
life into the first man. Another myth tells ~~about~~ how the
d   the two   left alive
godess Themis /after a great flood\ helped humans, She told them
living
to throw ~~some~~ stones ~~so~~ the stones turned into ~~other~~ humans.
Both of these
~~Greek~~ Myths tell how people needed the help of kind gods.

Proofreading Symbols

Symbol	Meaning	Example
∧	insert	god_ess
≡	capitalize	he
/	make lower case	Myths
∼	transpose (trade positions)	pepole
ℯ	omit letters, words	some
¶	make new paragraph	¶ Greek
⊙	insert a period	humans ⊙

Writing the Final Copy. As soon as you feel your writing is both clear and correct, write your final copy. Do it neatly and carefully. Indent paragraphs correctly. Then proofread your work again. Finally, look for any errors you might have missed.

Notice that in making this final copy, the student found and corrected an error in punctuation. She improved the wording of one phrase that had not been marked before. She added one more detail to complete her explanation.

Final Copy

> Greek myths say humans are alive because the gods were kind. In one myth, a god named Prometheus formed a human from the clay of the earth. He put the seed of life into the human shape and made the first man. Another myth tells how the goddess Themis helped the two humans left alive after a great flood. She told them to throw stones. The stones turned into living humans. Both of these myths say that people needed the help of kind and merciful gods.

Checklist for the Process of Writing

Pre-Writing

1. Choose and limit a topic.
2. Decide on your purpose.
3. Decide on your audience.
4. Gather supporting information.
5. Organize your ideas.

Writing Your First Draft

1. Begin writing. Keep your topic, purpose, and audience in mind at all times.
2. As you write, you may add new details.
3. Concentrate on ideas. Do not be concerned with grammar and mechanics at this time.

Revising

1. Read your first draft. Ask yourself these questions:

   a. Do you like what you have written? Is it interesting? Will others want to read it?
   b. Did you accomplish what you set out to do?
   c. Is your writing organized well? Do the ideas flow smoothly from one paragraph to the next? Are the ideas arranged logically?
   d. Does each paragraph have a topic sentence? Does every sentence stick to the topic? Should any sentence be moved?
   e. Should any details be left out? Should any be added?
   f. Does every sentence express a complete thought? Are your sentences easy to understand?
   g. Is every word the best possible word?

2. Mark any changes on your paper.

Proofreading

Ask yourself these questions as you check your writing for errors in grammar and usage, capitalization, punctuation, and spelling.

Grammar and Usage

a. Is every word group a complete sentence?
b. Does every verb agree with its subject?
c. Have you used the correct form of each pronoun?
d. Is the form of each adjective correct?
e. Is the form of each adverb correct?

Capitalization

a. Is the first word in every sentence capitalized?
b. Are all proper nouns and adjectives capitalized?
c. Are titles capitalized correctly?

Punctuation

a. Does each sentence have the correct end mark?
b. Have you used punctuation marks such as commas, apostrophes, hyphens, colons, semicolons, question marks, quotation marks, and underlining correctly?

Spelling

a. Did you check unfamiliar words in a dictionary?
b. Did you spell plural and possessive forms correctly?

Preparing the Final Copy

1. Make a clean copy of your writing. Make all changes and correct all errors. Then ask yourself these questions:

   a. Is your handwriting neat and easy to read?
   b. Are your margins wide enough?
   c. Is every paragraph indented?

2. Proofread your writing again. Read it aloud. Correct any mistakes neatly.

Guidelines for Study and Research

1. Using Reference Materials

The Dictionary

The dictionary lists words, in alphabetical order, along with their meanings. The **glossary** in a nonfiction book is like a dictionary. However, it limits its entry words to words from that book.

How To Find a Word. Guide words help you find the word you are looking up. Guide words are printed in heavy black type at the top of each page. They show the first and last words on the page.

For example, here are the guide words for two pages of a dictionary. On which page will *superficial* be listed?

suave—superior   supervise—sustain

You must examine the words to the sixth letter. Since *f* comes before *i, superficial* will appear between *suave* and *superior.*

What the Entry Word Tells You. The entry word, printed in dark type, tells how to spell the word correctly. It also tells how to break the word into syllables.

How To Find the Pronunciation. A respelling appears in parentheses after each entry word. It uses letters and symbols to stand for the sound of the spoken word. To understand how to pronounce these symbols, refer to the pronunciation key on that page or the page opposite it. (For the meaning of symbols in the respelling below, refer to the pronunciation key in the Glossary.)

> **su·per·fi·cial** (sōō′pər fish′əl) *adj.* of or on the surface; shallow.

Accent marks show which syllable or syllables to stress when you pronounce the word. Words with more than one syllable may have more than one accent. The heavy accent, the primary accent, is printed in dark type. The secondary accent is a lighter stress. It is printed in lighter type.

How To Find the Part of Speech. An abbreviation following the respelling tells the part of speech of the word. The definition, or meaning, of the word follows. Some words have many definitions listed. In addition, many words can be used as more than one part of speech. Definitions for each part of speech are grouped together.

After some entries, subentries are listed. Subentries are familiar phrases in which the entry word appears. The dictionary lists any special meanings of each phrase.

For more about using a dictionary, see pages 444, 466, and 474.

The Thesaurus

A thesaurus is a listing of words followed by related words. A thesaurus helps you locate the exact word you need to express your meaning. The related words are often synonyms for the listed word. Others are antonyms, words that have the opposite meaning from the entry word.

Suppose you needed a word to use instead of the word *happy*. You would find the listing for *happy* in the thesaurus. There would be listed such related words as *contented* and *glad*. You might also find antonyms for the word, such as *dejected*, or other words to look up such as *cheerfulness*.

Each thesaurus is organized a little differently. To use a thesaurus, you need to read the directions in that book. The index at the back of the thesaurus may also be helpful.

For more about using a thesaurus, see pages 355 and 617.

The Encyclopedia

The encyclopedia contains articles about a wide variety of topics. The articles are listed in alphabetical order, according to their titles. Many encyclopedias are several volumes long. An index telling what topics are discussed appears in the final volume.

The index of an encyclopedia is useful when you are looking for information. It tells which articles have information on each topic. It lists the volume and page where you can find each article.

For more about using the encyclopedia, see pages 244, 251, and 471.

The Nonfiction Book

A nonfiction book may be your best source of information concerning a specific topic. To decide whether a certain book will be useful to you, examine these parts:

The title page. Does the title mention your topic? Does the author or the editor have knowledge about the topic?

The copyright page. When was the book written and published? Some topics require up-to-date information.

The table of contents. Is the book organized clearly? Do the part titles or chapter titles suggest what you can find in each section of the book? Do they make it easy for you to find your topic?

The index. Does the index list terms or names that you need information about? Are the pages with maps, graphs, or illustrations indicated by boldface or italic type?

Readers' Guide to Periodical Literature

Magazines are a good source of information for anyone writing a report. They give current information on many interesting topics. To find magazine articles, use the Readers' Guide to Periodical Literature.

The Readers' Guide is an alphabetical listing of topics that have been discussed in magazine articles during a specific period of time. Under the topic, the guide lists the titles of articles on that subject and the magazines in which they were printed.

For more on using the Readers' Guide, see page 263.

2. Finding the Right Resource Material

The Library

The library contains many different sources of information. Among them are magazines, records, filmstrips, movies, microfilm, as well as books. The media specialist at your library can help you find any material you need.

Books are a major source of information. The books in a library are divided into two groups: fiction and nonfiction.

Fiction books are stories about imaginary events. These books are arranged alphabetically according to the author's last name. The author's name appears on the spine of the book.

Nonfiction books contain factual information. They are usually arranged according to the Dewey Decimal System. Each book is assigned a number in one of ten categories. That number is a call number and is printed on the spine of the book. The books are arranged on the shelves in numerical order. Biographies are usually in a separate section of the library. They are arranged by the last name of the person who the book is about.

THE DEWEY DECIMAL SYSTEM

000–099	General Works	encyclopedias, almanacs, handbooks
100–199	Philosophy	conduct, ethics, psychology
200–299	Religion	the Bible, mythology, theology
300–399	Social Science	economics, law, education, commerce, government, folklore, legend
400–499	Language	languages, grammar, dictionaries
500–599	Science	mathematics, chemistry, physics
600–699	Useful Arts	farming, cooking, sewing, radio, nursing, engineering, television, business, gardening, cars
700–799	Fine Arts	music, painting, drawing, acting, photography, games, sports
800–899	Literature	poetry, plays, essays
900–999	History	biography, travel, geography

The Card Catalog

The card catalog lists all the books in the library. The cards are arranged in alphabetical order according to the words on the top line of the card.

Each book has three cards: an author card, a title card, and a subject card. Each card contains the same information, but in a different order. The author card lists the author's name on the first line. The title card lists the title of the book on the first line. The subject card lists the subject or topic of the book on the first line. On the top left corner of each card; you will find the call number.

Your library may also have a catalog for audio-visual materials such as records or films. It is probably organized like the card catalog for books.

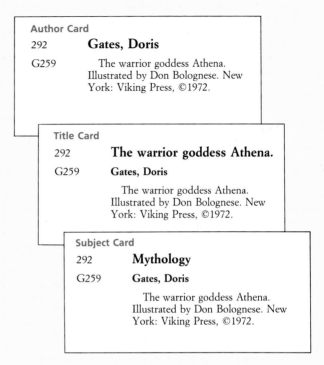

Author Card
292 **Gates, Doris**
G259   The warrior goddess Athena.
             Illustrated by Don Bolognese. New
             York: Viking Press, ©1972.

Title Card
292 **The warrior goddess Athena.**
G259   **Gates, Doris**
             The warrior goddess Athena.
             Illustrated by Don Bolognese. New
             York: Viking Press, ©1972.

Subject Card
292 **Mythology**
G259   **Gates, Doris**
             The warrior goddess Athena.
             Illustrated by Don Bolognese. New
             York: Viking Press, ©1972.

3. Preparing to Study

Preparations in Class

Before beginning an assignment, be sure you know what you are asked for. The first step to studying is listening carefully to directions.

1. Concentrate on only the directions about to be given.
2. Note how many steps there are.
3. Relate a key word to each step, such as *Read, Answer,* or *Write.*
4. If you do not understand a step, ask questions.

5. Repeat the directions to yourself and write them down.

An assignment notebook will help you keep track of what you must do. For each assignment, write the following:

1. The subject
2. The assignment and any details
3. The date the assignment is given
4. The date the assignment is due

Subject	Assignment	Date given	Date due

Your Schedule for Study Time

Plan ahead to complete assignments.

Some reading and writing assignments require a small amount of time. These are called short-term goals. Set aside time each day to work on these assignments.

Assignments that cannot be completed overnight are called long-term goals. They become more manageable when you break them down into smaller tasks. Estimate how long each small task will take. Then develop a plan for completing them.

A study plan will help you complete your work. On your plan, show what you will accomplish each day. Show the times you will work on your project.

4. Studying

Three Types of Reading

There are three types of reading that you will find useful in your studying. Each is used for a particular purpose.

Scanning is a kind of fast reading. It lets you find a specific piece of information quickly. Scanning means moving your eyes rapidly over the page. Look for key words that point out the information you need.

Skimming is another type of fast reading. It gives you an overview of the material you are about to read. Skimming means moving your eyes quickly over the material looking for titles, subtitles, and illustrations that will give you clues about the content of the material.

The third kind of reading is **study-type reading.** Take your time for this type of reading. Try to get as much meaning as you can from the words. Try to identify the order in which the information is arranged. Make connections between statements. The SQ3R study method is an example of effective study-type reading.

The SQ3R Study Method

The **SQ3R study method** is a good way to improve skills in reading and studying. SQ3R stands for five steps: Survey, Question, Read, Recite, and Review.

Survey. Get a general idea of what the material is about. Look at illustrations, such as pictures, maps, graphs, or tables. Read the titles and subtitles. Read the introduction and the summary.

Question. Read any study questions provided in the book or by your teacher. If there are none think of your own by turning titles and headings into questions.

Read. Read the material. Keep the study questions in mind. Keep track of main ideas.

Recite. After reading, recite the answers to the study questions. Write a few notes to help you remember any important ideas.

Review. Look back at the study questions and try to answer them without using your notes. Finally, study your notes to be sure you will remember them later.

Note-Taking

You will probably recognize main ideas and important facts as you read. Write them in a notebook or on cards.

Taking notes has two uses: 1) it helps you concentrate on the material and 2) it gives you something to study for a review.

Notes should be written clearly so you will be able to understand them later. They do not have to be written in sentences. Be sure to write down where your information came from. You may need to refer to that source again. Include the following source information in your notes.

Books. Give the title, the author, the copyright date, and the page number.

Magazine or Newspaper Articles. Give the name and date of the periodical, the title of the article, the name of the author, and the page numbers of the article.

Encyclopedias. Give the name of the set, the title of the entry, the volume number where the entry appears, and the page numbers of the entry.

Records. Write the title, the record company, and the date.

Direct Interviews. Write the name of the person you interviewed and the date of the interview.

Outlining

An **outline** is a way of organizing ideas and facts. It helps you see which ideas are main ideas and which ones are supporting details. When you make an outline, you begin to see the connections between ideas and facts.

To make an outline of some material you have read, first list the main ideas. The main ideas are often main headings. Under the main ideas, list any headings or subtitles that tell more about the main ideas. Under the subtitles, list smaller details.

Sample Note Card

Title of book	Copyright date
The Warrior Goddess Athena,	*1972*
Author	Page number
Doris Gates	*page 13*

Athena was the Goddess of Wisdom as well as the Goddess of War. She taught women the art of weaving and other crafts.

Outline Form

I. Main Idea
  A. Subtopic
    1. Detail
    2. Detail
  B. Subtopic
II. Main Idea
  A. Subtopic
  B. Subtopic
    1. Detail
    2. Detail

Summary of Skills in Critical Thinking

Analysis. Analysis is a process in which you study something carefully, piece by piece. It is often difficult to understand a piece of writing fully when you look at it all at once. That is why analysis is such a useful skill. When you analyze, you focus on each part individually.

For example, when you analyze a story, you may want to look at its characters, its setting, its dialog, or any other element.

As you study each part separately, you understand the whole selection better. Also, analysis helps you see the similarities and differences between selections.

Throughout this text, study questions in Developing Comprehension Skills, Reading Literature, and Developing Writing Skills focus the reader's attention on individual elements in the selections. In addition, questions under Developing Skills in Critical Thinking develop specific skills of analysis on pages 72, 111, 123, and 195.

Categorizing and Classifying. Categorizing and classifying mean grouping according to common elements. For example, imagine that you wanted to talk about an element of short stories, such as point of view. You would review short stories you have read. Then you might group together stories told from the first-person point of view together. Other short stories told from the third-person point of view would also be classified together.

Pieces of writing that are categorized or classified together have some element in common. That element could be similar characters, setting, or theme. It could be similar plots or point of view. When you classify literature, first decide on the element that the pieces have in common.

For more about classifying, see pages 90, 371, and 420.

Evaluation. To evaluate a piece of writing, you study it carefully and decide on its value. You must use certain standards to judge the worth of a selection.

Writing can be evaluated in two ways. First, you can judge the skills of the writer. Ask yourself questions such as these: How well has the writer achieved his or her purpose? Are the important elements in this type of writing developed well? Has the writer used effective methods of presenting ideas? Is the writing organized logically? Do the ideas make sense? Are the figures of speech clear?

The second type of evaluation is judging what the writer says, not only how he or she says it. Is the writing truthful and accurate? Is the writer qualified to write about this subject? Do you suspect that the writer is biased in any way? Has he or she left out important facts? What are the qualities that make this piece worth reading?

When you evaluate what writers write, watch for evidences of faulty thinking such as the following:

1. unsupported generalizations
2. confusion of fact and opinion
3. slanted writing

You know many of the elements that go together to make good writing. Apply the standards of good writing to everything you read.

For more about evaluation, see pages 401 and 558.

Fact and Opinion. Facts are statements that can be proved to be true. Opinions, on the other hand, are statements of a person's beliefs. They may or may not be supported by facts.

Fact: The sun rose at 6:05 A.M.
Opinion: The sunrise was beautiful this morning.

Opinions, although they cannot always be proved, should be based on evidence. You are often asked to give your opinion about an issue or question. You should be able to point to the reasons why you hold that opinion.

Throughout this text, study questions in Developing Comprehension Skills, Reading Literature, and Developing Writing Skills ask the reader to form and present opinions with supporting reasons. Some of these study questions are on pages 65, 243, and 409.

For more about separating fact and opinion, see pages 434 and 435.

Generalizations. A generalization is a statement about a group that is supposedly true of all members of the group. Although any generalization should be accurate and based on facts, readers should be aware that many generalizations are faulty. A generalization is faulty or inaccurate when it is not based on enough facts. Writers sometimes do not look at the facts in enough cases. They apply the generalization to more instances than the facts will support.

A fair generalization might be the following statement:

To be alert, all people need sleep.

The following is an example of a faulty generalization:

All people need eight hours of sleep to be alert.

If even one person does not need eight hours of sleep, the generalization is faulty.

Study questions about generalizations can be found under Developing Skills in Critical Thinking on pages 138 and 365.

Slanted Writing. Many times, statements that sound like facts are actually opinions. They cannot be proved. The writer uses these statements to make the reader think he or she must accept one view of the topic.

This is a type of slanted writing, writing that tries to present only one side of an issue. A second way that a writer can slant writing is by including certain details and leaving out any facts that do not support his or her opinion.

A third way a writer can express opinions is by careful word choice. Writers choose words with the meaning they want to express. They consider both the denotation and connotations of each word. Denotations are dictionary meanings. Connotations are the feelings or ideas a word brings to mind. In slanted writing, writers use many words with strong connotations. Connotations of some words may lead readers to feel strongly in favor of a point of view. The connotations of other words may make readers feel strongly against a subject.

For example, a speech could be described as "thorough and informative" by someone who enjoyed it. Someone who was bored by the speech might describe it as "overlong and rambling." A neutral observer might simply say the speech lasted thirty minutes.

Slanted writing is a powerful tool. It can make a reader agree with a writer without any good reasons. Be aware of its power as you read.

For more about slanted writing and connotations, see pages 28 and 117.

Glossary

The **glossary** is an alphabetical listing of words from the selections, with meanings. The glossary gives the following information:

1. **The entry word broken into syllables.**

2. **The pronunciation of each word.** The **respelling** is shown in parentheses. The most common way to pronounce a word is listed first. The Pronunciation Key below shows the symbols for the sounds of letters and key words that contain those sounds.

   A **primary accent ′** is placed after the syllable that is stressed the most when the word is spoken. A **secondary accent ′** is placed after a syllable that has a lighter stress.

3. **The part of speech of the word.** These abbreviations are used:

   n. noun   *v.* verb   *adj.* adjective   *adv.* adverb

4. **The meaning of the word.** The definitions listed in the glossary apply to selected ways a word is used in these selections.

5. **Related forms.** Words with suffixes such as *-ing, -ed, -ness,* and *-ly* are listed under the base word.

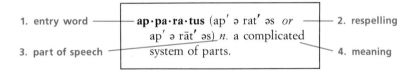

Pronunciation Key

a	fat	i	hit	o͝o	look		ə ⎰	a *in* ago	ch	chin
ā	ape	ī	bite, fire	o͞o	tool			e *in* agent	sh	she
ä	car	ō	go	ou	out			i *in* sanity	th	thin
e	ten	ô	law, horn	u	up			o *in* comply	*th*	then
ē	even	oi	oil	ur	fur			u *in* focus	zh	leisure
				'l	able		ər	perhaps	ng	ring

A

ab·stract (ab strakt′ *or* ab′ strakt) *adj.* thought of apart from a specific act or thing.

ab·surd (əb surd′ *or* ab zurd′) *adj.* so clearly untrue as to be something to laugh at. — **absurdity** *n.*

ac·com·pa·ni·ment (ə kum′ pə ni mənt) *n.* one thing that goes along with another thing; especially music played along with a solo.

ac·cord (ə kôrd′) *n.* consent, agreement.

a·cous·tic (ə kōōs′ tik) *adj.* to do with hearing or sound.

ac·quit·tal (ə kwit′ ′l) *n.* the freeing of an accused person by the verdict of "not guilty."

ad·min·is·ter (ad min′ ə stər) *v.* to carry out or give.

a·droit (ə droit′) *adj.* clever, skillful.

ad·vance (əd vans′) *v.* to lend.

ag·o·ny (ag′ ə nē) *n.* great pain in mind or body.

ale (āl) *n.* drink similar to beer, made from hops and malt.

am·bro·sia (am brō′ zhə) *n.* the food eaten by the ancient Greek and Roman gods.

am·i·ca·ble (am′ i kə b′l) *adj.* friendly.

am·phi·the·a·ter *or* **am·phi·the·a·tre** (am′ fe thē′ə tər) *n.* a round or oval building with rising rows of seats around an open area in which sports events and shows are held.

an·ces·tor (an′ ses tər) *n.* a person who comes before one in the family line, especially someone earlier than grandparents.

an·vil (an′ vəl) *n.* an iron or steel block on which heated metal things are hammered into shape.

ap·pall (ə pôl′) *v.* to cause to feel shock or upset.

ap·pa·ra·tus (ap′ə rat′ əs *or* ap′ə rāt′ əs) *n.* a complicated system of parts.

ap·pre·hen·sive (ap′rə hen′ siv) *adj.* feeling anxious or afraid about what may happen.

arch·er·y (är′ chər ē) *n.* the knowledge or sport of shooting with a bow and arrow.

a·re·na (ə rē′ nə) *n.* a building with an open space in the middle that can be used for events such as sports or concerts.

ar·ray (ə rā′) *v.* to dress in fine clothes.

as·cer·tain (as′ər tān′) *v.* to find out so as to be sure.

as·sas·sin (ə sas′ ′n) *n.* a murderer.

as·sault (ə sôlt′) *n.* a sudden attack made with tremendous force.

as·sem·blage (ə sem′ blij) *n.* a group of people or things gathered together.

a·sy·lum (ə sī′ ləm) *n.* a place that is a home for groups of helpless people such as orphans, the very old, or mentally ill.

a·tro·cious (ə trō′ shəs) *adj.* highly cruel or evil.

aus·tere (ô stir′) *adj.* very strict in the way one acts or looks.

au·to·mat·ic (ô′ tə mat′ ik) *adj.* done without thinking, as though by a machine.

a·vail (ə vāl′) *v.* to be of help or advantage.

av·a·lanche (av′ ə lanch) *n.* a large mass of rocks, snow, or ice, sliding rapidly down a mountain.

a·venge (ə venj′) *v.* to get revenge for; get even for a wrong or harm. — **avenger** *n.*

a·vert (ə vurt′) *v.* to turn away from something.

B

baf·fle (baf′ ′l) *v.* to confuse or perplex so as to keep from understanding or solving; puzzle.

bald (bôld) *adj.* plain and honest.

bam·boo (bam bōō′) *n.* a plant that grows in the tropics.

bank·rupt (bangk′ rupt) *adj.* unable to pay one's debts and freed by law from having to do so. — **bankruptcy** *n.*

bard (bärd) *n.* one who wrote and sang songs in ancient times.

bar·ra·cu·da (bar′ə kōō′ də) *n.* a large, ferocious fish found in warm seas.

bar·ren (bar′ ən) *adj.* unable to produce crops or fruit.

bat·ter·y (bat′ ər ē) *n.* an amount of heavy guns or cannons, used together in warfare.

bat·tle·ment (bat′ ′l mənt) *n.* a low wall on a tower, with spaces left open to shoot through.

bel·lows (bel′ ōz) *n. pl.* a device that blows out air by squeezing its sides together. It is often used to make fires burn hotter.

ben·e·dic·tion (ben′ə dik′ shən) *n.* blessing.

be·stow (bi stō′) *v.* to give as a present.

bit·ters (bit′ ərz) *n.pl.* a liquor containing bitter herbs, used for medicine and sometimes in cocktails.

biv·ou·ac (biv′ wak *or* biv′ ͞o͞o wak′) *n.* an outdoor camp for soldiers, set up with little or no shelter.

black·smith (blak′ smith) *n.* a person who makes or repairs iron things by heating them and hammering them into shapes.

blithe (blīth *or* blith) *adj.* happy; carefree.

boar (bôr) *n.* a male pig.

bol·ster (bōl′ stər) *n.* a long, narrow cushion or pillow.

boor·ish (b͞o͝or′ ish) *adj.* rude or awkward.

bor·ough (bʉr′ ō) *n.* one of the five main areas of New York City.

bough (bou) *n.* a large branch from a tree.

britch·es (brich′ iz) *n.pl.* trousers.

bul·ly (b͝o͝ol ē) *adj.* fine, wonderful.

bur·row (bʉr′ ō) *v.* to dig into a burrow.

C

cal·a·bash (kal′ ə bash) *n.* a bowl or tobacco pipe made from the dried shell of the calabash fruit.

ca·lam·i·ty (kə lam′ ə tē) *n.* an awful happening that brings great sadness; disaster.

cal·cu·late (kal′ kyə lāt) *v.* to discover by using arithmetic; to compute.

cal·lous·ly (kal′ əs le) *adv.* in an unfeeling or insensitive manner.

ca·pac·i·tor (kə pas′ ə tər) *n.* device used to store an electric charge.

cap·i·tal·ist (kap′ ə t′l ist) *n.* a person who has capital; owner of a large amount of wealth used in business.

ca·pit·u·late (kə pich′ ə lāt) *v.* to surrender or to give up to an opponent under various conditions. —**capitulation** *n.*

cap·ti·vate (kap′ tə vāt) *v.* to be very interesting or pleasing to someone; fascinate.

cap·tiv·i·ty (kap tiv′ ə tē) *n.* the state of being held as a prisoner.

car·pet·bag·ger (kar′ pit bag′ər) *n.* a Northerner who went South following the Civil War to make money by taking advantage of the confusion there.

car·tridge (kär′ trij) *n.* the metal or cardboard tube that contains the gunpowder and the bullet or shot to be used in a firearm.

cav·ern (kav′ ərn) *n.* a large cave.

cav·i·ty (kav′ ə tē) *n.* a hollow place, such as one caused by tooth decay.

cen·sus (sen′ səs) *n.* an official counting of all persons in a country or area to discover how many people there are and information such as sex, age, and occupation.

cen·taur (sen′ tôr) *n.* a mythical creature with the head of a man and the body of a horse.

chat·tel (chat′ ′l) *n.* property that can be moved, such as furniture or livestock.

chauf·feur (shō′ fər *or* shō fʉr′) *v.* to work as a driver of an automobile for another person.

civ·ic (siv′ ik) *adj.* of a city.

civ·i·li·za·tion (siv′ə lə zā′ shən) *n.* the stage in the progress of humans when they are no longer savages and when arts, sciences, and government are developed.

---

at, āte, fär; pen, ēqual; sit, mīne; sō, côrn, join, t͞o͝ok, f͞o͞ol, our; us, tʉrn; chill, shop, thick, *th*ey, si**ng**; **zh** *in* measure; ′l *in* idle; ə *in* alive, cover, family, robot, circus.

clar·i·on (klar′ ē ən) *adj.* clear, sharp, shrill.

clo·ven (klō′ v'n) *adj.* divided; sectioned; split.

coast·al (kōs′ t'l) *adj.* near or along a coast.

co·deine (kō′ dēn) *n.* a drug obtained from opium and used in medicines.

coil (koil) *v.* to wind around in circles.

com·mence (kə mens′) *v.* to start, to begin.

com·plex (kəm pleks′ *or* käm′ pleks) *adj.* consisting of different parts connected in a way that is difficult to understand.

com·po·sure (kəm pō′ zhər) *n.* self-control.

com·pound (käm′ pound) *n.* an enclosed place with a building or group of buildings in it.

con·ceal (kən sēl′) *v.* to hide or keep secret.

con·cen·tra·tion camp (kän′sən trā′ shən kamp) *n.* a prison camp for holding persons thought to be dangerous to the ruling group. These camps were used in Nazi Germany.

con·ces·sion (kən sesh′ ən) *n.* act of giving in.

con·cus·sion (kən kush′ ən) *n.* a shaking with force; shock.

con·fla·gra·tion (kän′flə grā′ shən) *n.* a large fire that does great damage.

con·tend (kən tend′) *v.* to compete in a contest. —**contender** *n.*

con·ti·nent (känt′ 'n ənt) *n.* any of the main big land areas of the Earth.

con·vey·ance (kən vā′ əns) *n.* anything used for conveying, such as a truck or car.

con·viv·i·al (kən viv′ ē əl) *adj.* enjoying a good time; loving fun; sociable.

cor·mo·rant (kôr′ mə rənt) *n.* a big sea bird that has webbed toes and a hooked beak.

cor·sage (kôr säzh′ *or* kôr säj′) *n.* a bunch of flowers for a woman to wear.

corse·let (kôrs′ lət) *n.* a piece of armor worn in the Middle Ages.

coun·sel (koun′ s'l) *n.* opinion or advice.

coun·te·nance (koun′ tə nəns) *n.* the face.

cour·ti·er (kôr′ tē ər) *n.* a person who attends at the court of a king or queen.

cow·er (kou′ ər) *v.* to bend over or tremble, as from fear or cold.

crafts·man (krafts′ mən) *n.* a person who works in a skilled trade.

crock·er·y (kräk′ ər ē) *n.* pots, jars and dishes which are made of baked clay.

croup (kroop) *n.* a childhood disease that causes hoarse coughing and hard breathing.

crown (kroun) *n.* a British coin.

crys·tal (kris′ t'l) *n.* clear, sparkling glass.

cul·ti·vate (kul′ tə vāt) *v.* to make ready and use land for growing crops; till.

cul·ture (kul′ chər) *n.* the ideas, customs, skills, and arts of a group of people in a certain time period.

D

dam·sel (dam′ z'l) *n.* a girl or maiden.

dank (daŋk) *adj.* uncomfortably damp; moist and cold.

daz·zle (daz′ 'l) *v.* to nearly blind with great brightness. —**dazzling** *adj.*

dec·la·ra·tion (dek′ lə rā′ shən) *n.* a public statement.

de·cree (di krē′) *n.* an official order or decision, often made by a government or court.

de·duc·tion (di duk′ shən) *n.* reasoning from given facts or general principles to a logical conclusion. —**deduction** *adj.*

de·i·ty (dē′ ə tē) *n.* a goddess or god.

de·mon (dē′ mən) *n.* an evil, cruel person or thing.

den·si·ty (den′ sə tē) *n.* the state of being dense, thick or crowded.

de·plete (di plēt′) *v.* to use up; exhaust.

de·pot (dē′ pō) *n.* warehouse or storehouse.

de·prav·i·ty (di prav′ ə tē) *n.* wickedness.

de·ri·sion (di rizh′ ən) *n.* ridicule; jeering or making fun of.

de·scend (di send′) *v.* to go down to a lower place. —**descent** *n.*

des·e·crate (des′ ə krāt) *v.* to use something sacred in an evil or wrong way.

des·o·late (des′ ə lit) *adj.* deserted.

des·tin·y (des′ tə nē) *n.* that which must happen; one's fate.

de·ter·mi·na·tion (di tur′mə nā′ shən) *n.* firmness of purpose; set aim.

de·vour (di vour′) *v.* to eat in a greedy way.

dex·ter·i·ty (dek ster′ ə tē) *n.* skill in using one's hands, body or mind.

di·men·sion (də men′ shən) *n.* measurement or size.

di·min·ish (də min′ ish) *v.* to make or become smaller in size, force, or importance. —**diminishing** *adj.*

dis·dain (dis dān′) *n.* scorn for a person or thing one considers beneath one's dignity.

dis·man·tle (dis man′ t'l) *v.* to make bare by taking out furniture or equipment.

di·vert (də vurt′) *v.* to turn aside.

di·vine (də vīn′) *adj.* coming from God; sacred; holy.

drought (drout) *n.* a long period of dry weather, with little or no rain.

drowse (drouz) *v.* to be almost asleep; doze.

du·al (dōō′ əl) *adj.* having or being two.

dupe (dōōp *or* dyōōp) *v.* to cheat or trick.

E

é·clair (ā kler′ *or* ē kler′) *n.* an oblong pastry shell filled with whipped cream or custard.

ed·dy (ed′ ē) *n.* a current of air or water that moves in circles against the main current.

e·go·tism (ē′ gə tiz′m) *n.* thinking or talking about oneself too often.

el·e·men·ta·ry (el′ə men′ ter ē) *adj.* having to do with the first or easiest things to be learned about something; basic.

e·man·ci·pate (i man′ sə pāt) *v.* to free from slavery or strict control. —**emancipator** *n.*

em·ber (em′ bər) *n.* a piece of wood, coal, or other fuel glowing in the ashes of a fire.

em·bold·en (im bōl′ d'n) *v.* to make daring or bolder; give courage to.

e·merge (i murj′) *v.* to come out; to be seen.

em·i·grate (em′ ə grāt) *v.* to leave one country or area and settle in another.

e·mit (i mit′) *v.* to send out; to give forth.

em·u·late (em′ yə lāt) *v.* to desire to be as good or better than another.

en·deav·or (in dev′ ər) *v.* to try hard; to make an effort.

en·gi·neer (en′jə nir′) *v.* to plan or direct skillfully.

en·twine (in twīn′) *v.* to twist together or around.

en·vel·op (in vel′ əp) *v.* to cover all around; wrap up or wrap in.

e·rup·tion (i rup′ shən) *n.* an explosion or throwing forth, as of lava from a volcano.

e·ter·nal (i tur′ n'l) *adj.* lasting forever; having no beginning or end. —**eternity** *n.*

e·vict (i vikt′) *v.* to require a person by law to move from a rented place, often for not paying the rent. —**eviction** *n.*

ewe (yōō) *n.* female sheep.

ex·hort (ig zôrt′) *v.* to urge or advise in a strong manner.

ex·pe·di·tion (ek′spə dish′ ən) *n.* a lengthy journey or voyage by a group of people, often to explore an area or take part in a battle.

ex·ploit (eks′ ploit) *n.* a brave or daring deed. *v.* (ik sploit′ *or* eks′ ploit) to use selfishly and cruelly. —**exploitation** *n.*

ex·po·sure (ik spō′ zhər) *n.* the act of being exposed.

ex·ten·sive (ik sten′ siv) *adj.* big, great, widespread.

ex·ter·mi·nate (ik stur′ mə nāt) *v.* to kill or destroy totally; wipe out.

ex·tin·guish (ik sting′ gwish) *v.* to put out or quench.

---

at, āte, fär; pen, ēqual; sit, mīne; sō, côrn, join, took, fōōl, our; us, turn; chill, shop, thick, *th*ey, sing; zh *in* measure; 'l *in* idle; ə *in* alive, cover, family, robot, circus.

ex·tol (ik stōl′) *v.* to praise highly.

ex·trav·a·gant (ik strav′ ə gənt) *adj.* wasteful; showy and ornate. —**extravagantly** *adv.*

ex·tri·cate (eks′ trə kāt) *v.* to set free from danger or difficulty.

ex·u·ber·ant (ig zōō bər *or* ig zyōō′ bər ənt) *adj.* lively and healthy; always in good humor.

F

fac·tor (fak′ tər) *n.* any one of causes or happenings that together bring about a result.

fang (fang) *n.* a long, pointed tooth with which animals catch and tear their prey.

fa·tigue (fə tēg′) *n.* a tired feeling.

fe·line (fē′ līn) *adj.* to do with the cat family.

fe·ro·cious (fə rō′ shəs) *adj.* mean or fierce in a wild way; savage.

fes·tal (fes′ t'l) *adj.* like a festival or holiday.

feud (fyōōd) *n.* a bitter quarrel, often one between two families.

flex·i·ble (flek′ sə b'l) *adj.* able to bend easily without breaking.

flit (flit) *v.* to fly or move in a quick, light way.

flout (flout) *v.* to ignore in an insulting or mocking way; to scorn.

fol·ly (fäl′ ē) *n.* foolish action or belief.

for·ay (fôr′ ā) *n.* a sudden attack or raid in order to capture or steal things.

ford (fôrd) *v.* to cross a shallow place in a stream or river.

fore·bod·ing (fôr bōd′ ing) *n.* a prediction that something bad will happen.

forge (fôrj) *v.* to mold metal in a furnace by heating and pounding.

for·lorn (fər lôrn′) *adj.* sad or unhappy, possibly due to loneliness or neglect; pitiful.

for·mal·i·ty (fôr mal′ ə tē) *n.* the condition of following rules or customs in an exact way.

fo·rum (fôr′ əm) *n.* the public gathering place of an ancient Roman city.

fren·zy (fren′ zē) *n.* a wild or uncontrollable outburst of emotion or action.

friv·o·lous (friv′ ə ləs) *adj.* not serious; silly.

fu·gi·tive (fyōō′ jə tiv) *n.* one who is running away, as from danger or officers of the law.

fur·tive (fur′ tiv) *adj.* acting in a sneaky way.

fu·tile (fyōōt′ 'l) *adj.* could not succeed; useless and hopeless.

G

gai·e·ty (gā′ ə tē) *n.* cheerfulness.

gait (gāt) *n.* a manner of walking or running.

gal·ler·y (gal′ ə rē) *n.* a balcony, especially the highest balcony in a theater.

gar·ri·son (gar′ ə s'n) *n.* a fort with soldiers and weapons; a military post.

gaunt (gônt) *adj.* very thin, so that the bones show through; worn and lean, as from sickness or hunger.

ghast·ly (gast′ lē) *adj.* awful or frightening.

gir·dle (gur′ d'l) *n.* a belt or sash worn on the waist, used mostly in earlier times.

glad·i·a·tor (glad′ ē āt′ər) *n.* a man, often a slave or prisoner, who fought animals or other men in ancient Rome, to entertain others.

glut·ton (glut′ 'n) *n.* one who eats too much in a greedy manner. —**gluttony** *n.*

gnash (nash) *v.* to grind the teeth together, often in anger or pain.

gon·do·la (gän′ də lə *or* gän dō′ lə) *n.* a railroad freight car that has low sides and no top.

gran·a·ry (gran′ ər ē) *n.* a place or building where grain is stored.

gris·ly (griz′ lē) *adj.* frightening; horrible.

grog (gräg) *n.* an alcoholic drink diluted with water.

grope (grōp) *v.* to find or seek by feeling about.

gro·schen (grō shən) *n.* a small silver German coin.

gro·tesque (grō tesk′) *adj.* looking odd and unreal in a wild way; fantastic.

guin·ea (gin′ ē) *n.* a gold coin that was used in England in earlier times.

H

hag (hag) *n.* an ugly and mean old woman.

hag·gard (hag′ ərd) *adj.* having a wild but weary look, often due to illness, hunger or grief.

hand·i·cap (han′ dē kap) *n.* something that makes things harder for a person or keeps them back; a hindrance.

ha·rangue (hə raṇg′) *v.* to give a long speech or talk to in a loud, scolding way.

har·ass (hə ras′ *or* har′ əs) *v.* to worry or bother.

hearth (härth) *n.* the floor of a fireplace.

her·e·tic (her′ ə tik) *n.* a person whose belief is different from that of others.

hid·e·ous (hid′ ē əs) *adj.* horrible; ugly or disgusting.

hoax (hōks) *n.* something that is intended to fool someone, especially a practical joke.

hoist (hoist) *v.* to lift or raise up; especially with a crane, pulley or rope.

hone (hōn) *v.* to sharpen objects by rubbing on a hard stone that has a fine grain.

ho·ri·zon (hə rī′ z'n) *n.* the line where the earth appears to meet the sky.

how·itz·er (hou′ it sər) *n.* a cannon that fires shells in a high curve.

hum·ble (hum′ b'l) *adj.* low in status or rank; simple and plain; lowly.

hu·mil·i·ate (hyoo mil′ ē āt) *v.* to take away one's pride or dignity; make ashamed. — **humiliation** *n.*

hy·po·der·mic (hī′ pə dur′ mik) *n.* a glass tube with a needle at one end and a plunger, used for forcing a medicine or drug under the skin.

I

il·lus·tri·ous (i lus′ trē əs) *adj.* famous; outstanding.

im·mac·u·late (i mak′ yə lit) *adj.* very clean.

im·mi·grant (im′ ə grənt) *n.* one who comes to a foreign country to make a new home.

im·mor·tal (i môr′ t'l) *adj.* never dying; living forever.

im·par·tial (im pär′ shəl) *adj.* not favoring one side more than the other; fair.

im·pa·tience (im pā′ shəns) *n.* the condition of not being patient; lack of patience.

im·pen·e·tra·ble (im pen′ i trə b'l) *adj.* something which cannot be penetrated or passed through.

im·pos·tor (im päs′ tər) *n.* one who cheats or tricks people, most often by pretending to be someone else or a different type of person.

im·pres·sive (im pres′ iv) *adj.* that affects the feelings or has a strong effect on the mind.

im·pu·dent (im′ pyoo dənt) *adj.* showing disrespect; very rude. —**impudence** *n.*

in·del·i·ble (in del′ ə b'l) *adj.* cannot be erased or rubbed out.

in·dig·nant (in dig′ nənt) *adj.* angry about something unfair or cruel. **indignation** *n.*

in·dis·crim·i·nate (in′dis krim′ ə nit) *adj.* not showing care in choosing.

in·dom·i·ta·ble (in däm′ it ə b'l) *adj.* unable to be conquered or overcome; unyielding.

in·ef·fec·tu·al (in′i fek′ choo wəl) *adj.* not having the desired result, or not being able to bring it about.

in·ev·i·ta·ble (in ev′ ə tə b'l) *adj.* that which must happen; unavoidable.

in·fest (in fest′) *v.* to swarm in or over, so as to damage or bother.

in·grat·i·tude (in grat′ ə too *or* in grat′ ə tyood) *n.* a lack of gratitude or thankfulness.

in·hab·it (in hab′ it) *v.* to live in or on.

in·hab·it·ant (in hab′ i tənt) *n.* person or animal that lives in a place.

in·jus·tice (in just′ tis) *n.* an unfair act.

---

at, āte, fär; pen, ēqual; sit, mīne; sō, côrn, join, took, fool, our; us, turn; chill, shop, thick, *th*ey, sing; **zh** *in* measure; ′l *in* idle; ə *in* alive, cover, family, robot, circus.

in·scrip·tion (in skrip′ shən) *n.* something written, printed or engraved, often on a coin, monument or in a book.

in·sig·nif·i·cant (in′sig nif′ ə kənt) *adj.* not important; of small value.

in·so·lent (in′ sə lənt) *adj.* not showing the proper respect; being rude.

in·stinc·tive (in stingk′ tiv) *adj.* done in a way that seems to be natural to one.

in·ter·cept (in tər sept′) *v.* to stop or cut off on the way.

in·te·ri·or (in tir′ ē ər) *adj.* of the interior; inner; inside.

in·tri·cate (in′ tri kit) *adj.* hard to understand or follow; complicated and full of details.

in·tu·i·tion (in′ too wish′ ən *or* in′tyoo wish′ ən) *n.* knowing something without actually thinking it out or studying; instant understanding.

ir·i·des·cent (ir′ə des′ ′nt) *adj.* showing a large amount of colors that keep moving and changing.

i·ron·ic (ī rän′ ik) *adj.* meaning the opposite of what is said.

J

jamb (jam)*n.* a side post of an opening for a door or window.

jav·e·lin (jav′lin *or* jav′ə lin) *n.* a light spear; nowadays one used in an athletic competition to see who can throw it the farthest.

jo·vi·al (jō′vē əl) *adj.* friendly and happy; playful and jolly.

K

ker·o·sene (ker′ə sēn) *n.* an oil made from coal or petroleum which can be used in some lamps or stoves.

knap·sack (nap′sak) *n.* a leather or cloth bag worn on the back, used for carrying.

knoll (nōl) *n.* a small rounded hill; a mound.

L

la·bo·ri·ous (lə bôr′ē əs) *adj.* taking a great deal of effort or work. —**laboriously** *adv.*

lab·y·rinth (lab′ə rinth) *n.* a place with twisting passages and dead ends that make it difficult to find one's way through; maze.

land·mark (land′märk) *n.* an easily seen building or tree that helps one to find a place.

lard·er (lar′dər) *n.* place in the home where food is kept.

lath·er (lath′ər) *n.* foam made by mixing soap with water.

le·git·i·mate (lə jit′ə mit) *adj.* reasonable; to be expected.

lev·er (lev′ər *or* lē′vər) *n.* a bar that can be turned or moved to make something work.

lib·er·a·tion (lib′ə rā′shən) *n.* the act of setting free.

lin·e·age (lin′ē ij) *n.* a person's ancestry; line of descent.

lin·tel (lin′t′l) *n.* the piece placed lengthwise along the top of a door or window to support the wall above the opening.

loom (loom) *n.* a machine that weaves thread or yarn into cloth.

lurk (lurk) *v.* to remain or be hidden, usually ready to attack or jump out suddenly.

lus·ter (lus′tər) *n.* a metallic appearance given to pottery by a glaze.

lyre (līr) *n.* an old instrument that looks like a small harp, used by the ancient Greeks.

M

mail (māl) *n.* armor for the body, made of metal rings or overlapping plates.

mal·ice (mal′is) *n.* the desire to hurt or harm someone; ill-will. —**malicious** *adj.*

mam·moth (mam′əth) *adj.* very large; huge.

ma·raud·er (mə rôd′ər) *n.* a person or animal that goes about attacking or plundering.

mar·i·ner (mar′ə nər) *n.* a seldom used name for sailor.

mar·row (mar′ō) *n.* the soft, fatty material in the hollow centers of most bones.

ma·son (mā′s′n) *n.* a person whose work is building using stone or brick.

mass (mas) *n.* a big amount or number.

me·di·e·val (mē′dē ē′v′l *or* med′ē ē′v′l) *adj.* of, like or part of the Middle Ages.

mel·an·chol·y (mel′ən käl′ē) *adj.* sad or gloomily thoughtful.

mer·ci·less (mur′si lis) *adj.* having or showing no kindness; cruel.

me·ringue (mə rang′) *n.* egg whites mixed with sugar that are beaten stiff and baked as small cakes or pie toppings.

mi·grate (mī′grāt) *v.* to move from one area or country to another, especially to make a new home.

min·strel (min′strəl) *n.* a person who entertained at the court of a lord during the Middle Ages, or one who traveled from place to place and sang or recited poetry.

mi·rac·u·lous (mi rak′yoo ləs) *adj.* magical; wonderful; marvelous.

mist (mist) *n.* a large mass of small drops of water in the air, similar to a fog.

mod·er·ate (mäd′ər it) *adj.* neither very big, good, or strong, nor very small, bad, or weak; reasonable or ordinary.

mo·lest (mə lest′) *v.* to bother so as to hurt or trouble.

mo·men·tous (mō men′təs) *adj.* of great importance.

mon·o·log (män′ə lôg) *n.* a lengthy speech made by one person during a conversation.

moor·land (moor′land) *n.* a large piece of open wasteland.

mor·tal (môr′t′l) *adj.* **1.** human. **2.** that must die at some time. **3.** extreme; great.

mur·mur (mur′mər) *v.* to make a soft, steady sound.

mu·ti·late (myoot′′l āt) *v.* to seriously hurt or damage by breaking or cutting off a necessary part or parts.

N

nape (nāp) *n.* the back area of the neck.

nar·ra·tive (nar′ə tiv) *n.* a story; tale.

nec·tar (nek′tər) *n.* what the gods drank in Greek myths.

nigh (nī) *adj.* near, close.

no·ble (nō′b′l) *n.* a person of noble rank or title.

non·de·script (nän′di skript′) *adj.* difficult to describe because not of any definite kind or class.

nov·el·ty (näv′′l tē) *n.* newness; something unusual.

O

ob·sta·cle (äb′sti k′l) *n.* something that gets in the way or prevents one from going ahead; an obstruction.

ob·sti·na·cy (äb′stə nə sē) *n.* the quality of not being willing to give in or change one's mind; stubbornness. —**obstinate** *adj.*

of·fen·sive (ə fen′siv) *adj.* making a person angry or annoyed; insulting.

op·pressed (ə prest′) *n.* people who are kept down by the cruel use of power.

op·pres·sion (ə presh′ən) *n.* the act of keeping down by the cruel use of power or the condition of being oppressed.

op·pres·sive (ə pres′iv) *adj.* difficult to put up with; a burden.

or·a·cle (ôr′ə k′l) *n.* a person through whom, the ancient Greeks and Romans believed, the gods spoke.

ord·nance (ôrd′nəns) *n.* cannon and artillery.

or·gan·dy (ôr′gən dē) *n.* a light, stiff cotton cloth, often used for dresses.

---

at, āte, fär; pen, ēqual; sit, mīne; sō, côrn, join, took, fool, our; us, turn; chill, shop, thick, they, sing; zh *in* measure; ′l *in* idle; ə *in* alive, cover, family, robot, circus.

P

pa·cif·ic (pə sif′ik) *adj.* not warlike; quiet and peaceful.

pag·eant (paj′ənt) *n.* a large, elaborate show or parade.

pal·pi·ta·tion (pal′pə tā′shən) *n.* a rapid beat or flutter.

pang (paṅg) *n.* a quick sharp pain or feeling.

par·a·dox (par′ə däks) *n.* person or thing that is full of contradictions. —**paradoxical** *adj.*

par·a·pet (par′ə pit) *n.* a low wall or railing found along a balcony or bridge.

par·tic·u·lar (pər tik′yə lər) *n.* a detail; fact.

peas·ant (pez′′nt) *n.* a person of the class of farm workers and farmers with small farms.

ped·es·tal (ped′is t′l) *n.* the base at the bottom that holds up a statue, column, or lamp.

pee·vish (pē′vish) *adj.* irritable; cross.

pen·e·trate (pen′ə trāt) *v.* to pass into or through by piercing; to enter.

pen·e·trat·ing (pen′ə trāt iṅg) *adj.* keen or sharp.

per·il (per′əl) *n.* something that could cause harm or injury. —**perilous** *adj.*

per·i·scope (per′ə skōp) *n.* a tube with mirrors or prisms inside it so that someone can look in one end and see the reflection of an object at the other.

pes·ti·lence (pes′t′l əns) *n.* a very contagious disease that infects a large group of people. —**pestilential** *adj.*

pe·tit four (pet′ē fôr′ *or* pet′ē fo͞or′) *n.* a small cake, a kind of French pastry.

pet·ri·fy (pet′rə fī) *v.* to change into a material like stone by replacing the normal cells with minerals.

pet·ty (pet′ē) *adj.* not very important; small; minor.

pil·lar (pil′ər) *n.* a long, thin, upright structure, used as support for a roof, or as a monument.

pi·ñon (pin′yən *or* pin′yōn) *n.* the seed of a small North American pine tree, which can be eaten.

pis·ton (pis′t′n) *n.* a disk or cylinder that goes back and forth in a hollow cylinder.

pit·tance (pit′əns) *n.* a small amount or portion, especially of money.

plac·ard (plak′ärd) *n.* a sign put up in a public place.

pla·cate (plā′kāt *or* plak′āt) *v.* to stop from being angry; soothe.

plac·id (plas′id) *adj.* quiet and peaceful; calm. —**placidly** *adv.*

plod (pläd) *v.* to work slowly and steadily, often in doing something dull. —**plodder** *n.*

plough (plou) *n.* British spelling of plow, a farming tool used to cut soil and turn it up.

plume (plo͞om) *n.* **1.** a feather, large and fluffy. **2.** an object shaped like a plume.

po·grom (pō gräm′, pō grum′, *or* pō′grəm) *n.* an organized persecution and slaughter of a group of people, as with the Jews in Tsarist Russia (until 1917).

pop·u·lace (päp′yə lis) *n.* the general public; the masses.

pop·u·la·tion (päp′yə lā′shən) *n.* people living in a certain area; especially, the total amount of these people.

pop·u·lous (päp′yə ləs) *adj.* a large amount of people; heavily populated.

pore (pôr) *n.* a tiny opening found in the skin or in the leaves of plants.

pound¹ (pound) *n.* the basic unit of money in the United Kingdom.

pound² (pound) *v.* to hit hard by using heavy blows.

pound³ (pound) *n.* a place for keeping animals.

prance (prans) *v.* to move with lively, strutting steps.

pre·dom·i·nate (pri däm′ə nāt) *v.* to be larger in amount or power; to prevail.

prem·ises (prem′is) *n. pl.* a building and the land that belongs to it.

pre·mo·ni·tion (prē′mə nish′ən) *n.* a feeling or instinct that something bad will happen; forewarning.

pre·pos·ter·ous (pri päs′tər əs) *adj.* so wrong or absurd as to be laughable.

pres·tige (pres tēzh′) *n.* fame or respect that comes from doing great deeds, having good character, riches, or success.

pre·sump·tu·ous (pri zump′chōō wəs) *adj.* daring or bold; taking too much for granted.

pre·tense (pri tens′ *or* prē′tens) *n.* an untrue claim, excuse or show.

prey (prā) **1.** *n.* a person or thing that becomes the victim of someone or something. **2.** *v.* to hunt other animals to eat for food.

pri·va·tion (prī vā′shən) *n.* the lack of things needed to exist or be comfortable.

pro·di·gious (prə dij′əs) *adj.* very great; large, enormous.

prod·i·gy (präd′ə jē) *n.* a person or thing so remarkable as to cause wonder; often a child who is unusually talented or intelligent.

proph·e·cy (präf′ə sē) *n.* **1.** The act or power of telling what will happen in the future. **2.** something told about the future, as by a prophet.

proph·e·sy (präf′ə sī) *v.* to say what will happen; predict.

prop·o·si·tion (präp′ə zish′ən) *n.* a task to be dealt with.

pros·trate (präs′trāt) *adj.* lying flat on one's face or back.

prov·ince (präv′ins) *n.* a region in or belonging to a country, having its own government.

pro·vi·sions (prə vizh′ənz) *n. pl.* a supply of food.

psych (sīk) *v.* a slang word referring to the use of psychological tricks or methods to outwit, control or overcome someone.

pum·mel (pum′′l) *v.* to hit again and again, especially with the fists.

put·ty (put′ē) *n.* a soft mix of powdered chalk and linseed oil, used to hold panes of glass in windows or to fill in cracks.

pyre (pīr) *n.* a stack of wood on which a dead body is burned; funeral pile.

Q

quar·ters (kwôr′tərz) *n. pl.* **1.** lodgings; a place to stay. **2.** mercy shown to an enemy.

quench (kwench) *v.* to put out; to extinguish.

quest (kwest) *n.* a search or hunt.

quiv·er (kwiv′ər) *n.* a container for holding arrows.

quoit (kwoit) *n.* any of the metal or rope rings which players throw in a game called quoits, a game similar to horseshoes.

R

raft·er (raf′tər) *n.* a sloping beam used to support a roof.

ram·part (ram′pärt) *n.* a mound of earth, often with a wall along the top, surrounding a place to defend it.

ran·cor (raŋ′kər) *n.* deep spite; a hate or bitter feeling that lasts a long time.

rap·ture (rap′chər) *n.* a feeling of joy, love, ecstasy. —**rapturous** *adj.*

rare·bit (rer′bit) *n.* a dish of melted cheese served on toast or crackers.

ra·tion·al·ize (rash′ən ə līz′) *v.* to give a good explanation without seeming to know that it is not the real one. —**rationalization** *n.*

rav·age (rav′ij) *v.* to destroy or wreck.

ra·ven (rā′vən) *n.* a large crow, with shiny black feathers and a large beak.

rav·e·nous (rav′ə nəs) *adj.* extremely hungry or greedy.

reb·el (reb′′l) *n.* a person who fights or struggles against authority or control.

re·cede (ri sēd′) *v.* to go, move, or tilt backwards.

re·coil (ri koil′) *v.* to jump or move back suddenly due to fear or surprise.

---

at, āte, fär; pen, ēqual; sit, mīne; sō, côrn, join, took, fōōl, our; us, turn; chill, shop, thick, they, siŋg; zh *in* measure; ′l *in* idle; ə *in* alive, cover, family, robot, circus.

rec·om·pense (rek'əm pens) *n.* something that is given or done in return for something else; a reward.

rec·on·cile (rek'ən sīl) *v.* to become friendly once more.

re·gal (rē'g'l) *adj.* of, like or suitable for a king or queen; royal; stately.

reg·is·ter (rej'is tər) *n.* a record or list of names, things or events, also a book in which such a list is kept.

re·ju·ve·nate (ri jōō'və nāt') *v.* to bring back to youthful appearance.

rel·e·vant (rel'ə vənt) *adj.* having to do with the issue at hand; to the point. —**relevancy** *n.*

rem·i·nis·cence (rem'ə nis''ns) *n.* the act of remembering experiences in the past; recollection.

re·nown (ri noun') *n.* a great amount of fame.

re·per·cus·sion (re'pər kush'ən) *n.* the bouncing back of sound from a surface; echo.

rep·u·ta·tion (rep'yōō tā'shən) *n.* good character in the opinion of others; a good name.

re·qui·em (rek'wē əm *or* rāk'wē əm) *n.* a Roman Catholic Mass for a person or persons who have died.

re·sil·ient (ri zil'yənt) *adj.* bouncing back into shape or position; elastic.

res·pite (res'pit) *n.* a time of rest or relief, as from pain, work or duty; a pause.

re·tal·i·ate (ri tal'ē āt) *v.* to hurt or do wrong in return for harm or wrong done.

rev·o·lu·tion·ar·y (rev'ə lōō'shən er'ē) *adj.* in favor of or causing a revolution, or overthrow of a government.

rheu·ma·tism (rōō'mə tiz'm) *n.* a disease where the joints and muscles become stiff, swollen and sore.

rogue (rōg) *n.* a person who is tricky or dishonest; scoundrel; rascal.

ru·in·ous (rōō'ə nəs) *adj.* causing ruin; highly destructive.

ruse (rōōz) *n.* a trick or scheme for fooling someone.

S

sa·cred (sā'krid) *adj.* having something to do with religion or put aside for some religious purpose.

sage (sāj) *adj.* wise; exhibiting good judgment.

sal·low (sal'ō) *adj.* pale yellow in a way that looks unhealthy.

satch·el (sach' əl) *n.* a small bag for carrying books or clothes, sometimes having a shoulder strap.

sate (sāt) *v.* to satisfy an appetite.

sav·age (sav'ij) *adj.* not tame; wild and fierce.

scheme (skēm) *n.* a plan, often a secret or dishonest one.

school (skōōl) *n.* a group of fish or water animals of the same kind that swim together.

scold (skōld) *n.* someone who frequently scolds or nags.

scorch (skôrch) *v.* to burn or be burned lightly.

scowl (skoul) *v.* to look angry or sullen by lowering the eyebrows and the corners of the mouth.

sea-nymph (sē'nimf) *n.* a minor nature goddess belonging to the sea.

sec·ond hand (sek'ənd hand') *adj.* used by another first; not new.

sem·i·bar·bar·ic (sem'ē bär ber'ik) *adj.* wild, crude, or unrestrained.

sem·i·hys·ter·i·cal (sem'ī his ter'i k'l) *adj.* emotionally uncontrolled.

se·nil·i·ty (sə nil'ə tē) *n.* weakness in body and mind caused by old age.

ser·pent (sur'pənt) *n.* a snake, especially a big or poisonous one.

shard (shärd) *n.* a fragment or a piece that has broken.

siege (sēj) *n.* the surrounding of a town or fortress by an enemy army trying to capture it.

sieve (siv) *n.* a strainer used to separate liquids from solids, or large pieces from small.

slaugh·ter (slôt'ər) *n.* the killing of people in a cruel way, or in large numbers.

slum·ber (slum'bər) *v.* to sleep.

sol·emn (säl′əm) *adj.* serious; very earnest.

sol·em·nize (säl′əm nīz) *v.* to carry out a ceremony.

sol·i·tude (säl′ə to͞od *or* säl′ə tyo͞od) *n.* the state of being alone; loneliness.

sor·tie (sôr′tē) *n.* a sudden attack made from a place surrounded by enemy troops.

spec·i·men (spes′ə mən) *n.* part of a whole, or one item of a group, used as a sample.

splay (splā) *v.* to spread out.

splin·ter (splin′tər) *n.* a thin, pointed piece of material such as wood or bone, broken off.

sprint (sprint) *v.* to run or move fast, as in a short race. —**sprinter** *n.*

squid (skwid) *n.* a sea animal with ten arms, two of which are longer than the rest.

stag (stag) *n.* a grown male deer.

stock quotations (stäk′ kwō tā′shenz) *n. pl.* daily lists showing stock market prices.

stock·bro·ker (stäk′brō′kər) *n.* a person who buys and sells stocks and bonds for other people.

strife (strīf) *n.* the act or state of fighting or quarreling; struggle.

strop (sträp) *v.* to sharpen on a strop, a leather strap on which razors are sharpened.

suav·i·ty (swä′və tē) *n.* smooth and graceful politeness.

sub·lime (sə blīm′) *adj.* of the highest kind; lofty, noble.

sub·merge (səb mʉrj′) *v.* to go, put or remain under water.

sub·side (səb sīd′) *v.* to sink to a lower level; to move down.

sub·stance (sub′stəns) *n.* property or wealth.

suit·or (so͞ot′ər) *n.* a man who is courting a woman.

sum·mon (sum′ən) *v.* to gather together; call or send for.

su·per·cil·i·ous (so͞o′pər sil′ē əs) *adj.* proud and scornful; haughty.

su·per·fi·cial (so͞o′pər fish′əl) *adj.* of or on the surface; shallow. —**superficiality** *n.*

sup·pli·cant (sup′lə kənt) *n.* one who begs or asks for something in a humble way.

sur·face (sur′fis) *n.* the outside or outer area.

swin·dle (swin′d′l) *n.* an act of cheating out of money or property; fraud.

symp·tom (simp′təm) *n.* a sign or indication showing that something else exists.

T

tack·ward (tak′wərd) *adv.* in a zig-zag motion.

taf·fe·ta (taf′i tə) *n.* a fine, stiff fabric made of silk or nylon, with a sheen.

tal·low (tal′ō) *n.* animal fat that is melted and used in candles or soap.

tal·on (tal′ən) *n.* the claw of a bird that kills other animals for food.

the·o·ry (thē′ə rē) *n.* an explanation of why or how something happens.

thun·der·head (thun′dər hed) *n.* a group of clouds that appear just before a rainstorm.

tid·al wave (tīd′l wāv) *n.* a large, destructive wave, caused by very strong winds or an earthquake.

tongs (tôngs) *n. pl.* a device for lifting things, often made with two arms hinged together.

ton·sil (tän′s′l) *n.* either one of the two soft oval masses of tissue at the back of the mouth.

tor·toise (tôr′təs) *n.* a turtle, usually one that lives on land.

tram (tram) *n.* British word for streetcar or trolley.

trance (trans) *n.* the state of being completely lost in thought.

tran·quil (traṅg′kwəl) *adj.* calm, peaceful, or quiet. —**tranquility** *n.*

---

at, āte, fär; pen, ēqual; sit, mīne; sō, côrn, join,
to͝ok, fo͞ol, our; us, tʉrn; **ch**ill, **sh**op, **th**ick, **th**ey,
si**ṅg**; **zh** *in* measure; ′l *in* idle;
ə *in* alive, cover, family, robot, circus.

tread (tred) *v.* to walk upon, in, along, or over.

trel·lis (trel′is) *n.* a frame of crossed strips, as of wood or metal, on which vines and other climbing plants are grown.

tres·pass (tres′pəs *or* tres′pas) *v.* to be on another property without permission or right. —**trespasser** *n.*

tri·fle (trī′f′l) *n.* **1.** something of small value or importance. **2.** a tiny amount; bit.

tu·mul·tu·ous (tōō mul′chōō wəs *or* tyōō mul′chōō wəs) *adj.* full of loud noises; confused.

ty·rant (tī′rənt) *n.* one who uses power in a cruel or unfair way.

U

un·a·mi·a·bly (un ā′mē ə blē) *adv.* in an unfriendly manner.

un·can·ny (un kan′ē) *adj.* so good as to seem unreal.

u·ni·verse (yōō′nə vʉrs) *n.* space and everything in it; earth, the sun and all things that exist.

V

va·can·cy (vā′kən sē) *n.* a job or position for which a person is needed.

va·grant (vā′grənt) *n.* a person that travels from place to place, doing odd jobs or begging; a tramp.

val·or (val′ər) *n.* bravery or courage.

van·i·ty (van′ə tē) *n.* the quality of being vain or conceited about oneself.

van·quish (vaŋg′kiwsh) *v.* to defeat or conquer.

vat (vat) *n.* a large tank or tub used to hold liquids.

veil (vāl) *n.* a piece of thin cloth worn by women over the face or head to hide the features, as part of a uniform or as decoration.

venge·ance (ven′jəns) *n.* the act of getting even for a wrong or injury; revenge.

ven·om·ous (ven′əm əs) *adj.* poisonous.

ven·tril·o·quist-dum·my (ven tril′ə kwist dum′ē) *n.* a puppet used in ventriloquism, the art of speaking so that the voice seems to be coming from somewhere else.

ven·ture (ven′chər) *v.* to go despite possible risk. *n.* an activity or undertaking in which there is some danger of losing something.

ve·ran·da (və ran′də) *n.* an open porch, found along the side of a building.

verge (vʉrj) *n.* the border, edge or brink.

vi·cin·i·ty (və sin′ə tē) *n.* a nearby region; neighborhood.

vict·uals (vit′′lz) *n. pl.* food.

vig·or·ous (vig′ər əs) *adj.* full of strength and energy.

vi·tal (vīt′′l) *adj.* very important.

vol·can·ic (väl kan′ik) *adj.* from or of a volcano.

W

wag·er (wā′jər) *v.* to place a bet. *n.* the act of betting or something bet.

warp (wôrp) *v.* to twist or to bend out of shape.

wel·ter (wel′tər) *v.* to be stained or soaked.

wheat·en (hwēt′n) *adj.* **1.** like the color of wheat. **2.** made from wheat.

whee′dle (hwē′d′l) *v.* to flatter or coax into doing something.

whirl·pool (hwʉrl′pōōl) *n.* water turning rapidly around and around.

whorl (hwôrl *or* hwʉrl) *n.* anything arranged in a circle or circles, such as the ridges that form a fingerprint.

wire·less (wīr′lis) *n.* a name for radio, used mostly by the British.

Z

zeal (zēl) *n.* strong, enthusiastic feeling, as in working for a cause; great interest.

Biographies of Authors

Joan Aiken

Isaac Asimov

Toni Cade Bambara

Joan Aiken (*born 1924*) has been writing stories and poems since the age of five. She was born in England, the daughter of an American poet, Conrad Aiken. When she was seventeen, Aiken sent one of her stories to a radio station. It was accepted for broadcasting. Later, she worked for that same station, as well as *Argosy Magazine*. Aiken is known for her imaginative books and stories, such as *The Whispering Mountain* and *The Wolves of Willoughby Chase*.

Isaac Asimov (*born 1920*) came to America from Russia at the age of three. As a youngster, Asimov developed a love of science-fiction magazines. This led to his deep interest in science. Asimov entered Columbia University at the age of fifteen. He eventually became a professor at Boston University's School of Medicine. He is the author of numerous professional texts and hundreds of articles and science-fiction fantasies. Some of Asimov's popular writings include *I, Robot* and *The Caves of Steel*.

Toni Cade Bambara (*born 1939*) is known for her stories, articles, and essays about black Americans. Her works have been included in anthologies and publications such as *The Liberator* and *Massachusetts Review*. Bambara's work experiences include welfare investigator, project director for social programs, and college instructor. She has served as the editor of *The Black Woman* and *Tales and Stories for Black Folks*.

Sally Benson (*1900–1972*) received an Academy Award nomination for her screenplay of the book, *Anna and the King of Siam*. The movie version was called *The King and I*. Benson was born in St. Louis, Missouri and attended school in New York City. A job with the *New York Morning Telegraph* provided her with experience as a feature writer, book reviewer, and film critic. She was also interested in mythology, as shown by her book *Gods and Heroes*.

William Blake

Ray Bradbury

Fredric Brown

William Blake (*1757–1827*) was one of the most imaginative of British poets. He began writing poems as a teen-ager in London. Blake claimed to have seen visions, which inspired his artistic creations, both poetry and illustrations. Two of his famous poetry collections are *Songs of Innocence* and *Songs of Experience*.

Philip Booth (*born 1925*) divides his time between teaching and writing. A graduate of Dartmouth College and Columbia University, Booth served with the Air Force in World War II. He is the recipient of two Guggenheim Fellowships and an award for his first book of poetry, *Letter From a Distant Land*.

Ray Bradbury (*born 1920*) had a passion for adventure stories, secret code rings, and comic strips as a boy in Illinois. When he was twelve years old, he was given a toy typewriter. Since then he has written over a thousand stories, as well as novels, plays, movie scripts, and television programs. Two well known collections of Bradbury's stories are *The Martian Chronicles* and *Dandelion Wine*. His novel *Farenheit 451* was made into a movie.

Fredric Brown (*1906–1972*) began his writing career as a journalist for a Milwaukee newspaper. Born in Ohio, Brown attended college in Indiana and then lived in Wisconsin, New York, and New Mexico. Brown's specialties are science fiction and mystery stories laced with irony. Two of his works, *Martians Go Home* and *The Lights in the Sky Are Stars*, have been translated into French.

Thomas Bulfinch (*1796–1867*) introduced generations of readers to Greek and Roman mythology. He also is known for rewriting Celtic, Scandinavian, and Oriental tales. Bulfinch worked as a banker for thirty years and did not begin his literary career until the age of fifty-seven.

Olive Burt (*born 1894*) grew up in Utah and has always had an interest in the Old West. *Petticoats West, First Woman Editor, Sarah J. Hale*, and *Negroes in the Early West* are historical books reflecting this interest. Burt has combined a writing career with jobs in teaching and library work.

Carl Carmer (*born 1893*) has shown his love for American history in a variety of ways. He has written poetry, novels, and collections of

Lucille Clifton

David Crockett

E. E. Cummings

Arthur Conan Doyle

folk tales and songs. Carmer's specialty is regional history and folkways. He has written about the South, the history of New York State, and life on the Hudson and Susquehanna Rivers. Carmer was born in New York and educated in Alabama. Besides being a writer, he has also been a professor of English.

Lucille Clifton (*born 1936*) grew up in New York and attended Howard University and Fredonia State Teachers College. She is the author of several collections of poetry, including *Good Times* and *An Ordinary Woman*. Clifton writes with warmth and humor about the vitality of black life. She won a 1974 Emmy Award for co-authoring a television program, *Free To Be You and Me*.

Olivia Coolidge (*born 1908*) grew up in England, the daughter of a newspaper columnist. After completing her studies at Oxford University, she came to the United States and taught English for several years. Coolidge has shown an interest in politics as well as the classics. Her books range from *Greek Myths* to *Makers of the Red Revolution*.

David "Davy" Crockett (*1786–1836*) was a famous frontiersman who became a folk hero during his lifetime. He was known not only for his marksmanship, but also for his humorous, exaggerated stories. After representing Tennessee in Congress, Crockett went to Texas in 1835. He joined the men who were fighting at the Alamo to establish an independent Texas, and he is thought to have died there.

E. E. Cummings (*1894–1962*) chose to sign his name e.e. cummings. This is one example of the many ways Cummings revised the rules of punctuation, capitalization, and verse form to create unusual shapes and sounds for his ideas. When his first book of poetry was published, critics were not sure if they should praise or condemn his style. Born in Massachusetts, Cummings received two degrees from Harvard University.

Sir Arthur Conan Doyle (*1859–1930*) was born in Scotland. He attended Edinburgh University and spent five years studying medicine. Upon returning to England, he set up a medical practice. While waiting for patients, Doyle created Sherlock Holmes, a "scientific" detective who was modeled after an actual professor. Doyle's stories became so popular that he was able to give up the medical career.

Biographies of Authors 649

T. S. Eliot

T. S. Eliot (*1888–1965*) gained wide recognition for his work in modern poetry. Born in the Midwest, Eliot eventually studied at Harvard and in Europe, then settled in London. There he worked as a teacher, lecturer, banker, and editor. Eliot's humorous poems about cats are in contrast to his serious works. His striking originality, shown in *The Love Song of J. Alfred Prufrock* and *The Wasteland*, was met with both criticism and praise.

Kathryn Forbes (*1909–1966*) was born in San Francisco, California. She wrote a semi-autobiographical account of her family history, *Mama's Bank Account*. That book was the basis for a Broadway play as well as a famous television series, "I Remember Mama." Forbes also wrote radio scripts and magazine articles.

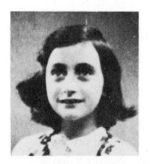

Anne Frank

Anne Frank (*1929–1945*) was born in Germany, but her family soon after moved to the Netherlands to avoid persecution of Jews. When the Nazis invaded Amsterdam, she and her family had to go into hiding. Anne wrote of those experiences in the diary she kept for two years. Eventually, the Frank family was discovered and sent to a concentration camp where all, except her father, perished.

Russell Freedman (*born 1929*) has written articles for magazines such as *Ranger Rick*, *Cricket*, and *Scholastic*. He researches and studies animal life, as reflected in his books *They Live with the Dinosaurs* and *Killer Fish*. Freedman was born and educated in California. He served in the Army, and then held jobs as a publicity writer for a television station and as a newswriter.

Robert Frost (*1874–1963*) had the honor of reading his poetry at the presidential inauguration of John F. Kennedy. Frost's works, often set in rural New England, are noted for their conversational style and realism. Before he achieved fame for his poetry, Frost worked at a variety of jobs—mill hand, shoe salesman, and farmer. He wrote more than a dozen volumes of poetry, and is the only American poet to win the Pulitzer Prize four times.

Robert Frost

Eloise Greenfield (*born 1929*) has written novels, short stories, biographies, and poetry. With the aid of her mother, Lessie Jones Little, Greenfield has written recollections of her childhood. She grew up in

Robert Hayden

O. Henry

Homer

North Carolina, attended Miner Teachers College, and worked for the U.S. Patent Office. Greenfield served as a director of the Black Writer's Workshop.

Marcie Hans (*1928–1975*) was a successful advertising copywriter when she wrote her two best-selling books *The Executive Coloring Book* and *The Executive Cut-Out Book*. The success of these books convinced her to devote all of her time to writing books. Later in life, she began writing poetry, publishing a collection of poems, *Serve Me A Slice of Moon*.

Sara Henderson Hay (*born 1906*) grew up in Pennsylvania and attended colleges in Georgia and New York. Hay's poetry is often about everyday subjects, such as nature and children. She also likes to write humorous verses about the role of women.

Robert E. Hayden (*1913–1980*) won many awards for his poetry. His themes emphasized black history and folklore. Born in Detroit, Hayden attended Wayne State University and the University of Michigan. He worked as an English professor at Fisk University and served as the poetry editor of a magazine.

O. Henry (*1862–1910*) was the pen name of William Sydney Porter. Before he achieved success as a writer, O. Henry worked as a bank teller, store clerk, and journalist. He served a prison term for bookkeeping irregularities at the bank, but always claimed innocence. Two popular collections of O. Henry's stories are *The Four Million* and *Of Cabbages and Kings*. His stories often have surprise endings.

Homer (*perhaps 800 B.C.*) was a Greek poet about whom we know little. His epics were probably recited for many years before being written down. Homer is credited with the authorship of *The Iliad* and *The Odyssey*. These epic poems relate events concerning the Trojan War, a battle between the cities of Greece and the city of Troy.

A. E. Housman (*1859–1936*) one of the major poets of the nineteenth century, was born in England and educated at Oxford University. He taught Latin to university students and translated the works of famous Roman authors. Housman's poetry is simple and direct, sometimes sad, often expressing the fleeting quality of love and beauty.

Langston Hughes

Naoshi Koriyama

Henry Wadsworth
Longfellow

Edwin Markham

Langston Hughes (*1902–1967*) was a playwright, poet, lecturer, and songwriter as well as an author of novels and short stories. He was employed at many other jobs before he achieved recognition for his writing talent. Hughes based much of his writing upon his varied experiences, including his travels in Africa. Many of his works reflect the speech patterns and jazz rhythms Hughes heard on the streets of Harlem. His first collection of poems was called *Weary Blues*.

Shirley Jackson (*1919–1965*) wrote many warm and humorous stories about family life, such as "Charles" and "Life Among the Savages." She is also known for her shocking tales of horror, which include the novels *We Have Always Lived in the Castle* and *The Haunting of Hill House*. Many of Jackson's stories have been adapted for stage, film, and television.

MacKinlay Kantor (*born 1904*) grew up in Iowa, where he helped his mother edit a newspaper. During World War II he joined the Royal Air Force in England, flew combat missions, and was awarded for his courage. He wrote about the Civil War in novels and stories for young people, such as "Lee and Grant at Appotomax" and "Gettysburg." His novel *Andersonville*, about a confederate prison camp in Georgia, won a Pulitzer Prize in 1956.

Naoshi Koriyama (*born 1926*) is a professor of English literature in Japan. Although his native language is Japanese, he set himself the challenge of composing his poetry in English. Koriyama's works can be found in anthologies, textbooks, and magazines.

Henry Wadsworth Longfellow (*1807–1882*) was one of the most popular poets of the nineteenth century. His narrative poem, "The Song of Hiawatha," sold more than a million copies in his lifetime. Longfellow was born in Maine and graduated from Bowdoin College. After traveling and studying in Europe, Longfellow returned to the United States to teach college. He continued to write poems and won fame for "Paul Revere's Ride" and "The Village Blacksmith."

Edwin Markham (*1852–1940*) became famous for his lectures and poems, especially those about Abraham Lincoln. Markham, a native of Oregon, lived most of his life in California. There, he became a teacher and superintendent of schools in several small communities.

Eve Merriam

Edna St. Vincent
Millay

Arthur Miller

Eve Merriam (*born 1916*) began writing as a child in Philadelphia, Pennsylvania. Her love of writing is shown in the large amount and variety of work she has produced—more than thirty books, as well as television scripts, song lyrics, plays, and magazine articles. Merriam's book *Growing Up Female in America* reflects her interest in the issue of women's rights.

Edna St. Vincent Millay (*1892–1950*) won recognition for her poem "Renascence," written at the age of nineteen. After graduating from college, Millay moved to New York City. She chose to live in Greenwich Village among other noted writers of the 1920's and 1930's. Millay was awarded a Pulitzer Prize for *The Harp Weaver and Other Poems*.

Arthur Miller (*born 1915*) is one of the most successful playwrights of this century. His dramas have been performed by amateur and professional groups all over the world. Miller began his career after his college graduation by writing radio scripts. Then he wrote a series of Broadway plays, including *A View From the Bridge* and *Death of a Salesman*, which won a Pulitzer Prize.

Lillian Morrison (*born 1917*) writes about a variety of subjects including jazz, dance, and sports. She was born in New Jersey and eventually moved to New York City, where she worked in the public library. Morrison is known for *The Ghosts of Jersey City*, a collection of her own poems, and *Sprints and Distances*, an anthology of sports poems which she edited.

Leroy Quintana was born and raised in New Mexico. After serving in the Vietnam War, he attended the University of New Mexico, Denver University, and New Mexico State University. Quintana went on to become a college instructor. *Hijo del Pueblo (Son of the Village)* is his first book of published poetry.

Theodore Roethke (*1908–1963*) was an original, imaginative poet and a professor of English, as well as a fine athlete and coach. His love of nature was based on his childhood experience growing up around a family-owned greenhouse in Michigan. Roethke was awarded a Pulitzer Prize in 1954 for his collection of poetry, *The Waking*. His works range from nonsense poems to serious verse.

Billy Rose (*1899–1966*) grew up in the Bronx, New York. A versatile individualist, Rose distinguished himself as a stenographer, song writer, and producer of Broadway shows. He enjoyed the role of a showman, owning a restaurant which featured lavish stage shows.

Catharine Sellew

Catharine Sellew (*born 1922*) has been interested in mythology since her mother read Greek myths to her as a child. After graduating from college, Sellew set about re-writing both Greek and Norse myths to make them easier to read. Two of her well-known collections are *Adventures with the Gods* and *Adventures with the Giants*.

William Shakespeare (*1564–1616*) was born in the English town of Stratford-on-Avon. Little is known of his youth, except for his marriage and the fact that he moved to London. There he established a successful career as an actor and playwright. Today he is considered one of the finest poets the world has ever known. Shakespeare is credited with the writing of thirty-seven plays and numerous sonnets. *Hamlet*, *King Lear*, and *Macbeth* are among his internationally-performed plays.

Robert Silverberg

Robert Silverberg (*born 1935*) has written over fifty science fiction and nonfiction books. His favorite subjects are archaeology, space exploration, and military history. *Needle in a Timestack* and *Lost Race of Mars* are two examples of his science fiction works. Silverberg was born in New York and attended Columbia University. He has also written under the name of Walker Chapman.

Isaac Bashevis Singer

Isaac Bashevis Singer (*born 1904*) came to the United States in 1935 from his native Poland. He is from a family of Jewish rabbis and pursued that vocation for awhile, until he decided on a writing career. Singer's stories, frequently set in nineteenth century Polish villages, are written in a clear, simple style. They often are a blend of superstition and the supernatural with everyday life.

Robert Louis
Stevenson

Robert Louis Stevenson (*1850–1894*), a Scottish author, was ill with tuberculosis as a child. That caused him to spend much time in bed, where he made up verses and stories long before he could write. Stevenson eventually traveled widely throughout Europe and the United States. He wrote *Treasure Island* to entertain his stepson, who loved adventure stories.

May Swenson

Sara Teasdale

Leo Tolstoy

Mark Twain

Frank Stockton (*1834–1902*) was born in Philadelphia, Pennsylvania. He first became known as an author because of his fairy tales, which were published in magazines and books. Stockton helped edit *St. Nicholas* magazine, a children's publication, and then began to write for adults. His best-known short story, "The Lady, or the Tiger?," has been translated into many languages.

May Swenson (*born 1919*) grew up and attended school in Utah. She taught at Purdue University and then served as a Poet-in-Residence there. Swenson's poems often take on unusual shapes. She wants her readers to enjoy the sight as well as the sound of her poetry. Two of her well-known collections of poems are *A Cage of Spines* and *Half Sun Half Asleep*.

Sara Teasdale (*1884–1933*), a native of St. Louis, Missouri, was a shy and delicate young woman. After she finished her formal education, she traveled all over the world. Teasdale's poetry often tell her personal feelings about love. She won a Pulitzer Prize for *Love Songs* in 1918. Other well-known works are *Rivers to the Sea* and *Strange Victories*.

Hernando Téllez (*born 1908*) is a Colombian diplomat and senator, as well as an author. He has written newspaper articles about social and political matters in South America. Téllez also writes short stories. A well-known collection of his works, *Ashes for the Wind and Other Tales*, reveals his love of justice and sympathy for the underprivileged.

Leo Tolstoy (*1828–1910*) was one of the greatest Russian authors. His writings have been translated into many languages. Tolstoy wrote about military experiences, religious themes, and humorous folk stories. One of his most famous works, *War and Peace*, has been filmed by both Americans and Russians.

Mark Twain (*1835–1910*) was the pen name of Samuel Clemens. He grew up in Hannibal, Missouri, where he had many adventures as a boy on the Mississippi River. He based his famous characters, Tom Sawyer and Huckleberry Finn, on people he knew in his childhood. In addition to his novels, Twain is also known for his humorous newspaper articles and lectures. One of his most successful books is *Innocents Abroad*, an account of his travels to Europe.

Mark Van Doren

Margaret Walker

Walt Whitman

Mark Van Doren (*born 1894*) is from Illinois. A graduate of the University of Illinois and of Columbia University, Van Doren became the editor of *Nation Magazine* and helped found the Great Books movement. His best-known works include poetry, fiction, essays, and biographies.

Margaret Walker (*born 1915*) won the Yale Younger Poets award at the age of twenty-seven for her book of poetry, *For My People*. She grew up in Birmingham, Alabama, lived in Mississippi and Louisiana, and then earned a degree from the University of Iowa. Walker has held jobs as a newspaper reporter, social worker, and English teacher.

Walt Whitman (*1819–1892*) had to pay for the printing of his first book of poetry because publishers were not interested in the free form and rhymeless style of the poems. That book, *Leaves of Grass*, eventually brought Whitman the recognition he deserved. During the Civil War, Whitman volunteered to nurse wounded soldiers. That experience was an inspiration for some of his finest poetry.

Reed Whittemore (*born 1919*) graduated from Yale University. He served in the Air Force during World War II, and then became a professor of English at Carlton College in Minnesota. Whittemore has written poetry and essays, as well as stories. He has been the co-editor of a magazine called *Furioso*.

Maia Wojciechowska (*born 1927*) is a native of Warsaw, Poland. She has lived in many countries and is fluent in French, Spanish, Russian, English, and Portuguese, as well as Polish. Wojciechowska's work experiences include detective, bullfighter, translator, editor, and literary agent. Her novel *Shadow of a Bull* won the Newbery medal in 1965.

Index of Titles and Authors

Index of Fine Art

Index of Skills

Skills in Comprehending Literature

Literature

Learning History Through Literature, 33, 47, 84, 474, 486, 495, 551

Relating Literature to Life, 79, 84, 89, 277

Logical Order See *Paragraphs, Organization.*

Main Idea 89, 166, 167, 189

Major Character See *Character.*

Metaphor 222–223, 337, 347, 417, 424, 604

Minor Character See *Character.*

Mood 256, 302, 331, 357, 399, 407, 417, 605

Motives 123, 130

Myth 2–3, 100–101, 164–165, 605

Narrator 267, 557, 577, 605

See also *Point of View.*

Nonfiction 432–433, 512–513, 605

See also specific types of nonfiction.

Omniscient See *Point of View, Third Person.*

Onomatopoeia 216–217, 368, 377, 605

Outcomes (Predicting) 235, 610

Paragraphs

Kinds, 166–167, 611

Organization, 166–167, 532, 611

Personal Recollections 432, 497, 605

Personification 224–225, 351, 605

Plays See *Drama.*

Plot 3, 57, 165, 232, 243, 557, 577, 606

Diagraming a Plot, 249, 277, 302, 324

Poetry 330–331, 374–375, 606

Concrete Poems, 331, 606

Structure, 343, 347, 389, 399, 409

See also *Rhyme, Rhyme Scheme, Rhythm.*

Point of View 267, 271, 357, 363, 606

First Person, Third Person, 267

Proverb 544, 606

Purpose See *Author's Purpose.*

Radio Play 585

Repetition 351, 359, 379, 391, 413, 419, 606

Resolution 233, 606

Rhyme 212–213, 375, 391, 414, 417, 607

Rhyme Scheme 213, 348, 354, 377, 422, 607

Rhythm 214–215, 347, 368, 407, 519, 607

Rising Action 127, 233, 317, 607

Science Fiction 311, 324

Sensory Images See *Imagery.*

Setting 3, 41, 57, 79, 101, 233, 277, 593, 607

Short Story 232–233, 266–267, 608

Simile 220–221, 405, 608

Slanted Writing 435, 444, 508, 519, 612

Sounds of Language 209–218, 228–229, 331, 353, 386–387, 394, 413, 424

See also *Alliteration, Assonance, Onomatopoeia, Rhyme, Rhythm.*

Speaker 331, 389, 391

Stage Directions 557, 608

Structure 486, 508, 513, 593 See also *Paragraphs, Organization; Poetry, Structure.*

Style (Literary) 357, 426, 509, 593

Suspense 233

Symbols 110, 333, 422, 547

Techniques See *Style.*

Theme 33, 57, 149, 267, 271, 331, 343, 465, 479, 501, 509, 547, 608

Third Person See *Point of View,*

Time Order 4–5, 16, 33, 64, 84, 111, 608

Identifying Signal Words, 21, 41

Making a Time Line, 71, 89

Tone 262, 351, 379, 433, 532, 608

Word Choice 366, 501, 509, 612

Vocabulary Skills

Affixes See *Prefixes; Suffixes.*

Allusions 523

Analogies 89–90, 410, 486

Antonyms 303, 614

Base Words 6, 7, 17, 110–111, 116, 136, 419, 613

Borrowed Words 334, 343, 371, 426, 616

Clipped Words 335, 426, 509, 616

Combined Words 335, 371, 426, 616

Writing Skills

Study and Research Skills

Speaking and Listening Skills

Skills in Critical Thinking

Acknowledgments

(*continued from copyright page*)

Gorilla, My Love by Toni Cade Bambara; copyright © 1972 by Random House, Inc. The Christian Science Publishing Society: For "Unfolding Bud" by Naoshi Koriyama, from *The Christian Science Monitor;* © 1957, all rights reserved. Crown Publishers, Inc.: For "We'll Always Sing His Songs" by Carl Carmer, from *Cavalcade of America;* copyright © 1956 by Lothrop, Lee and Shepard Co., Inc. Don Congdon Associates, Inc.: For "All Summer in a Day" by Ray Bradbury; copyright © 1954 by Ray Bradbury, renewed 1982 by Ray Bradbury. DC Comics, Inc.: For "Superman" by Jerome Siegel and Joe Shuster; Superman is a registered trademark of DC Comics Inc. and is used with permission; copyright © 1939, 1967 DC Comics Inc. Doubleday & Company, Inc.: For the "Kyklops" excerpts from *The Odyssey* by Homer, translated by Robert Fitzgerald; copyright © 1961 by Robert Fitzgerald. For "After Twenty Years," from *The Four Million* by O. Henry; copyright 1904 by Press Publishing Co. For excerpts from *Anne Frank: The Diary of a Young Girl* by Anne Frank; copyright 1952 by Otto H. Frank. For "Child on Top of a Greenhouse" by Theodore Roethke, from *The Collected Poems of Theodore Roethke;* copyright 1946 by Editorial Publications, Inc. For "The Third Wish" by Joan Aiken, from *Not What You Expected* by Joan Aiken; copyright © 1974 by Joan Aiken. E. P. Dutton, Inc.: For ninety-one pages of text (changing Roman names to Greek—the author chose to use Roman names in telling the stories) from *Stories of Gods and Heroes* retold by Sally Benson; copyright 1940, 1968 by Sally Benson, reprinted by permission of the publisher, Dial Books for Young Readers, a Division of E. P. Dutton, Inc. Farrar, Straus & Giroux, Inc.: For "The Washwoman," adapted from *A Day of Pleasure* by Isaac Bashevis Singer; copyright © 1963, 1965, 1966, 1969 by Isaac Bashevis Singer. For "Charles" by Shirley Jackson, from *The Lottery;* copyright 1948 by Shirley Jackson, copyright renewed © 1976 by Laurence Hyman, Barry Hyman, Mrs. Sarah Webster, and Mrs. Joanne Schnurer. Harcourt Brace Jovanovich, Inc.: For "Macavity: the Mystery Cat," from *Old Possum's Book of Practical Cats* by T. S. Eliot; copyright 1939 by T. S. Eliot, renewed 1967 by Esme Valerie Eliot. For "To Look at Any Thing," from *The Living Seed* by John Moffitt; copyright © 1961 by John Moffitt. For "Fueled," from *Serve Me a Slice of Moon* by Marcie Hans; copyright © 1965 by Marcie Hans. For "Mama and Her Bank Account," from *Mamma's Bank Account* by Kathryn Forbes; copyright 1943 by Kathryn Forbes; renewed 1971 by Richard E. McLean and Robert M. McLean. Harper and Row, Publishers, Inc.: For an adaptation of "People," from *Earth: Our Crowded Spaceship* by Isaac Asimov; copyright © 1974 Isaac Asimov, (John Day). For "Langston Terrace" (pp. 134–142), from *Childtimes: A Three-Generation Memoir* by Eloise Greenfield and Lessie Jones Little; copyright © 1979 by Eloise Greenfield and Lessie Jones Little (Thomas Y. Crowell). For "Punch, Brothers, Punch," from *Tom Sawyer Abroad* by Mark Twain. Sara Henderson Hay: For "For a Dead Kitten" by Sara Henderson Hay, from *A Footing on This Earth,* by permission of the author. Holt, Rinehart and Winston, Publishers: For "When I was One-and-Twenty," from "A Shropshire Lad"—authorized edition—from *The Collected Poems of A. E. Housman;* copyright 1939, 1940, © 1965 by Holt, Rinehart and Winston; copyright © 1967, 1968 by Robert E. Symons. For "Steam Shovel," from *Upper Pasture* by Charles Malam; copyright 1930, © 1958 by Charles Malam. For "The Road Not Taken" and "Stopping by Woods on a Snowy Evening," from *The Poetry of Robert Frost* edited by Edward Connery Lathem; copyright 1916, 1923, © 1969 by Holt, Rinehart and Winston; copyright 1944, 1951 by Robert Frost. Houghton, Mifflin Company: For "The Song of Beowulf," slightly adapted from *Legends of the North* by Olivia E. Coolidge; copyright 1951 by Olivia E. Coolidge, copyright © renewed 1979 by Olivia E. Coolidge. International Creative Management: For *Grandpa and the Statue* by Arthur Miller; copyright © 1945, 1973 by Arthur Miller. Little, Brown and Company: For Chapters 1–8, from *Adventures with the Giants* by Catharine F. Sellew; copyright 1950 by Catharine F. Sellew. For "Southbound on the Freeway," from *New and Selected Things Taking Place* by May Swenson; copyright © 1963 by May Swenson, first appeared in *The New Yorker,* by permission of Little, Brown and Company. Liveright Publishing Company: For "to be nobody-but-yourself" by E. E. Cummings, from "A Poet's Advice to Students"; copyright © 1955 by E. E. Cummings; copyright © 1965 by Marion Morehouse Cummings, from *E. E. Cummings: A Miscellany,* copyright © 1958, 1965 by George James Firmage. For "Those Winter Sundays," from *Angle of Ascent, New and Selected Poems* by Robert Hayden; copyright © 1975, 1972, 1970, 1966 by Robert Hayden. Macmillan Publishing Co., Inc.: For "Faces," from *Collected Poems* by Sara Teasdale; copyright 1920 by Macmillan Publishing Co., Inc., renewed 1948 by Mamie T. Wheless. For "The High School Band," from *The Self-Made Man and Other Poems* by Reed Whittemore; copyright © 1959 by Reed Whittemore. Frederic Brown and Scott Meredith Literary Agency, Inc.: For "The Weapon," from *Mad Scientists.* Norma Millay (Ellis): For "Lament" by Edna St. Vincent Millay, from *Collected Poems,* Harper & Row; copyright 1921, 1948 by Edna St. Vincent Millay. William Morrow & Company, Inc.: For twenty-seven proverbs from pp. 11, 13, 14, 15, 17, 21, 29, 35, 38, 40, 42, 44, 46, 48, 55, 58, and 59 in *Proverbs of Many Nations* compiled by Emery Kelen; copyright © 1966 by Emery Kelen, by permission of Lothrop, Lee & Shepard Books (A Division of William Morrow & Company). For "Nine Triads," from *The Sidewalk Racer and Other Poems of Sports and Motion* by Lillian Morrison; copyright © 1977 by Lillian Morrison, by permission of Lothrop, Lee & Shepard Books (A Division of William Morrow & Company). The New American Library, Inc.: For "The Life of Davy Crockett by Himself," from *The Life of Davy Crockett By Himself.* New Mexico Magazine: For "Piñones" by Leroy Quintana, from *New Mexico Magazine,* November/December 1974. The New Yorker: For "Central Park Tourney" by Mildred Weston, from May 9, 1953 issue of *The New Yorker* reprinted by permission; © 1953, 1981 The New Yorker Magazine, Inc. Harold Ober Associates, Inc.: For "Thank You, M'am" by Langston Hughes, from *The Langston Hughes Reader;* copyright © 1958 by Langston Hughes. The Organization of American States: For "Lather and Nothing Else" by Hernando Téllez, from

Art Credits

Cover

Virginia Site, 1959, Kenneth Noland.
Collection of Joseph Helman, New York.

Illustrations

Sarah Woodward, 58–59, 108, 114–115, 120, 121, 132–133, 148; David Cunningham, 204–205; Robert Masheris, 291, 293; Glenn Wolff, 396; Troy Thomas, 416, 564, 568–569, 576; William Cigliano, 443; Dale Bēda, 452.

Photographs of Authors

Arbor House Photograph, Susanne Lee Houfek: Robert Silverberg. The Bettmann Archive: William Blake, Arthur Conan Doyle, T. S. Eliot, O. Henry, Langston Hughes, Robert Louis Stevenson, Sara Teasdale, Mark Twain, Walt Whitman. Culver Pictures: E. E. Cummings, Homer, Henry Wadsworth Longfellow. Alex Gottfryd: Joan Aiken. Historical Picture Service: Robert Frost, Edwin Markham, Leo Tolstoy. Little Brown and Company: Catharine Sellew. National Portrait Gallery: David Crockett. Photo Researchers: Mark Van Doren. UPI/Bettmann: Anne Frank. Vassar College Library: Edna St. Vincent Millay.

Staff Credits

Editor-in-Chief: Joseph F. Littell
Project Director: Patricia Opaskar

Administrative Editor: Kathleen Laya
Managing Editor: Geraldine Macsai

Associate Editors: Geraldine Wall-DeGraff, Elizabeth Garber,
    Bernice Rappoport
Rights and Permissions: Irma Rosenberg
Associate Designer: Linda Schifano FitzGibbon

Special Contributors

Katherine Fischer; Roberta Knauf; Sister Margaret Murphy, O. P.;
Gerry Tremaine; Mary Ann Trost. Picture Research: Katherine Nolan.
Production: Dale Bēda; Carolyn Deacy.